JOSHUA

VOLUME 6

THE ANCHOR BIBLE is a fresh approach to the world's greatest classic. Its object is to make the Bible accessible to the modern reader; its method is to arrive at the meaning of biblical literature through exact translation and extended exposition, and to reconstruct the ancient setting of the biblical story, as well as the circumstances of its transcription and the characteristics of its transcribers.

THE ANCHOR BIBLE is a project of international and interfaith scope: Protestant, Catholic, and Jewish scholars from many countries contribute individual volumes. The project is not sponsored by any ecclesiastical organization and is not intended to reflect any particular theological doctrine. Prepared under our joint supervision, THE ANCHOR BIBLE is an effort to make available all the significant historical and linguistic knowledge which bears on the interpretation of the biblical record.

This project marks the beginning of a new era of co-operation among scholars in biblical research, thus forming a common body of knowledge to be shared by all.

William Foxwell Albright
David Noel Freedman
GENERAL EDITORS

THE ANCHOR BIBLE

JOSHUA

A New Translation
with Notes and Commentary

by ROBERT G. BOLING

Introduction by G. Ernest Wright

DOUBLEDAY & COMPANY, INC.
GARDEN CITY, NEW YORK
1982

ISBN: 0-385-00034-0
Library of Congress Catalog Card Number 79–6583

PREFACE

This book has been an unusually long time in preparation. The original division of labor called for the senior member of the team, G. Ernest Wright, to produce the Introduction and Comment, with Translation and Notes prepared by one of his former students. Sadly it was not to be so. Among the many promising projects under way at his death was an essentially completed manuscript of the Introduction to Joshua. We have published it here unrevised, except for updating references which have been published or republished since 1974.

In this case the relation of teacher and student goes deep, surviving many vicissitudes brought by a revised production plan and embracing the possibility of disagreement to which, here and there, the student's research seems to lead him. Such points are respectfully ventured in the body of the book and are appropriately introduced in the extensive NOTES and COMMENT on chapter 1. One of the marks of Wright's stature as scholar, teacher, and genuine human being was his satisfaction in achieving with students the very give-and-take that is the life pulse of scholarly enterprise.

There is not space here to name all those who have made possible the work on this volume: my family, former teachers, current colleagues, and McCormick Theological Seminary students over the past decade. One could find no more constant friend and persistent creative critic than Edward F. Campbell, Jr. I am also especially indebted to David Noel Freedman, Michael Patrick O'Connor, and Robert W. Hewetson—the first two for their primary editorial and thoroughly detailed review of the manuscript, the third for his incomparable copy-editing care. Doubleday's Eve F. Roshevsky, Anchor Bible Editor, has been of invaluable assistance all the way. Two major works not yet published were generously made available by their authors, Leonard J. Greenspoon and John L. Peterson. Special thanks also goes to Karen Summers, exceptional typist. Finally, however, my deepest and well-nigh inexpressible appreciation remains for the man in whose classroom one discovered the exhilaration and joy of learning, precisely because he so modeled the challenge of teaching—Professor G. Ernest Wright.

ROBERT G. BOLING
Chicago, IL

February 5, 1980

CONTENTS

* Chapter and verse spans *within parentheses* are those followed by Textual Notes, NOTES and COMMENTS.

LISTS OF ILLUSTRATIONS AND MAPS

Maps by John Morris

PRINCIPAL ABBREVIATIONS

1. PUBLICATIONS

AASOR	Annual of the American Schools of Oriental Research
ADAJ	Annual of the Department of Antiquities of Jordan
AJA	*American Journal of Archaeology*
ANEP	*The Ancient Near East in Pictures,* ed. J. B. Pritchard. Princeton University Press, 1954
*ANET*² and *ANET*³	*Ancient Near Eastern Texts Relating to the Old Testament,* ed. J. B. Pritchard. 2d ed. (1955) and 3d ed. (1969), Princeton University Press
ARM	*Archives royales de Mari*
ASOR	American Schools of Oriental Research
ATD	Das Alte Testament Deutsch
BA	*The Biblical Archaeologist*
BAR	*The Biblical Archaeologist Reader.* Garden City, NY: Doubleday Anchor Books. Volume 1, eds. G. Ernest Wright and David Noel Freedman (1961); vol. 2, eds. David Noel Freedman and Edward F. Campbell, Jr. (1964); vol. 3, eds. Edward F. Campbell, Jr., and David Noel Freedman (1970)
BASOR	*Bulletin of the American Schools of Oriental Research*
BWANT	Beiträge zur Wissenschaft vom Alten und Neuen Testaments
BZAW	Beihefte zur *Zeitschrift für die alttestamentliche Wissenschaft*
*CAH*²	*Cambridge Ancient History,* rev. ed., 1961-
*CAH*³	*The Cambridge Ancient History,* 3d ed., 1970-
CBQ	*Catholic Biblical Quarterly*
CMHE	*Canaanite Myth and Hebrew Epic,* by Frank Moore Cross. Harvard University Press, 1973
EA	The El-Amarna Tablets. *Die Al-Amarna Tafeln,* by J. A. Knudtzon. Leipzig, 1915 (reprinted 1964)

EAEHL	*Encyclopedia of Archaeological Excavations in the Holy Land,* ed. Michael Avi-Yonah. Jerusalem: Israel Exploration Society and Massada Press
GKC	*Gesenius' Hebrew Grammar,* ed. E. Kautzsch, tr. A. E. Cowley
GTOT	*Geographical and Topographical Texts of the Old Testament,* by J. Simons. Leiden: Brill, 1959
HTR	*Harvard Theological Review*
IB	*The Interpreter's Bible*
IDB	*The Interpreter's Dictionary of the Bible,* eds. G. A. Buttrick, et al., 4 vols. New York and Nashville: Abingdon Press, 1962
IDBSup	Supplementary volume to *IDB,* 1976
IEJ	*Israel Exploration Journal*
JAOS	*Journal of the American Oriental Society*
JBL	*Journal of Biblical Literature*
JEA	*Journal of Egyptian Archaeology*
JNES	*Journal of Near Eastern Studies*
JPOS	*Journal of the Palestine Oriental Society*
JSS	*Journal of Semitic Studies*
KAI	*Kanaanäische und aramäischen Inschriften,* eds. H. Donner and H. Röllig. Wiesbaden: Otto Harrassowitz, 1962-1964
LOB	*The Land of the Bible,* by Yohanan Aharoni. Philadelphia: Westminster, 1967
Mag Dei	*Magnalia Dei: The Mighty Acts of God.* Essays on the Bible and Archaeology in Memory of G. Ernest Wright. Editors Frank Moore Cross, Werner E. Lemke, and Patrick D. Miller, Jr. Garden City, NY: Doubleday, 1976
MLC	*Myth, Legend, and Custom in the Old Testament,* by Theodor H. Gaster. New York: Harper & Row, 1969
PEFQS	*Palestine Exploration Fund, Quarterly Statement*
PEQ	*Palestine Exploration Quarterly*
PTU	*Die Personennamen der Texte aus Ugarit,* by Frauke Gröndahl. Rome: Päpstliches Bibelinstitut, 1967
RB	*Revue biblique*
RevQ	*Revue de Qumrân*
SAYP	*Studies in Ancient Yahwistic Poetry,* by Frank Moore Cross and David Noel Freedman. Missoula, MT: Scholars Press, 1975

STBJ	"Studies in the Textual Tradition of the Book of Joshua," by Leonard Jay Greenspoon. Unpublished Ph.D. dissertation. Harvard University, 1977
Symposia	*Symposia Celebrating the Seventy-fifth Anniversary of the Founding of the American Schools of Oriental Research (1900-1975).* Volume 1, ed. Frank Moore Cross. Cambridge, MA: American Schools of Oriental Research, 1979
TDOT	*Theological Dictionary of the Old Testament,* eds. G. Johannes Botterweck and Helmer Ringgren. Volumes 1 (revised), 2 (revised), and 3. Grand Rapids: Eerdmans (1977, 1977, 1978).
Ten Gen	*The Tenth Generation: The Origins of the Biblical Tradition,* by George E. Mendenhall. The Johns Hopkins University Press, 1973
TWAT	*Theologisches Wörterbuch zum Alten Testament,* eds. G. Johannes Botterweck and Helmer Ringgren. Grand Rapids, MI: Eerdmans, 1974-
UF	*Ugarit-Forschungen*
UT	*Ugaritic Textbook,* by C. H. Gordon. Rome: Pontifical Biblical Institute, 1965
VT	*Vetus Testamentum*
*VT*Sup	*Vetus Testamentum,* Supplements
WHJP	*The World History of the Jewish People.* First Series: Ancient Times. Volumes II (1970) and III (1971), ed. Benjamin Mazar; vol. VI (1972), ed. Abraham Schalit. Tel-Aviv: Massada Publishing Co., 1970, 1971, 1972
YGC	*Yahweh and the Gods of Canaan,* by William F. Albright. Garden City, NY: Doubleday, 1968
ZAW	*Zeitschrift für die alttestamentliche Wissenschaft*
ZDPV	*Zeitschrift des deutschen Palästina-Vereins*
ZTK	*Zeitschrift für Theologie und Kirche*

2. VERSIONS

AT	Altes Testament
BH[3]	*Biblia Hebraica,* ed. R. Kittel. Privilegierte Württembergische Bibelanstalt: Stuttgart, 3d ed., 1937, and after

BHS	*Biblia Hebraica Stuttgartensia,* eds. K. Elliger and W. Rudolph. Deutsche Bibelstiftung: Stuttgart, 1977
D or Dtn	The bulk of Deut 4:44 - 28:68
EVV	English versions in general. (Chapter and verse numbers which differ in the Hebrew and English versions are designated by an "E" or an "H")
JB	*The Jerusalem Bible* here cited in the annotated edition, Garden City, NY: Doubleday, 1966
KJV	The Authorized Version of 1611, or the King James Bible
LXX	The Septuagint
*LXX^A	Codex Alexandrinus
*LXX^B	Codex Vaticanus
*LXX^{AL}	LXX^A and LXX^L (yet another manuscript) have the same reading
MT	Masoretic Text
NEB	*The New English Bible*
OG	The Old Greek
OL	The Old Latin
RSV	*The Revised Standard Version*
Syr	Syriac Version, the Peshitta
*Syr^h	The Syriac version of Origen's Hexapla
*Targ	Aramaic translations or paraphrases, the Targum
Vulg	The Latin Vulgate
AB	The Anchor Bible
J	Ancient Israel's national epic, the main Yahwist narrative stratum in the books of Genesis through Numbers, with at least two substrata: J$_1$, the more secular, and J$_2$, the more religious
L	The "lay" source in Genesis through Numbers, following the analysis by Otto Eissfeldt, *The Old Testament: An Introduction,* tr. Peter R. Ackroyd. New York: Harper & Row, 1965. This corresponds generally to J$_1$ in the earlier studies
E	The northern or Ephraimite version of the national epic, preserved only in part in the books of Genesis through Numbers; also known as the Elohistic epic, since it uses the generic noun for "God" (*^{e}lohim*), prior to the call of Moses in Exodus 3

* Other superscript letters in Textual Notes also identify manuscripts of these versions.

P	The priestly stratum in Genesis-Numbers
Dtr 1	Major edition of the historical work: Deuteronomy-2 Kings
Dtr 2	Final edition of the historical work: Deuteronomy-2 Kings

3. Other Abbreviations

NT	The New Testament
OT	The Old Testament
c.e.	Common Era; corresponds to A.D.
b.c.e	Before the Common Era; corresponds to B.C.
EB, MB, and LB	Early, Middle, and Late Bronze Ages
Kh.	Khirbet, Arabic word for a small ruin in contrast to a large ruin, a tell
mss	Manuscripts
K^{OR}	The *kethib* according to eastern Masoretes
Q^{OR}	The *qere* according to eastern Masoretes
	Half verses are represented in Textual Notes, Notes, and Comment by superscript letters, e.g. vv 1^a and 1^b.
†	The dagger before a place name (beginning with the Notes in 15:21) indicates that the place name in any form does not occur again in the Hebrew Bible

CHRONOLOGY OF

THE GREAT POWERS

Sumerian Age in Mesopotamia, c. 2800–2400
Pyramid Age in Egypt, c. 2700–2200
Akkad: first semitic dynasty in Mesopotamia, c. 2400–2200
Sumerian Revival in Mesopotamia, c. 2100–2000
Amorite dynasties: Babylonia to the Mediterranean, c. 2000–1700

Hyksos domination: Egypt and Canaan, c. 1710–1550

Asia Minor: Hittite Empire, c. 1600–1200
Egypt: New Kingdom, c. 1500–1200
Decline of Pharaonic power, c. 1400–1200
Crete: Golden Age of Minoan culture, fall of Crete, c. 1400

Greece: Dorian invasion, end of Mycenaean culture, c. 1200

Sea Peoples' invasion of Egypt and coast of Canaan, c. 1200–1125
End of Hittite Empire, c. 1200

Assyria quiescent, c. 1197–1125
Thessalian Federation in northern Greece, c. 1100

Neo-Assyrian supremacy, 727–633
Neo-Babylonian supremacy, 626–539

Persian supremacy, 539–334
Alexander's conquest of Egypt and Asia, 334–323

THE BOOK OF JOSHUA

ERAS

ERA OF THE PATRIARCHS
(Genesis 12–50)

2100	Middle Bronze I	Canaan effectively or nominally controlled from Egypt
1900	Middle Bronze II A	
1700	Middle Bronze II B	
1600	Middle Bronze II C	
1500	Late Bronze I	
1400	Late Bronze II A.	Amarna Age: Labayu at Shechem
1300	Late Bronze II B.	The Exodus and Sinai Wanderings c. 1250–1200

1200	Iron Age I.	Joshua's "Invasion" and the Shechem Covenant c. 1200–1175

ERA OF THE JUDGES

Gideon, Abimelech: sack of Shechem, c. 1150

ERA OF THE KINGS

Saul, c. 1020–1000
David, c. 1000–961
Solomon, c. 961–922
Yahwist epic (J), c. 950
Elohist epic (E), c. 800
Destruction of Samaria, end of the northern kingdom of Israel, 721
Josiah, c. 640–609
Deuteronomic Historical Work (Dtr 1), c. 615
First Babylonian invasion and deportation, 598
Second Babylonian invasion, destruction of Jerusalem,
   end of the southern kingdom of Judah, 587

ERA OF THE BOOK

Deuteronomistic Historical Work (Dtr 2), post–598

INTRODUCTION

The Book of Joshua is one of the Bible's critically important historical and religious works. It is one of Israel's greatest testimonies to the power and grace of the Sovereign Lord of all mankind. With Exodus it tells how the mighty God delivered a group of Egypt's state slaves to freedom in the wilderness of Sinai, then gave them a land, a place of "rest" and refuge. Slaves and wanderers for whom the world's justice and powers had no time were delivered, redeemed, rescued, formed into a nation, and given a land in which to live with their own government.

Here to old Israel was the supreme example of the grace of God. It was a normative, a newsworthy event about which parents spoke to their children because it explained the real meaning of their past. It was something to be recited and sung in worship because it identified the ultimate Power in the world as possessing a righteousness which was love and grace, releasing the weak and defenseless from bondage.

For this reason "you must love the strangers living in your midst, for you, yourselves, were once such strangers in the land of Egypt" (cf. Deut 10:19). "You shall not make it hard for the poor among you, because you were once the poor in Egypt. And do not be land profiteers for the land is God's who gave it and you are only temporary stewards of it" (cf. Exod 22:21-24; Lev 19:10; 25:23-24). "To me [God] the people of Israel are servants; they are my servants whom I brought out from the land of Egypt; I am the Lord your God" (Lev 25:55).

The New Testament uses the old theme of deliverance to explain God's work in Christ. It is explained to Christians, for example, that "you indeed are a chosen race, a royal priesthood, a consecrated nation, a people who are his special possession [Exod 19:5-6; Deut 7:6, etc.], so that you may proclaim the mighty acts of him who has called you out of darkness to his marvelous light—you who once were 'No-People' but now 'God's People,' you who were 'Not Pitied,' now 'Pitied' indeed [Hos 2:1,23]" (1 Pet 2:9-10).

Among the many themes drawn upon to interpret the American experience, one was crossing the Jordan (the Atlantic) to enter the Promised Land. In American revivalistic pietism this could be individualized eschatology, crossing the raging waters of the sea to enter the promised land of eternal life. In early New England, in the abolition movement before the

Civil War, and in the civil rights movement of the 1960s, however, the great word "freedom" had a concrete meaning for which Israel's ancient story functioned as archetype. "Free at last, free at last. Thank God Almighty, free at last!"—these words of Martin Luther King have intensity and depth of meaning because their immediate application to social issues is informed by the total range of the classic theme drawn from Israel.

Yet since the Enlightenment Western intellectuals have not generally read the Book of Joshua in this manner. Here one reads for himself in sacred writ about war, cruelty, and the killing of the defenseless, all evidently at God's command. If God is anything, his primary relation is to love and the good. How does one find such an idea in Joshua when what one reads appears to be another gross example of man's inhumanity to man, religion being used as its buttress? There thus has come about a rejection of the God of Joshua, and even more of the God of Israel, as a God of wrath, war, and judgment. Such a God contrasts with the God of love, the divine Father of the New Testament. Regardless of the fact that Judaism, not to speak of modern scholars of ancient Israel's life and faith in her own world, finds no such deity in the literature of Israel as a whole, many humanists and Christians have adopted this simplistic view of the Bible. The stories in chaps. 6-12 in Joshua are not liturgical reading for us, and the gap between the biblical understanding of them and our own is wide indeed.

As though this question were not difficult enough, the *historical* problem of Joshua is equally difficult. In the book ancient Israel recorded her belief as to how the nation came to live in ancient Palestine. Yet during the last century a majority of those attempting to apply the methods of modern historiography to Hebrew tradition have said the book is wrong; it never happened that way at all.

Clearly, he who would write a commentary on this book has a difficult task ahead. Not only does he have to attempt a presentation of the faith of Israel which is both exegetically correct and also of some sense to the modern ear, but he must comb through the layers of tradition, with his eye on the archaeological and historical situation as it is known today, in order to make some reconstruction of how Israel got into the land. What is the history of the tradition and what kind of a hypothesis can today best handle the evidence?

I. The God of Israel and the Conquest of Canaan

Israel's Way of Confession

The Bible as the record of the ancient Near East's most powerfully creative religious movement exhibits a richness in variety within it, but not
such as would enable us ever to class it as one of the world's idealisms—
to use that term in its technical meaning. It did not at any point define
some abstract entity as *The Good,* and then fit what was meant by deity
into the definition, so that the Reality and the rationally conceived Universal Good could be seen as identical. If one does this, then he will have
great difficulty in seeing evidence of the eternal, timeless Good in the
midst of the daily experience of human beings. The world of people as
they are has always been an unsolvable problem for Platonism, for example, and for all idealisms. From Hegel to Whitehead, the process of being
and becoming have been seen together as encompassing the good, which
emerges from conflict resolution so that evolutionary development can be
seen over a long period as providing examples of man's progress in
knowledge and appropriation of what is conceived to be good. Yet human
history has been and still is an enigma to a great portion of the human
race. "The terror of history" is precisely that "the more we try to sound
the inexhaustible meaning of the particular, the more devoid everything
seems to be of any meaning in particular."[1]

Israel had no idea of a two-realm theory of knowledge, one of a super-
nal, universal Good and one of the world of human beings where they
live. There was only one realm where significant knowledge was obtaina-
ble. That was their own, their own life as a people in the midst of the nations with whom they had contact. Yet in this world they indeed affirmed
that God is good, but they meant by this that definitive actions in their
history exhibited a mysterious Power who for his own reasons had acted
toward them with remarkable graciousness. They who had been a no-
people were now a people with land and law and government of their own.
Furthermore, the direction of movement of this Power had been against
the powers of earth on behalf of the defenseless, the slaves, the dispossessed, and for Israel this fact gave a quality of meaning to the term
"righteousness" which has become almost a classic norm in the western

---

[1] P. Leon as quoted by Geoffrey Barraclough in *The Philosophy of History in
Our Time,* ed. Hans Meyerhoff (Garden City, NY: Doubleday Anchor, 1959) 30.

world. All this did not mean for Israel that the world of human events was in itself good; rather a Power was affirmed, mysterious in its origin and purposes, which could be observed within history, within all human evil and ambiguity, which nevertheless favored human good.

For Israel, then, the basic data for theology, i.e. for the comprehension of human meaning, was derived from history, from an understanding of what was going on, and what Israel's collected tradition of past events signified. It bears constant repetition that this fact led them to an intense interest in the collection and preservation of historical traditions and even of a knowledge of the history of other peoples—and Israel was the first people in history to see their past in this manner. Tenth-century Israel in the Jerusalem courts of David and Solomon saw the *written* production of two remarkable historical works: the first written edition of Israel's epic story of her origins from the creation of the world to the creation of the nation on the soil of Palestine (called the work of the Yahwist or J by scholars) and the Court History of David as King. Neither work can be completely recovered, but nevertheless extensive portions of each can be identified so that we can judge their nature.

Contemporary Old Testament study has made much of the kerygmatic (proclamative) and confessional nature of Israel's epic story. The most brilliantly creative monograph on the question is that of Gerhard von Rad, *The Form Critical Problem of the Hexateuch*.[2] In seeking the oldest forms of Hebrew public confession as they are preserved in later literature, Von Rad points first to the old confession preserved in Deut 26:5-10. It surely derives from old times before the days of Israel's kings. It specifies that in the spring a worshiper shall take a basket of firstfruits from his land to the central sanctuary of Israel's tribes, hand it to the priest, and then recite a confession which spoke of his patriarchal ancestors migrating to Egypt, and there multiplying from few to many. Made slaves by the Egyptians, God saw their affliction, delivered them with a demonstration of great power and remarkable deeds, and then "brought us into this place and gave us this land, a land flowing with milk and honey" (v 9). Or again we are told that when a son in future generations asks what the whole tradition means, a father is to reply:

> Slaves were we to Pharaoh in Egypt, and the Lord with great power brought us out. And he gave great and hurtful signs and marvels in Egypt against Pharaoh and all his household before our eyes. And us it was that he delivered from there so that he might bring us in, to give to us the land which he swore to our fathers (Deut 6:21-23).

[2] First published in 1938 and available in English in *The Form Critical Problem of the Hexateuch and Other Essays*, 1-78. For summary of certain of the chief points, see also the Introduction to his commentary on *Genesis*, tr. John Marks; 3d ed. rev. (London: SCM Press, 1972).

In other words, it was characteristic of Israel to explain and expound their faith and allegiance to Yahweh (as the Lord's name was known) by a narrative of what he had done. In simplest form this consisted of two themes, rarely completely stereotyped in narration, exodus and conquest as deliverance and gift, both marvels for wonder and praise. To elaborate on this for an Israelite would simply be to tell more of the story, and especially more about the "fathers" or patriarchs (in Genesis). An old example, one perhaps showing signs of more extensive later editing than the confession in Deuteronomy 26, is Josh 24:2-13, where the divine guidance of the family of Abraham from beyond the Euphrates into Canaan (Palestine, the Lebanon region, and southern Syria) is narrated.

It is Von Rad's thesis that the first written edition of the epic by the Yahwist collected material from a variety of sources but drew its confession theme of the *magnalia Dei* (the mighty acts of God) from the old cultic confessions. It is this theme which provides the unity and continuity in the otherwise disparate material. Yet there are additional blocks of narrative with thematic treatment present in the epic which are not present in the credos. Working these together into the *magnalia Dei* outline they must represent reveals, suggests Von Rad, the originality and creativity of the Yahwist himself. The chief among these additional materials are these:

1. The working-in of the tradition about the covenant at Mount Sinai. That agreement or treaty was one in which the variety of people became "the people of Yahweh," accepted his lordship over them as their sovereign, and swore to obey his will as his "servants" or subjects. That is, the Sinai covenant held within it the picture of the world as a cosmic empire, ruled over by one divine sovereign, in which Israel was the people or vassal of this universal ruler. From him came indirectly the law within which Israel must live, mediated for the most part through Moses. The Sinai tradition is thus very important, because the sense of structure, of government and law, of ruler and service, furnished the context in which Israel lived. It is an old tradition, Von Rad believes, though the character of its transmission in the circles of ancient Israel is not clear. The old credos never mention the covenant. Yet when added to the story of God's marvelous deeds, there came together this early the two basic elements in all biblical religion: grace and law.

2. The old credos never mention the creation or anything alluding to early man in Genesis 1-11. This means, affirms Von Rad, that the Yahwist collected the old stories of the primordial period and recast them in such a way as to depict Israel's Lord, not only as the world's creator, but also as its sovereign with mankind given freedom and responsibility to accept service as Lord of earth. These are the conditions of life, but the story of man is a story of rebellion against the conditions of his creation to obtain

a freedom of action without restraint which characterizes only deity in this world ("You have made him little less than a divine being," Ps 8:5 [6H]). In this rebellion civilization and the nations have developed. With such an interpretation of human life placed as the introduction to the epic of Israel, the Yahwist has given a worldwide setting to the special dealing of God with Israel. The problem of mankind is to find its solution in the special work of God.

3. The Yahwist's elaboration of the theme of promise that had been an integral part of some of the old patriarchal traditions is the point where the tying of the prehistory into the traditions of Israel is most clearly seen. Gen 12:1-3 and 7 contain the developed tradition of the promises in the old epic which are repeated to each generation (22:15-18; 26:3-4; 28:13-14). They include the promise that Abraham's progeny will become a great nation, and will possess the land where they then were; furthermore all the nations of the earth will receive blessing through this blessed one. The first two of the promises, says Von Rad, were probably part of the old traditions, but the third was the contribution of the Yahwist. In any event, central now to the patriarchal narratives was the theme of promise, so that subsequent events will be seen as fulfillments, specifically the deliverance from slavery and the gift of the land. Thus, the inner theological coherence of Israel's epic, in Von Rad's view, came into being.

Of great importance in this analysis is Von Rad's presentation of the structure of the tradition, his highlighting of those themes which provide the essential literary and theological outline of the variety of traditional materials present in the epic. Here even the creation is narrated as though it were one of the glorious acts of God in history, although the first of the series. This type of narration is confessional and employs historical traditions for theological purposes. Israel's historical traditions were preserved for this reason, because the recitation of the story of her past was Israel's way of identifying both God and herself.

Certain elements in Von Rad's hypothesis are debatable. Two in particular have caused much discussion:

1. His method of showing that a vital relationship existed between Israel's public worship and her epic history is most rewarding and significant. The unproved assumption of the presentation is that the historian borrowed his basic themes from the recitations in the cultic liturgies. Yet when one studies the many recitations of the *magnalia Dei* which the Old Testament contains, whether in the historical literature, prophets, or psalms, one discovers such freedom and variety in narration that it is difficult to derive them from an originally limited selection of credos. As a hypothesis to explain the numerous variants it might be argued that

there once existed a rich oral tradition, whence a variety of cults drew inspiration. The small range of stereotypes and the great freedom in recitation apparently suggest a store of source material which was the living tradition of the people. Only to a severely limited extent can our tools of research provide the means of unraveling the early history of that tradition. The earliest written form of it appears in the Yahwist but it is difficult indeed to see how even the Yahwist's basic outline was drawn from the cultic recitations, rather than to consider both as drawn from a common source. So close to the Yahwist and so archaic are the surviving fragments of the northern Israelite variants of the tradition in the so-called Elohist sections, that in any case we are forced to assume that the Yahwist could not have been the creator of the epic in the sense that Von Rad suggested in 1938. Instead, behind all variants of the traditional history there must be projected something still earlier as its source.[3] That the source in question can be said to have a relation to the cult does not in itself say very much, because it is difficult to find anything that in one way or another has no relation to the worship of God. The point succinctly put is whether the cult was the originator of the traditions it celebrated. There is evidence that rites and centers of worship affected the transmission of epic materials, but our tools of research allow us to say little more than that.

2. A second assumption which can no longer be maintained is that the Sinai and exodus-conquest traditions did not originally belong together but had separate origins. One of Von Rad's three chief examples of the Israelite credo is Josh 24:2-13, but the context of that specific example is precisely a covenant ceremony. The other two are preserved in Deuteronomy, which centers its theology in the Mosaic covenant. In this theology the promises to the fathers are narrowed to an oath which God swore to the fathers to give them the land. While the conquest is the fulfillment of that oath, the question as to whether it will be kept in the future is now seen to be conditional on the keeping of the Mosaic covenant.

There must surely be another reason as to why the covenant is not mentioned in the recitations of the *magnalia Dei*. If the recitation were one part of the covenant renewal ceremony leading up to the vows, then there would be no necessary occasion to mention specifically a treaty in

---

[3] This is a position now so commonly held that the citation of a few authors is misleading. Nevertheless, for formal statements of the position, see W. F. Albright, *From the Stone Age to Christianity*, 249-254; Martin Noth, *Überlieferungsgeschichte des Pentateuchs* (Stuttgart: Kohlhammer, 1948) 40-44; D. N. Freedman, "Pentateuch," *IDB* 3, especially 726. For a recent presentation of older literary critical views, similar to those of Von Rad with regard to the Yahwist but for different reasons, see Otto Eissfeldt, *The Old Testament: An Introduction*, 129-143.

which the people took upon themselves obligations as a part of the vows which they themselves made. In the Abrahamic and Davidic types of covenants, where God himself for his own gracious reasons takes the obligations of the treaty upon himself, the event is celebrated as one of God's saving acts and it is frequently alluded to as such. This is not the case, however, with the covenant connected with the name of Moses.

Study of ancient treaty forms of the second millennium suggest that the above-mentioned solution is correct. The credo-form is a freely structured, never stereotyped, recitation of the benevolent acts of the suzerain or emperor toward the vassal with whom the treaty is being made. The purpose was clearly to place the sanctions for the obligations which followed in the context of gratitude for favor received, rather than as simply legal duty, the violation of which would bring about penalty. Hence covenant without credo in this setting is unthinkable.[4] The one is an inseparable part of the other, even though, in later literature which has survived, the recitations can be used for a variety of purposes outside of their original settings.

What, then, survives of Von Rad's presentation? Primarily it is his analysis of the structure of Israel's epic tradition and his theological penetration as to its meaning. Its history and formation is more complicated, and we lack the tools and contemporary information in order to unravel the story. We can present hypotheses, but how much weight they can carry will depend on future research and discovery. Two things, among others, are certainly clear. One is that the basic ingredients of Israel's epic as we now have it are much older than the Yahwist edition of it in tenth-century Israel. What was contributed by the individuality of the Yahwist is difficult to say, although the parabolic elements in Genesis 2-11 are among the best candidates. Another contention of Von Rad is most important; that is, the close relation of the epic material to public worship. With regard to the conquest tradition in Joshua, it is important to note its special and central role as a part of Israel's confession of the gracious work of God.

Conquest and Worship

The conquest as God's gift of land to those who had been landless appears in early as well as late sources. It thus cannot be understood as a

---

[4] See George E. Mendenhall, *Law and Covenant in Israel and the Ancient Near East=BAR* 3, 3-53, and "Covenant," *IDB* 1; Klaus Baltzer, *Das Bundesformular* (1959) tr. *The Covenant Formulary* (1971); James Muilenburg, "The Form and Structure of the Covenantal Formulations," *VT* 9 (1959) 347-365; John Bright, *A History of Israel* (1959) 132-137; and D. J. McCarthy, *Treaty and Covenant*.

primitive notion which Israel outgrew, nor as a later rationalization of something primitive.[5] The conception is primary to Israel's most primitive and most developed theology.

In Von Rad's three Hexateuchal credos embedded in later contexts the following is stated: "Us he brought out thence [from Egypt] for the purpose of bringing us in to give us the land which he promised by oath to our fathers" (Deut 6:23)—a formulation in thought and wording very much in Deuteronomic style. After the great deeds wrought by God for us in Egypt, "he brought us into this place and gave us this land, a land flowing with milk and honey" (Deut 26:9). These are the simplest of statements in which deliverance and gift are coupled without elaboration, the first using more explicit Deuteronomic language than the second. Equally simple is 1 Sam 12:8: after mention of Jacob, Egypt, Israel's cry to God for help, God's sending Moses and Aaron and his delivery of the fathers from Egypt, it is said, "he caused them to dwell in this place." This particular recital, however, is used for an occasion to confess Israel's rebellion. After these great acts of God in placing Israel in the land, "they forgot. . . ."

The covenant address of Joshua in Josh 24:2-13 is much more elaborate in drawing on various themes from the store of tradition. First it is stated that Israel's ancestors beyond the (Euphrates) River had served other gods. Then God took Abraham, led him through the land of Canaan, and gave him many offspring. Jacob went to Egypt. Then God sent Moses and Aaron, the plagues and the deliverance, with emphasis especially on the crossing of the sea and the darkness, followed by the long time in the wilderness. "I brought you to the land of the Amorites who lived on the other side of the Jordan, and they fought you. I put them in your power, and you took possession of their land" (v 8). Then comes the king of Moab's use of Balaam, the expert in divination and curses, whose oracles God turned into the blessing of Israel (cf. Numbers 23-24), so that Israel was saved from his power.

You crossed the Jordan and came to Jericho. The Jericho lords ganged up on you (the Amorites, the Perizzites, the Canaanites, the Hittites, and the

---

[5] In the analysis of the conquest theme which follows, I am indebted to a paper by Phyllis A. Bird, "The Theological Employment of the Conquest Events" (Harvard, 1966). For the monarchical images of God, including his involvement in earth's conflicts, as a purification of the ancient conception of the earthly emperor, see the writer's *Old Testament and Theology*, chaps. 3-5. This analysis suggests that the contention of Alfred North Whitehead, among others, that Christianity's greatest mistake was giving to God "the attributes which belong exclusively to Caesar" (*Process and Reality* [New York: Macmillan, 1929] 520) is an oversimplification and caricature.

Girgashites; the Hivites and the Jebusites),⁶ but I put them in your power. I sent before you The Hornet, and it drove them out on your behalf—the two Amorite kings. It was not by your sword or by your bow.⁷ I presented to you a land for which you had not labored and towns which you did not build, but on which you live. From vineyards and olive orchards which you did not plant, you eat (Josh 24:11-13).

Ezra's long prayer during his covenant renewal service has an even more complete group of traditional elements concerning the conquest. In Neh 9:22-25 Ezra, addressing God, says:

22 You gave them kingdoms and peoples; and you divided (the land among) them by parcel. They possessed the land of Sihon,⁸ king of Heshbon and the land of Og, king of Bashan. 23 Their progeny you multiplied as (the number of) the heavenly stars, and you brought them into the land which you promised our fathers they would possess. 24 ⁹You subdued before them those who lived in the land, (namely) the Canaanites. . . . 25 And they took fortified cities and a rich land. They took possession of houses full of every good thing, cisterns which had been dug out, vineyards, olive yards, fruit trees in great number. They ate, were filled, became fat and delighted in your great goodness.

Ezra's prayer is a confession of sin. Like Samuel in 1 Samuel 12, Ezra rehearses the great past events, including the conquest of Canaan, in order to contrast the righteousness of God with the unrighteousness of Israel within the good land. The result: "Lo, we today are slaves. On the land which you gave to our fathers to eat of its fruit and its good things, lo, we are slaves!" (v 36).

From these and other prose pericopes related to Israel's worship the following generalizations seem possible:

1. In Israel's worship the land is a Promised Land. The conquest is a fulfillment of promise. The old epic traditions and the Mosaic covenant theology of the Deuteronomic corpus emphasize the same theme.

2. The land was not won by Israel. It was a gift of God.

---

⁶ The original seems here to be making a specific reference to Jericho. An editor of the text appears to have taken it as including the whole of western Palestine, and thus inserted a stock list of the various peoples which tradition had preserved as the peoples of the land before Israel. The precise order and original contents of this list varies in E, D, Dtr, and LXX text traditions.

⁷ For Boling's translation of the same verses, turn to 24:12. The preceding verse, except for the editorial insertion of the list of peoples, speaks of the capture of Jericho. This verse is at least partially another editorial insertion which concerns the defeat of Sihon and Og under Moses in Transjordan (Num 21:21-35). It is a recensional variant, originally derived from the Covenant Code of tribal league times (Exod 23:28; cf. Deut 7:20), yet substituting "the two kings of the Amorites" for the list of the peoples west of the Jordan that existed in the original.

⁸ Omit "and the land of" as a mistake in the MT tradition, and instead follow 2 Esdr 19:22 (LXX).

⁹ The first two clauses are probably to be omitted, following the main uncials of the LXX.

3. In the liturgical references to the conquest noted thus far, there is little emphasis on particular battles and there are no human heroes or heroic acts mentioned. This way of recalling the conquest is uncharacteristic of most epic, which loves details of mighty deeds and battles. Sihon and Og from the Mosaic conquest in Transjordan are the only exceptions; these are mighty men who fought Israel but whom God defeated. In western Palestine no specific fighting is ever mentioned outside of the narrative in the Book of Joshua, except Jericho in Josh 24:11, and again it is the leading men (ba'ălê-yĕrîḥô) whom God subdues.

4. There is one hero, and one only. It is God himself and to him Israel must give all praise and credit.

5. In the late recitation of Ezra in Nehemiah 9, not only is the gift of the land to Israel present, but special mention is also made of God parcelling out the land to Israel, a reference to the tradition central in Joshua 13-19 in which God decides—the tribes learn the decisions by casting lots—which parts of the land are to go to the tribes in western Palestine.

6. When all of this is said, however, one is struck by the freedom and variety of expression. There are few stereotypes. Each confessional pericope shows the freedom and creativity of what was presumably already in the reservoir of oral tradition from which it was drawn, as well as the freedom individuals had in reciting from that reservoir.

In the New Testament one of the closest parallels to the old confession is to be found in the Apostle Paul's sermon in the synagogue at Antioch of Pisidia, summarized in Acts 13:16-19:

> 16b Men of Israel and you who fear God, hear (this): 17 The God of this people Israel chose our fathers and exalted the people during their day in the land of Egypt, and with uplifted arm (with great power) he led them from it. . . . 19 And when he had destroyed seven nations in the land of Canaan, he allotted them the land. . . ."[10]

The Conquest in Israel's Hymns and Psalms

Studying the references to the conquest in Israel's poetry, one becomes aware that the whole of Israel's epic story of promise (to the patriarchal fathers), deliverance from Egypt, wandering in the wilderness, and gift of

---

[10] Stephen's defense in Acts 7 has interesting variants which would lead one to suspect that it derives from a sectarian group of Jews. In vv 30-41 much is made of the greatness of Moses, reminding one of the work of Jesus ben-Sirach and II Baruch, in which much is made of the ancient human heroes of Israel in contrast to the old recitals of God's works in which human agency is scarcely mentioned. Verse 45, referring to the tent (tabernacle) of the wilderness wanderings of Israel, says most uncharacteristically that Israel's fathers with Joshua brought it "when they dispossessed the nations whom God drove out before our fathers. . . ."

a land is not always rehearsed in its entirety to make the point of God's greatness for purposes of praise or for confession of sin. It was sufficient to mention one or two items in the cluster of tradition to call to mind the whole. Further with regard to the exodus-conquest cycle, there seems to have been a tendency for the exodus event to gain the dominant position, especially in later literature. Thus, for example, the crossing of the sea (see below) appears to enfold into itself the crossing of the Jordan, the one event standing for the whole series.

In poetry Psalms 104-106 seem to be a trilogy with the most complete hymnic confession in ancient Israel's canon. Their date is presumably post-exilic, from the late sixth or fifth centuries, and thus of the same age as Ezra's prayer as recorded in Nehemiah 9. Psalm 104 is a hymn in praise of God the Creator; Psalms 105 and 106 rehearse the *magnalia Dei* for purposes of praise and confession of sin respectively. Psalm 105:7-42 presents a full statement of God's promise to the patriarchs as "an everlasting covenant"[11] and of the exodus events as fulfillment: "Indeed, he remembered his holy word and Abraham his servant" (v 42). The whole story is about what God did, not what Israel did. He made the promise, sent Moses and the plagues, led Israel from Egypt, and fed them in the wilderness. The conquest theme is briefly set within a hymnic conclusion:

> 43 He brought out his people (from Egypt) with joy,
>   With singing his selected (folk).
> 44 He gave them lands of the nations,
>   The toil of (other) people they possessed,
> 45 In order that they observe his decrees
>   And keep his laws. Hallelujah!

Psalm 106 goes over the same story again but confessing how at each juncture Israel sinned, forgot what God had done, rebelled. The only reference to the conquest here is an oblique one. The reason the event was not more successful, the reason there was still a hard time in the Promised Land, was that the people had not completed their task but polluted the good land by taking over the degrading customs of the people who remained:

> 34 They did not destroy the peoples,
>   As the Lord had commanded them to do;[12]

11 Hebrew *bĕrît 'ôlām* (in this text the words are reversed), which is the Jerusalem priesthood's (P's) understanding of the promissory covenant of God with Abraham (Genesis 17). Psalms 135 and 136 are sufficiently like Psalm 105 in date and emphasis that they will not be given separate treatment here.

12 This verse, together with the whole conception of God leading, defeating, etc., is drawn from the language of a special institution in early Israel: Holy War (see below).

35 But they mingled among the nations
And learned their customs.

36 So they served their (religious) images
Which became a snare to them.

37 They sacrificed their sons
And their daughters to the demons.

38 They poured out innocent blood,
The blood of their sons and daughters
Whom they sacrificed to the idols of Canaan

38d And the land was polluted with blood.

A much earlier psalm of an epic and confessional nature, in part comparable to Psalm 106, is 78. Yet its overall function is as an instruction, a meditation, on the fall of Israel (cf. the tent of Joseph, the tribe of Ephraim, v 67) at the battle of Shiloh (1 Samuel 4; cf. Jer 7:14) about 1050 B.C. This really meant the rejection of Joseph (the tribe of Ephraim) as the head of Israel; in his place and that of Shiloh David and Jerusalem were chosen (vv 67-72).[13] Ephraim was defeated because as a people they failed to keep God's covenant (the Mosaic rather than the Abrahamic),

11 They forgot his deeds,
His marvels which he had shown them.

After a recital of God's works on Israel's behalf in Egypt,[14] we read the following:

54 He brought them to his holy territory[15]
(To) this mountain his right hand had created.[16]

---

[13] The date is thus after the time of David (and probably during the Divided Monarchy because of the use of Ephraim for Israel), but there is no objective way otherwise to date it. The concentration of God's choice of David and of Zion (Jerusalem) means that it was composed among those in the Jerusalem court, probably sometime between the tenth and eighth centuries B.C. This dating lies between the extremes of Otto Eissfeldt's tenth-century dating (*Das Lied Moses Deut. 32:1-43 und das Lehrgedicht Asaphs Psalm 78* . . . [1958]) and the post-exilic dating of H.-J. Kraus, among others, in *Die Psalmen*, 535-548. For the use of Ephraim as a surrogate for north Israel, and for Manasseh virtually dropping from the tradition, see G. Ernest Wright, "The Provinces of Solomon," *Eretz Israel* 8 (1967) 58*-61*.

[14] These appear to include a list of seven plagues in agreement with Israel's epic sources (JE) in Exodus 7-11, in contrast to the later Psalm 105 which seems to rest on a tradition of ten plagues in agreement with Jerusalem's priesthood (P): so the writer and Joseph L. Mihelic, "The Plagues in Exodus," *IDB* 3, 822-824.

[15] The MT has gĕbûl, "border" i.e. with the border (of his land). LXX may possess the better reading since it preserves the parallelism and the mythological allusion: "he brought them to his holy mountain."

[16] A mythological allusion from Canaanite religion; see below. For this reason the verb is translated with both Canaanite and Hebrew as "created," instead of the pre-Ugaritic usual rendering, "purchased," "acquired," and thence "won" in battle (cf. for example, the old title of God as "Ēl 'Elyōn, Creator of Heaven and Earth," as rendered by all the versions of Gen 14:19).

55 He drove out nations before them;
   He allotted them (land) in a measured inheritance;[17]
   He settled the tribes of Israel in their tents.[18]

Two things about this passage may be noted especially. The first is the seemingly definite reference in a pre-exilic, and presumably early pre-exilic, poem to the tradition of the land as an allotment. We have noted the ubiquity of the theme of the land as promised and as a gift of God. Here we have a comparatively old description of the manner of the gift; God divided it among the tribes, evidently by lot. That is, the prose tradition in Joshua 13-19 rests on old pre-exilic tradition. The gift of the land does not fill out the tradition of the conquest without the mention also of God's parcelling the land among the tribes. The only way this could have been discovered by Israel was by the sacred lot. In Joshua this lot, administered by the (high) priest, Eleazar, by Joshua, and by the family or clan chieftains, is specifically referred to for those who lived in the Promised Land west of the Jordan in 14:1-5 and in 18-19.[19]

A second theme of special interest is the conquest as God's bringing Israel to the holy mountain which he himself has created (v 54). Here the allusion is mythological, originally referring to the sacred mountain in the far reaches of the north, at the juncture between heaven and earth, which is the abode of the gods in Canaanite religion. We will defer further discussion of this unusual allusion, however, until we have examined Exodus 15.

Both the J and E, southern and northern, versions of the epic of Israel included the Song of the Sea, as the psalm in Exodus 15 may be called. J attributes it to Moses and E to his sister, Miriam.[20] The weight of scholarship during the last century has viewed the poem as a comparatively late composition. In any case, it is argued, it could not date from the time

[17] This second colon of the verse is obscure, so that one cannot be entirely certain of its meaning. On the assumption that God's expulsion of the nations from his holy land should be followed by a statement concerning God's distribution of the people on the land by tribal allotments (cf. Joshua 13-19; Ezek 45:1; 47:21-22; 48:29; Neh 9:22; Acts 13:19; cf. Ps 105:44; Jonah 1:7), the passage is here so translated. The Hebrew literally is: "He made them fall, in a measured inheritance." The interpretation here given suggests that God made the sacred dice (Urim and Thummim) fall in such a way that the tribes learned which land was theirs. The term "cause to fall" was thus a technical term for "select," "allot," "make a grant of" a given piece of property. Alternate interpretations could be given, but none has the background in comparable contexts in such number.

[18] This is an archaic Hebrew expression using the verb škn in its primitive meaning, "to tent": thus literally, "he caused [was the agent in making] the tribes of Israel to tent in their tents." See F. M. Cross, BAR 1, 244.

[19] Josh 15:1; 16:1; and 17:1 all begin with the "lot" (gôrāl in MT, but strong LXX tradition has "border" gĕbûl).

[20] The J version is in vv 1b-18. E's version cites the poem only by its incipit, that is, by its first verse, or first two cola (v 21). The editors of the combined JE simply did not see the need of repeating the whole twice, but only of mentioning the divergent tradition as to authorship.

of Moses because of the mention of Philistia in v 14 and the sanctuary of Israel in v 17, which has been taken to refer to the Solomonic temple. The major settlement of the Philistines—the name of one group of peoples of the eastern Anatolian and Aegean world which Israel applied to them all—took place along Palestine's southern coastal plain about the second quarter of the twelfth century B.C. Hence one would not expect the name "Philistia" for that plain to be used until some time after the settlement.[21]

During the last two decades, following the lead of W. F. Albright,[22] attempts have been made to interpret Israel's earliest poetry by reconstructing the history of the Hebrew language. Evidence has been gathered from an ever-increasing list of inscriptions, Ugaritic and Amarna tablets, etc. This includes grammar, orthography, and prosody, and is a conscious attempt to find a more objective means of dating poetic compositions than the subjective methods based upon predetermined conclusions concerning the history of Israel's religious traditions and upon historical allusions. This method has yielded great success with tenth- and pre-tenth-century poetry and is beginning to promise equal success with late compositions, but thus far has not been of great help with the bulk of Hebrew poetry between the tenth and sixth centuries B.C. The Song of the Sea in Exodus 15 is one of the early poems which has been especially illumined by this method of analysis.[23] Cross has written:

[21] For the Ramesses III story and picture of his defeat of the Sea Peoples see *ANET*[3] 262-263, and *ANEP*, Fig. 341 (114). For the original texts and reliefs, which survive on the walls of this Pharaoh's temple at Medinet Habu at Thebes in Upper Egypt, see *Medinet Habu* I-II, by the Epigraphic Survey (Harold H. Nelson, Field Director), Oriental Institute Publications VIII-IX (University of Chicago Press, 1930-1932). For translation of the texts in these volumes, see W. F. Edgerton and J. A. Wilson, *Historical Records of Ramses III*. For a review of the current archaeological evidence, based upon personal topographical survey, and the new perspectives which it suggests, see G. E. Wright, "Fresh Evidence for the Philistine Story," *BA* 29 (1966) 70-86. The knowledge we now have for an earlier date of the Sea Peoples' destructive presence in Asia, and of the fall of the Hittite empire and of the cities of Ugarit and Alalakh during the reign of Pharaoh Merneptah (c. 1223-1211 B.C. or up to a decade earlier), does not mean that the settlement of the Philistines as military overlords of Philistia took place at the same time. Thus far the archaeological evidence requires a generation gap, though the presence of individuals from the Aegean area during the late thirteenth century B.C. has been noted from archaeological evidence: see Wright, ibid., 72-74; and for Mycenaean-type bench tombs in a thirteenth-century cemetery at Tell el-Fara (South), Jane Waldbaum, "Philistine Tombs at Tell Fara and Their Aegean Prototypes," *AJA* 70 (1966) 331-346. The standard archaeological treatment of the Philistines is that of Trude Dothan, *The Philistines and Their Material Culture*. For surveys of the final days of the Hittite empire and of Ugarit, see Albrecht Goetze, "The Hittites and Syria (1300-1200)," *CAH*[3], II, Part 2, chap. 24; and M. C. Astour, "New Evidence on the Last Days of Ugarit," *AJA* 69 (1965) 253-258.

[22] His methods were first expounded in print in his "The Psalm of Habakkuk," in *Studies in Old Testament Prophecy*, 1-18.

[23] See especially F. M. Cross and D. N. Freedman, *SAYP;* "The Song of Miriam," *JNES* 13 (1955) 237-250=*SAYP*, 45-65; and Cross, "The Song of the Sea and

The language of Exodus 15 is more consistently archaic than that of any other prose or poetic work of some length in the Bible.[24] The poem conforms throughout to the prosodic patterns and canons of the Late Bronze Age. Its use of mixed metrical structure, its baroque use of climactic repetitive parallelism, internal rhyme and assonance, place it alongside of the Song of Deborah (Judges 5). The latest comparable poems are Psalm 29 and the Lament of David (2 Samuel 1). The former is a Canaanite hymn borrowed by Israel probably in the tenth century but older in its original form. The Lament of David is doubtless a tenth-century work. While it uses an archaic elegiac meter, the patterns of climactic parallelism have wholly disappeared. In this regard it shares prosodic form with eleventh-century poems, especially Genesis 49 and Deuteronomy 33, and the tenth-century hymn, II Samuel 22=Psalm 18.[25]

We have collected some orthographic data which would suggest a tenth-century date or earlier for its being put first into writing.[26]

After celebration of the deliverance of Israel by Yahweh's drowning of Pharaoh and his army in a great storm at the Reed Sea, the last strophes of the poem (vv 13-18), as translated by Cross, recount the conquest as follows:[27]

13 You have faithfully led
　The people whom you have delivered.
　You have guided them in your might
　To your holy encampment.[28]
14 The peoples heard, they shuddered
　Horror seized the dwellers of Philistia. . . .[29]

Canaanite Myth," *Journal for Theology and the Church* 5 (1968) 1-25=*CMHE*, 121-144; Freedman, "Archaic Forms in Early Hebrew Poetry," *ZAW* 72 (1960) 101-107; and "Strophe and Meter in Exodus 15," in *A Light Unto My Path: Old Testament Studies in Honor of Jacob M. Myers*, 163-203.

Cf. also Norbert Lohfink, *Das Siegeslied am Schilfmeer*, 103-128; James Muilenburg, "A Liturgy on the Triumphs of Yahweh," in *Studia Biblica et Semitica*, 233-251.

[24] See fn 23.

[25] Cf. F. M. Cross and D. N. Freedman, "A Royal Song of Thanksgiving," *JBL* 72 (1953) 15-34=*SAYP*, 125-158.

[26] "The Song of Miriam" [fn 23], 243-250. The quotation just given is taken from "The Song of the Sea and Canaanite Myth" [fn 23], 10=*CMHE*, 121.

[27] I have taken the liberty of changing, among other things, Cross's "Thou" into contemporary idiom, though the latter fails in the distinction between the second person singular and plural which the Hebrew preserves.

[28] The noun here designates a tent shrine, and refers to Israel's "tabernacle" (*miškān* or *'ōhel 'mô'ēd*) as established at Mount Sinai, Kadesh, Shittim, or Gilgal.

[29] Cross believes that the prosody suggests a third colon has been lost from this line.

Verses 13-14 are the fourth strophe in the Cross reconstruction. The fifth strophe (vv 15-16) elaborates v 14: the leaders of Edom and Moab were immobilized by "terror and dread" and "struck dumb like a stone" —one of God's devices to ensure the safety of Israel. The final strophe (vv 16c-18) recounts the entry into the Promised Land, beginning with the crossing of the Jordan, as follows:

> 16c When your people passed over, Yahweh,
>   When your people passed over whom you created,
> 17 You brought them (in), you planted them
>   In the mount of your heritage,
> The dais of your throne
>   Which you made, Yahweh,
> The sanctuary, Yahweh,
>   Which your hands created.
>
> 18 Yahweh will reign
>   Forever and ever!

The conquest is God's bringing Israel into the Promised Land, his planting them there in the mountain of his "heritage," the place of his temple, either in the cosmic realm or its counterpart on earth, from which his sovereignty is to be exercised forever. Here again, as in Psalm 78, God's putting Israel in the land is recorded with allusions drawn from Canaanite myth. The "mount of your heritage" is, as Cross puts it, "a standard way for any poet, in Ugarit or in Israel, to specify the special seat of deity," the land which is the special property of a divine being.[30] In this case, the old mythical terms are used to refer to the Promised Land, the land or hill country of Canaan. This is Yahweh's land, his "heritage." There his "abode" or "sanctuary" exists as an earthly visible sign of his cosmic temple on the cosmic mountain, as Canaanite myth would understand it. Yet the temple is not simply an anthropomorphic concept of a place in space. Its primary connotation is political; it signifies sovereignty, the cosmic rule or kingdom of God.

The themes and language here are too old, too deeply a part of Israel's world, to allow one to see them as solely a reference to the Solomonic temple and Mount Zion (Jerusalem), though the same language was used of that temple. The mythic cosmogony begins with the divine warrior's victory over the dragon of chaos (also called Prince Sea, Judge River,

---

[30] Cross, "The Song of the Sea . . ." [fn 23], 23-24=*CMHE*, 125. See also Von Rad, "The Promised Land and Yahweh's Land in the Hexateuch," in *The Form Critical Problem* . . . , 79-93. For detailed treatment of *naḥălâh*, the Hebrew term for "heritage" or "inheritance," see the Harvard dissertation of Harold Forshey (1970).

Leviathan, Rahab, the Serpent [with seven heads]), and concludes with his erecting his sanctuary on his "mountain of inheritance" and the establishment of his eternal kingship.[31]

How could Israelite poets use Canaanite myth as an adequate exposition of the meaning of the conquest, when such myths meant little more to them in a literal sense than John Milton's elaborate use of Greco-Roman mythic themes meant to his contemporaries? What Israel celebrated in cultic tale and song was shaped by the historical experiences which were remembered and recited as the gracious acts of the God who created the new community, and even the world of the Canaanite deities. Covenant renewal festivals reenacted these epic events for community renewal. Yet Israel thought it meaningful to make poetic use of the age-old mythic patterns. The symbolic power of this pattern was evidently great indeed. Thus to speak of the conquest as God's bringing Israel to his holy mountain, or planting her in the "mount of his heritage," following which he will be known as eternal sovereign, is to take what to Israel was a pivotal event and set it apart from other earthly happenings. It was a deed of cosmic and eternal significance, the mythical expressions revealing the truly transcendent meaning of the event, without loss of its historical nature.

Another psalm, later than Exodus 15 though otherwise undatable, interprets the crossing of the Jordan as God's triumphant conflict with the Sea(-dragon of chaos)—an allusion to the Canaanite creation myth. This is Psalm 114, which may be read as follows:

> 1 When Israel went forth from Egypt,
>   The household of Jacob from a foreign-tongued nation,
> 2 Judah became his holy (place),
>   And Israel his royal dominion.
> 3 The Sea looked and fled;
>   The Jordan turned backwards.
> 4 The mountains danced like rams,
>   Hills like the young of sheep.
> 5 What is the matter, O Sea, that you flee,
>   O Jordan, that you turn backwards,
> 6 O mountains, that you dance like rams,
>   O hills, like the young of sheep?
> 7 Before the Sovereign tremble, O earth,
>   Before the God of Jacob,
> 8 He who transforms the rock into a pool of water,
>   Flint into a spring of water.

[31] For more detail with references, see Cross, "The Song of the Sea," 2-9, 24.

In vv 3 and 5 Sea and Jordan are in synonymous parallelism and are addressed as a person who fled, turned backward, in fear at Yahweh's approach. In Israelite historical tradition this can be seen as an allusion to the Jordan waters which are said to have stood still, rising in a hill or heap (Hebrew *nēd*), so that Israel crossed the Jordan bed "on dry ground" (Josh 3:16-17). On the other hand, the personalizing of Sea and River recall the several poetic allusions elsewhere to Yahweh's battle with the dragon of chaos, the latter under a variety of appellations.

Psalm 74 is a lament after a national defeat and a prayer to God for aid. The psalmist's confidence rests on his remembrance of God's great works of creation:

> 12 Yet God is my king of old,
>   A worker of saving deeds[32] in earth's midst.
> 13 (It is) you who divided Sea by your power;
>   You who shattered the heads of Tannin on the water;
> 14 You who crushed the heads of Leviathan,
>   You gave him for food to . . .[33]
> 16 Yours is day, yours also night;
>   (It is) you who created light and sun;
> 17 You who established all earth's bounds;
>   Summer and winter, you (it is who) has formed them.

In Ugaritic texts Baal defeats the Sea-dragon of chaos (*Yamm, Lōtān,* etc.) in order to establish his dominion and orderly government over earth:

> Sea fell,
>   He sank to earth;
> His joints trembled,
>   His frame collapsed.
> Ba'l destroyed,
>   Drank Sea;
>   He finished off Judge River.

The shout of victory then is heard and the statement of Baal's lordship:

> Sea verily is dead;
>   Ba'l rules![34]

Then follows the building of Baal's palace (temple) on Mount Zaphon (North) with a great feast of the gods celebrating Baal's installation as

---

32 Or "victories."

33 Hebrew obscure; literally, "to people, to wastelands."

34 Translation is that of Cross, "The Song of the Sea," 3-4=*CMHE*, 115-116, of Ugaritic text 2.4. 25-32, following the numbering of the Ugaritic texts by A. Herdner, *Corpus des tablettes en cunéiform alphabétique* (Paris: Paul Geuthner, 1963).

the world's suzerain and the inauguration of the regular services of his temple.[35]

The application of this theme to the crossing of the Reed Sea in Egypt and to the crossing of the Jordan suggests that Israel was not a simple desert folk, untutored in the ways of Canaan. In liturgy and hymns her poets evidently expected worshipers to understand rather sophisticated allusions to the neighbor's mythology, whereby her own creative and formative period was described mythically to suggest the manner of God's establishing of his sovereignty over Israel. The creation of the world represented that powerfully divine activity which was again seen in exodus and conquest traditions from Israel's own history.

Psalm 106, to which reference has already been made, personalizes the Egyptian Reed Sea that Israel crossed, as Psalm 114 does the Jordan:

> 8 He saved them for his name's sake
>   To reveal his mighty power.
> 9 He threatened [rebuked] Reed Sea and it dried up,
>   And he led them through Deep(s)[36] as through a desert.

Most vivid, for purposes of illustration of the use of myth for the Reed Sea crossing is the exilic (c. 540 B.C.) passage, Isa 51:9-11:

> 9 Awake, awake, dress in power, O arm of Yahweh!
>   Awake as in bygone days, the generations of antiquity!
>   Was it not you who cut in pieces Rahab, the writhing Tannin?
> 10 Was it not you who dried up Sea, the waters of the great deep?
>   Who made of Sea's depths a highway for the crossing of the redeemed?
> 11 Yahweh's ransomed shall return and enter Zion with a shout!

Here the creation battle with the chaos-dragon is the same battle as that which occurred in Egypt, the release into time of the same power which shall release the captives in exile for a second exodus, a second return to the holy city of Jerusalem.[37] The reference to the drying up of Sea here serves to bring to mind the whole epic story of Israel's deliverance and gift of a land, which is the ground for the confidence that God will bring those in exile back to their holy city again.

Psalm 66:5-7 has a similar single reference for the whole story whereby God established his dominion, his sovereignty forever:

[35] Following the generally accepted order of reading the Ugaritic texts. See Text 4 in Herdner, and Cross, ibid.

[36] The *Yam Suph* in Egypt is equated in the poetic parallelism with the great deep or deeps (sweet and salt) surrounding the universe in ancient thought which in myth were the chaos-dragon(s).

[37] For elaboration of this point, see Wright, *The Old Testament and Theology*, 70-81, 121-126. For a pre-exilic use of the creation theme in the context of Jerusalem's royal theology, see Ps 89:9-10[10-11H]. For the quieting of sea and the curbing of the uproar of peoples coupled in this background, see Psalm 65:7[8H].

5 Come and see the deeds of God
   The Awesome One in his work among the children of men.
6 He turned Sea to dry land;
   Through the Stream they passed on foot;
   There we rejoiced in him.
7 He is ruler by his power forever.
   His eyes watch over the nations—
   Let not the rebellious exalt themselves!

Since the personalizing of Sea can be used to exalt the meaning of both the Egyptian crossing of the Reed Sea and the crossing of the Jordan (cf. Psalm 65), we cannot tell in this case for certain which event may be in mind. Yet it does not matter, for the reference in this way to a single episode recalls the whole series, even as v 5 implies.[38]

The conquest as God's "planting" of Israel in the land was a figure of speech used as early as Exod 15:17. Two other comparable references are in Psalms 80 and 44. Verses 8-9 and 11[9-10 and 12H] of Psalm 80 read as follows:

8 A vine out of Egypt you removed;
   You expelled nations and planted it.
9 You cleared (the ground) for it,
   Made its root take root
   And fill the land. . . .
11 It sent its branches to the sea [Mediterranean],
   To the river [Euphrates] its suckers.

The context is a hymn of prayer by a people in trouble. The appeal for help is based upon the known power and mercy of God from past events, to which this verse is an allusion.[39] Psalm 44 is a comparable prayer from a similar context of trouble. Verses 1-8[2-9H] read as follows:

1 O God, with our ears we have heard,
   Our fathers have told us,
   How you worked in their days,
   You, in days of old, by your power;
2 How you dispossessed nations, but planted them [the fathers].
   How you hurt peoples, but saved them [the fathers].
3 Indeed it was not by their own sword that they possessed the land,
   Nor by their own arm did they save themselves;
   But it was by your right hand, your arm,

---

[38] For a comparable reference to that in Psalm 66, see Ps 77:16-20[17-21H].

[39] Otto Eissfeldt, "Psalm 80," in *Geschichte und Altes Testament*, 65-78, makes a good case for dating this psalm in north Israel after c. 733-732 B.C., when parts of Israel's "vine" had been amputated by Assyria. H.-J. Kraus also sees northern authorship but a century later in time, when under Josiah hope of restoration under the Davidic dynasty was present (see his *Psalmen*2 in *Biblisher Kommentar*).

Your good pleasure, that you showed them favor.
4 You indeed are my king, O God,
  Who commands the salvation of Jacob.[40]
5 By you we thrust back our adversaries;
  By your name we trample our assailants.
6 Indeed, not in my bow can I trust;
  My sword cannot save me.
7 But you have saved me from our adversaries;
  Those who hate us you have shamed.
8 God it is we praise every day;
  In your name forever do we glory.

In these passages we find another extension of meaning beyond the conquest event itself. While mythological allusion served to heighten the cosmic meaning and importance of the conquest as God's work as creator, and the release into the affairs of earth of a power working salvation, here reference to the past action of God against Israel's foes becomes the ground of hope and generalization concerning present and future. The turmoil of Israel on the Palestinian land-bridge is met by a faithful confidence in God's saving power, his protection against enemies. The setting for such confidence is early found in a reference to the conquest in a hymn of the eleventh century B.C. Deut 33:27-29 reads:

27 His refuge is the God of old;
   Under him are the arms of the Eternal One.
   And he drove out before you the enemy
   . . . .[41]
28 Israel encamps in safety;
   Securely apart dwells Jacob.
   Upon his land are grain and wine
   Yea, his heavens drip down dew.
29 How fortunate are you, O Israel!
   O Israel, who is like you!
   A people who found safety in Yahweh,
   Whose shield is your help,
   Whose sword your glory!
   Your enemies fawn upon you,
   But you upon their backs tread.[42]

The conquest as thus used becomes the ground for hymnic themes which assert faith and hope to later Israel caught within the imperialisms

[40] There is a textual problem here. The received text has the imperative "command," but the rendering given fits the context better and accords with certain versions; we read *mṣwh*, the *m* lost by haplography.
[41] Something appears to be wrong with the text of the second colon of this line.
[42] Translation from *SAYP*, 103. See also F. M. Cross and D. N. Freedman, "The Blessing of Moses," *JBL* 68 (1948) 191-210=*SAYP*, 97-122.

of the succession of powers during the first millennium B.C. We may thus
conclude this section with reference to one such hymn of praise, Psalm 9.
With backward look the Psalmist explains how God has to be praised in
song because he has defeated the enemies and their cities have vanished
in ruins. Now Yahweh is forever enthroned and judges the people of the
world in justice and equity. He therefore is a stronghold for all who are
oppressed or in trouble (vv 1-10[2-11H]). The final prayer of the psalm
is a plea (Hebrew vv 20-21):

> 19 Arise, O Yahweh! Let not man prevail;
>   May the nations be judged before thee.
> 20 O Lord, place fear within them;
>   Let the nations know that they are mere mortals.

In prophecy we may observe the use of the same themes in many of the
various ways already noted in Israel's psalms and hymns. Most frequent,
however, is the confession of God's beneficence as the background for the
indictment of Israel. Well known, for example, are the recitals in Hosea
11 about God's rearing his son who rebelled, and in Hos 13:4-6 about
God alone being savior in Egypt and in the wilderness, though when the
people had their hunger satiated, "their heart became proud; therefore
they forgot . . ." (cf. Deut 32:15). The contexts of Amos 2:9-10; Mic
6:4-5; Jer 2:6-7; 32:20-23; and Ezek 20:5-6 (cf. Isa 37:25-27=
2 Kgs 19:24-26) are similar. Hab 3:4-15, on the other hand, is a fresh
composition, filled with mythological allusions and ways of expression—
surely archaizing after the manner of some of Israel's earliest poetry. The
Egyptian salvation and the conquest are the actions of the Divine Warrior
in combat against the basic elements of the universe, with pestilence, sun,
and moon as his allies; River(s) (in parallelism with Sea), the eternal
mountains, and the deep are those who were shattered, who, terrified, had
surrendered. Here again the mythical serves to heighten the meaning of
what was singular and particular in the tradition. The epic events of
Egypt and Canaan are of universal significance, and the whole can be
spoken in terms which remind one of Canaanite cosmogony, while the
battles are generalized, so that Israel may understand the whole history of
earth's warfare as the divine battle for justice.[43]

In Micah 4-6 there are two items in the conquest traditions to which
allusion is made; the first and simpler is the Balaam story. The prophet
then uses the laconic expression "from Shittim to Gilgal, so that (there
be) knowledge of Yahweh's saving acts" (or "victories") (Mic 6:5).
Shittim was the place of encampment in the eastern Jordan valley at the
foot of the hills of Moab where Israel stayed after Moses' conquest of

---

[43] On this psalm, see W. F. Albright, "The Psalm of Habukkuk."

Transjordan and before the crossing of the Jordan (Num 25:1; cf. 36:13; Josh 2:1; 3:1). It is also the location of Israel when the idolatrous event of Baal-peor (Numbers 25) took place, to which Hos 9:10 alludes, and is implicitly the setting for the speeches of Moses in Deuteronomy. If one reexamines the various confessional recitals with these references in mind, he will recall one peculiarity. The conquest of western Palestine is almost always generalized as God's gift, God's warfare against the wicked, the gift of orchards, towns, and houses which Israel did not plant or build, the gift of a good land filled with food. The sole particularized events have to do with the Mosaic conquest of Transjordan, with the defeat of Sihon and Og, or more rarely with Balaam and Baal-peor. Nehemiah 9, which is a comparatively full listing of nearly all traditional elements, as would be expected in such a late composition, mentions Sihon and Og (v 22) before generalizing on the remainder of the conquest. So also do Pss 135:11 and 136:19-20. The confession of national sin in Psalm 106 mentions only the Baal of Peor.

While there is no possibility of proof, it can be supposed that these uneven characteristics of the tradition suggest a more complicated history than can now be recovered. In the time of Joshua and again in the time of the first king, Saul (Joshua 3-4; 9:6; 10:6-9,15; 1 Sam 11:15; 15:20-21), Gilgal in the Jordan valley near Jericho served as Israel's central sanctuary for special celebrations and convocations of the tribal league. It continued to serve as a sacred place where cultic rites were conducted at least as late as the eighth century B.C. (cf. Amos 4:4; 5:5; Hos 4:15; 9:15; 12:11[12H]). Even in the Byzantine period a church of the twelve stones existed at the site, commemorating the ceremony and sacred tradition of Josh 4:8 and 20, according to the Madeba map of the Holy Land.[44] Passover celebrations in Gilgal might be expected to commemorate the crossing of the Jordan, and the exodus and conquest events to that point, including only the Transjordan events in the latter. If so, then the disjuncture in the traditions of the conquest could find ready explanation by the incorporation of the special Gilgal celebrations into those of all Israel at Shiloh and Jerusalem.[45]

[44] Dating from c. the mid-sixth century B.C. See P. Palmer and H. Guthe, *Die Mosaikkarte von Madeba* (Leipzig: K. Baedeker, 1905) for the best reproduction. For up-to-date discussions of it, see R. T. O'Callaghan, "Madaba, Carte de," *Dictionnaire de la Bible, Supplement* V, cols. 627-704; M. Avi-Yonah, *The Madaba Mosaic Map;* and V. R. Gold, "The Mosaic Map of Madeba," *BA* 21 (1958) 50-71=*BAR* 3, 366-389.

[45] On an attempt to assess the importance of a Gilgal cult and its manner of incorporation in the worship of Israel, see F. M. Cross, "The Divine Warrior in Israel's Early Cult," in *Biblical Motifs: Origins and Transformations, Studies and Texts* III (Harvard University Press, 1966) 11-30=*CMHE*, 91-111, especially 103-104. Cf. also Von Rad, *The Form Critical Problem . . . ,* especially 41-48; and especially H.-J. Kraus, *Worship in Israel,* 152-165.

The first exodus as the model for the second exodus from exile of eschatological hope in prophecy and apocalyptic (cf. Zech 10:8-12) has already been mentioned. Of special interest is the new allotment of the land based on the old tradition of allotment of the land of promise in the idealized portrayals of past and future by the Jerusalem priesthood (Numbers 34 and Ezekiel 48). This again must be assumed to indicate how deeply set in the tradition was God's gift of the land to individual tribes, as a human determination by lot. The result was that the language of the lot became specialized for the divine distribution of the land by parcels, not merely to all Israel, but also to individual tribes and families. Thus, in theory, the priests held that land capitalism and land profligacy were absolutely forbidden because the land was God's (Lev 25:23).

The Divine Warrior

Throughout the confessional use of the conquest theme, as well as in the Book of Joshua itself, the central background model for conceiving the meaning of the tradition was the sovereign Lord acting in his role as Warrior against forces opposing his will and in behalf of his chosen agent, Israel. The march through the wilderness from Egypt to Canaan is pictured in poetry as well as in prose as a triumphant march of the divine commander in chief leading his earthly and heavenly forces from the Sinai wilderness to victory,[46] having chosen to do this for the most lowly of people, a group of state slaves in Egypt. The whole power of the universe is his, and he works for his own, often mysterious, will. He has set his course to create a new people and to provide them a land, and those on earth, including the newly liberated people, were expected to follow. Lack of faith-faithfulness had its penalties, one of which was the lost generation of those who came out of Egypt. All of them save Joshua and Caleb died in the wilderness, and the conquest was achieved only with a new generation (see especially the old epic narrative in Numbers 13-14; and the interpretation of the affair by the Deuteronomic historian, Deut 1:19-46).

In other words, the conception of active power here cannot be equated with Israel's nationalism after the manner described by Ludwig Feuerbach as follows:

> Man—this is the mystery of religion—projects his being into objectivity, and then makes himself an object to this projected image of himself thus converted into a subject. . . .[47]

---

[46] See Cross, "The Divine Warrior . . ." [fn 45] *passim.*
[47] *The Essence of Christianity,* tr. George Eliot, introductory essay by Karl Barth (New York: Harper, 1957) 29-30.

While this generalization could be defended in the roughest of terms,[48] it is problematic as a satisfactory answer to the particular forms of any world religion, and certainly of the manner in which Israel's God was perceived. He was conceived to be entirely independent in his exercise of power, one who set his own course which customarily did not coincide with Israel's willingness to follow. Slaves freed but still the responsible vassals of a cosmic emperor who tolerated no rivals, no materializations, no sharing of power or religious attention—is Feuerbach's expectation the normal one for a motley group of the world's dispossessed who were projecting their own being into objectivity? Certainly the free independence of the deity means that his being cannot be related to the American "Uncle Sam," the British "John Bull," or Hitler's *Das Reich,* projections of a sense of nationality.

The specific context of the Divine Warrior motif—with its concomitant component for the Israelite of a radical faith-faithful response, or, on the part of God's foes, of terror, dread, becoming dumb, incapable of fighting so that the victory was always Yahweh's—was early Israel's institution which modern scholars have been calling "Holy War." The term at this point should not be generalized through our frequent observations that all wars are thought by the participants to be sanctified by the sacred institutions of both sides of the conflict. The Crusades are a great Christian example of warfare deemed sacred, for the true God was using the Crusaders against the infidel. The modern Muslim *jehad,* with which leaders frequently attempt to mobilize a united Arab war against Israel, has likewise become too generalized as a comparison. Nevertheless, the *jehad* was originally a direct borrowing of Islam from Jewish traditions. The original institution survives to this day among the *Hasidim,* or ultra-orthodox of Judaism. The Dead Sea scroll of the "War Between the Children of Light and the Children of Darkness" is an elaborate description of how the final war before the Kingdom comes is to be waged. The Essenes of the scrolls lost life and their Qumran center because they chose the wrong war, supposing the one with the Romans in A.D. 66 to be the final one. In theory the modern *Hasidim* of Israel maintain a position similar to that of the Essenes. They do not recognize the modern state of

[48] For example, along the lines of Bultmann's demythologizing program, that actually turns into a de-symbolizing process of frames of reference of which an individual in his individualized experience of life may disapprove, and resymbolizing in the specific terms of Heidegger's existentialism; or along the lines of a much older understanding of the nature of religious language which began in the biblical period itself; e.g. Wright, *The Old Testament and Theology,* chap. 6 and references there cited; J. L. Moreau, *Language and Religious Language* (Philadelphia: Westminster, 1961); S. M. Ogden, *Christ Without Myth* (New York: Harper, 1961); G. D. Kaufman, *Systematic Theology,* especially 117-133.

Israel because it is not God's final government in the time of his ultimate Kingdom.

Some data have been assembled about early Israelite institutions, but our knowledge is limited.[49] We can certainly say that with the introduction of the monarchic state and its professional army during the course of the tenth century, the *institution* of sacred war faded away, though later prophets, the north Israelite "Deuteronomic" theology, as well as many of the passages dealing with the exodus and conquest cited above, retain its ideology as the background of their thought. It is central to both Jewish and early Christian apocalyptic. Early Christians had a mission comparable to that assigned the Servant in Second Isaiah (e.g. Isaiah 42:1-9; 53), but behind the scenes God himself was carrying on warfare against his enemies with the result that men could have hope, even in a dismal history. The little apocalypse of Mark 13 (cf. Matthew 24; Luke 21:5-36) and the Apostle Paul's picture of divine warfare against Satan or the principalities and powers of darkness are illustrations of this conflict as the setting of the early church. Certain branches of that church loved to elaborate more explicit and detailed pictures of the last days before the inbreaking of the new heavens and the new earth. The Book of Revelation is an example, and it has had its successors from that time to this.

The books of Deuteronomy and Joshua preserve the flavor and even some details about the institutions of Holy War more than other Old Testament literature, especially if we except certain hymnic and prophetic poetry. Note these instructions in Deuteronomy 20, for example: when you encounter an army larger than your own, do not be afraid for the God who brought you out of the land of Egypt is with you. When you draw near to battle, a priest shall address you, presumably to make the official declaration, "This is God's war; therefore, do not fear or tremble or be in dread of your enemies, for God goes before you. He is the warrior and will give the victory." Then officers shall pass through the army asking: "Who is afraid; who has a new house, a new vineyard, a waiting one betrothed, or a new bride? Let him return home!" As in the story of Gideon (Judges 7), numbers mean nothing in this type of war. God is the Warrior, and what is needed on Israel's part is a radical faith-faithfulness to follow him without any fear whatever. Before battle the army evidently underwent some sort of ritual cleansing (cf. Josh 3:5) and among the re-

---

[49] Contemporary discussion of Israel's early institution of Holy War was started by Gerhard von Rad, *Der Heilige Krieg im Alten Testament* (1951), which was summarized in the same writer's *Studies in Deuteronomy* (1953), and in part in G. E. Wright, "Deuteronomy," *IB*, vol. 2 (1963). See also Cross, "The Divine Warrior" [fn 45]. The most complete treatment, including evidence outside the Bible for a similar phenomenon, is P. D. Miller, Jr., *The Divine Warrior in Early Israel.*

quirements one was to refrain from sexual intercourse (cf. Uriah's remarks to David in 2 Sam 11:11). When Israel approached a city in the conquest, according to the tradition of Deut 20:10-18, peace was first offered. If rejected, and if that city was within the Promised Land where Israel was herself to live, then it was under the dreaded ban (*herem*). No living person or animal was to be taken as booty. No profit whatever was permissible because all was ritually unclean. All must be killed in a holocaust offered up as a purification ceremony so that the land might be "cleansed" for Israel's occupation.

Needless to say, this sounds to us today like a particularly vivid example of primitivism and fanaticism. To make sense of it in biblical terms, one must recall two central points in biblical theology: (1) God works in this world mediately, through chosen agents whether they know it or not; and (2) the divine use of an agent confers no special righteousness or merit on the agent. God uses people as they are. Thus, he chose Jacob instead of his brother Esau, but Jacob's morality, or lack of it, was certainly not the ground of choice. The sin of Israel, God's agent against the Canaanites, is constantly emphasized. The specially vivid passage in Deuteronomy 9 is one place where the conquest ideology is explicit on this point. God had his own purposes in choosing Israel. The people were certainly not to think that God was rewarding their superior righteousness in defeating the Canaanites. Quite the contrary! Indeed, the chapter gives detailed specification that Israel had been rebellious from the very beginning of God's actions in her behalf. Ezekiel 16 is even more vividly explicit on the point. At the same time God used the Aramean ("Syrian"), Assyrian, and Babylonian armies as his agents against covenant-breaking Israel. Yet that did not make the agents righteous by any means (cf. Isa 10:5-19 for the classic statement in prophecy on the point).

War is a miserable business in a world of men who live in rebellion against the conditions of their creation. Yet God as Suzerain is not defeated. He uses people as they are, to further his own, often mysterious, ends. Hence by implication, we must say that God's use of Israel and her early institution of Holy War does not invest either war or Israel with sanctity or righteousness. On the contrary both are evil; yet God used Israel as she was for his own purposes. And among the results was the creation of the seedbed for Judaism, Jesus Christ, and the Christian movement.

The Holy War ideology which gave all credit to Israel's Lord is precisely the reason for the omission of battles and heroes and the emphasis on Yahweh as sole actor, the sole Warrior. Thus whether in narrative or cultic confessions and hymns it is always God's goodness and justice which are the assumed context of the conquest. Whether the language speaks of God's gift of the Promised Land, of God planting his vine, of his assuming the cosmic kingship on his holy mountain, of his leading his people across Sea or River, of his conquest of the chaos-dragon, of his use of Balaam's magic to praise Israel, of his defeat of Pharaoh and his armies or of great and mighty kings, or of all his terrestrial enemies—it is always within the context of the conception of cosmic government, of world order and the rule of law. War and conflict, to which biblical people were more individually and continually associated than the individual American, were thus always assumed to fall within God's active government of the world. Though in later literature many an Israelite found it hard to discern what individual experiences meant, and conceptions of innocent and vicarious suffering came into being—and even a suffering love in God himself—there was never an assumption that providence could be unjust, though Job and his friends debated the issue. Hence even Holy War as an institution of early Israel cannot be separated from the larger conceptions of divine justice and the divine use of human agencies for his own purposes, without conferring righteousness on the agent or detracting from the righteousness of the Divine Warrior.

It must be assumed that basic themes in Israel's hymnic literature—such as the enthronement of Yahweh as creator-lord over the world, the conquest of his enemies, the procession of the Ark symbolizing the crossing of the Jordan ("from Shittim to Gilgal") and/or the bringing of the Ark to Jerusalem (2 Samuel 6), regardless of their particular order in the variety of special services, together with the vows of Israel and the promised blessings and the threatened curses of God in the Mosaic covenant and/or the eternal promise of God in the Abrahamic (Genesis 15 and 17) and Davidic (cf. 2 Samuel 7) covenants, again depending upon particular times and places—all of these must have been material from which Israel drew the motifs that were central in services of worship.

If so, then one such theme must have been the "ritual conquest," whether of the Promised Land, or in more generalized form of the enemies of God's work in the world. To point out the importance of this "ritual conquest," and to establish a hypothesis on its history and transformation from Gilgal, to Solomonic Jerusalem, to exilic and post-exilic apocalyptic, is a central purpose of Frank M. Cross in his work cited above.[50]

A particularly vivid example of the ritual conquest is found in Ps 24:6-10, which Cross believes to be "a tenth century B.C. liturgical piece." His translation is as follows:

[50] Cross [fnn 23 and 45]=*CMHE*, 77-114. The seriousness with which such discussions are taken, whether full agreement on every statement in them is reached or not, depends upon the seriousness with which one takes contemporary work in the reconstruction of Canaanite grammar and prosody and the insight it has given into early Israelite prosody. On Psalm 24, see also *CMHE*, 91-99.

This is the "circle"[51] which seeks your presence, Yahweh,
Which desires the presence of the Bull of Jacob:

Lift up, O Gates, your heads,
Lift yourselves up, ancient doors,
And the king of glory will enter.

Who is this king of glory?
Yahweh mighty and valiant,
Yahweh the warrior.

Lift up, O Gates, your heads,
Lift yourselves up, ancient doors,
And the king of glory will enter.

Who is this king of glory?
Yahweh of [Heavenly] armies,
He is the king of glory.

On one side, one can see reflected here the reenactment of the creation victory of God and his entrance into his city and (cosmic) temple as victorious king to be enthroned. Yet at the same time as the Canaanite mythical pattern can be noted, it is improbable that the Israelite would have been thinking primarily in mythical terms. On the contrary, the psalm probably celebrated for the Israelite the return of Yahweh as Warrior-Emperor from victorious conflict with his enemies—or liturgically after a procession with the Ark and at the entry in spring or fall New Year's service into the temple courts. The preceding verses thus specify who can properly follow into the courts: he who has "clean hands and a pure heart."

For another liturgical aspect, we recall the final verses of Exodus 15 already quoted above:

When your people passed over, Yahweh,
    When your people passed over whom you created,
You brought them (in), you planted them
    In the mount of your heritage, . . .
The sanctuary, Yahweh,
    Which your hands created.

Yahweh will reign
    Forever and ever!

The Canaanite background in these verses has been mentioned. Yet the Israelite worshiper would have been thinking of something more concrete: Israel's crossing the Jordan under the leadership of the Divine

---

[51] Meaning, as in Canaanite, "council" or "assembly": see F. M. Cross, "The Council of Yahweh in Second Isaiah," *JNES* 12 (1953) 274 n. 1, and references there cited.

Warrior, "the glorious King" who established his rule over the conquered Promised Land forever as a foretaste of his eternal kingdom. Old epithets of this glorious King were *gibbôr milḥāmâ*, literally, "mighty warrior in war," and Yahweh Sabaoth, literally "He (who) creates the Armies" (celestial primarily, for those of earth were merely followers). One of the lost sources of Israel's early poetry is the "Songs of the Wars of Yahweh" (Num 21:14), evidently about "the wars of Canaan" (Judg 3:1).

The passage of Israel through the wilderness has been mentioned as poetically a picture of a processional march of Yahweh and his cosmic army. The Song of Deborah from the period of the Judges begins with this theme (Judg 5:4-5):

> When Yahweh went forth from Seir
> In his stridings from the steppes of Edom,
> Earth shook, mountains shuddered . . .
> Before Yahweh, the One of Sinai,
> Before Yahweh, God of Israel.[52]

From the same period is the hymn in Deut 33:2-3 as reconstructed by Cross and D. N. Freedman:[53]

> Yahweh from Sinai came,
> He beamed forth from Seir to us,
> He shone from Mount Paran.
> With him were myriads of holy ones,
> At his right hand proceeded the divine ones,
> Yea, the purified of the peoples.

In this passage there is no question but that the wilderness wandering is conceived as the introduction of the Divine Warrior marching on his way to Canaan with his heavenly host.

In early or proto-apocalyptic, the dominance of the "ritual" conquest, procession of the Divine Warrior (symbolized by the procession of the Ark), and the exultant acknowledgment of Yahweh's sovereignty over the world play important thematic roles. Second Isaiah's place in this development has already been noted when Isa 51:9-11 was quoted. Isaiah 40:3-6 and 52:7-12 are further examples of the highway prepared for the return of the Divine Warrior, bringing captives he has released by his victorious conquests. The procession returns to Zion to celebrate the kingship of Yahweh. "For Yahweh goes before you, the God of Israel your rear guard" (Isa 52:12).

The end of the biblical path on the influence of the conquest theme can

---

[52] Translation of Cross in "The Divine Warrior" [fn 45], 25. Cf. *CMHE*, 101.
[53] Ibid. Cf. Num 10:35-36; 23:22-24; 24:8-9; Ps 68:7-8[8-9H]; Hab 3:3-15.

be summarized without going into detailed exposition of Christian adaptation of the apocalypticism of certain Jewish communities.[54]

> Late Prophetic eschatology was born of this wedding of the kingship and the Conquest themes in the cultus. The Day of Yahweh is the day of victory in holy warfare; it is also the Day of Yahweh's festival, when the ritual Conquest was reenacted in the procession of the Ark, the procession of the King of Glory to the Temple, when "God went up with the festal blast, Yahweh with the sound of the horn . . . for Yahweh is king of the whole earth" (Ps 47:6,8).
>
> In apocalyptic, the battle of the sons of light and darkness—the Second Conquest—becomes a central feature of the last days. At the same time it is the time of the manifestation of the kingdom of God, when the dark powers of chaos and evil are subdued, and the new heavens and earth created. Here mythic and historical themes are recombined in a radical tension.

> Arise, O Warrior,
> Take thy captives, O Glorious One,
> And gather thy spoil, Doer of Valor.
> Put forth thy hand on the neck of thy enemies,
> And thy foot on the heaps of the slain
> . . . .
> O Zion, rejoice exceedingly.
> Break forth with joyful song, O Jerusalem,
> And exult, all ye cities of Judah.
>
> Open thy gates forever,
> That [men] may bring to thee the wealth of nations,
> And their kings serve thee.[55]

As one considers the range of the material surveyed, it is not an exaggeration, therefore, to say that the traditions of the Book of Joshua must stand in the very center of any consideration of biblical religion. A proper commentary on the book is centrally a theological task, one made the more difficult by the fact that no such commentary has been produced in modern times. During the last two centuries, when the movement of historical criticism reached maturity, the theological counterpart of historical evolution was "progressive revelation." During this period the Book of Joshua has been considered the most primitive rung on the ladder of progress. Even during the resurgence of the biblical theology movement under the neo-orthodoxy of recent decades, the conquest has received little theological study, though, of course, it has been of great importance

[54] Ibid., 30. Detailed exposition is provided in P. D. Hanson, *The Dawn of Apocalyptic* (1975).
[55] 1QM xii 9-10,12-13 (*Order of the War Between the Children of Light and the Children of Darkness*, a scroll among those found in Cave 1 at Qumran). Translation is that of Cross, *CMHE*, 111.

for Palestinian and biblical archaeologists because of the apparent opportunity of an external check on both biblical and archaeological chronology (see below). The more sensitive literature on war in modern times has generally come from pacifist humanists and Christians, to whom Joshua, and for that matter most of the Old Testament, make poor reading indeed. In one of the best modern surveys Roland H. Bainton concludes a few paragraphs about the Deuteronomistic school on war with the words: "War is more humane when God is left out of it."[56] This may well be true with regard to the fanaticism of a holy war crusade, but it contributes little to the attempt to comprehend the Bible's own views on the subject, which are anything but simplistic and are the very antithesis of doctrinaire pacifism. The latter has its roots in modern idealism (in the technical sense of the term), rather than in a biblical "realism" which insists upon seeing the providence of God in the mixed good and evil of human activity on earth.

We have thus returned to our point of beginning. No one can make any sense out of the biblical attempt to comprehend the role of God in conflict and war when he starts from an idealistic basis in which his own definition of God as love or the Good, as he understands or thinks love and the Good are or should be, in a projected Utopia beyond our current history. Such a basis excludes at the very beginning the mystery and tension between good and evil, love and justice, gospel and law, which form the core of our human experience so that at one and the same time man is a child of nature and a child of God.[57]

Neither, of course, can any modern see any sense to biblical religion if, like so many intellectuals of our day, he approaches it with the childlike literalism of Sunday School children, having never applied the same critical criteria to religious language that he applies to the variety of other languages that he daily uses. Religious language is always connotative, not denotative; it alludes to what is otherwise not to be described in words, any more than the precise nature of the "ultimate" in physical reality, i.e. in the creation, as the Bible would understand it, can be described. Neither can one make any sense out of much of the Bible without the use of all the modern tools of the historian. With study of a few simple works, however, even the non-specialist can get the main points of the biblical approach to reality as a special phenomenon among the other

---

[56] *Christian Attitudes Toward War and Peace, A Historical Survey and Critical Re-evaluation* (New York: Abingdon, 1960) 49.

[57] If anyone in modern American theology was the enemy par excellence of idealism as a guide to proper ethical action or an understanding of man and God in favor of the biblical perspective, the Niebuhr brothers were. Reinhold Niebuhr's *Nature and Destiny of Man* (1941-1943) and *Moral Man and Immoral Society* (1932) remain as prophetic and explosive for contemporary America as they were for their own generation.

chief religious possibilities of the world. Briefly, at this point, only a few generalizations can be made.[58]

It is basically important to understand that in the biblical outlook as a whole the problem of the world is precisely the problem of man. It is not simply an incomplete evolution; it is not simply that parents do not rear their children correctly and perfectly; it is not simply that a few bad people have ruined so much for so many. Rather no one of us is born into a world that is other than corrupt. And this corruption at bottom lies in the human will which is capable of instigating the most noble and the most ignoble of acts. Both become institutionalized as ideal and as actuality. The fault, therefore, lies not in the creation itself, nor in the Creator, but in the misuse of that freedom which is a part of the mystery of the self. We are not automatons; we are given freedom to rule over the world as our kingdom. Indeed, our responsible vocation is precisely to rule wisely since our freedom is under authority. Having failed to do so, the human succession of generations is heir to accumulated folly, institutionalized in every conceivable way. Hence, good actions are continually compromised by their opposite, and human wisdom can become institutionalized self-interest.

The biblical manner of making this situation vividly clear is by the use of language and pictures drawn primarily from the ancient world's highest achievement in government—the Suzerain and the empire. The Lordship of God over the world is the first and basic proposition of the Bible. Its corollary is that men, their institutions, nationality, and individuality, find their true freedom and purpose fulfilled only in the Suzerain's service. This service is not forced upon us, but is held before us as goal and salvation. It is its own reward. To those who object to this picture with a shudder, thinking that we have long grown out of such primitivism, one can reply by asking what and where are the signs of growth. Our perpetual struggle for democracy is simply to balance human powers because unchecked human authority becomes autocratic, or at best paternalistic. The sole guarantee of human freedom is the common recognition that a higher than purely human law is its source and requirement. The freedom of man is protected by the absolute freedom of the Suzerain to preserve it.

The use of the Divine Warrior theme is unwelcome to our ears. Yet, consequent to the basic language of the Bible, "the fighter for justice" is a human way of stating the Suzerain's concern for universal order and his active role in the world in its support. God the Redeemer and God the Warrior are not contradictory terms, for the love of God is always two-

---

[58] See further, Wright, *The Old Testament and Theology*, 129-131. For a presentation of the basic symbolism which is the source and primary coherence of biblical language, see chaps. 3-5 of the same book.

edged. Power actively at work in the world for redemption is something
we all have experienced in both its positive and negative aspects.

That men fight and war follows war is not the purpose of the Creator
and Lord, but the folly of men and their conflicting self-wills. That man
hopes for peace even in war is to hope that God the Lord will exert his
authority. Conflict in history and the authority of God in action are to be
seen, not as necessary contradictions, but as possible signs of God the
Warrior. Yet always from the partiality of any human perspective, the
view is "through a glass, darkly."

God as Suzerain works among people as they are, using them as he
will, as his agents, but in conferring agency he does not also confer righteousness. It is always man who, unhumbled by the Suzerain, absolutizes
his own agency as he interprets it. "Holy War" and early Israel were used
by God for his own purposes (cf. Deuteronomy 7 and 9), but so also
were the empires of the Arameans, Assyrians, and Babylonians *against*
Israel—indeed in her very destruction as a nation—between 900 and 587
(586) B.C. God does not sanctify war any more than he does murder, for
his purpose is universal peace where none shall learn war and none need
be afraid. Yet in the world as it is there can be no peace without justice.
Hence a world without conflict and judgment must be a new world, filled
with a newly remade people (Jer 31:31-34; Ezek 36:22-32, etc.).

The action of God as Lord and as active Judge (Warrior) is the theme
that spells hope for man in this world. Conflict can be comprehended
without being hallowed, and human vocation becomes meaningful because its purpose has a direction formed by the Suzerain's activity and intention. Human life was not created in the present world to seek a haven
of rest, but to engage in the divine struggle for purposes beyond immediate fulfillment. Yet through it all we must treat our neighbors with respect and love; indeed, the whole meaning of economic and social life is
love of neighbor, against whom hate, vengeance, curse, or grudge are not
permitted "lest you bear sin because of him" (Lev 19:9-18).

It may be objected that various passages have been cited from various
parts of Israel's literature, without historical considerations. Yet as
previously stated, the Book of Joshua stands at the top, not at the bottom
of Israel's confessional literature. Its confession and proclamation of
God's great gift is not primitivism. Its surrounding structure of meaning,
therefore, has to be referred to the bulk of later biblical literature.

II. The Book of Joshua in Modern Study

The first formal view of the canon of Scripture was initiated by Jewish
scholars during the Babylonian exile. They had available to them a con-

siderable body of literature, part of which was set aside from all other literature as the special revelation of God to Israel, and was therefore normative for all of Jewish life. The background for this view of a "canon" of a body of literature, considered as a normative guide to life and faith, must have been in pre-exilic covenant renewal services, wherein the law was read by the leader or covenant mediator and the participants in the services vowed to be faithful to it.

The form used for the great variety of legal materials appearing in the books of Exodus, Leviticus, and Numbers is typically God speaking to Moses on Mount Sinai (or Horeb), who in turn transmitted God's "Words" (the Ten Commandments) and Ordinances (Exod 20:1; 21:1; 24:3; Deut 5:6; 6:1; etc.) to the people or to Aaron and the priests. From the form of the literature, therefore, the law was all conceived to be God's revelation to Moses at the time of the covenant at the sacred mount. Deuteronomy, on the other hand, is different in form, being a "second" presentation of the law, Moses himself proclaiming or *expounding* it (*bē'ēr*) to Israel (Deut 1:5b). In Deuteronomic circles, wherever its material was used in covenant renewal services, both before and after it achieved its present written form, the recitation of the Deuteronomic Code as the center of the covenant renewal service (Deuteronomy 5-28, the legal part being chaps. 12-26) was termed "the Book of the Law of Moses" (Josh 23:6; cf. 1:8; Deut 4:44; 17:18-20).[59]

When Ezra returned from exile to Jerusalem with power to reform religious life according to "the law of your God which is in your hand" (Ezra 7:14; cf. v 25 where the document is called "the wisdom of your God"), it has been assumed by most modern scholars, as well as by ancient rabbinic authorities, that a complete edition of the first five books, the Pentateuch, was meant. In Ezra's covenant renewal service he read from "the book of the law of Moses" (Neh 8:1ff). He himself is accorded a new epithet as a scholar "skilled in the law of Moses" (Ezra 7:6). In other words, the phrase Dtr used for the Deuteronomic covenant renewal code was adopted by exilic priestly scholars as the technical name for the whole Pentateuch.

In Part I of this Introduction we have noted how Israel herself in confession, in hymns, and in worship saw the great acts of God in creating, forming, saving, and settling the people of Israel in the Promised Land to be the central content of her epic. The post-exilic community, formed

---

[59] Neither this phrase nor any shortened form of it appears in core material of Deuteronomy 5-28, except in the law of the king (17:18-20), which nearly all scholars attribute to the seventh (or sixth) century. Dtr (the Deuteronomic historian of Israel) used Dtn as the theological platform for his survey in the books Deuteronomy-2 Kings. For the phrase "book of the law" in Dtr see Deut 28:61; 29:20; 30:10; 31:26; Josh 1:8; 23:6; 2 Kgs 14:6; 22:8,11 (cf. 2 Kgs 17:13; 21:8).

from scattered remnants of the destroyed kingdom of Judah, was forced to place central concern on survival, because the prophets had been proved correct in announcing destruction as the result of breach of the divine treaty or covenant. Survival, then, required a more absorbed attention to the will of God; and where was it to be found but in the legal materials preserved for covenant renewal services? Hence, the Pentateuch as the divine constitution for the Jewish community was what came to be emphasized as the central content of the epic. It was the *Torah*.

The first view of the canon of Scripture, therefore—and the one which is that of the Jewish community to this day—is that its central core is the Torah which holds around it the prophets and the hagiographa (sacred writings). While this tripart division of Israel's canonical literature appears to be first mentioned in the Book of Ecclesiasticus,[60] dating from the second century B.C., the basic conception must be pushed back much earlier than a previous generation of scholars had thought possible. Of great importance in this shift of scholarly opinion has been the study of the Dead Sea scrolls. By the second century B.C. highly trained scribes had long experience and a long tradition behind them in copying sacred texts in which the Hebrew consonants were considered fixed and not to be altered, in which scholarly textual study and commentary were the environment for work, in which what was sacred and old was distinguished by script and quality of leather from what was not. Since the oldest manuscripts of Qumran (4QEx^r and 4QSam^b) of this type date from the third century B.C. and a second-century copy of the canonical Psalms (4QPs^a) is easily distinguished from a contemporary collection of psalms (1QH), we are forced to conclude that a canon of Law, Prophets, and Writings must have existed at least as early as the fourth century B.C. In other words, we are forced back to the Persian Age for the major collections of the canonical literature, even though marginal books like Daniel, Esther, Ecclesiastes, and the Apocrypha were either not yet composed or agreement on their status was not yet attained.[61]

[60] Or *The Wisdom of Jesus ben-Sirach*. In the Prologue to the Greek translation of the book, the grandson, writing c. 132 B.C., says that his grandfather, Jesus (or Jeshua), had devoted himself for a long time "to the reading of the Law and the Prophets and the other books of our forefathers." This division appears to correspond to the order of books in the Hebrew Bible, except that it does not specify what the "other books" were, or whether they were considered canonical in a strict sense of the term. Consequently, a previous generation of scholars was accustomed to consider the Torah or Pentateuch "canonized" c. 400 B.C., the prophets completed c. 200 B.C., and the sacred writings around the end of the first century A.D. Yet the conception of a special group of "other writings" studied by Jesus ben-Sirach certainly points to a third category of especially important sacred literature, even though agreement among Jewish sects upon its exact content was not attained until after the destruction of the Second Temple.

[61] On this problem contrast what was considered fairly certain before the study of the Dead Sea scrolls was far advanced (e.g. Robert H. Pfeiffer [d. 1958], "Canon

The Book of Joshua in the Jewish canon is the first book of the Former
Prophets, as the "prophetic" histories, Joshua, Judges, 1-2 Samuel and
1-2 Kings, are called. The designation indicates a rabbinic concern with
the special character of these "histories" which put them together in a
special group immediately following the Torah. In that sense the early
rabbinic position and that of modern scholars have a central concern in
common, as shortly will be indicated. As for the listing of these books
among the prophets, it is to be noted that as early as 900 B.C. the practice
of extending the term "prophet" to include every great leader of Israel's
past tradition was well fixed.[62] Ben-Sirach is within this perspective when
he speaks of Joshua as "the successor of Moses in prophesying," and of
Samuel who established the kingdom as "a prophet of the Lord"
(46:1,13).

Joshua himself has been traditionally considered the book's author.
The modern scholar who comes nearest to tradition at this point is
Yehezkel Kaufmann, who believed that with minor exceptions, such as
Josh 24:1-27, the book is a unity "composed by a recorder of events at
the beginning of the period of the Judges, at the time of Dan's migration
to the north. This author wrote in an ancient Deuteronomistic style. He
collected the stories from living tradition and wrote them down in his
own style," though he "also possessed various written sources."[63] John
Calvin, on the other hand, among others, argued that the name Joshua
appended to the book implies nothing more concerning authorship than
Samuel's name does for 1-2 Samuel. Calvin continues: "Joshua died before the taking of Hebron and Debir, and yet an account of it is given in
the 15th chapter of the present Book. The probability is that a summary

---

of the OT," *IDB* 1, 498-520) with F. M. Cross, *The Ancient Library of Qumran*,
163*ff*. Of central importance for our point is the fact of the LXX, a canonical
translation of the third (and second) centuries B.C. Also important has been the
redating of the Chronicler from the early third to early fourth century, and the
abandonment of commonly held views regarding Maccabean psalms in the Psalter
and of widespread editing and additions to the canon of the Former and Latter
Prophets during the third and second centuries B.C. For summary of this viewpoint,
see G. Ernest Wright, *The Old Testament and Theology* [fn 5], 173-176; *Biblical
Archaeology*, 214-220.

[62] Prophecy as a formalized institution in Israel's religious and political life
began late in the period of the Judges, presumably with Samuel as its creator:
see William F. Albright, *Archaeology, Historical Analogy and Early Biblical Tradition*, 42-65; *YGC*, 208-213; and, independently, G. Ernest Wright, "The Lawsuit
of God," 26-67; and "The Nations in Hebrew Prophecy," *Encounter* (Christian
Theological Seminary, Indianapolis) 26.2 (Spring 1965) 225-237. Yet the use of
the term "prophet" for Moses and even Abraham is firmly fixed in Israel's epic
traditions and would appear to be a special characteristic of the northern traditions;
e.g. Gen 20:7; Num 12:1-7; Deut 34:10.

[63] For a rabbinic statement that Joshua was the book's author, though Eleazar,
son of Aaron, recorded Joshua's death, while Phinehas added the final verse, 33,
about the death of his father Eleazar, see *Baba Batra* 14b-15. For Kaufmann's
view as quoted, see his *The Biblical Account of the Conquest of Palestine*, 97.

of events was framed by the high priest Eleazar, and furnished the materials out of which the Book of Joshua was composed. . . . Let us not hesitate, therefore, to pass over a matter which we are unable to determine, or the knowledge of which is not very necessary." Such views were too strong for Calvin's editor of a century ago, who in a long footnote defends the possibility of Joshua having written the book bearing his name.[64]

Joshua as a Deuteronomic Book

Modern scholarship's conclusion concerning Joshua, which parallels the rabbinic listing of it at the head of the "former prophets," is the statement that, before anything else one must say about it, the book is a part of the Deuteronomic corpus of literature. The hortatory style and the theological perspective of the Book of Deuteronomy are so distinctive as to separate it sharply as literature from the rest of the Pentateuch. While a certain amount of Deuteronomic editing was once assumed to have taken place in the books of Genesis and especially in Exodus, another view now prevails. Deuteronomy surely arose from a theological school in ancient Israel which was much larger than one or a few writers. It appears to have been the same school of north Israelite religious emphasis from which the Elohist material in Genesis, Exodus, and Numbers derived earlier and in which the prophet Hosea was reared. It lived on after the fall of Israel to the Assyrians in 724-721 B.C. While Ezekiel was trained as a priest in the Jerusalemite priestly tradition, it is clear that Jeremiah came from a priestly family trained in the once northern theology.[65]

At the center of the Deuteronomic theology, as it is presented in the Book of Deuteronomy, is the relationship of two facts in the received tradition: the divine promise of the land to the Fathers of Israel—which in the epic sources (JE) was an unconditioned promise (Genesis 15)—and the Sinai (Horeb) covenant. The first is referred to as the oath, covenant, or word, which God swore to the Fathers (cf. Deut 6:23; 7:8; 8:1,18; 9:5; 10:11; 11:9; etc.). Yet in the north Israelite school, as in prophecy generally, the divine commitment of the land was qualified by the Mosaic

[64] *Commentaries on the Book of Joshua*, by John Calvin; translated by Henry Beveridge (Grand Rapids: Eerdmans, 1949) xvii-xviii.

[65] For a summary of this viewpoint see G. Ernest Wright, "Deuteronomy," in *IB* 2, Introduction; and "Exodus, The Book of," *IDB* 2, especially 194; James Muilenburg, "Jeremiah," *IDB* 2, especially 825; Freedman, "Pentateuch," *IDB* 3, especially 714-717; Artur Weiser, *The Old Testament: Its Formation and Development*, 111-135; Alan Jenks, "The Elohist and North Israelite Tradition"; Gerhard von Rad, *Deuteronomy*, 26-27.

covenant, so that permanent possession of the Promised Land depended upon Israel's fidelity to obligations vowed to the Divine Suzerain. One quotation from Deuteronomy 8 will suffice for the point:

> [1] Every commandment which I command you this day you must keep and do, so that you may live and multiply. . . . [18] You must remember the Lord your God because he is the one who gives you power to become wealthy so as to confirm his covenant which he swore to your Fathers, as (is the case) this day. [19] But if you indeed forget the Lord your God and go after other gods, serving and worshiping them, then I bear witness against you this day that you will certainly perish. [20] Like the peoples which God is causing to perish before you, so you shall perish because you would not listen to the voice of the Lord your God.

The old core of Deuteronomy (chaps. 5-28) comes from a period when Israel's life in the land given her by God had become problematic. Hence, the literature is filled with warnings, like those of the prophets, that safety even in the Promised Land is no certainty. Remember the covenant obligations, listen, serve, be obedient—or else!

The Deuteronomic historian of Israel in the Promised Land (Dtr) uses a similar viewpoint, especially in the books of Judges and 1-2 Kings,[66] and he sets forth his prolegomena clearly in additions to Deuteronomy. Pivotal is the "song" in chap. 32 which Dtr's tradition attributed to Moses. The essential content is interpreted as an expression of warning and commitment to "this book of the law" which in Jerusalem evidently was placed beside the Ark of the Covenant (31:26) in the temple. The "song" was thought to have been written by Moses, taught to Israelites that it might "be a legal witness for me against the people of Israel" (31:19). Moses calls an assembly of tribal elders and military leaders to hear the reading and to call "heaven and earth" as witness against them should they breach the covenant after his death (v 28). Following the recital Dtr quotes Moses as saying that this is fundamental to Israel's life if they are to live long in the land being given (32:44-47). That is, the framework which Dtr places around the "song" virtually announces the main theme and concern of his history of Israel in the land which God is

---

[66] Following a unitary view of the final compilation of this history in Joshua, Judges, 1-2 Samuel, and 1-2 Kings as set forth by Martin Noth, *Überlieferungsgeschichtliche Studien* I, though against Noth presuming a first edition c. 625-610 B.C. and a final updated edition (c. 560-550 B.C.) after Jerusalem's destruction. Whether, however, one must consider "Dtr" as one person (with Noth) or two persons (as here assumed), or whether the source comes from a theological school, is a matter to which we shall return at the end of this section. "Dtr" is used as personalistic in the following pages for purposes of simplicity in presentation, but this writer sees no possibility of proving that we are not simply concerned with a theological school which had evolved a unitary plan for the work. Further specification of the identity of Dtr seems impossible and, in any event, is not necessary for what is written below.

giving Israel. The "song" has as its central theme the covenant lawsuit (*rîb*). This in turn, it has been argued, is a reformulation of the covenant-renewal theme, one that took place in north Israel among those who zealously preserved the tribal league traditions but for whom also the new office of the prophet was central in the rule of God. The prophet was counselor of kings, the announcer on earth of the decisions of the court of the Divine Suzerain, and beginning in the ninth century, the one who proclaimed the Suzerain's legal suit against Israel for breach of covenant.[67]

The lawsuit form recites the great acts of God in forming Israel and giving her a bounteous land. It then turns, however, to expound Israel's

[67] So Wright, "The Lawsuit of God," 26-67. In other words, this treatment with regard to the date of the "song" argues against Eissfeldt's attempt to date the psalm by applying the enemy allusions in it to those of the fall of Shiloh in Psalm 78, in order to obtain a late eleventh-century date for its composition. The argument instead is that such a psalm must be dealt with form-critically, and the only hope of dating it lies in the possibility of dating the use of the form, the time of its origin and evolution as a form. The trouble is that while the form central to this psalm is central also to pre-exilic prophecy (except that of Ezekiel, who as a Jerusalemite priest did not use the form until the post-exilic period [cf. above Psalm 106 and Stephen's sectarian review of Israel's history in Acts 7]), it never occurs as pure liturgy at any point. Psalm 82 is related but is not strictly analogous because it uses the form to sentence the world's gods to death like mortals: cf. G. Ernest Wright, *The Old Testament Against Its Environment*, 30-41; and James S. Ackerman, "Psalm 82." Consequently, the approach of Kraus, *Die Psalmen*, 535-548, while instructive is as unconvincing regarding date (late or post-exilic with Gunkel-Begrich because of the mixture of elements and lack of seemingly "pure" form, which make it a *mischgedicht*) as the approach of Eissfeldt. It must be stated that the method of looking at the covenant lawsuit here employed, while informed by Gunkel's work, begins with the significant article of H. Wheeler Robinson, "The Council of Yahweh," *Journal of Theological Studies* 45 (1944) 151*ff*; his *Inspiration and Revelation in the Old Testament* (1946) 167*ff*; through Wright's treatment of Psalm 82, see above; Cross [fn 51], 274*ff*=*CMHE*, 186-194—all further developed in the light of Mendenhall [fn 4]=*BAR* 3, 3-53. In this perspective the discussion of the covenant lawsuit takes on added dimensions and a more precise setting than the discussions which bypass Robinson and Mendenhall and continue directly with Gunkel's *Gerichtsreden*. Theoretically the covenant lawsuit could have been, and probably was, in existence in theological conception throughout the period of the tribal league as well as later: cf. Julien Harvey, "Le 'Rîb-Pattern,' réquisitoire prophétique sur la rupture de l'alliance," *Biblica* 43 (1962) 172-196; and *Le plaidoyer prophétique contra Israël après la rupture de l'Alliance;* Artur Weiser, "Samuels 'Philister-Sieg,' " *ZTK* 56 (1959) 253-272; *Die Psalmen, ATD* 14 (1959) 21, 30-35; in *The Psalms*, translated by H. Hartwell, 52-60; *The Old Testament: Its Formation and Development* [fn 65], 81-125; Ernst Würthwein, "Die Ursprung der prophetischen Gerichtsrede," *ZTK* 49 (1952) 1-16. To find a proper life setting for the judgment oracle Würthwein has to resort to the enthronement psalms where God appears as judge of the peoples of the world—a different theme from that presumed here. Yet possible as the covenant lawsuit is at any time because of the covenant curses, the fact is that the first fully datable use of it is during the Aramean wars of the ninth century (cf. 1 Kgs 19:15-18; 22:13-23). For a date half a century later, see John S. Holladay, Jr., "Assyrian Statecraft and the Prophets of Israel," *HTR* 63 (1970) 29-51.

actions as base ingratitude and infidelity, so that God has sentenced Israel
to dire punishment at the hands of an external enemy, not to speak of
various calamities from the natural order, all included in the curses listed
at the end of the treaty stipulations (cf. Deuteronomy 28).[68] It is in the
atmosphere of the lawsuit as the continual threat over Israel that Dtr
compiled his history. In the final address of Joshua to Israel (Joshua 23),
Dtr includes a new statement of the conditional nature of the covenant
and the threat of expulsion from the land if the covenant is broken. In
vv 15-16 we read:

> And as surely as everything good which Yahweh your God promised
> you has come true for you, so Yahweh will also bring upon you everything
> harmful, until he has obliterated you from this good land that Yahweh
> your God has given you. When you violate the covenant . . . , then Yah-
> weh's wrath will be kindled against you. . . .

In Judges 2-3 Dtr attempts a generalized interpretation of the whole
period of the Judges as a time of repeated covenant violations, punishments, acts of repentance which God repeatedly followed by raising up a
new savior ("judge") and giving Israel another chance, whereupon the
people fell back into covenant violation again. In the books of Samuel it
is difficult to distinguish definitely between Dtr's editorial expansions and
his multiplicity of sources. In 1 Sam 12:6-25, whether from Dtr or from
an older Israelite anti-monarchic source from which 1 Samuel 8 was also
taken, the story of God's great acts is followed by a narration of Israel's
rebellion and God's response in supplying saviors ("judges"). His latest
act of the same nature is to supply a king at Israel's request. Yet the people are warned that safety under kingship is not assured. God will turn
against both people and king if they rebel. The author adds (vv 22,24,
25):

> Indeed, Yahweh does not cast away his people because of his great name,
> for Yahweh has determined to make you into a people for himself. . . .
> Yet fear Yahweh and serve him [or give Yahweh reverent service] with
> fidelity, with your whole heart, for look how greatly he has acted in your
> behalf! But if you persist in doing wrong, both you and your king will be
> swept away.

[68] Because Deuteronomy 32 has Wisdom elements from the teacher form at the
beginning and a holy war hymn added to the end, Wright, "The Lawsuit of God,"
argued that its form was that of a "broken *rîb*"—i.e. the lawsuit theme is mixed
with other teaching or liturgical devices. Yet whether we should expect to find a
liturgically complete and "pure" form is doubtful before the fall of Jerusalem,
at least, because of the *ad hoc* character of each specific use, to interpret current
crises. Deuteronomy 32 appears originally to expound the meaning of a specific
crisis (that of the ninth-century Aramean problem?) and subsequently to have been
generalized, its initial and final portions furnishing the framework for the specificity of the "no people . . . a foolish nation" as enemy in v 21b.

When the United Kingdom split into two parts after Solomon's reign, Dtr knows of God's informing Solomon about it before the latter's death. Though God had appeared to Solomon twice with instructions, Solomon had not obeyed. For that reason God is going to split the kingdom. Yet for the sake of David, he will only do it in the time of Rehoboam, Solomon's son. Furthermore, because of David and of Jerusalem "which I have chosen," God will not tear everything away from the dynasty of David; he will leave Solomon's son one tribe (1 Kgs 11:9-11). Furthermore, to the high official, Jeroboam, whom God through the prophet Ahijah selected as king of the northern ten tribes which kept the name "Israel," the conditions are repeated. God explains:

> You I am taking to reign over all you desire, and you will be king of Israel. If you listen to all I command you and walk in my ways . . . , then I will build for you a secure dynasty [Hebrew "house"] as I did for David (1 Kgs 11:37-38).

Yet before Jeroboam's reign ended Dtr explained that the king's obligations had been so flagrantly violated as to ensure the complete destruction of Jeroboam's dynasty "from the surface of the earth" (1 Kgs 13:34; 15:27-30). Every king of the northern kingdom is equally condemned, usually for following the same path as Jeroboam, until the Assyrian destruction of Israel in 724-721 B.C. At that point Dtr inserted an exposition in defense of the righteousness of God in the tragic story (2 Kings 17). God's prophets at every step of the way had warned both Israel and Judah of the consequences of rebellion, that they not forget the covenant, and now Israel has been swept away and only Judah is left. Yet even Judah has walked in the ways of Israel. Meanwhile, the new inhabitants of Israel, a mixture including people drawn from various parts of the Assyrian empire, worship Yahweh, but they also worship a variety of their own deities, thus turning Yahwism easily into a polytheism because subsidiary divine beings are identified and given cults of their own. "Just as their fathers did, so they are doing to this day" (2 Kgs 17:41).

This statement, taken with a number of others similar to it, suggests that Dtr must have lived and written his great work before the fall of Jerusalem to the Babylonians (597-587 B.C.) because the conditions are described as existing at the time the work was being written. While Martin Noth simply held to the position that Dtr composed his great work c. 550 B.C. after the last events recorded in 2 Kings 25, most scholars have believed that the main work was composed before the exile and that after the exile 2 Kgs 23:26 - 25:30 was added to update the work; there are suggestions of exilic editing elsewhere.[69]

---

[69] For Noth's views see his *Überlieferungsgeschichtliche Studien* I. The more common view, to be found as early as Kuenen and Wellhausen, survives in our

Yet the virtually unsolvable problem of Dtr has been the main theme and purpose of Noth's writing, especially his final section about the last years of the kingdom of Judah (2 Kings 18-25). From the material so far surveyed, and more unmentioned, it is clear that, while a central thesis of Dtn is that the original unconditioned promise of the land to the patriarchs is to be taken as conditional on the maintenance of the Mosaic covenant, Dtr is interpreting Israel's history of trouble in the good land as occasioned by the breach of the covenant and the consequent continual threat of the covenant curses befalling the whole people.

Through it all the most remarkable fact is the grace of God in continually giving the people another chance in the land, though their perversity constantly brings upon them dire hardships of every sort. Saviors ("judges," šōpᵉṭîm), one after another, were provided in the days of the tribal league. Then in the days of Samuel a transition to kingship as a more stable governing force to save the nation from the Philistine menace was again a gift of God to grant the nation life when it was threatened with death.

One old source which Dtr uses is clearly not enthusiastic or optimistic about the value of the monarchic institution. Human kingship is something borrowed from neighboring nations and is not indigenous to Israel's covenant system. It poses a severe conflict of interest and authority between the rule of God and the rule of the king (1 Samuel 8). Nevertheless, Samuel is ordered to accede to the people's request, and to warn them what the king is going to be like. Samuel then proceeds to give a precise description of the autocracy of Solomon according to Dtr's sources (1 Sam 8:11-18): forced military service, a standing army, a huge servant establishment, fields and vineyards given to favorites, the institution of the tithe as a state tax, and forced service in state labor battalions, until "you will cry out in that day [for relief] from your king . . . but Yahweh will not answer you in that day" (v 18). The source behind 1 Samuel 8 must be old, therefore, and not too far removed from the events and hot temper in the north which caused the kingdom to be divided at the death of Solomon (1 Kings 12).

At the same time Dtr also has available and includes another tenth-century tradition, this one from the Jerusalem court, rather than from north Israel. That is 2 Samuel 7, a much reworked piece of literature which in its final form says that God, through the prophet Nathan, denies permission for David to build a temple in Jerusalem, but instead promises

---

era in such works as Eissfeldt, *The Old Testament: An Introduction,* 241-303, especially 284-285; John Gray, *I & II Kings, A Commentary,* Introduction; Robert H. Pfeiffer, *Introduction to the Old Testament* (New York: Harper, 1941) 277*ff;* (E. Sellin and) G. Fohrer, *Introduction to the Old Testament* (tr. D. E. Green; New York and Nashville: Abingdon, 1965) 227-337.

David peace, a great and prosperous nation, and a dynasty which will continue forever. "Your dynasty [Hebrew "house"] and your kingdom shall be secure forever before me [LXX; MT has "before you"]; your throne shall be set up forever" (2 Sam 7:16). This unconditioned divine commitment to David is the basis of the royal theology of the Jerusalem court by the time of Solomon, in all probability, even though this theology must be reconstructed from a variety of sources, especially from the psalms. Among the sources is the "Last Words of David," probably from the tenth century, which speaks of the commitment to David's dynasty as "an everlasting covenant" (2 Sam 23:1–7).[70] In the post-exilic age the divine promise to David became a center of hope for the future of Judaism, the leading motif for the Chronicler, for example, while the theology of Dtr had played out its role in the destruction of Jerusalem.

Two themes are present in the books of Kings and are left in tension with one another. The first is the constant threat and warning that the national covenant-breaking will result in the Divine Suzerain's suit for breach of contract (rîb) with the sending of the covenant "curses" (Deuteronomy 28). Indeed, after the institution of monarchy and its marvelous success under David following initial failure with Saul, Dtr composes the books of Kings as God's controversy (rîb) against kings, providing a fairly stereotyped evaluation of each one, while giving us the king's name, telling when and how long he reigned, and reporting some pertinent information about him abstracted from sources, to two of which Dtr usually refers the reader for more information, either "The Book of the Deeds of the Kings of Israel" or "The Book of the Deeds of the Kings of Judah."[71] The story Dtr presents of kings is a sad one, every king of Israel being condemned, and only Hezekiah and Josiah receiving unqualified praise in Judah.[72] The second theme, God's promise to David, has been re-

[70] For attempts to state what we know about the Jerusalem theology of monarchy, see Gerhard von Rad, *Old Testament Theology* I, 306-354; Keith R. Crim, *The Royal Psalms;* Bernhard W. Anderson, *Creation Versus Chaos*, 60-77; Kraus, *Worship in Israel*, 179-236; Helmer Ringgren, *Israelite Religion*, 220-238; Martin Noth, "God, King and Nation in the Old Testament," in *The Laws of the Pentateuch and Other Essays*, 145-178; Albrecht Alt, "The Monarchy in the Kingdoms of Israel and Judah," in *Essays on Old Testament History and Religion*, 311-335.

[71] In the case of Solomon, he refers one to "the Book of the Deeds of Solomon" (1 Kgs 11:42[41H]). At the death of David no such reference to a source is given (1 Kgs 2:10-11), perhaps because Dtr in 1-2 Samuel and in 1 Kings 1-2 had used so much of the early "official" biography, with little condensation or alteration. 1 Chronicles 29:29 refers to biographies covering both the early and latter part of David's reign by Samuel, Nathan, and Gad. Three histories of Solomon are also alluded to, by Nathan, Ahijah, and Iddo, the last having written the history of Jeroboam (2 Chr 9:29). It is characteristic of the Chronicler, however, to refer to a number of sources not mentioned by Dtr.

[72] Asa, Jehoshaphat, Jehoash, Amaziah, Uzziah, and Jotham, however, receive qualified praise: "He did what was right in the eyes of Yahweh . . . but . . ." 2 Kgs 14:3-4; 15:3-4,34-35. Cf. 1 Kgs 15:11-15; 22:43-44.

ferred to as the ground for hope in the work of Dtr, the theme of grace, which points to a messianic future and the reestablishment of the Davidic dynasty after the exile (Von Rad), or to the restoration of a covenant people, though not necessarily of the monarchy (H. W. Wolff).[73] On a few occasions Dtr, looking back on the history of Judah, explains that God did not cause more harm to such and such a king, or to the people of Judah, because of his servant David (cf. the programmatic statement in 2 Sam 7:14-15; then Ahijah to Jeroboam, 1 Kgs 11:32,34; Abijam, 1 Kgs 15:4; Jehoram, 2 Kgs 8:19; cf. Ps 89:30-37). Yet, owing evidently to the complexity of Dtr's sources, he preserves two references to God's special mercy shown to Israel also. Hazael and the Aramean power were not permitted to destroy Israel. Yahweh was gracious and compassionate to Israel: "For the sake of his covenant with Abraham, Isaac, and Jacob he was unwilling to destroy them and throw them away from him until now" (2 Kgs 13:23). Again following the amazing victory of Jeroboam II in conquering Aram and restoring the Davidic northern border of Israel, Dtr or more probably one of his sources explains: Yahweh had seen the terrible situation of Israel, that no one was left to help her. "Indeed, Yahweh had not said to blot out the name of Israel from under the heavens. So he saved them [gave them victory] by the hand of Jeroboam ben Joash" (2 Kgs 14:26-27). This second explanation of a victory sounds precisely like a formula used in the Book of Judges. It is apparently employed here to mitigate the picture of unremitting judgment (*rîb*) against Israel in order to show that Yahweh was still compassionate and that what happened to Israel at Assyrian agency a few years later was not a necessary fate.

Recently, Frank M. Cross has turned again to Dtr's use of the divine promise to David in 2 Samuel 7, and maintains it to be "the persistent, and in many ways major, theme of the Book of Kings." Once this is seen to be the true center of Dtr's perspective in the juxtaposition of the two themes, then pre-exilic Dtr "may be described as a propaganda work of the Josianic reformation and imperial program. In particular the document speaks to the North calling Israel back to the Lord's ancient Shrine in Jerusalem. . . . It speaks equally or more emphatically to Judah. Her restoration to ancient grandeur depends on her return to the covenant of Yahweh, and on the wholehearted return of her king to the ways of David, the beloved of the Lord. In Josiah is centered the hope of a new Israel and the expectation of the 'covenant fidelities' of David."[74]

[73] G. von Rad, *Studies in Deuteronomy*, 74-79; *Old Testament Theology* I, 334-347; and H. W. Wolff, "Das Kerygma des deuteronomistischen Geschichtswerkes," *ZAW* 73 (1961) 171-186.

[74] Frank M. Cross, "The Structure of the Deuteronomic History," *Perspectives in Jewish Learning* III: *Annual of the College of Jewish Studies* (Chicago, 1968) 9-24=*CMHE*, 274-289. Quotations from 11 and 16-17=*CMHE*, 278 and 284.

The clue to the disentangling of the pre-exilic Dtr (seventh century) from the exilic Dtr (sixth century), Cross continues, is to be found at those points where the original edition has been reworked for the exiles. Just as the sin of Jeroboam I was the crucial event in the history of the northern kingdom, so for Judah, as exilic Dtr reworked 2 Kings 21, the sin of Manasseh was so terrible that not even Josiah's reform was sufficient to withhold the judgment (cf. 2 Kgs 23:26b-27). The prophecy of Huldah was probably also reworked in that it speaks of the delay of the disaster to Judah until after Josiah's death because of the latter's obedience (2 Kgs 22:18-20). A number of passages also appear to be addressed to exiles, calling for their repentance, providing assurance that Yahweh will not forget his covenant with the patriarchs, and in one case promising restoration. Such passages are: Deut 4:27-31; 28:36,63-68; 29:28[27H]; 30:1-10; 1 Sam 12:25; 1 Kgs 8:46-53; 9:6-9; 2 Kgs 17:19-20; 20:17-18; 23:26-25:30. Other passages, such as Deut 30:11-20 and Josh 23:15-16, may be suspected as exilic.

This lucid treatment provides a clear platform on which to judge more precisely the nature of the exilic Dtr's work. Whether, however, one can be so certain that the original history of Dtr was primarily a propagandistic work for the Josiah reform is much more doubtful. (1) The promise to David is certainly not the central theme for the Dtr editing of Dtn, or for the books of Joshua or Judges. (2) In 1 Samuel 8 a north Israelite source is fully quoted which interprets the monarchy after the manner of the judges. Kingship is God's concession to the rebellion of Israel, to provide life instead of destruction, but that it is a promise of salvation for the future is most emphatically denied. At the same time Dtr also includes the unconditioned promise of God to the Davidic dynasty (2 Samuel 7), but nonetheless constructs the books of Kings as God's controversy with the kings. Inasmuch as it is central to both the theology of Dtn and Dtr that the "unconditioned" covenant of God with the patriarchs was indeed conditioned by the Mosaic covenant, a view shared by the Jerusalem priesthood (Genesis 17), it is legitimate to infer that in Deuteronomic theology, in both early and late versions, God never commits himself to eternal security for any institution or people without regard to the conditions he upholds for life and security.[75]

In any event, the passage to be found in Dtr which says that Yahweh

---

[75] Cf. Jeremiah, trained in the Deuteronomic or northern theology (contrast Ezekiel, the Jerusalem priest who shares much in common with Tetrateuchal P), especially his temple sermon in 608 B.C., directed against priests who, apparently on the basis of Isaiah's precedent, proclaimed the eternal inviolability of the temple institution. See Jeremiah's violent reaction in the interpretation of God's true covenant (chaps. 7 and 26): cf. G. Ernest Wright, "Security and Faith," *The Rule of God*, 77-92; and Walther Eichrodt, "The Right Interpretation of the Old Testament: a Study of Jeremiah 7:1-15," *Theology Today* 7 (April 1950) 15-25.

will never remove his support from a Davidic king as he removed it from
Saul, even when the king does evil and is chastened (2 Sam 7:14-16), is
shortly followed by the removal of ten tribes from the Davidic dynasty,
leaving only one, Judah (which had already absorbed Simeon), "because
of my servant David" (1 Kgs 11:32,34). This would appear to be a severe qualification of the overt meaning concerning the everlasting prosperity, peace, and secure dynasty promised in 2 Sam 7:8-16. The term
"secure" (ne'man), used as a verb to describe God's intentions regarding
the dynasty of David (2 Sam 7:16), is used participially to describe the
secure dynasty promised by God to Jeroboam through the prophet Ahijah
(1 Kgs 11:38), but the dynasty was destroyed in its second generation.
Abijam walked in the evil ways of his father, Rehoboam, but God saved
him for David's sake (1 Kgs 15:4), while Jehoram, married to a daughter of the Omri dynasty and walking in the evil ways of that dynasty, did
not bring judgment upon Judah because of the divine promise to David
(2 Kgs 8:19).

These four passages are the sole evidence in the books of Samuel and
Kings for the attitude of pre-exilic Dtr toward the Davidic dynasty. Did
he consider the divine promise in any light different from exilic Dtr who
knew that the promise was a conditional one (e.g. 1 Kgs 9:4-9)? The
passages mentioned are insufficient to provide us a certain answer. Given
the north Israelite theological attitude toward monarchy as one can reconstruct it from Deut 17:14-20; 1 Samuel 8; Hos 8:10,[76] we cannot be
sure at all that original Dtr was written as Josianic propaganda. It is much
more likely that for Dtr, as for Jeremiah, while radical reform was Judah's
only answer if safety were to be found, the tension between God and nation, intrinsic to the Mosaic covenant, remained. 1 Samuel 8 and 2 Samuel
7, both essentially old sources reworked in Dtr, are thus left in tension with
one another and provide a dialectic in the Dtr theology which is not resolved and could not be resolved except by God himself in future events.

Thus far Dtr, following Noth, has been referred to in personal terms as
though he were one person, or two persons, a pre-exilic Dtr and an exilic
Dtr. Noth has argued for the singularity of authorship of the block of
Deuteronomic literature (Deuteronomy-2 Kings), because the overall
unity of theme and theology is not something a committee would produce
but is better conceived as the work of one personality. Yet other scholars
have felt such a view too constraining because of the different manner in
which the books were constructed. Are the differences to be explained by
differences in the source material available to Dtr, or are different person-

---

[76] See also A. Alt on Israel's rejection of the Jerusalemite theology: "The
Monarchy in the Kingdoms of Israel and Judah."

alities also involved? There seems to be no objective way of solving this question, nor does its answer alter in any significant manner what has been said above.

Dtr is simply a convenient symbol for a theological school of thought that had its origin in north Israel before moving to Judah after 724-721 B.C. and the destruction of Israel. The Josiah reform in 622 B.C. meant its triumph for a time in Judah. The remarks which are occasionally made to the effect that the Lachish and Arad letters "prove" that Dtr's prose was the common literary tradition of seventh-century Judah, slim as the evidence for this position is, should not be used to obscure the fact that other schools of theology existed in Jerusalem at the same time. These included the royal Davidic theology, the theology of the Jerusalem temple priesthood, even perhaps a small group who still liked to use the old tabernacle terminology for the temple, and the complex theology of the Wisdom movement. In any event, whether Dtr is a symbol for one person, two as here assumed, or a group, can neither be proved, nor does it make a significant difference as one attempts to assess the theology of the school.

What, then, is the role which the Book of Joshua plays in the total Dtr historical work? Joshua is God's charismatic leader for the task of leading the people in the conquest. He is especially chosen and empowered; he was not a son of Moses nor did his office pass to his sons. Yet the honor of the great victories does not fall to Joshua. He is merely an instrument of God's power. The victories are God's alone. Israel can claim no credit; the book does not enable one to fashion hero stories, nor traditions of the great fighting prowess of the men of Israel. Quite the contrary! The victory and the credit belong to God alone. In this way the traditions Dtr employs and the manner in which he uses them correspond to the confessional use of the conquest theme in the Bible as a whole.

The Dtr editor constructed the final address of Joshua in Joshua 23, like the speeches of Moses in Deuteronomy, to make it clear that the great victories lead not to exultation, but rather to warning. God has done this for you, but beware of your future. The gift bears great responsibilities, nothing less than the creation of the covenant society, a revealed order, in the land given. This you have promised to do, and your security in the land depends upon your fidelity to your oaths. God has been gracious, and no doubt you can continue to rely on that grace. Yet divine forgiveness and salvation do not mean that he acquits the guilty without judgment (cf. Exod 34:6-7; Deut 10:12-22). "Watch yourselves very carefully, so as to love Yahweh your God. But if in fact you turn away . . . !" (Josh 23:11-12).

Objections to the Theology of Dtr

A common attitude toward the historical perspective of the Deuteronomic theologian is that it results in an extremely moralistic and unrealistic interpretation of human life. That is, if Israel is good, the nation will be rewarded. If not, then punishment and the threatened destruction will follow. The reward-and-punishment ethic of the Dtr application of covenant theology to Israel's history is surely simplistic, and by regarding all evil or hardship as punishment for wrongdoing the author overlooks all innocent suffering. Furthermore, Israel on that small corridor between continents could not remain "pure and unspotted" from the world without constant influence from foreigners who throughout human history, to this day, find life or business there an imperative. The Palestinian corridor, by its very geographic situation, has always been one of the world's most critically important spots, where mixture of peoples, customs, commerce, and traffic are inevitable. Empires expanding in any direction, from south or north, have been attracted to the potentially wealthy Syrian, Anatolian, and Mesopotamian lands, or conversely to the riches of the Nile Valley. How can any people's history at that spot avoid the strong currents of the whole world? Any ideological exclusivism there is bound for sore trial and almost inevitable defeat.

It must be remembered, however, that the perspective of Dtr must not be equated with that of the friends of Job. The latter have simply elevated into an almost metaphysical system the view that the power directing all life works in a completely moralistic way. Thus in common with so many ordinary people the world over, they believe that if misadventure befalls a person, then he simply must confess sin or error somewhere in past actions or attitudes and hope that the confession may be sufficient to bring a change in his fortunes.

Dtr has not evolved such a moralistic theory for *individual* life. His concern is with a whole people and their life in a land of promise. Implicit in his perspective of the covenant is a revealed order of life under the direct rule of God. Israel is responsible for a whole social order wherein loving fidelity to the Suzerain involves, not simply a proper cultic life, but an order of justice and fidelity, which excludes service to any other powers, divine or human, but specifically includes fair dealing in all conceivable paths of the common life. Idolatry is especially stressed because it breaches covenant and all the loyalties based upon inner assent. These alone can bring wholeness of life and a wholesome society which make up the meaning of the term *shālôm* ("peace"): e.g. Deuteronomy 6 and 10.[77]

With this as firm conviction and presupposition, Dtr examines Israel's history in the Promised Land of peace and rest. The story is not a good one; there has been little peace and plenty of danger and disorder. He thus concludes that Israel's vows have been violated and he has plenty of illustrations of that fact. Thus his work cannot be looked upon as a prescriptive theology of individual rewards and punishment in this present life. It is instead an interpretative theology, which justifies God's acts with and against Israel and Judah over more than six hundred years of history. It cannot be shown to be a programmatic theology for the reign of Josiah or for anyone else. To a country in dire danger (Dtr 1, the first edition, predates the destruction of Jerusalem) or to a ravaged and destroyed country and political entity after the destruction of Jerusalem (Dtr 2, the final, completed work), the Dtr history, using the great variety of old sources available, writes an *interpretative* account of the past actions of God and Israel, using as its main basis of interpretation the promises and warnings of blessing and curse in the Deuteronomic tradition of the Mosaic covenant. It is a national document, providing a justification of God's action in first giving his people a land, and then destroying them and giving a surviving remnant to a foreign conqueror. It was surely this theology, expounded also by the pre-exilic prophets, which preserved faith in Israel's God during the kind of disaster which spelled death to the gods of nature and culture among Israel's neighbors.

Still another popular line of approach to the theology of Dtr is to write it off as meaningless from a viewpoint like the following. The destruction of Israel and of Judah with Jerusalem meant that the days of God's mighty acts are far in the past and they provide no basis on which to sustain a future hope, or a life of meaning for a hopeless present. Neither does the exposition of Dtr. Instead, one of the most important theological documents of the hopeless period of the exile was the Book of Job. There the whole past providence and justice of God, as expounded by Dtr, are denied, and a new revelation of God from the whirlwind is provided. Suffering cannot be explained but God's providence can be affirmed on the basis, not of his activity in the history of Israel, but as creator of the universe, and ruler of Leviathan, that archetypal symbol of eternal chaos threatening the world.

Needless to say, this as answer to Dtr, if such it is, is very close to Canaanite sources. It deals with the myth of the eternal return to the creation of order to obtain the assurance of providence in the present disor-

[77] For an inner psychological description of this "peace," see Johannes Pedersen, *Israel, Its Life and Culture*, Part I-II, 263-335.

der. That Job was created as the theological answer to Dtr in sixth-century Jerusalem or elsewhere must certainly be denied. The complexity of the book's structure shows that it has a literary history. This is also suggested by the archaism of names and language and the fact that a close thematic parallel to the book exists in a piece of Mesopotamian Wisdom literature which cannot be confined to a date as late as the sixth century. In other words, the Wisdom literature in Israel does not belong to one period. Wisdom is Israel's "humanistic" *movement,* possessing an international flavor, presumably taught, as elsewhere in the Near East, by scholars in the centers of bureaucracy to the children of royal officials and of the royal family. This literature shows no interest whatever in the Mosaic covenant, or the meaning of Israel's society in relation to past, present, or future. Its sole concern is with the individual's way to a happy and successful life. In Proverbs 8 it can even assert that Wisdom is a part of the creation, grounded in the very order of things. In Job's protest the "friends" stand for an interpretation of individual success and failure in this life as reward and punishment for the individual's moral or immoral actions. The writer provides a classic denial of this worldwide reaction of the common man to his lot by setting forth the case of the innocent sufferer, insisting that righteous Jobs do indeed exist, and that worldly wisdom's typical answer is wrong.

The suggestion here being made is that Wisdom theology and its skeptical attitude toward observable providence in an individual's life are both old, if we argue from parallels in literature outside Israel. Consequently, the royal theology of monarchy in Jerusalem, the priesthood's theologies of the meaning of the Jerusalem temple, the theology of Dtr, and the Wisdom theologies are all present in one form or another in seventh-century Jerusalem. After the fall of Judah to the Babylonians, the Wisdom collections were preserved and during the next two centuries or so were given virtually their final form. At the same time one normative form of future expectation appears in the work of an exiled priest-prophet from the Jerusalem temple (Ezekiel 40-48) which seems to have formed a background for the attempt to reconstitute Jerusalem and rebuild the temple in the period between 538 and 515 B.C. (cf. Ezra-Nehemiah and the prophets Haggai and Zechariah). Among this group a second exodus and a second conquest are ardently hoped for. In Isaiah 56-66, on the other hand, another school of prophetic (and probably also priestly) insight is to be observed. This seems not to agree with the majority of the community, but affirms that preceding the new exodus, and the new heavens and new earth, there must be a new judgment which is to fall again upon the Judean community because it is still not the true Israel (cf. Isaiah 57-59; 64-66). This clue to a sectarian development among the returned exiles is reinforced by the probability of other sects also, as is suggested by the Jewish colony at Elephantine in Upper Egypt.

During the sixth century, in other words, successors of the prophetic and Dtr viewpoints became increasingly "otherworldly" or visionary, seeing and hoping in God's future, cast in the forms of second exodus and second conquest, but increasingly unable to relate such a viewpoint to actual happenings in the world. Haggai and Zechariah, promising the dawn of the glorious new era with the rebuilding of the temple under the anointed Zerubbabel and Jeshua, evidently met such a disaster in prediction that the process of positively uniting current history and expectations concerning its end ceased to be explicit. Prophecy as an active institution with a vigorous role in current affairs also ceased. This is the community which preserved the Wisdom literature, even identifying wisdom with God's law (cf. Ezra 7:14,26; Ps 119:34,73; etc.). Whether in this period there was ever a true Joban school of theology we do not know. We have only the book itself, testifying in poetry and in the prose prologue and epilogue to different ways of thinking about providence and the individual who suffers misfortune.

To treat Job simply as a theology for a bankrupt nation is scarcely true to the many suggestions of variety of viewpoint at every stage of the way. Post-exilic Judaism, as it developed, was undoubtedly a complex phenomenon. Dtr, on the other hand, along with the pre-exilic prophets, enabled a destroyed nation to cling to meaning in disaster because the past was understood and provided the models out of which new forms of community were preserved and developed.

Literary Criticism of the Book of Joshua

The late nineteenth- and early twentieth-century critics of Joshua, while convinced of the Deuteronomic character of the book, concluded that its contents were more or less artificially separated from the first five books or Pentateuch. Consequently, while "Pentateuch" was the separation of the Torah for theological reasons as the central core of the Jewish canon, the literary critics for literary reasons did not think one could deal with the first five books without at the same time working with Joshua. The same Pentateuchal sources continued through the book and indeed only found their fulfillment there.[78] Thus literary critics worked with a unit named the Hexateuch.

[78] For a few "classical" statements of the position see Julius Wellhausen, *Die Composition des Hexateuchs und der historischen Bücher des Alten Testaments* (1876-1877); Samuel R. Driver, *Introduction to the Literature of the Old Testament* (1891); Carpenter and Harford-Battersby, *The Hexateuch* II (1900) 303-359; George Foot Moore, "Joshua (Book)," in *Encyclopaedia Biblica* II (1901)

The Deuteronomic editing of Joshua consisted of providing the frame-work and editing of older epic sources, to which later additions of the Jerusalem priesthood (P) were made. Thus in chap. 1 the first two verses continue Dtr's edition of the story from epic sources of Moses' death in Deuteronomy 34. Verses 3-9 continue with the solemn charge to Joshua which Dtr had already introduced with practically identical language in Deut 31:7-8 plus 7:24 and 11:24. The ceremony of blessings and curses at Mounts Ebal and Gerizim commanded in Deuteronomy 27 is carried out according to Josh 8:30-35. The address to the Transjordan tribes in Josh 1:12-18 is based on Deut 3:12,18-20 and is concluded with the dismissal of these tribes to return to their settlements in Josh 22:1-6. Joshua 23 is a final address of Joshua to an assembly of all the tribes, directly parallel in language and theology to Moses' series of final addresses in Dtr and Dtn (Deuteronomy 1-4; 5-11; 29-31). Virtually all literary critics were agreed that the original Deuteronomic Joshua consisted at least of Joshua 1-12; 21:43 - 22:6; and 23.

Yet the basic narrative in Joshua 2-11 seems to be drawn from older sources, related to those in Genesis, Exodus, and Numbers. Indeed, it is the fulfillment of the promise of the land and the climax expected for the story in the epic sources. While some hesitance existed as to whether the old sources used in Joshua were the same as the JE found in the earlier books, the majority of scholars assumed that they were the same and con-tinued their analysis at least through Joshua, while some continued to find the same sources continuing through Judges, 1-2 Samuel, and 1 Kings 1-2. Yet we should note the caution of certain pioneers which others did not observe. Wellhausen wrote:[79]

> If I include the book of Joshua here, I must affirm, first of all, that unlike Judges, Samuel and Kings it is an appendix to the Pentateuch which presupposes the Pentateuch on all points, *yet not that what is to be under discussion is the same material handled in the same manner* [italics this writer's].

The careful and balanced British scholar Samuel R. Driver expressed sim-ilar warnings.[80]

These warnings went largely unheeded, and scholars generally found J and E in Joshua's narrative material. As in all such epic traditions, vari-ous ways of telling the old stories often have left a certain unevenness

---

cols. 2600-2610; Heinrich Holzinger, *Das Buch Josua* (1901); Otto Eissfeldt, *The Old Testament: An Introduction* (1965) 248-257 (first published in Ger-many in 1934); (E. Sellin and) G. Fohrer, *Introduction to the Old Testament* (1968) [fn 69], 196-205.

[79] *Die Composition des Hexateuchs* (3d ed., 1899) 116.
[80] *Introduction to the Literature of the Old Testament* (13th ed., 1913) 104.

in the narrative, apparent in some places more than in others, depending upon the preliterary history of the material. For example, in Josh 3:17 - 4:8, "all Israel" crosses the Jordan while the priests carrying the Ark of the Covenant stand in the midst of the riverbed. Joshua then issues instructions that twelve men take twelve stones, according to the number of the tribes of Israel, and set them up where they encamp that night as a memorial of the crossing. This was done (v 8). Yet in 4:9 we read that the stones were set up in the middle of the Jordan itself where the priests had stood, "and they are there to this day" (whenever the time to which this dating alludes). Where, then, were the twelve stones put?

Still another narrative, duplicating the first, says that the twelve stones out of the Jordan were set up at Gilgal (4:20). Since Joshua 3-4 are especially important, written as the story of how the sanctuary of Israel at Gilgal was originally established, one must presume that the first and third versions must be close to correct, but this leaves no explanation for the tradition in 4:9, which can hardly be accurate. One way of handling the problem is that of Carpenter-Battersby which ascribes the first account to J and the third to E, while the peculiar v 9 has to be ascribed to an unknown, presumably Deuteronomic, redactor; the authors regard the analysis of these chapters (Joshua 3-4), however, as most difficult.[81] On the other hand, it is easy to find scholars who offer radically different analyses. W. H. Bennett, for example,[82] regards the basic narrative as E, the mysterious 4:9 being a J tradition, and the statement in 4:20 that the twelve stones were set up in Gilgal being added by the redactor who combined J and E into one document.

Indeed, the attempt to analyze the basic epic narrative into J and E in Joshua cannot be said to be successful. While often done, the results contain variant and individualistic conclusions because the criteria for this type of analysis are simply not clear, even as Wellhausen stated. In addition to the ease by which what is E for one scholar will be J for another, extreme positions will deny the presence of either J or E entirely in the book. In such cases the number of additions by redactors is simply increased to account for the obvious unevenness in the old material. Thus, while a basic assumption of literary critical source analysis has been that the Hexateuch is a unity because the Pentateuchal sources are present, it is evident that divergence of opinion regarding the analysis of the epic narrative in Joshua is so great that the Book of Joshua on this point presents special problems and, indeed, has peculiarities belonging only to itself.

Literary criticism has felt itself to be on more certain ground when it came to the identity of material added to the book from the sources of

[81] Carpenter-Battersby, *The Hexateuch* II, notes on 325-326.
[82] *The Book of Joshua*, 3.

the Jerusalem priesthood (P). In Joshua 1 the divine commissioning of Joshua was noted above to have had its precedent in Deuteronomy 31 by the Dtr editor(s). It is also known and related earlier by P in Num 27:18-23. The promise of the Transjordan tribes to assist in conquest of western Palestine and their own settlement east of the Jordan is reviewed by P in Numbers 32. The distribution of the land, the designation of the Levitical cities and the cities of refuge, carried out in Joshua 13-21 is fully provided for by Moses, according to P, in Numbers 34-35. Even the inheritance of the daughters of Zelophehad appears in P's Numbers 36 and Josh 17:3.

Thus, the Book of Joshua seems as much a fulfillment of previous promises and expectations of P as it is for the Deuteronomic school and for the old epic sources in Genesis, Exodus, and Numbers. Yet if for the literary critical school P had a story of the conquest, it is not preserved. The entry into Canaan was known since most scholars ascribe Josh 4:19 to P. The story of keeping Passover and the note in 5:10-12 that manna ceased when Israel crossed the Jordan reflects a P concern. Otherwise only faint traces of P were found in Joshua 1-12, as in the reference to "the ark of the testimony" (4:15), P's name for the portable symbol of the covenant (Exod 25:22), the box containing the Decalogue, which in Deuteronomic circles was commonly called "the ark of the covenant."[83]

It is in the territorial allotments to the tribes (chaps. 13-19) that the clearest evidence of P was believed to be present. The formulaic character of the lists, as well as the naming of the cities of refuge and of the Levites (20-21), contain so many terms and verbal clichés characteristic of P in the Pentateuch that the resemblance is unmistakable. Thus, the Transjordan settlement in 13:15 - 14:5, the settlements of Judah in 15:1-12, 20-62, of Ephraim and Manasseh in 16:4-9 and 17:1-10, of the remaining tribes in 18:1,11 - 19:46,48, and of the cities of refuge and of the Levites in chaps. 20 and 21, together with the Jordan altar story (22:9-34), are all believed to have come from the Jerusalem priesthood's archival sources, some of them probably old.

Yet the introduction to the P material in 13:1-14, indeed the setting for it, is that of Dtr. The conclusion to the allotments is also provided by Dtr in 21:43-45. So is the introduction, 22:1-8, to the supposedly P story of the Transjordan settlement and of the altar called "Witness" in the Jordan valley in 22:9-34. The final chapter, the original conclusion of the Dtr book, is 23, Joshua's farewell address to all Israel.[84]

---

[83] It is now realized that "testimony" ('ēdût), used by P for the Decalogue, was an archaic term for "covenant." See Delbert R. Hillers, *Covenant: The History of a Biblical Idea*, 161-162.

[84] Chapter 24 is almost pure E with some Deuteronomic reworking. It was considered practically a summary of the Elohist version of the Hexateuchal story,

Here, then, as with epic sources in chaps. 2-12, the situation is different in Joshua from what it is in the Pentateuch. In the latter P furnishes the framework, but in Joshua Dtr furnishes the framework for P. In the first half of the book little of P can be discerned; it becomes prominent only in the second half of the book. In addition, Dtr has so many evidences of P phraseology within it, while P has so many of Dtr, that the phenomena are of a most perplexing kind for the literary critic. In any event, it can only be argued "that the combination of P with JED was not effected in Joshua by the same hand or on the same method as in the Pentateuch."[85]

Instead of supplying a detailed review of the variety of discussions among literary critics about the problem, we shall instead turn to the discussion of Martin Noth, whose commentary on Joshua is probably the most important, original, and influential in our time.[86]

The Analysis of Martin Noth

As indicated earlier, Noth's analysis of the major collections of historical traditions in Israel is based, first of all, upon the sharp distinction of Deuteronomic material in Deuteronomy through the books of Kings (1) from the Jerusalem priesthood's editing of the old epic of Israel after the fall of Jerusalem (c. 587 B.C.) in the first four books—Genesis-Numbers—and (2) from the Chronicler's history of Judah written for the small restored post-exilic community (c. 400 B.C.; 1-2 Chronicles, Ezra, and Nehemiah).[87] One other modern analysis should also be mentioned: the work of Volz and Rudolph which systematically attempted to show that no such thing as E ever existed in the Hexateuch. The basic original narrative is J, a work

---

a special source appended by a redactor to the original Dtr book in order to preserve it. Literary critics considered it particularly valuable as a check on the nature of the E epic as derived from literary analysis in Genesis, Exodus, Numbers, and Joshua.

[85] So Carpenter in Carpenter-Battersby, *The Hexateuch* II, 316 (see 315-319 and vol. I, 176-179 for discussion). For a similar viewpoint, see Holzinger, *Das Buch Josua*, xi, though with none of the detailed discussion provided by Carpenter. For a more standard treatment, though with some reservation, see S. R. Driver, *Introduction* . . . (13th ed.) 103-116. Eissfeldt, *The Old Testament: An Introduction*, 248-257, introduces his L (Smend's J$_1$, and with modifications Pfeiffer's S; and in Exodus, Morgenstern's K—see Eissfeldt, 169-170, for discussion and bibliography) into the pre-Dtr analysis of Joshua 2-7. Eissfeldt does not regard P as present in Joshua 1-12; and as for chaps. 13*ff*, he believes that "P, as has already been stressed (pp. 206*f*), does not really offer narrative for its own sake, but a programme of demands concealed in the form of narrative" (252).

[86] Martin Noth, *Das Buch Josua* (1938; 2d ed., 1953).

[87] Noth, *Überlieferungsgeschichtliche Studien* I (1943). For analysis of the problem from another perspective, see Sigmund Mowinckel, *Tetrateuch-Pentateuch-Hexateuch* (1964).

prepared for the United Monarchy in the tenth century B.C. This work
had a number of editings and additions, they believed, before its final incorporation and editing by P, but there never existed in their opinion a
parallel and distinct work in the northern kingdom which one could designate as the Elohist document.[88]

Volz and Rudolph gained few converts, but one effect of their work
was a change in emphasis from an equal weight given J and E to the realization that J was all that Volz and Rudolph claimed for it, the primary
epic of Israel, while the north Israelite version of that epic (E) was so
close to it that all we can detect of it are those sections where, after the
fall of Israel in 724-721 B.C., editors deemed it superior to J or to possess
supplementary or parallel material that was felt important to preserve.
This viewpoint influenced Noth, and, though he differs from it, it is important for the understanding of his analysis of the epic narrative in
Joshua 2-11.[89]

Building on the difference in the way in which the epic sources appear
in Joshua, Noth believes that the basic failure of literary critical research
was its assumption that the contents of the book are simply a continuation of those in the Pentateuch. Thus for Noth there never existed such
a thing as the "Hexateuch" in any form or period of the tradition. The
main difficulty with the common past assumption is the primary fact that
the traditional stories of Joshua are simply a different type of material
from those of the Pentateuch. For the most part these stories are *orts-
gebunden;* that is, they are the type of thing preserved as traditional
memories at places or about places in traditional lore. They are not centered about individual personalities as in Genesis, but about events
remembered in relation to specific sites. The framework of these stories is
not priestly, but in the language and conception world of the Deuteronomic creator of Israel's history in the Promised Land, as is shown by
introductory and concluding passages (1:1-18 and 21:43 - 22:6 with 23)
and by the frequent evidences of Deuteronomic editing within the epic
material. Because of the book's clear relation to Deuteronomy before it
and to Judges after it, it is part of Dtr which originally was created as a
work, having knowledge of, but independent of, the Pentateuchal narrative
tradition.

Yet in Joshua there are two distinct Deuteronomic sections. The first is
the conquest narratives in Joshua 1-12 and the second is the tribal geography in 13:1 - 21:42. In the past the second has been thought to have
been a production of P, but wrongly so. This section with so many lists

[88] Paul Volz and Wilhelm Rudolph, *Der Elohist als Erzähler: Ein Irrweg der
Pentateuchkritik?* (1933); Wilhelm Rudolph, *Der "Elohist" von Exodus bis Josua*
(1938).
[89] For what follows see Noth, *Das Buch Josua.*

has a special, singular prehistory which is no proof whatever of its priestly compilation. Certain formal introductory and concluding formulae of lists are a fragile basis for a demonstration of a P style and vocabulary. The picture of the tribal occupation of Transjordan under the leadership of Moses in Joshua 13 and that of the tribal occupation after the division of the land under Joshua's leadership clearly has a Deuteronomic basis. Even the cities of refuge in chap. 20 are tied to Deut 19:1*ff*.

At the same time, Noth believes with earlier literary critics that the tribal geography (13:1-21:42) had its own independent history of redaction and transmission before it was introduced into the basic Dtr book. The same is true with regard to the covenant ceremony which created "all Israel" (that is, the Twelve Tribe League) at Shechem on the soil of the Promised Land (chap. 24). Both show inner evidence of Deuteronomic redactional history, though neither belonged to the original Dtr book which must have concluded with the farewell address to a great national assembly of Israel as related in chap. 23. Thus, we have to reckon with a Deuteronomic Joshua to which additional Deuteronomic material has been added.

Yet having stated his position, Noth then explains that there are numerous later additions to both the primary and secondary portions of the book. At this point, one discovers that Noth regards what other scholars have deemed priestly words or phrases as *Zusätze*, additions, comparatively small in quantity, however, and insufficient to be regarded as a separate source. Since this sort of thing happened in other books, it is not surprising, Noth says, that we should find it also in Joshua. Yet we now see that the analysis becomes so minute as to make it indistinguishable in method from that of the literary critical school. From the standpoint of historical conclusions based upon such literary analysis, however, the following should be noted especially.

1. The picture of a united Israel meeting together to parcel out the land by lot is Deuteronomic and not historical. This means that 14:1b and a portion of the eleven Hebrew words of v 2; 19:51a; 21:1-2 are additions.

2. The place of the meeting at Shiloh, and the erecting of the "Tent of Meeting" there, belongs only to the latter part of the period of the Judges and not to the early part of the period. This means that all references to Shiloh must be omitted, though there is no considered analysis of the passages in question as to whether in each the location "in Shiloh" is not demanded by the context or whether some other location was originally present.

3. Deletion, in the first point above, of references to the distribution of the land by lot means that all references to Joshua and the priest Eleazar who are in charge must be deleted. And for other reasons of historical reconstruction the figure of Joshua is considered by Noth as a secondary

unification of disparate traditions, as was Moses; this happened in the pre-literary stage of the tradition.

These are only a few examples of the exceedingly complex and minute literary analysis of Noth. It is almost impossible to ascertain from it any coherent picture of the mentality, oral and scribal, which could have worked upon the literature after such a manner to produce the result we have, one of high literary quality. The solution to the question of material of P type in Joshua 13-21 is different from that of the most astute pioneers of a previous generation of literary critics: the presence of a P "document" fitted into a framework of epic sources edited by Dtr is denied by Noth. There was no such "document." Yet Noth, having argued for this view, then takes the same markers of priestly style initially recognized, and considers them as additions to the series of homilies and lists written and collected by Dtr. Without arguing the individual cases one must query whether a close analysis of literary style can so simply leave out words, phrases, or sentences which get in the way of a theory and still have a coherent literary style.

It would seem that earlier critics, who analyzed the problem and indicated the difference between the way P appears in Joshua and in the Pentateuch and then left the matter largely unsolved by the methods used, were on less subjective grounds.

If one must provide some hypothesis for the phenomenon as a working platform, this writer would prefer something like the following: Dtr worked in Jerusalem and for him Zion was the center of his world, even as it was for the Jerusalem priesthood. The royal Davidic theology and the theology and teaching practice of the wise men also were present in the same comparatively small city. Where known pre-exilic documents of one school or another are isolated, it is seldom that the influence of other schools of thought are not present. Pure, unadulterated forms and styles may exist, but usually in short pericopes only, before elements that in theory do not belong to the form appear. Currently, there is great interest in the Wisdom literature and numerous articles are being written about Wisdom elements in the royal psalms, in a number of the prophets, in the Joseph story, and in the court history of David. Form critics have often worked with the theory that mixed forms are late on the assumption that only pure forms could be early. Yet Deuteronomy 32 has to be considered a comparatively early psalm, as does Psalm 78, but both are clear examples of mixed forms.[90]

From the discernible pre-exilic mixture of forms, why then would not Dtr have the possibility, assuredly in the long reign of Josiah at least, to gain access to the temple and court archives of which the priests (P) in

---

[90] See Wright, "The Lawsuit of God," 26-27, with references there cited.

the exilic and post-exilic periods were the heirs because they were the group who possessed what was saved from temple archives? In the Book of Joshua, as already indicated by Carpenter and others, the mixture of material is so great that the criteria for disentangling the sources in Genesis-Numbers cannot solve the problem of the literary history of the Book of Joshua. That Joshua 13-21 is basically P-type material in a Dtr-edited framework is most difficult to deny, for Noth's denial involves him in a minute and subjective assumption of *Zusätze* as complicated as those of Rudolph when he attempted to even out the narrative by his elimination of E. The basic problem is the analysis of this P-type material. Once Noth has removed his P and other *Zusätze,* his views are as follows.

A great amount of material which had already been fixed was used by Dtr in Joshua. Chapters 2-9, Noth believed, were for the most part etiological sagas tied to specific places. They had their original setting in the sanctuary at Gilgal which belonged to the central Palestinian tribes, specifically to the tribe of Benjamin. The broadening of this local tradition to an all-Israelite or tribal league tradition is to be discovered in the history of the Gilgal sanctuary before the monarchy and certainly before it had become the central sanctuary for all tribes in the time of Saul. The close relation of these traditions to Joshua is due to the proximity of Ephraim, where Joshua was buried (Josh 24:29-30). Joshua 10-11 are two war narratives which originally were of merely local importance. Secondarily they were elevated to a status involving all Israel in which Joshua was the central figure. In the present book they serve to show how the Judean south and the Galilean north were conquered. The etiological saga about the occupation of Ai (chap. 8) and of Gibeon and related cities (chap. 9) indicate that the Samarian middle of the country was also captured by the Israelite tribes.

The outline of this whole narrative complex, Noth states, is present in the oldest literary forms (cf. especially 5:1; 6:21; 9:3, part of 4; portions of chaps. 10 and 11). Noth names the author of this oldest narrative *der "Sammler,"* the "Collector." He frankly says that it is difficult to "prove" his authorship of individual verses and pericopes. Most certainly, however, one can attribute to him the introduction of the figure of Joshua into the narratives. And one must suppose that the "Collector" was not late in time. Judging from 11:10-15 he knew that before Solomon rebuilt Hazor it was a city laid waste and unoccupied (cf. 1 Kgs 9:15). On the other hand, he appears to know nothing of the resettlement of Ai, which according to archaeological discovery was reoccupied by Israel in the tenth century (8:28).[91] The "Collector's" manner of expression in 11:16

[91] This archaeological datum has been corrected by more recent excavation, which has discovered that the presumed Israelite reoccupation, after some twelve

("Joshua took all this land: the Highlands, all the southern desert, all the territory of Goshen, the foothills, the Arabah [the Highlands of Israel and its foothills]") presupposes the two states of Israel and Judah which had come into being in the time of the United Monarchy. Hence, Noth believes the "Collector" must have worked about 900 B.C. His viewpoint was Judean as his language indicates (11:2, "the northern kings . . . ," and 11:16 cited above).

This appeal to geographical reference and archaeology is surely not a strong argument for the date of anything, especially since both types of evidence are so lacking in specificity and could be used for other types of arguments, considering the variety of ancient information and usage at Dtr's disposal.

With regard to the literary prehistory of the tribal geography (chaps. 13-21), Noth believes that two main sources can be isolated in the literary prehistory of the section. Both were originally recognized by Albrecht Alt.[92] The first is an old list of tribal boundaries which must depict the tribal claims on the basis of which boundary disputes could be settled during the period of the Judges. It thus must derive from a pre-monarchical document. What the Deuteronomic editor has preserved from this are the detailed boundaries for Judah with Simeonite territory unmentioned but included (15:1-12), Ephraim (16), western Manasseh (17:7-11), and Benjamin (18:11-20)—that is, the hill country, coastal plain, and Negeb, lacking Galilee and the Transjordan settlements.

The second document is a list of the cities of the kingdom of Judah during the Divided Monarchy, listed within twelve groups which must have represented the administrative districting of the separate Judean kingdom during the Divided Monarchy. It includes, besides Judah, the territory of Simeon and Benjamin, with the chief towns in each province listed with appropriate divisions and concluding enumeration formulae (15:20-62; 18:21-28). Alt initially, followed by Noth, dates this document to the second half of the seventh century; that is, to the period of Josiah (c. 640-609 B.C.).

In 1956 Frank M. Cross and G. Ernest Wright introduced a new study of the second document, employing fresh historical-topographical and archaeological information. Because the province list includes an eastern Benjamin which takes in Bethel and a small portion of Ephraimite territory around it, and because the only information we have about such a

---

hundred years in which there was no settlement of "the Ai" (Hebrew; "the Ruin" is the meaning of the tell's title in the Bible), consisted of two strata of the earliest Iron Age, c. 1200-1000 B.C., there being no evidence of a tenth-century occupation. See below NOTES and COMMENT on 7:1 - 8:29.

[92] See Albrecht Alt, "Das System der Stammesgrenzen im Buch Josua," in *Kleine Schriften* I, 193-202; "Josua," ibid., I, 176-192; "Judas Gaue unter Josia," ibid., II, 276-288; and "Eine galiläische Ortsliste in Josua XIX," *ZAW* 45 (1927) 59-87.

Judean occupation of Bethel comes, not from Dtr, but from passages in 2 Chronicles dating from the end of the tenth through the ninth century, the Judean province list was dated to that era, with a probable eighth-century updating by a summary listing of the Philistine city-states (15:45-47)—unless the latter was simply an idealization of Dtr, representing claims but not necessarily possession when the province document was adapted to a use in Joshua 15 and 18, whereby the original tribal allotments could be described.[93] This treatment has been subjected to two major critiques, the first of which would date the list to the reign of Uzziah in the mid-eighth century, while the second would date it into the reign of Hezekiah in the late eighth century.[94]

These two documents have been used to depict the territory claimed by the original twelve tribe system. There remain Galilee and the division of the allotments in Transjordan to be described. The Galilean list for Noth in 19:10-39 is simply a list of places, artificially put together to appear to be like the southern border place and town lists. This was done by a Redactor (*Bearbeiter*) who put the whole together with formulae so that each tribe received its land as an "inheritance." While Sigmund Mowinckel, *Zur Frage nach dokumentarischen Quellen in Joshua xiii-xix* (Oslo: Jacob Dybwads, 1946), had attempted to solve the problem here by a perpetuation of the old theory of documentary sources, Noth rejects that view as incorrect because it cannot solve the peculiar and individualistic problems of each group of lists.

The list of Levitic cities (chap. 21), Noth believes, following Alt, belongs to the seventh century B.C., the era of Josiah, and is an indication of Josiah's attempted reconstruction of the Davidic state.

The next literary stage was to take this material about tribal occupancy and transfer it into a context of possession of the land achieved by a united, twelve tribe Israel and a great campaign led by Joshua. The presence of Dan in 19:40-48, even though Dan had early migrated to the far north near Mount Hermon (v 47) and was originally not part of the Josianic list, the addition of Simeon (19:1-9), and of the Transjordan town lists of Reuben and Gad, are editorial indications of the attempt to adjust the use of the old border list and the Judean province list for the purpose of reconstructing the situation presumed to have existed in the time of Joshua. The presence of the name "Joshua," Noth believes, is the clear indication of the final literary stage, since it, like Moses in the Penta-

---

[93] Frank M. Cross and G. Ernest Wright, "The Boundary and Province Lists of the Kingdom of Judah," *JBL* 75 (1956) 202-226.

[94] Zechariah Kallai-Kleinmann, "The Town Lists of Judah, Simeon, Benjamin and Dan," *VT* 8 (1958) 134-160; and Yohanan Aharoni, "The Province-List of Judah," *VT* 9 (1959) 225-246. See for further analysis the NOTES to the text, where the general point of view, with modifications of the original Cross-Wright analysis [fn 93], will be presented anew.

teuchal material, is the sole factor which unites material of such disparate origin. Old material is present throughout, having been drawn especially from the document in Judges 1. Finally, the cities of refuge in chap. 20 are added, though the origin of this six-city list is unknown except that it must go back to Deut 19:1ff.

Thus does Noth account for the complicated history of chaps. 13:1 - 21:42, a history separate from that of chaps. 1-12; 21:43 - 22:6; and 23. The two parts of Joshua were only put together during the exile as a part of the whole Dtr work on Israel in the Promised Land.

With regard to 24:1-33, we have here a pre-Deuteronomic tradition which underwent Dtr redaction. It is a special addition to the Book of Joshua, but it has no relation to the remainder of the book. The story of the assembly at Shechem is a special tradition which cannot be recovered.

Conclusions Regarding Joshua in Modern Source Criticism

The following comments will indicate the reaction of this writer to Noth's position.

1. Noth's case for stressing the special Dtr nature of Joshua seems well taken. The book possesses, as he says, a type of Deuteronomic editing not to be found in the Pentateuch. On the other hand, the pre-Deuteronomic materials in chaps. 13-21 have an independent history which is entirely unrelated to the Pentateuchal sources. As for the pre-Deuteronomic material in chaps. 2-11 the question as to whether they are a continuation of Pentateuchal JE can only be raised; it cannot be answered. Indeed, the mixture of elements crucial to the analysis, where they exist, is so different as to lead one to be skeptical. The relation to Pentateuchal sources, as Noth maintains, simply cannot be demonstrated. The formula for the wonders at the Egyptian Reed Sea in 2:10 and 4:23, for example, connects with nothing in Exodus 14. Overriding every other consideration is the fact that Joshua is an integral part of the Dtr history of Israel in the Promised Land.

2. As indicated above, however, severe reservations have to be expressed regarding Noth's handling of P in Joshua. Within chaps. 1-12 usual P indicators are so occasional and isolated that one hesitates to say that within the Jerusalem of Dtr a P editor has to be posited to explain these occasional expressions. Certainly one must agree with Noth that one cannot posit a complete P source for Joshua. For that matter, it is exceedingly difficult to posit P as a complete narrative source in the Tetrateuch. Much simpler is the hypothesis that P is only the exilic editor of the JE epic in the Tetrateuch, at a time when the urge was most strong to

preserve Jerusalem archives for prehistory, and the Patriarchal, Exodus, Sinai, and Wilderness eras of the epic narrative.[95]

Yet the situation is different in chaps. 13-21. As indicated above, the older literary analysis found so much individualistic phraseology of P in 13:15-32; 14:1-5 and in parts of each of the other chapters from 15 through 22 that the question is not easy to overlook. Nor can one be satisfied with the often minute excising of these indicators after the manner of Noth in order to maintain a pure Dtr text, using older material.

Previously, it has been here argued that the primary Dtr was a first or pre-exilic edition, dating from the end of the seventh century, following the Josianic adoption of Dtn as the basis of a massive state reform. We have also made a special point of the fact that a basis for a portion of Noth's views had already been made by certain pioneers in the literary critical movements, who had pointed out the difference of the use of P in Genesis-Numbers and in Joshua. In the former P provides the outline and setting for the epic narrative, whereas in the latter P is encountered in a framework provided by Dtr's editing of the epic narrative. Hence in the Jerusalem of the late seventh century B.C. it is not a difficult hypothesis to assume that Dtr drew on the same temple and/or state archives to which the Jerusalem priests were the sole heirs in the exilic and post-exilic periods after the destruction of both state and temple.

3. The view of Alt that there once existed an old pre-monarchic document specifying tribal boundaries, and that this is the source of the detailed boundaries given for Judah, Ephraim, Manasseh, and Benjamin in chaps. 15-18, is difficult to counter. Chapters 13-21 must have behind them a conception of tribal allotments derived from actual tradition and probably temple archives which preserved the knowledge of the tribal claims of the tribal league before the monarchy.

A question arises, however, whether Dtr would have constructed from the sources at that school's disposal a story of the conquest without at the same time a story of how God granted each tribe its "inheritance." As pointed out repeatedly in Part I of this Introduction, the gift of the land in Israel's hymns and confessions involved both an act of God in using the Holy War institution to "cleanse" and ready the land for occupation, and also the distribution of the land to the tribes so that each tribe and family understood the particular portion of land falling to it to be a divine determination over which the Suzerain was the real owner and ruler. Thus as early as the psalm in Exodus 15 mythical language is used to speak of the Promised Land as God's creation, the mountain of his inher-

---

[95] Here I follow Cross, *CMHE*, 301-321. Volz also denies that P was a narrative source; he considered P, like E, simply as an elaboration of J (see Volz-Rudolph, *Der Elohist . . .* , and Eissfeldt, *The Old Testament: An Introduction,* 167).

itance (*naḥălâ,* v 17). Yet the land was also Israel's "inheritance," a possession of which the nation had ownership and control. At least as early as Psalm 78—we cannot date it precisely except that it is surely early pre-exilic—the two are stated together as part and parcel of the same event: God's gift of and his allotting the land to individual tribes and clans as their "inheritance." Verse 55 reads:

> He drove out nations before them;
>   He allotted them (land) in a measured inheritance;
> He settled the tribes of Israel in their tents.

As was explained in Part I it is most difficult to dissociate the Hebrew term "allot" from the old custom of casting lots to determine divine will. That is, the only way Israel could have ascertained the will of God regarding the land distribution was to have carefully surveyed the land in advance and then to have seen what God wanted by the official "dice," the Urim and Thummim. If the theme of allotment cannot be separated from conquest as gift, then the tradition in Josh 14:1-5 and in chaps. 18-19 about Joshua and the high priest assigning the land by lot cannot be assumed to be a secondary embellishment of the narrative, enlarging individual tribal conquests into an all-Israel setting. Surely the actual course of events must have been more complicated.

4. Noth's view of the conquest of Canaan accepts without question the older literary critical view that the unified conquest of Canaan cannot have happened as described in the Book of Joshua. Judges 1, it is believed, gives a glimpse of what must have been the real situation: an individual clan or tribal grouping conquering this piece of territory, another conquering that at another period, and still others initially failing in this or that place. For Alt and Noth, then, great importance is attached to Joshua 24 as deriving from that Shechem assembly when "all Israel" of the twelve tribe league actually came into being. But the conquest itself was a long drawn-out affair, while the unity of Israel was a final result of a gradual amalgamation and struggle. Historically the version of the conquest presented by Dtr is a myth concocted by the later tradition developed in "all Israel." Thus, in Noth's analysis described above, it is the "Redactor" who secondarily introduced the lot and the tribal assemblies of "all Israel" at Shiloh into the lists to bind them together. Furthermore, the man Joshua, whose name appears everywhere, is the sure sign of the final stage of editing since that name binds the whole together.

Yet in point 3 above conquest and "allotment" are seen to be so deeply embedded in the confessional and hymnic traditions of Israel that one cannot simply accept this old view of the conquest without serious reservations. Its basis is extremely fragile in literary evidence and one must be impressed with the mounting evidence from old poetry, as we are enabled to date it on more objective grounds, that the situation was far more complex than the historical conclusions drawn from Judges 1 by literary critics would suggest. The basic problem of the literary critical view of the conquest that centers its case on Judg 1:1-2:5 is the assumption that the latter is a coherent, unified source which most critics assume to be the J account of the conquest (Eissfeldt attributes it to his L, his name for J_1). Yet how can such a congeries of individual tribal items be considered a unified narrative source such as the Yahwist of Genesis-Numbers would be expected to produce? If the Yahwist's version of the climax of the story of God's mighty acts (whether "J_1" or "J_2") in the formation of Israel in the Promised Land were actually preserved, would it not more likely be a basic narrative such as presently exists in Joshua 2-11? It surely would not be such a congeries of individual items of different tradition-history background such as Judg 1:1-2:5 represents. What is the history of the tradition behind the peculiar story of the Judean capture of Jerusalem (Judg 1:3-8), when all agree that Jerusalem did not come into Israelite possession until David made it his capital (2 Sam 5:6-9)? If the former is a tradition dependent upon the latter, it is most peculiar, to say the least, from the presuppositions of literary criticism. Similarly, the traditions about the capture of Debir and about Caleb, Hebron, and the Kenites (Judg 1:9-20) certainly read like another piece of ancient folklore, like the comparable Jerusalem pericope in Judg 1:1-8. The capture of Luz, renamed Bethel, by the tribal groups of Joseph (Judg 1:22-26), has no parallel in any narrative source, unless with Albright it is considered the true and parallel tradition to the Joshua tradition about the nearby "Ruin" (Ai), a town of unusual importance between c. 3000-2300 B.C., with a small Israelite settlement of short duration during the twelth and eleventh centuries B.C.[96]

There follows the only part of the chapter which seems to have derived from a coherent document: vv 27-36, a list of tribal claims which could not be realized. Manasseh could not occupy the plains of Jezreel or Dor; Ephraim could not take the city-state of Gezer; Zebulon, Asher, and Naphtali could not take all of Galilee, while Dan was unable to occupy its claim, outside the lowlands, in the plain (where the city-state of Gezer, and the city of Ekron, founded by the Philistines in the twelfth century, prevented the tribe's expansion and forced its twelfth-century migration to Upper Galilee below Mount Hermon).

How can such an uneven gathering of materials, from different sources and tradition-histories, including differing types of literature, be considered a single source, presenting the true picture of the original conquest?

[96] See G. Ernest Wright, "The Significance of Ai in the Third Millennium B.C.," in *Archäologie und des Altes Testament*, 299-319, and NOTES and COMMENT on 7:1-8:29.

The only reason, surely, is that the critic reacts negatively to the overly enthusiastic pictures of total conquest believed by the Dtr school (cf. Josh 10:40-42; 11:16-23). Yet in spite of these glorifications of the work of Joshua, Dtr knew perfectly well that for one reason or another God did not permit "all Israel" to succeed in the conquest completely, and this information is given by Dtr explicitly in Josh 13:1-6; Judg 3:1-6, in addition to his interspersion of the negative notes of Judg 1:27-36 within Joshua 15-19, including the statement in 15:63 (not an original part of the province list, but a Dtr addition) that Judah could not expel the Jebusites from Jerusalem "to this day"—the last indicating that an old pre-Davidic source was being quoted.[97]

5. Chapters 13-21 make up a complex document about tribal allotment which uses several pre-existent sources and traditions in order to reconstruct the post-conquest tribal territories to which Israel laid claim. With a Dtr introduction and conclusion the following sources have been detected:

a) The old detailed boundary lists preserved for Judah (15:1-12), Joseph (Ephraim and Manasseh: 16:1-8; 17:7-11[12-13H]), and Benjamin (18:12-20). These are felt probably to derive from a pre-monarchical boundary document, prepared and used by members of the tribal league.

b) The province list of the cities of the kingdom of Judah from a period after the death of Solomon when Benjamin belonged originally to the southern kingdom, as did also the territory of Bethel (15:20-61; 18:21-28). The provinces can be detected because the towns are listed by geographical sub-areas under four main headings: Southland (Negeb: 15:21), Lowland (Shephelah: 15:33), Hill Country (15:48), and Wilderness (15:61). Each district is concluded by the number of towns in each with the dependent villages. This regular form is interrupted by the list of Philistine cities, named from north to south: Ekron, Ashdod, and Gaza (15:45-47). Omitted are Gath (under vassal treaty to Judah during the tenth century at least) and Ashkelon. In any event, these verses are not in the form of the rest of the province list and have been added to it, either by Dtr or an earlier editor, perhaps during the eighth century when, under King Uzziah, Judah for a time controlled the whole southern coastal plain.

c) A list of the remaining tribes in chap. 19 which uses the lists of towns, provides the total numbers in each tribe, after the pattern of the province list of the kingdom of Judah, but also uses the town list to suggest borders, after the pattern of the old tribal boundary descriptions

---

[97] See further G. Ernest Wright, "The Literary and Historical Problem of Joshua 10 and Judges 1," *JNES* 5 (1946) 105-114; see also Part III below of this Introduction.

(e.g. "Their border went up westward . . ." 19:11, etc.). Alt saw here the preservation of a *document* describing the Galilean allotments by means of a list of Galilean places.[98] Noth rejected this claim for a more radical view of the editorial, artificial, and secondary construction of a boundary listing for the remaining tribes about which nothing had been said up to that point.[99] In the NOTES to the text the question will be raised as to whether Alt's view should not be revived. In any event, the editor or author of the chap. 19 material is probably not Dtr, but it can be argued that the *final* compiler is Dtr, who thus did not compose his Book of Joshua *without* chaps. 13-19.

d) The listing of the territorial claims of the Transjordan tribes in chap. 13 is superficially like the tribal allotments in chap. 19, except we are told they were specifically given by Moses, and were not parcelled out by lot as was the case with the Promised Land, which originally had been Canaan west of the Jordan (see further below).

e) From Jerusalem archives were drawn the lists of cities of refuge and of the Levites (chaps. 20-21).

At the end Dtr summarizes the conclusion of the allotment by saying (21:43-45) that all was finished. God had given the land to Israel as he had promised (sworn to) the patriarchs, and not one of these wonderful promises had Yahweh failed to keep. All had been fulfilled. Dtr continues then with an introduction (22:1-6) to the story of the altar of witness (22:7-34), in which Joshua gives a final admonition to the Transjordan tribes and sends them back to settle in their homes, now that the whole conquest was complete. Later, after many years, when Joshua had become old, a league assembly was called, according to Dtr, at which Joshua gave his final instructions and covenant warning to the whole people (chap. 23). Thus Dtr concludes his book with the end of a great era and of a series of remarkable events. Chapter 24 is a separate, old and valuable tradition, not fitting precisely at any earlier point. It has been preserved as an appendix.

6. Finally, what should be said about Noth's view that the person of Joshua is the latest introduction into all the narratives, thus binding together the various disparate elements of the tradition? Noth, of course, made the same claim for the figure of Moses in the books Exodus-Numbers.

Noth believes that Joshua is unquestionably the primary figure only in the account of his grave tradition in Ephraim (24:29-30), and probably also in the Shechem covenant story of 24:1-28 where the league is consti-

---

[98] *ZAW* 45 (1927) [fn 92], 59-81.
[99] "Studien zu den historisch-geographischen Dokumenten des Josuabuches," *ZDPV* 58 (1935) 188-255. Cf. Cross and Wright [fn 93], 203-211, where Cross carefully reviews Noth's arguments and is persuaded by them.

tuted. By the time of Dtr he had become the central figure of the whole conquest tradition. Yet a closer examination of individual traditions in Joshua 2-9 suggests to Noth that these are primarily etiological sagas of the tribe of Benjamin, preserved in the Gilgal sanctuary. The Benjaminite and Galilean battle stories (chaps. 10-11), originally local, nevertheless assumed an all-Israel setting very early. When the event of Joshua 24 became an all-Israel tradition then Joshua also as leader became an all-Israel figure.

In the study of the text each pericope will have to be examined in the light of Noth's presuppositions. Most seriously to be challenged, however, is the role of *Ortsgebundenheit* (traditions tied to natural phenomena, or places, such as a grave or a peculiar topographical feature). John Bright has challenged the assumption that this plays a *primary* role in the creation of historical tradition.[100] Perhaps, on the contrary, its primary role is in myth. The question thus concerns the *presuppositions* which are brought to the form and tradition-history methodologies, rather than the methods themselves. If one finds other presuppositions welling from the narratives, then, as a matter of course, different conclusions regarding the role of Joshua in the narratives will be reached.

For example, the story of Josh 5:13-15 (Joshua's encounter with the head of Yahweh's cosmic army) is unique and without parallel. Yet it is surely not a composition of Dtr, but an ancient tradition in which place-attachment plays no role. Instead, the story derives from Holy War traditions. Yet Joshua's encounter with the cosmic commander near Jericho is clearly an account in which the centrality of Joshua in the narrative is pivotal. So also is the tradition's statement of the pivotal place Joshua has in the sight of the unseen cosmic forces behind the conquest events. A strong *presupposition* is immediately created, therefore, that Joshua is not a secondary figure in the Gilgal-Jericho pericopes or, for that matter, in the remainder of the narratives.

III. HISTORICAL PROBLEMS OF THE BOOK OF JOSHUA

As observed above, scholars of the nineteenth and twentieth centuries who have dealt primarily with the inner biblical literary traditions only, and whose avowed purpose has been "truth," without first stating or assuming dogmatic or doctrinal considerations as presuppositions, have almost unanimously rejected the historicity of the conquest as Dtr has re-

[100] John Bright, *Early Israel in Recent History Writing.*

lated it in Joshua.[101] The primary figure in modern times who created the opposition to this "classical" opinion was William F. Albright.[102] His reaction was both emotional and empirical—emotional primarily because of what he believed to be the *ad hoc* character of presuppositions long ago formulated but scarcely reexamined in a modern setting. He felt strongly about this because his education was German-oriented, where new perspectives were being developed which were largely unknown in the United States. He was also empirical because, as distinct from the average biblical scholar, he was trained primarily in classics and in the literary and archaeological worlds of Mesopotamia and Egypt. Beginning in 1920, his self-training in Palestinian and Syrian archaeology led him to become the dominant creative figure in the attempt to place the Bible in a perspective of the whole of ancient history as it was taking shape following a century of exploration and excavation.

The Graf-Wellhausen reconstruction of Israel's history, he believed, had been formulated by those who lived in the pre-archaeological era and who breathed the atmosphere of German idealism. In our time we must gather together the known facts and base our theoretical reconstructions upon them, rather than upon a pre-existing ideology of history as always and only an evolution from the simple to the complex, and of religion as the emergence primarily of ethical ideals and ethical monotheism in an ascending progression within the historical process.[103]

For a majority in the biblical world Albright's work established the basic chronology for the events related in Joshua (a thirteenth-century date for the conquest) and the historical support for the background of the narrative. Yet a carefully defined statement of what archaeology is and is not, does and does not do, has been hard to articulate. Such a statement must follow the experiments of reconstruction, and first at-

[101] Sufficient citations of the literary critical school on the points at issue have been given in Part II; for review, cf. Wright, "The Literary and Historical Problem of Joshua 10 and Judges 1." For Noth's last stated views, other than those contained in his commentary, *Das Buch Josua,* see "Hat die Bibel doch Recht," in *Festschrift, Günther Dehn,* W. Schneemelcher, ed. (Neukirchen: Kreis Moersverlag, 1957) 8-22; "Der Beitrag der Archäologie zur Geschichte Israels," in *VT*Sup 7 (1960) 262-282; *The History of Israel* (1960) 68-80.

[102] See especially Albright's pioneer article, "The Israelite Conquest of Canaan in the Light of Archaeology," *BASOR* 74 (1938) 11-23. For treatments by his students, see Bright, *Early Israel in Recent History Writing* (1956); *A History of Israel* (1959) 117-120; 3rd edition (1981) 129-133; Paul W. Lapp, "The Conquest of Palestine in the Light of Archaeology," *Concordia Theological Monthly* 38 (1967) 283-300. Wright's latest treatment is in *Biblical Archaeology,* 69-84.

[103] Albright's most forthright statement of this perspective was his presidential address before the Society of Biblical Literature, "The Ancient Near East and the Religion of Israel," printed in *JBL* 59 (1940) 85-112, an important article for views which were not repeated in the same pertinent way in the following book: his *From the Stone Age to Christianity* (1940) can be said to be the greatest and most classical treatment of biblical archaeology from his perspective ever written.

tempts may need future modification when the polemical period which is always created when general assumptions are badly shaken is past.[104]

What Archaeology Can and Cannot Do

While the term "archaeology" was first used by classical authors simply to mean "ancient history," its revival in modern times had led to a narrowing of its meaning to the ruins of past civilizations and cultures, especially their excavation. For Albright and his students archaeology has included both epigraphic and non-epigraphic discoveries, even though the investigation of the two must each develop its own set of disciplines. Yet in the antiquarian field philologists and archaeologists are usually separate, the former studying documents and the latter the methodologies of conducting an excavation and the study and presentation of what is found. The field has suffered from too much compartmentalization at this point.

Furthermore, archaeologists themselves have suffered from too great a separation from one another in their various fields, and usually too great a separation from humanistic disciplines on the one hand and from the natural sciences on the other. Anthropological archaeology, for example, starting from its primary point of reference, primitive man, has developed methodology and cooperation with natural sciences more quickly than other fields, because the very nature of most of the deposits studied required it to do so in order to extract a maximum of information from a minimum of deposit. On the other hand, the humanistic aspects of the subject have often been shortchanged and the results impoverished by overzealous attempts to remain non-historical and "scientific" by scholars who are actually trying to reconstruct all they can about human beings, to whom "science" has only limited application.

Classical and most of early Near Eastern archaeology has been dominated by a museum mentality which requires objects for display to a contributing public primarily interested in art and art history. Archaeologists from this background have been slowest of all to develop an interest in ever more precision and control in methodology. They have, to their credit, maintained their full humanistic interest, but, with exceptions, separation from the natural sciences has been most notable in the information derived from the queries put to their material.

[104] For outstanding attempts at such statement, see especially Roland d. Vaux, "On Right and Wrong Uses of Archaeology," in *Near Eastern Archaeology in the Twentieth Century*, 64-80. For a treatment of the same subject from the standpoint of a classicist, see M. I. Finley, "Archaeology and History," *Daedalus* (Winter 1971) 168-186, reprinted in *The Use and Abuse of History* (New York: Viking, 1975) 87-101.

Excavation of the great Near Eastern tells has brought such wealth of architecture and objects that there seemed no need to ask further questions than those of the historian regarding chronology, interconnections, and typological history.

The conceptual framework and methodology of excavation has been most highly developed and refined in the historical period by a few exceptional persons whose primary training has been in other countries, but who for one reason or another began excavations in Palestine: Flinders Petrie and Kathleen Kenyon from England, George A. Reisner and William F. Albright from the United States. That small corridor between continents has few natural resources, and thus was very poor as compared with the centers of world power in antiquity. To gain any positive result from work in that area requires one's turning his attention away from an expectation of rich stores of anything, especially great palaces and a wealth of inscriptions, the latter forming the primary guide to where in time one is located while digging. Pottery chronology and the stratigraphy of the deposits of earth have to be the primary concentration. It was Petrie who in 1891 left Egypt for a short period of work at Tell el-Ḥesī in the southern coastal plain. There he proved that ceramics could be a primary chronological tool by demonstrating the differences in pottery between levels cut into the steep cliff of the tell eroded by a winter stream. It was Reisner who left Egypt in 1909 and 1910 for two seasons of work at Samaria and encountered an intricate jumble on the tell which required an entirely different strategy from anything he had used in Egypt.

It was Albright, beginning in 1920, who developed the pottery tool into an instrument of some precision by taking it out of the mists of oral tradition, articulated its use in writing, and provided a critical assessment of the whole discipline in the light of his knowledge of the entire Near East. Following his work one could begin to write archaeological histories of the country—something impossible before the discipline had been subjected to his critical work and his ceramic sequences.

Reisner's methodological principles were generally not followed, except for the new care with which recording and find spots were handled. Thus there evolved the ideal of being able to reproduce a tell's stratigraphy and pinpoint the exact location of all artifacts. It was with Kenyon's reintroduction of Reisner's principles independently, as they had been developed in the archaeology of England, that the new revolution in precision and field control was put in practice for all to see in eastern Mediterranean archaeology. The key to this control lay in digging and distinguishing the soil layers as a geologist would do, rather than focusing primarily on building or wall sequences, following the lead of the chief interests of the expedition's architect.

Palestine west of the Jordan is the most intensively dug and explored area of its size in the world. Its very poverty has been a major factor in the development of precision in archaeological field work to a degree seldom reached in the historical periods anywhere else in the classical and Near Eastern worlds. The proper use of archaeology as a "scientific" tool in biblical study was impossible before the work of Albright, while the period of the 1960s was the time of a revolution in controlled archaeology, following the period 1952-1958 of the Kenyon expedition to Jericho.[105]

Even these new methodologies fail to extract a maximum of information from the occupational debris of antiquity. Beginning in Palestine in 1970, certain American explorations were able to staff their expeditions with a more or less full complement of natural scientists. Such cross-disciplinary approaches were a "first" in the Near East's historical period. They were modeled after the great pioneering prehistoric enterprises of Robert J. Braidwood in the 1950s, which have refocused our knowledge of human prehistory with regard to what happened before, during, and after *the Neolithic revolution* when the first villages were established in the Near East. Hence it can be predicted that the 1970s and '80s will see a far greater amount of controlled information made available to the biblical student than the archaeologist has hitherto been able to provide.

With regard to biblical events, however, it cannot be overstressed that archaeological data are ambiguous. Fragmentary ruins, preserving only a tiny fraction of the full picture of ancient life, cannot speak without someone asking questions of them. And the kind of questions asked are part and parcel of the answers "heard" because of predispositions on the part of the questioner. Archaeology can *prove* very little about anything without minds stored with a wide-ranging variety of information which carefully begin to ask questions of the remains in order to discover what they mean. It is all too easy for lack of information and imagination to gain less than the remains can supply, or for fertile imaginations to suppose that the ancient trash heaps tell one more than a very controlled mind can believe they do. It is small wonder, then, that disagreement and debate arise. A destruction layer in the ruins does not tell us the identity of the people involved. Indeed, we know that certain black soot and charcoal layers do not necessarily mean destruction. An accidental fire in one part of the town or city, certain industrial pursuits, or even an earthquake may be the answer.

Yet the nature of the remains does not mean that archaeology is useless. It simply means that ancient cultural and political horizons and sequences can only be reconstructed by hypothesis from every kind of critically

[105] Cf. Kathleen M. Kenyon, *Beginning in Archaeology; Digging Up Jericho;* and G. Ernest Wright, "Archaeological Method in Palestine—An American Interpretation," *Eretz Israel* 9 (1969) 120-133.

sifted evidence available. At some points more data are available than at others. Hence historical reconstructions have varying degrees of probability. In studying antiquity it is important to recall that models and hypotheses are the primary means by which reconstruction is possible after the basic critical work is done. And, furthermore, it takes a great deal of humility to say frankly what the physical sciences have had also to say; predisposition of minds at any one period frame the type of questions asked of the material and become a part of the "answers" we suppose we have obtained from our investigations. Final *proof* of anything ancient must be confined to such questions as how pottery was made, what rock was used, what food and fauna were present, etc. Certainly that proof does not extend to the validity of the religious claims the Bible would place upon us, and we must remember that the Bible is not a mine for scientifically grounded certainties about anything. It is instead a literature that places before us one of history's major religious options.

What archaeology can do for biblical study is to provide a physical context in time and place which was the environment of the people who produced the Bible or are mentioned in it. Inscriptional evidence is of exceptional importance for biblical backgrounds and even for occasional mention of biblical people and places. For the rest, archaeology provides evidence which must be critically sifted. It then is used along with other critically assessed data, where it exists, in order to form *hypotheses* about the how, why, what, and when of cultural, sociopolitical, and economic affairs in thirteenth-century Palestine, for example. These hypotheses will stand or be altered as new information makes change necessary. Final and absolutely proven answers are impossible to provide. One generation's questions may not be another's, and in every case the questions asked are integral to the answers. Thus one generation's research differs from another's.

Noth's predisposition led him to a negative view of the historical background of the confessional events surveyed above in Part I. To this writer, such a negative assessment, deriving from the last century's criticism, is not only a defensible, but an indispensable tool in historical *methodology*. But when the tool becomes the dominant item of the conclusion, it then is most often a bias or predisposition of the author. There is no reason whatever, as previously indicated, that the opposite predisposition should not be held, namely one toward a positive view of the evidence, even though the actual course of events may have been far more complex than tradition has remembered. Whether optimism or pessimism is taken as predisposition, the fact is that we have a dominant and central confessional and literary theme of conquest both in the Book of Joshua and in parallel liturgical statements. This requires explanation. A necessity is upon us to explain its presence in the earliest literature (e.g.

Exodus 15) as well as in the latest. Something formative to Israel's world view happened in her earliest historical experience. Can a hypothesis be suggested which explains without claiming too much or too little? By definition such a hypothesis is devised to explain most completely what we *now* know, *not* what it may be necessary or possible for another generation to say.

The situation with regard to Joshua, ranging from extreme negative assessment to positive, has numerous parallels in other fields where scholars assess literary tradition, philological analysis, tradition-history, form, language, text, archaeology, and historical background—and then try to come up with a story of what *really* happened! Faulty analysis or overemphasis at the wrong place can throw the resulting hypothesis "out of gear" entirely. Yet one must forge ahead, under the critical light of one's peers, in the knowledge that the work has to be as carefully done in this time as possible, and then restudied a generation later, if not sooner!

Roland de Vaux reviewed the evidence for the Trojan War and for the Phoenician colonization of the Mediterranean, and found precisely the same problems being struggled with in the same way, with the same radically different conclusions.[106] With regard to the Phoenicians ancient authors assert that Cadiz and Utica, for example, were founded as early as 1100 B.C., while Carthage was founded in 814 B.C. and became the Phoenician power of the west *par excellence* for centuries. Yet Rhys Carpenter in 1958, basing his results on purely archaeological evidence, disregards the literary tradition completely and says that the cities in question were not founded much before c. 700 B.C., and that only gradually during the next two centuries did the Phoenicians spread to Sicily, Sardinia, Cadiz, Spain, and the Balearic Islands. Now with tenth- and ninth-century B.C. inscriptions existing on Cyprus and in Spain, which Carpenter had no training to handle critically, and eighth-century specimens in Sicily, Sardinia, and Malta, the skeptics can only defend themselves by challenging the archaeologist's methods, especially the disciplines of paleography, etc. Nevertheless, the basic point has been made by the archaeologists in general agreement with the ancient authors: Phoenician colonization preceded the arrival of the Greeks.

What can be said about the tradition made immortal by Homer in the *Iliad* and the *Odyssey?* Schliemann evidently found the ruined tell of Troy, but then came the debate as to which stratum was destroyed and by what agency at the site. Carl Blegen, the latest excavator, accepts the city's identification, and claims the city destroyed in Homer's traditions must be identified with Stratum VII A, in which Mycenean pottery still occurs in abundance. Thus Homer's story of the expedition against Troy

---

[106] See De Vaux, "On Right and Wrong Uses of Archaeology."

must have a historical basis. Archaeology for Blegen "proves" that there must have been some kind of coalition of Achaens or Myceneans who fought Troy and its allies and defeated them.

Yet a more "judicious" answer has been that Troy VIIa was destroyed by human violence, but the excavations have provided not one scrap of evidence of a Greek coalition or any identification whatever to answer the question of "Who did it?" Perhaps it was destroyed by the Sea Peoples. The best procedure of all, in this viewpoint, is to dissociate the whole archaeological discovery from myth and poetry, and even from the legend of Troy itself.

Yet in both instances still other scholars raise basic questions with regard to both viewpoints as to whether the two extremes are really in methodological tune with the use of archaeology as "proof" or as evidence. The skeptic always has the advantage because archaeology speaks only in response to our questions and one can call any tradition not provable. Thus since no proof can be attained anywhere, one extreme simply asks that archaeological data be presented and the attempt to prove anything in literary tradition cease forthwith.

Both sides of the controversy use the term "proof" in ways inadmissible, even absurd, with regard to cultural, political, and socioeconomic history.

Whether it is Trojan history, Phoenician history, or what history remains in the Book of Joshua, we must begin with the fact that we have *actual texts*. These must be interpreted by all the means of literary analysis available to us. Then we must reconstruct the archaeological and ecological context as best we can both in the given area and in the widest possible context. Then we must examine the question as to whether the one illumines the other, or whether a reasonable hypothesis can be reconstructed which best explains what we know at this time. The dictum of De Vaux is axiomatic: "Archaeology does not confirm the text, which is what it is; it can only confirm the interpretation which we give it."[107] Conversely, archaeology, dealing with the wreckage of antiquity, proves nothing in itself. Its results must be analyzed in a variety of ways and then, with all other data available, their meaning in the overall picture of a cultural continuum is expressed by interpretation. Here again it is the interpretation that is at all usable, and that is the product of a human brain with the use of tools available, not of a pure vacuum mistakenly called by some "science." Instead the brain belongs to a limited person, living and working in a given time and space. A person is not more infallible than his sources and predecessors. Ambiguity and relativity enter every sphere of human activity. Some minds rise above others as masters

[107] Ibid., 78.

of their peers, but the solid *proofs,* which so many assume possible at the end of either scientific or historical work, cannot be attained by finite beings. We are historical organisms by intrinsic nature, and ambiguity is always a central component of history, whether of the humanities, of social science, or of natural science.

The Historical Background of Thirteenth-Century Palestine

The Eighteenth Dynasty of Egypt (sixteenth-fourteenth centuries B.C.), with its series of great generals, administrators, artists, and architects, is one of the world's extraordinary phenomena, never repeated or repeatable. Crucial to Palestine's history is the inclusion of that area, Lebanon, and much of Syria in the Egyptian empire. The Egyptians left intact the local political system composed of autonomous city-states who were continually making alliances of smaller or greater numbers for this purpose or that. The local "king" (*melek*) of each city-state was responsible to the Pharaoh through local Egyptian commissioners. Gaza and Beth-shan were or became Egyptian points of control with administrative and military missions in each.

Besides the great coastal cities (Gaza, Ashkelon, Ashdod, Dor, Akko, Tyre, Sidon, Beirut, Byblos) the second quarter of the fourteenth century witnesses the hill country controlled by a small number of fairly major city-states: Lachish, Gezer, Shechem, and Megiddo play major roles, while Jerusalem and presumably Hebron were smaller and played less important parts. In the Jordan valley Jericho is unmentioned and unoccupied as a city, while only Pella, well-protected on the eastern side of the valley just south of the Sea of Galilee, is important. Most of Transjordan south of the Yarmuk reverted to nomadism after c. 1900 B.C. and played no significant role in affairs west of the Jordan. Yet a small square temple at Amman, dated c. 1400 B.C., like one at Tananir on a low eastern spur of Mount Gerizim dating two centuries earlier, provides a hint of what life there was like then, as from time immemorial. The temple with its sacred pillar in the exact middle of a square open sanctuary furnished the central shrine and divine presence which created a covenant stability among the tribes who belonged to its compact.[108]

---

[108] See Robert G. Boling, "Excavations at Tananir, 1968," in *Report on Archaeological Work at Ṣuwwānet eth-Thanīya, Tananir, and Khirbet Minḥa (Munḥata)*, ed. George M. Landes, *BASOR* Supplemental Studies 21 (Missoula, MT: Scholars Press, 1975); "Bronze Age Buildings at the Shechem High Place," *BA* 32 (1969) 81–103; and Edward F. Campbell, Jr., and G. Ernest Wright, "Tribal League Shrines in Amman and Shechem," *BA* 32 (1969) 104-116.

Opposite page, Map A

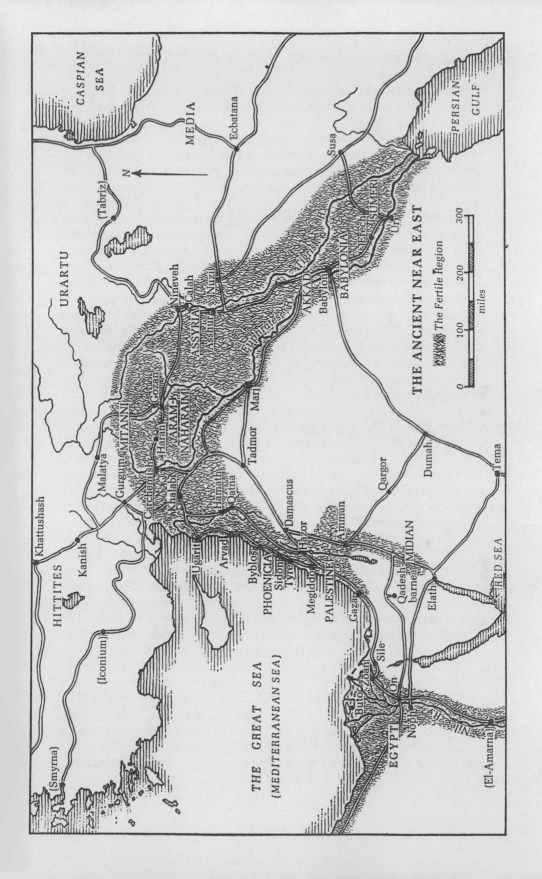

CASPIAN SEA

MEDIA

Ecbatana

N

(Tabriz)

URARTU

PERSIAN GULF

Susa

SUMER

Erech

Ur

THE ANCIENT NEAR EAST

Nineveh

Calah

Nuzi

Ashur

ASSYRIA

BABYLONIA

Babylon

AKKAD

Tigris R.

Euphrates R.

The Fertile Region

0   100   200   300

miles

Khattushash

Kanish

HITTITES

Malatya

Gurgum

Carchemish

Khalab

MITANNI

Haran

ARAM-NAHARAIM

Gozan

Mari

Tadmor

(Iconium)

Hamath

Qatna

Qadesh

Damascus

Qarqar

Dumah

Tema

Ugarit

Arvad

Byblos

Sidon

PHOENICIA

Tyre

Hazor

Megiddo

Amman

PALESTINE

Gaza

MIDIAN

Qadesh-barnea

Elath

RED SEA

THE GREAT SEA
(MEDITERRANEAN SEA)

(Smyrna)

Sile

Zoan

On

Buto

Noph

EGYPT

Nile R.

(El-Amarna)

West of the Jordan, Eighteenth Dynasty Palestine appears to have had nothing equivalent to third-millennium Ai, which like Nippur in southern Iraq formed the religious center which held together a number of the city-states in a religiously sanctioned unity. With only the Egyptian administration forming a loose unity, intrigue, rivalry, and covert fighting to enlarge one's territory at the expense of others gave the land an incredible instability, the Egyptian overlords interested mainly in satisfying their own greed.

The most important single event affecting the Levantine area was the conquest of northern Syria and the kingdom of Mitanni (east and north of the great Syrian bend of the Euphrates) by the Hittite army under its king, Shuppiluliumash, about 1370 B.C. It is remarkable that for one hundred fifty years Hatti and Egypt maintained a fairly stable border at approximately the northern part of modern Lebanon and along a southeastward line below the great city-state of Hamath on the Orontes and north of Damascus. Here the border was the territory, not precisely definable, named Amurru, whose energetic kings played an expansionist role in the Amarna period (second quarter of the fourteenth century), according to diplomatic correspondence found in Egyptian foreign office archives. The only head-on clash between the Hittite and Egyptian powers was at the Battle of Kadesh on the Orontes (i.e. near the border) c. 1285 B.C., an eloquent account of which is provided by Ramesses II. There was no victory by either side, and in due course a formal treaty was drawn up stabilizing the border approximately where it had been.

This situation, providing the external stability which allowed the city-states freedom for their internal bickering, suggests at least two major influences on later Israel. For one thing, the Egyptian possession in Asia seems to have included a geographical entity called "the land of Canaan." It is this entity which became Israel's "Promised Land." It is carefully described in Jerusalem priesthood sources as the land west of the Jordan, including Lebanon to the north and extending into Sinai as far as "the River of Egypt" (Wadī el-Arish): Num 34:1-12; Ezek 47:15-20; cf. also Gen 10:15-19. Why Israel never planned occupation of the Lebanon region cannot be known. Yet Canaan was a definite geographic entity, and a "Canaanite" was considered a foreigner farther north in the city of Ugarit, according to documents found there in the palace precincts.

The second contribution to our knowledge of this period has been the discovery in Hittite archives of the vassal treaties which the Hittite emperor made with the states and regions which he had conquered south of Asia Minor. George E. Mendenhall first brought this type of vassal treaty, with its special form confined to the period in question, to the attention of the biblical scholar as a datum of primary importance. In the treaty the vassal's obligations were set within a context of the freely narrated, non-stereotyped story of the suzerain's history of good deeds to the vassal in the past. Mendenhall's contention that it is the closest form yet found to depict Israel's relation to Yahweh has been the most stimulating, provocative, and constructive new insight into Israel's world view and how she understood the nature of Yahweh and her relation to him in the last half century of Old Testament study.[109]

Another factor of considerable importance belongs to the nature of the country. Large numbers of people formed a shifting population in, among, and on the fringes of the developed sociopolitical framework of the Fertile Crescent. They were independent, not entirely bound to the existing legal entities. In the highly urbanized, even rapidly developing technology of modern Israel and Jordan, this phenomenon still exists. Bedouin from the Beersheba area fill the uncultivated hills and valleys of the Gezer area each spring when flora is abundant, but they disappear for the most part by the end of June. In the great Shechem plains outside the large city of Nablus, some 64 km north of Jerusalem, Bedouin suddenly appear following the grain harvest. By an immemorial rule their flocks glean the harvest fields for a time; then as suddenly as they appeared they are gone, generally during August.

Taking his cue from the frequent mention of a people called *'Apiru* throughout western Asia during the second millennium (prounced *Ḥab/piru* in Akkadian, the diplomatic language of the day), and especially from the letters found at Tell el-Amarna in Egypt, Mendenhall has pointed to a probable sociological factor in Palestine which may be one way of envisaging the Israelite conquest of Canaan.[110] The *'Apiru* cannot be pinpointed as a special ethnic element, even though the term is certainly related to "Hebrew" (*'ibrî*). Almost any known national, and many who had no nationality, could be called by the term. Furthermore, they can and did hire themselves out in a large variety of capacities to the settled "establishment" of a given area. Most of those mentioned in the

[109] Mendenhall, *Law and Covenant in Israel and the Ancient Near East=BAR* 3, 3-53. For close inspection and comparison with the biblical materials, as well as for translations of the relevant Hittite texts, see Dennis J. McCarthy, *Treaty and Covenant,* a dissertation written under the direction of William L. Moran. McCarthy accepts Mendenhall's thesis, but then proceeds to point out meticulously the differences between the Hittite and Israelite treaty (covenant) forms. This part of McCarthy's work does not come off well in the view of this writer. What is needed is a first-rate theological mind to examine these differences from the standpoint of Israelite and Hittite theologies and differing world views. Obviously an international treaty form had to be radically altered for depicting Yahweh and his relation to Israel, thus defining Israel's whole sense of identity, view of obligation, vocation, etc. Many student papers passing through my hands have radically criticized McCarthy at precisely this point, i.e. the technical side of his work is not complemented by theological sensitivity.

[110] George E. Mendenhall, "The Hebrew Conquest of Palestine," *BA* 25 (1962) 66-87=*BAR* 3, 100-120.

Amarna letters were of a warlike capacity, although the term 'Apiru declines in the letters of the local city-state monarchs to mean little more than "rebel" against the Egyptian overlord. Each kinglet in his letters is a good, faithful, righteous subject, while his enemies are all 'Apiru!

A previous generation saw in this frequent mention of 'Apiru in the Amarna letters evidence of a great invasion of the region from the east. Now the evidence is interpreted more generally in relation to the instability of the area, with its rival factions accusing each other of infidelity to the Egyptian foreign office, while roving bands of displaced people, many probably unpaid mercenaries of Egyptian outposts in the country, were seizing people for ransom, stealing whatever they could, and in general making a prosperous life in the land impossible for almost everyone. For Mendenhall the Hebrew conquest of Canaan can be interpreted as a gradual shifting of power from the landholders to the landless, as the latter gradually gained power in this area or that. How such a view can be seen as a vital part of the complex events will be dealt with below.

The Decline and Fall of Civilization, c. 1250-1200 B.C.

The second half of the thirteenth century witnesses the climax of the chaos in Palestine, and also the decline and fall of empires and whole civilizations. For reasons which cannot be detailed, the great Mycenean civilization in Greece came to a sudden end during the second half of the thirteenth century. Violence and invasion seem to have been the causes. In any event, a vast dark age suddenly descended upon the whole Aegean while Late Mycenean IIIb pottery was still being made. On Rhodes and Cyprus colonies seem to have escaped and continued to make pottery in this tradition during the twelfth and eleventh centuries.

On the Upper Tigris there was a small revival in the "Middle Assyrian" period, as it is called, while foreigners called Kassites continued a moribund rule in Babylon, devoid of political or cultural energy. Yet of greatest significance and profound effect on the whole Levantine coastline was the collapse of the brilliant Hittite empire and several of its north Syrian satellites. This was accompanied by the sudden weakening of Egypt at the end of the Nineteenth Dynasty, with only two kings exhibiting any energy, Merneptah (high chronology: c. 1236-1223 B.C.; low: c. 1223-1211 B.C.) and Ramesses III, first king of the Twentieth Dynasty (high: 1196-1164 B.C.; low: c. 1175-1144 B.C.).* It is within the very complex series of local events all over the ancient world in this time of disaster and chaos that we must formulate hypotheses to account for

* "High" and "low" here are different assessments of evidence.

the epic of Israel, the presence of a people by that name in Palestine during an Asian campaign of Pharaoh Merneptah during his fifth year (c. 1230 or 1220 B.C.), and the presence of Israel settled in her Promised Land by the twelfth century according to the typology of prosodic canons whereby the hymns in Exodus 15, Numbers 23-24, and Judges 5 can be dated among other early literary compositions in the Old Testament.

Fortunately, new information from Hittite archives, and from the important satellite city of Ugarit in northern Syria, near the coast a few miles south of the Orontes as it enters the Mediterranean, enables a more detailed picture of the downfall of the Hittite empire. The fatal problem lay with the people of western Anatolia, who long had been prepared to take any advantage of weakness of the power centered in the great plateau which today is the region of Ankara. By the middle of the thirteenth century, or within a decade or so thereafter, the last of the great Hittite monarchs, Tudkhaliash IV, had been forced to make raids deeper into his western neighbors' territory than ever before and for the first time to take enough interest in Cyprus to attempt to control it. As long as Cyprus was only an important trading port between Syria and the Aegean, the Hittites were uninterested. As soon as the empire's rear was threatened and Cyprus became a possible military threat to control of western Anatolia and Syria, it was subjected to military invasion.

In the time of the next monarch, Arnuwandash III, a contemporary of Pharaoh Merneptah, the western Anatolians were linked in an alliance and took over control of Cyprus. The Middle Assyrians, taking advantage of the situation, were able to advance to the Euphrates River in northwestern Mesopotamia. Merneptah in his second year sent a shipment of grain to the Hittites to assist in a period of shortage and famine. The Great King appears not to have lived long and his younger brother, the last Hittite king, Shuppiluliumash II, presided over the empire's fall, for during his reign the written archives cease.[111]

Tablets found in the palace at Ugarit, and especially the vivid pictures left on the "oven tablets," fill in a few bits of information that enable us to imagine what happened.[112] The vassal king of Ugarit was called upon, obviously against his will, to fulfill his military duties to his suzerain. While he, his army, and his fleet were in Anatolia, his own city, undefended, was successfully attacked and plundered by sea-raiders. The "oven tablets" are letters and documents dealing with almost every phase of life in the city, clay documents which were being baked before permanent filing. The city was destroyed before they were removed from the

[111] For review see especially Goetze, *CAH*³, II, Part 2, chaps. 17, 21a, and especially 24.
[112] See Astour, "New Evidence on the Last Days of Ugarit," *AJA* 69 (1965) 253-258.

oven. They picture the Hittite king and his allies falling back before his attackers, until they reached the mountain borders of Syria. The king of Ugarit wrote back to his mother: "And you, my mother, be not afraid and do not put worries into your heart." Still another letter, found in another place in the city, and not in the oven, may refer to the final battle. It says, "Our food in the threshing floors is sacked [or burned?], and also the vineyards are destroyed. Our city is destroyed, and you should know it [or and may you know it]." There were houses in the excavated city which were not burned. The inhabitants evidently fled the enemy and never returned. Like biblical Ai, the enemy made Ugarit "a tell forever" (Josh 8:28). The chronological indicators in the clay archives suggest that the city and the Hittite empire fell perhaps late in the reign of Merneptah, or within the era 1230-1215 B.C.

Meanwhile, from Egyptian sources we obtain information which suggests the identity of the enemies who destroyed the Hittite empire and Syrian coastal cities like Ugarit and even Alalakh in the inland plain of Antioch. Merneptah's father, Ramesses II, having reigned for sixty-seven years, had lived too long to maintain his army and frontier patrols, and the strong control of empire which characterized his younger years. The storm broke against his son Merneptah in the fifth year of his reign, when Libyans from the west and "people of the sea," named Sherden, Sheklesh, Tursha, and Akawasha, in a coalition led by one general, attacked. These names remind one of the second invasion of the "Sea Peoples" during the reign of Ramesses III. If they are the same people—and surely they must be—who had wrought the great victories in destroying the Bronze Age civilization of the Hittites and the wealthy north Syrian city-states, then we must surmise that the "Sea Peoples" are western Anatolians, using both land and sea lanes which they had secured. Aegean folk were certainly a minority element since they were dominated by the Mycenean civilization, which at the same time was in process of elimination. The later biblical identification of the Philistines and all other "Sea Peoples" as *Kaphtôrîm* ("Cretans") cannot be considered, therefore, as a precise identification. The conquerors of the Hittites must surely be the same as those whom the Egyptians called "peoples of the Sea," and the Israelites named "Philistines" from the name of one of the groups.[113]

One has usually assumed that Merneptah's engagement with the "peoples of the Sea," the conquerors of Hittites and north Syrians, took place in the Delta of Egypt or near its borders. Yet that is not something to be assumed, nor can one assume that the battles with the Libyans occurred

[113] See, among many sources, Raymond O. Faulkner, "Egypt: From the Inception of the Nineteenth Dynasty to the Death of Ramesses III," in *CAH²*, II, Part 2, chap. 23; William F. Albright, "Some Oriental Glosses on the Homeric Problem," *AJA* 54 (1950) 162-176; and *CAH³*, II, Part 2, chap. 33.

at the same time, rather than beforehand and/or afterward. The Pharaoh claims to have killed six thousand of the enemy, to have taken much booty, and to have captured the Libyan chieftain.

In addition to the long inscription at Karnak about the war and the stela from Athribis, we must come to terms with the so-called Israel stela. This is a hymnic and lyrical panegyric about the war. The important point is that the Pharaoh has definitely been in Asia. As a result of his victory the poet claims that the virtual restoration of world order was achieved—surely a considerable exaggeration! At any rate, within the document occur these words: "Men come and go with singing, and there is no cry of men in trouble. . . . The [enemy] chieftains are prostrate. Destruction is for Tjehenu. Khatti [Hittite Land] is at peace. Canaan is plundered with every evil. Ashkelon is carried off, Gezer captured, Yanoam is made non-existent, Israel is waste and has no seed, Khor [Palestine and lower Syria] has become a widow because of Egypt."[114]

This certainly sounds as though Merneptah, in the time of the next-to-last Hittite king, Arnuwandash III, found Canaan, the Egyptian possession in Asia, threatened. Hence, his campaign was to lift the threat and to assist the one to whom he was bound by treaty, the Hittite king. Consequently, Merneptah's war can safely be assumed to have included a campaign into Palestine, and perhaps Lebanon, at any rate into Asiatic Canaan at the time when the enemies of the Hittites had retaken Cyprus and were looting in Syria behind the Hittite armies. This would have been an excellent moment for various strong Palestinian city-states to withhold tribute and attempt independence. Yet their actions were costly, though the Egyptians were unable to make another vigorous effort to maintain control of Palestine until probably late in the reign of Ramesses III.

Late thirteenth-century destructions at Gezer and Ashdod are possible candidates for the Merneptah raid. At Gezer the cultural sequence can only be said to be temporarily interrupted, because it picked up promptly again with no basic change observable in the culture.[115] The Yanoam

114 From Faulkner [fn 113], 220.
115 See William G. Dever, H. Darrell Lance, and G. Ernest Wright, "Gezer I. Preliminary Report of the 1964-1966 Seasons," *Annual of the Hebrew Union College Biblical and Archaeological School in Jerusalem* I (1970) 22-24. The probability in the view of this writer is that one of the early phases of the thirteenth-century stratum can be described as the interruption caused by the pharaoh at a time when sea lanes were open at least as far as Cyprus, and Cypriote White Painted ware was still being imported. In Field VI during the 1968–1969 seasons a major building was unearthed in the acropolis area which, though it had a succession of phases, continued in use from the thirteenth century into that period of the twelfth century when Philistine pottery was first introduced.

mentioned in the "Israel Inscription of Merneptah" is evidently in the northern Jordan valley, but we have no certain idea of its location, or of the reason for its importance to Pharaoh.

G. ERNEST WRIGHT

Lexington, MA
December 1973

SELECTED BIBLIOGRAPHY

See also Principal Abbreviations; titles there are not repeated here.

I. COMMENTARIES

A. Book of Joshua

Bennett, William Henry. *The Book of Joshua*. The Sacred Books of the Old Testament, ed. Paul Haupt. Leipzig, London, and Baltimore: J. C. Hinrichs; Dodd, Mead, 1895 and 1899.

Bright, John. "Joshua, Introduction and Exegesis," in *The Interpreter's Bible* 2. New York and Nashville: Abingdon, 1953.

Calvin, John. *Commentaries on the Book of Joshua*. Grand Rapids: Eerdmans, 1949.

Garstang, John. *Joshua-Judges*. The Foundations of Bible History. London: Constable, 1931.

Gray, John. *Joshua, Judges and Ruth*. The Century Bible, New Edition. London: Nelson, 1967.

Hertzberg, Hans Wilhelm. *Die Bücher Joshua, Richter, Ruth*. Göttingen: Vandenhoeck und Ruprecht, 1953.

Holzinger, Heinrich. *Das Buch Josua*. Kurzer Hand-Commentar zum AT. Tübingen: J. C. B. Mohr, 1901.

Miller, James Maxwell, and Gene M. Tucker. *The Book of Joshua*. The Cambridge Bible Commentary on the New English Bible. Cambridge University Press, 1974.

Noth, Martin. *Das Buch Josua*. Second Edition. Handbuch zum Alten Testament. Tübingen: Mohr, 1953.

Robinson, Henry Wheeler. *Deuteronomy and Joshua*. The Century Bible. Edinburgh: T. C. & E. C. Jack, 1907.

Soggin, J. Alberto. *Joshua*. Philadelphia: Westminster, 1972.

de Vault, Joseph J. *The Book of Josue*. Pamphlet Bible Series II. New York: Paulist Press, 1960.

B. *Other Biblical Books*

Boling, Robert Gordon. *Judges.* AB 6A. Garden City, NY: Doubleday, 1975.

Brown, Raymond Edward. *The Gospel According to John.* 2 vols. AB 29 and 29A. Garden City, NY: Doubleday, 1966 and 1970.

Burney, Charles Fox. *The Book of Judges.* Second Edition. London: Rivingtons, 1930; reprinted with Prolegomenon by W. F. Albright. New York: Ktav, 1970.

Campbell, Edward Fay, Jr. *Ruth.* AB 7. Garden City, NY: Doubleday, 1975.

Dahood, Mitchell. *Psalms,* 3 vols. AB 16, 17, 17A. Garden City, NY: Doubleday, 1966, 1968, 1970.

Goldstein, Jonathan. *I Maccabees.* AB 41. Garden City, NY: Doubleday, 1976.

Gray, John. *I & II Kings, A Commentary.* Philadelphia: Westminster, 1962.

Kraus, Hans-Joachim. *Die Psalmen.* Second Edition. Biblischer Kommentar, AT XV. Neukirchen: Neukirchener Verlag, 1961.

Myers, Jacob Martin. *I Chronicles.* AB 12. Garden City, NY: Doubleday, 1965.

Pope, Marvin H. *Song of Songs.* AB 7C. Garden City, NY: Doubleday, 1977.

von Rad, Gerhard. *Deuteronomy,* tr. Dorothea M. Barton. Philadelphia: Westminster, 1966.

Speiser, Ephraim Avigdor. *Genesis.* AB 1. Garden City, NY: Doubleday, 1964.

Weinfeld, Moshe. *Deuteronomy and the Deuteronomic School.* Oxford: Clarendon Press, 1972.

Weiser, Artur. *The Psalms,* tr. Herbert Hartwell. Philadelphia: Westminster, 1962.

Wright, George Ernest. "Deuteronomy," in *The Interpreter's Bible* 2 (1953).

II. TEXTS AND VERSIONS

Allegro, John Marco. *Qumran Cave 4.* Discoveries in the Judaean Desert of Jordan V. Oxford: Clarendon Press, 1968.

Brook, Alan England, and Norman McLean. *Joshua, Judges, and Ruth.*

The Old Testament in Greek, vol. I, part IV. Cambridge University Press, 1917.

Cross, Frank Moore. *The Ancient Library of Qumran.* Revised Edition. Garden City, NY: Anchor Books, 1961.

────── "The Evolution of a Theory of Local Texts," in *1972 Proceedings of the International Organization for Septuagint and Cognate Studies,* ed. Robert A. Kraft. Society of Biblical Literature, 1972.

Holmes, Samuel. *Joshua: The Hebrew and Greek Texts.* Cambridge University Press, 1914.

Jellicoe, Sidney. *The Septuagint in Modern Study.* Oxford: Clarendon Press, 1968.

Margolis, Max. *The Book of Joshua in Greek.* Paris: Geuthner, 1931-1938.

Orlinsky, Harry Meyer. "The Hebrew *Vorlage* of the Septuagint of the Book of Joshua," *VTSup* 17 (1968) 187-195.

Strugnell, John. "Notes en Marge du Volume V des 'Discoveries in the Judaean Desert of Jordan,'" *RevQ* 7 (1969-1971) 163-276.

Swete, Henry Barclay. *An Introduction to the Old Testament in Greek.* Cambridge University Press, 1900.

III. Literature and History

A. General Studies

Albright, William Foxwell. "The Ancient Near East and the Religion of Israel," *JBL* 59 (1940) 85-112.

────── "From the Patriarchs to Moses: I. From Abraham to Joseph," *BA* 36 (1973) 5-33; "II. Moses Out of Egypt," ibid., 48-76.

────── *From the Stone Age to Christianity: Monotheism and the Historical Process* (1940). Second Edition. Garden City, NY: Doubleday, 1957.

────── "Syria, the Philistines and Phoenicia," *CAH*³, Part 2, chap. 33.

Alt, Albrecht. *Essays on Old Testament History and Religion,* tr. R. A. Wilson. Garden City, NY: Doubleday, 1967.

────── *Kleine Schriften,* 3 vols. Munich: C. H. Beck, 1959.

────── "Das System der Stammesgrenzen im Buche Josua," in *Kleine Schriften* I. 193-202.

Anderson, Bernhard W., and Walter Harrelson, eds. *Israel's Prophetic Heritage.* New York: Harper & Row, 1962.

Astour, Michael C. "New Evidence on the Last Days of Ugarit," *AJA* 69 (1965) 253-258.

Ben-Shem, Israel. *The Conquest of Transjordan.* Hebrew with English summary. Tel Aviv University, 1972.

Benvenisti, Meron. *The Crusaders in the Holy Land.* Jerusalem: Israel Universities Press, 1970.

Bream, H. N., Ralph Daniel Heim, and Carey A. Moore, eds. *A Light Unto My Path: Old Testament Studies in Honor of Jacob M. Myers.* Pittsburgh: Temple University Press, 1974.

Bright, John. *Early Israel in Recent History Writing.* Studies in Biblical Theology. London: SCM Press, 1956.

———— *A History of Israel.* Second Edition. Philadelphia: Westminster, 1969.

Campbell, Edward Fay, Jr. "The Amarna Letters and the Amarna Period," *BA* 23 (1960) 2-22; reprinted *BAR* 3 (1970) 54-75.

Carpenter, Joseph Estlin, and George Harford-Battersby. *The Hexateuch.* Two volumes. London: Longmans, Green, 1900.

Dever, William G. "The Peoples of Palestine in the Middle Bronze I Period," *HTR* 64 (1971) 197-226.

Driver, Samuel Rolles. *Introduction to the Literature of the Old Testament* (1891). *Revised Edition.* New York: Scribners, 1950.

Edgerton, William Franklin, and John A. Wilson. *Historical Records of Ramses III.* Studies in Ancient Oriental Civilization 12. University of Chicago Press, 1936.

Eissfeldt, Otto. *The Old Testament: An Introduction,* tr. of third German ed. by Peter R. Ackroyd. New York and Evanston: Harper & Row, 1965.

Faulkner, Raymond Oliver. "Egypt: From the Inception of the Nineteenth Dynasty to the Death of Ramesses III," *CAH³,* Part 2, chap. 23.

Fohrer, Georg. *Introduction to the Old Testament,* tr. David E. Green. New York and Nashville: Abingdon, 1965.

Freedman, David Noel. "Pentateuch," in *IDB* 3. 711-727.

de Geus, C. H. J. *The Tribes of Israel.* Amsterdam: Van Gorcum, 1976.

Glueck, Nelson. *The Other Side of the Jordan.* Cambridge, MA: American Schools of Oriental Research, 1940, reprinted 1970.

Goetze, Albrecht. "The Hittites and Syria (1300-1200)," *CAH³,* Part 2, chap. 24.

Gurney, Oliver Robert. *The Hittites.* Second Edition. Harmondsworth: Penguin, 1962.

Hayes, John Haralson, and James Maxwell Miller, eds. *Israelite and Judaean History.* Philadelphia: Westminster, 1977.

Hillers, Delbert R. *Covenant: The History of a Biblical Idea.* Baltimore: Johns Hopkins University Press, 1969.

Jacobsen, Thorkild. "The Cosmos as a State," in *Before Philosophy,* eds. H. and H. A. Frankfort, John A. Wilson, and Thorkild Jacobsen. New York: Penguin, 1954. 137-199.

Kaufmann, Yehezkel. *The Biblical Account of the Conquest of Palestine,* tr. M. Dagut. Jerusalem: Magnes Press, 1953.

McKenzie, John L. *The World of the Judges.* Englewood Cliffs, NJ: Prentice-Hall, 1966.

Mayes, Andrew D. H. *Israel in the Period of the Judges.* London: SCM Press, 1974.

Mendenhall, George Emery. "The Hebrew Conquest of Palestine," *BA* 25 (1962) 66-87; reprinted *BAR* 3 (1970) 100-120.

Moore, George Foot. "Joshua (Book)," in *Encyclopaedia Biblica* II, eds. T. K. Cheyne and J. S. Black. London: A. & C. Black, 1901; cols. 2600-2610.

Mowinckel, Sigmund. *Tetrateuch-Pentateuch-Hexateuch.* Beihefte *ZAW* 90. Berlin, 1964.

Nilsson, Martin Persson. *Geschichte der griechischen Religion.* Second Edition, vol. I. Munich: Beck, 1941.

Noth, Martin. *The History of Israel,* tr. Peter R. Ackroyd. New York: Harper, 1960.

—————— *A History of Pentateuchal Traditions,* tr. Bernhard W. Anderson. Englewood Cliffs, NJ: Prentice-Hall, 1972.

—————— *The Laws of the Pentateuch and Other Essays,* tr. D. R. Ap-Thomas. Edinburgh and London: Oliver & Boyd, 1966.

—————— *Das System der zwölf Stämme Israels.* Stuttgart: W. Kohlhammer, 1930.

—————— *Überlieferungsgeschichtliche Studien* I. Halle: Max Niemeyer Verlag, 1943.

Pedersen, Johannes. *Israel, Its Life and Culture.* Copenhagen and London: Oxford University Press, 1926-1940 (reprinted 1959).

von Rad, Gerhard. *The Form Critical Problem of the Hexateuch and Other Essays,* tr. E. W. T. Dicken. Edinburgh and London: Oliver & Boyd, 1965.

—————— *Old Testament Theology,* tr. D. M. G. Stalker. Two volumes. New York: Harper & Row, 1962 and 1965.

Ringgren, Helmer. *Israelite Religion,* tr. D. E. Green. Philadelphia: Westminster, 1963.

Robinson, Henry Wheeler. *Inspiration and Revelation in the Old Testament.* Oxford: Clarendon Press, 1946.

Rowley, Harold Henry. *From Joseph to Joshua.* London: Oxford University Press, 1951.

de Vaux, Roland. *Ancient Israel: Its Life and Institutions,* tr. John McHugh. New York: McGraw-Hill, 1961.

Weippert, Manfred. *The Settlement of the Israelite Tribes in Palestine,* tr. James D. Martin. Studies in Biblical Theology, Second Series, No. 21. Naperville, IL: A. R. Allenson, 1971.

Weiser, Artur. *The Old Testament: Its Formation and Development,* tr. D. M. Barton. New York: Association Press, 1961.

Wellek, René, and Austin Warren. *Theory of Literature.* Third Edition. Harmondsworth, Middlesex, England: Penguin University Books, 1973.

Wellhausen, Julius. *Die Composition des Hexateuchs und der historischen Bücher des Alten Testaments* (1876-1877). Fourth Edition. Berlin: Walter De Gruyter & Co., 1963.

———— *Prolegomena to the History of Ancient Israel,* tr. W. Robertson Smith. New York: Meridian Books, 1957.

Westermann, Claus. *Forschung am Alten Testament.* Munich: Kaiser, 1964.

Wolff, Hans Walter. "Das Kerygma des deuteronomistischen Geschichts-werkes," *ZAW* 73 (1961) 171-186.

Wright, George Ernest. "Fresh Evidence for the Philistine Story," *BA* 29 (1966) 70-86.

———— *The Old Testament Against Its Environment.* Chicago: Henry Regnery, 1950.

———— *The Old Testament and Theology.* New York: Harper & Row, 1969.

———— *The Rule of God: Essays in Biblical Theology.* Garden City, NY: Doubleday, 1960.

B. Archaeology

Aharoni, Yohanan. "Hebrew Ostraca from Tel Arad," *IEJ* 16 (1966) 1-7.

———— "Nothing Early and Nothing Late: Re-writing Israel's Conquest," *BA* 39 (1976) 55-76.

———— et al. *Investigations at Lachish.* Tel Aviv: Gateway Publications, 1975.

———— ed. *Beer-Sheba I: Excavations at Tel Beer-Sheba, 1969-1971.* Tel Aviv University: Institute of Archaeology, 1973.

Albright, William Foxwell. *Archaeology, Historical Analogy and Early Biblical Tradition.* Baton Rouge: Louisiana State University Press, 1966.

———— "The Israelite Conquest of Canaan in the Light of Archaeology," *BASOR* 74 (1938) 11-23.

Alt, Albrecht. "Josua," BZAW 66 (1936) 13-19; rpt. *Kleine Schriften* I. Munich: Beck, 1959. 176-192.

Bar-Adon, P., Claire Epstein et al. *Judaea, Samaria, and the Golan: Archaeological Survey, 1967-1968,* ed. M. Kochavi. In Hebrew. Jerusalem: Carta, 1972.

Bennett, Boyce M., Jr. "The Search for Israelite Gilgal," *PEQ* 104 (1972) 111-122.

Boling, Robert Gordon. "Excavations at Tananir, 1968," in *Report on Archaeological Work at Ṣuwwānet eth-Thanīya, Tananir, and Khirbet Minḥa (Munḥata)*, ed. George M. Landes. *BASOR* Supplemental Studies 21. Missoula, MT: Scholars Press, 1975. 28-85.

Boraas, Roger Stuart, and Siegfried H. Horn. *Heshbon 1973: The Third Campaign at Tell Hesban, A Preliminary Report*. Berrien Springs, MI: Andrews University, 1975.

Callaway, Joseph A. "Excavating Ai (Et-Tell): 1964-1972," *BA* 39 (1976) 18-30.

Campbell, Edward Fay, Jr. "The Shechem Area Survey," *BASOR* 190 (April 1968) 19-41.

———— James F. Ross, and Lawrence E. Toombs, "The Eighth Campaign at Balâṭah (Shechem)," *BASOR* 204 (1971) 4.

———— and George Ernest Wright. "Tribal League Shrines in Amman and Shechem," *BA* 32 (1969) 104-116.

Condor, C. R. "Notes on the Antiquities of the Book of Joshua," *PEFQS* (1899) 161-162.

Dayton, J. E. "Midianite and Edomite Pottery," in *Proceedings of the Fifth Seminar for Arabian Studies*. London: Seminar for Arabian Studies, 1972. 25-33.

Dever, William G. "The MB II C Stratification in the Northwest Gate Area at Shechem," *BASOR* 216 (December 1974) 31-52.

———— H. Darrell Lance, and George Ernest Wright. "Gezer I: Preliminary Report of the 1964-1966 Seasons," *Annual of the Hebrew Union College Biblical and Archaeological School in Jerusalem* I (1970).

Dornemann, Rudolph Henry. "The Cultural and Archaeological History of the Transjordan in the Bronze and Iron Ages." Unpublished Ph.D. dissertation. The University of Chicago, 1970.

Dothan, Trude. *The Philistines and Their Material Culture*. In Hebrew. Jerusalem: Bialik Institute and Israel Exploration Society, 1967.

Finley, Moses I. "Archaeology and History," *Daedalus* (Winter 1971) 168-186; reprinted in *The Use and Abuse of History*. New York: Viking, 1975. 87-101.

Franken, Hendricus Jacobus. *Excavations at Tell Deir 'Alla* 1. Leiden: Brill, 1969.

Glueck, Nelson. "Explorations in Eastern Palestine," AASOR 14 (1932-1934), 15 (1934-1935), 18-19 (1937-1939), and 25-28 (1945-1949).

————— "Three Israelite Towns in the Jordan Valley: Zarethan, Succoth, Zaphon," *BASOR* 90 (1943) 2-23.

Hoftijzer, Jacob. "The Prophet Balaam in a 6th Century Aramaic Inscription," *BA* 39 (1976) 11-17.

Huesmann, John E. "Tell es-Sa'idiyeh," *RB* 75 (1968) 236-238.

Kenyon, Kathleen. *Beginning in Archaeology*. New York: Praeger, 1952.

————— *Digging Up Jericho*. New York: Praeger, 1957.

Kochavi, Moshe. "Khirbet Rabûd=Debir," *Tel Aviv* 1 (1974) 2-33.

————— ed. *Judaea, Samaria, and the Golan: Archaeological Survey 1967-1968*. Jerusalem: Carta, 1972.

Kuschke, Arnulf, and Ernst Kutsch, eds. *Archäologie und des Altes Testament*. Tübingen: Mohr, 1970.

Landes, George M. "The Material Civilization of the Ammonites," *BA* 24 (1961) 65-86; =*BAR* 2 (1964) 69-88.

————— "Report on an Archaeological 'Rescue Operation' at Ṣuwwānet eth-Thanīya in the Jordan Valley North of Jericho," *BASOR* Supplemental Studies 21. Missoula, MT: Scholars Press, 1975. 1-22.

Lapp, Paul Wilbert. "Bab-Edh-Dhra', Perizzites and Emim," in *Jerusalem Through the Ages*. Jerusalem: Israel Exploration Society, 1968. 1-25.

————— "The Conquest of Palestine in the Light of Archaeology," *Concordia Theological Monthly* 38 (1967) 283-300.

————— *The Dhahr Mirzbaneh Tombs*. New Haven: American Schools of Oriental Research, 1966.

————— "Late Royal Seals from Judah," *BASOR* 158 (April 1960) 11-22.

————— "The 1968 Excavations at Tell Ta'annek," *BASOR* 195 (October 1969) 2-49.

Mazar, Benjamin. "Excavations at the Oasis of Engedi," in *Archaeological Discoveries in the Holy Land*. Compiled by The Archaeological Institute of America. New York: Bonanza Books, 1967. 67-76.

————— *The Mountain of the Lord*. Garden City, NY: Doubleday, 1975.

Muilenburg, James. "The Site of Ancient Gilgal," *BASOR* 140 (1955) 11-27.

Noth, Martin. "Der Beitrag der Archäologie zur Geschichte Israels," VTSup 7 (1960).

Oren, E. D., and Ehud Netzer. "Tel Sera' (Tell esh-Shari'a)," *IEJ* 24 (1974) 264-266.

Parr, Peter J., G. Lankester Harding, and J. E. Dayton. "Preliminary Survey in N.W. Arabia, 1968," *Bulletin of the Institute of Archaeology* 8/9 (1970) 219–241.

Paul, Shalom M., and William G. Dever. *Biblical Archaeology.* Jerusalem: Keter Publishing House, 1973.

Pritchard, James Bennett. *Gibeon Where the Sun Stood Still.* Princeton University Press, 1962.

Rainey, Anson Frank. "A Hebrew 'Receipt' from Arad," *BASOR* 202 (April 1971) 23-29.

Rothenberg, Beno, and Yohanan Aharoni. *God's Wilderness.* London: Thames and Hudson, 1961.

Seger, Joe Dick, and Oded Borowski. "The First Two Seasons at Tell Halif," *BA* 40 (1977) 156-166.

Sellers, Ovid Rogers. *The Citadel of Beth-zur.* Philadelphia: Westminster, 1933.

——— et al. *The 1957 Excavations at Beth-zur.* AASOR, Cambridge, MA: American Schools of Oriental Research, 1968.

Toombs, Lawrence E. "Problems of the Early Israelite Era," in *Symposia* I. 69-84.

Tushingham, A. Douglas. "The Excavations at Dibon (DHIBAN) in Moab, 1952-1953," AASOR 40 (1972).

de Vaux, Roland. "On Right and Wrong Uses of Archaeology," in *Near Eastern Archaeology in the Twentieth Century,* ed. J. A. Sanders. Garden City, NY: Doubleday, 1970. 64-80.

Vriezen, Karel J. H. *"Hirbet Kefīre—*eine Oberflachenuntersuchung," *ZDPV* 91 (1975) 135-158.

Waterhouse, S. Douglas, and Robert Ibach, Jr. "The Topographical Survey," *Andrews University Seminary Studies* 13 (1975) 235-248.

Wright, George Ernest. "Archaeological Method in Palestine—An American Interpretation," *Eretz Israel* 9 (1969) 120-133.

——— *Biblical Archaeology.* Revised Edition. Philadelphia: Westminster, 1963.

——— *Shechem: The Biography of a Biblical City.* New York: McGraw-Hill, 1965.

Yadin, Yigael. *The Art of Warfare in Biblical Lands in the Light of Archaeological Study,* tr. M. Pearlman. New York: McGraw-Hill, 1963.

——— *Hazor* I-IV. Jerusalem: Magnes Press, I (1958), II (1960), III-IV (1961).

C. Geography and Topography

Abel, Felix-Marie. *Géographie de la Palestine,* 2 vols. Paris: J. Gabalda, 1933 and 1938; rpt. 1967.

Aharoni, Yohanan, and Michael Avi-Yonah. *The Macmillan Bible Atlas*. New York: Macmillan, 1968.

Avi-Yonah, Michael. *The Madaba Mosaic Map*. Jerusalem: Israel Exploration Society, 1954.

Boling, Robert Gordon. "Where Were Debir 2 and Gilgal 3?" ASOR *Newsletter* (July-August 1976) 7-8.

Demsky, Aaron. "Geba, Gibeah, and Gibeon—An Historico-Geographic Riddle," *BASOR* 212 (1973) 26-31.

———— "The Genealogy of Gibeon (1 Chron 9:35-44): Biblical and Epigraphic Considerations," *BASOR* 202 (April 1971) 16-23.

Elliger, Kurt. "Michmethath," in *Archäologie und des Altes Testament*. Kurt Galling Festschrift, eds. Arnulf Kuschke and Ernst Kutsch. Tübingen: Mohr, 1970. 91-100.

Har-El, Menashe. "The Pride of the Jordan—The Jungle of the Jordan," *BA* 41 (1978) 65-75.

Ibrahim, Moʻawiyah, James Abbot Sauer, and Khair Yassine. "The East Jordan Valley Survey, 1975," *BASOR* 222 (April 1976) 41-66.

Kallai, Zecharia. *The Tribes of Israel: A Study in the Historical Geography of the Bible*. In Hebrew. Jerusalem: Bialik Institute, 1967.

———— and Haim Tadmor. "Bīt Ninurta=Beth Horon—On the History of the Kingdom of Jerusalem in the Amarna Period," *Eretz Israel* 9 (1969); Hebrew, 138-147; English summary, 138.

Kempinski, A. "Tell el-ʻAjjul—Beth-Aglayim or Sharuhen?" *IEJ* 24 (1974) 145-152.

May, Herbert Gordon et al. *Oxford Bible Atlas*. Second Edition. London and New York: Oxford University Press, 1974.

Miller, James Maxwell. "Jebus and Jerusalem: A Case of Mistaken Identity," *ZDPV* 90 (1974) 115-127.

Noth, Martin. "Studien zu den historisch-geographischen Dokumenten des Josuabuches," *ZDPV* 58 (1935) 185-255.

Orni, Efraim, and Elisha Efrat. *Geography of Israel*. Jerusalem: Program for Scientific Translations, 1966.

Parunak, H. Van Dyke. "Geographical Terminology in Joshua 15-19." Unpublished Harvard seminar paper, 1976.

Peterson, John L. "A Topographical Surface Survey of the Levitical 'Cities' of Joshua 21 and 1 Chronicles 6: Studies on the Levites in Israelite Life and Religion." Unpublished Th.D. dissertation. Seabury-Western Theological Seminary, 1977.

Rainey, Anson Frank. "The Identification of Philistine-Gath," *Eretz-Israel* 12 (1975) 63*-76*.

Schunck, Klaus-Dietrich. *Benjamin, Untersuchungen zur Entstehung und Geschichte eines israelitischen Stammes*. BZAW 86. Berlin: Töppelmann, 1963.

Simons, J. *Handbook for the Study of Egyptian Topographical Texts Relating to Western Asia.* Leiden: Brill, 1937.

Smith, George Adam. *The Historical Geography of the Holy Land,* London: Hodder & Stoughton, 1894. Twenty-fifth revised edition, 1931; reprinted Harper Torchbooks/The Cloister Library; New York and Evanston: Harper & Row, 1966.

Wright, George Ernest. "A Problem of Ancient Topography—Lachish and Eglon," *HTR* 64 (1971) 437-488.

———— and Floyd Vivian Filson. *The Westminster Historical Atlas.* Revised Edition. Philadelphia: Westminster, 1956.

D. Various Discrete Units

Aharoni, Yohanan. "The Province-List of Judah," *VT* 9 (1959) 225-246.

Albright, William Foxwell. "The List of Levitic Cities," in *Louis Ginzberg Jubilee Volume,* eds. Saul Lieberman et al. New York: American Academy for Jewish Research, 1945. 49-73.

Auld, Graeme. "Judges 1 and History: A Reconsideration," *VT* 25 (1975) 261-285.

Bartlett, John Raymond. "The Conquest of Sihon's Kingdom: A Literary Re-examination," *JBL* 97 (1978) 347-351.

Blenkinsopp, Joseph. *Gibeon and Israel.* Cambridge University Press, 1972.

Cross, Frank Moore, and George Ernest Wright, "The Boundary and Province Lists of the Kingdom of Judah," *JBL* 75 (1956) 202-226.

Emerton, John Adney. "The Priests and Levites in Deuteronomy: An Examination of Dr. G. E. Wright's Theory," *VT* 12 (1962) 129-138.

Fensham, Frank Charles. "The Treaty between Israel and the Gibeonites," *BA* 27 (1964) 96-100.

Fritz, Volkmar. "Das Ende der spätbronzezeitlichen Stadt Hazor Stratum XIII und die biblischer Überlieferung in Josua 11 und Richter 4," *UF* 5 (1973) 123-139.

Gevirtz, Stanley. "Jericho and Shechem: A Religio-Literary Aspect of City Destruction," *VT* 13 (1963) 52-62.

Giblin, Charles Homer. "Structural Patterns in Joshua 24:1-25," *CBQ* 26 (1964) 50-69.

Grintz, Jehoshua M. "The Treaty of Joshua with the Gibeonites," *JAOS* 86 (1966) 113-126.

Halpern, Baruch. "Gibeon: Israelite Diplomacy in the Conquest Era," *CBQ* 37 (1975) 303-316.

Hanson, Paul D. "The Song of Heshbon and David's NÎR," *HTR* 61 (1968) 297-320.

Haran, Menahem. "Studies in the Account of the Levitical Cities," *JBL* 80 (1961) 45-54 and 156-165.

Holladay, John Scott, Jr. "The Day(s) the *Moon* Stood Still," *JBL* 87 (1968) 166-178.

Hulse, E. V. "Joshua's Curse and the Abandonment of Ancient Jericho: Schistosomiasis as a Possible Medical Explanation," *Medical History* 15 (1971) 376-386.

Kallai-Kleinmann, Zechariah. "The Town Lists of Judah, Simeon, Benjamin and Dan," *VT* 8 (1958) 134-160.

Kraus, Hans-Joachim. "Gilgal. Ein Beitrag zur Kulturgeschichte Israels," *VT* 1 (1951) 181-191.

Langlamet, F. *Gilgal et les récits de la traversée du Jourdain (Jos. III-IV)*. Paris: Gabalda, 1969.

L'Heureux, Conrad E. "The *yĕlîdê hārāpā'*—A Cultic Association of Warriors," *BASOR* 221 (February 1976) 83-85.

Liver, Jacob. "The Literary History of Joshua IX," *JSS* 8 (1963) 227-243.

Lohfink, Norbert. "Die deuteronomistische Darstellung des Übergangs der Führung Israels von Moses auf Josua," *Scholastik* 37 (1962) 36-38.

Long, Burke O. *The Problem of Etiological Narrative in the Old Testament*. BZAW 108. Berlin: Töppelmann, 1968.

McCarthy, Dennis J. "The Theology of Leadership in Joshua 1-9," *Biblica* 52 (1971) 165-175.

Malamat, Abraham. "Hazor 'The Head of All Those Kingdoms,'" *JBL* 79 (1960) 12-19.

Noth, Martin. "Die fünf Könige in der Höhle von Makkeda," *Palästinajahrbuch* 33 (1937) 22-36.

Porter, Joshua Roy. "The Succession of Joshua," in *Proclamation and Presence,* eds. John L. Durham and Joshua Roy Porter. London and Richmond: SCM Press and John Knox Press, 1970. 102-132.

Rösel, Hartmut. "Studien zur Topographie der Kriege in den Büchern Josua und Richter," *ZDPV* 91 (1975) 159-196.

Soggin, J. Alberto. "Gilgal, Passah und Landnahme. Eine neue Untersuchung des kultischen Zusammenhangs der Kap. III-VI des Josuabuches," *VTSup* 15 (1966) 263-277.

Tucker, Gene M. "The Rahab Saga (Joshua 2): Some Form-Critical and Traditio-Historical Observations," in *The Use of the Old Testament in the New and Other Essays: Studies in Honor of William Franklin Stinespring,* ed. James M. Efird. Durham, NC: Duke University Press, 1972. 66-86.

Van Seters, John. "The Conquest of Sihon's Kingdom: A Literary Examination," *JBL* 91 (1972) 182-197.

Wilcoxen, Jay A. "Narrative Structure and Cult Legend: A Study of Joshua 1-6," in *Transitions in Biblical Scholarship: Essays in Divinity* 6, ed. J. Coert Rylaarsdam. University of Chicago Press, 1968. 43-70.

Wright, George Ernest. "The Literary and Historical Problem of Joshua 10 and Judges 1," *JNES* 5 (1946) 105-114.

——— "The Provinces of Solomon," *Eretz Israel* 8 (1967) 58*-68*.

Yadin, Yigael. "And Dan, Why Did He Remain in Ships?" *Australian Journal of Biblical Archaeology* 1 (1968) 9-23.

E. Treaty and Covenant

Aryaprateep, Kamol. "Studies in the Semantics of the Covenant Relationship in Deuteronomic Teaching." Unpublished Th.D. dissertation. Seabury-Western Theological Seminary, 1974.

Baltzer, Klaus. *The Covenant Formulary,* tr. David E. Green. Philadelphia: Fortress Press, 1971.

Fitzmyer, Joseph A. *The Aramaic Inscriptions of Sefire.* Biblica et Orientalia 19. Rome: Pontifical Biblical Institute, 1967.

Gerstenberger, Erhard. "Covenant and Commandment," *JBL* 84 (1965) 38-51.

Harvey, Julien. *Le plaidoyer prophétique contra Israël après la rupture de d'Alliance.* Paris and Montreal: Desclée de Brouwer and Bellarmin, 1967.

Hillers, Delbert R. *Treaty-Curses and the Old Testament Prophets.* Rome: Pontifical Biblical Institute, 1964.

Isaac, Erich. "Circumcision as Covenant Rite," *Anthropos* 59 (1964) 444-456.

Kraus, Hans-Joachim. *Worship in Israel,* tr. Geoffrey Buswell. Richmond: John Knox Press, 1966.

McCarthy, Dennis J. *Treaty and Covenant.* Rome: Pontifical Biblical Institute, 1963.

Mendenhall, George Emery. *Law and Covenant in Israel and the Ancient Near East.* Pittsburgh: The Biblical Colloquium, 1955; reprinted *BAR* 3, 3-53.

——— "Social Organization in Early Israel," in *Mag Dei.* 132-151.

Moran, William L. "The Ancient Near Eastern Background of the Love of God in Deuteronomy," *CBQ* 25 (1963) 77-87.

Muilenburg, James. "The Form and Structure of the Covenantal Formulations," *VT* 9 (1959) 347-365.

Petersen, David L. "Covenant Ritual: A Traditio-Historical Perspective," *Biblical Research* 22 (1977) 7-18.

Widengren, Geo. "King and Covenant," *JSS* 2 (1957) 1-32.

Wright, George Ernest. "The Lawsuit of God: A Form-Critical Study of Deuteronomy 32," in *Israel's Prophetic Heritage,* eds. Bernhard W. Anderson and Walter Harrelson. New York: Harper & Row, 1962.

———— "The Nations in Hebrew Prophecy," *Encounter* (Spring 1965) 225-237.

F. Special Studies

Ackerman, James Stokes. "Psalm 82." Unpublished doctoral dissertation, Harvard University, 1966.

Albright, William Foxwell. "Midianite Donkey Caravans," in *Translating and Understanding the Old Testament,* eds. Harry Thomas Frank and William L. Reed. Nashville: Abingdon, 1970. 197-205.

———— "The Psalm of Habakkuk," in *Studies in Old Testament Prophecy,* ed. H. H. Rowley. Edinburgh: T. & T. Clark, 1950. 1-18.

Andersen, Francis I. *The Hebrew Verbless Clause in the Pentateuch. JBL* Monograph Series 14. Nashville and New York: Abingdon, 1970.

Anderson, Bernhard W. *Creation Versus Chaos.* New York: Association Press, 1967.

Avigad, Nahman. "The Priest of Dor," *IEJ* 25 (1975) 101-105.

Boling, Robert Gordon. "In Those Days There Was No King in Israel," in *A Light Unto My Path,* eds. Howard N. Bream, Ralph D. Heim, and Carey A. Moore. Philadelphia: Temple University Press, 1974. 33-48.

———— "Some Conflate Readings in Joshua-Judges," *VT* 16 (1966) 293-298.

Bright, John. "The Apodictic Prohibition: Some Observations," *JBL* 92 (1973) 185-204.

Campbell, Edward Fay, Jr. "Moses and the Foundations of Israel," *Interpretation* 29 (1975) 141-154.

Childs, Brevard S. *Memory and Tradition.* Naperville, IL: Allenson, 1962.

———— "Unto This Day," *JBL* 82 (1963) 279-292.

Clifford, Richard J. *The Cosmic Mountain in Canaan and in the Old Testament.* Harvard Semitic Monographs 4. Cambridge, MA: Harvard University Press, 1972.

———— "The Tent of El and the Israelite Tent of Meeting," *CBQ* 33 (1971) 221-227.

Crim, Keith Renn. *The Royal Psalms*. Richmond: John Knox Press, 1962.

Crisler, B. Cobbey. "The Acoustics and Crowd Capacity of Natural Theaters in Palestine," *BA* 39 (1976) 128-141.

Cross, Frank Moore. "Epigraphic Notes on Hebrew Documents of the Eighth-Sixth Centuries B.C.," *BASOR* 163 (1961) 12-14.

——— "The Priestly Tabernacle," *BA* 10 (1947) 45-68; reprinted *BAR* 1, 201-228.

Davies, Gwynne Henton. "The Ark in the Psalms," in *Promise and Fulfillment* (S. H. Hooke Festschrift), ed. F. F. Bruce. Edinburgh: T. & T. Clark, 1963.

Dumbrell, William J. "Midian—a Land or a League," *VT* 25 (1975) 323-337.

Eissfeldt, Otto. "Gilgal or Shechem?" in *Proclamation and Presence,* the G. Henton Davies Volume, eds. John L. Durham and Joshua Roy Porter. London and Richmond, VA: SCM Press and John Knox Press, 1970. 90-101.

——— "Psalm 80," in *Geschichte und des Altes Testament*. Beiträge zur historischen Theologie 16; Alt Festschrift, 1953. 65-78.

Elliger, Kurt. "Josua in Judäa," *Palästinajahrbuch* 30 (1934) 47-71.

Flanagan, James W. "Court History or Succession Document? A Study of 2 Sam 9-20 and 1 Kings 1-2," *JBL* 91 (1972) 172-181.

Forbes, Robert James. *Studies in Ancient Technology* II. Leiden: Brill, 1955.

Forrer, E. O. "The Hittites in Palestine: Part I," *PEQ* 48 (1936) 190-203; "Part II," *PEQ* 49 (1937) 100-115.

Freedman, David Noel. "Archaic Forms in Early Hebrew Poetry," *ZAW* 72 (1960) 101-107.

——— "Divine Names and Titles in Early Hebrew Poetry," in *Mag Dei*. 55-107.

——— "Early Israelite History in the Light of Early Israelite Poetry," in *Unity and Diversity: Essays in the History, Literature and Religion of the Ancient Near East,* eds. H. Goedicke and J. J. M. Roberts. The Johns Hopkins University Press, 1975. 3-35.

——— "Early Israelite Poetry and Historical Reconstructions," in *Symposia* (1979). 85-96.

Ginsberg, Harold Lewis. "Judah and the Transjordan States from 734 to 582 B.C.E.," in *Alexander Marx Jubilee Volume: English Section,* ed. Saul Lieberman. New York: Jewish Theological Seminary, 1950. 347-368.

Glock, Albert Ernest. "Warfare in Mari and Early Israel." Unpublished Ph.D. dissertation, University of Michigan, 1968.

Gottwald, Norman. *The Tribes of Yahweh.* Maryknoll, NY: Orbis, 1979.

Halpern, Baruch. "Levitic Participation in the Cult of Jeroboam I," *JBL* 95 (1976) 31-42.

———— "Sectionalism and Schism," *JBL* 93 (1974) 519-532.

Hanson, Paul D. *The Dawn of Apocalyptic.* Philadelphia: Fortress, 1975.

Huffmon, Herbert Bardwell. *Amorite Personal Names in the Mari Texts.* The Johns Hopkins University Press, 1965.

Hurvitz, Avi. "The Evidence of Language in Dating the Priestly Code," *RB* 81 (1974) 24-56.

Japhet, Sara. "Conquest and Settlement in Chronicles," *JBL* 98 (1979) 205-218.

Jenks, Alan. "The Elohist and North Israelite Tradition." Unpublished doctoral dissertation, Harvard University, 1965.

Jones, Gwilym H. " 'Holy War' or 'Yahweh War'?" *VT* 25 (1975) 642-658.

Kaufman, Gordon D. *Systematic Theology: A Historicist Perspective.* New York: Scribners, 1968.

Keel, Othmar. *Wirkmächtige Siegeszeichen im Alten Testament,* Orbis Biblicus et Orientalis 5. Göttingen: Vandenhoeck und Ruprecht, 1974.

Kraus, Hans-Joachim. *Worship in Israel,* tr. G. Buswell. Richmond: John Knox Press, 1966.

Kupper, Jean Robert. *Les nomads en Mesopotamie au temps des rois de Mari.* Paris: Les Belles Lettres, 1957.

Lambdin, Thomas Oden. *Introduction to Biblical Hebrew.* New York: Scribners, 1971.

L'Heureux, Conrad. *Rank Among the Canaanite Gods: El, Ba'al, and the Repha'im.* Harvard Semitic Monographs 21. Missoula, MT: Scholars Press, 1979.

Lohfink, Norbert. *Das Siegeslied am Schilfmeer.* Frankfurt am Main: J. Kecht, 1965.

McEvenue, Sean. *The Narrative Style of the Priestly Writer.* Analecta Biblica 50. Rome: Pontifical Biblical Institute, 1971.

Malamat, Abraham. "The Ban in Mari and in the Bible," in *Biblical Essays: Proceedings of the Ninth Meeting of Die Ou-Testamentiese Werkgemeenskap in Suid-Afrika (1966).* 44-45.

———— "Conquest of Canaan: Israelite Conduct of War According to Biblical Tradition," in *Encyclopaedia Judaica Year Book 1975/6.* Jerusalem: Macmillan, 1977. 166-182.

———— "Doctrines of Causality in Hittite and Biblical Historiography: A Parallel," *VT* 5 (1955) 1-12.

———— "Northern Canaan and the Mari Texts," in *Near Eastern Archae-*

ology in the Twentieth Century, ed. James A. Sanders. Garden City, NY: Doubleday, 1970. 20-33.

Martin, W. J. " 'Dischronologized' Narrative in the Old Testament," *VT* Sup 17 (1969) 179-186.

Matthews, V. H. *Pastoral Nomadism in the Mari Kingdom.* ASOR Dissertation Series. Cambridge, MA: American Schools of Oriental Research, 1978.

Mayes, Andrew D. H. "Israel in the Pre-Monarchy Period," *VT* 23 (1973) 151-170.

Mazar, Benjamin. "The Cities of the Priests and the Levites," *VT*Sup 7 (1960) 193-205.

Mendenhall, George Emery. "The Census Lists of Numbers 1 and 26," *JBL* 77 (1958) 52-66.

Meyers, Carol. "The Roots of Restriction: Women in Early Israel," *BA* 41 (1978) 91-103.

Milgrom, Jacob. "Sancta Contagion and Altar/City Asylum," forthcoming.

——— "The Shared Custody of the Tabernacle and a Hittite Analogy," *JAOS* 90 (1970) 204-209.

Miller, Patrick D., Jr. *The Divine Warrior in Early Israel.* Harvard Semitic Monographs 5. Harvard University Press, 1973.

——— "Faith and Ideology in the Old Testament," in *Mag Dei.* 464-479.

Moran, William L. "The End of the Unholy War and the Anti-Exodus," *Biblica* 44 (1963) 333-342.

Muilenburg, James. "A Liturgy on the Triumphs of Yahweh," in *Studia Biblica et Semitica,* eds. W. C. van Unnik and A. S. van der Woude. H. Veenman en Zonen N.V.: Wageningen, 1966. 233-251.

Neufeld, Edward. "Insects as Warfare Agents in the Ancient Near East (Ex. 23:28; Deut. 7:20; Josh. 24:12; Isa. 7:18-20)," Orientalia 49 (1980) 30-57.

Noth, Martin. *Israelitischer Personennamen im Rahmen der gemein-semitischen Namengebung,* BWANT III, 10. Stuttgart: W. Kohlhammer, 1928.

O'Connor, Michael Patrick. "The Grammar of Getting Blessed in Tyrian-Sidonian Phoenician," in *Rivista di Studi Fenici* 5 (1977) 5-11.

———*Hebrew Verse Structure.* Winona Lake, IN: Eisenbrauns, 1980.

Ottoson, Magnus. *Gilead: Tradition and History.* Lund: Gleerup, 1969.

Pardee, Dennis. "An Overview of Ancient Hebrew Epistolography," *JBL* 97 (1978) 321-346.

Priebatsch, Hans Y. "Jerusalem und die Brunnenstrasse Merneptahs," *ZDPV* 91 (1975) 18-29.

von Rad, Gerhard. *Der Heilige Krieg im Alten Testament.* Zürich: Zwingli Verlag, 1951.

———— *Studies in Deuteronomy,* tr. David Stalker. Studies in Biblical Theology 9. London: SCM Press, 1953.

Roth, Wolfgang. "The Deuteronomic Rest Theology: A Redaction-Critical Study," *Biblical Research* 21 (1976) 4-14.

Rudolph, Wilhelm. *Der "Elohist" von Exodus bis Josua.* Berlin: Töppelmann, 1938.

Sakenfeld, Katherine Doob. *The Meaning of Hesed in the Hebrew Bible.* Harvard Semitic Monographs 17. Missoula, MT: Scholars Press, 1978.

Sasson, Jack M. *The Military Establishment of Mari.* Rome: Pontifical Biblical Institute, 1969.

Sellers, Ovid Rogers. "Musical Instruments of Israel," *BA* 4 (1941) 33-47; reprinted *BAR* 1 (1961) 81-94.

Soggin, J. Alberto. "Kultätiologische Sagen und Katachese im Hexateuch," *VT* 10 (1960) 341-347.

Speiser, Ephraim Avigdor. "People and Nation in the Old Testament," *JBL* 79 (1960) 157-163.

Stager, Lawrence E. "Ancient Agriculture in the Judean Desert: A Case Study of the Buqei'ah Valley in the Iron Age." Unpublished Ph.D. dissertation, Harvard University, 1975.

———— "Farming in the Judean Desert During the Iron Age," *BASOR* 221 (February 1976) 145-158.

Stolz, Fritz. *Jahwes und Israels Kriege: Kriegstheorien und Kriegsfahrungen im Glauben des alten Israels.* Zürich: Theologischer Verlag, 1972.

Talmon, Shemaryahu. "The Gezer Calendar and the Seasonal Cycles of Ancient Canaan," *JAOS* 83 (1963) 177-187.

Thomas, David Winton. "KELEBH 'DOG': Its Origin and Some Usages of It in the Old Testament," *VT* 10 (1960) 410-427.

———— "The Meaning of the Name Hammath-Dor," *PEFQS* (1934) 147-148.

Volz, Paul, and Wilhelm Rudolph. *Der Elohist als Erzähler: Ein Irrweg der Pentateuchkritik?* Giessen: Alfred Toppelmann, 1933.

de Vries, Simon J. "Temporal Terms as Structural Elements in the Holy War Tradition," *VT* 25 (1975) 80-105.

Westermann, Claus. *The Praise of God in the Psalms,* tr. Keith R. Crim. Richmond: John Knox Press, 1965.

Wijngaards, Joanne N. M. "The Dramatization of Salvific History in the Deuteronomic Schools," *Oudtestamentische Studien* 16 (Leiden: Brill, 1969) 1-132.

Wilson, Robert R. *Genealogy and History in the Biblical World.* Yale University Press, 1977.

Wright, George Ernest. "The Levites in Deuteronomy," *VT* 4 (1954) 325-330.

Zyl, A. H. van. "Chronological Deuteronomic History," in *Proceedings of the Fifth World Congress of Jewish Studies* I. Jerusalem: World Congress of Jewish Studies, 1969. 12-26.

———— *The Moabites.* Leiden: Brill, 1960.

Note on the Hebrew Text

Two companion works in this series have described recent developments and current trends in the textual criticism of the historical books of the Old Testament. The reader who has not been initiated in these mysteries is referred to our discussion in *Judges,* AB 6A (1975) 38-42 and 297-301; and to Edward F. Campbell, Jr., *Ruth,* AB 7 (1975) 36-41. In those pages the basic terminology is defined and the breakthrough which has followed the discovery of the Qumran scrolls is described, so that here we may summarize briefly.

Considerations of style and internal organization in many differing manuscripts give evidence of classes for which the technical term is "recensions." The best text must be reconstructed by comparing the recensions known. In biblical studies the terminology of recensional classes has been based on Jerome's description of the three principal Greek recensions known to him at the end of the fourth century A.D.—the Hesychian, the Lucianic, and the Origenic. All three had developed from an Old Greek translation of the OT (from the Hebrew) produced during the third and second centuries B.C.

The first of the three is probably to be connected with a martyred Alexandrian bishop of the third century A.D. Not much is known about this recension.

The second is associated with Antioch where Lucian was martyred c. 311. A full-scale attempt to reconstruct the Lucianic text was initiated by Lagarde in the nineteenth century; principal carriers of Lucianic readings, it is generally agreed, are manuscripts boc_2e_2 and the Old Latin version. Subsequent refinements have questioned the precision with which Lagarde grouped manuscripts, but in the main his approach has been validated.

Origen (185-253), the head of the catechetical school of Alexandria, set himself the task of producing a single work in which the principal Greek texts available in his day were arranged in parallel columns, with another column for his critically reconstructed Greek (LXX) text, and diacritical marks to indicate how it was related to his main sources. Three of the latter were Aquila, Theodotian, and Symmachus. The first two scholars were probably Jews, while Symmachus was an Ebionite Christian. Each of them had worked in his own way to bring the Greek text of his day into closer conformity with a developing Hebrew text.

Scholars in our century, working their way back, inductively, through the maze, have discovered two main stages on the way from the Old Greek and its Hebrew original (*Vorlage*) to the fully developed LXX which came to stand alongside the single Hebrew text type that had been selected by the rabbis to be authoritative (MT), in the early centuries A.D. It is now clear that the text of the Hebrew Bible was being developed by scholars in each of three great centers of Jewish population (Egypt, Palestine, Babylonia), not in total isolation but with a high degree of independence. In addition to continuing cultivation of the text in Egypt, which had produced the Old Greek, there was a distinct Palestinian text which in the last century B.C. was used as the basis for revising the Greek. The result was a recension now termed "Proto-Lucianic" because it precedes by several centuries the man whose name was later assigned to one distinct family of manuscripts.

In Babylonia, too, a Hebrew text was being carefully cultivated and perpetuated. It was the Babylonian text which in the first century B.C. served as the basis for another revision of the Greek, to bring it into line with the developing Hebrew text. This has become known as the *kaige* recension, because of its standard use of that compound in the Old Greek where the simple conjunction *kai* normally suffices. There are, at the latest count, ninety-five additional characteristics of usage which serve to distinguish and trace the influence of the *kaige* recension. Stemming probably from the last third of the first century A.D. (thus also appropriately nicknamed "Proto-Theodotian"), the *kaige* stands as close to a developed Hebrew text as did Proto-Lucian to the Old Greek.

The preceding remarks are for the most part only made possible by the pioneering work of Frank M. Cross and his students, over the first thirty years with the materials from Qumran, where a considerable variety of Hebrew and Greek texts is represented. In preparation of this volume, I have had the benefit of the dissertation by Cross's student, Leonard Jay Greenspoon, "Studies in the Textual Tradition of the Book of Joshua," Ph.D. thesis, Harvard University, 1977.

Greenspoon begins his thesis with an exhaustive study of the readings of Theodotian in Joshua. He shows unmistakably that Theodotian corrected his Greek to a Hebrew text that was almost identical to the MT.

A second focus of Greenspoon's thesis is the relationships between Theodotian, Aquila, and Symmachus. He concludes that Theodotian was in turn the basis for Aquila's further revision and that Aquila had no independent knowledge of the Old Greek. Symmachus had both and used both the work of Theodotian and the Old Greek, and perhaps other recensions (and/or translations) as well.

Finally, Greenspoon enters into a complete investigation of the *kaige* recension in Joshua. "The accumulated evidence leaves no doubt that Th. [Theodotian] in Joshua is to be included in the general *kaige* recension. He does occupy a position midway between (a form of) the OG and Aquila (also Symmachus), he does revise the OG to a Hebrew (almost) identical to the MT, and he does share a number of *kaige* equivalences and especially the tendency to standardize the Greek rendering of individual Hebrew words and phrases" (495).

Among the multitude of lettered scraps of leather from Qumran Cave 4 are fragments from two manuscripts of Joshua (Cross, *BA* 19 [1956] 84), on which Cross is at work and which he will publish in due course along with the rest of Historical Books fragments from Cave 4. In a presentation at the southeastern regional meeting of the American Academy of Religion and Society of Biblical Literature (1978), Professor Greenspoon reported that the 4Q fragments cover portions from each of chaps. 2-8, plus portions of chaps. 10 and 17. The greatest part of the legible material is described as belonging to a manuscript of the Hasmonean period, c. 100 B.C. Greenspoon's study of the fragments leads him to the conclusion that the 4Q Joshua manuscripts are in the same tradition of the full, expansionistic text as Joshua in the MT, the type which Cross labels Palestinian. This clearly suggests relationships very different from those seen, for example, in Samuel fragments from Qumran which display a Hebrew text much more closely related to the *Vorlage* of the Old Greek translation.

And this makes the establishment of the text in a particular passage often even more difficult than "before Qumran." The trail not infrequently branches, leading, so far as the critic can tell, to equally genuine variant readings.

R.G.B.

JOSHUA

Translation
Textual Notes
Notes
&
Comments

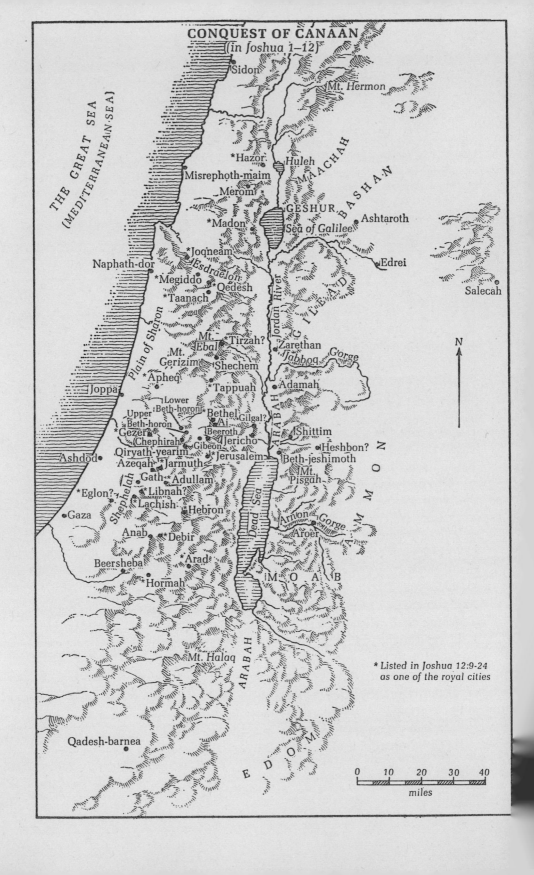

CONQUEST OF CANAAN
(in Joshua 1–12)

THE GREAT SEA
(MEDITERRANEAN SEA)

Sidon

Mt. Hermon

*Hazor

Huleh

MAACHAH

Misrephoth-maim

Merom

BASHAN

*Madon

GESHUR

Sea of Galilee

Ashtaroth

*Joqneam

Esdraelon

Naphath-dor

Edrei

*Megiddo

Qedesh

Salecah

*Taanach

GILEAD

Plain of Sharon

Mt.
Ebal

*Tirzah?

Zarethan

Jabbog

Gorge

Mt.
Gerizim

Shechem

*Apheq

Jordan River

*Tappuah

Adamah

Joppa

Lower
Beth-horon

Bethel

Gilgal?

ARABAH

Shittim

Upper
Beth-horon

*Ai

Beeroth

Jericho

Heshbon?

*Gezer

*Chephirah

Gibeon

Beth-jeshimoth

Qiryath-yearim

Jerusalem

AMMON

Ashdod

Azeqah

*Jarmuth

Mt.
Pisgah

Gath

*Adullam

*Eglon?

Shephelah

*Libnah?

*Lachish

*Hebron

Arnon

Gorge

Gaza

Aroer

Anab

*Debir

Dead Sea

Beersheba

*Arad

*Hormah

M O A B

N

Mt. Halaq

ARABAH

* Listed in Joshua 12:9-24
as one of the royal cities

Qadesh-barnea

E D O M

0   10   20   30   40

miles

I. MOBILIZATION AND INVASION
1:1-5:12

A. MARCHING ORDERS
(1:1-18)

Joshua and Israel

1 ¹ After the death of Moses, the Servant of Yahweh, Yahweh said to Joshua ben Nun, Moses' lieutenant:

² "My servant Moses is dead. Proceed to cross this Jordan at once —you and all this people—to the land that I am giving to them, to the Bene Israel! ³ Every place on which you will set the soles of your feet I have given to you, exactly as I promised Moses. ⁴ From the wilderness and this Lebanon all the way to the Great River, the river Euphrates (all the land of the Hittites), and to the great sea where the sun sets, shall be your territory.

⁵ "No one shall hold his ground before you as long as you live. As I was with Moses, so I will be with you. I will not abandon you; I will not desert you! ⁶ Be strong and courageous, for you will enable this people to inherit the land that I promised on oath to their ancestors to give them. ⁷ Only be very strong and courageous, careful to implement the entire Treaty-Teaching which Moses my Servant commanded you. Do not in any way deviate from it, to the right or left, that you may succeed wherever you go. ⁸ This Book of the Treaty-Teaching shall never be missing from your lips, and you shall recite it day and night that you may be sure to do all that is recorded in it. For then shall you profit in your pilgrimage and have success. ⁹ Have I not commanded you? Be strong and courageous! Be not frightened or dismayed! Yahweh your God is indeed with you, wherever you go!"

¹⁰ Joshua gave the order to the officers of the people:

¹¹ "Go throughout the camp and give the order to the people,

Opposite page, Map B

'Prepare supplies for yourselves, for within three days you will cross this Jordan to enter and possess the land that Yahweh, God of your ancestors, is giving to you as a possession.' "

All Israel

12 And to the Reubenites, the Gadites, and half the tribe of Manasseh, Joshua said:

13 "Remember the charge with which Moses the Servant of Yahweh commanded you saying 'Your God Yahweh grants you rest and is giving you this land.' 14 Your wives, your little ones, and your livestock shall remain in the land which Moses gave you—in the region across the Jordan. But you shall cross over in battle array before your kinsmen—all you burly warriors—and help them 15 until Yahweh your God grants a place of rest for your kinsfolk, as he has done for you, and they too shall take possession of the land which Yahweh your God is giving to them. Then you may return to your own holding, which Moses the Servant of Yahweh gave to you, beyond the Jordan where the sun rises."

16 They answered Joshua, "All that you have commanded us we will do. Wherever you send us we will go. 17 As in everything we obeyed Moses, so we will obey you. Only may Yahweh your God be with you as he was with Moses! 18 Whoever disputes your rulings and does not obey your words, whatever order you give him, shall be put to death. Only be strong and courageous!"

TEXTUAL NOTES

1 1. *the Servant of Yahweh*　There is considerable textual variety and no general pattern where this title is involved. Here and in v 15 it is lacking in LXX, but homoioteleuton in the Hebrew *Vorlage* of LXX stimulated a haplography: *mš[h 'bd yhw]h*.

Nun　This is the Hebrew spelling, in place of which LXX regularly reads *Nauē*. See NOTE.

2. *this*　Cf. "this Lebanon" in v 4. LXX lacks the demonstrative adjective in both places. The difference must go back to traditional variants, since there is no mechanism to explain introduction of the pronoun into one text or loss of it from the other.

to the Bene Israel   Martin Noth in the critical apparatus of *BH*³ recommends omission of this phrase, which was not represented in the Old Greek. To be sure, the shorter reading cannot here be explained by any common kind of scribal error. The longer reading may be the result of glossing, but it does not add much clarity. The text is probably a conflation of variants, both of which use an emphatic particle. The critical apparatus for the Book of Joshua in *BH*³ represents a balanced use of the LXX in the era of scholarship preceding the Qumran finds in the late 1940s and subsequent discoveries. For review of the treatment of LXX in Joshua, see H. M. Orlinsky, "The Hebrew *Vorlage* of the Septuagint of the Book of Joshua," *VT*Sup 17 (1968) 187-195. Recent discoveries have greatly clarified the early history of the text. In *BH*³ the citation of variant readings in the upper rank of notes (those using Greek letters for *sigla*) is necessarily limited and sometimes misleading because of partial quotation. In every case the text must be checked, using especially the works of Samuel Holmes, *Joshua: The Hebrew and Greek Texts,* and Max Margolis, *The Book of Joshua in Greek*. The latter, unfortunately, was finished only as far as 19:38. "The remainder of the manuscript (Part V and the Introduction) must be numbered, it would seem, among the literary casualties of the Second World War, since repeated inquiries have failed to elicit any trace of it in Paris and it must be presumed to have been irretrievably lost or destroyed." Thus Sidney Jellicoe in *The Septuagint and Modern Study,* 278, reports on the basis of communication from Orlinsky.

The reader will observe that not infrequently we have disagreed with the critical judgments of *BH*³, found in the second part of its apparatus (notes using Latin letters as *sigla*). This is due to the sharp redefinition of the text-critical situation since Qumran, which is reflected in the simpler apparatus of the newest edition (1977), *BHS*. The latter is, however, not cited fully in our notes because it appeared while our work on Joshua was far advanced.

4. *Lebanon*   Here and elsewhere in Joshua, LXX regularly reads *antilibanon,* referring perhaps to the Anti Lebanon range and everything west of it to the coast, and omits the demonstrative.

(*all the land of the Hittites*)   Lacking in LXX, which is usually taken to mean that MT is glossed. We suspect, however, that it is a very ancient marginal comment which dropped out of LXX because it no longer made sense.

5. *you*   The pronoun is singular in MT (referring to Joshua), plural in LXX (referring to the Israelites: the next is singular in both texts, so the guarantee of success is still tied to the figure of Joshua).

6. *their*   LXX reads second person plural: "your ancestors." See NOTE.

7. *very*   LXX seems to reflect a lack of *m'd* in its *Vorlage,* perhaps lost under the influence of v 6. But if *oun* can be taken as the Greek equivalent of *m'd,* then *rq,* "Only," may have been lost by homoioteleuton at the beginning of v 6. Michael Patrick O'Connor, private communication.

careful to implement   MT has the two infinitives juxtaposed, but they are separated by the conjunction in LXX:

$$l\check{s}mr \begin{cases} l'\check{s}wt & \text{MT} \\ wl'\check{s}wt & \text{LXX} \end{cases}$$

LXX lacks *the entire Treaty-Teaching*. The differences are possibly to be resolved into two variants stemming from oral tradition.

lšmr   *kl-htwrh*   '*šr*   to be careful [   ] the entire Treaty-Teaching
l'šwt k-   '*šr*   [   ] to act according to [   ]

Do not in any way deviate   This is the Hebrew: *'l-tswr*. LXX has a
prefixed conjunction ("and do not . . ."). Both texts of v 8 show the same pattern at the beginning, but MT uses the more emphatic negative: *lō'*.
   8. *all*   LXX, Syriac, Vulgate support this shorter reading *kl*, against MT
kkl, "according to all." The latter may be due either to a simple dittography or
contamination from *kkl* in the preceding verse.
   in it   The phrase is missing from LXX. *hktwb[bw]* may reflect dittography
in MT.
   then   Hebrew '*z* is here repeated with both verbs in MT, but the initial *ky*,
"For," is not reflected in LXX.
   profit   The verb is *hṣlḥ*, "to prosper." LXX renders both *qal* and *hiph'il*
forms of the verb.
   your   The Hebrew is *děrākekā*, a singular pausal form, which many medieval manuscripts together with LXX and Targum took to be plural *děrākêkā*,
"your pilgrimages." Vulgate supports the singular.
   11. *camp*   LXX reads "the camps of the people," in what is apparently a
scribal lapse anticipating the same word just three words away.
   for yourselves   Lacking in LXX.
   you   LXX^BL read a prefixed conjunction which is anomalous unless it
preserves an archaic emphatic usage. But the latter would require a finite verb,
not the participle.
   God of your ancestors   This agrees with LXX, where MT shows a
haplography: *'lhy ['bwty]km*, "your God."
   as a possession   This is lacking in LXX, probably because of haplography
l[ršth wl]r'wbny.
   13. *charge*   There is support in the Greek, though not uniform, for "word
of the Lord."
   14. Medieval Hebrew manuscripts and Versions reflect "and" before "your
little ones."
   Moses and *in the region across the Jordan*   Lacking in LXX.
   15. *your God*   This follows LXX. In the MT, the first occurrence of
'lhykm was dropped when a scribe's eye jumped to the similar consonant cluster immediately following it: *l'hykm*.
   holding   This follows LXX where MT continues: "and take possession of
it." But that reading (*wyrštm 'wth*) may have arisen through partial dittography of the preceding (*yrštkm*). The awkward repetition results in a certain rhetorical similarity to passages such as Deut 3:18 and 3:20 (likewise concerned with the Transjordan tribes), as well as Deut 4:1 and 4:5.
   the Servant of Yahweh   Lacking in LXX. See Textual Note at v 1.

17. *so*   Hebrew *ken* seems to be lacking in the *Vorlagen* of LXX and Syr.ᵂ which are thus less emphatic.

your   LXX reads "our."

NOTES

The purpose of these sections in our book is to show the basis for the translation and to focus attention on matters of internal organization and literary history. The NOTES are dedicated to the proposition that "One of the first tasks of scholarship is . . . the careful undoing of the effects of time" (René Wellek and Austin Warren, *Theory of Literature,* 57). We shall bear in mind that the "effects of time" may be found in the reader and the commentator as well as in the text.

1:1-11. This is the introduction to the Book of Joshua, in the first and major edition of the work. It emphasizes the qualities required of Joshua, and the leadership he must provide in taking over the land. These are stressed in vv 1-9, and in the next two verses he issues his first command to the officers.

1-9. The unit has a sermonic sound to it, with many items of vocabulary and rhetorical style in common with Deuteronomy. The passage is not merely exhortation. There is here a regular formula for divine installation of a person into a public office. Three elements stand out: a. the encouragement given to the new officer; b. the statement of task or function; c. an assurance of divine help or presence. For the prior commissioning of Joshua, see Deut 31:1-8,14-15,23 and compare Deut 1:38; 3:21-22,28. J. R. Porter, "The Succession of Joshua," in *Proclamation and Presence,* 102-132. See also McCarthy, *Treaty and Covenant,* 143-144 n. 6. It has been argued that Joshua's figure is here based upon the reforming King Josiah who proclaimed the law and represented the people in covenant renewal before Yahweh. So, G. Widengren, "King and Covenant," *JSS* 2 (1957) 1-32. It would be better to say that Joshua is here portrayed as a military model for King Josiah. See COMMENT.

1. *After the death of Moses.* The formula *wyhy 'ḥry mwt NN,* where *NN* stands for a personal name, is significant in Dtr (Judg 1:1; 2 Sam 1:1; and, slightly modified, in 2 Kgs 1:1), but rare in the Tetrateuch (only in Gen 25:11). Moses, Joshua, Saul and David, and Ahab are crucial figures in Dtr and the author-compiler has used them to divide the time span treated in the work into four eras:

     A. Conquest under charismatic leadership (Joshua);
     B. Possession of the land under charismatic leadership (Judges-1 Samuel);
     C. Possession of the land under monarchical government (2 Samuel-1 Kings);
     D. Loss of the land under monarchical government (2 Kings).

In terms of literary proportions, A and D are comparable as are B and C. Rhetorically the corpus thus displays one large chiastic pattern. See A. H. van Zyl, "Chronological Deuteronomic History," in *Proceedings of the Fifth World Congress of Jewish Studies* I, 12-26. It should be emphasized that this is the organization of the finished work.

the death of Moses. This presupposes the old epic story of the death of Moses in Transjordan (Deut 34; cf. Num 20:12; 27:14; Deut 3:26; 31:1-8), which was detached from its original context when the Tetrateuch and subsequent works were connected to complete the Primary History (the books of Genesis-2 Kings). See D. N. Freedman, "Pentateuch," *IDB* 3, 711-727; and "Canon," *IDBSup.*

Moses. Despite the popular Hebrew explanation of this name in the epic source of Exod 2:10, it is Egyptian. It is the shortened form of a sentence name, of a class beginning with the name of a deity: *X-mōse,* "the god X is born" (for example, *Thutmōse, Ahmōse, Ramōse*). The authenticity of Hebrew connections with Egypt of the Seventeenth and Eighteenth Dynasties where these names cluster is confirmed many times over by other Egyptian names in the early *Israelite* onomasticon, for example: Hophni, Phinehas, and Merari. See especially Bright, *A History of Israel,* Third Edition 121 and n. 30 with bibliography; and W. F. Albright, *YGC,* 165 and n. 36.

Servant of Yahweh. Although it is applied honorifically to each of the major patriarchs (Abraham, Isaac, Jacob), Moses was no doubt the first to bear this description (Deut 34:5). "Servant" becomes a favorite term throughout the entire Dtr-corpus where it is virtually a title. See also "my servant" in vv 2 and 7. Joshua will be the next to bear the title, in 24:29 and Judg 2:8. Elsewhere in the early era, only Caleb is called Yahweh's servant, and that in a confidential communication to Moses in the epic (Num 14:24). In one story Samson will take the title to himself (Judg 15:18). The title "servant" is applied in Dtr with special frequency to the Jerusalem kings. Thus 2 Sam 3:18; 7:5; 1 Kgs 11:13,32,34,36,38; 14:8; 2 Kgs 19:34; 20:6 (see also Jer 33:21,22,26 and so on); Cross, *CMHE,* 253. The distinctive OT career of this title attains its climax in the exilic Songs of the Second Isaiah (*Isaiah* 40-55, AB 20, 1968) where the title is applied to Israel the Suffering One as Yahweh's ambassador in that new day. See our observations in *Judges,* AB 6A, 71-72.

Yahweh. The first and most basic definition of this name as used throughout the Book of Joshua is given by the deity himself in the context of the covenant with which the book ends—"God of Israel" (24:2), which in archaic poetry goes back at least as far as the composition of the Song of Deborah (Judg 5:3). The people here dealt with are constituted by covenant—not by blood kinship, social class, or any inherited pattern of social organization, including religious heritage. What is the background of the divine name?

The divine name parses as a causative imperfect of the verb **hwh>hyh,* "to be, become," thus meaning approximately, "He creates." Objections that such a meaning is too abstract for primitive Yahwism are adequately refuted by Albright (*YGC,* 169) and others. See D. N. Freedman and Michael Patrick O'Conner, "Yahweh," forthcoming in *TWAT.* But *Yahweh* is the verbal element only. What or who were subject and object?

In a series of recent studies, David Noel Freedman acknowledges a continuity in the history of religion from the patriarchal era to Moses, but he emphasizes radical distinctiveness and novelty in Yahweh and the Mosaic movement that in fact was the first reformation of Israel. See especially a trilogy of essays by Freedman: "Early Israelite History in the Light of Early Israelite Poetry," in *Unity and Diversity, Essays in the History, Literature and Religion of the Ancient Near East* (1975) 3-35; "Divine Names and Titles in Early Hebrew Poetry," in *Mag Dei* (1976) 55-107; and "Early Israelite Poetry and Historical Reconstructions," presented to the American Schools of Oriental Research Seventy-Fifth Anniversary Symposium, Jerusalem, 1975, and published in *Symposia* (1979) 85-96. On this view, Yahweh has emerged from obscurity within the old family of El. That is, in the period of the Judges, elements of the older El-religion and the younger Yahwism flow together to produce the religion of Israel.

At the same time, Frank M. Cross has sought to explain the name Yahweh as part of a liturgical epithet originating in the old pre-Mosaic cult of the deity El going back to patriarchal times and recalled especially in later priestly lore as Shaddai. On this view the original would be: "(It is) El who creates." Moreover, the full sentence name would include an object of the action, for which Cross argues we may understand "the armies" (*ṣĕbā'ôt*). Thus the full appellation would have been: El is The One Who Creates the (Heavenly) Armies (*CMHE*, especially Part I, 1-75). On this view, as well, Yahwism emerges as a radical reformation out of an old El-religion.

In any case, our new translation given below in 3:10 becomes virtually certain, in light of the foregoing.

The name *Yahweh* occurs in ostraca of the seventh and sixth centuries from Lachish and Arad and in an eighth-century seal reported by Cross, but its earliest appearance is in Egyptian topographical lists from the reigns of Amenophis III (1417-1379 B.C.) and Ramesses II (1304-1237 B.C.). *CMHE*, 61-62, with special reference to Raphael Giveon, "Toponymes Ouest-Asiatiques à Soleb," *VT* 14 (1964) 239-255, especially 244. Presumably, the full place name would have been *bêt Yahweh*, as observed by Freedman in the first article of the trilogy cited above. This place has been identified with Qurayyah, a site 70 km northwest of Tabuk and 26 km west-southwest of Bir Ibn Hirmas, the Saudi Arabian customs station on the Hejaz Railway, a little more than 60 km from the Jordanian frontier at Mudawwara. Two things stand out from the initial survey of the site. One is the distinctive painted ceramic and the related wares which elsewhere have been variously described as "Edomite" or "Midianite" and which at Qurayyah are "local and common." The other is the remains of an extensive irrigation system which is "amongst the earliest known from the entire area of Arabia and the Levant," that is, two or three centuries earlier than systems in the Negeb which date to about the tenth century. Peter J. Parr, G. L. Harding, and J. E. Dayton, "Preliminary Survey in N.W. Arabia, 1968," *Bulletin of the Institute of Archaeology* 8/9 (1970) 219-241. See also J. E. Dayton, "Midianite and Edomite Pottery," in *Proceedings of the Fifth Seminar for Arabian Studies* (1972) 25-33.

If an ancient Beth-Yahweh is to be located at the Late Bronze Age site of

Qurayyah, then it was probably a Midianite sacral-center, with Yahweh as patron deity.

Yahweh said to Joshua. Hebrew *wy'mr yhwh 'l yhwš'*. This expression occurs six times before the capture of Jericho, five times as an introductory formula (1:1; 3:7; 4:1b,15; 6:2). In 5:9 it occurs within a narrative unit, and there the introductory statement shows the disjunctive variation of the formula *b't hhy' 'mr yhwh 'l yhwš'* (5:2).

Joshua. Hebrew *yĕhôšūa'*, alternate form "Hoshea" (as in Num 13:8,16 and Deut 32:44). The name is also borne by a great eighth-century prophet and by the last king of north Israel. The name becomes *yēšūa'* in a later period (Chronicles, Ezra-Nehemiah), whence the Greek transcription (*Iēsous*) and Latin (*Iosue*).

ben. The spelling *bin* in MT is *ben-n* "remorphologized as one word, yielding a geminate *n*, which stimulates vowel-lengthening or raising." M. P. O'Connor private communication. Other examples of *bin* for *ben* are collected in GKC ※96. A literal translation is "son of" but probably here not originally designating genealogical descent. It was only later that Joshua was incorporated into genealogical systems (1 Chr 7:20-27). The word *ben* often designates a category; in this case it stands for membership in a subgroup named *Nun.*

Nun. The name is *Non* in 1 Chr 7:27. Therefore it is probably not "Fish"; LXX spells it *Nauē*, which may retain awareness of an old clan name that was spelled in Hebrew with an enclitic: *nawe-n*. See J. A. Soggin, *Joshua*, 1, on the authority of J. R. Kupper, *Les nomads en Mesopotamie au temps des rois de Mari*, 12*f*.

The new leader is introduced as though he were well-known. It is notoriously difficult to assess the significance of the scattered references to Joshua in Tetrateuch sources. See Exod 17:8-16; 24:13; 32:17; 33:11; Num 11:28; 13:8,16,17-33 (by implication); 14:6,30,38; 26:65; 27:15-23; 32:12,28; 34:17; and Deut 34:9. To the Dtr historical work belong the references to Joshua in Deut 31:14,23 and 32:44.

lieutenant. Or "minister" in older translation. The same word describes Joshua's relationship to Moses (Exod 24:13; 33:11; Num 11:28) and Elisha's "service" to Elijah (1 Kgs 19:21). The common denominator to these traditions is formed by the image and value system of service to the Divine Warrior. The word also describes the boy Samuel's service of God (1 Sam 3:1).

2. *Proceed to cross.* Literally, "Arise! Cross!" but the two imperatives form a verbal hendiadys. Thomas O. Lambdin, *Introduction to Biblical Hebrew*, 238-240. See also 6:26 and NOTE.

at once. Hebrew *w'th* (literally, "And now") at the very beginning of the clause in Hebrew belongs with "today, this day," etc., as a freighted time expression; see below, NOTE on 3:7. Only with the death of Moses had the time arrived for the invasion. This belongs to the "Unholy War" presentation in the latest work on Deuteronomy 2. See William L. Moran, "The End of the Unholy War and the Anti-Exodus," *Biblica* 44 (1963) 333-342.

this people. Hebrew here uses the basic and lasting identification of ancient Israel: *'ām*. Each level of redactional work in the material (Dtn, Dtr 1, and Dtr 2) selects from a variety of other terms that are complementary to this one. But nothing displaces this word. The result is that in the bulk of the material *'ām* resists mere ethnic or nationalistic definition. Israel was, as the earliest prose sources put it, *'am sĕgullâ,* "a particular (KJV 'special' or 'peculiar') people" (Deut 7:6; 14:2; 26:28; cf. Exod 19:5). From the international treaties, which use the strict linguistic equivalent of *sĕgullâ,* we know that this people's peculiarity was specifically its constitution by covenant with Yahweh. It will be important throughout Joshua to watch for the usage of this word *'ām,* "people."

the land. Here it can only be entered by crossing the Jordan; it is the old Egyptian definition of the province Canaan which later coincided with King Josiah's claims for his realm.

I am giving. On the primacy of this theme in ancient Israel's worship, see Wright's Introduction, especially 10-13. The gift is "in fief," not an outright grant. The roots of Israel's military organization have been clearly traced back to the old Amorite society of northwestern Mesopotamia known best from the eighteenth-century Mari letters. See Jack M. Sasson, *The Military Establishment of Mari;* and especially Albert Ernest Glock, "Warfare in Mari and Early Israel" (Ph.D. dissertation, University of Michigan, 1968). The latter makes it clear that "the sequence is land grant-warfare-land use" (46). Soggin, *Joshua,* thinks that the use of the participle *nôtēn* denotes intention and renders "I prepare to give." The Mari evidence suggests precisely the reverse; the gift is made at the outset in exchange for the promise of service in the future. It is not a merely academic distinction: "Here lies the basis of the biblical concept of the power of God, not in metaphysical speculation or ontology." George E. Mendenhall, "The Hebrew Conquest of Palestine," *BA* 25 (1962) 78=*BAR* 3 (1970) 111. "By making the struggle for power an illicit assumption of the prerogatives of God alone, the early Israelite religion laid the foundations for an internal peace which Canaanite society evidently could not do." Ibid.

to the Bene Israel. Hebrew *lbny yśr'l.* The book begins with a strong declaration of the relation between Yahweh, people, and land. The last is a gracious gift in trust from the deity. We have decided to transliterate *bĕnê* rather than to translate (literally, "sons of"). "Israelite" is a gentilic term and should be reserved for translation of the ancient *yśr'ly.* The latter is almost nonexistent in biblical usage but is ubiquitous in later and modern Hebrew, whence the transliteration "Israeli." Cf. French *Israëlite* and *Israëlien.* The point here is that the contrast in ancient texts between gentilic formations (for example, "Amorite," "Canaanite," "Jebusite") and tribal or clan organization using kinship terminology (Bene Israel, Bene Yehuda, etc.) is often intentional and meaningful and so ought to be retained wherever possible in translation. The "Bene Israel" here being addressed are the participants in the Moab covenant, which is presented in Deuteronomy as the sequel to Sinai. Memory of the Moab covenant was preserved mainly in materials stemming from Shechem.

3-9. Deuteronomy 31:7-8 plus 7:24b and 11:24 add up to the same thematic total in almost identical language.

3. *Every place.* Hebrew *kl mqwm.* Cf. Deut 11:24.

your foot. Suddenly the pronoun suffix is plural (while the verb is singular), as though all Israel were being addressed. The forms will in fact shift back and forth disconcertingly: plurals are "to you" in v 3, "your border" in v 4, and "before you" in v 5 (LXX). Such variation is characteristic of orally formulated and orally transmitted material, such as the old covenant-renewal materials behind Deuteronomy certainly were. No attempt is made in this commentary to record all such fluctuations.

exactly as I promised. Classical Hebrew has no one-word equivalent for the verb "to promise." Rather, Hebrew uses simply the verb "to speak" (*dbr*) and relies on context for the nuance of promise. Here "promising" is contained within "speaking." To give special emphasis to the promissory dimension, biblical usage has *nšb'*, "to swear," that is, "promise on oath." See above, Wright's Introduction, 10-12.

4. See Map A, 81, "The Ancient Near East," where Aram-Naharaim is also the territory of the Neo-Hittite kingdoms.

wilderness. It is not clear that this *mdbr* refers to both the Negeb and southern Transjordan as is sometimes claimed. The conjunction preceding "this Lebanon" seems to leave no room for much distance between them. The remainder of the description suggests an east-west axis to the original description, unlike the monarchical tradition ("J") in Gen 15:18 which reflects the northwest-southeast claims and aspirations of the Davidic empire: from the Wadi of Egypt "to the Great River, the river Euphrates."

this. If, as seems likely, the language of the introduction to the book is ultimately rooted in covenant-renewal ceremonies, *this* was perhaps accompanied by a sweeping gesture.

Lebanon. In biblical usage this generally includes both the Lebanon and Anti-Lebanon ranges together with the rich Beqa-plain separating them. On this unclaimed gift, see the remarks of Wright, above, 82.

(all the land of the Hittites). Elsewhere in Scripture there are references to Hittites, located especially in Hebron (Genesis 23), Beersheba (Gen 26:34), Bethel (Judg 1:22-26), Jerusalem (Ezek 16:3,45), among David's confederates (1 Sam 26:6) and in his army (Uriah), and in Solomon's harem. That is, there were enough of them scattered widely enough to understand how someone might have referred to the whole region as "land of the Hittites." Numbers 13:29 and related lists are especially important in this respect. An example of how Hittites came to be in Canaan, far south of the great Hittite empire and its successor "Neo-Hittite" kingdoms in northern Syria, is to be seen in the resettlement of the Kurushtama people, known from the Plague Prayer of Mursilis II (c. 1339-1306 B.C.). These were the inhabitants of a city in northern Anatolia, who had been transferred by the Hittites or had emigrated to "the land of Egypt." The latter seems to have been rather in the northern reaches of Egypt's Asiatic realm, identical with "the land of Amka," that is, the Lebanese Beqa! See E. O. Forrer, "The Hittites in Palestine: Part I," *PEQ* 48 (1936) 190-203, and "Part II," *PEQ* 49 (1937) 100-115. For translation of the Plague Prayer, see *ANET*², 394-396.

We also know, from the annals of Ramesses III, of Hittites among refugees who are fleeing into Syria. Thus, it is not beyond the realm of possibility that the nucleus of this entire description in Josh 1:4 is the phrase *all the land of the Hittites,* referring specifically to the hill country west of the Jordan, as acknowledged by O. R. Gurney, *The Hittites.* See now A. Kempinsky, "Hittites in the Bible," *Biblical Archaeology Review* 5 (1979) 21–45. But it would then be necessary to explain the expansion of the description into its received form. In the last analysis, Gurney concludes, the phrase is most easily explained as a gloss, by one to whom "Hittite" meant one of the Syrian successors to the former empire. Ibid., 60. Since none of those kingdoms extended south of Hamath, and the latter involved no part of Palestine, being separated from it by the Aramean kingdom of Damascus, it was probably a marginal query. Hence the parentheses in our translation.

5-9. This larger part of the speech has been compared with the events and concerns surrounding an ancient near eastern royal coronation and installation, at which the new king "was presented with a written document that set forth the righteousness that he was to maintain." Jay A. Wilcoxen, "Narrative Structure and Cult Legend: A Study of Joshua 1-6," in *Transitions in Biblical Scholarship: Essays in Divinity* 6 (University of Chicago Press, 1968) 43-70.

5. The verse is deeply rooted in the earliest Yahwist confession, using language that is characteristic of Dtn.

No one shall hold his ground before you. Word for word this is also said in Deut 7:24 and again but with plural pronouns in 11:25.

As I was with Moses, so I will be with you. To be said again in 3:7. Joshua hears at the very outset the words which originally had been needed to overcome Moses' objections at the burning bush in Exod 3:12—*'ehyeh 'immāk.* The antiquity of this expression in the Moses story is guaranteed by its role in the comic introduction to Judge Gideon in Judg 6:16. Boling, *Judges,* AB 6A, 129 and 132.

The idiom *yhwh 'mk/w,* "Yahweh is with you/him," affirms Yahweh's presence or support of the leader. Taken over from epic sources as noted above, this became a favorite expression echoing throughout the Deuteronomic material—2 Sam 5:10; 7:3; 2 Kgs 18:7, and so forth; 2 Sam 7:9 repeats the words of Exod 3:12. These references are collected by Cross, *CMHE,* 252.

I will not abandon. The root is *rph,* as in Deut 4:31; 31:6,8. See also the plea of the men of Gibeon in 10:6.

I will not desert. Third person equivalent is in Deut 31:6,8.

6. *Be strong and courageous.* These imperatives occur again in v 9, thus framing the most emphatic formulation with the same words in v 7. The forms echo Deut 31:7,23. Plural forms occur in Josh 10:25 and Deut 31:6.

to inherit. This presupposes both the warfare (chaps. 1-11) and the land distribution (chaps. 12-21). Here the Hebrew uses the technical term for military compensation that is implicit in the promise of land by Yahweh in v 2. The verb *nḥl* and its cognate noun at Mari were regularly used to denote the sovereign's grant of a plot of ground in return for the warrior's promise of military service. See Boling, *Judges,* AB 6A, 16-17.

the land that I promised on oath. See above, third NOTE on v 3. Here it is explained that the promise (v 3) to Moses was in order to confirm a prior oath to the fathers. The land grant motif that had been indigenous to patriarchal cults is thus assimilated to the sovereignity of Yahweh alone. Here the divine promise appears to be unconditional, as in Deut 1:8,39, as pointed out by Cross, *CMHE,* 251. The territory in question is only rarely referred to as "the land of Canaan," so that the latter expression provides a clue to the redaction-history. See below on 14:1.

their. In LXX "your fathers" presumably reflects an original covenant-ceremony setting for the speeches in Deuteronomy 5-29, upon which the Dtr framework-speeches are modeled.

ancestors. Literally, "fathers." These would seem to be the parents and grandparents of the Joshua generation, but in the larger corpus they are the three patriarchs of the United Monarchy tradition: Abraham, Isaac, and Jacob (Deut 1:8; 6:10; 9:5,27; 29:12; 30:20; 34:4).

7-9. Compare Deut 17:18-20 in the "law of the king." The latter is surely an addition to the nuclear edition of Deuteronomy (Dtn) which otherwise shows not the slightest awareness that "Israel" will ever have a human king. It is clear that the bulk of Deuteronomy represents legal practice from some community in Israel that had escaped or evaded the changes in law which the monarchy brought with it. See George E. Mendenhall, "Ancient Oriental and Biblical Law," *BA* 17 (1954) 26-46, reprinted in *Law and Covenant in Israel and the Ancient Near East* (1955) and in *BAR* 3 (1970) 3-24.

The incorporation into Deuteronomy of the "law of the king" must be related to the Dtr enterprise in this introductory chapter of Joshua. Within this chapter, some scholars regard vv 7-9 as secondary, a later addition to the original. Noth, *Überlieferungsgeschichtliche Studien* I, 41, n. 4; *Das Buch Josua,* 28-29. Norbert Lohfink, "Die deuteronomistische Darstellung des Übergangs der Führung Israels von Moses auf Josua," *Scholastik* 37 (1962) 36-38. However, to subtract these verses is to blunt the rhetorical structure described above in the first NOTE on v 6.

7. *Only . . . very.* Hebrew *raq . . . mĕ'ôd.* This is not a radical editorial disjunction in the address, but an emphatic imperative at the center of it.

Treaty-Teaching. Simultaneous discovery made in the early 1950s, by Klaus Baltzer in Germany and G. E. Mendenhall in the United States, finding the origin of biblical covenant forms and covenant-semantics in international diplomacy, is still reverberating. Here it has shaken loose a good English equivalent for *tôrâ,* where the root meaning "teaching" says too little and the later theological development of "law" says too much. What this word signifies for the ancient historian is best seen in the reaction to its rediscovery in 2 Kgs 22:11-13.

Moses. His name used in relation to this "Treaty-Teaching" together with the "Book of the Treaty-Teaching" in the following verse, combines with "the Book of the Mosaic Treaty-Teaching" (23:6) to form a prominent framing device in the finished book.

which Moses my Servant commanded. Wright took the Treaty-Teaching as thus described to refer to the Deuteronomic Code. The same term, then, was adopted in priestly circles as the technical term for the entire Pentateuch, the five "Books of Moses." See above, 37-40.

commanded. Yahweh is Commander in Chief.

8. *Book*. Hebrew *sēper* is a "written document" or "treaty" in Exod 24:7; Deut 27:2-8; 2 Kgs 23:2,21; Isa 34:16. Soggin, *Joshua*, 225, with special reference to Joseph Fitzmyer, *The Aramaic Inscriptions of Sefire*.

shall never be missing from your lips. Literally, "shall not depart from your mouth."

and you shall recite it day and night. Compare Ps 1:2 on the same subject with some of the same vocabulary.

then. Hebrew *'āz*, repeated with both verbs, is another "freighted time expression." See above.

then shall you profit in your pilgrimage. Literally, "make your way prosperous." For a clear view of this interesting idiom, see how it recurs in Gen 24:21,40,42,56. With a negative prefixed to it, the same statement can serve as a covenantal curse (Deut 28:29).

and have success. Hebrew *tśkyl.* Plural in Deut 29:8. This is also a favorite word in the circles of "the wise." A historian includes it in David's last words to Solomon (1 Kgs 2:3). See also the conditional use in the "lawsuit" Song of Moses (Deut 32:29).

9. *Have I not commanded you?* Here the Hebrew uses the form of the rhetorical question to express an emphatic declaration. The proof that this is so is seen in LXX, which translates *hălô'*, the negative interrogative, in the same way it generally renders *hinnēh*, the exclamatory particle.

indeed. Hebrew *ky* here has asseverative force, balancing the first segment of the verse.

Yahweh . . . with you. Hebrew *'mk yhwh* emphatically echoes the promise first announced in v 5, *'hyh 'mk*, "I will be with you."

10. *Joshua gave the order.* His first act as successor to Moses.

to the officers. Hebrew *šōṭĕrê* which LXX translate as *grammateusin*, "recorders." Essentially they must have been muster officers.

11-15. This has been treated as the first of a series of speeches by public officials, which Noth recognized as marking the editorial framework in the books of Joshua through Kings. Especially prominent in the series are the "farewell address" of Joshua in chap. 23, the speech of Samuel in 1 Sam 12:1-25, and the prayer of Solomon in 2 Kgs 8:12-53. Cross adds to this list the Nathan prophecy in 2 Sam 7:5-16 and the prayer of David in 2 Sam 7:18-29. *CMHE*, 274-275. The speeches show signs, however, of two main redactions.

Actually here in Joshua 1, it is Yahweh who makes the first, longest, and most distinctively "Deuteronomistic" speech, whereas the elements of vv 11-15 separate into two units, so distinct that they may originally have been unrelated. See below on vv 12-18.

11. *supplies.* Hebrew *ṣēdâ.* It has been claimed that the "conquest" as here reported was "something very peaceful, like a cultic procession, where it is necessary to carry provisions, but where one has nothing else to worry about, as the liturgy has laid down everything" (Soggin, *Joshua*, 32). But it is clear that whatever action was presupposed by the liturgical sources, the ancient historians used them to relate what they believed was as violent as anything can

be. Judges 20:10 proves that *ṣēdâ* covers everything needed for a military campaign.

three days. To be resumed in 3:2, here it must mean "part of today, tomorrow, and part of the next day." Wilcoxen, "Narrative Structure . . . , in *Transitions in Biblical Scholarship* . . . , 62. For other examples of such inclusive reckoning of three-unit periods, see the work of Edwin R. Thiele, *The Mysterious Numbers of the Hebrew Kings,* 2d ed. (Grand Rapids: Eerdmans, 1965): for example, Gen 40:13,19,20; 42:17-18; Exod 19:10-11,15-16; and 2 Kgs 18:9-10.

Compare the following exhortation from the description of the siege of Megiddo in the war of Thutmose III some two and a half centuries earlier: "Prepare ye. Make your weapons ready, since Pharaoh will engage in combat with that wretched enemy in the morning . . ." *ANET*[2], 236. See also Yigael Yadin, "Warfare in the Second Millennium B.C.E.," in *WHJP* II, 141.

12-18. These verses pick up the thread of Deut 3:12-20, which comprise a distinct block within the introduction to that book, a self-contained summary of the Transjordanian scene which might simply be lifted out of its context in Deuteronomy 3, leaving a smooth transition from v 11 to v 21. Similarly, the last segment of Joshua 1 gives the impression of being an east-bank appendage. Georg Fohrer similarly regards this unit as belonging to the second, i.e. exilic, of "two Deuteronomistic recensions." *Introduction to the Old Testament,* 202. Likewise, Soggin following Hertzberg has come out for two editions in Joshua, military (older) and cultic (younger) versions of the conquest. Soggin, *Joshua,* 33. The latter description of the contrast, however, is too simplistic, as will be seen below.

12. *And to.* Here the disjunctive syntax of *waw* + non-verb marks the beginning of the second large unit in the chapter, a special introduction to the Transjordan tribes.

Reubenites, . . . Gadites. Gentilic formations are used here, in contrast to the more characteristic form of tribal names (Bene Reuben, Bene Gad, etc.), as in 4:12 and elsewhere. According to the epic sources preserved in Numbers 32, the Bene Reuben and the Bene Gad had negotiated with Moses for their plots of territory east of the Jordan (Num 32:1-27). Moses had given the order accordingly, to Eleazar the priest and Joshua ben Nun (mentioned in that order, as in Josh 21:1), contingent upon the pledge of military service west of the Jordan (Num 32:28-32).

and half the tribe of Manasseh. In Numbers 32 they are not mentioned in the two important paragraphs described in the preceding note, but appear for the first time in 32:33, "and Moses gave to . . . the Bene Gad and the Bene Reuben and to half the tribe of Manasseh. . . ." Only at the end of that chapter is it explained why they too are included in this special Transjordan settlement: the Bene Machir (who were a branch of the Bene Manasseh) "went to Gilead and took it . . ." (see Num 32:39-42). See also Deut 3:12-20.

It is a striking fact that these three Transjordan tribes of Reuben, Gad, and eastern Manasseh are *the only ones* of the familiar twelve ever to be mentioned by name in the warfare sections of the book. See 4:12 and especially the story of the altar by the Jordan in chap. 22, where again these three have the starring tribal roles; all others are anonymous in chap. 22. Within the narrative units, "Judah" is mentioned in 7:1,18, but with no special significance; the process of elimination used in uncovering Achan had to begin there. The story of the "Bene Joseph" in 17:14-18 is unique, and calls for separate treatment; see the NOTES and COMMENT on it. We may thus suspect that in the Book of Joshua, the specific mention of the three tribes settled east of Jordan in any passage means that we are on literary terrain which is different from the bulk of the book. There are other indicators of this, to be noted below.

13. *Remember.* In contrast to the commissioning speech of Yahweh (vv 2-9) and the first order issued by Joshua (vv 10-11), which used the imperative form repeatedly, here the command is expressed in the form of infinitive absolute, which has most emphatic force. This imperative force is then continued by imperfects ("Your wives . . . shall remain. . . . But *you shall cross*") and converted perfects ("and *help* them . . . and *they too shall take* possession"). The stylistic contrast with vv 1-11 could scarcely be sharper.

Moses the Servant of Yahweh. This is the favorite name and title in all strata of the "Deuteronomic" literature.

grants you rest. Hebrew *mēnîăḥ*, the causative participle used as a noun. Repeated in v 15, this verb is a key term. *NEB* translates as "grants security," which it is explained "does not refer so much to peace of mind or spiritual calm as to the external conditions of national security and peace which prevail when Israel is obedient to the law" (J. M. Miller and G. M. Tucker, *The Book of Joshua,* 24). This explanation begins with an important point, but says too much, for it prematurely resolves an ambiguity. That Yahweh's activity in granting *rest* involves peace from surrounding enemies is clear. Thus 21:44; 22:4; 23:1. It is a characteristic idiom in all strata of the corpus (see Cross, *CMHE,* 252, ※1), but from the distribution of texts it looks like an emphasis of the final editor. And it is not at all clear that the final editor was hoping for a national restoration.

The activity of Yahweh in granting *rest* is not exercised exclusively toward Israel and in fact may on occasion be exercised against Israel (Judg 3:1). As the ground of hope it is found originally in the relationship between Yahweh and Moses (Exod 33:12-16). For the subsequent history of theologial *rest,* see G. von Rad, "There Remains Still a Rest for the People of God," in *The Form Critical Problem of the Hexateuch, and Other Essays,* 94-102; and now, Wolfgang Roth, "The Deuteronomic Rest Theology: A Redaction-Critical Study." We would question, however, that *rest* ever referred to "complete and final occupation . . . on *both* sides of the Jordan" (13). Here it would seem to refer to the completion of the conquest under Joshua.

14. *in battle array.* Hebrew *ḥămušîm* occurs again in 4:12 and clearly has something to do with military organization. See Exod 13:18; Num 32:17 (so read with LXX; the Transjordan negotiations!); Judg 7:11. The word is related to the numeral "five." Mari text VII:161 lists accessories furnished for weapons and chariots. The list includes "wheels, seat-holders, harnesses, bridles, eye-patches(?) of leather, rings, four teams of *ḥumušūm* (five donkeys?). . . ." Sasson, *The Military Establishment of Mari,* 32.

burly warriors. Hebrew *gbwry ḥḥyl.* It occurs again in 6:2; 8:3; and 10:7. Elsewhere it is rarely used to refer to warriors of Israel because it also denoted "landed gentry" within the feudal society of Canaan. Compare the stories of Gideon and Jephthah, both of which made inverted use of this formula in its only occurrences in the Book of Judges, 6:12 and 11:1. It is not coincidental that half of the Gideon story and all of the Jephthah story take place in Transjordan. That was where the Yahwist movement was initially most successful. That the formula *gbwry ḥḥyl* is more frequent in the Joshua book probably reflects the social restratification which was largely taken for granted in monarchic Israel.

15. *rest.* By this time it sounds like military "leave, furlough," or even "honorable discharge from active duty," that is, "retirement."

16-18. The eastern tribes have the last word in this opening scene.

17. *Only.* Hebrew *raq,* a skillful use of the same particle, in concluding declarative statement, that had previously been used at the rhetorical center of the imperative section (see above on v 7).

be with you. The ability of "Yahweh your God" to do this is most deeply rooted in the call of Moses, which here again is clearly evoked (Exod 3:12). This concluding emphasis of Joshua 1 is often related to a profound anxiety resulting from the crisis of leadership at the end of the monarchy, an anxiety which has the people here insisting upon "letters of credit." Soggin, *Joshua,* 34. Our analysis indicates more than this. The verses read like the response to a crisis which took shape during the reign of Josiah. It is the response advocating return to the religion of Moses, not merely to the "book" of Moses.

COMMENT

When, in negotiations with Gibeonites in 9:8, Joshua at last gets to ask the historical question, he says: "Where do you come from?" The same question today often has a different sense, in colloquial usage. To ask, "Where are you coming from?" is to ask about a point of view, presuppositions of method, hypothetical models, and anything else implicit that will help to follow the analysis and interpretation. Readers of this commentary will ask both kinds of questions: general historical ones (because it is an ancient book), and specific "methodological" ones (concerning critical study). The commentator owes it to his readers at the outset to let them know where he is coming from.

What do you mean: Early Israel?

It was within the span of one long generation—at most the half-century c. 1225-1175 B.C.—that the twelve tribe organization known in the Old Testament as the Bene Israel emerged in control of the wooded hilly regions east and west of the Jordan River. The tribal organization came to control most of the narrow corridor linking Africa and Asia, between the desert and the sea. Remaining outside the control of the Bene Israel were the heavily populated and fertile plains of the coast and the Esdraelon Valley, dominated by strongly fortified cities, as well as strongly fortified enclaves in the hill country, most notably Jerusalem. Except for these pockets and the stronger power fringe, an old order was replaced by one totally new and radically different, within the equivalent of one person's lifetime. This is the view most widely credited in university departments of history, and the same conclusion would have to be maintained even in the absence of any biblical traditions in the area. Archaeology documents the fact of rapid and radical change, as we shall have occasion to note, in the land of Canaan at the beginning of the Iron Age there (c. 1200 B.C.). As the pottery chronology for Transjordan has been refined, it has become clear that the emergence of the kingdoms of Edom and Moab happened well along in the thirteenth century. On the other hand, the mid-twelfth-century destruction of Shechem, which is surely reflected in the story of Abimelech (Judges 9), marks a reactionary move that was remembered as especially tragic. In fact it must have been regarded as nearly the end of Israel, among Yahwist "old-timers." See *Judges,* AB 6A, 165-185.

Precise definition of early Israel continues to challenge scholarship. A nearly contemporary parallel to the formation of Israel may be seen in the old Thessalian League of northern Greece—an alignment of newcomers who resisted cultural assimilation and attained a wide-ranging political and economic domination. The Thessalian League clearly triggered the formation of rival leagues and eventually it formed the nucleus and most powerful constituency in the great Delphic Amphictyony. Yet the comparison with the earlier Thessalion League is only partial; see Norman Gottwald, *The Tribes of Yahweh,* 753-754 n. 284. Objections to the analogy of amphictyonies in the later Aegean world are also well founded; see *Judges,* AB 6A, especially 18-23. The objections go much too far when they also rule out "any other sort of federation of all or most of the Israelite tribes." Thus A. D. H. Mayes, "Israel in the Pre-Monarchy Period," *VT* 23 (1973) 167. There can be no substitute for sociological reconstruction based primarily upon ancient Israel's own testimony.

If we are left with little more than half a century between the arrival of Yahweh covenanters in southern Transjordan and the near demise of a vastly larger Yahwist League at Shechem, how can we make any sense of the biblical traditions? Returning to the trail of historical reconstruction, as it emerges from Wright's Introduction, we will be testing throughout this commentary the hypothesis that in the beginning of the Book of Joshua there was a simultaneous process of religious reformation and political revolution. There was a mythological symbiosis between palace and temple in the ancient Near East, and that is what posed the perennial plight of the Late Bronze Age people.

> If the major functions of religion in the Late Bronze Age were the guaranty of political legitimacy of the state and the correlative quality of economic abundance, why the entire process [the growth of Yahwism] constitutes a religious revolution is then apparent. Something had to take precedence over and destroy the religious ideology, the myth, upon which political legitimacy rested. Similarly, a concept of the process of productivity had to emerge that would liberate the population from the age-old tutelage of the great fertility goddess and the rituals associated with her. (Mendenhall, *Ten Gen,* 24.)

The religion of Moses brought to Canaan the long-needed and seldom repeated liberation movement. And on this view it is the displacement of myth by ethic at the motivating center of religious behavior that best describes the rapid change. In terms of an organismic philosophy of history, it was a societal *mutation* (Albright, *From the Stone Age to Christianity;* see especially chap. 2). For some two centuries the Bene Israel effectively displaced the competing and malfunctioning mini-monarchies that were the spin-offs of Egyptian imperialism.

To be sure, not all scholars are persuaded by the reconstruction that works with ideological revolution as hypothetical model. But most of the objections fail really to join the issue, as may be seen in the otherwise excellent review of Joshua-Judges problems by Manfred Weippert, *The Settlement of the Israelite Tribes in Palestine.* Most notably Weippert has not comprehended the emphasis upon ethical obligation and individual decision-making as an ultimate concern in the constitution of early Israel. On the subject of Ḫabiru/Apiru as *linguistic cognate* of "Hebrew," and as label for a most productive societal *source for converts* to Yahwism, see Wright's remarks above (80-84) and Mendenhall's chapter on "The 'Apiru Movements in the Late Bronze Age," *Ten Gen,* 122-141.

The consolidation of the Bene Israel in control of the hills east and west of the Jordan early in the twelfth century—the nucleus of this organization being the Sinai group who had arrived via southern Transjordan, with many of their own roots not more than two generations away in state slavery in Egypt, but some of them with ultimately north Mesopotamian ancestry—this is what we might call the secular transcript of the ancient Israelite confession (Deut 26:5-9). As far as the historian can tell, there is nothing seriously wrong with the memory and much to commend it. If Yahwism was a missionary movement that was spawned and spread by the rejection of an entire political order together with its mythological support system, this will make sense of much in the Bible that is otherwise obscure and unexplainable.

On the other hand, it will not suffice simply to set ethic over against myth in the genesis of Yahwism. The Divine Warrior in Israel's oldest poetry is fully in control and is not a static "symbol." Indeed, the early poets made free, selective, and highly creative use of inherited mythic themes and rhetorical structures to give expression to their experience with Yahweh. How shall we understand this?

Three striking phenomena leap out, as one scans the archaeological horizon. First is the rapid collapse of international order, the end of "the first internationalism," to use James Henry Breasted's phrase for the Late Bronze Age. The most prominent feature of this decline is the breakup of the mighty Hittite empire which had radiated out from Asia Minor. See Map A, 81. Second, the same wider period saw, presumably as a reflex of the chaos elsewhere, the establishment of many more and smaller city-states in the lower Canaanite corridor. This had been an international fringe-area since time immemorial. The political fragmentation of the land in the fourteenth century is vividly reflected in the linguistic variety of the Amarna-letter scribes and their masters. Third, there is the fact that "no later than the fourteenth century B.C. in north Syria, the cult of Ēl was declining, giving place to the cult of Baʻl Haddu . . . more supportive of kingship and of agriculture as opposed to cattle-keeping economy." Cross, *CMHE,* 48. In other words, there were two very different kinds of mythic heritage. One was related to the cult of the venerable god El, the cosmic patriarch. Noted for his practical wisdom and kindliness, El was also the exceedingly lusty Father of gods and of humankind, and in that sense he was their creator, whose characteristic mode of revelation was the wise decree of the clan head, handed down in dream or vision. His cult was originally at home in the countryside, supportive of rural and village life at least from the time of the patriarchs in Genesis, with whose God the Canaanite El might be readily confused, except that the God of the patriarch has no consort in Scripture.

The other mythic stream, and one that had flooded the land in the middle centuries of the second millennium, was that of the vigorous *young* warrior, King of the gods by right of conquest, who usurped the center so that old El was "promoted upstairs," as it were. Haddu, better known in Scripture by his title *baʻal* ("Lord") is also master of the fertility cult and mighty warrior whose victory sustains the created order and brings annual renewal of physical productivity to humanity, beast, and field. His cultus is especially supportive of city-state reality. When Baal the Warrior speaks, it is in lightning and thunder.

In the events at Sinai (Exodus 19-24), Yahweh manifests himself as the Divine Warrior in the manner of Baal. The fire and smoke at the mountain are imagery rooted in descriptions of a terrifying electrical storm with its black clouds and white steam and jagged lightning. Such divine speech is in the manner of Baal, but the content is something else. The covenant stipulations (the Decalogue) would elsewhere be regarded more specifically as El's kind of subject matter—a common-sense teaching of ethical guidelines rooted in the everyday experience of home and village life—clan wisdom. To this extent we agree with Erhard Gerstenberger, "Covenant and Commandment," *JBL* 84 (1965) 38-51. But this is the heart of the Sinai-covenant maneuver; Yahweh the Sovereign of Israel governs the Bene Israel directly, as they subscribe to the guidelines given in his covenant. Thus John Bright responds to Gerstenberger. "The Apodictic Prohibition: Some Observations," *JBL* 92 (1973) 185-204. We conclude that at Sinai the ancient heritage of the Divine Patriarch is radically reformed, so as to appear brand new, putting ethic in place of power. At the same time the Baal myth gets hoist with its own petard.

What do you mean: Dtn, Dtr 1, Dtr 2?

There have been few developments since Wright wrote his thoughtful review of these matters, "Joshua as a Deuteronomic Book" (above, 41-51). It will suffice here to mention that the contribution of Cross to the discussion is now generally available in expanded form as part of a larger synthesis: "The Themes of the Books of Kings and the Structure of the Deuteronomic History," *CHME*, 274-289. In the same interim we have completed our analysis of the Book of Judges as part of the long historical work. Here is the way we will use the symbols in NOTES and COMMENT.

Dtn

This stands for the nucleus of one book, the bulk of Deut 4:44 - 30:20, minus those passages which were added to turn it into an introduction to the historical work.

Provenance: Northern, rural, Levitical. It is unrelated, so far as we can tell, to any Israelite royal sanctuary. It preserves lore and "legislation" that stem ultimately from an old fall-festival at the Shechem sanctuary in the time before the monarchy (Deuteronomy 27; Josh 8:30-35; 24:1-28). The carriers of this tradition were most likely reform-minded northern Levites who had been alienated by the policies of the royal houses, beginning as early as the reign of Solomon (see our discussion of the Levitical Towns in chap. 21) and by the early abandonment of Shechem as capital of the northern kingdom. Dtn is their literary output, probably first appearing in relation to the reforms of King Hezekiah, following the destruction of the northern kingdom in 721 B.C. (2 Kgs 18:1-8; 2 Chr 29:1-36).

Dtr 1

This is the bulk of the material in Joshua through 2 Kings (also called "Deuteronomic" in *Judges,* AB 6A). The old work Dtn, here and there retouched, served as theological introduction to the historical work, and the entire corpus was given a new preface in Deut 1:1 - 4:43.

Provenance: The Jerusalem establishment of King Josiah (640-609 B.C.). These were the circles of southern Levites who found in the theology of Dtn an explanation for the demise of the old northern kingdom and the justification for their own profound influence at the Jerusalem court.

Dtr 2

This is supplementary material added in the last major edition (previously called "Deuteronomistic"). It was produced in the wake of Josiah's death at Megiddo in 609 B.C., with the collapse of his program and reforms, and finally updated after the spiraling political chaos that issued in the exile. In this last substantial work on the corpus, the introduction was overwritten in Deuteronomy 1-3 to make inverted use of the "Holy War" language—Yahweh versus Israel!—in the account of the Qadesh Rebellion. Elsewhere, especially in major framework passages, there is a tragicomic transformation of the tradition (e.g. Judges 19-21), or inverted presentation (e.g. Judges 1 in contrast to the "mainline" traditions of Joshua). Probably it was Dtr 2 that pulled together the whole Primary History, from Genesis to 2 Kings (D. N. Freedman, private communication).

Provenance: Certainly not the same circles who produced the first edition. Dtr 2 here and there adds material that had survived independently. We suggest that the carriers of this supplementary tradition were the Levitical refugees from the north after 721 B.C., who in the wake of 587 B.C. had the last word. See our study of the contrasting Levite-stories in Judges 17-21. AB 6A, 254-294.

The evidence for such a redactional history is structural. There is semantic clustering that correlates with various themes and rhetorical devices which are clear signs of stratification in the book. The stratification makes best sense if the two main layers are late monarchical. The topmost layer, however, is like an archaeological "fill" layer; it reuses very old material. The purpose of Dtr 2 was not merely to continue the story but to set it all in broader perspective. Both Dtr 1 and Dtr 2 would rightly claim to be rooted in Dtn. But the first looks forward to a great new day of righteous nationhood that seemed to be dawning in the reign

of King Josiah, while the second had to adapt the material to be somehow supportive of life in exile. Together the two strata illustrate how
difficult it is, if not impossible in historical description, for any one work
to tell all of the truth. In the Book of Joshua: Dtr 1 emphasizes Joshua's
leadership and the loyalty of the people as army of Yahweh, while Dtr 2
puts emphasis on ingenuity and a sense of humor as *the best response to
violence*. The final edition lifts up truth that had not been suppressed, but
neither had it been shown so poignantly.

Does it all hang together?

That will be for the reader to determine. The descriptive method to be
followed in our work must be both analytic and wholistic. It will highlight
grammatical, semantic, and thematic relationships asking at every point
how the transitions were supposed to be intelligible. There is a logic
which holds a single story or archival unit together; but it may be quite
another logic which holds various units together in the larger configuration. See our treatment of the end of the era (*Judges*, AB 6A, 294).
Here we shall focus on how it holds together, and try not to get lost in
the task of taking it apart.

What's the use of history?

If history is best defined as the totality of human experience, it would
seem to follow that "historical work" is not in fact the best descriptive
label for the product of the Dtr-writers. They are rather narrowly restricted in their focus and selection of data. On the other hand, comparisons with classical epics (the *Iliad,* the *Odyssey,* the *Aeneid*) have a certain validity. Notably they help in understanding the processes and
materials of oral tradition. Ironically, there is probably more of reliable
historical memory in Joshua than in the classical epics.

> A more enlightening parallel might be drawn between Joshua and the less
> well-known Pharsalia of Lucan or the *Punic War* of Silius Italicus in
> which a solid sub-stratum of fact is presented in a manner deliberately
> very different from that of textbooks and for a different purpose. An even
> closer . . . and more enlightening comparison might be drawn between the
> Book of Joshua and Shakespeare's *Henry V* in which dramatic form only
> thinly veils the epic quality.

Thus, P. Giffin, "The Epic of Joshua," *Scripture* 14 (1962) 77. That is,
Giffin argues, the purpose is to make use of the past in such a way as "to
inspire emulation of the heroes of the past." This will hold for Dtr 1. But
elsewhere the description would obscure a dialectic that runs throughout
the entire corpus, a dialectic that is rooted in the people's despair. Dtr 2

would have the people remember all of the past, but to remember it as "passed."

What do you mean: Framework?

The reader is encouraged at this point to scan rapidly the contents of two "books"—Joshua and Judges. The conclusion to the first one, Joshua 24, leaves the Bene Israel united in possession of the land and poised for life there. How will Israel in fact live in the land which is Yahweh's gift?

At the end of Judges, Israel has come full circle. In Judges 21, Israel is perilously close to self-destruction, after a tragic and costly civil war. Yet the end is still a long way off—2 Kgs 22:1 - 23:25.

If the first edition (Dtr 1) was produced in the reign of the great reforming King Josiah (2 Kings 22-23), the astonishing thing is that the first edition survived at all. It was simply supplemented. It was given a laconic ending which reports abruptly the release of the exiled King Jehoiachin from his Babylonian prison cell, to be royally clothed and henceforth fed for the rest of his days at the table of the pagan king of Babylon. This is a weak basis for finding in Dtr 2 a hope for national restoration. But it forms a rhetorical inversion with the boast and treatment of another pagan king (the lord of Bezeq in Judges 1) at the outset of the long and problematic period (Israel in the land). It adds up to a liberated implication that it is possible to live as Yahwists, though far from the ruined Temple and the devastated land of Canaan.

1:1 - 5:12   Mobilization and Invasion

To judge from the proportions of space allotted to the subject (five of the first eleven chapters!) entering the land was as important as leaving Egypt (which takes up fifteen of the twenty-five "action" chapters in the Book of Exodus). This event of entering the land is "solemn, even ritual in character, and it is told in hieratic style. . . . Human agents are passive in the account of the entrance; Yahweh does all." John L. McKenzie, *The World of the Judges,* 45-46.

That these sections display internal relations which they do not share with the chapters that follow has been demonstrated clearly by Wilcoxen, "Narrative Structure and Cult Legend: A Study of Joshua 1-6," in *Transitions in Biblical Scholarship: Essays in Divinity* 6, 43-70. As indicated by his title, he also includes chapter 6 as the culmination of all that takes place in chaps. 1-5. But the success at Jericho has high symbolic status as Victory Number One for Yahweh's army in the land. It stands in abrupt contrast to the failure at Ai in chap. 7. The clearest pause is at the culmination of the Gilgal preliminaries and the end of the Wanderings-food, manna (5:12).

1:12-18   It began in Transjordan

After the announcement of marching orders for entrance into the Promised Land, given in the most general terms in vv 1-11, the abrupt shift to specificity in vv 12-18 is arresting and evocative. This section recalls events that are known mainly from epic sources in the Book of Numbers, sources that were not subjected to "Deuteronomic" editing. The reason for this is not far to seek. In the first and major editing of these materials the focus is on Moses as the one who with Yahweh as Sovereign readies Israel for its entrance and life *in the land,* that is, *west of the Jordan.* Despite the imperial sweep of the land limits in v 4, it is necessary according to the main story line of the book to cross the Jordan River so as to enter the land. It appears here and elsewhere that the first and main edition of this work paid scant attention to the situation and tribes east of the Jordan. If so, the addition of these final verses is a gentle reminder that "Israel" was a cooperative movement, something much more than the tiny west-bank remnant to which Judah had shriveled under Assyrian vassalage, greater even than the larger west-bank realm to which it had recently expanded once again, thanks to the vigorous policies of King Josiah.

In other words, we hear a conversation taking place in the production of the Book of Joshua as individuals struggled to understand what it had originally meant to be Israel, especially in the wake of shattering setbacks such as the demise of the north and the death of Josiah.

A leading Israeli scholar has written that "the historiosophic approach of the Bible is conditioned by the belief in Israel's uniqueness, and accordingly from the very outset its history constitutes the realization of God's word." Jacob Liver, "The Bible and Its Historical Sources," in *WHJP* II, 48. But this approach obscures the struggle; it is doubtful that the Bible as a whole displays a single historiosophic approach.

One effect of the sudden collapse of Josiah's imperial future was to focus again on the parameters or borders of Yahwistic territory in the period prior to statehood. We may infer that for Dtr 2, the Israel of the future will be like the Israel of Moses and will not have territorial definition. But here at the outset we must ask about the memory of Israel in Transjordan.

The relevant archaeological work is that of Nelson Glueck, in his pioneering surveys of Transjordan in the 1930s and 1940s, published over the years as "Explorations in Eastern Palestine," AASOR 14 (for 1932-1934), 15 (for 1934-1935), 18-19 (for 1937-1939), and 25-28 (for 1945-1949). Glueck discovered a small and scattered, and therefore presumably "nomadic," population pattern in central and southern Transjordan throughout the middle centuries of the second millennium. Subsequent discoveries have forced revisions but in general Glueck believed the pattern to be confirmed. Nelson Glueck, *The Other Side of the Jordan*.

Archaeological discoveries made over the last twenty years, together with restudy of linguistic evidence, indicate an exploding population in Transjordan in the Late Bronze Age, which was not all locally begotten. "The amount of foreign pottery present in the Transjordan during this period is greater than at any other time prior to the Hellenistic period." Rudolph Henry Dornemann, "The Cultural and Archaeological History of the Transjordan in the Bronze and Iron Ages" I, 55. The claims and history of the Transjordan tribes will, of course, be studied in detail in chap. 13. Here it will suffice to recall the two main sources of rapid increment to the population of Transjordan: from the west bank of Canaan and from the northern arc of the Fertile Crescent. Prior to the wide-scale domestication of the camel at the close of the Late Bronze Age, there could have been no sizable invasions from the desert oases. Biblical tradition clearly recalls such a plight (Judges 6-8) posed for the first time by the Midianite raids in the time of Gideon. See *Judges*, AB 6A, 122-161.

But the area was no more stable than elsewhere. "The international commerce which apparently was still at a high point in the thirteenth century B.C. . . . came to a very abrupt end" (Dornemann, ibid., 425). This sud-

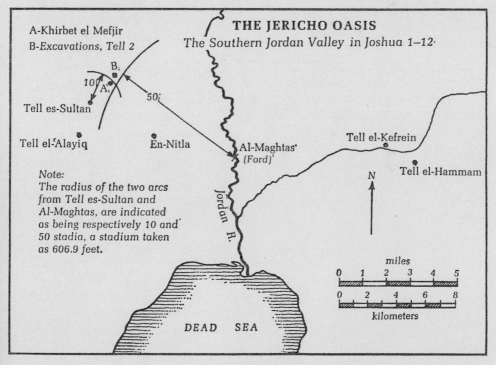

Map C

den change is probably not unrelated to Egyptian efforts at reclaiming the area; an expedition to Moab early in the reign of Ramesses II captured sites even to the north of the Wadi Arnon. Abraham Malamat, "The Period of the Judges," in *WHJP* III, especially 152-154.

Summary

We have recognized in Joshua 1 the contribution of two historiographical and redactional stages. The relationship between the original bulk of the material (henceforth for convenience Dtr 1) and the much briefer but varied additions (Dtr 2) is both complementary and dialogical. It is possible that this hortatory chapter has displaced an older "epic introduction" to Joshua. In any case, in the next chapter, we step out onto very different literary terrain.

B. RECONNAISSANCE
(2:1-24)

2 ¹ Joshua ben Nun quietly sent two men as spies from Shittim: "Go, have a look at the land—and Jericho!"

So they set forth, and the two men came to Jericho. They entered the house of a prostitute by the name of Rahab and rested there. ² And it was reported to the king of Jericho: "Here some men have come this very night—from the Bene Israel—to explore the land!"

³ So the king of Jericho sent word to Rahab, "Bring out the men who came to you, who entered your house this very night. For they came to explore the whole land!"

⁴ Although the woman had taken and hidden the two men, she said, "That's right. The men came to my place, but I did not know where they came from! ⁵ And when at dusk the gate was about to close, the men went out. But I don't know where they went. Pursue them quickly! You can still overtake them!"

⁶ But she had shown them to the roof and hidden them among stalks of flax which were arranged for her on the roof. ⁷ So the men chased after them, along the Jordan road, toward the fords. They closed the gate.

As soon as the posse had gone out after them, ⁸ and before they had rested, she came to them on the roof ⁹ and said to the men, "I know that Yahweh has given you the land. Indeed, dread of you has fallen upon us, and all the land's rulers grow faint because of you! ¹⁰ Indeed, we have heard how your god Yahweh dried up the waters of the Reed Sea for your sake when you came out of the land of Egypt, and what he did to the two Amorite kings on the other side of the Jordan—Sihon and Og—whom you put to the ban. ¹¹ We heard and our hearts melted. There was no spirit left in anyone among us, because of you! Your god Yahweh is indeed God in the heavens above and on the earth below. ¹² Swear to me now, by Yahweh, that you will show mercy to my father's house because I have shown mercy to you. And give me some reliable sign. ¹³ Let the house of my father and mother live—that is, my brothers and sisters—and all my 'house' with all who belong to them. Deliver our lives from death!"

14ᵇ And she said to them, "When Yahweh gives the land into your hand, show confident mercy toward me!"

14ᵃ The men said to her, "Our life for that of your family! If you do not disclose this mission of ours, then, when Yahweh gives us the land, we will show confident mercy toward you."

15 She had lowered them by a rope through the window, for her house was between the double walls and she was living in the wall-system. 16 She said to them, "Head for the hills, or else the posse may discover you! Hide out there for three days until the posse has returned. And after that, you can be on your way."

17 The men said to her, "We are guiltless in this oath of yours which you have made us swear. 18 Look, when we enter the city, you will give a sign. Tie this band of scarlet cord in the window through which you have lowered us. And your father, your mother, your siblings—all your father's household—you shall gather round you in the house. 19 Whoever goes out the doors of your house into the street has responsibility for his blood on his own head; we will be guiltless. As for anyone who is with you in the house, responsibility for his blood will be on our heads if a hand is laid upon him. 20 But if you disclose this mission of ours, we will be guiltless with respect to your oath which you have made us swear."

21 Said she: "Whatever you say is the way it will be." And she sent them on their way. They went on their way and she tied the scarlet cord in the window.

22 They went on their way and entered the hill country, remaining there for three days, until the posse had returned. The posse had inquired all along the road but got nowhere. 23 Then the two men returned. They came down from the hills, crossed over, and went in to Joshua ben Nun. They reported to him everything that had befallen them. 24 They said to Joshua, "For sure Yahweh has given the whole land into our hands. And what's more, all the land's rulers grow faint because of us!"

TEXTUAL NOTES

2 1. *quietly*   Hebrew *ḥereš* shows no reflex in LXX, Syriac. Perhaps the translators no longer understood the archaic word.

and the two men came to Jericho. They entered   This follows LXX where MT shows a sizable haplography: *wyb'w* [*šny h'nšym yryḥw wyb'w*].

2. *Here some men have come this very night*   With three of five successive words beginning and ending in *h*, the situation was ripe for scribal accidents. LXX reflects a text in which two words were lost: [*hnh*] *'nšym b'w hnh* [*hlylh*]. "[   ] some men came here [   ]."

3. *who came to you, who entered your house*   LXX lacks the end of one phrase and the beginning of the other: *hb'ym* [*'lyk 'šr b'w*] *lbytk*. It is possible that the repetition of the root *b'* triggered a haplography. But the endings are not identical. The LXX may be tendentious, trying to avoid any ambiguity about what the two men were doing there.

this very night   This is LXX, where it may have been added under the influence of v 2, however.

the whole   Hebrew *kl* is not reflected in LXX.

4. *hidden*   This reading adopts the editor's proposal in *BH*³, which treats the anomalous suffix as the result of dittography: *wtṣpn*[*w*] *wt'mr*.

two   The numeral is lacking in LXX^A and Vulgate.

but I did not know where they came from(!)   This statement was lost by haplography in LXX *Vorlage*: *w*[*l' yd'ty m'yn hmh w*]*yhy*.

5. *But*   Reading the conjunction before the negative, as in the preceding verse, with which this is grammatically parallel. Either the conjunction was lost by haplography or else a single letter is doing double duty: *yṣ'-w-l'*. This reading is supported by several Hebrew and Greek manuscripts and Syriac.

they went   This follows LXX, Syriac, Vulgate, where MT specifies the subject: *h'nšym*, "the men." The uniformly shorter reading in the versions cannot be traced to any common scribal lapse. The longer reading is probably a repetition of the same form six words earlier.

quickly   Lacking in LXX.

7. *As soon as*   This is LXX. The key here is *'aḥărê ka-'ăšer*, which occurs nowhere else in the OT. It probably represents a conflation of variants, one of which is intact in LXX, as follows:

LXX	*sgrw*	*wyhy*		*k'šr*	*yṣ'w*
*	*sgrw*		*'hry*		*yṣ'w*

9. *to the men*   Hebrew *'l h'nšym*. LXX *'lyhm*, "to them."

and all the land's rulers grow faint because of you(!)   This follows MT, where a situation ripe for haplography has yielded the shorter LXX text: *'lynw* [*wky nmgw kl-yšby h'rṣ mpnykm*] *ky*. This is vital information which the spies will report in v 24 and for which Rahab is the only source.

10. *your god Yahweh*   This follows LXX where MT has only the divine name, after haplography: *yhwh '[lhykm ']t.*

the land of   In agreement with LXX^B. Haplography may account for the shorter text: *m['rṣ] mṣrym.*

he   This follows the leading LXX recensions. MT has assimilated to the person and number of the final verb in the sentence; thus, "you (plural) did."

11. *in anyone among us, because of you(!)*   In agreement with LXX^B and Syriac, where MT has suffered haplography: *b'yš m[mnw m]pnykm.*

12. *Yahweh*   LXX continues with *'lhym,* and the Lucianic family of manuscripts show the pronoun: "your god." But unlike v 10, the context here does not give a mechanism for haplography. Here the longer reading probably represents the Lucianic tendency to level throughout uniform translation equivalents.

And give me some reliable sign   Lacking in LXX, after haplography: *w[nttm ly 'wt 'mt w]hhytm.*

13. *the house of*   The word for house was lost by haplography in MT, but survived in LXX *Vorlage:* *'[t by]t 'by.*

and all my "house"   This is restored from LXX which, on the other hand, lacks "and sisters." As often happens, the original was longer than any of the survivors:

MT	*'hy*	*w't*	*'hwty*	[			]	*w't*	*kl*	*'šr*
LXX	*'hy*	[			]	*w't*	*kl*	*byty*	*w't*	*kl*	*'šr*
*	*'hy*	*w't*	*'hwty*	*w't*	*kl*	*byty*	*w't*	*kl*	*'šr*	

14b. The text is a jumble. The reconstruction is not much more than a guess, although it shows the mechanism for a lengthy haplography in the Hebrew, restored at the wrong place (14b) in LXX: *mmw[t 14b wlhm 'mrh btt yhwh bydk 't h'rṣ 'š 'my ḥsd w'm]t 14a wy'mrw lh h'nšym.* See now Katherine Doob Sakenfeld, *The Meaning of Hesed in the Hebrew Bible.* Harvard Semitic Monographs 17 (Missoula, MT: Scholars Press, 1978) 39-40, 64-68.

14a. *you*   Read the singular ending *y,* in agreement with several Hebrew and Greek manuscripts, against the MT plural ending *w.* The letters *w* and *y* were easily confused in some (later) forms of the script.

15. *by a rope*   This is missing from LXX, after a haplography in its *Vorlage: b[ḥbl b]'d.*

16. *the posse*   Literally, "those who pursue you." The pronoun is restored from LXX, to fill a lacuna in MT: *hrdpy[m 'ḥryk]m w'ḥr.*

17. *which you have made us swear*   LXX here shows another haplography in its *Vorlage: hzh ['šr hšb'tnw] hnh.* The Masoretic voweling (*hišba'tānû*) seems to treat Rahab as masculine (as again at the end of v 20). Cf. *hwrdtnw* in v 18.

18. *city*   This agrees with LXX, where MT has "the land." But it is clear that the Hebrew in this verse is not intact and "the land" may be a correction of a mutilated text. See below.

you will give a sign   Restored from LXX, after haplography in MT: [*w't ttn 't h'wt*] *'t htqwt ḥwt.*

19. *guiltless*   LXX is longer as in both texts in comparable expressions in

vv 17 and 20; but with no mechanism for haplography, the shorter reading is to be preferred.

20. *But if you disclose*   LXX is longer: "But if you do wrong (*adikēsē* and disclose. . . ." The Hebrew equivalent is not clear.

oath   There follows in LXX the word for "this" (cf. the similar phrase in v 17). But here the context lacks a consonant sequence that might have triggered haplography. The shorter reading is to be preferred.

21. *They went on their way*   The major Greek recensions show a lapse, omitting the second half of the verse: *wylkw* [. . . *wylkw*].

22. *until the posse had returned*   Missing in LXX, another lapse behind the Greek: *ym*[*ym 'd šbw hrdp*]*ym*.

23. *and went in*   Missing in LXX, another lapse: *wy'br*[*w wyb'*]*w*.

NOTES

2:1-24. Like the longer story of another famous non-Israelite woman, Ruth, this story belongs to a large collection of historical tales. Few if any of them can be dated later than the ninth century B.C. and many of them are still pervaded by a pre-statehood perspective. "By classifying together such stories as the episodes in Judges, the Court History of David in 2 Sam 9-20, and the J and E strands of Genesis, we must conclude that there is no boundary to be found which clearly divides fiction from historical narrative." Edward F. Campbell, Jr., *Ruth,* AB 7, 9.

This story is probably related to old sources which surface in Numbers 32 and not at all in Deuteronomy. The observation that there is a general stylistic relation between "the narrative sections of the Pentateuch and Joshua" is as old as the Protestant Reformation. See Fohrer, *Introduction to the Old Testament,* 25-26. The problem is that specific relations with the source-strata of Genesis-Numbers are exceedingly difficult to pin down and no clear pattern has emerged. See Wright's remarks above, 55-59.

1. *Joshua ben Nun.* This is a new beginning, as indicated by use of the longer name (as in 1:1), not simply "Joshua" (as in the intervening verses).

men as spies. The Hebrew has two terms juxtaposed, *'nšym mrglym;* hereafter either term alone will suffice. When the story at last concludes in 6:23, they are "the young men who serve as spies," which is the LXX reading here as well (*hn'rym hmrglym*). The ancient audience would already know in general what the story was about, and would be waiting to see how the storyteller would weave a new creation out of it. The roots for "spy, explore" (*rgl,* "to go about on foot, to hoof it"; *ḥpr,* "to explore"), are used three times at the outset (vv 1,2,3), so that there will be no misunderstanding the nature of their mission west of the Jordan. They are not used again in the chapter.

Shittim. This place is not previously mentioned in any "Deuteronomic" reference to the wilderness experience. In Num 33:49, the camp is described as ex-

tending "from Beth-yeshimoth as far as Abel-shittim in the plains of Moab."
The latter is clearly a place name, and scholars have thought the most likely
site identification to be Tell el-Hammām. See Map C, 137.

In this story the name has the definite article and might be translated literally, "The Acacias," reminding the reader of the harsh desert terrain and cli-
mate at the southern end of the Jordan valley, roughly 0.4 km below sea level.
Here for the bulk of the year the shade of these beautiful trees is a welcome
relief and it is not surprising that they should have given their name to a small
region. This opening also sets the tone of adventure and risk. In such desert
terrain, getting from "The Acacias" to Jericho means crossing not only the
river, but a lot of open country.

Go, have a look at. lěkû rě'û, literally, "Go! See!" in a verbal hendiadys.

the land. This is the ultimate objective. For a fuller example of such a commission, and therefore of what the spies might have expected to do, see Num
13:18-20. Here, however, Joshua's instructions are pared to the minimum, because the narrator's interest does not center, really, in military reconnaissance.
Compare the commission in 7:2 and what follows there. In the latter passage,
the men will do the true work of spies, but the result for Israel will be disastrous. Here, on the other hand, Israel's first victory in Canaan begins with a
spy story that is touch and go from start to finish.

and Jericho(!) Are the words a "limping addition"? So D. J. McCarthy, "The
Theology of Leadership in Joshua 1-9," *Biblica* 52 (1971) 174. The three references to Jericho in quick succession here (vv 1-3), but not again in the chapter, serve to tie this story of reconnoitering the land together with the story of
the fall of Jericho in chap. 6. When the spies report back to Joshua in v 24,
they mention only the land in general, with no reference to Jericho.

We conclude that the *RSV* reading in v 1, "and especially Jericho," is inac-
curate. The words are an effort to be sure we understand that Rahab lived at
Jericho.

The site of Tell es-Sultan is about 8 km west of the meandering riverbed
today. See Map C, 137.

came . . . entered. Two senses of the verb *b'*, which is used exactly seven
times in rapid succession at the outset (vv 1-4), then not again until late in the
unit, when it occurs another three times (vv 18,22, and 23).

a prostitute. Hebrew *'šh zwnh,* literally, "a woman, a prostitute." This can be
compared to the construction of *hn'r hlwy,* "the young Levite" (Judg 18:3)
and *'yš lwy,* "a man, a Levite" (Judg 19:1).

The Hebrew *zōnâ* may refer to either secular or cultic prostitution. The latter was an almost invariable element of Canaanite religious practice. The language has, however, for use by a narrator who wished to avoid ambiguity, a
special term for the cultic variety: *qĕdēšâ.* Interpretations based on the notion
that Rahab was a cultic prostitute are adequately answered by Soggin, *Joshua,*
89. See below on 6:25, the resumption of this story. Toward the end of the
pre-monarchy period is the story of Jephthah, who is introduced right at the
outset, Judg 11:1, as son of *'šh znh,* "a prostitute." His thorough, self-con-
ducted reconnaissance and laborious diplomatic exchanges will contrast sharply
with the approach of Joshua and his two spies. Vows in both stories set condi-

tions in almost identical wording (see below on v 19), but they lead to quite opposite conclusions. If the Jephthah story in Judges 11 has a tragic ending, the genre here in Joshua 2 is more like comedy.

Rahab. This is presumably the shortened form of a sentence name: *rāḥāb-N*, "the god *N* has opened/widened (the womb?)." Compare the names Rehoboam and Rehabyahu, the latter being clearly a Yahwistic name on the same root. See Martin Noth, *Israelitischer Personennamen im Rahmen der gemeinsemitischen Namengebung,* BWANT III, 10, 193.

Rahab has exercised a special fascination, well into NT times, where she is reckoned among the ancestors of Jesus (Matt 1:5); she is lauded as an example of living by faith (Heb 11:31), and justified by her works (James 2:25). See Raymond E. Brown, *The Birth of the Messiah* (Garden City, NY: Doubleday), 71-74.

It has been pointed out that going to Rahab's establishment was not necessarily a deviation from orders, for "the inn and the brothel have been found in one establishment often in the history of mankind," and where better to get information than a bar? McKenzie, *The World of the Judges,* 48. It remains true that the visit to her house was the sum total of the men's reconnaissance activity. Probably the narrator intends to titillate by reminding readers of an immemorial symbiosis between military service and bawdy house. It is reliably reported that at the height of the 1948 warfare, morale in the desperately besieged Jewish quarter of Jerusalem was considerably bolstered by the arrival of a barber and a prostitute. Larry Collins and Dominique Lapierre, *O Jerusalem* (New York: Pocket Books, 1973), 196.

2. *the king of Jericho.* He remains anonymous.

Here. The particle *hinnēh* often signals a statement that is a logical deduction from the circumstances described or presupposed. See Lambdin, *Introduction to Biblical Hebrew,* 168-171.

this very night. As in Ruth 3:2, we are probably to think of "the twilight hours." Campbell, *Ruth,* AB 7, 119.

The evening here seems to belong to the first of the three days which are given special emphasis by repetition (vv 16 and 22). In other words, the story presupposes a reckoning of the day from morning to morning. The consistent morning-to-morning reckoning of the day in the Hebrew text of these chapters was noted by Wilcoxen, "Narrative Structure and Cult Legend: A Study of Joshua 1-6," 62 n. 30.

3. *Bring out the men.* Processes of interrogation are known from sources such as descriptions of the Battle of Qadesh, between forces of Egypt and Hatti, where "the extortion of information from prisoners was, of course, carried out in the usual manner." Yigael Yadin, "Warfare in the Second Millennium B.C.E.," in *WHJP* II, ed. Benjamin Mazar, 145.

the whole land(!) Far more was at stake than the great Jordan valley oasis alone.

4. *had taken and hidden.* The text seems to read most simply "The woman took and hid." The problem of verbal tenses is explained by some as an indifference to logical details in Hebrew storytelling. H. W. Hertzberg, *Die Bücher Joshua, Richter, Ruth,* 2a. But this is to avoid the issue. The translation

as pluperfects here is warranted by context alone. McCarthy, "The Theology of Leadership . . . ," 170-171.

came to my place. This is the seventh occurrence of the root *b'* in this story.

but I did not know. They were, after all, just a couple of patrons from whom it was not customary to require credentials.

5. *Pursue.* The Hebrew root *rdp* occurs six times in the chapter. Rendered "chased" in v 7, the participial form is "posse" in vv 7,16 (*bis*), and 22.

6. *But.* The syntax is disjunctive.

flax. This would probably have been regarded as quite providential, since it is most likely that flax was not being cultivated in that early period. See Shemaryahu Talmon, "The Gezer Calendar and the Seasonal Cycles of Ancient Canaan," *JAOS* 83 (1963) 177-187. It was, rather, more likely wild flax, the relative scarcity of which would heighten the sense of escape "by the skin of your teeth."

7. *the men.* Hebrew *h'nšym,* the common noun. But the men are probably not commoners. They represent the king. In the old account of the Shechem Valley Covenant in chap. 24, when Joshua recounts the history of grace that will motivate acceptance of the treaty, he refers to Jericho without mentioning either a "king" or "the men." There the opposition comes rather from "the lords of (*ba'ălê*) Jericho" (Josh 24:11). The latter term is clarified from the story of Abimelech in Judg 9:2,3,7 (*et passim*) where it points to oligarchic rule. But the Shechem nobility in Judges 9 are in fact reinstituting a monarchy there! Canaanite social organization was pyramidal, with a numerically small but economically powerful and socially privileged elite. In most cases, the elite was first established militarily, but would rapidly acquire commercial control as well; they hold the temple treasury in Judg 9:4. It can hardly be doubted that the prerogatives and interests of such groups were seriously threatened by the collapse of kingdoms and the outlandish egalitarianism of the Transjordan Yahwists. See below on 12:1-6 and 13:8-32.

9-11. The pagan prostitute is the first one to recite saving history in the final edition of the book. "Rahab is quoted as being rather well read in the Deuteronomic tradition of the exodus and the wilderness." McKenzie, *The World of the Judges,* 48. Compare also the argument of the Gibeonites in 9:6-15. On the prime importance of the themes of Rahab's speech as preamble to the constitution of ancient Israel, see Wright's remarks above, 5-9.

9. *I know.* The verb *yd'* often has specifically covenantal nuance, signifying the active acknowledgment that establishes a formal relationship, not merely a passive cognitive condition. Amos 3:2 is the classic text.

dread. Hebrew 'êmâ. The victory of the Divine Warrior is not achieved by the weapons in human hands. See Exod 15:16; 23:27; Job 20:25; Jer 50:38.

rulers. An echo of Exod 15:14, where Hebrew *yōšĕbîm* refers to the occupants of thrones, not the entirety of a land's inhabitants, as recognized by D. N. Freedman.

faint. The root is *mwg,* "to melt," another effect of activity by the Divine

Warrior, as in Exod 15:15-16. See also 1 Sam 14:16; Isa 14:31; Jer 49:23; Ezek 21:20; and Nah 2:7. D. J. McCarthy, "Some Holy War Vocabulary in Joshua 2," *CBQ* 33 (1971) 230.

10. *when you came out of the land of Egypt.* The most probable date is around the turn of the twelfth century. See Edward F. Campbell, Jr., "Moses and the Foundations of Israel," *Interpretation* 29 (1975) 141-154.

Sihon and Og. It is a striking fact that these are the only kings mentioned by name in the story or, for that matter, anywhere in the first nine chapters of the book! This should be understood in terms of the special character of the early Gilgal-sanctuary, when there was only the East Jordan phase of conquest to recall and celebrate. See Wright's discussion above (24-26), with special reference to the studies of Gerhard von Rad and Hans-Joachim Kraus.

11. *Your god Yahweh is indeed God.* Compare Deut 4:35,39; 7:9; 10:17; 1 Kgs 8:60; cf. 18:39 (*bis*). See Moshe Weinfeld, *Deuteronomy and the Deuteronomic School,* 331.

in the heavens above and on the earth below. Weinfeld calls attention to Deut 4:39; 1 Kgs 8:23; and compares Exod 20:4 and Deut 5:8. Ibid.

12. *Swear to me now, by Yahweh.* The only way, apparently, to avoid the ban is to make a covenant. Here it is done openly. In chap. 9 the covenant with Gibeon involves subterfuge. Both of these traditions must be pre-Deuteronomistic in origin. McCarthy, "The Theology of Leadership . . . ," 174. However, the Gibeon treaty was clearly regarded as an exception for which some explanation had to be found in the first Dtr-edition. See below, NOTES and COMMENT on chap. 9. Not so chap. 2, which tells the story with a high sense of humor and lets Rahab be the one to recite the saving history. It is very difficult to see how these stories of negotiations at Jericho and Gibeon could belong originally to the same history-writing enterprise. But they make good sense as independently redacted stories. We suggest that the Rahab story was only incorporated into the final edition of the book. At that stage, as we shall see in chap. 9, the Gibeon story in the first edition was also expanded in such a way as to reflect a sense of humor.

mercy. The noun is *ḥsd,* a word for covenant-loyalty that is notoriously difficult to translate (*KJV* often renders it "kindness" or "loving kindness"). Rahab is the first to use the word in this book. The semantic nucleus is responsible caring. See Campbell on the theology of the Book of Ruth, AB 7, 28-32; and the Harvard University dissertation by Katherine Doob Sakenfeld, *The Meaning of Hesed in the Hebrew Bible,* Harvard Semitic Monographs 17.

13. *our lives.* LXX reads "my life," under the influence of the preceding sentence.

14b. For this restoration of sentence sequence, see above, Textual Note.

show confident mercy. KJV "deal kindly and truly." She insists that they "do *ḥsd* and *'mt,*" a hendiadys for covenantal integrity. The NT Greek equivalents are *charis* and *alētheia,* "grace and truth."

14a. *family.* This word is supplied for clarity, where MT has simply the second person plural pronoun.

when Yahweh gives us the land. Hebrew *btt yhwh lnw.* Compare the certainty of success voiced here with the anxiety expressed by Jephthah in his vow: "If . . ." (Judg 11:30-31).

15. *She had lowered them.* As in v 4, the only clues to the tense of the verb must be wrested from context. It has been suggested that the converted causative imperfect *wattôrîdēm* is inchoative (so-called *futuram instans*), but it would help to be shown other examples. McCarthy, "The Problem of Leadership . . . ," 171. Probably a better solution is to be sought in the storytelling characteristic which W. J. Martin has dubbed "'Dischronologized' Narrative in the Old Testament," in *VT*Sup 17 (1969), discussing this passage on 182. A classic example is Judg 1:1-3 where the English past perfect must be used in order to understand the verses in the wider context. See *Judges*, AB 6A, 50, 53-54, 63-64. In the Rahab story, Martin thinks that the brief flashback continues into v 16: "The situation, the sleeping city, the silence of the dead of night, makes it evident that Rahab's instruction must have preceded the descent from the wall." This is one possible understanding of the narrative.

for her house was . . . This entire explanation (v 15b) is lacking in LXX which may in fact preserve an original reading since the context shows nothing that might have caused a haplography. On the other hand, these differences may stem from the adaptation of the story, about the expedition to Rahab's house, as preparation for the story of the attack against the great mound of ancient Jericho.

between the double walls. In the *qyr* of the *ḥwmh*, literally, "in the wall of the wall." The expression seems to refer to defensive fortifications of the casemate type, in which parallel walls are divided by cross-walls into chambers which may be rubble-filled for added strength or be used for residence and storage. Since the Early Bronze Age in the third millennium, casemate construction had been "an integral part of the fortifications in the Near East and constituted an efficient protection from the battering-ram." Yadin, "Warfare in the Second Millennium B.C.E.," *WHJP* II, 155. The supposed "double wall" found at Tell es-Sultan and dated by the Garstang expedition to the Late Bronze Age is actually composed, in part, of successive Early Bronze Age walls. Line Drawing, 213. See below on 6:1-27.

16. *She said to them.* "We are left with the picture of the spies pausing to complete their agreement with Rahab as they cling to the rope from her window." Gene M. Tucker, "The Rahab Saga (Joshua 2): Some Form-Critical and Traditio-Historical Observations," in *The Use of the Old Testament in the New and Other Essays*, 76. Tucker takes what we consider signs of the "dischronologized" narrative as evidence of successive redactions. However, in the absence of clear criteria for redaction, it is better to recognize such incongruities as part of the narrative design.

"Head for the hills . . . be on your way." She speaks in an envelope construction with two forms of the verb *hlk*, "to go," framing two references to the posse. The word order at the beginning *hhrh lkw*, with verb last and *daghesh forte* in the *l*, emphasizes that this westward direction is the opposite of what might be expected by a posse. It is interesting, in view of so many other points of comparison with the Jephthah story, that the latter uses the same verb in a feminine imperative (*lky*) when he releases his daughter to lament her destiny on "the hills" (Judg 11:38).

the hills in question are those of eastern Benjamin, according to the land divisions described in chaps. 13-19. By NT times they are part of the "wilderness of Judah." Towering high above Jericho is Jebel Qarantel, the Mount of Temptation, named after the gospel story (Matt 4:1-11 and parallels).

for three days. In the final form of the book, this period of time is apparently to be understood as identical with the period of preparation for the crossing of the river (1:11). Within the old self-contained story unit, it was simply a period long enough for the posse to become weary and/or satisfied with searching the badlands between Jericho and the river.

has returned. The infinitive absolute form is here an elegant substitute for a finite form and it does not need to be emended as proposed by *BH*³.

17-21. It has been objected that these verses occur "too late in the narrative." *The Jerusalem Bible* annotator suggests that they "seem to derive from a different tradition (v 20 is parallel with v 14) and there is no further mention of the scarlet cord." This is not impossible.

17. For the sentence structure in Hebrew, cf. Num 6:8. Francis I. Andersen, *The Hebrew Verbless Clause in the Pentateuch*, 68.

this. MT *hzh* (anomolous masculine form with feminine referent) resists explanation.

18. *Look.* See third NOTE on v 2.

19. *Whoever goes out the doors of your house.* Hebrew *kl 'šr yṣ' mdlty bytk.* Compare Judg 11:31, *hywṣ 'šr yṣ' mdlty byty* in Jephthah's tragic vow. There is clearly an inverted relationship between these stories as they now stand: (1) the Yahwists pledge themselves to an enterprising pagan harlot, and later keep their word for a happy ending; (2) the one Israelite who was otherwise remembered as the greatest negotiator of his era, and son of a harlot, becomes a tragic figure who sacrifices his virgin daughter in fulfillment of an anxious vow.

20. *your oath.* See above, on v 17. The two occurrences form an inclusio.

which you have made us swear. This anticipates the contrasting situation in the story of Jephthah's negotiations with the elders of Gilead (Judg 11:4-11).

21. *Whatever you say.* Literally, "According to your words" (or "word" in LXX and Syriac). On the formula structure, compare Gen 44:10 and 1 Sam 25:25. Andersen, ibid.

23. *Joshua ben Nun.* The name forms an inclusio with v 1, closing off the old story of reconnaissance across the Jordan. We must reckon with the possibility of a non-Jericho Rahab story. The later editor was able to use her story with very little adaptation other than to make Rahab a resident of Jericho, but also a prophet like Moses.

all that had befallen them. Rahab was their only informant, but she had told them all that they needed to know. The young men had stumbled onto the truth.

24. *given . . . into our hands.* This is the equivalent of a scene found often in ancient art (Plate III) and analyzed in detail by Othmar Keel, *Wirkmächtige Siegeszeichen im Alten Testament.* The Akkadian equivalent, *ina qāti nādānu,* "he gave into the hand," is used of a god granting victory over enemies,

as early as the Old Akkadian period. Moran, "The End of the Unholy War
. . . ," 337 n. 1.

COMMENT

The first story told in the Book of Joshua is in many ways the least characteristic. In fact it resembles much more closely the stories in the Book
of Judges, which are for the most part self-contained units, with few internal signs of "Deuteronomic" editing. In Judges the signs of Dtr-editing
occur in the connections between stories. There, in other words, the editor tells how it was, in the old stories handed down from the pre-monarchy period. In Dtr 1, the old stories of the Judges served mostly to illustrate the new problems posed by the rapid expansion of Israel and the
need for a strong central government.

In the Book of Joshua, on the other hand, the stories were largely
rewritten in such a way that they present the relation between Israel and
Joshua, between Joshua and Yahweh, in exemplary and idealistic terms.
That is, the figure of Joshua, in contrast to the tumultuous careers of the
judges, is held up for emulation by the later officials of Israel. Hence the
pattern of commissioning and exhortation in chap. 1. In contrast to the
use of unrevised stories in Judges, the stories are recast in Joshua to show
"how it is" or how "it is going to be," thanks to the rise of Josiah, a king
who takes with utmost seriousness the Book of the Treaty-Teaching, that
is, the old Deuteronomic code.

Yet there is a glaring internal contradiction between the warfare
guidelines in Deut 20:10-20 and this negotiated exception, which makes
the Rahab story stick out like a sore thumb. Moreover, this contradiction
is the Achilles heel of every attempt to explain the spy story as anciently
legitimated by a holy war ideology. The shape of the story is said to be
determined by that pattern: "The war cannot begin without the assurance
that Yahweh is with the people to give them victory" (Tucker, "The
Rahab Saga . . . ," 78). But this has already been made explicit in chap.
1, several times over, so that the story is redundant and superfluous if such
is its purpose. If it is so, why did the editor, who elsewhere in Joshua had
no reservations about retelling stories with his own idiom, not do the
same in chap. 2?

There is a similar problem with the explanation that views this story as
an "illustration of faith," a genre that is said to have its origins in a per-
vasive ideology of holy war, stemming from the pre-monarchy period. On
this view the spies "are saved and their mission is accomplished because
of Rahab's intervention inspired by faith in Yahweh. They are entirely

passive, the classic illustration that Yahweh and not men wins wars. Further Rahab's speech is loaded with holy war vocabulary. . . ." McCarthy, "The Theology of Leadership . . . ," 173-174. This is surely on the right track, to begin with; but it gets derailed precisely in the attempt to harmonize elements of the Dtr corpus by appealing to a single holy war theology dominating the scene.

Although it has had enormous heuristic value, the holy war construct must be carefully delimited. It has recently been shown that the holy war idea in Israelite tradition was a *"post eventum* interpretation and schematization of past events," although it was "built on a tradition that already existed in the Yahweh War experience. The theory was an attempt to define and formulate what was regarded as fundamental to the old tradition. . . ." Gwilym H. Jones, " 'Holy War' or 'Yahweh War'?" *VT* 25 (1975) 656. This carries us further along the right track, for it focuses on actual human experience in the Yahweh Wars and the values that were at stake in them.

So far as institutions are concerned, most features of warfare in early Israel have a parallel in the Mari texts, "sources not overlaid with theological interpretations" (Glock, "Warfare in Mari and Early Israel," 230 n. 115). Equally important: "neither the formal language of the tradition nor the separate elements identified as components of 'holy war' require a cultic interpretation" (ibid.). In light of all this, it is increasingly difficult to force all parts of the corpus into a continuous Deuteronomic "school" with some members more articulate, and others less articulate, spokesmen for essentially the same point of view.

But if some of the tensions in the material are seen to be of the essence, and if they can be analyzed as reflecting a "dialogue" taking place as the old story is supplemented under the press of experience in new and very different historical contexts, then a great many texts and indeed larger narrative units suddenly snap into focus. The distribution of spy stories is a case in point. The story in Joshua 2 is only broadly reminiscent of the earlier reconnaissance of Canaan from the south, during the wilderness period based at Qadesh-barnea, in which Joshua himself had participated (Numbers 13). Much more directly it anticipates the negotiations with a prominent citizen of Bethel in Judg 1:22-26, which in itself unfolds as a commendable example of keeping treaty-faith but stands in strong tensions with its larger context! The "reconnaissance of Bethel" is best understood as another contribution by Dtr 2.

On the other hand, the spy story in Judges 18 leads to the migration of the tribe of Dan and its conquest in the far north. That was regarded as a particularly tragic exploitation of the *ḥrm,* in the work of Dtr 1. The story in Judges 18 illustrates a situation of "every man doing what is right in his own eyes," viewed negatively.

These observations reinforce the awareness that has been evoked by other evidence that the Rahab story was only rescued from oblivion and put in place by the later redactor, Dtr 2 (a conclusion also argued by Jon D. Levenson, "Who Inserted the Book of the Torah?" *HTR* 68 [1975] 220). For this spy story clearly shows two men of Israel doing what is right in their own eyes; and that is viewed positively! This in fact anticipates the very end of the Book of Judges, where the story of tragic civil war which resulted in the suppression of Benjamin is nevertheless brought to a positive conclusion. The warfare at the very outset of the era also had been concentrated in the territory of Benjamin.

This story together with its conclusion in 6:22-25 is the reader's first confrontation with the problem of etiological narrative in Joshua. The classic definition of such narrative has been imported from the study of Greek mythology. As formulated by M. P. Nilsson, an etiology is "a narrative which seeks to explain why something has come to be, or why it has become such and such" (*Geschichte der griechischen Religion*² I, 25). Recognition of etiological elements in the books of Joshua and Judges has led to extremely low estimates of their historicity, especially in Joshua, by highly respected scholars, headed chiefly by Albrecht Alt and his student, Martin Noth. The vigorous rebuttal by John Bright won a concession that even material in etiological form might preserve historical content. See M. Noth, "Der Beiterag der Archäologie zur Geschichte Israels," in *VT*Sup 7 (1960) 278*ff*. Yet the debate seems to have achieved a stalemate, to judge from the survey of the problems in Weippert, *The Settlement of the Israelite Tribes in Palestine*.

At the same time, recent form-critical studies may offer a way out of the impasse. Here it will suffice to mention the work of I. L. Seeligmann, "Aetiological Elements in Biblical Historiography," *Zion: Quarterly for Research in Jewish History* 26 (1961) 141-169 (Hebrew with English summary); Claus Westermann, *Forschung am Alten Testament,* 39–47; Brevard S. Childs, "Unto This Day," *JBL* 82 (1963) 279-292; and especially Burke O. Long, *The Problem of Etiological Narrative in the Old Testament,* BZAW (1968). The presence of an etiological element reflects didactic interest—the narrator would be a teacher. But the etiological element will most often be recognized as marginal, or secondary, to the structure of the story. It derives from a later antiquarian motivation and explains the preservation, not the creation, of the story.

Joshua 2 does not by itself reflect any etiological motivation. Rather here a new era gets under way. All merely antiquarian curiosity is ruled out, and the narrator includes only what is essential to the action—two young men of Israel clearly not going "by the book," but finding their mission crowned with success.

C. FROM SHITTIM TO GILGAL
(3:1-4:18)

Opening the Jordan

3 1 Joshua got busy next morning, and set forth from Shittim. With him all the Bene Israel came as far as the Jordan and camped there before crossing over. 2 Then at the end of three days, the officers moved throughout the camp 3 and gave the order to the people:

"When you see the Covenant-Ark of Yahweh your God with the Levite-priests carrying it, then you will set forth from your position and follow it. 4 Be very sure that there is a distance between you and it, about a kilometer (Hold position! Do not get near it!), so that you may know the route by which you are to proceed, for you have not previously passed this way."

5 Joshua said to the people, "Make yourselves ritually ready for tomorrow, because tomorrow Yahweh will work wonders in your midst."

6 Joshua said to the priests, "Take up the Covenant-Ark, and proceed before the people." So they took up the Covenant-Ark and proceeded before the people.

7 Yahweh said to Joshua, "Today I will begin to magnify you in the eyes of all the Bene Israel, so that they will know! For I am going to be with you, as I was with Moses. 8 You are to give orders to the priests bearing the Covenant-Ark: 'When you come to the brink of the Jordan's waters, you will stand still in the Jordan.' "

9 Then Joshua said to the Bene Israel, "Come here and hear the words of Yahweh your God. 10 By this you will know! For El the living is in your midst; and he will utterly dispossess before you the Canaanites, Hittites, Hivites, Perizzites, Girgashites, Amorites, and Jebusites! 11 Here is the Covenant-Ark; the Lord of all the earth is passing before you across the Jordan. 12 Take for yourselves now twelve men from the tribes of Israel, one man from each tribe. . . . 13 When the soles of the feet of the priests carrying the Ark of Yah-

weh, Lord of all the earth, rest in the Jordan's waters, the Jordan's waters will be cut off. The water coming from upstream will stand up in one heap!"

14 And so it happened, when the people set out from their tents to cross the Jordan, with the priests carrying the Covenant-Ark in front of the people, 15 and when those carrying the Ark came to the Jordan and the feet of the priests carrying the Ark were dipped at the brink of the water (The Jordan overflows its banks throughout the harvest), 16 the water coming down from above stood still. It arose in one heap a great distance from Adam the city which is beside Zarethan.

And the stream going on down toward the Arabah Sea (the Salt Sea) was entirely cut off. The people crossed, opposite Jericho.

To the National Memorial

17 The priests carrying Yahweh's Covenant-Ark stood firmly on dry ground in the middle of the Jordan; and all the Bene Israel crossed on dry ground, until finally the entire nation had crossed the Jordan.
4 1 When finally the entire nation had crossed the Jordan, Yahweh said to Joshua, 2 "Take for yourself twelve men from the people, one man from each tribe, 3 and command them: 'Take with you from this place, from mid-Jordan—from the place where the feet of the priests were firm—twelve stones. Take them across with you and deposit them at the place where you camp tonight.'"

4 Joshua called the twelve men whom he had appointed from the Bene Israel, one man from each tribe. 5 He said to them, "Move out before the Ark of Yahweh your God toward the middle of the Jordan, and each of you lift one stone to his shoulder, according to the number of the twelve tribes of the Bene Israel. 6 So that this may be a sign to you, in your midst he is setting it up. When your children ask in the future, 'What are these stones to you?' 7 you will explain to your children that the Jordan's waters were cut off before the Covenant-Ark of Yahweh, when it crossed over the Jordan. Thus these stones shall be an everlasting reminder to the Bene Israel."

8 And the Bene Israel did exactly as Yahweh commanded Joshua. They picked up twelve stones from the middle of the Jordan, as Yahweh had instructed Joshua, when the Bene Israel had completed the

crossing. They took them across with them to the campsite and deposited them there.

In Other Words

9 (Twelve other stones Joshua had set up in the middle of the Jordan, as platform for the feet of the priests bearing Yahweh's Covenant-Ark. They are there to this day.)

All the People

10 While the priests bearing the Ark continued standing in the middle of the Jordan until Joshua had completed everything that Yahweh had commanded to tell the people, the people hurried across.
11 When finally all the people had crossed over, then the Ark of Yahweh and the priests crossed over before the people. 12 The Bene Reuben, the Bene Gad, and half the tribe of Manasseh crossed over in battle array before the Bene Israel, just as Moses had instructed them. 13 About forty contingents of armed warriors crossed over before Yahweh for the battle—to the Jericho plains.
14 On that day Yahweh magnified Joshua in the eyes of all the people Israel. They revered him, just as they had revered Moses, all his life.

Closing the Jordan

15 Yahweh said to Joshua, 16 "Command the priests carrying the Testimony-Ark of Yahweh to come up, out of the Jordan." 17 So Joshua commanded the priests, "Come up, out of the Jordan." 18 And as the priests carrying Yahweh's Covenant-Ark came up from the middle of the Jordan, the soles of the priests' feet reached dry ground, and the Jordan's waters returned to their position and flowed as before along its banks.

TEXTUAL NOTES

3 1. *and set forth*   The singular verb (*wys‘*) is found in LXX[BL] and Syr[A]. The plural in MT (*wys‘w*) has assimilated to the number of the next verb in the sentence (*wyb’w*).

With him all the Bene Israel   This is lacking in LXX, while Syriac shows no reflex of the first three words and begins the sentence with "The Bene Israel."

3. *the Levite-priests*   The juxtaposition in MT is to be retained, as in 8:33. In both passages the Versions insert a conjunction; see fourth NOTE on v 3.

4. *Hold position!*   The translation adopts the proposal of *BH*[3], that Greek *stesesthe* stands for Hebrew *‘imĕdû*. MT is unidiomatically redundant, in giving *bmdh*, "by the measure," after the distance; the reading may be an attempt to make sense out of a mutilated copy. Vulgate omits, for the smoothest text of all.

5. *for tomorrow*   Restored from LXX.

7. *the Bene*   Thus LXX. MT has "all Israel." So also v 17. The readings are clearly alternates.

9. *words*   The plural of MT is surely original. LXX and Vulgate, under influence of later prophetic tradition perhaps, read singular. Or the singular may have originated in a haplography: *dbr*[y] *yhwh*.

10. The better LXX recensions omit "and Joshua said," which in MT is perhaps a vertical dittography from the beginning of v 9.

11. *before you*   Lacking in LXX.

12. *now*   Lacking in LXX.

tribes   LXX reads "sons."

13. *the soles of*   MT is perhaps conflate. LXX lacks "the soles of."

will stand up in one heap!   The only serious problem in the Hebrew is the conjunction before the verb: *wy‘mdw*. This can be parsed as an archaic use, the *waw*-emphatic, which marks a verb located toward the end of the sentence. Mitchell Dahood, *Psalms III*, AB 17A, 400-401. The archaic usage was lost on LXX translators who smoothed things over by omitting "from upstream" and "a single heap," ignoring the emphatic conjunction and supplying another one at the very beginning: "and the waters coming down. . . ."

The archaic usage was also lost on the Masoretes, who gave the *athnach* to *mlm‘lh*, "from upstream." Other versions reflect various modifications of this.

15. *those carrying the Ark*   LXX specifies "the priests" as subject, and has "ark of the covenant."

water   LXX has "waters of the Jordan."

16. *It arose in one heap a great distance from Adam the city which is beside Zarethan*   LXX is quite different: "forming a single heap over a very wide area, as far as the frontier of Qiryath-yearim."

17. *the Bene*   Thus LXX, where MT reads: "all Israel," as in v 7.

4 1. *When finally the entire nation had crossed the Jordan*   Lacking in LXX^L, which however reflects a haplography: *w[yhy . . . w]y'mr.*

2. *Take for yourself*   Context requires the singular verb as in the Versions, against MT. The plural verb is explained by the following word which shows a dittography, as a result of which the singular pronoun became plural: *lk[m] mn.* Translators of the Vulgate no longer understood the form and so dropped it. The Greek recensions also avoid the preposition *lkm,* "with you," in v 3, even though the plural poses no problem there. On the other hand, LXX shows the reflex of *lkm,* "to you," in v 6, where it is the predicate of the sentence.

twelve   LXX^B lacks the numeral.

3. *command*   The imperative must be singular (*wṣw*) as in the Versions. The plural in MT (*wṣww*) is either dittography or contamination triggered by the shift to plural imperatives only three words away in MT ("Take with you").

from this place, from mid-Jordan   The first phrase is missing in LXX^B, because of haplography *m[zh m]twk.*

from the place where the feet of the priests   Lost by haplography from LXX *Vorlage,* framed by words which begin and end with the same letters: *hyrdn* and *hkyn.* On the latter, see first NOTE on 4:3.

5. *He*   Thus LXX, where MT repeats the name "Joshua" under influence of the preceding verse.

before the Ark of Yahweh your God   LXX shows a dittography at the outset: *lpny lpny-'rwn,* "before me, before the ark." The major Greek recensions lack "your God," reflecting haplography: *'l[hykm 'l-]twk.*

twelve   This is LXX. Haplography dropped the numeral from MT: *š[nym h'śr š]bṭy.*

6. *to you*   Based on LXX. MT seems to represent a revised text, after the occurrence of the haplography to be described next.

in your midst he is setting it up   MT is fragmentary. The Greek *keimenon dia pantos* must reflect Hebrew *bĕqirbĕkem mēqîm* or the like. The participle (*mēqîm,* cf. *hēqîm* in v 9), placed last for emphasis, was also a prime candidate for omission: *bqrbk[m mqy]m ky.*

7. *you will explain to your children*   Based on LXX, where the verb is *dēloō* (most likely for Hebrew *yd'* or *yrh;* MT has *'mr*). The Hebrew formula represented by LXX would be *w* + Perfect + *bnykm* + *l'mr.* MT is an awkward attempt to make sense after the loss of *bnykm,* "your children."

Yahweh   LXX reads "Lord of all the earth."

when it crossed over the Jordan   Thus MT, where LXX lacks the final reference to the Jordan. But then MT continues: *nkrtw my hyrdn,* "the Jordan's waters were cut off." This is either a conflation or a nearly complete dittography of *nkrtw mymy hyrdn* from the preceding line; the lopsided *chiasm* of MT is not convincing. Without these words, the lapse which produced the still shorter LXX text becomes clear: *b'brw [byrdn] whyw.*

8. *Yahweh*   Based on LXX, where haplography dropped the divine name from MT: *ṣwh y[hwh 't y]hwš'.*

when the Bene Israel had completed the crossing   The *BH*[3] note is misleading. *bny yśr'l* is clearly reflected in LXX. The problem is the two preceding words in MT: *lmspr šbṭy,* "*according to the number of tribes of.*" These words are syntactically disconnected from what precedes them. But LXX makes good sense and shows a mechanism for the haplography after which MT was awkwardly filled out. The Greek *en tē sunteleia tēs diabaseōs tōn huiōn Israēl* translates Hebrew *bĕ[tōm la'ăbōr bĕ]nê yiśrā'ēl.* The equation of the verbs is established by vv 1,10, and 11.

9. *other stones*   LXX is clear. The crucial modifier, however, was dropped from MT by haplography: *'bn[ym 'ḥr]ym*

Yahweh's   Thus LXX.

10. *Ark*   LXX reads "Covenant-Ark."

until Joshua had completed everything that Yahweh had commanded to tell the people   Thus LXX, probably traceable to an oral variant. Cf. MT, "until everything was completed that Yahweh had commanded Joshua to tell the people, as with everything that Moses had commanded Joshua." The last phrase is a corruption based on a scribe's anticipation of the reading in v 12.

11. *Ark of Yahweh*   LXX reads "Yahweh's Covenant-Ark." See second NOTE on 3:11.

priests   With MT. LXX reads "the stones," surely a contamination from vv 3-9.

before the people   Thus MT: *lpny h'm.* LXX reflects *lpnyhm,* "before them," after the loss of one letter.

14. *the people Israel*   This agrees with LXX. See NOTE.

16. *of Yahweh*   With LXX.

NOTES

3:1 - 4:18. In these stories about the crossing of the Jordan River, we move onto new literary terrain, different from the first two chapters. The origin of the basic story line was in the experience of the successful penetration of Canaan by the Yahwist movement. The odds against it must have appeared formidable. And so the surprisingly rapid success of the movement came soon to be celebrated with dramatic reenactment at the early sanctuaries. The language and organization of chaps. 3-6 is shaped to a great extent by a dramatization, a "liturgical conquest." In other words, the ancient historians here used what we would call secondary cultic sources to describe primary historico-theological events.

3:1-6. Joshua makes preparations for invasion, told now in lively narrative form.

1. *got busy.* As also in 6:12 and 7:16, the verb *hškm* construed with *bbqr,* "in the morning," does not mean merely "to rise," but is "to act persistently,

diligently," or the like. E. A. Speiser, *Genesis*, AB 1 (1964) 138, n. on Gen
19:2. Contrast the uses of this verb in Josh 6:12 and 6:15.

morning. The distance to be traveled that day was not great (see Map C,
137) from the vicinity of Tell el-Hammām to the Jordan.

set forth. The Hebrew verb means literally "to pull up tent stakes, break
camp."

from Shittim. See the indictment-speech of Yahweh in Mic 6:5 where the
phrase "from Shittim to Gilgal" occurs, unfortunately in a difficult context.
Nevertheless, it is clearly a context of saving historical events, which begins
"from the land of Egypt" and which has transpired so "that you may know the
saving acts of Yahweh" (Mic 6:4-5).

all the Bene Israel. That is, it included both east-bank believers and those
who would settle on the west bank. See 4:11-12.

the Jordan. The verbal root in this name means "to descend." The ending of
Yardēn belongs with various -*ān* endings which generally in Hebrew become
-*ōn*, as in Simeon, though in the far north they sometimes show the further
Tyrian-Sidonian Phoenician shift to -*ūn*, as in Zebulun. See, for example,
F. Gröndahl, *PTU*, 51-53, and for related Arabic broken plural patterns,
W. Wright, *A Grammar of the Arabic Language I* (Cambridge University
Press, 1896) 216-218. We owe these references to M. P. O'Connor, in a private
communication. The name of the river occurs some twenty-eight times in chaps.
3 and 4 (in which curiously the Jordan is never called a river).

crossing over. This is another pivotally important root that is used with considerable variation in meaning, twenty times in this section, 3:1 - 4:18. In this
story of the opening waters, the root is used exactly seven times. Thus 3:2
("moved throughout"), 3:4 ("passed"), 3:6 ("proceed"), 3:11 ("passing"),
3:14, and 3:16.

2. *at the end of three days.* Why this brief period of encampment at the last
station outside the land? To the redactor this would be the same time interval
as in the spy story (2:16 and 22). In this way, preformed narrative units could
easily be connected. Here it is not simply a matter of "dischronologized narrative," discussed above at 2:15. The fact that there are so many time references
in chaps. 3-6 suggests that in the background is an extended complex of cultic events. See Wilcoxen, "Narrative Structure . . . ," 60.

the officers. See NOTE on 1:10.

3. *When you see. . . .* One of the officers is quoted at length, yielding a
vivid scene.

the Covenant-Ark. This is the first reference to this venerable institution in
the Book of Joshua. Elsewhere we catch only a glimpse of its early importance
as war palladium (Num 10:35). It is known best from traditions of the late
pre-monarchy period, where it is associated with Shiloh. From there it goes
forth to the battlefield with Israel's volunteer forces (1 Samuel 4-6). It had not
always been at Shiloh, as other texts make clear: Josh 8:30-35 (Shechem) and
Judges 20 (Bethel); and did not return there after the Philistine captivity:
1 Samuel 7 and 10 and 2 Samuel 6 (Qiryath-yearim, Mizpah). As the portable
throne of the Divine Suzerain of all the earth, it occupied the holiest place in
the Tabernacle or "Tent of Meeting," the Divine King's portable palace.

Whether there (as presupposed in the final phase of land allotment, at Shiloh in Josh 18:1) or traveling (as presupposed in Judg 20:27; cf. 1 Sam 7:16), the Ark was the place of highest legitimate oracular inquiry. There Yahweh spoke the commands necessary to the undertaking of war in this early period. See now Fritz Stolz, *Jahwes und Israels Kriege: Kriegstheorien und Kriegsfahrungen im Glauben des Alten Israels*.

The Ark that was later installed in the Holy of Holies of the magnificent Jerusalem Temple was surmounted by the awesome figures of the Cherubim, where the sight could be a most evocative one (Isa 6:1-8). The monarchy had brought massive changes. The rise of a large and permanent military establishment, concurrent with the flowering of the new Jerusalem cultus had meant that the Ark went into semi-retirement, so to speak, seldom going forth except on high holy days. The older ritual reenactments of the conquest came to have less and less to do with the convenantal revival of ethic. At the same time, in the matter of divination before battle, the kings beginning with David were scrupulous about making their wars look holy (see the story of Micaiah ben Imlah in 1 Kings 22), but the Ark stayed at home, far too valuable now as a symbol of national unity to be risked by carrying it into battle. After the account of Absalom's rebellion (2 Samuel 15-19), it rapidly drops from view, except when its presence must be assumed in connection with the reconstruction of the Jerusalem liturgy. See Cross, *CMHE*, especially chaps. 4-6, 79-144.

In the priestly lore that was at last assembled to serve, it was hoped, as constitution for the restored community after the disaster of 587 B.C., the focus of attention was on the Ark as divine throne, which meant above all the seat of mercy and place of annual atonement.

If then the symbolic value of the Ark changed with the rise of monarchial institutions and ideology, this probably explains why the Ark is (1) inseparable from the conquest period and (2) mentioned most frequently in passages that are dependent upon liturgical action at some place other than Jerusalem.

But the material was at last assembled by Jerusalem personnel. And those personnel were very interested in the holy object, to which in this chapter a distinctive modifier clings. It is not simply the war palladium of the Divine Warrior, nor yet essentially the throne of the Divine Forgiver. It was rather the one place where you could be sure to find a copy of the "constitution." See Deut 31:26.

Yahweh your God. Inasmuch as Ark-like objects are known in other religions (see COMMENT), it is the Covenant with "your God Yahweh" that makes this Ark distinctive. The relationship behind the Covenant was established by virtue of the individual's decision to accept the offer which is extended with far better motivation than coercion (Exod 20:2; Josh 24:2-13).

the Levite-priests. Literally, "the priests, the Levites." The second half of the expression can hardly be explained away as a late annotation. It is a distinctive label, the grammatical peculiarity of which is obscured by the usual rendering: "the levitical priests." It is clear enough from references to their duties and prerogatives in Deut 17:9,18; and 27:9 that the phrase does not refer to a large class of lower-ranking personnel that served in the Second Temple as some have alleged. Certainly in the Josianic period and later, the label "the priests, the Levites" might mean "priests claiming true Levite lineage as opposed to other priests." John Bright, *IB* 2 (1953) 564. Is this what it meant in the original Deuteronomic milieu? Probably not.

In Dtn the phrase stands in contrast with other references to "the tribe of Levi" or "the Bene Levi," or "the Levites." (Deuteronomy 18:1 can be read "the Levite-priests out of all the tribe of Levi," restoring an *m* after *lywm*.)

According to Deut 10:8, it is "the tribe of Levi" (in Deut 31:25 "the Levites") which has the important responsibility of transporting the Ark of Yahweh's Covenant. This association between the Ark and the Levites in the milieu of Deuteronomy cannot be dissociated from the sustained militancy of Deuteronomy, its "martial spirit" which G. von Rad found to be such an imposing feature of the book. See his *Studies in Deuteronomy* (1953) and subsequent works.

In contrast to the general category of "the Levites" or "all the tribe of Levi," Dtn also uses the unusual collocation "the Levite-priests." This label, Wright argued, refers to a smaller group of high-ranking clergy who officiated at the altars of the various sanctuaries which were to be found in many of the towns, prior to Josiah's reform. From study of the list of Levitical towns in chap. 21, it becomes clear that a rivalry of two old priestly houses, one claiming descent ultimately from Aaron and the other from Moses, continued throughout the First Temple period. See Cross, *CHME*, especially chaps. 8, 10, and 11, 195-215, 274-287, and 293-325. The rivalry has in fact helped to shape the historical books in their final form. See below on "Eleazar" in 14:1 and "Phinehas" in 22:13,30,31.

What is the basis of Deuteronomy's distinction between "the priests, the Levites" and the great number of poor Levitical personnel scattered throughout the tribes? The latter Deuteronomy ranks with the widow, the orphans, and the stranger—as especially requiring the benevolence of the believer. In contrast to these rural and itinerant teacher-preachers, dispersed from one of the most militant of the early constituencies having roots in the pre-Mosaic Israel (Genesis 34 and cf. 49), there were the altar-clergy. These are called "the priests, the Levites." G. Ernest Wright, "The Levites in Deuteronomy," *VT* 4 (1954) 325-330. This is as far as Wright pursued the distinction in that article. The idea of the dispersed client-Levites as teacher-preachers in the period of the monarchy was rejected by some scholars because of the total lack of any direct references to them in the books of Samuel and Kings. We suggest, however, that there is a reason for this neglect, and that historical as well as genealogical distinctions within the category of Levitical persons will help to explain a tension that runs throughout the Dtr corpus, the tension between the prestigious character and high responsibility of "the priests, the Levites" and the repeated preoccupation in Dtn with the poverty of "the Levite." In an unpublished paper by Wright's student, Merlin Rehm, the problem is reviewed once again. Rehm proposes the theory that "the two names do not represent two different groups living and working at the same time, but they represent (essentially) the same group working at two different times. . . . The situation of the poor country Levite who is to be helped by the Israelites coming to the central sanctuary reflects the time between Jeroboam and Josiah." It also would reflect the decline or disappearance of the system of Levitical towns (see chap. 21). Regarding the other usage in Dtn "the priests, the Levites," since it cannot be derived from anything later, Rehm concludes that it must be older. It must stem from the heyday of Levitical prestige and responsibility—the pre-mon-archy period.

In striking contrast with the frequencies and usages in Dtn, there are amaz-ingly few references, in any form, to Levitical persons in Dtr. The title is "the Levite-priests" here and again in the brief report of the Shechem Valley Cove-nant (8:33). In these passages, it is the title of the more restricted and presti-gious group that has responsibility for the Ark, whereas in Dtn that respon-sibility was given to the whole militant tribe!

On the other hand, the larger class of Levites is mentioned in Joshua only to emphasize its unique base of support, having no self-contained territory (13:14,33; 14:3) but only residential privileges and access to pasturelands at towns scattered throughout the other divisions of the Bene Israel (14:4 and 21:1-42).

The surprising thing to note, after all this literary trouble to prepare for the assignment of Levitical towns in Joshua 21, is the almost total silence on the subject of Levites in all of Judges through 2 Kings! Levites are present at the recovery of the Ark from the Philistines in 1 Sam 6:15, and "all the Levites" transport the Ark during David's evacuation of Jerusalem in 2 Sam 15:24. Apart from these two passages, there is no other reference to Levites in Dtr except for a pair of contrasting stories at the end of the Book of Judges. In the first of those stories, a young client-Levite from the south (Bethlehem of Judah, in fact) finds employment at the Ephraimite Micah's place and is finally exploited at the far northern sanctuary of Dan (Judges 17-18). The pro-Judahite character of the story, with a bias against the itinerant Levite work-ing in the north, could hardly be clearer. The story comes from the Jerusalem establishment.

The story of Micah's Levite is followed in the final edition by the story of a well-heeled Levite from Ephraim who follows his offended concubine when she goes home to her father in Bethlehem. This Levite later mobilizes the entire might of the Bene Israel to avenge the gang-style rape and murder of his con-cubine (Judges 19-20). In this story the disapproval of those northern Levites who sought to avail themselves of "southern hospitality" is equally clear. The story makes sense if it was appended to Judges by Levites coming from the north but remaining unassimilated in the south, amid the mounting chaos that follows Josiah's death.

Where does all this leave "the Levite-priests" in Dtr 1? The title expresses a self-understanding of Jerusalem priests who were doing their best to implement the newly discovered Dtn and to compile a history of the nation in light of Dtn. But the radical torah-teaching client-Levites, with their old-style Mosaic militancy, are mentioned not at all, except to be dismissed in a polemical story. The Ark, however, continues to be of the highest significance as symbol of the Covenant which the Jerusalem king renewed.

follow it. The idiom is *hlk 'ḥr,* "to walk behind," describing here a liturgical procession. See Judg 2:12, where it means much more.

4. *Be very sure.* The syntax is disjunctive and the force is emphatic.

a distance between you and it. As in other religions, holy objects have a power, somehow akin to what the anthropologist calls "mana," which can manifest direct action of deity. In Yahwism the deity transcended this holiness in such a way that entertaining and edifying stories might be told about the Ark. Yahweh used his Ark both to refute Philistine superstition concerning it and to confound false Israelite optimism based on it (1 Samuel 4-7). Such attitudes were so deeply rooted from the early days that when, in the move to bring the old Ark to Jerusalem, Uzzah touched it to steady it behind the stumbling oxen, he died (2 Sam 6:6-9).

about a kilometer. 2,000 cubits=3,000 feet=⅝ of a mile. This is also a sabbath day's journey.

Hold position! Keep a constant distance from the Ark.

that you may know the route. The distance appears to be too great for this to be explained in terms of steep and dangerous riverbanks (Soggin, *Joshua*, 56). The narrator plays on the verb "to know." See below.

5. *Joshua said.* Presumably this speech takes place in a convocation of the tribes which followed from the work of the officers in vv 3 and 4. It is time to complete the preparations in anticipation of Yahweh's direct participation in the crossing.

Make yourselves ritually ready. Literally, "Make yourselves holy." That is, prepare to be in the presence of The Holy One; see 7:13 and Deut 23:13-15. Neither of the translations, "Sanctify" (*RSV*) or "Hallow" (*NEB*), does justice to the range of prescriptions, which includes abstinence from sexual activity and from certain foods as well as participation in purification rites (Exod 19:10-15; Num 11:18; and the story of Uriah in 2 Samuel 11). "Because the war was sacral, a sphere of activity in which Israel's God was present, the camp and warriors had to be ritually purified." Miller, *The Divine Warrior in Early Israel*, 157.

tomorrow. Hebrew *māḥār* is indefinitely future and can also mean "henceforth," or the like.

wonders. Hebrew *npl'wt* is a favorite of the Yahwist storytellers, as in the climax to the promise of Samson's birth, when Yahweh is titled "Wonder Worker." Judg 13:19, AB 6A, 218 and 222. Now that Joshua had given the warning and announced the promise, it was time for the procession to set forth.

6. *the Covenant-Ark.* In LXX, it is "the Ark of Yahweh's Covenant" (twice), but the divine name seems to be an addition. See also v 14.

7. *Yahweh said to Joshua.* The statement occurs six times in chaps. 1-6. See 1:1; 4:1; 4:15; 5:9; 6:2. Joshua acted upon Yahweh's initiative, not his own!

Today. Not in some indefinite "tomorrow." This is the second time the narrative has used the device of interruption. Yahweh resolves an ambiguity by giving specificity to the miracle-schedule that was "predicted" by Joshua in v 5. This day will be remembered as a decisive one. On the stylistic importance of time expressions like "today," see Simon J. DeVries, "Temporal Terms as Structural Elements in the Holy-War Tradition," *VT* 25 (1975) 80–105; and above, NOTE on 1:2.

I will begin to magnify. This promise will be fulfilled in 4:14. The reader is thus encouraged to ignore the Masoretic division between chaps. 3 and 4.

will know. Hebrew *yēdĕ'ûn.* An archaic "energic" form which retains its emphatic force. See also the second person form in v 10 and *yikkārētûn* in v 13. Each of these three is in a pausal position.

with you, as I was with Moses. This is the second occurrence of the promise in a Yahweh speech (see 1:5 and NOTE). For Dtr 1 this puts Joshua in a category quite distinct from that of the savior-judges whose stories follow his story. The stories of the judges give a certain legitimacy to the sociological description of them as charismatic leaders, although the meager references to the "spirit of Yahweh" cannot be used as uniformly positive evidence in that regard. See the discussion in *Judges,* AB 6A, 25-26, and NOTES on passages cited there. After Joshua, there are only two persons in the entire Deuteronomic corpus that came anywhere near his stature—King David and King Josiah. On the other hand, there is a clear basis for comparison with the so-called "minor judges" and Jephthah (Judges 10-12) in Josh 17:14-18 (probably from Dtr 2). See below.

8. *You.* Hebrew *'th,* where LXX reflects *'th,* "now." But it is Joshua who commands the people (v 9), not the priests. The syntax is disjunctive, with the independent pronoun preceding the finite verb for emphasis. It was important to specify that Joshua would be giving orders, even to the priests; unlike Moses he was not related to any of the priestly houses.

waters. Mentioned ten times in chaps. 3 and 4. The old mythic overtones of *nhr,* "river," are almost completely lost, in part because of the use of the plainer term "waters."

stand still. The verb is *'md,* used in a significant pattern: introduced by the officers (v 4, "Hold position!"), used by Yahweh (v 8), repeated by Joshua (v 13, "stand up"), and again by the narrator (v 16).

9. *words of.* The form is plural construct of *dbr,* in usage which is very reminiscent of the use of "word" in the sense of "commandment" or "stipulation." See especially the reference to "ten words" in Deut 4:13 and 10:4. Joshua's usage is no doubt a reflection of liturgical usage in covenant-renewal ceremonies of the early period.

your God. As above in v 3, the possessive pronoun has only covenantal legitimacy.

10. *By this you will know!* Hebrew *bz't td'wn* is a distinctive phrase, elsewhere used only once in the Old Testament, Num 16:28, where Moses is the speaker and he will leave it to Yahweh to authenticate the fact that Yahweh has indeed sent him. The crossing of the Jordan River will be a sign? Yes, and more. As in the past, the experience of the Sovereign's gracious initiative will ground the renewal of the relationship. The Hebrew verb *yd'* has a wide semantic range: from "comprehend" to "experience." But the meaning that best fits a text drawing upon a covenant-liturgy source is the act of recognition in the establishment of relationships between Sovereign and subjects. This makes plausible narrative based on liturgical action, precisely because the liturgical action is derived from historical experience as interpreted by common-sense wisdom in the treaty form.

El the Living. Hebrew *'l ḥy* appears to be poetic (no definite article), referring to the old god of the pre-Mosaic league. Cf. *'ēl 'ĕlôhê yisrā'ēl,* "El, God of

Israel," in Gen 33:20. Freedman, private communication. The appellative '*l ḥy* occurs in parallelism with "Yahweh Sebaoth" in Ps 84:2-3. Cf. also Ps 42:3,9; Hos 2:1; Job 27:2. For "the living God" (*'lhym ḥyym*), see Deut 5:23; 1 Sam 17:26,36; Jer 10:10; 23:36. On the relation between Canaanite or Amorite El and Yahweh, see above, NOTE on 1:1. This archaic appellative immediately evokes a contrast with the annually dying and rising deity of the pagan context.

is in your midst. For the syntax of the non-verbal sentence here, compare Lev 21:23; Gen 8:9; 25:28; Exod 10:10; 17:16; Deut 3:19. Andersen, *The Hebrew Verbless Clause in the Pentateuch*, 87.

he will utterly dispossess. The Hebrew infinitive absolute reinforces adverbially the finite form: *wĕhôrēš yôrîš*. What is apparently envisaged is an act of divine expropriation modeled upon similar human actions in efforts at land reform. The God of Sinai had said "All the earth is mine" (Exod 19:5) to those who would enter into the Covenant with him. See also Judg 1:27-33, which catalogues tribal failures at land reform.

Canaanites. The Greeks called them "Phoenicians," a name related to the purple dye produced from the murex shellfish and exported to all parts of the Mediterranean. Whether the name was first applied to the land or the people is not clear; but gentilics usually derive from place names. "Canaanite" can be used as a blanket word to cover the entirety of the highly mixed local population at the time of the Yahwist movement, most of whom, however, spoke the same language. Because a major livelihood was trade, "Canaanite" came much later to mean "merchant." In the distinction between "Canaanites" and six other relatively newcomer peoples, we have the background of the remarkable maritime merchant empire later based at Tyre and Sidon.

When the term "Canaanites" contrasts with "Amorites," as it does in this list, it probably refers to the older centers of indigenous population located primarily in the plains of the coast, Esdraelon, and the Jordan valley. This is the first name in a list of seven nations, or better, "peoples," granted each name is a gentilic formation. See above, fourth NOTE on 1:2. The Old Testament has some twenty-one such lists, more or less stereotyped (Gen 10:15-18=1 Chr 1:13-16; 15:19-21; Exod 3:8,17; 23:23; 33:2; 34:11; Deut 7:1; 20:17; Josh 3:10; 9:1; 11:3; 12:8; 24:11; Judg 3:5; 1 Kgs 9:20=2 Chr 8:7; 1 Chr 1:13-16; 2 Chr 8:7; Ezra 9:1; Neh 9:8). In these lists the names and order fluctuate. The total of seven is a mnemonic device. "The century of confusion which followed the disintegration of the Hyksos suzerainty left the country open to a migration of mixed peoples who set up literally dozens of tiny principalities and city-states." McKenzie, *The World of the Judges*, 23-24.

The Amarna archive (c. 1400-1350) is especially instructive. From those 379 documents it is clear that a half-dozen city-states dominate central and southern hill country and plains: from north to south these were the "realms" of Biridiya of Megiddo, Labayu of Shechem (by far the largest domain, ranging to points bordering the next two), Milkilu of Gezer, Abdu-Hepa of Jerusalem, Zimreda of Lachish, and Shuwardata of Keilah. This is the situation about 150 years before the "seven nations." These were only the most powerful overlords. A sharper focus on the political fragmentation of the land is provided in the list of some thirty-one kings west of the Jordan who lost their thrones (Josh 12:7-24). With one or two exceptions, the names in this list do not have "national" status outside the Bible in the literature of the second millennium. They had only recently become nations in the very turmoil that preceded the formation of Israel. "The 'nations' had their bases in the various city-states which did not become a part of the Israelite confederation. . . ." Mendenhall, *Ten Gen*, 155. They represent a fluctuating political reality which did not fully disappear until the establishment of the Davidic empire.

Hittites. In the list of the seven peoples, this term is probably to be understood in relation to the Hittites of Hebron, Beersheba, Bethel, Jerusalem, and elsewhere. See NOTE on 1:4. That this list of cities where Hittites lived is far from complete is suggested by the presence of Anatolian traditions in sanctuary architecture at Tell-Balatah (Wright, *Shechem: Biography of a Biblical City*, 97, 107, and 121) and in linguistic and cultural connections with the next group in the list.

Hivites. For extended discussion of this people, see the story of Gibeon in 9:3-27 and NOTES, especially on 9:7. Here it will suffice to indicate the explicit biblical connection with Shechem (Gen 34:2) and the Lebanese Beqa (Josh 11:3), as well as the tetrapolis headed by Gibeon.

Perizzites. Identity uncertain. The term may be ethnic (Hurrian) or appellative (cf. *pĕrāzôt*, "unwalled villages," Esth 9:19; Ezek 38:11; Zech 2:8). Stylistic considerations favor the latter in passages such as 16:10 (LXX), Judg 1:4, and Gen 34:30, where they are paired and presumably contrasted with Canaanites (see *Judges*, AB 6A, 54). Where did they come from? Paul W. Lapp argued that they were to be found among the population of Canaan at the dawn of the EB/MB period and descended from invaders who came in waves throughout the Early Bronze Age and during the dark age between the collapse of EB and the rise of MB (c. 2300-1900 B.C.). Specifically he sought to identify them as the folk who introduced the distinctive shaft tomb burial customs, with some artifactual evidence to trace their background in the central Asian regions of Tashkent and Samarkand. Paul W. Lapp, *The Dhahr Mirzbaneh Tombs*, 86-116; *Biblical Archaeology and History* (New York: World Publishing Company, 1969) 164; "Bab Edh-Dhra', Perizzites and Emim," in *Jerusalem Through the Ages*, 1-25. Most scholars continue to find better arguments for the roots of the MB I culture in northern Syria and Mesopotamia, among a general "Amorite" movement. In their view the population groups in question would be related to the earlier wave of seminomadic people from the fringes of Syria, as distinct from the later wave of migration which introduced the distinctive urban culture of MB IIA. William G. Dever, "The Peoples of Palestine in the Middle Bronze I Period," *HTR* 64 (1971) 197-226; "The Beginning of the Middle Bronze Age in Syria-Palestine," in *Mag Dei*, 3-38.

Girgashites. The most obscure of the seven, these "have been found in both Ugaritic and Egyptian sources of the Late Bronze Age, and constitute therefore a historically attested social group of some sort which we cannot further define or locate." Mendenhall, *Ten Gen*, 145.

Amorites. Hebrew *'ămōrî* is etymologically "Westerner," a meaning that survives in Judg 1:34-35 and 6:10. While the term could also be used as a synonym or substitute for "Canaanite," it has here a well-attested narrower meaning: cities in the central mountains and the kingdoms of north and central Transjordan that the Old Testament calls "Amorite." These cities are smaller and farther apart than the great Canaanite centers of the coastal plain and the valleys of Esdraelon and the Jordan. See further 13:10-13,21 and NOTES.

Jebusites. People of Jerusalem. See 15:8; 18:28; Judg 19:10-11. Virtually, the entire linguistic and cultural rainbow represented by the five preceding names was to be found in the Jerusalem of Joshua's day, which was then known by a clan name as "Jebus." Linguistically, the name correlates with Amorite *yabusum* and the name of a town in Transjordan, Jabesh(-Gilead). Herbert B. Huffmon, *Amorite Personal Names in the Mari Texts,* 38 and 178. The older name, however, was Urusalim, as known from the fourteenth-century Amarna letters and the mid-third-millennium documents from Ebla. In the Amarna period Jerusalem had a native-born king bearing a name compounded with that of a well-known Hurrian goddess (*Abdu-Hepa,* "servant of Hepa"). It has been suggested that the Jebusites were basically Hurrian (E. A. Speiser, *Cahiers d'histoire mondiale* 1 [Paris, 1953] 321), but this is unlikely. Despite early successes against "Jerusalem" claimed in Joshua 10 and Judg 1:8, a new group had arrived which could not be evicted by Benjamin, according to Judg 1:21. The Jebusites were "possibly allies or vassals of the Hittites." Benjamin Mazar, *The Mountain of the Lord,* 149. With King David's capture of the city, still another name for it will acquire pride of place in hymnic material: Zion.

Because of continuous and dense occupation across the centuries, not many structures from the Jebusite period had been discovered in the limited areas which were available for excavation south of today's Old City in Jerusalem before 1967. Mazar can mention only "some foundations of the eastern slope of the hill and remains of supporting walls on the higher slopes . . ." (ibid., 50). However, recent discoveries by Yigal Shiloh add substantially to our understanding. Y. Shiloh, "Jerusalem: the City of David, 1978," *IEJ* 28 (1978) 274-276; "City of David Excavations, 1978," *BA* 42 (1979) 165-171; "Jerusalem: the City of David, 1979," *IEJ* 29 (1979) 244-246, Plate 33.

11. *Here is.* Hebrew *hinnēh.*

the Covenant-Ark; the Lord of all the earth is. Hebrew *'rwn hbryt 'dwn kl h'rṣ* is ungrammatical, unless there is a major pause. Misunderstanding at this point led to confusion in vv 14 and 17. There LXX supports variant readings where MT has "Ark" and "Covenant" in ungrammatical combination. But each occurrence may be understood as the result of contamination, the longer readings being influenced by the far more frequent shorter readings with which the context swarms. R. G. Boling, "Some Conflate Readings in Joshua-Judges," *VT* 16 (1966) 293-298.

passing. Hebrew *'ōbēr.* The participle indicates that the action is current and not to be translated as infinitive as in EVV.

12. *Take for yourselves now.* The verse seems to be a fragment of an instruction. It very possibly once continued with a command to carry twelve

stones into the river to provide firm footing for the bearers of the Ark. This thread of the story resumes in 4:4.

one man from each tribe. It is emphatic, *'yš 'ḥd 'yš 'ḥd lšbṭ.* Literally, "one man, one man, to a tribe."

13. Though not directly quoting it, this verse clearly reflects the language of Exod 14:21-22 and 15:8. "The miracle of the Red Sea is realized once again in the present in the cult" (Soggin, *Joshua,* 60). In the cultic action the reenactment would precede and thus motivate the reaffirmation of the ethical guidelines. The cultic action was not at first an end in itself. The historian is not commending the defunct cultic experience as such. Rather, the historian is using cultic texts as, apparently, the best available sources for telling this part of the story.

one heap! Again in v 16. Hebrew *nēd 'eḥād* may be secondary here, since it is not found in the Old Greek. Cross, *CMHE,* 138 n. 90. The word for heap (*nēd*) shows that the text has definitely been influenced by the Song of the Sea in Exod 15:8. Albright, *YGC,* 45.

14-16. The language and style suddenly become expansive and full in an effort to match the majesty of the event. But the lengthy recapitulation was not clear to one scribe whose marginal comment has been drawn into the text, interrupting the rhetorical flow at the end of v 15.

14. *the Covenant-Ark.* It is "the ark of the Lord's covenant" in LXX. See 3:6 and NOTE.

15. *at the brink.* Reference to the position of the porters "at the brink" turns back upon the same expression in v 8; this *inclusio* indicates we are near the end of a unit. But the rhetorical force of this repetition is obscured by the parenthetical contribution of a later commentator. The commentator was trying to explain a contradiction between this unit, where the Ark-bearers seem to stand near the riverbank, and the next one, where they clearly stand in midstream. How could this have been? Answer: In this first unit, they had entered the water but not the river channel. They could do this because the river was in flood. In fact, during most of the year, the Jordan can easily be forded (Judg 3:28; 8:4; 1 Sam 13:7; 2 Sam 17:24). See COMMENT.

The Jordan overflows its banks. The overflow is associated with late winter to early spring, when the river is at its fullest, swollen by the long winter rains first and later by the melting of snows in the Anti-Lebanon range.

harvest. Early summer is when the first crops come in and the river is still high. LXX secondarily specifies "wheat harvest."

The scribe who contributed this harmonizing parenthesis understood that the miracle began when they stepped into the floodwaters, before entering the riverbed proper. This has the effect of heightening the miracle. Yet it is proper to ask how the stopping of the river might have occurred. The collapse of very soft limestone banks temporarily damming this meandering stream is recorded for 7 December 1267 and again in 1906. Preceded by an earthquake, it was observed again on 11 July 1927. See John Garstang, *Joshua-Judges,* 136. There is one long geological fault line which has created the valley of the northern lakes, the Jordan River, the Dead Sea, the Arabah, and Gulf of Aqabah in the south. It is in fact not hard to understand how some have taken the present form of the story to reflect a temporary damming of the Jordan in order to accommodate an extensive liturgical procession. Hans-Joachim Kraus, "Gilgal. Ein Beitrag zur Kulturgeschichte Israels," *VT* 1 (1951) 181-189; *Gottesdienst in Israel* (München: Kaiser Verlag, 1962) 179-189=*Worship in Israel* (Richmond, VA, 1966). The subsequent discussion is well represented in J. A. Soggin, "Gilgal, Passah und Landnahme . . . ," *VT*Sup 16 (1966) 263-277; *Joshua*, 43-76.

16. *stood still.* Thus fulfilling the prediction of Joshua (v 13).

Adam. Also called "Adamah." Map B, 112. The site is Tell ed-Dāmiyeh, just south of the mouth of the Jabboq, some 27 km north of Jericho in an area which was militarily restricted at the time of our search for a number of Transjordan sites in the summer of 1975. It is known from previous surveys to show evidence for occupation in Late Bronze II and Iron I-II. Glueck, *AASOR* 25-28 for 1945-1949 (1951), Part I, 329-334. The place may be mentioned in Hos 6:7; see Andersen and Freedman, AB 24.

Zarethan. A strategic and very important town, to judge from its appearance as a point of reference in the list of Solomonic provinces (1 Kgs 4:12) and in the notice about the casting of bronze implements for the Jerusalem Temple "between Succoth (=Tel Deir 'Allah) and Zarethan" (1 Kgs 7:46). The Jerusalem Talmud (*Soṭa* 7.5) locates Zarethan 19.2 km from Adam, which fits well the great site of Tell es-Sa'idiyeh, just 18 km north of the Dāmiyeh bridge. Nelson Glueck, "Three Israelite Towns in the Jordan Valley: Zarethan, Succoth, Zaphon," *BASOR* 90 (1943) 2-23. Some have held out for a west-bank site, in the vicinity of Qarn Ṣarṭabeh, where however the recent Israeli survey shows nothing between the Chalcolithic and Iron ages at the site and no other likely prospect in the vicinity. P. Bar-Adon, Claire Epstein, et al., *Judaea, Samaria, and the Golan: Archaeological Survey, 1967–1968*, 102-104. For the archaeology of Tell es-Sa'idiyeh, see the various brief reports of the excavator. J. P. Pritchard, "Excavating a Biblical Site in Jordan: Joshua's and Solomon's Zarethan Identified," *Illustrated London News* (28 March 1964), 487-490, figs. 1-15; "Reconnaissance in Jordan," *Expedition* 6 (1964) 3-9; "Excavations at Tel es-Sa'idiyeh," *ADAJ* 8-9 (1964) 95-98; "Excavations at Tell es-Sa'idiyeh," *Archaeology* 18 (1965) 292-294; "A Cosmopolitan Culture of the Late Bronze Age," *Expedition* 7 (1965) 26-33; "The Palace at Tell es-Sa'idiyeh," *Expedition* 11 (1968) 20-22. See also J. E. Huesman, "Tell es-Sa'idiyeh," *RB* 75 (1968) 236-238.

Especially noteworthy is the massive waterworks at Tell es-Sa'idiyeh, with impressive parallel at Boghazkale in Turkey, which is suggestive of Late Bronze Age influence from Anatolia. Mendenhall, *Ten Gen*, 158.

If this identification of Zarethan holds up, then the stretch of river from there to Adam covers in fact the natural point of entry to the north-central hill country, the area which centers in Shechem. This has led to some interesting speculation. "We have here an echo of . . . tradition that the entrance into the land was not only by way of Jericho, but along the whole length of the Jordan from Adam the city until Jericho. . . . It seems reasonable to assume that one of the entrances in one of the stages, in one of the waves, was from there to

Shechem. . . ." Yigael Yadin, "Military and Archaeological Aspects of the Conquest of Canaan in the Book of Joshua," in *El Ha'ayin*, Third Edition, I (Jerusalem: 1965) 7-8.

A more sophisticated but less convincing hypothesis is that the entire tradition "from Shittim to Gilgal" is the transformation of a prior tradition "from Succoth to Shechem." Joanne N. M. Wijngaards, "The Dramatization of Salvific History in the Deuteronomic Schools," *Oudtestamentische Studiën* 16 (1969) 1-132.

the Arabah. As used here it is the longer rift which contains the Jordan River and Dead Sea. More often the term refers to the southern extension of the rift, from the Dead Sea to Aqabah. This is the ancient Atika in the list of Ramesses III (Papyrus Harris I, 408). See *ANET²*, 260-262, for references.

The people crossed. The goal is attained. It is the end of a literary unit.

opposite Jericho. The most satisfactory point, considering all indicators, would be the ford that Arabs call al-Maghtas, 12 km southeast from T. es-Sultan and 13 km due west from T. el-Hammam. See Map C, 137.

3:17 - 4:8. This unit appears to be separate from the main story by virtue of a vocabulary that is otherwise rare in these historical books and a special interest in the twelve stones at Gilgal. The various approaches to this complex section from the standpoint of documentary analysis are well summarized in Wright's discussion above, 56-57 in the Introduction.

The most up-to-date effort to trace the Tetrateuch sources in this material is by F. Langlamet, *Gilgal et les récits de la traversée du Jourdain (Jos. III-IV)*. He distinguishes two major redactional phases, drawing upon a variety of materials and transformations.

Langlamet's detailed analysis has had high heuristic value; but it is difficult to understand how elements with such very different meanings in the reconstructed originals could all contribute finally to a single configuration. The reconstructions are in fact only possible on the basis of older methodological assumptions in literary analysis and in the evolution of religion that most scholars find increasingly inadequate.

When all is said and done, the bulk of the peculiarities in this section is accommodated by the observation of the basic dichotomy of the hypothetical sources, an observation that critical scholars have often made. In 3:1 - 4:18 there are essentially two blocks (not interwoven "strands") of material. One block told of the crossing "from Shittim to Gilgal" without highlighting the latter or even mentioning the twelve-stone memorial (3:1-16 + 4:10-18). Into this was inserted another block (3:17 - 4:8) which made up for that lack. The first and major version (Dtr 1) supportive of the Jerusalem establishment would not need to mention the Gilgal memorial at this point. This is quite comparable to the similarly low status of Shechem in the south, despite the contribution which Shechem clearly made in the formation of Dtn!

The insertion of a preformed "parallel" out of another file (Dtr 2) does what that redactor characteristically does elsewhere, tells more of the truth: Gilgal had very early been a *national shrine*, with a public reminder there visible of the wonder-working God of "all Israel," not merely the west-bank Israel of the late monarchy period.

The only direct reference to the stones in the middle of the Jordan, which is supposed by many critics to be a rival etiological tradition (4:9), now reads as an explanatory parenthesis which makes sense because the redactor was working with largely preformed units.

It is advisable to enter at this point a caveat concerning P in chaps. 3-5. Because of the obvious interest in cultic institutions (Ark, circumcision, Passover), these chapters are alleged to show the hand of an exilic or post-exilic editor who had much in common with those who gave us the "Priestly Code" in the books of Genesis through Numbers. In addition to the arguments marshalled against this notion by Wright (Introduction, 57-67), there is now strong linguistic evidence against (or lack of evidence for!) a post-587 date for the Priestly Code. On the basis of the books of 1 and 2 Chronicles, Ezra-Nehemiah, and Ezekiel (i.e. indisputably exilic and post-exilic literature) and rabbinic texts, it emerges that "P is totally unaware and independent of the terminology characteristic of distinctly exilic and post-exilic literature, in regard to fundamental priestly practices and regulations." Avi Hurvitz, "The Evidence of Language in Dating the Priestly Code," RB 81 (1974) 24-56. The material in Dtr 1 and Dtr 2, reflects only pre-exilic archives, not later ones. There are, on the other hand, significant linguistic contrasts to be noted between Dtr 1 and Dtr 2, on the basis of Hurvitz's study. See below on 9:15; 13:15,23; 15:12; and 18:20.

3:17. *The priests carrying Yahweh's Covenant-Ark.* This excerpt from a parallel telling of the story starts well past the beginning, and so the transition here is abrupt. Since both 3:8 and 3:15 specify that the waters stop flowing when the priests step in at the brink of the stream, the redactor assumes that the priests have here already moved to midstream. The difference in any case is minimal (perhaps no more than 7 to 15 meters), if the present narrow channel is any reliable indicator. The Jordan is but a narrow ditch compared, say, to the majestic Nile. It is, in fact, not easy to see how anyone who had actually seen the Jordan would compare its crossing with the crossing of a large papyrus marsh, much less a Red Sea! Actually, in the present context the focus is not on the miracle or even the crossing of the people. There would be many more problems on the shore than in the river. The center of attention is the Ark and the twelve stones carried to the other side, from the middle of the river. See Menashe Har-El, "The Pride of the Jordan—The Jungle of the Jordan," *BA* 41 (1978) 65-75.

stood. The usage of '*md* here and in 4:10 has nothing to do with the usage noted above in 3:8,13, and 16.

firmly. Hebrew *hkn* is the infinitive absolute used adverbially, a stylistic nicety not reflected in LXX which seems not to have understood, perhaps because of the old-fashioned spelling, without a vowel letter (see NOTE on 4:3). Thus LXX obscures the point, which has to do precisely with the irreplaceable value of the Covenant-Ark to the incoming Yahwists.

on dry ground. Hebrew *bhrbh.* Compare Exod 14:22 which uses a synonym *bybšh.*

in the middle of the Jordan. Hebrew *btwk hyrdn.* The transition from one unit to another was easily effected by insertion of these two words.

nation. Hebrew *gôy,* not strictly synonymous with *'ām,* "people," as argued by E. A. Speiser, "People and Nation in the Old Testament," *JBL* 79 (1960) 157-163. Speiser assumes an overarching, uniform pattern of biblical thought which it is impossible to maintain any longer. The word *gôy* is very rarely used with reference to Israel in the Deuteronomic corpus. In Joshua-Judges, excluding the archaic poetic couplet in Josh 10:13 where the *gôy* may not refer to Israel at all, there are a mere five occurrences (see Josh 4:1; 5:6,8; Judg 2:20). The distribution in Deuteronomy is significant; *gôy* is found twice in the introduction to the larger corpus (Deut 4:6 and 34). It occurs again in 9:14 where, after the Horeb rebellion of the "stiff-necked people," Yahweh wills to make Moses into a *gôy* that is mightier and greater than Israel. But the context here is a distinctive unit, which Von Rad compared form-critically to Deuteronomy 1-3. Von Rad, *Deuteronomy,* 77. Thus we may assign Deut 9:14 to the historical corpus (or even to J) and not to the nuclear Dtn. For otherwise in Dtn Israel is never a *gôy.* Not once. Deuteronomy 26:5 (the famous credo) recalls that in Egypt "your father became a great *gôy";* but the outcome of the covenant ceremony in which one recites the credo is that "you will become a people (*'ām*) consecrated to Yahweh"! Finally in Deut 32:38, in the archaic Song of Moses in the indictment form, Israel is indeed a *gôy,* "without understanding." The reason for this distribution in Deuteronomy is not far to seek; Israel in Dtn was first of all and above all Yahweh's *'ām* ("people") and as such was to be Yahweh's answer to the problem of the *gôyîm,* ("nations"). Yet what had begun as the covenantal *'ām* had itself become a *gôy;* and for Dtr 1 there could be no turning back. Yet this historian very rarely referred to Israel as a *gôy.* In fact the word is used so consistently in a pejorative sense, for the enemies of Yahweh and Israel, that it will be a good idea to be alert for double meaning when Israel is called a *gôy,* and to watch to see what synonyms or parallel words cluster with it. Focus is here clearly on the concept of the entry of the *entire nation,* and the reader momentarily forgets about the Ark, which presumably is still out there in midstream.

crossed . . . crossed. This repetition signals a heightened interest in the verb *'br* which will be used six times in this section. See 4:1,3 ("take them across" ="cause them to cross"), 5 ("move out"), 7, 8 (twice).

4:1. *the entire nation.* Repetition of the long phrase using this word yields a chiastic arrangement of clauses, and indicates that the narrator is here more interested in achieving rhetorical effect than in avoiding redundancy. Verse 1a is missing from LXX^L, but that reflects a sizable haplography.

Yahweh said to Joshua. It was important to emphasize repeatedly the divine initiative in these events.

2. *twelve.* The numeral occurs five times in vv 1-8, thus driving home the lesson that the entire nation was represented in the events under Joshua's leadership.

3. *were firm.* Hebrew *hkyn* here seems to be infinitive absolute (normally spelled without vowel letter *hkn*); as indeed LXX understood it (*hetoimous*).

twelve stones. Compare the "twelve standing-stones for the twelve tribes of Israel," commemorating the Covenant at Sinai in Exod 24:4.

Take them across with you. Twelve stones from the middle of the river will direct attention to the miracle which had happened when the Covenant-Ark first entered the land.

deposit them. For the legitimating story (foundation legend) of a national sanctuary, this is distinctly low-key. Here the old story serves another purpose.

at the place where you camp. Hebrew *bmlwn 'šr tlynw*, literally, "the lodging place where you lodge." The noun is repeated in v 8, but is not used again in Joshua-Judges. The verbal root is rare in Dtr (Josh 3:1; 6:11; 8:9; Judg 18:2), except for eleven occurrences in the tragicomic story of the Levite and his concubine (Judg 19:4,6,7,9 [*bis*],10,11,13,15,20; 20:4), which was put in place by Dtr 2.

4. *called.* The Hebrew idiom is *wyqr' 'l.*

he had appointed. Hebrew *hēkîn* is the finite form in an obvious wordplay with the infinitive *hākîn*, "firm," in the preceding verse. The antecedent of this verbal action must be the imperative sentence fragment noted above in 3:12, where the beginning of a command is all that survives; the account of its implementation has been lost. The idea in the final edition is that Joshua turns to the same twelve men whom he had previously appointed to carry stones into the river from the east bank to make a platform for the porters of the Ark. The same twelve men are now directed to return from the west bank to midstream and bring back twelve stones. They are to do this for a poetic-didactic purpose, as stated in the following verse.

6. The first half of the verse is an old didactic saying, around which the story has been told. The general catechetical form of vv 6 and 7, and comparisons with similar recitations or liturgical responses (Exod 12:26-27; 13:14-15; Deut 6:20-25), has been stressed by J. A. Soggin, "Kultätiologische Sagen und Katachese im Hexateuch," *VT* 10 (1960) 341-347.

So that this may be. Hebrew *lm'n thyh z't* may be taken either as a clause of purpose or of result. It is not the common idiom *hyh l-*, "become."

a sign. Hebrew *'wt*, occurring nearly eighty times in the Old Testament, has a broad semantic range: (1) referring to a prophetic sign-act, for example, Ezek 4:1-3; (2) referring to an event predicted by a prophet as "sign," for example, 1 Sam 10:1,7,9 and Isa 38:7; (3) referring to an event predicted but which consists of miraculous, extraordinary happenings, for example, the plagues and wonders in Egypt, recounted in Exod 4-11; (4) referring to an event not connected with prophecy, but a miraculous deed performed by Yahweh alone, for example, in theophany stories such as Judg 6:11-24; (5) referring to an event in the heavens, for example, Jer 10:2 and Gen 9:12-17; (6) referring to a cultic practice or regulation, for example, Gen 17:11; (7) referring to an event in the *Heilsgeschichte*, or an object which recalls the same, for example, Josh 4:6. Long, *The Problem of Etiological Narrative*, 65.

The word for "sign" is not used here in the sense that it has when it is paired with another wonder-word (*mptym*) in the old confession of faith (Deut 26:8) and where it refers to the traditions of the ten "smitings" (EVV "plagues") administered to Egypt through the agency of Moses and Aaron (Exodus 4-11). Here, rather, the word *'wt* refers to a physical reminder, a longstanding visual aid to historical memory.

your children. See especially the concern of Deut 6:2,7,20-25. Such education was no doubt the daily responsibility of "the sons of Levi" who are so pivotally important and especially deserving of benevolence throughout Dtn.

ask. Hebrew *yš'lwn*, another example of the old energic ending (see above on 2:8; 3:7,10,13). Children will be persistent, we might say pesty, with their questioning.

What are these stones . . . ? Compare the child's question in Deut 6:20— "What is the meaning of the testimonies and the statutes and the ordinances . . . ?"

to you. Inclusion of this phrase (see Textual Notes) transforms the question from a merely catechetical (memorizable) to a truly didactic (dialogical) one.

7. *waters were cut off before the Covenant-Ark.* This is the midpoint of the whole larger block of material from 3:1 - 5:12. Noth was surely perceptive when he argued that, since the waters disappear only once, there is only one basic tradition of the crossing that has been elaborated. He found that basic tradition to be represented in 4:1b-2, most of v 3, most of vv 8-10, vv 13, 18b,19-21a,23. This nuclear tradition explained the twelve Gilgal stones in relation to the Jordan crossing; vv 4-5 and 6-7 represent progressively later material. Noth, *Das Buch Joshua,* 31ff. Long, *The Problem of Etiological Narrative,* is a sympathetic updating of this view, but with a more truly critical approach to the significance of etiology (see 83).

reminder. Hebrew *zikkārôn.* On the theological career of the root *zkr,* see Brevard S. Childs, *Memory and Tradition.*

8. *commanded . . . instructed.* Here in parallel, to wrap up the unit, are two basic words for Levitical teaching method, construed with Yahweh as both sovereign and teacher: *ṣwh* and *dbr.*

campsite. Hebrew *mlwn,* an *inclusio* with the same word in v 3.

and deposited them. Likewise turning back upon v 3.

9. *Twelve other stones.* This is an editorial explanation. See above, Textual Note.

Joshua had set up. The past perfect tense in translation is clearly suggested by the disjunctive syntax. The antecedent is obscured by the lacuna, noted above, at the end of 3:12. The verse makes sense as a parenthetical explanation by an editor or commentator caught between two equally authoritative but somewhat disjointed units. This interpretation is preferable to the variations on the documentary hypothesis reviewed as problematical by Wright in the Introduction.

in the middle. It has been suggested that there is a relation between this midstream platform and the altar that is said to be "by the Jordan" in the odd story at the end of this era (22:7-34). Wijngaards, "The Dramatization of Salvific History in the Deuteronomic Schools," 5. This may be, but it will have to be argued on different grounds. The interesting point of comparison here is the emphasis on the midstream location in Joshua 4 and the lack of precision in locating the problematical altar either to the east or west of the river in chap. 22!

there to this day. An invisible underwater stone platform could scarcely have attained much symbolic value. Perhaps the redactor is manipulating the etiological formula to indicate that, in contrast to the defunct sanctuary at Gilgal, at least these stones are safely beyond the reach of vandals and secure from anyone seeking an easy source of building material. C. R. Conder also rejected the notion that the building of a monumental stone heap where it would never be seen could have made any sense. See his "Notes on the Antiquities of the Book of Joshua," *PEFQS* (1899) 161. But a practical stone platform is another matter and makes excellent sense as a subject of didactic interest here.

10-14. Despite the appearance of a hodgepodge here, there is a logic that holds things together. For one thing, the verb *'br* is used five more times. Such repetitions are not coincidental, but represent a pedagogical concern behind the formation of the narrative, making it easier to commit to memory and so to perpetuate.

10. *While the priests bearing the Ark continued standing.* After the interruption for recapitulation, with special attention to the Ark and the entry of the nation on the one hand, to the Ark and the Gilgal memorial on the other, the similarity with 3:17a makes this verse something special. It looks like the editorial device called "repetitive resumption," that has been studied in detail by Shemaryahu Talmon (paper presented to the Biblical Colloquium, 1970). He shows how, frequently, when the compiler inserts material, the last matter before the interruption is repeated at the end, most often in a slightly different form. The classic example is formed by the two lists of David's officials framing the old "Court History" in 2 Sam 8:15-18 and 20:23-26. A good example in Joshua-Judges is the notice of Joshua's death and burial (Josh 24:29-31 and Judg 2:6-9). See also the statement "and the land was at rest from war" (Josh 11:23, cf. 14:15). See also our NOTE on the minor-judge formula in Judg 15:20 and 16:31. *Judges,* AB 6A, 252. This device will be found frequently in the Book of Joshua.

the people hurried across. Or "crossed hurriedly." Hebrew *wymhrw h'm wy'brw* forms a verbal hendiadys.

11-14. Here, in stark contrast to its wider context, there is no mention of "the Jordan" or its "waters."

11-12. After the repeated statements to the effect that all the people, the entire nation, had crossed over, the specific mention of the three Transjordan tribes appears somewhat superfluous. In that respect these verses go with 1:12-18. Together with the story of these same tribes and the altar "by the Jordan" in 22:7-34, the passages form a framework in which we may recognize the hand of Dtr 2.

11. All is very orderly. The Ark reviews the parade through the water after which the people then line up to view the removal of the Ark to the west bank.

12. *in battle array.* As specified in 1:14.

before the Bene Israel. In chap. 22, the three Transjordan tribes are represented as even more emphatically distinct from the Bene Israel. See especially 22:9,11-13,32. But why the emphasis here? Are the three Transjordan tribes being presented here as the military escort, pending the full formation of the Yahweh army upon the performance of circumcision and observance of the Passover (5:2-12)? See Wilcoxen, "Narrative Structure and Cult Legend," 68. In any case the final redactor would emphasize that the initial west-bank successes of Yahwism were not won without the service and effectiveness of east-bank Yahwist militiamen. It was a contribution which Dtr 2 considered to have been seriously slighted by Dtr 1.

just as Moses had instructed them. This reference to the authority of Moses contrasts sharply with his absence in 3:1 - 4:8.

13. *contingents.* Not originally "thousands." The word *'elep* shows a complex semantic history. It is etymologically connected with "head of cattle," like the letter *'aleph,* implying that the term was originally applied to the village population unit in a pastoral-agricultural society. From that it came to mean the quota supplied by one village or "clan" (Hebrew *mišpāḥâ*) for the military muster. Originally, the contingent was quite small, five to fourteen men in the muster lists of Numbers 1 and 26, as shown conclusively by Mendenhall, "The Census Lists . . . ," *JBL* 77 (1958) 52-66. Finally the word became a technical term for a military unit of considerable size, which together with the use of the same word for the number "1,000" has obscured its semantic range. See *Judges,* AB 6A, 17, the stories of Gideon's "muster" (Judg 7:2-8), and the odds in the war with Benjamin (Judg 20:12-48).

before Yahweh. That is, before the Ark. It evokes the picture of the reviewing stand and the Commander in Chief reviewing the troops.

for the battle. We agree with Noth that the explicitly military expectation that suddenly appears here, in contrast to the wider context, most likely represents an older and independent piece of tradition. This is true of most Dtr 2 material.

14. *On that day.* Here is another "freighted time expression." See 1:2; 3:7; 8:30; 11:6.

Yahweh magnified Joshua. As promised in 3:7. This may be taken as a fair statement of the major theme in the primary edition of the material—Dtr 1. It is never said of anyone else.

people Israel. The translation is based on LXX which employs the noun *genous,* "people," as determinative, presumably to bracket out any specifically geographical or political sense of the name *Israel.* The use of *genous* in LXX where MT has no comparable word, which also occurs in 11:21, there, too, serves to define Israel as a people.

revered. The verbal root is *yr'* in a special sense for which "to fear" is most inadequate. With repetition of this verb, the verse points ahead to another climax, in 24:14.

Moses. This turns back upon 3:7, tightly closing off one rhetorical unit.

15-18. This concluding section is distinctive, both for a crucial item of vocabulary and its style, the best illustration in the book of what has been happily called a "hieratic recital." McKenzie, *The World of the Judges,* 49-50.

15. *Yahweh said to Joshua.* This introduces the third speech of Yahweh to Joshua in this larger unit. See 3:7 and 4:1.

16. *Testimony-Ark.* It is a distinctive expression, using for the only time in Joshua the Covenant-synonym *'ēdût.* Elsewhere in Dtr this word occurs only in 2 Kgs 11:12; but it is common in Psalms and in specifically priestly literature as alternative for *bĕrît.* Scholars have often deduced from the absence of the latter in P that the Sinai covenant is somehow less significant for P than for

other streams of Mosaic tradition. Nothing could be further from the truth, as now shown conclusively by Cross, *CMHE*, especially the section entitled, "The P System of Covenants," 295-321.

18. *the Jordan's waters returned*. The gates are closed. The divine king and his subjects have entered into the royal estate.

position. The word is a link with 3:3.

COMMENT

In dealing with material such as this section 3:1 - 4:18, there can be no substitute for a clear picture of the geography involved (see Plate I and Map C, 137) and accurate description. The Jordan, whose name means the Downcomer, is some 213 meters below sea level where it enters the Lake of Galilee; and from there south to the Dead Sea, 104 km away, it descends another 186 meters. The Jericho oasis, with its own abundant water source, is today several miles west of the river, in the broad outer valley known to Arabs as the Ghor (and called in Greek, *aulōn*, "Groove"). The primordial channel varies from two to fourteen miles (3.3 to 23 km) in width, as one travels north to the Galilee. It was most densely settled in antiquity along the east bank. This has recently been shown most dramatically by the Jordan Valley Survey, begun in the spring of 1975, which has more than doubled the number of known archaeological sites in the northern valley proper, between the Lake of Galilee and the Jabboq. See M. Ibrahim, J. Sauer, and K. Yassine, "The East Jordan Valley Survey, 1975," *BASOR* 222 (April 1976) 41-66. The southern half of the valley was under survey as this was being written, reports to be forthcoming.

Our story is set in the inner channel of the Jordan, which has never been a useful river for irrigation. Since there is currently no photography allowed at the Allenby Bridge, and exploration on foot is entirely out of the question, we have good reason to quote a classic at some length:

> Down this broad valley there curves and twists a deeper, narrower bed—perhaps 150 feet deeper, and from 200 yards to a mile broad. Its banks are mostly of white marl, and within these it is packed with tamarisks and other semi-tropical trees and tangled brush. To those who look down from the hills along any stretch of the Valley, this Zor, as it is called, trails and winds like an enormous green serpent, more forbidding in its rankness than open water could be, however foul or broken. This jungle marks the Jordan's wider bed, the breadth to which the river rises in flood. . . . But it is floods which have made the rankness, they fill this wider bed of Jordan every year; and the floor of the jungle is covered with

deposits of mud and gravel, dead weed, driftwood and the exposed roots of trees.

Penetrating this unhealthy hollow you come soon to the Jordan itself. Remember that it is but a groove in the bottom of an old sea-bed, a ditch as deep below the level of the ocean as some of our coal-mines, and you will be prepared for the uncouthness of the scene. . . .

The river itself is from 90 to 100 feet broad, a rapid, muddy water. . . . The depth varies from 3 feet at some fords to as much as 10 or 12. . . . The swiftness is rendered more dangerous by the muddy bed and curious zigzag current which will easily sweep a man from the side into the centre of the stream. In April the waters rise to the wider bed, but for the most of the year they keep to the channel of 90 feet. (George Adam Smith, *The Historical Geography of the Holy Land* [1894]. Twenty-fifth edition [1966] 312-313.)

For additional illustrative detail, cf. Menashe Har-El, "The Pride of the Jordan—The Jungle of the Jordan," *BA* 41 (1978) 65-75.

Such is the physical setting in relation to which one should read the narrative and measure for probability every liturgical reconstruction, since some form of worship seems to be behind the text. Such a liturgical reenactment need not have been associated with the river itself, but might as appropriately have been found at a religious sanctuary.

Yet a prior question is very much in order, concerning the relation between historical experience and liturgical celebration in the formation of the story as we have it. Is the "history" based exclusively on cultic texts? And has something of true historical memory regarding an actual crossing of the Jordan *for the first time* been mediated to the ancient historian (Dtr 1?) by the cultic texts? We suggest that the answer to both questions is "yes." We are confronted here with the perennial problem posed by sacral tradition when it is not consistently examined for its own value system and its role in the continuous process of value formation. A prime example is the phrase "from Shittim to Gilgal," which we borrowed from Mic 6:5 as heading for this long section. If the referent of Micah's phrase is the larger epic unit of Genesis through Joshua (the Hexateuch), then the phrase will also bracket the infamous affair of Baal-peor (Numbers 25). H. McKeating, *Amos, Hosea, Micah;* The Cambridge Bible Commentary on the *NEB* (Cambridge: University Press, 1971) 184. However, since the Hexateuch cannot be said ever to have had independent existence, it is assumed above in NOTES that Micah uses "from Shittim to Gilgal" to evoke only gracious memories, in the introduction to his poem on the Divine Suzerain's indictment of Israel.

That is to say, for interpreting the phrase "from Shittim to Gilgal" in Mic 6:5 the immediate formal context seems more reliable than the scholarly construct, Hexateuch.

The crossing of the Jordan must be seen in the broadest possible context. The sources used by the ancient historians in producing this version already had a complex history, as indicated above in the first NOTE on 3:17-4:8. Unlike the rather simple and straightforward narratives that are taken up in the Book of Judges, this is material that relates to the founding of a major politico-religious center in the pre-monarchy period. It was a sanctuary which seems to have flourished again in the eighth century, when it was roundly denounced by prophets (Amos 4:4; 5:5; Hos 4:15; 9:15; 12:12). Such materials are "not immediately clear and intelligible on a first reading; they presuppose a setting in which explanation by knowledgeable men was readily available and was orally transmitted from generation to generation." Wilcoxen, "Narrative Structure and Cult Legend . . . ," 55. Such persons at other sanctuaries comprise "the tribe of Levi" in Dtn. Yet Gilgal is not included in the system of Levitical towns in Joshua 21. All of this suggests that the teachers at Gilgal later had little in common with the old Yahwist tribe of Levi. Some of the latter were, at the same time, busily assembling their teaching—to become at last the Book of the Treaty-Text—which would be adopted as public agenda by King Hezekiah. Probably it is in their circles too that we ought to look for the beginnings of a historical corpus, the ending of which is now to be seen at 2 Kgs 17:41, immediately preceding the introduction to Hezekiah. Kamol Aryaprateep, "Studies in the Semantics of the Covenant Relationship in Deuteronomic Teaching," 149-162. We have previously referred to this as the "Pragmatic" work, a didactic collection of historical narratives. *Judges,* AB 6A, especially 29-38.

But it is above all the reign of Josiah and its abrupt end which have left their marks on the formation of the collection. In this light Josh 3:1-4:18 can be viewed as four segments.

1) The opening of the river for the crossing of the people into the land (3:1-16). Rhetorical structure as pointed out in our NOTES strongly suggests that v 16 with mention of Jericho is the end, the clincher. Thanks to the presence of the Covenant-Ark at the river, the people made their way into the land. There is no mention of twelve stones in the river, or on either side of the river; there seems to be a gap at the end of v 12. Gilgal is not mentioned, perhaps for the same reason (but unlike the twelve stones there is otherwise no hint of it).

The impression is unavoidable that the story belongs to a celebration of entry into the land, wherein "the land" lies entirely west of the Jordan. That is to say, the statement reflects the post-Solomonic shrinking of the Israelite empire.

Verse 10 indicates, however, that the story is ultimately rooted in the earliest successes of Yahwism east of the Jordan from which point Yahwism was introduced into Canaan as a radical reformation of the patriarchal religious heritage. In terms of the history of religion, this is the connection which gave legitimacy to Yahweh's claim to be owner of the land. It must have brought many of the old El-worshiping clans of the villages and countryside into the movement, over against the ethnic solidarities and city-state coalitions that came to be known as "the seven nations." There can be no doubt that all this is rooted in a Jordan valley celebration of the Yahweh-covenant, its periodic renewal. This explains the peculiar semantics of the pivotal action-word that is repeated in vv 7 and 10, "know," that is, acknowledge Yahweh as sole Sovereign, precisely on the basis of his mighty act in opening the river to the incoming Bene Israel. Except for the fact that there is neither opposition nor pursuit, the comparison with the Exodus-Sinai events is striking and there has been some lexical assimilation. "The passage through the Sea of Reeds was so much more important than the crossing of the Jordan that borrowing must have taken place along the normal stream of literary activity." Albright, *YGC,* 45-46.

The total lack of any reference, or even any allusion, to Gilgal here is striking; and it calls for some explanation. It is true that after the destruction of Jericho in chap. 6 the Ark is never again mentioned in a "conquest" narrative. And it never appears in other texts at Gilgal. However, in the early chapters of 1 Samuel, there is a link between the Ark and Gilgal. The link is that the people who follow the Ark from Shiloh into battle fall back to Gilgal in defeat! This is very old, genuinely self-critical Yahwist tradition.

But the Ark in Josh 3:1-16 is the Ark as put to use during the monarchy—a symbol of "sanctuary-presence" of the Divine Warrior. And Yahweh as Divine Warrior was more and more conceived, during the monarchy, in the standard terms of the ancient Near East. See Cross, *CMHE,* 219-265. The story in 3:1-16 makes excellent sense as a fragment of the religious heritage which was originally antimonarchical but was finally put to nation-reforming use. The sponsor of the reform was a royal administration which believed that it could impose the authority of Moses and the style of Joshua in the interest of national survival. In any case the story in 3:1-16 displays a somewhat restricted perspective on the origins of the ancient Israelite nation, and so this was remedied by the inclusion of the next segment.

2) It was while the priests stood bearing the Ark—not at the edge of the water but in difficult midstream—that the entire nation had crossed safely into the land (3:17-4:8). And Yahweh in direct address had then suggested that they commemorate the firm midstream footing for the Ark-bearers by laying down twelve riverbed stones at the unnamed campsite. That unnamed camp must have been very crowded indeed, since it is reported that all the nation was there. This is in truth an etiological story;

it explains why in Israel there was the saying quoted in 4:6. But the sanctuary involved had been long since in ruins and neither Dtr 1 nor Dtr 2 may be suspected of wanting to reactivate the place. These verses reflect a sense of humor in recounting the entry of all "the nation." Their children will forever after be reminded of the Jordan-crossing miracle by looking upon the twelve-stone configuration at the campsite somewhere west of the river and not far from Jericho.

It is no wonder that with two such very different blocks of material placed end to end someone (perhaps even the Dtr 2 compiler) felt obliged to add the explanatory comment in 4:9, no part of which seems now to have any etiological significance. We have treated this verse as parenthetical because a third major segment of text clearly begins with v 10.

3) The bulk of 4:10-14 follows directly upon segment 1 discussed above; 4:14 turns back upon 3:7, tying the two blocks together. In other words, the first edition was broken open to insert segment 2. Within this third segment the redactor's presence is signaled by what seems to be superfluous mention of each of the three Transjordan tribes, in language echoing 1:12-18. For the most part, however, the final redactor had no improvements to make in segment 3.

4) In this segment (4:15-18), the final redactor had still less to contribute, once the tone had been set by the insertion of segment 2. Here the one distinctive item is a covenant-word introduced in v 15 (*'ēdût*), which serves to focus thought on the other word (*bĕrît*), in danger of being taken for granted in its repeated usage and of being preempted in the reader's mind by the river and the stones. By just so simple a maneuver as the use of this word once, the effect is to suggest that what had always been most important about the Ark was not its alleged wonder-working power, but the modifier that is used repeatedly with it to indicate its covenantal function—that is, creating unity without destroying diversity.

According to this ancient view, it was the covenantal and therefore reconciling dimensions of the religion that had made the entrance of Yahweh and his army, crossing the Jordan into their "inheritance" around the turn of the twelfth century B.C., one of the most wonderful events in history. It is a conclusion that wears well.

D. THE CULTIC ENCAMPMENT
(4:19-5:12)

Reminder: the People for all Peoples

4 19 The people came up out of the Jordan on the tenth day of the first month, and the Bene Israel camped at The Circle on the eastern border of Jericho. 20 Those twelve stones, which they had taken from the Jordan, Joshua set up at The Circle. 21 And he said to the Bene Israel, "When in the future your children ask their fathers, 'What about these stones?' 22 then you shall teach your children: 'On dry ground Israel crossed this Jordan!' 23 For Yahweh your God dried up the Jordan's waters before you until you had crossed, as Yahweh your God did to the Reed Sea, which he dried up before them until they had crossed, 24 so that all the earth's peoples might discover how strong the hand of Yahweh is, and so that you might fear Yahweh your God for ever."

The Royal Reaction

5 1 Now all the Amorite kings who were across Jordan to the west and all the kings of the Canaanites by the sea, when they heard how Yahweh God had dried up the Jordan's waters before the Bene Israel, until they had crossed over, their hearts melted and there was no longer any courage in them before the Bene Israel.

A Renewal: Circumcision

2 At that time Yahweh said to Joshua, "Make for yourself some flint knives, and circumcise the Bene Israel a second time." 3 So Joshua made for himself some flint knives and circumcised the Bene Israel at Foreskins Hill.

4 This is the reason Joshua circumcised them: all the males who came out of Egypt, all the fighting men, had died en route in the wil-

derness since their departure from Egypt. 5 To be sure, all the people who came out had been circumcised, but all those of the people born en route in the wilderness since their departure from Egypt had not been circumcised. 6 In fact, the Bene Israel had migrated for forty years in the wilderness, until the entire nation had died out, that is, the fighting men who had come out of Egypt, who disobeyed the voice of Yahweh, and of whom Yahweh vowed that he would never let them see the land Yahweh had promised on oath to their ancestors to give us, a land flowing with milk and honey. 7 But their children he raised up in place of them. They were the ones whom Joshua circumcised because they had been uncircumcised, since no one had circumcised them en route.

8 When finally all the nation had been circumcised, they stayed in the camp until they were healed. 9 And Yahweh said to Joshua, "Today I have rolled away from you the Egyptian reproach." Thus the name of that place is Circle, to this very day.

A Resumption: Passover

10 The Bene Israel camped at The Circle and celebrated the Passover on the fourteenth day of the month, in the evening, out on the Jericho flats.

11 Right after the Passover they ate some of the land's produce: unleavened bread and parched grain (on that very day). 12 The manna ceased after that. When they ate from the land's produce, there was no more manna for the Bene Israel. They ate from the crops of the land of Canaan that year.

TEXTUAL NOTES

4 19. *the Bene Israel*   Thus LXX, where MT shows a haplography: *b[ny yśr'l b]glgl*.

20. *they*   The major Greek recensions show an assimilation to the next verb in the sentence and read the singular: "he had taken."

21. *And he said to the Bene Israel*   LXX shows a sizable haplography here: *bglg[l wy'mr 'l bny yśr']l l'mr*.

their fathers   Thus MT. LXX reads "you." These look like genuine variants going back to oral beginnings.

23. *them* and *they*   Thus LXX. MT reads "us" in both places.

24. *you might fear*   On the form *yĕrā'tem,* see NOTE.

5 1. *all* and *all*   Both lacking in LXX.

Yahweh God   Thus LXX. The shorter MT reading may be the result of haplography: *yhwh '[lhym ']t.*

they   This has the support of the bulk of ancient witnesses, including MT's *qere,* against MT's *kethib* "we."

and   LXX is corrupt. *kataplagēsan* may be due to a dittography of *b't* (v 2) read as a verb.

2. *circumcise*   The Hebrew juxtaposes two imperatives: *šûb,* "repeat," and *môl,* "circumcise." LXX reads the former as *šēb,* "sit down." But in view of the end of the verse, MT is to be retained.

a second time   Hebrew *šēnît* has no reflex in LXX, which avoids the redundancy of MT.

4. *en route in the wilderness*   Haplography will account for the absence of this phrase in LXX: *b[mdbr bdrk b]ṣ'tm.* An incorrect restoration of it might account for the confusion of LXX in the next verse. Problems of this section are more fully discussed in the NOTES to the translation.

6. *forty*   LXX reads "forty-two" (*'arbā'îm ušĕnayim*), which however may have arisen from a partial dittography of the next word "year" (*šānâ*).

wilderness   In LXX the wilderness has a name, *Madbaritidi,* which looks like an incorrect restoration of the phrase seen to be missing in v 4. O'Connor, private communication.

9. *Joshua*   LXX has "Joshua ben Nun."

Circle   Hebrew *gilgāl.* Here in the chief LXX recensions begins an omission extending to the same word in v 10.

11. *Right after the Passover*   Missing because of haplography in LXX[AB]: *m[mḥrt hpsḥ m]ṣwt.*

NOTES

4:19 - 5:12. With the Covenant-Ark and all the people safely across the Jordan, this section reports on a variety of matters which remain to be carried through in preparation for the takeover of Canaan by the Bene Israel. Several units, drawn from a variety of "sources," are easily distinguishable, so that there is no need for elaborate documentary analysis. Here the basic ingredients were epic (5:1,10-12), archival priestly lore (5:2-7), and a didactic or catechetical activity (4:19-24; 5:8-9) which had the last word. An editorial repetition in reference to the camp of the Bene Israel at The Circle (4:19 and 5:10) signals interruption of an original story line, in order to introduce a variety of material. This is the ancient framing device, discussed above at 4:10, of "repetitive resumption." The clarity of this device elsewhere strengthens its recognition here. And here it correlates with a touch of humor. The incongruity of a divine command to resume the practice of circumcision, as appropriate response to the cowardliness of the pagan kings, suggests that it is the final redactor (Dtr 2) who has made the largest contribution to the sequence of units. Thereby he hoped to prepare his people better for life in exile, ruled again by pagan kings.

4:19-24. This unit would follow rather directly upon 4:8 without leaving any signs of a gap.

19. *people*. Hebrew *'ām*. The unit speaks to their relationship with all the "peoples of the earth" (*'my h'rṣ*), as becomes clear in the concluding v 24.

out of the Jordan on the tenth day. There have been three days of preparation for this event (1:1 - 3:4), and there will follow three days more of preparation, before the celebration of the Passover on the fourth day after the crossing (5:10-12). The fall of Jericho will fill another seven-day period. See Wilcoxen, "Narrative Structure and Cult Legend . . . ," 60-61.

first month. Events are pegged to the beginning of the New Year in the spring.

camped. It is interesting and perhaps significant that the place in question, though famous and frequently mentioned, is never called a "city" (Hebrew *'yr*); and nowhere is there mention of "the inhabitants of Gilgal" or any similar expression. George M. Landes, "Report on an Archaeological 'Rescue Operation' at Ṣuwwānet eth-Thanīya in the Jordan Valley North of Jericho," BASOR Supplemental Studies 21 (Missoula, MT: Scholars Press, 1975) 11.

at The Circle. Hebrew *bag-gilgal* is voweled to reflect the definite article, repeated in the next verse (also 10:15-43), in contrast to the indefinite form which is coming up in 5:9. This suggests that here the meaning of the name is important to rhetorical structure. For the approximate location of this "Gilgal," see Maps B and C (112 and 137). On the candidacy of several sites in the neighborhood of Jericho, see COMMENT. This "Gilgal" is not to be confused with others that are mentioned, such as the border point between Judah and Benjamin in 15:7 (called "Geliloth" in 18:17), which lies elsewhere. Gilgal is presumably an example of an isolated league shrine such as the Amman Airport and Mount Gerizim sanctuaries. Edward F. Campbell, Jr., and G. Ernest Wright, "Tribal League Shrines in Amman and Shechem," BA 32 (1969) 104-116. For the Tananir building, see Robert G. Boling, "Excavations at Tananir, 1968," in *Report on Archaeological Work at Ṣuwwānet eth-Thanīya, Tananir, and Khirbet Minḥa (Munḥata)*, ed. George M. Landes. BASOR Supplemental Studies 21 (Missoula, MT: Scholars Press, 1975) 25-85.

eastern border. See Map C, 137. The best candidate (Kh. el-Mefjir) is more to the north than east of Jericho (Tell es-Sultan).

20. *twelve stones*. One per tribe, in the league which celebrated the heritage of Moses and Joshua at The Circle. Other installations of twelve that immediately come to mind are the pillars set up by Moses at the mountain of the covenant (Exod 24:4) and the twelve stones used by Elijah to build the Yahweh altar on Mount Carmel (1 Kgs 18:31-35). A less likely parallel is the reference to the "images" which were "near The Circle" in Judg 3:19,26. Soggin assumes this equation and refers without further explanation to "the twelve columns of the sanctuary." *Joshua*, 60. But the "images" or "carvings" in Judg

3:19,26 belong to another semantic field, and those texts probably refer to idol gods which were supposed to serve as treaty witnesses, as we have suggested in *Judges*, AB 6A, 86.

had taken. Beginning with the direct object in Hebrew, the syntax of the sentence is disjunctive. We may therefore recognize the work of a redactor at this point, making an identification between the stones which gave The Circle its name and the twelve stones hauled out of the river to commemorate the crossing.

Joshua set up. Unlike many other stone circles and cairns in the land, it is claimed that this one at least did not have a pagan origin.

21-23. The form is didactic, or catechetical, question and answer. Here "the prescribed answer summarizes the tradition events with which twelve stones were associated." The recital "neither identifies the stones nor explains their origin. Rather it capsulates that which the stones memorialize, and to this extent explains them as a memory sign." Long, *The Problem of Etiological Narrative*, 80.

21. *"What about these stones?"* Compare the form of the questions in v 6 and in Deut 6:20. The latter is another catechetical context, and the answer refers the inquiring children specifically to "signs and wonders, great and grievous," while concentrating the recital of Yahweh's benevolence in two themes: deliverance from state-slavery and gift of the land as fulfillment of an old promise (Deut 6:21-23). There can be no doubt that at this point in Joshua the teacher has in fact been taught by Dtn. Its preoccupations immediately become explicit.

22. *you shall teach*. Compare Deut 6:7. If this had been a special Levitical responsibility in the past, it would become a prime parental duty in the future, when there would no longer be access to the great Yahweh sanctuaries and the festivals, which were the major institutions for public education in the ancient world.

23. *Reed Sea*. This is the meaning of the Hebrew *yām sûp*. The familiar "Red Sea," still to be found in *NEB*, is based on an ambiguous translation in the LXX. Here it is asserted that the entry into the land was so similar to the escape from Egypt that it may surely be taken as a sign of the reliability of Yahweh. Such is the teaching which was to be put to work in the world, according to the following verse.

he. In place of the Hebrew relative particle *'šr*, LXX reads "the Lord our God."

24. *so that*. Run-on sentences are perhaps the most striking characteristic of Deuteronomy's style, which is here being imitated.

all the earth's peoples. They are the objective of the divine concern, for whom the crossing of the Reed Sea, and later the Jordan, will have evidentiary value. The plural here (*'my h'rṣ*) balances the singular (*h'm*) at the very outset (v 19) in this unit, focusing on the relation between the one and the many in the family of peoples.

might discover. The verbal root is *yd'*, but not in the covenantal sense discussed above at 3:7 and 10 where it is implicit that the object of the act of knowing is Yahweh. Here, rather, the object of the knowing is a demonstration of Yahweh's power.

hand. LXX avoids the anthropomorphism with an entirely satisfactory substitute: "power."

fear. That is, "give allegiance." MT *yĕrā'tem* is a form unique to the OT. But it parses as the perfect. There is no strong reason for revoweling to read the suffixed infinitive **yir'ātēm*, which is sometimes proposed. 1 Kings 15:4 is another Dtr text in which a perfect (the verb is *ntn*) is governed by *lĕma'an.* There too the usage has to do with perpetuation of a kingdom. This verse turns back upon v 14 where the same distinctive verb is used twice. That this is "the key word for understanding the whole section (Jos iii 1 - v 1)," is shown by Kamol Aryaprateeb, "A Note on YR' in Jos. IV 24," *VT* 22 (1972) 240-242. In her unpublished dissertation, Aryaprateeb has isolated this so-called "fear" of the Lord as the prime covenant stipulation in Dtn (see Deut 5:29; 6:2,13,24; 8:6; 10:12,20; 13:5; 14:23; 17:19; 28:58; 31:12,13) and something no less important to the Dtr historians (see Deut 4:10; 1 Sam 12:14,24; 1 Kgs 8:40,43; 2 Kgs 17:32,33,34,39,41). Aryaprateeb, "Studies in the Semantics of the Covenant Relationship in Deuteronomic Teaching." The setting of this verb within the treaty form, in Deuteronomy and dependent texts, makes it clear that what is meant is neither "fear" nor "reverence," but something like single-minded and exclusive loyalty.

5:1. At this point the literary terrain shifts briefly from catechism to epic, just long enough to describe the response of the ancient kings, upon the arrival of the covenanters, accompanied by Yahweh and his Ark. This verse might in fact be read immediately after 4:18 with no indication or sense of a gap.

Amorite. See above in 3:10. Here the term seems to stand generally for the rulers of the hill country.

Canaanites. They are *phoinikēs,* "Phoenicians," in LXX. In this verse, two names out of the famous "seven nations" listed in 3:10 are used to summarize the variety previously described. This is the biblical echo of an older political fragmentation going back at least as far as Hyksos hegemony and its breakup. In the years c. 1468-1436, Thutmoses III sponsored no fewer than sixteen military campaigns into the Asiatic domains. Lists commemorating his victories and naming the opponents yield about 350 place names, with 119 Canaanite names alone. There is no indication that the situation thereafter changed significantly, until the rapid emergence of Joshua's Israel.

their hearts melted. This is the second such melting in the book. Rahab uses identical language in 2:10-11. There could be no more forceful echo or reminiscence of Exod 15:13-17, on which this story is modeled, but the result in the present context is surprising. It was in this way, by immobilizing the pagan kings through use of the traditions in psychological warfare, that Yahweh purchased the time for Joshua's attention, in the following verses, to some important ritual matters. For those who had ears to hear while the nation-state was disintegrating all around them, it would be an instructive account of preparations for conquest.

2-9. Instead of an order to attack, Yahweh issues the order to circumcise the males. This turns back upon the final editing of the introduction to the entire collection, in Deuteronomy 1-3. There the language of sacral warfare is ironically turned against Israel; it is Yahweh versus Israel until an entire generation of fighters has died out (Deut 1:34-46). Only "when all the men of war had perished and were dead from among the people" (Deut 2:16) was Israel ready for the conquest. Such an air of unreality is characteristic of a good many Dtr 2 texts. It must be so by design.

In this respect the layout of the re-circumcision story is significant: "terse narrative" in segments (vv 2-3,8-9) framing "verbose explanation" (vv 4-7). Miller and Tucker, *The Book of Joshua*, 46.

2. *At that time.* Another use of a freighted time expression, such as is noted above in 1:2; 3:7; and 4:14. In other words, this event begins while the kings are still in a state of shock at the news.

Yahweh said. Hebrew '*mr yhwh.* Because the clause is disjunctive, this corresponds to the converted imperfect (*wy'mr yhwh*) in 1:1; 3:7; 4:1,15; 5:9; and 6:2).

flint knives. LXX specifies knives of *petras akrotomou,* "worked [or polished] flint." Cf. Exod 4:25. Why the material is specified is not clear. Perhaps it means simply that flint was locally available in some abundance. These knives will be buried with Joshua in 24:30.

circumcise. Two backdrop texts are directly pertinent here. One gives the basis for the practice of infant circumcision, which later became normative (Gen 17:10-14). For the ultimate origins of this the normative practice, the balance of evidence in fact tips in the direction of northern Syria in the era of the patriarchs of Israel, as presupposed in Genesis 17. Jack M. Sasson, "Circumcision in the Ancient Near East (Jos. 5:2, 9; Ex. 4:25)," *JBL* 85 (1966) 473-476. The other pertinent passage here is Exod 12:44-48, where it is stipulated that only those households whose men were circumcised could participate in the celebration of Passover.

a second time. This is clearly what the text says. What does it mean? Rashi (R. Shelomo Yitzhaki of Troyes, A.D. 1040-1105) in his commentary says: "Our rabbis said that 'a second time' refers to the tearing off which was not demanded of our father Abraham." There now appears to be a critical basis for a very similar answer. The combination of evidence from ancient texts, plastic art, and mummified bodies shows "a basic difference between the Israelites and the Egyptians in the surgical practice. . . . Whereas the Hebrews amputated the prepuce and thus exposed the corona of the penis, the Egyptian practice consisted of a dorsal incision upon the foreskin which liberated the glans penis." Sasson, "Circumcision . . . ," 473-476. On this view the text originates in the allowance for those who had previously undergone an Egyptian circumcision to complete it in the Israelite (originally Mesopotamian) manner. This is entirely credible if early Israel was a religious movement rapidly expanding as it moved again into Canaan.

The trouble with this explanation is that the narrative deals with the second generation of those who came out of Egypt, none of whom presumably were old enough to have been included in the first circumcision. The story clearly understands that only adults were circumcised; it implies that they had all been born in the desert but that is not necessary or likely. In the Numbers account the implication is that all children are exempt, not just those born since leaving Egypt. The story in Exodus 4 implies the same things (Zipporah's action was an emergency one). The conclusion is that the Abraham infant circumcision is an old tradition which only later became normative practice. While the Joshua story is interpreted as special because of the wilderness interval, it probably reflects standard practice, that is, a group rite at some stated occasion for all who had come of age, presumably marital age as the terms *ḥātān* and *ḥōtēn* suggest (see below and COMMENT).

3. *Joshua . . . circumcised*. With an infant the rite was performed on the eighth day after birth (Lev 12:3), by the father (Gen 21:4), or rarely the mother (Exod 4:25). In later times there were male specialists who did this (1 Macc 1:61). It was "never done in the sanctuary or by a priest." Roland de Vaux, *Ancient Israel: Its Life and Institutions*, 46.

at Foreskins Hill. The interruption of narrative for the leisurely explanation which follows has the effect of elevating this name to a position of prominence. But its function is at most pedagogical; the narrator is interested in explaining another name (v 9). The name "Foreskins Hill" may have been a pre-Yahwist name of one of the little tells or hillocks in the vicinity of Kh. el Mefjir. See description by James Muilenburg, "The Site of Ancient Gilgal," *BASOR* 140 (1955) 11-27. The name in turn may reflect an originally pagan custom of performing circumcision there, not in infancy but as a rite of passage upon reaching the age of eligibility for marriage and military service. For comparative ethnological data, see Bernhard Stade, "Der 'Hugel der Vorhäute' Jos. 5," *ZAW* 6 (1886) 132-143; Holzinger, *Das Buch Josua*, 12. The story might thus make sense as reflecting the Yahwist takeover and reform of an old shrine and its rite, which was remembered thereafter as a one-time exception to the normative Israelite practice of infant male circumcision. That adult circumcision at Gilgal was a recurring Israelite rite is to be seriously doubted, in the total absence of any hint of such practice elsewhere in the tradition.

4-7. These verses are an explanatory digression which does not once use a verb in the standard narrative tense of the converted imperfect. They explain the act, however, as a first circumcision, for those who entered the land.

4-6. The translation of these verses is based on MT. The LXX is considerably shorter, and the differences here cannot be assigned to scribal accidents in transmission. It appears in fact that in these verses the Greek, although some of the differences are scribal, is based on a Hebrew text that escaped the final redaction. See further in the COMMENT.

5. *the people*. Hebrew *hā'ām* is used twice in the verse. It is a favorite Deuteronomic word for Israel, together with *qāhāl*, "assembly," and, in special cases, *'ēdâ*, "congregation."

6. *nation*. Hebrew *gôy*, used again in v 8, is rarely found with Israel as referent in the Deuteronomic collection. See above on 3:17-4:1, where the word occurs twice in rapid succession, thus calling attention to itself and contributing to a sense of irony. That the word was not considered straightforward Deuteronomic usage seems to be reflected in the reading *had-dōr*, "the generation," in several manuscripts.

a land flowing with milk and honey. Is it entirely coincidental that this phrase is here used for the first time in the Book of Joshua? The evocative power which it would accumulate by the end of the seventh century is suggested by the following distribution: Exod 3:8,17; 13:5; 33:3; Lev 20:24; Num 13:27; 14:8; 16:13,14; Deut 6:3; 11:9; 26:9,15; 27:3; 31:20. Outside these old epic and Deuteronomic texts, the phrase occurs twice in Jer 11:5 and 32:22, and twice in Ezek 20:6,15, but not again in the Old Testament.

8. *When finally all the nation had been.* Hebrew *k'šr tmw kl-hgwy.* Compare the expression *'d 'šr tmw kl-hgwy* at the Jordan crossing in 3:17 and 4:1. This verse is the splice, connecting the explanation and the epic once again.

until they were healed. The edited narrative seems to allow at most three days for the healing to take place.

9. *reproach. NEB* follows Targum, reading the plural "reproaches," but this is questionable; the precise referent is unclear but has somehow to do with freedom from the scorn for and indignity of slavery.

place. Hebrew *māqôm* often, as here, evokes the sense of "holy place," "sanctuary."

Circle. Hebrew *gilgāl,* without the definite article, in contrast to 4:19,20 and 5:10. The contrast is scarcely coincidental. It is comparable to another naming of a place called "Weepers" (*bôkîm* in Judg 2:5, but using the definite article in 2:1 to introduce the form). *Judges,* AB 6A, 53, 61-63, 66-67. The form *gilgāl,* with reduplication of the biconsonantal root, is iterative—going 'round and 'round. In other words, the story is not truly etiological. It explains neither the name "Foreskins Hill" nor the rite of circumcision. It seems instead to be a wordplay (another sense of the verb is "to roll away") using the name of an old and defunct cultic place as an aid in teaching the tradition and something of its value.

10-12. The first celebration of the Passover in the land marks a point of transition, from the long account of entrance into the land to the account of the razing of Jericho.

10. *the Passover.* Exodus 12:1-27.

the fourteenth day. This completes the first seven-day period, which may be reviewed as follows:

> Day 8—Joshua announces the crossing three days in advance and dispatches the spies.
>
> Day 9—Joshua and the Bene Israel advance to the Jordan while the spies are hiding out in the hills (another incongruity, proceeding without waiting for the intelligence report).
>
> Day 10—This is implied for the return of the spies; the Jordan is forded.
>
> Days 11, 12, 13—Setting up The Circle, and the circumcision.
>
> Day 14—Passover.

11. *Right after the Passover.* Although this is not in the best LXX recensions, the probability favors scribal error as the explanation, not glossing as was supposed by De Vaux, *Ancient Israel: Its Life and Institutions,* 487-488.

Right after. Hebrew *mim-maḥărat,* literally, "the morrow," but used indefinitely here. Its importance is signaled by the repetition in v 12 ("after that"). Not everything important could be accommodated by the seven-day schema. The spillover at this point tries to avoid specific mention of another "day."

some of . . . produce. Hebrew *mē'ăbûr.* The prefix is partitive, which may account for the indefinite objects "unleavened bread and parched grain." The word order, however, does not inspire confidence.

unleavened bread. Hebrew *maṣṣôt.* This is presumably a reference to the feast day which was originally separate from and sequel to Passover (Exod 12:15-20). It was so understood by the one who added the parenthesis, if we have rightly divined the significance of that dangling temporal phrase.

(on that very day). Our guess is that this is the contribution of someone trying even harder to protect the seven-day schema, by referring all the eating in the verse, including Passover, to the same day.

12. *manna.* Exodus 16 and Deut 8:3. This substance was excreted by two species of insects on the branches of tamarisk trees. The latter were far more common then than now, due to centuries of environmental exploitation. W. F. Albright, "Moses in Historical and Theological Perspective," in *Mag Dei,* 125.

land of Canaan. Here is the first occurrence of this designation, which is used only sparingly in the Book of Joshua (see 14:1 and 21:2), until it is found four times in the altar story (22:9,10,11,32) and finally in 24:3.

COMMENT

In this section dealing with the final preparations for the Yahweh wars in Canaan, we recognize the hand of an editor living late in the monarchical period. That editor was attempting to resurrect some pre-monarchic traditions centering upon Gilgal, in preparation for a post-monarchical situation which was rapidly approaching, or perhaps had already arrived.

The old Gilgal catechism is recast in narrative form for the benefit of those who no longer have access to the place itself. This presupposes the reign of Josiah, with his systematic suppression of all possible rivals to the Jerusalem Temple (2 Kings 22-23; 2 Chronicles 34-35). In any case a re-paganized Gilgal cultus had been flourishing as late as the mid-eighth century when it was denounced by prophets from both the south (Amos 4:4; 5:5) and the north (Hos 9:15; 12:12). It is curious that Gilgal is denounced only *in* the north. Does that mean that Gilgal belonged to northern traditions? We owe this question to Freedman (private communication). It is among the descendants of alienated northern Levites that we ought to look for the contributors of Dtr 2.

Gilgal figures prominently in the historical traditions only in the stories of Samuel and Saul, that is, the tradition of the introduction of monarchy to Israel in response to Philistine pressures (1 Sam 7:16; 10:8; 11:14,15; 13:4,7,8,12,15; 15:12,21,33). The poem in 1 Sam 15:21 is closely related to Hos 6:6 and Hosea is certainly interested in Gilgal. The place is mentioned twice in the story of Absalom's rebellion (2 Sam 19:16,41) and twice in connection with Elijah (2 Kgs 2:1; 4:38). Otherwise the Deuteronomic corpus rarely mentions Gilgal. In Deut 11:30 Gilgal is merely a point of geographical reference, and a notoriously obscure one. In Judg 2:1 the angel of the Lord goes up "from the Circle" and in Judg 3:19 Gilgal has passed into Moabite control. It was regained, thanks to Ehud; and it became the place to which the priests retreated and erected a sanctuary which became a rallying point in the days of Samuel.

The finished form of the Book of Joshua offers a corrective to the tradition concentrating upon the king-making role of Gilgal by going all the way back to its importance at the very outset, in the days of Joshua.

It can be said with confidence that the Gilgal in question was never a very large place. One recent study would find it at Tell es-Sultan. Carl Umhau Wolf, "The Localization of Gilgal," *Biblical Research* 11 (1966) 42-51. See Map C, 137. This would substitute one large problem for another! Of the several more likely sites, Tell en-Nitla is still favored by *The Jerusalem Bible* annotation on Josh 4:18-19, and this perhaps best fits the reference to a point on the "eastern" border of Jericho. But excavation at Nitla has yielded no evidence of any town or village earlier than the Byzantine period. Muilenburg, "The Site of Ancient Gilgal," 19-20. The second of two small tells found about 150 meters north of Kh. el-Mefjir continues to offer the only positive archaeological evidence, as indicated by Muilenburg in the report on his soundings there. More recently a site lying about 330 meters west-southwest of Kh. el-Mefjir has been proposed by Boyce M. Bennett, Jr., "The Search for Israelite Gilgal," *PEQ* 104 (1972) 111-122. The results of the 1968 excavations there were inconclusive. Landes, "Report on an Archaeological 'Rescue Operation' at Ṣuwwānet eth-Thanīya in the Jordan Valley North of Jericho," BASOR Supplemental Studies 21 (1975) 1-22.

Despite the continuing uncertainty about the correct location of Gilgal, there have been provocative reconstructions of the Gilgal cultus, pioneered by Kraus, "Gilgal. . . . ," *VT* 1 (1951) 181-191; *Worship in Israel,* 152-165. See also Soggin, "Gilgal, Passah und Landnahme. . . . ," *VT*Sup 15 (1966) 263-277, with exhaustive bibliography.

The reconstructed festival is compactly described by Cross, in the following sequence:

> 1) The people are required to sanctify themselves, as for holy war, or as in the approach to a sanctuary (Josh 3:5).
>
> 2) The Ark of the Covenant, palladium of battle, is borne in solemn procession, which is at the same time battle array, to the sanctuary of Gilgal.
>
> 3) The Jordan, playing the role of the Red Sea, parts for the passage of the Ark and the people of Israel. . . .

4) At the desert sanctuary of Gilgal, twelve stones were set up, memorial to the twelve tribes united in the covenant festival celebrated there; we must understand this festival to be the festival of the old spring New Year. It is explicitly called Passover. . . .

Cross then notes the circumcision story and the abrupt appearance of the angelic army commander (5:13-15) and concludes: "In these fragments of cultic tradition we recognize the use of the ritual procession of the Ark as a means of reenactment of the 'history of redemption,' of the Exodus-Conquest theme, preparatory to the covenant festival of the spring New Year." *CMHE,* 103-105.

This, then, was the festival that had fallen into disrepair—if it had not in fact been carefully revised in the interests of monarchy—at least by the time of Amos and Hosea. Dtr 1 drew upon the materials of this defunct festival in order to highlight the unparalleled role of Joshua in the past. Dtr 2 drew further upon the same resources so as to emphasize, for the future, two marks of the people whose fear of Yahweh might provide for all the earth's peoples a demonstration of Yahweh's power. Circumcision and the Passover are at last presented as the divinely ordained preparation for going to war against the combined might of all the kings.

It will be helpful at this point to compare the shorter version of vv 4-6a which is preserved in LXX:

> [6] in this manner Joshua purified the Bene Israel: all who had been born on the way and all those who were uncircumcised at the Exodus from Egypt —[5] Joshua circumcised all of them. [7] For forty-two years Israel had wandered through the Madbaritide desert. That is why most of the warriors were uncircumcised, who came out of Egypt, the ones who disobeyed the commandments of God. Concerning them. . . .

Except for the curious "Madbaritide," which seems to be based on misreading of a reduplicated *mdbr,* "desert," this is a good text. In diametrical opposition to MT which insists that all who came out of Egypt had been circumcised, the LXX candidly allows that some had not. There could not be any stronger testimony to the event that each is trying to explain. Both explanations are in tension with the narrative specification that this was, literally, "a second time." The shorter explanation of LXX is presumably the earlier version (Dtr 1?), which was favored by the Greek translator.

The original significance of circumcision is elusive. The Bible is in general strongly opposed to every practice of mutilation or deformation of the body, practices which are common in other ancient religions. Because the Israelites are "children of Yahweh," all such practices as tattooing and scarification are explicitly forbidden to them (Deut 14:1). See also Lev 19:28; 21:5. These are precisely the practices with which circumcision is associated in other cultures. What did circumcision in Israel stand for?

To judge from the distribution in biblical and extra-biblical texts, as well as in ancient artistic representations, the significance of circumcision is not to be defined along ethnic lines. See De Vaux, *Ancient Israel: Its Life and Institutions,* 46-47. While the practice of infant circumcision, as the distinctive mark of the male who belonged to Israel and to Yahweh, came at last to prevail in Judaism, our story in 5:2-9 indicates that some of the earliest Israelites knew of adult circumcision and had participated in it. This correlates as well with the nuclear lexical cluster. In Hebrew the words for "bridegroom," "son-in-law," and "father-in-law" are all based on the same verbal root *ḥtn,* which in Arabic means "to circumcise." In Genesis 34 circumcision is associated with marriageable age. In non-Israelite societies, whether ancient or modern, where it appears, circumcision generally occurs at puberty in relation to initiation procedures, interpreted anthropologically as *rites de passage.* But Genesis 34 also illustrates what is distinctive about circumcision in the Old Testament—it is a covenantal rite, "a special case of general cutting or dismembering rites by which covenants or treaties were established." Erich Isaac, "Circumcision as Covenant Rite," *Anthropos* 59 (1965) 444. Moreover, in early Israel it is in covenant with the Divine Warrior that circumcision became important. If puberty-rite it was that which made a man fit for normal sexual life, as covenant-rite it was to be a reminder of ethical obligation; only the circumcised could celebrate the Passover. One might speak of an "uncircumcised heart" (Jer 9:25), meaning one that does not comprehend. An "uncircumcised ear" (Jer 6:10) is one which is no good at listening. And "uncircumcised lips" (Exod 6:12,30) are inarticulate.

There remains one final event in the mobilization of the Yahweh army for the takeover in Canaan: Passover. As instituted in Exodus 12, it is a uniquely familial celebration, which to this very day is done best at home, and which King Josiah had tried mightily to reestablish at the capital city after it had apparently long since fallen into disuse (2 Kgs 23:21-23). Josiah's attempt to exploit the old Gilgal pattern of Passover at the main sanctuary failed. But the family-centered celebration would be successful together with circumcision, as one of the few marks of the believer, apart from a distinctive ethic. Along some such line of reasoning, we may reconstruct the thought of Dtr 2.

All is at last in readiness for the warfare.

II. THE WARFARE
5:13-11:23

A. THE COMMANDER
(5:13-15)

5   13 It happened while Joshua was in the vicinity of Jericho. He looked up, and right there a man was standing before him, holding his sword already drawn. Joshua walked toward him and said to him, "Do you belong to us or to our enemies?"

14 He said to him, "Neither one! As commander of Yahweh's army I have now arrived!"

Joshua fell face down on the ground, doing homage, and said to him, "What does my lord have to say to his servant?"

15 Yahweh's army commander said to Joshua, "Take the sandal off your foot, for the place where you are standing is holy." And Joshua did just that.

TEXTUAL NOTES

5 13. *and right there*   Hebrew *whnh*, missing in LXX *Vorlage*, where a scribe's eye jumped from one *'aleph* to another: *wyr' [whnh] 'yš*.

14. *"Neither one!"*   Hebrew *lō'*. This is the more difficult reading, which must be retained against the bulk of ancient witnesses. The latter reflect instead "to him" (*lô*), perhaps as *BHS* suggests as a result of contamination by *lô* in the second half of this verse and the previous verse.

on   This is the reading of oriental MSS, *'l*, against MT *'l*.

doing homage   Hebrew *wyštḥw* is not represented in some major LXX MSS, presumably reflecting haplography in the *Vorlage*.

15. *army*   This is lacking in LXX, probably as a result of an inner-Greek haplography: *archistratēgo[s dunameō]s*.

off your foot   Both sandals and both feet are, of course, implicit. Several manuscripts and versions read the plural, in strict conformity to the MT of Exod 3:5; more read "feet" as plural than "sandal," oddly. The Exodus passage shows similar textual differences for both words in versions and manuscripts.

And Joshua did just that   Missing from LXX^AB by haplography: *wy['s yhws' kn wy]ryḥw*.

NOTES

5:13-15. This is distinctively not a late monarchical composition, but we have here to do with the result of "an effort to preserve the remains of a fuller account which had suffered in transmission, not with a deliberate selection from a lengthier episode." Harold J. Wiener, "The Conquest Narratives," *JPOS* 9 (1929) 4.

13. *It happened while*. Hebrew *wayhî bihyôt*, in contrast to the temporal construction with preposition *k* ("when") used in 5:1.

in the vicinity of. The preposition is *b*, usually "in," which indicates that Joshua was in the area controlled from Jericho, not necessarily within the walled town! In 4:19 the Israelite camp at The Circle (Gilgal) is said to be "on the eastern border of Jericho." See Map C, 137. The ambiguity here is very likely intentional. It was not at a holy place (Gilgal) or another famous town (Jericho), but in the course of a reconnaissance mission, that the manifestation occurred.

He looked up. Literally, "He lifted up his eyes and saw," a verbal hendiadys. Given the Jordan valley location, Psalm 121:1-2 immediately suggests itself:

> I lift up my eyes to the hills.
> From whence does my help come?
> My help comes from the LORD
> Who made heaven and earth.

Such poetry is to be read against the background of standard epic material, in this case the usual inchoative construction of gods spying gods, e.g. *UT* 51:II:12-14

> When she lifts her eyes, she sees.
> Asherah spies Baal's progress,
> The progress of Batultu Anat,
> The march of Nations' Forebear.

and of people seeing gods, e.g. II Aqht v:9-11.

When he [Danel] lifts his eyes, he sees.
Over thousands of fields and myriad hectares
He spies Kothar's progress.
He sees the march of Hasis.

In the first case, the person looking should be scared out of her wits; and in the second, the person is very, very happy, while at the same time hard at work adjudicating the case of the orphan and the widow. We owe this comparison and these translations to O'Connor (private communication).

right there. Hebrew *hnh*, KJV "behold." Joshua is suddenly put on alert.

a man was standing before him, holding his sword already drawn. Compare the angel seen by Balaam and his ass (Num 22:23,31), and one beheld by King David (1 Chr 21:16). The latter is especially instructive: "When David lifted up his eyes he saw the angel of Yahweh standing between the earth and the heavens with the drawn sword in his hand, stretched out over Jerusalem. Then David and the elders covered themselves with sackcloth and fell down upon their faces." Translation by Jacob M. Myers, *I Chronicles,* AB 12, 144.

his sword. Hebrew *ḥarbô.* It is an effective weapon, but it is to be doubted that it was subsequently presented to Joshua as the sign *par excellence* of sovereignty. Rather, it was a matter of utmost importance that Joshua should know for whom that sword was to be wielded. Thus the drawn sword here should be kept distinct from the *kîdôn* (probably "sicklesword") which Joshua holds out at the defeat of Ha-Ai in 8:18 and 26. See Othmar Keel, *Wirkmächtige Siegeszeichen im Alten Testament.* Keel's point about Joshua 8 is well taken, but it may be stretching things to say these three verses narrate Joshua's commissioning.

Joshua walked toward him. An indication of Joshua's bravery facing, so he thought, a merely human warrior. David's reaction to the vision of a comparable warrior stationed "between heaven and earth" was to collapse in sackcloth and make his confession (1 Chr 21:16b-17). In this scene, however, Joshua's bravery is paired with a slowness of discernment. He must proceed to determine the loyalty of this person who seemed to be blocking his way.

to us or to our enemies? Who goes there, friend or foe? This is challenge by sentry, as in the first scene of *Hamlet.* The answer takes everyone by surprise.

14. *"Neither one."* Hebrew *lō'.* This sense of the negative is rare but not impossible. An alternative solution proposes to read the emphatic *lamed:* " 'Indeed; but because I am commander of the army of the Lord, I have now come . . .' And Joshua fell on his face to the earth and gave him worship." Soggin, *Joshua,* 76-77. The interrupted sentence in Soggin's translation is effective, with the superior cut off by the subordinate. Yet it is difficult to see how the originally affirmative answer could have been so completely and consistently misunderstood as either the negative or the suffixed preposition.

Yahweh's army. Hebrew *ṣb' yhwh.* The heavenly contingents have thus far been overlooked or omitted in the account of the mobilization. But one of the oldest names of the deity is Yahweh Sabaoth, "He Creates the (Heavenly) Armies." See above, NOTES on 1:1. The activity of the heavenly troops is celebrated in the Song of Deborah (Judg 5:20):

From the heavens fought the stars
From their courses they fought against Sisera.

They were probably regarded as the source of rain on that occasion. *Judges,*
AB 6A, 103 and 113. See also the victory at Gibeon in Josh 10:12-13.

now. On the whole, our impression is one of a somewhat breathless response
to Joshua's question. Has the commander arrived only in the nick of time?

doing homage. The verbal root is *ḥwh* and parses as an archaic *š*-causative
with infixed-*t,* forms of which survive regularly with this verb. The semantic
field is that of etiquette in the royal audience hall, greatly clarified from usage
of this verb in the Amarna Letters. There the prince repeatedly addresses himself to Pharaoh in stereotyped expressions of behavioral homage: "I fall,"
"bow," etc. The old story of Gideon's nighttime reconnaissance of the
Midianite camp makes comparable narrative use of the Yahwist court custom
in describing Gideon's reaction to the divine assurance that Yahweh had so
elaborately arranged for him to overhear (Judg 7:15).

"What does my lord have to say to his servant?" Noth has shown that the
commander's first response might be taken to announce an official visit and intended to introduce a message (Dan 9:22), *Das Buch Josua,* 23. The omission
of any detailed message, then, has an interesting effect here. Joshua is simply
told, in so many words, to pattern his response after that of Moses.

15. The verse is a partial parallel to the scene at the burning bush, even in
wording. Compare Exod 3:5. But Joshua does not here deal directly with Yahweh. He is not being presented as another Moses.

place. The encounter has made it holy. But everything about the story
indicates the encounter was unexpected. Therefore it is to be doubted that
māqôm here means "sanctuary," with specific reference to either Gilgal or
Jericho. It is questionable that place-attachment has any significance for the
text in its present form. See Wright's remarks, 59-61, 71-72.

COMMENT

This is another fragment of epic. No time reference is given, so it is probably to be understood as occurring on or during the night preceding the
first of the seven days involved in the capture of Jericho. Wilcoxen, "Narrative Structure and Cult Legend," 62-63.

Only with the arrival and involvement of Joshua's heavenly counterpart
could the true Yahweh warfare begin.

The unnamed, and probably unknown, spot where Joshua had encountered the angel must ever after be remembered as especially holy. Interest
centers on the action, not the place.

The commander of Yahweh's army is also known in Scripture as the
mal'ak Yahweh, "envoy/angel of Yahweh," which explains Joshua's be-

havior at the introduction. It is not quite true that Yahweh and the commander are always identified, with the later as hypostasis of the former (Soggin, *Joshua,* 78). Rather, often the angel/commander is a forerunner, as is clear in the story of the enlistment of Gideon to be savior-judge (Judg 6:11-32, AB 6A, 128-134) and explicit in Mal 3:3. The angel bears the word of the one who sends him, just as a messenger has the authority of his sender; it is not a metaphysical question but a juridical one, as in the Gospel of John which treats the authority of Jesus as that of one sent by God with the latter's word (cf. Isaiah 55).

B. Phase One. MOSTLY MIRACLE 6:1-10:43

1. JERICHO: INITIAL SUCCESS
(6:1-27)

6 1 Jericho was shut up tight because of the Bene Israel. No one was coming out. No one was going in. 2 Yahweh said to Joshua: "Attention! I have given into your hand Jericho, its king in it, and the seasoned warriors. 3 You are to march around the city, all the fighting men going around the city once. Thus you are to do for six days. 4 Seven priests are to carry seven ram's horn trumpets ahead of the Ark. And on the seventh day you are to march around the city seven times; and the priests are to blow the trumpets. 5 At the blast of the ram's horn, when you hear the sound of the trumpet, all the people are to give a tremendous shout. The city wall will collapse on the spot, and all the people are to go up, every man straight ahead."

6 So Joshua ben Nun summoned the priests and said to them, "Take up the Ark of the Covenant! Seven priests are to carry seven ram's horn trumpets ahead of Yahweh's Ark." 7 And he said to them, "Command the people: 'Move out. March around the city. The armed guard is to move out ahead of Yahweh's Ark.'"

8 Now seven priests, carrying the seven ram's horn trumpets before Yahweh, had moved out! They blew the trumpets, with the Ark of Yahweh's Covenant coming after them. 9 The armed guard was marching ahead of the priests who were blowing the trumpets, and the rearguard was marching after the Ark—marching while blowing the trumpets!

10 To the people Joshua had given orders, "You are not to shout or let your voice be heard. Not a word is to come from your mouth, until the day I say to you: Shout! Then you shall shout." 11 So he sent Yahweh's Ark around the city. It went around once, then they entered the camp and spent the night in the camp.

12 Joshua got busy next morning; and the priests took up Yahweh's Ark. 13 The seven priests, carrying the seven ram's horn trumpets

ahead of Yahweh, keeping step marched forth. They blew the trumpets! The armed guard was marching ahead of them, and the rearguard was marching after Yahweh's Covenant-Ark—marching while blowing the trumpets! 14 Thus on the second day they marched around the city once and returned to the camp. So they did for six days.

15 Then on the seventh day they got up at daybreak and marched around the city, in the usual manner, seven times. Only on that day did they march around the city seven times. 16 Then at the seventh time the priests blew the trumpets, and Joshua said to the people:

"Shout! For Yahweh has given you the city! 17 The city with all that is in it is to be under the ban to Yahweh.

"Only the harlot Rahab and all who are in the house with her are to live, because she hid the messengers whom we sent. 18 But as for you, keep clear of the ban, lest you covet and take something banned, thus placing the camp of Israel under the ban and making trouble for it! 19 All silver and gold, any vessels of bronze and iron, are holy to Yahweh. They are to go into Yahweh's treasury."

20 The priests blew the trumpets.

When the people heard the sound of the trumpets, the people gave a tremendous shout. The wall collapsed on the spot. The people went up into the city, every man straight ahead, and took the city. 21 They put everything in the city under ban—man and woman, young and old, ox and sheep and ass—at the mouth of the sword!

22 To the two men who reconnoitered the land, Joshua had said, "Go into the harlot's house and bring out the woman, with all who belong to her, as you swore to her." 23 So the young spies went in and brought out Rahab and her father and mother and brothers and all who belonged to her. All her relatives they brought out, and they quartered them outside the camp of Israel.

24 The city they burned, with everything in it. But the silver and gold, and the vessels of bronze and iron, they put into the treasury of Yahweh's house.

25 And the harlot Rahab, with her father's household and all who belonged to her, Joshua let live. She dwells in Israel to this very day, because she hid the messengers whom Joshua sent to reconnoiter Jericho.

26 Joshua administered an oath, at that time, before Yahweh: "Cursed be the man who proceeds to rebuild this city, Jericho:

With his firstborn he shall lay its foundations
With his youngest he shall set up its gates."

27 Yahweh was with Joshua, and his fame was country-wide.

TEXTUAL NOTES

6 1. *because of the Bene Israel*   Lacking in LXX.

2. *in it*   Restored from LXX, omitted from MT by haplography due to *homoioteleuton* after *mlkh*.

3. LXX v 3 is much shorter: "And the army shall form a circle around the city." The plural second person form in the MT of v 3 extends the singular of the previous verse. The Israelites are *'nšy mlḥmh* while the Jericho people are *gbwry ḥyl*.

you second occurrence.   Greek plural, Hebrew singular.

4. The verse is lacking in LXX^AB, probably by haplography in the *Vorlage:* *w[šb'h . . . w]hyh*.

5. *when you hear the sound of the trumpet*   Lacking in LXX. MT probably preserves variants.

6. *summoned*   In LXX he "went to" the priests.

"Take up the Ark of the Covenant! Seven priests are to carry seven ram's horn trumpets ahead of Yahweh's Ark."   Lacking in LXX.

7. *he*   This follows the *qere wy'mr*, against the plural spelling of the *kethib wy'mrw*. For the latter LXX seems to read an imperative *w'mrw*.

them, "Command   This agrees with LXX, from which the shorter text of MT may be derived, but not vice versa, *wy'mr 'l[yhm ṣww 't] h'm*. Odds in favor of the haplography would have been even greater if the text were written in pre-exilic orthography, without internal vowel letters such as the *y* in **'lyhm*. The plural form of the verb in MT (*wy'mrw*) would thus be an attempt to clarify after the accident. The *qere* (*wy'mr*) supported by Syriac, Targum, and Vulgate is to be preferred.

Ark   LXX lacks reference to the Ark, but this looks like an internal Greek haplography: *k[ibotos k]uriou*.

8. *Now . . .*   In agreement with LXX, this omits the first phrase in MT: "And when Joshua had spoken [MT *k'mr, mss b'mr*] to the people." The latter is perhaps best explained as a secondary development, after the corruption which shifted the object of Joshua's address from the priests to the people in v 7.

seven priests   The indefinite noun is found in LXX, where the seven priests have not been previously mentioned. The ram's horn trumpets are definite also only in Hebrew, not in Greek.

Yahweh   "Yahweh's Ark" in some manuscripts and versions is euphemistic.

them   Verse 9 follows MT, where LXX reflects a complex history of corruption and "correction," approximately as follows. A haplography, skipping from the first to the second occurrence of *šōpārôt*, dropped all reference to the rearguard. The verse was subsequently improved to read in the Greek text: "The armed guard marched ahead, with the priests marching after the Ark of the Lord's Covenant—blowing continually."

9. *who were blowing*   This is the *qere,* supported by Syriac and Targum, against the *kethib,* "they blew."

10. *Not a word is to come from your mouth*   This is lacking in LXX[AB], which also lacks the mechanism for haplography here. MT is perhaps a conflation.

11. *he sent*   The form is *hiph'il* (MT), not *qal* (as reflected in LXX, Syriac, and Vulgate).

they entered the camp and spent the night   LXX reads both verbs as singular, with the Ark as subject.

12. *morning*   LXX specifies "on the second day" at the beginning of the verse.

13. *ram's horn trumpets*   This renders MT *šōpĕrôt hay-yôbĕlîm.* In place of the second word, LXX[AB] and Syriac translate *hōlĕkîm,* "marching," which comes four words later in MT but is missing at that point in the versions!

Yahweh   "Yahweh's Ark" in some mss and versions; cf. v 8.

14. *on the second day*   In LXX[AB] this specification occurs at the beginning of v 12.

they   LXX has both verbs in the singular.

15. *at*   MT *k*=K[Or] *b.*

in the usual manner   Hebrew *kmšpṭ hzh* has no reflex in LXX.

seven   "Six," both times, in LXX[B].

Only on that day did they march around the city seven times   Because of haplography, LXX[AB] show no reflex of this: *p'mym*[. . . *p'mym*].

17. *because she hid the messengers whom we sent*   LXX lacks this entire explanatory clause, due to haplography: *rq* [*rḥb* . . . *wrq*] *'tm.*

hid   The form is *heḥbî'ah* as in v 25. The anomalous *heḥb'ātāh* results from a partial dittography of the following particle *'t,* before final vowel letters (*h* in this case) were added.

18. *lest you covet*   This is LXX, which reflects *tḥmdw* against MT *tḥrymw.* The latter presumably arose out of a scribal preoccupation with the Achan story which comes next and to which this is introduction. The letters *d* and *r* were not infrequently confused, especially in worn manuscripts.

19. *They are to go*   Hebrew *yābô'* is here used impersonally and might be properly rendered as passive in Greek. There is no need to posit a form *yûbā'* behind LXX.

20. *The priests*   This is LXX. In MT the priests are displaced by a conflation of two ways of referring to the shouting of the people: *wyr' h'm* (singular) and *wyry'w h'm* (plural).

and took the city   Missing in LXX due to haplography: *wy*[*lkdw* . . . *wy*]*ḥrymw.*

21. *They*　In LXX^B the subject is singular and explicit: "Joshua."

22. *the land*　This is missing in LXX^{AB}, thanks probably to haplography in the *Vorlage*, '[*t h'rṣ* ']*mr*, although it might also be internal to the Greek where there are four consecutive words ending in *n*, to account for the loss of *tēn gēn*.

harlot's　Because of a haplography in LXX *Vorlage*, she is not "the woman, the harlot" (so the Hebrew literally), but simply "the woman": *h'š[h hzwn]h*.

as you swore to her　Here LXX reveals another haplography: '*t kl 'šr* [*lh k'šr nšb'tm*] *lh*.

23. *in*　LXX continues "to the city and to the harlot's house," compensating for the loss from the previous verse.

all who belong to her. All her relatives　LXX has the two phrases reversed: "all her relatives and all who belonged to her."

they brought out　Lacking in LXX, this may well be secondary in MT.

24. *house*　Lacking in LXX.

25. *her*　LXX has "all" her father's house, possibly contamination from the next phrase, which was subsequently lost by haplography in the Hebrew *Vorlage: w't-bt-'by[h w't kl 'šr l]h*. But conflation cannot be ruled out.

messengers　This is the Hebrew *hml'kym*, in place of which LXX reflects *hmrglym*, "the spies," under the influence of the root *rgl* later in the sentence.

26. This verse also appears in the remarkable sectarian document from Qumran, now known as 4Q Testimonia. J. M. Allegro, *Qumran Cave 4*, 1 (4Q 158-4Q 186), No. 175, lines 22-23. See especially John Strugnell, "Notes en Marge du Volume V des 'Discoveries in the Judaean Desert of Jordan,'" *RevQ* 7 (1969-1971) 228.

before Yahweh　This agrees with LXX, which omits these words from the quotation but includes them in the rubrics.

Jericho　This is Hebrew '*t yryḥw*, lacking in LXX^A. It was perhaps originally a marginal note.

gates　LXX is longer, showing how the curse "came true," in a variation of 1 Kgs 16:34.

NOTES

Here begins a long and major part of the book (6:1 - 10:43), where everything turns upon the interventions of Yahweh to produce three pivotal victories: Jericho (chap. 6), Ha-Ai (chaps. 7 and 8), and Gibeon (chaps. 9 and 10). Such stories are "through and through embodiments of the idea of the miraculous sign." Kaufmann, *The Biblical Account of the Conquest of Palestine*, 78.

6:1-27. This is a highly polished story which became peculiarly stylized long before it was taken up into the Dtr-history. The first victory of the Yahweh army west of the Jordan had symbolic importance out of all proportion to the size of the actual enterprise; of this we may be quite sure. Tell es-Sultan, the site of Bronze Age and Iron Age Jericho, dominated an extensive oasis, but it was not a large city at any time within the biblical era, covering only about eight and a half acres. "A large city might cover an area of about 20 acres and accommodate more than 3000 inhabitants. Cities of medium size had from several hundred to a thousand inhabitants." Shalom M. Paul and William G. Dever, *Biblical Archaeology*, 18. Given the incommensurability of the military achievement and its theological import, it is not surprising that the bulk of the action in the chapter appears to be liturgical.

1-17a. In these verses there is no carryover from the spy story in chap. 2; indeed, there is no hint of awareness that the reconnaissance story has been told. The proclamation of the ban in v 17a admits of no exception; the city and all within it are to be destroyed.

1. *was shut up tight.* Hebrew *sôgeret uměsuggeret,* literally, "had shut and was shut," a cliché used for emphasis.

The regulations for Yahwist siege warfare distinguish between cities which lie outside the inheritance (Deut 20:10-15) and those which have belonged to one of the "seven nations" (Deut 20:17, in the Versions). In the latter "you shall save alive nothing that breathes" (Deut 20:16) because of what they might teach you to do (Deut 20:18). This story concerns ostensibly a city in the second category.

The story begins well past the beginning of the action, a favorite narrative device.

2. *Yahweh said to Joshua.* This is the sixth occurrence of the identical formula (1:1; 3:7; 4:1,15; and 5:9). A similar formula occurs in 5:2, where the formulation is disjunctive, making a total of seven times that Yahweh addresses his field commander, in preparation for the capture and destruction of Jericho.

I have given into your hand. The Akkadian equivalent, *ina qāti nadānu,* "give into the hand," is used with reference to a god granting victory over enemies, as early as the Old Akkadian period. Moran, "The End of the Unholy War . . . ," *Biblica* 44 (1963) 337 n. 1. It was also clearly represented in art (Plate III).

3. *You.* The subject is plural in the first verb form (*to march*) but singular in the second one (*to do*). Such variation is characteristic of orally transmitted material. The early Versions (LXX^L, Syriac, Vulgate) solve the problem by reading both verbs as plural.

march around. The translation is governed by context. Hebrew *sabbōtem* can also mean "encircle," as in the shorter LXX *Vorlage*. In MT the assonance with forms of the cardinal numerals, "six" (*šēšet*), "seven" (*šib'â* and *šeba'*), as well as the ordinal "the seventh" (*haš-šěbî'î*), suggest that perhaps "the sabbath" ought to be in mind here, although it is not mentioned. There can be no doubt that the final articulation of this story was made for folk facing threat of exile, where circumcision, Passover, and sabbath would be central to the practices of the faithful.

around the city. How long would that take? Instructions for marching in orderly fashion around the city once a day for six days, and then seven times on the seventh day, presuppose a situation in which the way would not be encum-

bered with defensive towers, houses, and the various outbuildings such as surrounded the typical city; in fact the bulk of the population of an ancient town
lived outside the walls. In other words, these instructions presuppose that
Jericho is mostly ruins at the outset. It has been suggested that the practice involved is based on "the widespread custom of laying claim to territory by so
tracing out its bounds. Such circulatory marches often formed part of the
ceremonies at the installation of kings." Theodor H. Gaster, *MLC*, 411-412
and notes, with abundant documentation. In this case the speaker in these
verses would be the Divine King, marking out the first piece of Canaan to be
recovered with the cooperation of the Bene Israel.

4. The absence of anything corresponding to v 4 is another indication that
LXX shows here a less "liturgical" source, a tradition of what was consistently
regarded as a military takeover, in line with the spy story and the LXX version
of the second circumcision.

ram's horn trumpets. Hebrew *šôpĕrôt hay-yôbĕlîm.* See Ovid R. Sellers,
"Musical Instruments of Israel," *BA* 4 (1941) 42-43; reprinted in *BAR* 1
(1961) 81-94. As military instrument, the shofar was used to rally the troops
(Judg 3:27; 6:34), to halt the fighting (2 Sam 2:28; 18:16; 20:22), and to
signal victory (1 Sam 13:3). Glock, "Warfare . . . ," 218 n. 9. Here, as in
Gideon's use of ram's horns (Judg 7:16-22), the narrator seems to exploit the
use of the shofar to begin battle. No doubt the horns also serve a certain magic
function. For extra-biblical examples of magic horns, the blast of which can
raze walls, and for the use of noise to expel hostile powers in general, see
Gaster, *MLC*, 413. This possibility is especially attractive in view of the medical theory to be discussed below in NOTES and COMMENT.

the Ark. See NOTE on 3:3.

5. *all the people.* That is, the militia; *NEB* translates as "the whole army."

7. There is no basis for the *NEB* translation in this verse, which has simply
interpolated a reference to the Transjordan contingents: "Then he said to the
army, 'March on and make the circuit of the city, and let the men drafted
from the two and a half tribes go in front of the Ark of the Lord.'"

8. The inverted Hebrew word order in the first sentence (*wšb' hkhnym . . .
'brw*) ends with a verb in the perfect: "moved out." This is disjunctive syntax
which indicates non-sequential action.

They blew. A non-converted perfect used at the outset here yields a chiastic
relationship in the two sentences.

9. *was marching.* The shift to the participial form in Hebrew signals action
that is contemporaneous with the several non-sequential actions reported in the
preceding verse. It is a very busy scene.

marching while blowing. Hebrew *hālôk wĕtākôă'.* Two infinitives absolute.
Varied use of the infinitive absolute is one of the stylistic niceties of this chapter. Here the first of the two may refer not to a simultaneous action but to ac-
celeration; the blowing became louder and louder.

11. *he sent . . . around.* Other Ark stories display the same usage (*hiph'il* of
sbb); cf. 1 Sam 5:9-10. In those stories earthshaking shouts greet the Ark as it
enters the camp of Israel (1 Sam 4:1-9).

the camp. The ancient editor assumes this was at *hag-gilgāl* ("The Circle") throughout this and the following stories. See usage in 10:15 and 43.

12. *got busy.* See above on 3:1, and below on v 15.

13. *keeping step marched forth.* Hebrew *hôlĕkîm hālôk.* Here the finite verb is followed by its own infinitive absolute used adverbially, evoking a sense of a solemn procession.

15. *they got up at daybreak.* The verb *hškm* is here construed with *k'lwt hšhr,* literally, "rising of the dawn," in contrast to v 12, and means "to arise early." The seventh day would be the busiest of all, and they would need to get an early start.

17. *ban.* Hebrew *ḥērem.* This is the biblical equivalent of an old Amorite expression, "to eat the *asakkum*" of a god or king. At Mari it had to do with certain spoils of war marked for the treasury of the royal house or for sacrificial offering to the deity. Execution of the *ḥērem* in biblical texts is frequently associated with destruction by fire, and the latter has been interpreted as a response to epidemic disease, especially bubonic plague. See Mendenhall's treatment of the Beth-Baal Peor story in Numbers 25 (*Ten Gen,* 105-121); and Carol Meyers, "The Roots of Restriction: Women in Early Israel," *BA* 41 (1978) 91-103. The latter concludes that ". . . the unconscionable *ḥērem* perhaps can be seen as a kind of plague control" (96). The practice of the *ḥērem* existed in Israel alongside the taking of spoil (8:26-27; 11:14), and so presumably both were originally regulated by ad hoc decree. For the magnitude of implication where the *ḥērem* is involved, see the story of the break between Samuel and Saul in 1 Samuel 15. It is not a uniquely Israelite word or practice. The ninth-century Moabite king Mesha speaks thus of "devoting" the Israelites to his god Chemosh. *ANET²,* 320 after line 15. By that time, however, the same institution in Israel seems to belong to the past. In the Book of Judges, the *ḥērem* is mentioned in the introduction (1:17) and conclusion (21:11) and otherwise clearly figures only once within the period (Judg 8:22-27). This last is the conclusion to a scathing portrayal of Gideon after his use of the people's militia in a war of private vengeance. This use is clearly regarded as irregular in this period. See *Judges,* AB 6A, 16, 58 (NOTE on 1:17), 161 (COMMENT on 8:22-29), 292 (NOTE on 21:11). When the *ḥērem* at last became passé, with the establishment of the monarchy, the distribution of booty became the prerogative of the king (1 Sam 30:23-25) in Israel as elsewhere.

Yahweh. LXX reads "Yahweh Sabaoth," reflecting again a more literally militant version of events at Jericho.

17b-25. In this segment the siege of Jericho is connected in two directions. The narrative picks up the thread of the spy story in chap. 2 and lays the groundwork for the story of Achan in chap. 7.

17b. *Only.* The syntax is sharply disjunctive.

18. *something banned.* The important word *ḥērem* is here used three times (four in MT) in quick succession so as to establish a relation with the final verb in the sentence. A remarkable Canaanite illustration of this practice was excavated by Sir Flinders Petrie near Tell el-'Ajjul and dated to the early sec-

ond millennium, roughly the era of the biblical patriarchs. Discovered in a pit were:

> an immense quantity of black ash, the remains of burnt garments. Amid the ash was goldwork which had obviously been most carefully destroyed. Bracelets had been cut into scraps, and the terminals, in the shape of serpents' heads whose eyes still gleamed when found, had been severed. The bright plating of gold had been stripped from everything and broken into the smallest fragments. Gold-plated studs and nails were all loosed from woodwork which had been burnt. Lumps and globules of gold were found, the melted remains of the inferno. Found together with the gold were two basalt tripod stands which had been smashed on the spot, as shown by the fact that not a single fragment was missing. Many horses' teeth and chips of bone were also found. There must have been a complete destruction of property, gold and silver, at the spot. (Paul and Dever, *Biblical Archaeology,* 202-203.)

making trouble for it! Hebrew *w'krtm 'wtw.* The same root will be used in the naming of a famous place, Trouble Valley, the story of which follows next (7:1-26). In these two words at the end of 6:18, the compiler furnishes another example of Joshua's "prophetic" competence.

19. *treasury.* Hebrew *'ôṣar.* For a vivid description in later prophecy of the way Yahweh's wealth is to be acquired (by expropriating the proceeds from the harlot Tyre's international "hire") and not kept stored (*lō' yē'āṣēr*) but used "for those who dwell before the Lord," see Isa 23:18.

20. *The priests blew the trumpets.* From that point things would seem to go forward without a flaw.

In ancient military theory, there were five ways (to be used separately or in various combinations) to reduce a fortified town: (a) to penetrate the town over the wall; (b) to penetrate the town through the wall or the gates; (c) to penetrate the town from beneath the wall; (d) to subdue the town through siege: (e) to overpower the town by a stratagem. Yigael Yadin, "Warfare in the Second Millennium B.C.E.," in *WHJP* II, 155.

The wall collapsed. Against efforts to analyze the several processions, horn blasts, and war whoops as reflecting two or more documentary sources is the fact that after all the repetitive buildup this great and colossal happening is only "reported in one very brief and unadorned statement." Wilcoxen, "Narrative Structure and Cult Legend," 49-50. He would see, instead of literary sources, a variety of cultic patterns contributing to the narrative. But a cultic explanation does not account for the chapter as connected narrative. Nor does it account for the genesis of the story. Was it an earthquake? The Jordan valley-Dead Sea-Arabah rift is part of a long and very unstable fault line. If walls on the tell were already in a state of disrepair (stumps of abandoned MB and early LB Age construction), it would not have taken much of a tremor to bring them down. In some such vein we may reconstruct an experience which gave credibility to the prose story. There is also a poetic version, where the crossing of the Jordan is parallel to the deliverance at the sea in Psalm 114:3-7:

> When the sea saw him, it fled,
>   the Jordan turned back.
> The mountains leaped like rams,
>   the hills like lambs of the flock.
>
> . . .
>
> In the presence of the Lord writhe, O land.
>   (Dahood translation, AB 17A, 133.)

21. *at the mouth of the sword!* The exact meaning is not clear. Ancient swords in which the blade comes out of a shaft to form the tongue of an animal whose head appears at the handle have been excavated. T. J. Meek, "Archaeology and a Point of Hebrew Syntax," *BASOR* 122 (1951) 31-33. On the other hand, the frequency of the expression construed with the verb "to smite" suggests that the expression originated in the use of the sicklesword. The latter was sharp only on the convex side, so that one neither cut nor stabbed, but hit with it (see Plate III). Yigael Yadin, "Military and Archaeological Aspects of the Conquest of Canaan in the Book of Joshua," *El Ha'ayin* 1 (1965) 4. In a response to this article, Abraham Malamat in the same issue (22) makes the interesting suggestion that mention of the sword implies the activity of Qenites ("smiths") as suppliers of armaments.

22. *had said.* The form is *qal* perfect and the syntax is disjunctive.

23. *the young spies.* Hebrew *hn'rym hmrglym*, literally, "the young men, the spies"; cf. "two men" in 2:1.

24. *The city they burned.* This is like the treatment of Hazor in the far north (11:11), which is presented as an exception to the general rule that "all the cities standing on mounds" the Israelites did not burn. Archaeology in fact documents a broad continuity of cultural elements from LB into Iron I (thirteenth to twelfth centuries B.C.). There is a later but distinct parallel in the Arab conquest which inherited Byzantine culture and preserved it with the aid of Byzantine artists and craftsmen.

Yahweh's house. Hebrew *byt yhwh.* The Gilgal sanctuary? This is not necessarily a reference to the Jerusalem Temple, built nearly two hundred years later. An ostracon from the later Israelite temple at Arad also mentions a *bêt-yahweh*, namely, the building in which it was found. There was a *hykl yhwh*, "temple/palace of Yahweh," at Shiloh late in the pre-monarchical period as we know from 1 Sam 1:9.

25. *the harlot Rahab.* See especially her speech in 2:9-13. ". . . While her precise profession of faith in Yahweh may be an anachronism, there can be no doubt of her conversion and eventual assimilation into the Israelite community." Joseph J. de Vault, *The Book of Josue,* 11.

She dwells. In her descendants.

to this very day. In a majority of cases, this is a secondary formula, added to the text as a redactional comment on the preformed unit. Brevard S. Childs, "Unto This Day," *JBL* 82 (1963) 289*ff.* When M. Noth understands Joshua 2 and 6:17b,22,23,25 as a story which seeks to explain the presence of a family or "House of Rahab" (regarded as Canaanite) in the midst of Israel, "it is clear that he has implicitly imposed an inferential model on an extensive narrative which in fact contains no inferential statement." Long, *The Problem of Etiological Narratives in the Old Testament,* 89. The interest of the narrator lies elsewhere. "By emphasizing the survival it points up the effectiveness of Joshua's directions. . . ." McCarthy, "The Theology of Leadership in Joshua 1-9," *Biblica* 52 (1971) 170. More specifically, what the etiological formula does at this point is to signal a shift of interest by a redactor (Dtr 2, most likely) away from the story of the fall of Jericho per se and onto the story of covenant-keeping with Rahab, the former pagan. The fall might be of little direct value to life in exile, whereas the story of covenant-keeping with the pagan harlot would be directly relevant in the chaos that followed the reign of Josiah.

the messengers. Hebrew *ham-mal'ākîm,* which elsewhere may stand for "angels" and is sometimes deliberately left ambiguous. The word is used only here with reference to the spies. Along with disjunctive syntax, all this suggests the activity of a redactor bringing together the largely preformed story units.

26. The event described here is unique in the Old Testament. Nowhere else in the Hebrew Bible is a city's rebuilder proleptically cursed.

administered an oath. Hebrew *way-yašba',* "caused a swearing."

at that time. Since no specific day reference is given, it is assumed that all the events of chap. 6, excluding of course the flashback to Rahab's activity in chap. 2, belong to the second period of seven days.

before Yahweh. On this reading see Textual Note above.

"Cursed be the man." As here presented, it is an invective designed to prevent Israelite settlement at the newly conquered site. Since presumably Joshua gave the whole people the oath it was a self-imprecation.

who. Hebrew *'šr.* No doubt originally the archaic form *šā* stood here.

proceeds to rebuild. Hebrew *yāqûm ûbānâ,* a verbal hendiadys. See NOTE on 1:2.

With and *With.* Hebrew *bĕ-* is here to be taken directly and emphatically. Here it seems to mean "at the cost of." Within the parameters of early Yahwism the saying defies understanding as any sort of prescriptive curse referring to the practice of infant sacrifice. But it would make very good sense as a descriptive curse if it reflects the reality of a high infant mortality rate in the area watered by the Jericho spring. See COMMENT.

set up its gates. This happens in 1 Kgs 16:34. "Prophecy and Fulfillment" is a favorite organizing device in Dtr 1.

27. *with.* Hebrew *'t* is used here, forming an inclusion with the more common *'m,* which occurs as part of a promise in Yahweh's introductory speech (1:9), and the Transjordan tribes' introductory hope (1:17). This demonstrated divine support culminating in the self-discipline shown by the act of cursing Jericho was electric in effect.

his fame was country-wide. Whose fame? Joshua's or Yahweh's? Probably Joshua's since Rahab has already testified that Yahweh's fame had preceded him.

COMMENT

In late June and early July of the year 1099, the Crusader preparation for the capture of Jerusalem entered the countdown phase:

> The Crusaders erected three moving siege-towers which were higher than the wall. . . . When the towers had been erected the Crusaders began a fast of three days, at the conclusion of which they moved in procession around the city's walls, led by the clergy carrying sacred banners and pictures of saints, the entire host walking barefoot and bareheaded. The Moslems, who saw the procession from the walls, mocked the Christians and shot arrows at them; the Crusaders, having encircled the walls of the city like the Israelites at Jericho, expected them to fall, but they remained whole and menacing as before. (Meron Benvenisti, *The Crusaders in the Holy Land* [Jerusalem: Israel Universities Press, 1970] 37.)

The comparison seems valid, on the surface. And if it is accurate, it is also clear that the Crusaders rapidly managed to transcend their reliance upon deity and besieged the city directly.

> The Crusaders, drunk with victory, conducted a massacre in the city such as has seldom been paralleled in the history of war; the troops ran amok through the streets, stabbing and slaying everyone they encountered. . . . The Jewish community, gathered in the central synagogue, were shut in by the Crusaders and burnt alive. . . . The massacre aroused horror among the Crusaders themselves. . . . (Ibid., 38)

This presumed continuity with Joshua 6 is only superficial. Let us begin with the problem of the missing "city wall."

No traces of a fortification wall have been found at Tell es-Sultan (the only known candidate for Old Testament Jericho) which might have collapsed late in the Late Bronze Age or early in Iron I (that is, somewhere in the late thirteenth to mid-twelfth centuries B.C.) to admit the Bene Israel. By that time Jericho was already a city that was many millennia old, with a history of human habitation, reflecting a high level of social organization in an early (pre-pottery) phase of the Neolithic or New Stone Age. The earliest excavated fortifications at the site consist of a massive circular stone tower (8.5 meters diameter; 7.75 meters high) abutting the inner face of a town wall. See sketch plan of the Walls of Jericho. See *ANEP*, ⚔863. Material for dating the Tower has yielded radiocarbon dates ranging from 8340 B.C. ±200 years to 6935 B.C. ±155 years. These earliest fortifications give evidence of a population which must have made considerable use of irrigation agriculture, for the nearby spring "in its natural state could not have watered an area large enough for the fully grown town." Kathleen Kenyon, "Jericho," in *EAEHL* II (1976) 554.

In Joshua's day these earliest structures lay deeply buried under an accumulation of debris around and over defense walls of the later periods. The innermost of these (see below) is the wall which in past decades has been mistakenly associated with the Israelite invasion, on the basis of earlier excavations. Thanks to the greatly improved techniques for stratigraphical digging and recording introduced at Jericho by the late Dame Kathleen Kenyon, it is clear that "City Wall 1" was built, used, and destroyed, all within the Early Bronze Age, the third millennium B.C.

When in the following Middle Bronze period Jericho revived, it was provided at last with an elaborate fortification system. Near the foot of the tell was a stone retaining wall, which supported a sloping surface heavily packed with hard lime plaster (see the line drawing for both features), which in turn was surmounted by a screening wall on its summit. In such a system it is only the upper screening wall that is capable of collapse.

It is not beyond the realm of possibility that it was the destruction of the MB fortification at Jericho that lies at the basis of a number of details in Joshua 6. Whether MB Jericho was destroyed by Egyptian forces in connection with the expulsion of the Hyksos or as part of the later prelude to the Amarna Age chaos is a moot question. It is doubtful that we have enough evidence to reduce the chapter to nothing more than a "reminiscence of an earlier capture of the city by pre-Israelite Hebrews (*Ḥabirû*)," as claimed by Gaster, *MLC,* 411.

What is clear from extensive excavations at Tell es-Sultan and from the substantial probes at every known candidate for a nearby Gilgal is that the LB occupation of the area around the oasis was extremely sparse! Especially in the post-Amarna period, conditions at the southern end of the Jordan valley seem to have reverted to something like those preceding the Neolithic development of the oasis, except for the scattered concentrations of "wealth" represented by a handful of LB tombs excavated by John Garstang. On the mound itself the scant evidence points to something which might at most have been the unfortified hangout of a local strongman. It is likely therefore that the story owes much to older accounts among the Hebrews of violent reduction of a walled town.

But why would Jericho have been considered to be worth the effort, especially if the region were as depressed as the archaeological evidence suggests? It is not quite accurate to say that Jericho commands the approaches to the central highlands. "There are a number of routes" which invaders could take without being blocked by forces based at

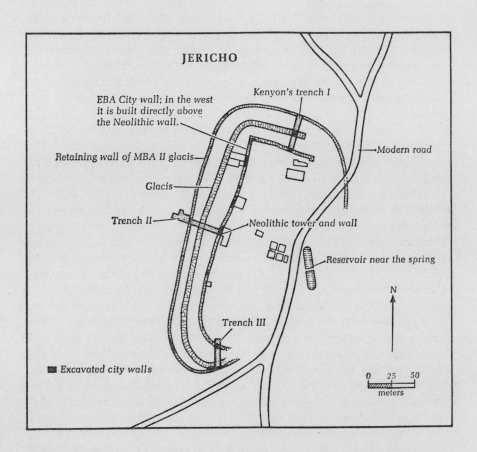

JERICHO

EBA City wall; in the west
it is built directly above
the Neolithic wall.

Kenyon's trench I

Retaining wall of MBA II glacis

Modern road

Glacis

Trench II

Neolithic tower and wall

Reservoir near the spring

N

Trench III

■ Excavated city walls

0   25   50
meters

Jericho, unless those forces were superior in number, "and this is not suggested by the account" (McKenzie, *The World of the Judges*, 47).

And finally, there is the curse. Why go to the trouble to capture a townsite that is not going to be settled? Is it possible, since the cursing at Jericho is the culmination of the chapter, that it was from the outset the goal of the expedition and is thus the key to the whole story?

This cursing of a captured city is unique in the Old Testament, but it is not unknown elsewhere. Examples have been collected by S. Gevirtz, "Jericho and Shechem: A Religio-Literary Aspect of City Destruction," *VT* 13 (1963) 52-62. He concludes that there is a relationship between this prohibition of resettlement in the destroyed town and the act of consecrating it. What is lacking in this interpretation, however, is any clue to a motivational factor for singling out this particular place for such a purpose.

In view of all this, a recently published medical approach to the tradition deserves serious attention.

Schistosomiasis is caused by a blood fluke parasite whose intermediate host, a species of snail (*Bulinus truncatus*), has been found in excavations at Tell es-Sultan. This host organism is known to thrive best in water that is contaminated during usage by human beings, a process for which the single Jericho spring at the foot of the tell is unusually well situated. Moreover, genito-urinary schistosomiasis causes dramatic external signs of which an informant such as Rahab would presumably know quite a lot. Its debilitating effects in attitudes of defeatism and despair (leaving "fortifications" in dilapidated disrepair?) and especially in reduced fertility follow quite naturally.

If the reason for the prohibition of Yahwist settlement there was in fact knowledge of high infant mortality, the terms of the poetic "curse" suddenly make sense, as do the remarks made to Elisha at Jericho in 2 Kgs 2:19, "Behold, the situation of this city is pleasant, as my lord sees, but the water is bad and the land is unfruitful" (*RSV*). Is it mere coincidence that there is a four-hundred-year gap in settlement at Jericho, just where geography, historical movements, and climatological conditions in the Middle Bronze and Late Bronze ages might have all converged for the flourishing of this disease whose etiology is clear? For a complete statement of the proposal, although it perhaps seeks to explain too many details, see E. V. Hulse, "Joshua's Curse and the Abandonment of Ancient Jericho: Schistosomiasis as a Possible Medical Explanation," *Medical History* 15 (1971) 376-386.

The possibility that Jericho was in fact known to be such an unhealthy place sets the whole manner of its "capture," and the narrative peculiarities of chap. 6, in an entirely new light. It is not stated in the text, nor is it clearly implied, that the marching around the city for six days and the shouting and horn-blowing are related to the collapse of the walls. Rather, the tradition may perhaps more plausibly have originated in a series of protective ritual exercises which were accompanied or soon followed by an unexpected seismic event. The solemn procession around the city would indeed be providentially "Israel's participation in the manifestation of the power of Yahweh" (McKenzie, *The World of the Judges,* 52).

The story of the river crossing suggests that this was a period of such seismic tremors. All of this would then, very properly, be interpreted in such a way as to establish The Circle as an especially holy place, developing its own liturgy but without much permanent settlement. The celebration there was seasonal, a spring New Year covenant-renewal feast.

The editor leaves us in v 27 with the impression that the capture of Jericho had been flawless. In any case it served to secure the wide-ranging reputation of Joshua. With Joshua in charge, what could possibly go wrong?

2. ACHAN AS EXPLANATION
(7:1-26)

7 ¹ The Bene Israel committed a treacherous violation of the ban. Achan ben Carmi ben Zabdi ben Zerah, of the tribe of Judah, had taken some of the devoted goods. And Yahweh's wrath was kindled against the Bene Israel.

² Joshua sent some men to The Ruin, which is near Beth-aven (that is, to the east of Bethel). He said to them, "Go up and reconnoiter the land." So the men went up and reconnoitered The Ruin.

³ They returned to Joshua and said to him, "Do not deploy all the people, for about two or three contingents of men can go up and defeat The Ruin. Do not weary all the people there, where they are few in number."

⁴ So there went up thither, from the people, exactly three contingents. But they ran away in defeat before the men of The Ruin! ⁵ The men of The Ruin struck down thirty-six of their men, whom they chased from in front of the gate as far as The Quarries, and striking them down at the descent. The people's heart melted—turned to water!

⁶ Joshua rent his clothes and fell face down on the ground before the Ark of Yahweh and stayed that way until evening—he and Israel's elders—throwing dust on their heads. ⁷ Said Joshua: "Ahh! Lord Yahweh, why did you persist in bringing this people over the Jordan? To give us into the power of the Westerners? To destroy us? If we only had been content to live in the region beyond the Jordan! ⁸ Please, my Lord, what can I say after Israel has shown its neck to its enemies? ⁹ When the Canaanites and all the land's rulers hear of it, they will surround us and will cut off our name from the earth. What will you do about your own great name?"

¹⁰ And Yahweh said to Joshua:

"Get up. Why are you prostrate? ¹¹ Israel has sinned! They have violated my covenant which I commanded them. They have taken some of the condemned goods. They have stolen and they have covered up the theft. They have put it with their own gear. 12 The Bene Israel are unable to stand before their enemies. They turn back in the face of their enemies because they have become banned themselves! I shall not continue to be with you if you do not destroy what is condemned in your midst.

13 "Get on with the preparation of the people; say, 'Make yourselves ritually ready for tomorrow. For thus says Yahweh, God of Israel: There is condemned stuff in your midst. You will not be able to stand before your enemies until you have removed what is condemned from your midst.

14 " 'In the morning you will be summoned by tribes. The tribe which Yahweh designates shall approach by clans. The clan which Yahweh designates you shall bring near by households. And the household which Yahweh designates shall approach one by one. 15 The one who is taken with the condemned goods will be burned, he and all that belongs to him, because he has violated Yahweh's covenant and has committed an outrage in Israel.' "

16 So Joshua got busy next morning and summoned Israel by tribes. The tribe of Judah was designated. 17 He summoned the clans of Judah, and he took the Zerahite clan. He summoned the Zerahite clan, one by one, and the Zabdi family was designated. 18 He summoned his household, one by one, and Achan ben Carmi ben Zabdi ben Zerah was designated.

19 Joshua said to Achan, "My son, glorify Yahweh, God of Israel, and give praise to him. Let me know what you have done. Do not hide anything from me."

20 Achan answered Joshua. "In truth, I have sinned against Yahweh, God of Israel. It happened about like this. 21 When I saw among the booty a fine Shinar-cloak, and two hundred shekels' weight of silver, and a gold bar weighing fifty shekels—I coveted them and took them. They are hidden underground inside my tent, with the silver at the bottom of it."

22 So Joshua sent messengers who ran to the tent. And there it was, hidden inside his tent, with the silver at the bottom of it. 23 They took the things out of his tent and brought them to Joshua and all the Bene Israel. They spread them out before Yahweh.

24 Joshua took Achan ben Zerah together with the silver, the cloak, the gold bar, his sons, his daughters, his ox, his ass, his sheep, his tent, and everything that belonged to him. All Israel was with him. They brought them up to Devastation Valley.

25 Said Joshua, "Why have you devastated us? Yahweh will devastate you this very day."

And all Israel stoned him. They burned them and stoned them. 26 They erected over him a stone cairn. Then Yahweh relented from his hot wrath. (Therefore the name of that place is called Devastation Valley, down to this day.)

TEXTUAL NOTES

7 1. *Achan*   Hebrew *'kn*. His name is *'kr* in LXX^B, Syriac (so also in vv 18-20,24) and 1 Chr 2:7. This represents assimilation to the name of the valley which his story was at last thought to explain (v 26).

Zabdi   The name is "Zabri" in LXX^A (whence Zambri in LXX^B), reflecting the not infrequent scribal confusion of *d* and *r*. Cf. Zimri in 1 Chr 2:6.

against the Bene Israel   For *bbny yśr'l* some manuscripts read *byśr'l*, "against Israel."

2. *men*   Thus LXX. MT specifies "from Jericho," but there is no way to show haplography in the Greek or its *Vorlage*. The prepositional phrase was perhaps originally a marginal note.

Beth-aven (*that is, to the east of*   Lacking in LXX, after a long haplography: *'m byt*[*-'wn mqdm lbyt*]*-'l*.

He said to them   In LXX^AB the text is shorter, after haplography: *lbyt-'l* [*wy'mr 'lyhm*] *l'mr*.

"Go up and reconnoiter the land." So the men went up and reconnoitered The Ruin   The text is much shorter in LXX, where a scribe's eye jumped from *r* to *r* and from *wrglw* to *wyrglw*: *l'mr* [*'lw w*]*rglw* [*'t-h'rṣ wy'lw h'nšym wyrglw*] *'t-h'y*.

3. *for about*   This is LXX, where in MT the consonantal sequence **ky'm'lpym* (or **ky'lpym*) has been telescoped to *k'lpym*.

The Ruin   Hebrew *h'y*, where LXX and Vulgate reflect a difference of one letter: *h'yr*, "the city."

4. *thither, from the people*   LXX^A omits *from the people*, while LXX^B lacks the entire expression. These look like inner-Greek developments.

5. *thirty-six*   Thus LXX^A and Syriac, where MT reads "exactly thirty-six" (*kšlšym wššh*). The *k* is understood as a vertical dittography from "exactly three units" (*kšlšt 'lpym*).

as far as The Quarries   This translates Hebrew *'ad haš-šĕbārîm*, which is lacking in LXX^B. Syriac and Targum read the same consonants as *'ad hiššābĕrām*, "till they were shattered"; but context leads us to expect a place name.

6. *the Ark of Yahweh*   Major Greek recensions read simply "before the Lord," which seems to reflect an inner-Greek haplography: *k*[*ibōtos k*]*uriou*.

However, the form occurs so frequently in LXX that it may be a different tradition.

7. *persist in bringing this people over*　The Hebrew *h'brt h'byr* uses the infinitive absolute following the finite form of the verb to emphasize continuous aspect of the action. The LXX may reflect confusion of *r* and *d* reading: "Why did your servant [*h'bd*] bring this people over . . ." Less likely is the suggestion that the Greek represents a tendentious theological development.

in the region beyond　Hebrew *b'br yrdn*. LXX seems to reflect *'l hyrdn*, "along the Jordan."

8. *Please, my Lord*　LXX omits. See NOTE.

9. *our name*　For Hebrew *'t šmnw* LXX has "us," presumably *'tnw*.

11. *Israel*　In LXX not *Israel*, but "the people." See NOTES.

They have stolen and they have covered up the theft　LXX shows a haplography: *lqḥw mn hḥrm* [*wgm gnbw wgm kḥšw*] *wgm šmw bklyhm*.

13. *thus*　Lacking in LXX, by haplography: *ky* [*kh*].

your midst　For the pronoun, LXX retains the original plural form, in keeping with the context. MT adds a vocative "Israel" which triggered a shift to singular pronoun suffixes. Leonard Greenspoon, private communication.

14. *you shall bring near*　This is the second plural *hiph'il* addressed to the people, following LXX, where MT shifts abruptly, with a specific instruction addressed to Joshua, "you shall approach."

15. *with the condemned goods*　Hebrew *bḥrm*. This is not represented in LXX^AB, probably preserving the original.

16. *next morning*　Hebrew *bbqr* has no reflex in LXX, which also reads "the people" in place of *Israel* (as in v 11).

17. *clans*　This agrees with a small collection of manuscripts, against MT's singular form. We would expect either the plural or else a word for "tribe."

he took　Thus MT, referring to Yahweh. In this verse it was the fluctuation of mood, in orally transmitted material, that was puzzling to the Greek translators. They leveled the passive throughout this section.

18. *ben Zerah*　Thus LXX. MT continues: "belonging to the tribe of Judah." But this is probably the result of contamination from the full genealogical form which, as we should expect, occurs at the outset (v 1). Here in v 18 there is no mechanism to explain haplography in either Hebrew or Greek.

19. *"My son*　This is lacking in LXX^AB, with nothing to explain the loss.

to him　Thus MT, which is not clearly reflected in LXX, unless it is implicit in the verb: *eksomologēsin*.

21. *When I saw*　This is the *kethib: wā-'er'eh*.

weighing　Thus MT, where LXX^AB and Syr^h show a haplography: *ḥmšym šqlym* [*mšqlw*] *w'ḥmdm*.

underground　In a perfect setup for haplography, LXX lacks the *underground* reference: *b['rṣ b]twk*.

my　The original was perhaps *'hly* (so LXX), contaminated by anticipation of *h'hlh*, "to the tent," in the following verse, to yield the anomalous form in MT: *h'hly*. Or the reading may be a conflation of "the tent" and "my tent."

23. *all*   Lacking in LXX, by haplography: *'[l k]l*.

Bene   LXX reads instead "elders" (*ziqnê*). Syriac lacks both.

24. *Zerah*   Instead of the following list of plunder, LXX has a redundancy: "They brought him to Devastation Valley."

25. *They burned them and stoned them*   The versions show haplographies omitting all of this (LXX^AB) or only the last half of it (Syriac, Vulgate). Losses triggered by the ubiquity of converted imperfects in Hebrew narrative are, of course, the most common kind of scribal lapse. The apparent redundancy in MT, followed here, may have an explanation other than mere conflation. See NOTES.

26. *stone cairn*   Thus LXX. In MT a scribe has anticipated the end of the verse and written in an extra occurrence of the formula "down to this day."

NOTES

In this chapter the first of two attacks on a place called The Ruin is repulsed and the defeat of the Bene Israel is traced to one man's violation of the *ḥērem*-decree. The foundation for the story has been laid by the inclusion of a *ḥērem*-proclamation at Jericho in 6:17-18. As it now stands, the story of Achan (7:1,6-26) is interrupted, and the defeat at The Ruin (7:2-5) is given as the cause of his discovery and undoing. The story displays the tension between individual guilt and corporate responsibility to Yahweh.

7:1. *The Bene Israel*. All of them? It is an effective opening which arrests attention. Special guard units would have been posted with responsibility for protecting booty. Yigael Yadin, "Warfare in the Second Millennium, B.C.E.," 141, referring to ARM, I, 43, lines 4-12.

committed a treacherous violation. The root *m'l* is here repeated, in the construction of verb + cognate accusative, a device that is especially characteristic of popular narrative. The same verb and noun are used in the altar story (22:16) where the noun occurs again (22:22) in the context, and where the subject is the sin of Achan! Otherwise the story of Achan is never mentioned again in OT (there may be allusions to it, such as Hos 2:7, Freedman suggests). This is the first of a series of lexical and rhetorical connections with the story in chap. 22.

This forceful introduction to the story diverts attention away from Joshua, the hero of the era, and onto the violation of his decree.

the ban. It is going too far to make the *ḥērem* into the central feature in holy war. N. Gottwald, *Review and Expositor* 61 (1964) 299-305. Yet there is no doubt that the *ḥērem* was important enough to focus all attention upon the guilty one.

Achan. The name is "Achar" in 1 Chr 2:7. He is mentioned exactly five times in this chapter.

ben. The Hebrew word for "son" has a wide range of social and idiomatic usage. For example, Bene Israel could not originally have meant "children of Israel" in a strictly genealogical sense. It meant simply "members of the large, multi-tribal association: Israel."

Carmi. 1 Chronicles 2:7; 4:1. It is an occupational name, related to the word for "vineyard." This is also an important "family" in Reuben (Gen 46:9; Num 26:5-6; 1 Chr 5:3). The abrupt introduction of so much genealogical information in one of these stories from the early period must be carefully surveyed, with a view to both form and function in the narrative unit. See Robert R. Wilson, "The Old Testament Genealogies in Recent Research," *JBL* 94 (1975) 169-189; *Genealogy and History in the Biblical World* (New Haven and London: Yale University Press, 1977); "Between 'Azel' and 'Azel': Interpreting the Biblical Genealogies," *BA* 42 (1979) 11-22.

Zabdi. The name is also found among the Levitical musicians of a later era (Neh 11:17) and in Benjamin (1 Chr 8:19; 27:27). Most interesting is one royal official who is "over the produce of the vineyards for the wine cellar." The name is a shortened form of the sentence name: Zabdiel, "El has endowed me" (Neh 11:14; 1 Chr 27:2), or Zebadyah, "Yah(weh) has endowed" (1 Chr 8:15,17; 12:8; 26:2; 27:7; 2 Chr 17:8; 19:11; Ezra 8:8; 10:20).

Zerah. Twin brother of Perez in the genealogy that became authoritative (Gen 38:30; 46:12; 1 Chr 2:4). The full sentence name is Zerahyah (Ezra 7:4; 8:4; 1 Chr 5:32; 6:36). The name also occurs as a "son" of Simeon (Num 26:13; 1 Chr 4:24) and among the Levites (1 Chr 6:6,26; cf. Ezrahite in Pss 88:1; 89:1). A gentilic form of the name is found in the Chronicler's list of the monthly divisions as organized by King David (1 Chr 27:11,13) and here in v 17.

Judah. This is the only west-bank tribe that is mentioned by name in the supposedly Benjaminite war stories, as rightly stressed by Kaufmann, *The Biblical Account of the Conquest of Palestine,* 67.

Yahweh's wrath was kindled. Against Israel, it happened only once in this period, in striking contrast to the next one (Judg 2:14,20; 3:8; 10:7).

2. *Joshua sent some men.* This repeats the wording of the first reconnaissance story (2:1), of which there will be many reminiscences in this story. But this story is in a very different category because here the warfare in Canaan has already begun. With the surprising Jericho victory behind him, Joshua proceeds to reconnoiter a new target.

Did Joshua on this occasion neglect to consult the oracle? Attention has been called to this possibility (which had already suggested itself to the writer) by Othmar Keel, *Wirkmächtige Siegeszeichen im Alten Testament,* 18 n. 4. "Divination" before battle was an invariable concomitant of ancient warfare, including Israelite warfare, where the means of discovering the divine will were, however, severely restricted. It is at least interesting that one of the few places where Urim (one of the sacred dice) is mentioned is in the account of Joshua's commissioning: "And he shall stand before Eleazar the priest who shall inquire for him by the judgment of the Urim before the Lord; at his word they shall go out, and at his word they shall come in, both he and all the people with him, the whole congregation" (Num 27:21).

The Ruin. See Ai, Map D, 260. This is a most unusual type of place name; and it occurs here five times in rapid succession—another twenty-two times in the sequel (8:1-29)! The meaning of the name is thus profoundly important, but not for any superficially etiological reasons. The site that has proved to be the most likely location of The Ruin is in Arabic simply called et-Tell, "The Hill." Similarly in antiquity there were many other ruins, so that in 12:9 the consistent form of the list of overthrown kings is violated in order to make it clear that The Ruin in question is the one near Bethel. The Ruin is not included as such in the towns of Benjamin (18:21-28). Here the narrator assumes the relevance of "What's in a name." And a certain rhetorical effect is achieved by the extended effort to fix the exact location of this ruin at the outset.

Beth-aven. "House of Iniquity" is obviously a distortion (which could be used polemically of Bethel), perhaps for an original *Beth-'Ôn*. Bright, *IB* 2, 584. The best candidate is Tell Maryam 5 km south of Deir Dibwan. See also Benjamin's border in 18:12.

that is. These words are not represented in the Hebrew, which simply places phrases in apposition.

Bethel. "House of El" or "House of God." The story of its recognition by the patriarch Jacob is told in Gen 28:10-22. Following the split of the tribes at the death of Solomon, Bethel became the important southern border sanctuary of the northern kingdom, Israel. Unfortunately, excavations have not succeeded in locating the sacred area, which no doubt now is covered by modern structures in the village of Beitin.

Bethel's priests were probably of a house that claimed Aaronite descent, a rival lineage to other Aaronites whom David had brought to Jerusalem from Hebron. The latter rapidly won out, ousting even the Mushite lineage (i.e. one which claimed descent from Moses) which had come from Shiloh into the monarchical establishment. For this reconstruction of the history of rival priestly houses, we are indebted to Cross, *CMHE* (especially chap. 8, "The Priestly Houses of Early Israel") 195-215. Against this background, the history of our chapter begins to come into focus. The first "edition" used the scornful name Beth-aven; this was the Dtr 1 (or Josianic) version. But it was reworked by someone, as the parenthetical identification with Bethel shows. There are a number of pointers to groups such as alienated and disaffected Levites from the north as the contributors of "Dtr 2."

3. *contingents.* Not "thousands." The military semantics of *'ălāpîm* in early narrative is much clearer than it used to be. See above, first NOTE on 4:13. This reference to contingents is another point of similarity with the altar story at the end of the period (22:14 and 21). Another example of the same semantic confusion is 2 Sam 10:18, where *RSV* reads "seven hundred chariots and forty thousand horsemen." We should read instead "seven hundred chariots, that is, forty equestrian units." The proportions become entirely credible.

4. *exactly three contingents.* Hebrew *kšlšt 'lpym*. The *k* is emphatic, matching the precision of the numeral thirty-six in the next verse.

5. *thirty-six.* There is no way of knowing how large these contingents were. If the *'lp* was, for example, fifteen soldiers, then there was an 80 per cent loss; if twenty soldiers, then 60 per cent loss; if thirty soldiers, then 40 per cent loss.

The smaller units have the higher credibility for this early period. The stylistic phenomenon represented by these numbers is strictly comparable to the one involved in the stories of Gideon's muster (Judg 7:1-22) and the Benjaminite Civil War (Judg 20:1-48). See *Judges*, AB 6A, 142-149, 280-288. A loss of thirty-six out of a force of three thousand would surely not be considered all that decisive. But thirty-six dead or disabled out of three contingents means in any case a resounding defeat. And Joshua's reaction likewise becomes credible.

in front of the gate. Why this precise location is specified is not clear. The city gate was the most important element in city fortifications, usually massively built, with flanking guardrooms in towers that were two or more stories high, the entire structure roofed over and surmounted by battlement platforms. From Mari we know that the gate might commemorate a powerful monarch (e.g. "the Gate of Itūr-Mer") or deity (Nergal, Hišamitum). Sasson, *The Military Establishment at Mari*, 4. To attack a city gate head-on, with a small force, would not be wise. This element of the story belongs to its rhetorical elaboration, since et-Tell was at most an unwalled village, settled later in this period (Iron I A).

The Quarries. Thus NEB renders *hšbrym*, precise location unknown.

at the descent. A *môrād* is a place for "going down," in this case, into the wadi system leading back to Jericho. See Plate II. For detailed description of the geographical features, see now Hartmut Rösel, "Studien zur Topographie der Kriege in den Büchern Josua und Richter," *ZDPV* 91 (1975) especially 164-168.

heart melted. With the same language previously used by Rahab (2:11) and a redactor describing the panicked reaction of the kings (5:1), the situation is now completely reversed.

6. *Joshua rent his clothes and fell face down.* For these and related rituals of mourning and penitence, see Joel 1:8-14; Jer 16:6-7; Job 1:20; 2 Sam 12:15-16.

fell . . . and stayed that way. Here the text has only one verb, *wypl*, combining inchoative and continuous senses in a situation where the combination is impossible in English.

before the Ark of Yahweh. This is the first indication, in this book, of the Ark's well-known oracular function. As portable throne of the Divine King, it was also the place of highest legitimate inquiry. The sudden reference to the Ark here places it in rhetorical relationship to the introduction of the Ark at Bethel (*sic!*) as the place of successful inquiry, after two rounds of failure at Mizpah (Judg 20:18,23,26-27). The relation of narrative motives in Joshua 7-8 and Judges 19-21 is clearly inverted. Here the first setback in Canaan finds Joshua inquiring before the Ark; in Judges 20 it is only after two severe drubbings, at the hand of tiny Benjamin, that the militia will make inquiry where "the Ark of God's Covenant" was "at that time." See *Judges*, AB 6A, 281-282, with NOTES and COMMENT.

until evening. In verbatim agreement with Judg 20:26. The impression is that all this is happening quickly. And this is credible. Unlike the social organization of the larger city-states, Israelite warfare was not based on strong fortifications and heavy armaments. It was waged by a people's militia based on family and tribe. There are few instances of siege warfare in the pre-monarchy tradition and the actual fighting that constitutes a "war" often lasts less than a full day.

and Israel's elders. The elders are not otherwise mentioned here, and they appear just as abruptly in 8:10 (see NOTE). This is another sign of rhetorical relationship with the end of Judges where, just as abruptly, the elders propose the final solution to the problem of wives for Benjamin (Judg 21:16-22).

7-9. These verses break up into complaint (v 7) and petition (vv 8-9), a cultic pattern which is seen to be reflected in many psalms of lament. In the Jerusalem Temple cultus, there was generally an "assurance of being heard," either expressed or implied, in many a lament. Claus Westermann, *The Praise of God in the Psalms,* tr. Keith R. Crim (Richmond: John Knox Press, 1965) 64-81. It is a pattern which Joshua's language would immediately call to mind for the reader of Dtr 1 or Dtr 2. Yet the impression here is something of a harangue.

7. *"Ahh! Lord Yahweh.* Upon discovering the identity of his partner in dialogue, Gideon uses exactly the same expression (Judg 6:22). The element *'āhāh* is here best rendered as a guttural sigh, since English "Alas!" has largely gone out of use. Compare Jephthah's lament in Judg 11:35.

why. Moses had performed similar intercessary functions. Exodus 32:11; Num 14:13-19; Deut 9:26. But Joshua's inquiry here also has much in common with the people's "murmuring" in Exod 14:11-12 and 16:2-8, as well as Moses' complaint to Yahweh in Num 11:11-15.

Westerners? Hebrew *hā-'ămōrî,* used in its etymological sense, apparently as a synonym for "Canaanites" in v 9. The same usage occurs in Judg 1:34-35; 6:10.

we only had been content. A glance at the lexicon suffices to show that the *hiph'il* verb *hw'l* occurs far more frequently in Dtn and Dtr texts than in all others combined. See especially Deut 1:5; Judg 1:27,35; 17:11; 19:6; 1 Sam 12:22; 17:39; 2 Sam 7:29; 2 Kgs 5:23; 6:3.

the region beyond the Jordan! This is a distinctive Dtr 2 interest, as noted above at 1:12-18 and 4:12.

8. *Please, my Lord.* Hebrew *bî 'ădōnî.* The phrase puts Joshua, for the moment, in the company of Gideon (Judg 6:13) and Manoah (Judg 13:8).

9. *our name . . . your own great name?* Here a most central conception of biblical theology is invoked. The name is an effective extension of the self, as may be most clearly seen in the dialogue at the burning bush, where Moses holds out to know the name of God (Exod 3:13). Then, as now, the name can also be a metaphor for "reputation." Here at the climax of his complaint Joshua means to hit where it will hurt the most. And it brings a response.

10. *"Get up.* Hebrew *qûm lāk,* literally, "get yourself upright." The imperative is here to be taken literally, reinforced by the pronoun, in contrast to the usage of the same verb form in Yahweh's speech to Joshua at the very outset in 1:2 (where it is translated "Proceed" in a verbal hendiadys) and in 7:13. The first two occurrences have a periodizing effect: the first introduces Joshua the famous military leader, and the second introduces Joshua as "judge." Apart from the notice about the territorial demands of the Bene Joseph in 17:14-18,

there are not many examples of Joshua in this unidealized role; and so we may confidently recognize here the supplementary activity of Dtr 2.

Why are you prostrate? Literally, "Why is this: you have fallen on your face?"

11. *Israel.* LXX reads instead "the people," which as a collective term for the fighting force might be considerably less inclusive and more accurate. Once again the LXX seems to display a text which here and there escaped the final redaction of Dtr 2.

has sinned! Is this hyperbole? It is a standing biblical theme that the entire community may suffer for the sin of one of its members. Consider, for example, the famine in David's day (2 Sam 21:1-10), traced to Saul's crime. Is the punishment of Achan "a ritual of purification," so that "by removing the guilty party (and his family) Joshua removes the guilt . . ."? Miller and Tucker, *The Book of Joshua,* 62. Yes, and more. For unless it is a matter of something like plague-bearing contamination, the story as it stands seems oddly out of phase with the value system of early Yahwism. There justice assumes the ethical responsibility and value of the individual and is blind to lines of family and social distinction.

They have violated my covenant. No specific treaty stipulation can be cited. The covenant is a relationship of living wills, a relationship that is to be regulated by the stipulations as guidelines.

some of the condemned goods. Literally, "from the ḥērem."

12. *They turn back in the face of their enemies.* Unfaithfulness is offered as the explanation for the last-minute development of battlefield fears. The man who was "fearful and fainthearted" was to be exempted, from the outset, according to Deut 20:8.

they have become banned themselves! It is an abrupt experiential lesson on the reliability of Yahweh as head of the Israelite organization.

what is condemned. Both the goods and the guilty ones are banned. That is, if there is disease involved, not only are the objects likely to be infected; the people are, too.

I shall not continue to be with you. After the repeated exhortations and promises of the opening chapters and the emphatic last words of the Jericho phase (6:27), this statement describes an especially grave and totally frustrating crisis.

13. *"Get on with the preparation.* Hebrew *qûm qādēš.* It is a verbal hendiadys. Compare 1:2.

preparation . . . ritually ready. The "holiness" root *qdš* is here used twice, calling attention to itself. In contrast to 3:5, where everything was going smoothly and Joshua had issued the same command, here it appears he must be prompted to do it again.

14-18. The elimination perhaps proceeded by decision of the sacred lot, which is explicitly mentioned in the definition of tribal territories (14:2 and 18:6).

The three concentric circles within which the individual identified himself— house, clan, tribe—are the basis of the proceedings. Compare the process of elimination in selecting Saul as *nāgîd,* "leader," later *mélek,* "king" (1 Sam 10:17-24); and the determination of Jonathan as guilty of unknowingly violating an ad hoc decree during warfare (1 Sam 14:37-42). The latter suggests that the use of the lot was to evoke confession of guilt, but not to determine guilt without interrogation.

14. *tribe.* Hebrew *šēbeṭ* is originally "staff," or "club," as symbol of authority (Judg 5:14), and then is extended to refer to "that over which the staff of office rules. It is an administrative unit within the federation, though it is most probable that such units correspond to already existing social groupings. . . ." Mendenhall, *Ten Gen,* 185. The word *šēbeṭ* is used in the Bible only with reference to one of the twelve Yahwist units which indeed suggests that they are not "tribal" in the same sense as the *'ummôt* elsewhere in ancient society (Gen 25:16; Num 25:15).

clan. Hebrew *mišpāḥâ* is sometimes rendered "family." The closest anthropological term is "phratry." Abraham Malamat, "Tribal Societies: Biblical Genealogies and African Lineage Systems," in *Archives Européennes de Sociologie* 14 (1973) 126-136. This is "'the basic tribal unit. Its members live together, migrate together, and most of them are descended from the father of the family whose name they bear. . . . It includes to a smaller or larger extent additions from without as also the offspring of servants and slaves, whose position is at first inferior to that of the actual members of the family, but who are in the course of time absorbed by it either by marrying into the family or by claiming genealogical descent from one of its fathers." J. Liver, "The Israelite Tribes," *WHJP* III (1971) 188. The problem with the term "phratry" is that it is drawn from the classical Greek setting where it represents a much larger subdivision of the "tribe." For a new look at the socio-economic and political significance of the "clan," interpreted instead as a voluntary local protective association of extended families ("father's houses"), see Norman Gottwald, *The Tribes of Yahweh,* Part VI, 237-343.

household. Hebrew *bayit.* To judge from the account of the actual process in vv 17-18, this is probably the same unit, narrower than "family," that is elsewhere referred to as the "father's house." For example, Deut 29:17; Judg 6:15. This is the smallest unit of "patriarchal rule, all the offspring—including the adults—being subject to the father's authority, and all together forming a compact social unit during his lifetime. Upon his death, the 'father's house' disintegrates." Liver, "The Israelite Tribes," 184. Thus, with appropriate qualification, the "house" or "father's house" may be understood sociologically as the extended family. As the smallest unit for the muster it also has military use. Glock, "Warfare in Mari and Early Israel," 220-221 n. 32.

15. The death penalty for a breach of covenant is known from other texts (Exod 21:12,15-17; 22:18-20). Only burning is mentioned here, with no reference to death by stoning.

violated. The verb is *'br,* "to cross over," "transgress." With *bĕrît* as object, see 23:16; Judg 2:20; 2 Kgs 18:12. With "commandment(s)" as object, see Deut 26:13; 1 Sam 15:24.

has committed an outrage in Israel." This statement is ancient exegesis of what it means to transgress Yahweh's covenant. The outrageous or sacrilegious act is *něbālâ*, as in Judg 19:23-24 where the word occurs twice in the old man's complaint, and in Judg 20:6,10 where it refers to the rape. See Wolfgang M. W. Roth, "NBL," *VT* 10 (1960) 394-409; and especially Robert A. Bennett, "Wisdom Motifs in Psalm 14=53—*nābāl* and *'ēṣāh*," *BASOR* 220 (1975) 15-17. The effect of pairing this statement with the preceding Deuteronomic cliché is to give unmistakable emphasis to the "all Israel" interests of the story's adaptor.

16. *got busy*. For this sense of Hebrew *hškym*, see NOTE on 3:1.

17. *he took*. The subject is presumably Yahweh although Joshua is grammatically possible. Such ambiguity is not surprising if the story is rooted in oral composition and/or transmission.

18. *ben Zabdi*. This must be the name of the "father's house" to which Achan's parents belonged.

20. *It happened about like this*. Hebrew *wkz't wkz't 'syty*, literally, "thus and thus I did."

21. *booty*. Hebrew *šālāl*, a word which may also stand for plunder quite distinct from the *ḥērem*. Is he confessing to a different crime from the one of which he is accused? In a Mari document, one writer complains to his superior about unfair distribution of booty. The army officers are accused of appropriating in addition to their own shares those portions which had been properly reserved for the troops and for the viceroy at Mari, as well as for the writer. He claims that what has happened is "a violation of the *asakku* of the gods, the king, and his viceroy." Abraham Malamat, "The Ban in Mari and in the Bible," in *Biblical Essays: Proceedings of the Ninth Meeting of Die Ou-Testamentiese Werkgemeenskap in Suid-Afrika* (*1966*) 44-45, discussing ARM II, 13 among other examples. Such may well have been the concern of the old Achan story, if it was only secondarily referred to Jericho and used to divert attention from Joshua's strategic responsibility in the first battle of The Ruin.

Shinar-cloak. The exact referent is not clear. The name "Shinar" is applied to part of Babylonia in post-biblical tradition. The garment in question might conceivably be either an import or a local imitation.

two hundred shekels' weight. The shekel was 11.4 grams=4.03 ounces. Thus the silver had a total weight-value of 2,285 grams=2.25 kilos=81 ounces=5.9 lbs.

fifty. The gold bar weighed 571 grams (over half a kilo) or 20 ounces (1.25+ lbs.).

at the bottom of it." Apparently the silver was considered the most valuable of all.

24. *All Israel was with him*. This parenthetical statement perhaps serves to explain the logistics of the execution which may have taken place some considerable distance from both the base camp and the scene of the debacle. "All Israel" was there to effect the move.

his and *him*. The third person pronoun suffix occurs a total of seven times in the series.

Attempts to rationalize this story in terms of the "corporate personality" of the one and the many, a distinctive ancient idea of solidarity in sin and salvation, are not very convincing. While the OT has great texts concerning the grace of vicarious suffering, and atonement, this is not one of them. But neither should it be used as a foil for such texts. Here it appears rather to be a serious problem of physical contamination and disease which becomes possible through the offense of Achan.

They brought. Joshua's investigation leads to action by "all Israel" which disposes not only of Achan and the plunder but also of sons, daughters, ox, ass, sheep, tent, and all personal possessions.

Devastation Valley. The region is better known from English versions as the Valley of Achor (as on Map G, 364). The region is today known in Arabic as the Buqei'ah, a small and isolated plain just west of Qumran on the high escarpment above the Dead Sea. Running north-south, the area is about 8 × 4 km. The region became a center of several desert-farming communities, later in the monarchy (see below on Judah Province XII, in 15:61). After working there in the September heat of 1975, we concluded that from the harshness of existence the area was appropriately named.

25. *devastated.* The verbal root is '*kr*.

all. The specification, where the community removes one member, prefigures Judges 20, where the federation will be mobilized against one of its constituencies, on behalf of one Levite. See "all" in Judg 20:1,2,8,11.

stoned him. Here the verb is *rgm.* Achan was executed as a result of a judicial finding.

burned them. The referent is presumably the stolen objects.

stoned them. The verb is *sql* and the object, presumably, is the family implicated by contagion (probably literal). In other words, this execution does not reflect excessive and disproportionate retaliatory "justice" but a serious concern for public health. We owe this suggestion regarding the verbal contrast to O'Connor, private communication.

26. *stone cairn.* The king of The Ruin will be buried in the same way (8:29), as also will be Absalom (2 Sam 18:17).

(*Therefore.* This final statement appears to be secondary. The explanation which this chapter provides for this name is so tortuous and full of incongruities that it is doubtful that very many persons would have taken it as straightforward narrative with the purpose of explaining the name. "One might even suppose that the etymological elements, given their lack of unity, are later accretions onto fixed *traditions which served some other end.*" Long, *The Problem of Etiological Narrative in the Old Testament,* 25-26 (italics ours).

Some have concluded on the basis of geography that the Achan story was originally a bit of Benjaminite polemic against Judah, "the purpose of which seems to have been mainly to give an etiological explanation" for a stone cairn in the Judahite Buqei'ah. Soggin, *Joshua,* 98. But the question arises of what familiarity in detail a Benjaminite audience might be expected to have with that out-of-the-way place where life was so difficult that it was one of the last regions to be developed for subsistence farming. Rather, here it is the meaning of a previously established name that serves the historian's interests. Used twice in v 24, the name Achor prepares the way for Joshua's attempt at a wordplay, using the same root '*kr* twice in v 25.

COMMENT

Chapters 7 and 8 together might be appropriately subtitled, "How to Make an Everlasting Ruin." The chapters afford a comparatively clear view of the entire process of the formation and redaction history of such material. In the beginning was an old story of the crime and punishment of Achan. Chapter 7 itself contains no direct statement of the origins of Achan's plunder. The execution and burial in Devastation Valley take place in Judahite territory, a considerable distance from either of the Benjaminite areas that are pertinent, namely The Circle near Jericho and The Ruin near Bethel. But an editor understood that Achan's offense had occurred at Jericho, and so his story comes right after chap. 6, where it serves to explain a most serious setback to Joshua and the Bene Israel. Setback is an understatement. A defeat of such proportions is a tragedy for the people and a debacle for the officers.

The story of Ha-Ai is truly etiological (fascinated by the meaning of a name), but it is not merely etiological (designed to explain the name). What chap. 7 does is to explain away the fact that somewhere in Benjamin the great leader of Yahweh's guerrilla forces suffered a resounding and thoroughly embarrassing setback. In other words, a true story was told etiologically. The fact that three contingents comprised a force from which the loss of thirty-six was considered to be devastating brings the story into believable focus alongside the small unwalled twelfth-century village (8,094 sq. meters!) excavated at et-Tell in recent years. The small village nestles in the large-proportioned ruins of a great Early Bronze Age city. As unoccupied place of rendezvous for the Israelite militia, the site displays all the elements needed for the creation of the story. See the preliminary report by Joseph A. Callaway, "Excavating Ai (Et-Tell): 1964-1972," *BA* 39 (1976) 18-30.

The story of Achan in chap. 7 displays a tendentious use of the etiological principle. This is a most important distinction, and one that is much neglected in the voluminous discussions of etiology. The latter are compactly summarized and evaluated by Wright in his Introduction to this volume.

The key to the etiological tension in the present chapter is the contradiction observed in the NOTES on the specific offense of Achan. The context and indictment of "Israel" emphasize the sin of *ḥērem*-violation (6:17-19,21; 7:1,11-15); yet the old narrative core must have been too well known to be revised. Achan confesses to having stolen from the "booty" (Hebrew *šālāl*), no doubt understanding it as marked for distribution as compensation to the fighters. This was an interpretive move, from "booty" to "ban," coinciding with the shift from focus upon one man to indictment of "all Israel." The result is to give a tendentious "legalistic" rationalization for a most serious tactical blunder on Joshua's part. The use to which the Achan episode is put is a diversionary tactic. An ancient awareness of "corporate personality" is used to explain away the individual responsibility for defeat at The Ruin—namely, Joshua's lapse of good military judgment. The Achan story was thus very important to Dtr 1, in the Josianic heyday, for whom Joshua was a primary model.

In other words, it appears that memories of (1) a contaminating *ḥērem*-violation at Jericho and (2) Achan's theft of *šālāl,* "booty" (the latter given a Jericho setting), have been combined by a historian in such a way as to protect Joshua from any charge of poor military judgment in the debacle of the first battle for The Ruin.

The story of Achan offers a vivid example of that situation which is viewed negatively in the expression, "In those days there was no king in Israel; every one did what was right in his own eyes." From the perspective of Dtr 1, where we first encounter that cliché in Judg 17:6, the goings-on at Micah's place make indeed a bad scene. And yet at the end of the era, because of a radically different context, the same statement becomes a positive affirmation (Judg 21:25; see *Judges,* AB 6A, 254-256, 289-294), this is Dtr 2.

In the NOTES above we have observed many indications of the later redactor, who was living in the collapse of all hopes that had centered on the great reforming king. From this beginning it will become doubly clear in chap. 8 that Dtr 2 has been able to recall two of the most painful true happenings in Israel's past, the defeat at The Ruin and the execution of Achan, and face the possibility of exile without despair, thanks to a healthy sense of humor.

3. YAHWEH AS VICTOR
(8:1-29)

8 1 Yahweh said to Joshua:

"Be not afraid or dismayed. Take with you all the fighting force and go back up to The Ruin! Attention! I have given into your power the king of The Ruin—with his people, his city, and his land!

2 "You shall do to The Ruin and its king as you did to Jericho and its king, except that its booty and cattle you may plunder for yourselves. Place an ambush against the city to its rear."

*3 *So Joshua and all the fighting force rose to go up to The Ruin. Joshua chose thirty, a man from each contingent (the burly warriors) and sent them out at night.* 4 *He commanded them:*

"Attention! You are to be an ambush against the city—to the rear of the city. Do not go too far away from the city, so that all of you will be ready! 5 *I and all the people with me will approach the city. When they come out to confront us as on the first occasion, we will flee from them.* 6 *They will come after us until we have enticed them away from the city. For they will say: 'Fleeing from us, as on the first occasion!'* 7 *Then you are to rise up from the ambush, approach the city, and take possession of it. Yahweh your God will give it into your power.* 8 *When you have seized the city, you are to set it on fire. According to Yahweh's word shall you act. Attention! I have commanded you!"*

9 *Joshua sent them out. They went to the place of ambush and waited between Bethel and The Ruin, to the west of The Ruin. Joshua spent that night in the midst of the people.*

10 *Joshua got busy next morning and mustered the people. He went up, together with Israel's elders, at the head of the people, toward The Ruin.* 11 *All the militia who were with him made the ascent and approached until they had arrived opposite the city. They camped*

* The italicized portions are from Dtr 2; the remainder, from Dtr 1. See NOTES for discussion.

*north of The Ruin, so that the valley was between them and The
Ruin.*

12 He had taken exactly five contingents and stationed them in ambush between Bethel and The Ruin, west of the city. 13 Thus they stationed the people: the main camp which was north of the city, and its "rearguard" west of the city. Joshua went out that night into the valley.

14 When the king of The Ruin saw it, the townsmen hastily made preparations and went forth to confront Israel for the battle. He and all his people were at the assigned place facing the Arabah! He did not know there was an ambush against him, to the rear of the city.

15 Joshua and all Israel let themselves be routed before them and fled toward the wilderness. 16 All the people in The Ruin were called out to pursue them. They pursued Joshua and were maneuvered away from the city. 17 There was not a man left in The Ruin, or even the sanctuary, who did not go out after Israel. They left the city wide open and pursued Israel.

18 Yahweh said to Joshua, "Point the sicklesword in your hand toward The Ruin, for I am giving it into your power."

So Joshua pointed the sicklesword in his hand toward the city. 19 The ambush arose swiftly from its position and ran while he stretched out his hand. They entered the city and captured it. And they swiftly set fire to the city.

20 *When the men of The Ruin turned around to see, the city was visibly going up in smoke!*

They were unable to flee either backward or forward when the force that had retreated to the wilderness turned back upon the pursuers. 21 *When Joshua and all Israel saw that the ambush had captured the city and that the city was going up in smoke, then they turned to strike down the men of The Ruin.*

22 *They had gone out from the city to encounter them, so that they were in the very midst of Israel, scattered hither and thither. They struck them down until at last he left for them neither refugee nor survivor,* 23 *except the king of The Ruin whom they captured alive and brought up to Joshua.*

24 *When Israel had finished killing all the inhabitants of The Ruin (on the open plateau! in the hills by the descent! where they pursued them until they were wiped out and all had fallen to the sword!), then all Israel turned to The Ruin and put it to the sword.*

25 *The casualties on that day, both men and women, were twelve contingents—all the inhabitants of The Ruin.*

26 Joshua did not withdraw his hand, with which he pointed the sicklesword, until all the inhabitants of The Ruin had been executed under the ban.

27 The Bene Israel plundered for themselves only the cattle and spoils of that city, in accordance with Yahweh's word, with which Yahweh had commanded Joshua.

28 Joshua burned The Ruin and made it an everlasting tell, a devastation to this very day. 29 The king of The Ruin he hanged on a tree until evening. At sunset Joshua gave the command, and they took his corpse down from the tree and threw it down at the city gate.

They erected over him a stone cairn—to this very day.

TEXTUAL NOTES

8 1. *with his people, his city*   These words were lost by haplography in LXX^AB: *w't ['mw w't 'yrw w't] 'rṣw*.

2. *and its king*   This is lacking at the first occurrence in LXX^AB, not the second, as indicated in the apparatus of *BH*³.

4. *"Attention!*   This may be secondary. It is lacking in LXX, and there is no mechanism for such a loss.

against the city   Lacking in LXX, which is most likely original.

too   Lacking in LXX^AB, probably a haplography due to easy confusion of *r* and *d: mn h'yr [m'd]*.

6. *They will come after us until we have enticed them*   Hebrew *wyṣ'w 'hrynw 'd htyqnw 'wtm*. LXX however reflects the temporal construction with infinitive construct: *wbhwṣ'm 'hrynw wytyqnw 'wtm*, "When they come out after us, we will entice them. . . ." Syriac is confined to a brief declarative statement: "They will come after us."

'Fleeing   See NOTE.

occasion!   Thus LXX. MT continues: "and we will retreat before them." This is most likely a dittography of v 5.

7. *from the ambush*   Hebrew *mē-hā-'ôrēb*. Use of the same noun three times in Judg 20:37-38 argues against the emendation in this verse proposed by *BH*³ and *BHS*. That is, one telling of this story had used the form *hamma'rāb* ("the place of ambush" in v 9), another this form in relation to Judges 20.

approach the city   Hebrew *wngštm 'l h-'yr*, restored on the basis of LXX.

and take possession of it   Hebrew *whrštm 'th*, missing in LXX. After the loss of the preceding phrase in MT, the object pronoun after the verb here was expanded to read *'t hyr*, "the city." LXX was not adjusted.

Yahweh . . . power. [8] *When you . . . on fire*   Here there is a large lacuna in LXX^AB, which looks like an inner-Greek development.

8. *According to Yahweh's word*   Hebrew *kdbr yhwh*. LXX *kdbr hzh*, "according to this word."

9. *The Ruin*   Syriac reads "the city," a difference of only one letter, but the result is ambiguity in the narrative.

Joshua spent that night in the midst of the people   Missing by haplography from LXX^AB or the *Vorlage: wy[ln . . . wy]škm*. "The people" (*h'm*) is often emended in light of v 13 to "the valley" (*h'mq*), but there is no textual evidence and literary analysis does not support it. See NOTE.

10. *Israel's elders*   LXX reads "the elders" and omits "Israel."

11. *opposite the city*   This specification is not in itself sufficient to understand the relative positions. LXX continues *ap' anatolōn*, presumably to indicate that this large force arrived "from the east." This may be an addition to LXX, attempting to clarify the situation following the lapse which dropped the last half of the verse. See below.

They camped north of The Ruin, so that the valley was between them and The Ruin   The second half of this verse seems to have been lost by haplography in LXX or its *Vorlage: wy[hnw . . . wy]qh*.

12. The bulk of vv 12-13 is not reflected in LXX. Since it is a recapitulation, it might have been intentionally omitted, if it was not the victim of another haplography: *wy[qh . . .* [14] *wy]hy*.

Bethel   "Beth-aven" in K^Or, LXX^L.

west   This follows MT, where Q^Or, LXX^L, Targum, Vulgate, and several Hebrew manuscripts all reflect "west of Ai." The latter is best explained as contamination encouraged by the same phrase in v 9.

city   LXX is extremely brief: "and the ambush was west of the city." Combined with the LXX addition at the end of v 11a ("from the east"), this looks like clarification after the lapse whereby all of vv 11b-13 were lost.

13. *went out*   Hebrew *wylk*. Several manuscripts read *wyln*, "spent the night," as in v 9. But there is no need to emend here. See NOTE on v 9.

into the valley   This is MT (*b'mq*). Syriac reads "among the people" (=Hebrew *b'm*) as in v 9. But emendations are unnecessary. See NOTE on v 9.

14. *the townsmen*   LXX omits and reads the verbs as singular. It is not quite accurate to say that the Greek shows no reflex of the *hiph'il* verb *wyškm* pace *BHS*. Rather this verb is used adverbially when coordinated with another verb. Speiser, *Genesis*, AB 1, NOTE on Gen 19:2 (see above, NOTE on Josh 3:1). LXX in our verse clearly shows the adverbial reflex in specifying that he went "straightway," that is "hastily."

Israel   Thus MT. LXX "them."

were at the assigned place   This is lacking in LXX, where the absence cannot be explained as any ordinary kind of scribal lapse. See NOTE.

15. *and fled . . . the wilderness.* [16] *All the people . . . to pursue them*

LXX has here a long lacuna, due presumably to haplography in the *Vorlage*: *wkl yśr'l lpn[yhm . . . lrdwp 'ḥr]yhm.*

16. *The Ruin*   This is the *qere*, strongly supported by the versions, against the *kethib h'yr*, "the city."

Joshua   LXX "the Bene Israel."

17. *or even the sanctuary*   Lacking in LXX. See NOTE.

18. *power."*   LXX continues "and the ambush will arise promptly from its position." Cf. v 19.

20. *when the force that had retreated to the wilderness turned back upon the pursuers*   Lacking in LXX^{AB}, which reflect a haplography: *w[h'm . . . w]yhwš'.*

22. *so that they were in the very midst of Israel*   Hebrew *wyhyw lyśr'l btwk* shows two idioms used together. Literally, "They were Israel's in its midst." LXX lacks "Israel" and reads "in the midst of the camp."

he left for them   There is no need to revocalize *hš'yr* as infinitive construct. The negative *blty* can govern a finite verb. Cf. GKC, 152x. Here context requires a plural pronoun (*lāhem* for MT *lô*). The idiom is clear in 11:8. Here it appears to be contaminated by the singular form that is appropriately used in 10:33. Compare Num 21:35; Deut 3:3; and 2 Kgs 10:11, all of which have the same form as our text.

24. *Israel*   LXX "the Bene Israel."

in the hills by the descent!   This follows LXX where MT shows haplography, probably triggered by a misreading of the last word "descent" (*mwrd*), where MT has instead "wilderness" (*mdbr*). The differences can be blocked out as follows:

| LXX | *bśdh* | *bhrym* | *bmwrd* |
| MT | *bśdh* | *b[* | *]mdbr* |

until they were wiped out   This is LXX, which however lacks the next clause, "*and all had fallen to the sword,*" where MT may be conflate.

25. *The*   This agrees with LXX, where MT reads "all," before the "casualties." The latter can perhaps be connected with a misunderstanding of *'lp* as "one thousand" so that the total would have appeared much larger.

inhabitants   This is LXX, reading *yšby*, against MT *'nšy*, "men," as more apt.

26. The verse is lacking in LXX. See NOTES.

27. *with which Yahweh had commanded Joshua*   This repetition of the divine name occurs in LXX, but it was lost by haplography in MT: *'šr ṣw[h yhw]h.* This tends to support LXX which reflects the prefix *k* at the very beginning of the phrase: "according to which [*k'šr*] Yahweh had commanded Joshua." This would then be recognized as a variant within the conflate text.

28. *The Ruin*   LXX and Vulgate read "the city."

29. *the city gate*   This is Hebrew *š'r h-'yr*, with no reflex in LXX. We have omitted the word that precedes this, and which the Masoretes pointed as "door" (*ptḥ*). This presumably goes back to a variant of *š'r*, but was read by LXX as "pit" (*pḥt*), which in turn precipitated the short text. LXX preserves "and they threw him into the pit."

NOTES

In this chapter Yahweh takes charge and leads Israel because of its flawless obedience to victory in the second assault on The Ruin. In these verses The Ruin is mentioned twenty-two times. Other frequencies cast this one in high relief: Joshua is mentioned sixteen times, Israel ten times, Yahweh five times. Recurring phrases serve to tie the whole together: "the king of The Ruin" (vv 1,14,23,29), "all Israel" (vv 15,21,24). The clustering of references to The Ruin gives evidence that two narrators have, successively, contributed to the formation of the unit:

Dtr 1   Dtr 2

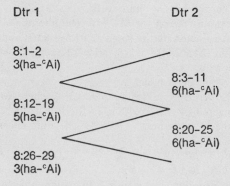

8:1–2
3(ha-ᶜAi)

                                         8:3–11
                                         6(ha-ᶜAi)

8:12–19
5(ha-ᶜAi)

                                         8:20–25
                                         6(ha-ᶜAi)

8:26–29
3(ha-ᶜAi)

Three segments which together mention The Ruin exactly eleven times alternate with two units, each of which name The Ruin six times. That this is not merely fortuitous pattern is clear from two additional observations. First, the three segments (vv 1-2,12-19,26-29) can in fact be read in the Hebrew as continuous narrative, without any sense of a gap. This is not true of vv 3-11 and 20-25. Secondly, the inclusion of the two blocks 3-11 and 20-25 turns the story of the victory of The Ruin into a preview of the victory in the civil war at the end of the Book of Judges! In the latter story, "Gibeah" is mentioned eighteen times in Judges 20, which also teems with words, phrases, and indeed whole sentences that make it a companion piece to Joshua 8.

In other words, it appears that what the final contributor to the stories of The Ruin and the civil war has done is to use the same story line in developing the battle scenes. The surrounding terrain of Bethel and Gibeah is similar enough (both are atop the watershed ridge, though Bethel is nearer to the eastern brink of the rapid descent into the Jordan valley) that it would not be surprising to have the ambush at one place sound so much like the other one. It would have clear didactic value. For in this way the final redactor could let the point be made that there is no defeat of Israel that cannot be at last turned around if Yahweh is truly allowed to take command.

8:1. *"Be not afraid.* Hebrew *'al tîrā'.* It is the "familiar word of encouragement and battle cry of holy war." P. D. Miller, Jr., *The Divine Warrior in Early Israel,* 133. See especially Exod 14:13; Deut 1:21; 3:2 (with the negative *lō',* Deut 7:18; 20:1; 31:8). This is the first occurrence in the Book of Joshua. See also 10:8,25; 11:6.

dismayed. Echoing the commissioning of Joshua in 1:9.

with you. In 1:9 the ground of Joshua's courage was to be the promise that Yahweh your God is "with you."

all the fighting force. Do not make the same mistake twice. The contrast with 7:3 is obvious.

go back up. Hebrew *wĕqûm 'ălēh.* This verbal hendiadys begins with an echo of 7:10.

"Attention! This usage of *r'h* echoes 6:2.

the king . . . with his people. In a major city, the latter would include all the royal household, the family and attendants, together with a battery of civil servants and whatever garrison of permanent troops and mercenaries were maintained and the families of the officials and upper social strata. Archaeology has shown, however, that the king of ha-'Ai ruled, if anything, rather a small village. Presumably he was the Suzerain (his home base forgotten) of kings rallying at The Ruin.

2. *Jericho and its king.* The king of Jericho has previously been mentioned only in 2:2-3. The Book of Joshua is built up from preformed narrative units. This comparison with Jericho is the only hint of the relative strength of the opposition.

except. Some kind of distinction between "booty" (*šālāl*) and "ban" (*ḥērem*) is clearly implied. The basis of the distinction is not clear.

ambush. Hebrew *'ôrēb.* This is the strategy that would at last be adopted for the defeat of Gibeah, after the Israel militia had been trounced twice, but a favorable and reliable oracle had at last been secured at Bethel (Judg 20:29,36,37, *et passim*). There, however, the idea of the ambush seems only to have been prompted tardily (by the memory of Joshua 8?). Here it originates with Yahweh in direct command.

The threat and reality of ambush in Canaan is a major theme of the Egyptian scribe Hori, in the satirical letter with which he seeks to educate another aspiring scribe, in a period very nearly contemporary with Joshua. *ANET*[2] (1955) 477.

to its rear." Which side of the city would that be? Presumably the west, if it is spoken from the Jordan valley perspective. But it would be to the north, if spoken from the Devastation Valley position. Logical locations for such an ambush have been suggested; in the caves of the next gully to the north (Wadi el-Gāye) and on the higher, boulder-strewn hill called Burǧmus on the west of et-Tell. See Plate II. Rösel argues convincingly for the second of these alternatives. "Studien zur Topographie der Kriege . . . ," *ZDPV* 91 (1975) 169-170.

3. *thirty, a man from each contingent.* This translation treats *m* as doing double-duty (or perhaps the result of haplography) in the sequence *šlšy-m-'lp 'yš.* "Three thousand" (EVV) is too wildly discordant with v 12. Likewise "thirty contingents" (roughly three hundred men perhaps) would be an impossibly large ambush in such terrain. "Thirty" is also an important number in

Judg 20:31 and 39; and the misunderstanding of numbers on the part of Masoretic scribes is another area of common ground between these stories of the battle for The Ruin and the civil war in Benjamin. See Judg 20:2,15,17, 25,34,35,44,45,46. Judges, AB 6A, 283-288. In the present instance the confusion may have been spurred on by the construction *kḥmšt 'lpym 'yš*, "some five contingents," in v 12.

(*the burly warriors*). Hebrew *gbry ḥḥyl*, as in 1:14 (see NOTE) and 10:7. They were "men of substance," economic and/or physical. The latter must be intended here. An interesting illustration for comparison from a much later era is the Crusader place name of Beit-guvrin, "House of Freemen," which involves the same root *gbr*. Beit-guvrin was one of sixteen military-administrative centers, originally a frontier fortress. Each of the Beit-guvrin settlers received a "house and a plot of seven hundred dunams," in exchange for a tenth of the crop plus an additional fixed payment. "The settlers owed military service and received a share of the spoils. . . ." Benvenisti, *The Crusaders in the Holy Land*, 173,185-188.

at night. A not implausible march, from the Jordan valley near Jericho. Calculations from the Egyptian record of the Battle of Qadesh indicate that the vastly larger and cumbersome Egyptian army could cover, on an average, some 20 km (a dozen miles) in a day.

5. *as on the first occasion*. Hebrew *k'šr br'šnh*, repeated in v 6; it is a signal. Compare *kbr'šnh*, "as at first," and *kmlḥmh hr'šnh*, "as in the first battle," in Judg 20:32 and 39. Cross recognizes here a Dtr idiom and cites also 2 Sam 7:10; cf. *kbr'šnh* in 1 Kgs 13:6; Jer 33:7,11; and Isa 1:26. *CMHE*, 254.

6. *'Fleeing*. LXX and Syriac reflect also an independent subject pronoun: "They are fleeing . . ." This reflects the continuing influence of the related texts in Judg 20:32 and 39.

7. *Then you*. Hebrew *w'tm*. The pronoun is emphatic.

8. *set it on fire*. The same signal is used in Judg 20:40.

9. *that night*. That is, the night previously mentioned in v 3. This is the first of two nights. During this night the men who comprise the ambush are sent on ahead, so as to be already in a concealed position when the main force arrives the next day in full view of the defenders. There is thus no contradiction between vv 9 and 13; these refer to successive nights. The first night Joshua spends with the main force; the second night he is in the valley.

10. *got busy next morning*. For the meaning of *wyškm . . . bbqr*, see NOTE on 3:1.

Israel's elders. In this book the elders are rarely mentioned, appearing for the first time in 7:6, where they are seen to be lamenting with Joshua after the defeat at The Ruin. Except for these two occurrences they will be mentioned only in 20:4; 23:2; 24:1,31. This pattern is striking and must be significant. In ancient village and countryside, as well as in the smaller "cities," the elders were the ones responsible for law and order and for maintaining the ethic of obligation toward the disadvantaged—the widow, the orphan, the resident alien, and the like. The elders were the ones who in time of war determined who would have to go to battle. They were "authorized to deal primarily with legal and religious matters within the sphere of family law—with bloodshed and murder, landed and other property, marriage and levirate marriage." Thus Liver, "The Israelite Tribes," *WHJP* III (1971) 191.

This very important institution is most notable in Joshua for its relative absence; this absence reflects the dominant interest of Dtr 1 in presenting and elevating the leadership of Joshua as model for the era of monarchy. The elders would become pivotally important for any continuing solidarity of community in the post-Josianic era. References to the elders here and there will properly be recognized as part of the preparation for life in exile—contribution of Dtr 2.

11. *the militia.* The term is *'m hmlḥmh*, but contaminated by the much more frequent *h'm* (vv 5,9,10,13, *et passim*). Boling, "Some Conflate Readings . . . ," *VT* 16 (1966) especially 298 n. 2.

north of The Ruin. Some have wondered whether this might not be a survival of an older and more original narrative, with Israel coming down from the north (that is, from Shechem), rather than from Gilgal. So Soggin, *Joshua*, 100. However, it is much more likely, in light of the foregoing, that this verse too belongs to the more expansive story that is rhetorically related to Judges 20. It may be significant here that in the civil war the punitive action against Gibeah had originated a few miles north of Gibeah, at the Mizpah sanctuary.

12. *He had taken.* Without vv 3-11, it would most naturally translate as simple past tense, "He took," following directly upon the order given him in v 2! After incorporation of the parallel account in vv 3-11, the same verb would be understood as past perfect, referring back to the previous action. Cf. Judg 1:1-2. AB 6A, 50, 54, another contribution of Dtr 2.

exactly. Another example of emphatic *k.*

five contingents. This is another way of referring to the the "thirty" (v 3). That is, the ambush was composed of an elite group formed into five contingents, each one at perhaps half the strength of the three units lost in the first battle. Such small units, especially for concealment in this terrain, are entirely plausible. The units in Numbers 1 and 26 range from five men per unit (Simeon) to over fourteen men per unit (Gad). Mendenhall, "The Census Lists . . . ," *JBL* 77 (1958) 62-63.

between Bethel and The Ruin. The smaller units might plausibly be concealed there but not all concentrated at one spot. To do the same with a force of thirty thousand or even five thousand would be physically impossible. This interpretation involving the much smaller numbers makes immaterial the question as to whether or not Bethel was still in Canaanite control.

west. Hebrew *miyyām.* In Judg 20:33 (LXX and related versions) the ambush is likewise "west" (*mimma'ărab*) of Gibeah.

13. All is in readiness, with the main camp, as recently arrived decoy, in place north of the city and diverting attention from the previously stationed "rearguard."

Joshua went out. This time he will do the scouting in person and be ready to direct maneuvers in the morning.

14. *hastily made preparations.* A hendiadys formed by two especially "busy" words, *mhr* and *hškm*, the latter noted above at v 10.

the assigned place. Hebrew *ham-mô'ēd.* In Judg 20:38 the same word stands for the agreed-upon strategic signal. The same word may also mean "assembly (-place)." The recommendation in *BH³* to emend and read *ham-môrād*, "to the descent" (see 7:5), does not commend itself in view of what follows, especially in v 18. It was when they were as far away as the brink of the descent, so that the king and his warriors must have thought it was going to be a rerun of chap. 7, that Joshua is credited with a most symbolic action. See NOTES on v 18.

15-17. The tantalizing narrative here interrupts the action line for a recapitulation. These verses heighten the suspense and supply a detail which was not mentioned first time around.

17. *the sanctuary*. Hebrew *bêt-'ēl*. It is generally assumed that this is the place name Bethel, as in 7:2 and 8:9,12; but in those verses it is merely a geographical reference point. The narrator has implied all along that Bethel, for whatever reason, posed no threat; for the ambush was stationed virtually at Bethel's doorstep. This problem is solved if we recognize here an intentional ambiguity, which will be echoed in usage with the same double meaning in the civil war story: *bêt-'ēl* is "the sanctuary" at Mizpah in Judg 20:18 but "Bethel" in Judg 20:26. See *Judges*, AB 6A, 281-282, 285-286, NOTES on 20:18 and 26. Here it means that the king of The Ruin was so confident of a second victory that he did not even leave a contingent in town to defend the sanctuary there. In this general period sanctuaries often had to do double-duty as last-ditch fortresses. See especially the story of Abimelech's destruction of Shechem in Judges 9.

LXX lacks any reflex of this reference to the sanctuary at The Ruin; LXX in fact often shows a more sober formulation of a Joshua story, in this respect no doubt standing more in line with the first edition.

18. *sicklesword*. See Plate III. There must be some reason for the use of the rare word *kîdôn* (*RSV* "javelin"), which refers to a weapon that is distinct from the "sword" (*ḥereb*), and "spear" (*ḥănît*). Except for this story, the *kîdôn* does not appear to be in use in ancient Israel. Goliath had one (1 Sam 17:6,45: "scimitar," McCarter, AB 8), as did the troops of a mighty nation "from the north" in the prophecies of Jer 6:23; 50:42. Otherwise the *kîdôn* is found only in Job 39:23 among other equipment such as quiver and spear which rattle and flash from the prancing war horse, and in Job 41:21. That the *kîdôn* is the obsolete curved sword is the proposal of Othmar Keel, *Wirkmächtige Siegeszeichen im Alten Testament*, 11-82. On the evolution of the curved sword, see Yadin, "Warfare in the Second Millennium, B.C.E.," *WHJP* II (1970) 131. The weapon has prototypes found as early as the Third Dynasty of Ur, if not earlier, and was widely used throughout the Near East during the second millennium. It was replaced by the straight sword at the end of the second millennium.

By the time of its retirement from "active duty," the sicklesword had attained high symbolic importance, as a sign of sovereignty. In Mesopotamian and Egyptian art, it is ubiquitous (Keel includes seventy-eight figures as illustrations).

On this view, the outstretched *kîdôn* is an "ideogram," a powerful sign, not originally a signal to the ambush. The advance briefing session with the men of the ambush says nothing about a signal (vv 4-8). In other words, the story shows Joshua fleeing until the entire opposing force has been enticed to a point where all together they are trapped, as Joshua with sicklesword in hand strikes a pose that enacts a venerable sign of divine sovereignty. The difference is that he in no way exercises divine power.

In LXX, on the other hand, the outstretched weapon is merely a signal to the ambush. This is less and less credible, the more one learns about the topography. For there is no way that one man's flashing of a weapon, among all those retreating downhill to the east of The Ruin, would have been visible to the ambush crouched in hiding behind The Ruin. See Plate II.

19. *while.* Not "when." The sentence is clearly disjunctive and (like 5:13) uses the preposition *k* as distinct from *b*.

20. This long verse is constructed chiastically, beginning and ending with temporal clauses, neither one of which uses a temporal particle. The construction of the first (beginning with a converted imperfect) is well enough known. For the disjunctive final clause, see Lambdin, *Introduction to Biblical Hebrew*, 162-164.

the city was visibly going up in smoke! Compare Judg 20:40, "there it was, the whole city going up in smoke" (AB 6A, 283).

22. *They.* At the beginning of the verse this pronoun is emphatic, with antecedent in the immediately preceding phrase, "the men of The Ruin."

24-26. *inhabitants.*   Used three times in a short space. Hebrew *yōšĕbê* can also evoke the sense of royalty, "ones enthroned."

24. (*on the open plateau! in the hills by the descent!* Compare the description of the Midianites in retreat before Gideon, "To Beth-shittah! Towards Zererah! To the border of Abel-meholah, near Tabbath!" Judg 7:22 (AB 6A, 143).

the descent! An echo of 7:5.

25. *The casualties.* Literally, "And those who fell were . . ." See Judg 20:46 for the same idiom.

twelve contingents. We are given no indication how large the units of the opposition were, whether closer to the larger size of Israel's first attack, or closer to the smaller units in the subsequent ambush. But the losses of Israel in the first battle ("thirty-six") probably set the limits for a total loss of seventy-five to 150 people dead and disabled in the Israelite victory.

The relatively small numbers involved, as analyzed here, correlate very nicely with the extremely modest proportions of the Iron I village at et-Tell, one of the later settlements in a pattern to be found repeatedly in the wider neighborhood in this period. See COMMENT.

26-27. Here it is explicit that there was a clear distinction between *ḥērem* and booty. See 6:17-19.

26. Absence of this verse from LXX, together with the expansion noted above in v 18, is clear indication that the LXX tradition did not understand the outstretched sicklesword as "ideogram" and assumed, rather, that with it Joshua too was busily smiting the opposition. In LXX the "sign" is reduced to a signal.

Comparison with the outstretched arms of Moses at the battle with Amaleq at Rephidim (Exod 17:11) is surely in order. Likewise reference to the "arm" of Yahweh at Israel's deliverance (e.g. Ps 44:3; Deut 26:8), and in Israel's hope (Isa 51:9-11).

27. *The Bene Israel.* This reading is the uniform witness of the versions, where MT reads simply "Israel" as subject of its plural verb.

in accordance with Yahweh's word, with which Yahweh had commanded Joshua. It makes an enormous difference who is in fact in charge. This time it went off without a hitch.

28. *made it an everlasting tell.* "The Ruin" would be just that, ever after. The narrator is living sometime after the final decline and abandonment of the village late in the eleventh century. See COMMENT.

29. *hanged on a tree.* The verbal root is *tlh* and will be used again to describe the treatment of five royal corpses in 10:26. It must be that some highly formalized custom is involved. See Mendenhall, *Ten Gen,* 117 n. 49.

until evening. Hebrew *'d 't h'rb.* Joshua 10:26 has nearly identical wording. This reflects legal precedents such as survive in Deut 21:22-23, according to which the corpse displayed on a tree is not to be left there overnight but is to be buried the same day. The law was later extended to the crucified. See Raymond E. Brown, *The Gospel According to John,* AB 29A, 933-934. Compare Matt 27:57-60; Mark 15:42-46; Luke 23:50-53; John 19:31-41.

his corpse. Hebrew *nbltw.* The same letters might be taken as a mock title "His Folly." O'Connor, private communication.

at the city gate . . . a stone cairn. Disposal of the corpse gives a redactor the occasion to tie things together. The location "at the city gate" is an *inclusio* with 7:5. And *"stone cairn"* turns back upon 7:26.

to this very day. Since the finished book is prepared for people who will be living in exile, it is scarcely probable that the cairns are any longer supposed to have evidentiary value. It is an ironic conclusion to the story of Joshua's second victory.

COMMENT

The work of The Joint Archaeological Expedition from 1964 to 1972 at et-Tell and neighboring sites has greatly clarified the history of that neighborhood. Already on the basis of earlier excavations, it was known that et-Tell had been a large and powerful city-state center in the Early Bronze Age but that it had been destroyed and lay in ruins throughout the Middle Bronze and Late Bronze periods. And it appeared that this situation continued on into Iron I. It was a very puzzling state of affairs. On the one hand, the thousand-year gap in occupation might well explain the origin of a place named "The Ruin" (Hebrew *hā-'Ai;* cf. Arabic *et-Tell*). But whence came the story that was supposed to be ancient Israel's explanation of the name? In this situation many scholars were attracted to the suggestion of W. F. Albright that a confusion between Bethel and Ai had entered into the tradition. For it was known from the excavations at Beitin that the town there was destroyed toward the close of the Late Bronze Age. This tended to underscore the tradition which reported the Israelite takeover at Bethel, somewhat later, at the beginning of the judges era (Judg 1:22-26). Moreover the thirteenth-century destruction at Beitin was followed almost at once by resettlement. Albright considered this to be the Israelite settlement. It was perfectly logical, then, to suspect that in the normal process of oral transmission a story of the destruction of Bethel (which however was immediately rebuilt) became fixed on a nearby site already called The Ruin.

That approach may no longer be necessary. The recent excavations have established that a very small village existed on the mound of et-Tell, which began in the last quarter of the thirteenth century (c. 1220 B.C. according to Joseph A. Callaway in *EAEHL* I [1975] 49) and continued through two phases in Iron I, until it was abandoned about 1050 B.C. Callaway suggests that the artifactual evidence points to "the north or east," more specifically to Hivite homelands, for the origins of some of these settlers. This is precisely a period when old sites are being resettled and new sites are being occupied throughout the wider region of the south-central hill country. In addition to Ai, the excavator lists Tell en-Nasbeh (Mizpah?), el-Jib (Gibeon), Mukhmas (Michmash), Rammun (Rimmon), et-Taiyiba (identification uncertain), Kh. Raddana in Bireh, Tell el-Ful (Gibeah), "and many small campsites on hilltops in the region. The Iron Age village at Ai, therefore, was settled as part of a large influx of newcomers, who apparently met with little or no resistance" (ibid.).

The last statement, about newcomers in large numbers, seems to be going beyond the evidence. A local population mustering at The Ruin in the late thirteenth or early twelfth century would not have been large. There can be no doubt that there were newcomers on the scene. But for the most part the new settlements show a strong continuity of local city-state culture. What they seem overall to demonstrate is a new and different political and social reality. It was becoming safe for the first time in history to live in unwalled villages throughout this rich upland terrain (the heart of "Benjamin").

The archaeological data encourage a fresh approach to the relationship between the stories of The Ruin and of the civil war with Benjamin (Judges 19-20). Wellhausen's idea that Joshua 8 was the "model" for Judges 19-20 is now generally turned around by critical scholars. But the similarities and differences cannot all be comprehended as a result of unilinear development or as polemical challenge and response concerning the same events.

The similarities and differences can only be explained in terms of continuing reflection and dialogue concerning the role of Joshua, as best formulated in the following couplet:

> How splendid he was when he raised his arms
> to brandish his sword against cities!
>   (Ecclus 46:2-3, JB)

There are two views on this subject clearly reflected in the Book of Joshua. The first view focused on Joshua as bearer of the sicklesword on behalf of his commander in chief Yahweh and who, like Moses of old, had produced an "effective victory-sign" in the second battle for The Ruin. The story made a point that should not be forgotten, but it was set at last in another context. The latter, expressing yet another vision, told the story of The Ruin as ironic preview of Gibeah's defeat in the costly civil war with Benjamin at the end of the era. In this way the large picture, of Israel's life in its land without monarchy, was at last framed.

In these two views we may surely recognize the historians we have been calling Dtr 1 and Dtr 2 respectively.

Why did the latter thus expand upon the old story of The Sign enacted at The Ruin? Presumably it was for didactic reasons, in order to emphasize the impact of *Yahweh's* participation in the second surprising victory of the Yahwists, and thus provide motivation for what comes next. The scene now shifts abruptly to the north-central hill country.

4. THE SHECHEM VALLEY COVENANT
(8:30-35*)

8 30 Then it was that Joshua built an altar for Yahweh the God of Israel near Mount Ebal, 31 as Moses the Servant of Yahweh had commanded the Bene Israel, as described in the book of the Treaty-Teaching of Moses: "an altar of whole stones against which you have wielded nothing of iron." They offered upon it burnt offerings to Yahweh and they sacrificed peace offerings.

32 And there he wrote on the stones a copy of the Treaty-Teaching of Moses which he recorded in the presence of the Bene Israel. 33 All Israel (that is, its elders, officers, and its judges) were standing on opposite sides of the Ark, before the Levite-priests who carry Yahweh's Covenant-Ark; both the resident aliens and the aborigines, one half were in front of Mount Gerizim and the other half were in front of Mount Ebal, as Moses the Servant of Yahweh had originally commanded, to bless the people Israel.

34 After that, he read all the stipulations of the Treaty-Teaching, the Blessing and the Curse, everything as inscribed on the Stele of the Treaty-Teaching. 35 There was not a word of all that Moses had commanded which Joshua did not read before the general assembly of the Bene Israel: the men, women, youngsters, and aliens who journeyed in their midst.

TEXTUAL NOTES

8 31. *the* second occurrence.   Instead of Hebrew *'t,* the direct object marker, a few manuscripts read the preposition *'l,* "to."

the book of   Lacking in LXX.

They offered upon it burnt offerings to Yahweh and they sacrificed peace offerings   LXX here reflects only one verb with singular subject and com-

* In LXX this follows 9:1-2.

pound object: "and he sacrificed to Yahweh burnt offerings and peace offerings."

32. *he*   LXX has "Joshua." Also in v 34.

which he recorded   Lacking in LXX[B]. See NOTES.

33. *officers*   This is MT *wšṭrym*, where a few Hebrew manuscripts plus LXX[A], Syriac, and Targum attest the suffixed form *wšṭryw*.

the Levite-priests   This follows MT which is the more difficult text. LXX supplies a conjunction ("the priests and the Levites"), but that reflects the post-exilic ranking of religious functionaries.

the people Israel   This is perhaps a conflation, since "Israel" is lacking in LXX[B].

34. *Stele of the Treaty-Teaching*   This is MT. LXX has "Mosaic Treaty-Teaching" but no mention of the text.

35. *commanded*   LXX adds, curiously, "to Joshua."

before   Hebrew *ngd*. LXX reflects *b'zny*, "in the ears [hearing] of."

the Bene   With LXX, lacking in MT.

men   Restored from LXX, after haplography in MT: *wh['nšym wh]nšym*.

in their midst   This is MT *bqrbm*, for which LXX reflects a slightly expanded text: *bqrb yśr'l*.

NOTES

8:30-35. This unit fits loosely into its context. It appears to be based on a liturgical fragment relating to events that are described with more detail in chap. 24. If it was originally an incipit of chap. 24, the redactor moved it here so that the reader would think about that event in relation to the victory at The Ruin and the treaty-defense of Gibeon which is the next large unit (chaps. 9 and 10). The clear implication is that what happens in 8:30-35 makes possible the progress from one to the other.

In LXX[B] this unit follows, instead of preceding, the reaction of the western kings (9:1-2). In fact the formation of royal coalitions and the rapid coalescence of a reformed Israel must have happened more or less concurrently, each giving reciprocal impetus to the other, so that both the Hebrew and Greek text traditions are in part accurate. In any case the importance of the events represented in these verses has to do with the fact that the next round of fighting will not be against another relatively small village force. Joshua's Israel is about to come up against a coalition of major city-state forces.

8:30. *Then it was that Joshua built.* The unit begins with another freighted time expression, such as were noted above in 1:2 and 3:7. Hebrew *'āz yibnēh* is here strongly disjunctive. Normally the pattern *'āz* + finite verb is used to pinpoint action within a larger narrative unit (for example, 10:12 and 33), but twice in Joshua this pattern is used to introduce units: here and in 22:1. Thus the two altar-building stories in the book are rhetorically related. The Shechem altar is the legitimate one; the Jordan altar is the problematical one.

near. The preposition *b* has the same sense here it has in Deut 27:4 and in Josh 5:13. To say "on" Mount Ebal and "on" Mount Gerizim, Deuteronomic usage is *'al* (Deut 11:29; 27:12-13).

Mount Ebal. This is the northern and higher of the two mountains flanking the important east-west pass through the north-central hill country. It is opposite Mount Gerizim (v 33) and looks down on the city of Shechem. See Map B, 112. Ebal is an unavoidable reference point:

> Looking south, you have at your feet the pass through the range . . .
> the site of ancient Shechem; then over it the mass of Gerizim, with a
> ruin or two; and then twenty-four miles [38.4 km] of hill-tops, at the back
> of which you dimly discern a tower. That is Nebi Samwil. Jerusalem is
> only five miles [8 km] beyond, and to the west the tower overlooks the
> Shephelah. Turning westwards, you see—you almost feel—the range
> letting itself down by irregular terraces to the plain; the plain itself
> flattened by the height from which you look, but really undulating to
> mounds of one and two hundred feet [30.3 and 60.6 meters]; beyond the
> plain the gleaming sandhills of the coast and the infinite blue of the sea.
> Joppa lies south-west thirty-three miles [53 km]; Caesarea north-west
> twenty-nine [46.4 km]. Turning northwards, we have the long ridge of
> Carmel running down from its summit perhaps thirty-five miles [56 km]
> distant, to the low hills that separate it from our range; over the rest of
> this the hollow that represents Esdraelon; over that the hills of Galilee in a
> haze, and above the haze the glistening shoulders of Hermon, at
> seventy-five miles [120 km] of distance. Sweeping south from Hermon, the
> eastern horizon is the edge of Hauran above the Lake of Galilee, continued
> by the edge of Mount Gilead exactly east of us, and by the edge of Moab
> away to the south-east. . . . It is only twenty-five miles [40 km] away, and
> on the near side of it lies the Jordan Valley—a wide gulf, of which the
> bottom is out of sight. On this side Jordan the foreground is the hilly
> bulwark of Mount Ephraim, penetrated by a valley coming up from
> Jordan . . . to meet the pass that splits the range at our feet. (G. A.
> Smith, *The Historical Geography of the Holy Land*, 94-95.)

From Ebal the only part of the land not in view is the Negeb. Throughout the second millennium B.C., whoever commanded the pass around Ebal could control all the hill country from a point not far north of Jerusalem almost to the plain of Esdraelon.

From The Ruin to Ebal is about twenty miles [32 km] in a straight line. In the narratives we hear nothing of any military resistance to the movement of Joshua and his force in this region.

It is an interesting fact that the great city-state center at Shechem is not mentioned by name in this unit or in any of the Deuteronomic background texts (Deut 11:29-32; 27:1-8,11-13). Probably this is a reflex of the course of actual history as it is now known from excavations. Shechem was destroyed in the mid-twelfth century B.C. What had been a briefly flourishing Yahweh-

Covenant cultus became a cyclical pilgrimage place, attracting only a few worshipers to the ruined sanctuary. This would be quite analogous to what was happening at about the same time in the Jordan valley, where there was no sizable settlement but an important pilgrimage sanctuary—Gilgal. The difference is that Shechem, unlike Gilgal, was not a new Israelite foundation, but had a history going deep into the patriarchal past. See COMMENT.

31. *Moses Servant of Yahweh.* He is mentioned exactly five times, in this compact unit. As in 1:13,15; cf. 1:2.

> Perhaps the tradition which associates Joshua with the oracle of the Tent of Meeting in the desert (Exod 33:11) and with Moses himself in the original Covenant at Sinai (Exod 24:13) should be taken more seriously than Alt has treated it ("Johsua," *Kleine Schriften* I, 176-177), though we must respect his caution in the paucity of evidence. (John Gray, *Joshua, Judges, Ruth*, 45-46.)

book. Hebrew *sēper*. Whether the word here refers to inscribed documents carried in the Ark or to the oral teaching perpetuated by "the Levite-priests" is moot.

Treaty-Teaching. As in 1:7.

whole stones. Exodus 20:25. This perhaps means that altars of hewn stones such as the great horned altar found in the Beersheba excavations (from the monarchy period) were regarded as standing in the pagan tradition. For the Beersheba altar, see Yohanan Aharoni, "Nothing Early and Nothing Late: Rewriting Israel's Conquest," *BA* 39 (1976) 65. The same shape altar in smaller form was found at Megiddo. See *ANEP*, ⁂575. The prophet Amos denounced the cult of Beersheba, bracketing it with the northern royal sanctuaries in his day at Dan and Bethel (Amos 5:5; 8:14).

burnt offerings. Hebrew '*lwt*, sacrifices which were consumed entirely by the fire of the altar.

peace offerings. Hebrew *šlmym*. The latter can be rendered as "communion-sacrifices." This was a joyous offering, partly eaten by the one who presented it. It "implies the idea of a tribute offered to God to maintain or to establish good relations between him and his worshippers"; De Vaux, *Ancient Israel*, 427.

32. *he wrote on the stones.* The stones of the altar? More likely it refers to sacred pillars which had been divested of their old fertility-cult significance, to serve somehow as treaty witnesses (24:26-27; cf. Exod 24:4). Three large standing stones associated with Fortress-Temples of MB-LB Shechem were found there. Treaty inscriptions were written on a plaster surface (Deut 27:2-3) on such stones. Examples of writing on plaster have been found at Deir 'Alla in the Jordan valley and at Quntillet 'Ajrud in the northern Sinai.

a copy of the Treaty-Teaching of Moses. Hebrew *mšnh twrt mšh*, which LXX took to be "a second law, the law of Moses" (*deuteronomion nomon Mōusē*), and which in turn gave a name to the fifth part of the Torah: Deuteronomy. What the original intends, however, is that Joshua found the precedents for the Shechem Valley treaty—and no doubt its basic ethical guidelines —in the Sinai agreement.

which he recorded. Lacking in LXX, this may be secondary. It counters any lingering uncertainty that it was the same teaching that Moses had sponsored. The sudden clustering of words and phrases having to do with Moses and *tôrâ*, which have not been used since chap. 1, suggests that this has been the goal of all the intervening narrative, in the finished book.

33. *All.* Hebrew *wĕkōl*. Disjunctive use of explicative *w*.

elders. See above, on 8:10.

officers. Hebrew *šôtĕrîm*.

judges. Probably the best comparison here is with the so-called "minor judges" listed in Judg 10:1-5 and 12:8-15, plus Jephthah, whose story is framed by those two units.

Ark. This was last mentioned in 6:13, and is otherwise not explicitly associated with Shechem; it has therefore been suggested that this reference also belonged originally to a Gilgal story. Otto Eissfeldt, "Gilgal or Shechem?" in *Proclamation and Presence,* 91.

the Levite-priests. Mentioned here for their responsibility in transporting and protecting the Ark.

the resident aliens. Hebrew *gr* used as a collective here presumably stands for all the Hebrews present, most of whom had long been resident in the area.

the aborigines. Hebrew *'zrḥ*, a collective term for persons who are native to the area. We get a picture of two groups facing each other in the narrow pass, while the leaders are gathered around Joshua as he executes the text. The idea was to create a new bond between them.

and the other half. The unusual form with double determination (*wehaḥeṣyô*) continues to resist explanation. A supposed parallel in the Karatepe inscription has been disproved by M. Patrick O'Connor, "The Grammar of Getting Blessed in Tyrian-Sidonian Phoenician," in *Rivista di Studi Fenici* 5 (1977) 5-11. Notable for its absence here is any listing by tribes, such as is found in Deut 27:12-14. The latter derives from a period when the twelve administrative districts ("tribes") of the covenant league had been more or less clearly defined, presumably along the lines described below in chaps. 13-19. At this point, however, the population of Israel is only in the process of being united.

to bless. The covenant liturgy is patterned on the order of historical experience with Yahweh: blessing comes first, to be followed by obligation.

34. *After that.* Prior benevolence sets the context.

stipulations. Literally, "words" in a well-known Deuteronomic usage.

the Blessing and the Curse. See especially Deuteronomy 27-28 and cf. Leviticus 26. Blessing and Curse are two standard elements in the treaty form used in Israel to provide a model for the community's relationship to God and to order its internal affairs. Without that context Blessing and Curse have been seriously misunderstood to bespeak an ancient doctrine of legalistic rewards and punishments. But these two elements especially belong to Yahwism's answer to the pagan power monopoly, reinforced as it was by the mythic and cultic interfacing of heaven and palace sanctuary. In contrast, where Yahweh was acknowledged to be king, "His authority was exercised in the first place by the community's obedience to His commands, and secondly by His control over all those powers of nature and history that man individual and corporately could neither control nor predict" (Mendenhall, *Ten Gen*, 25). Considered from this angle there could be no more appropriate abbreviation for the new constitution in the region west of the Jordan than "The Blessing and the Curse."

Stele. Hebrew *sēper* is here clarified from the strictly analogous use of the Aramaic cognate in the Sefire treaty inscription. Delbert R. Hillers, *Treaty-Curses and the Old Testament Prophets*, 46 and 85. The *inclusio* with *sēper*, translated "book" in v 31, is most effective. See also Dennis Pardee, "An Overview of Ancient Hebrew Epistolography," *JBL* 97 (1978) 331 n. 50.

35. *assembly.* Hebrew *qāhāl*. In the Book of Joshua this is our first introduction to an institution that was extremely important to Dtn (see Deut 5:19; 9:10; 10:4; 18:16; 23:2,3,4,9; 31:30; cf. *qhlt* in 33:4). In those passages the *qāhāl* is the deliberative and decision-making assembly of the people or their representatives (see also the verb forms of *qhl* in Deut 4:10; 31:12,28; and again in the literature from the exilic and post-exilic period). The word *qāhāl* is ubiquitous in Chronicles where it stands for the post-exilic worshiping community. This is the revival of a word from the early days when the *qāhāl* that gathered to renew the covenant was to include all categories of persons in the population.

It is highly significant that these *qhl*-words occur only rarely in the books of Samuel and Kings, which afford the oldest historical description of the entire monarchy period. The verb occurs twice where Solomon is in direct control (1 Kgs 8:1-2, a context which is notoriously blatant in its effort to undergird the Solomonic reaction!) and one where the son of Solomon is the subject (1 Kgs 12:21). The only other occurrence is 2 Sam 20:14, which describes the rally in support of Sheba's rebellion! This passage is part of the famous "Court History," an old document which Dtr 1 did not revise.

The noun *qāhāl* in Samuel and Kings shows a strikingly similar distribution. With one exception it is confined to contexts where David (1 Sam 17:47) or Solomon (1 Kgs 8:14,22,55,65) is the center of attention. The exception is 1 Kgs 12:3, where "all the assembly of Israel" supports Jeroboam against the son of Solomon. This is the last reference to a *qāhāl* in the old style or any other style during the entire period of monarchy in Dtr.

This telltale distribution was overlooked by Weinfeld in his monumental work, *Deuteronomy and the Deuteronomic School*. He attempts to dissociate the use of *qāhāl* in Deuteronomy from the "amphictyonic assemblies" and understand it simply as pedagogical rhetoric. The very low frequency of Deuteronomy's favorite assembly-words in the work of the pre-exilic Jerusalem historians indicates that they made *selective use* of Dtn. Those historians make it quite clear that the reforming king Josiah had very wide popular support among the *'am-hā-'āreṣ*, "the people of the land." But there is a vast difference between a covenant renewed by the power of the throne (2 Kings 22-23) and one which would arise out of popular initiative, making monarchy largely irrelevant. Dtn's covenant is of the second type. (Scholars regularly recognize the "law of the kingship" in Deut 17:14-20 as secondary.)

That the *qāhāl* in Israel was for so long eclipsed may surely be traced to administrative design. Solomon had sought to transform Israel into a full-fledged Oriental monarchy and was prepared to ignore or to flout older institutions in his determination to centralize powers and to consolidate his realm. In his ambition to raise the outlandish little kingdom to an exalted place among the sophisticated states . . . he overreached. . . . That is another story, however, and we are here interested in the shattering of Solomon's empire only as it illuminates the extent and violence of his innovations. (Cross, *CMHE*, 241.)

It was, however, Dtr 2—who lived through the final "shattering of Solomon's empire"—that first pointed out all of this by inserting older material such as these verses about the Shechem Valley Covenant.

COMMENT

These verses cannot be considered apart from chap. 24, which recapitulates at much greater length a covenant ceremony explicitly located at Shechem. That chapter is a self-contained literary unit, which scholars generally regard as older than the bulk of the literary work to which it is related. Placed at the end of the era of Joshua (see 1:5, *kl-ymy-ḥyyk,* "as long as you live") as a liturgically based conclusion to all the fighting and dividing of the land, chap. 24 looks like the redactional contribution of Dtr 1. The insertion of 8:30-35 is, in this view, a corrective made to indicate that the important Shechem tradition had been launched very early in the career of Joshua. There was, as indicated above, a deeply rooted teaching that Moses had said, in effect: Once you get into the land of Canaan, go to Shechem. Why Shechem?

According to the patriarchal traditions in Genesis 34, it was at Shechem that Levi and Simeon had sabotaged the agreement by which their sister Dinah might have been happily married to another newcomer in the area. Hamor is called a "Hivite" in MT. This points to a homeland in Cilicia (see below on 9:7). A rival tradition in LXX calls Hamor "the Horite," which would point to the Middle Euphrates Valley. The names Simeon and especially Levi are best explained as non-Semitic, with closest parallels in Anatolia. See below on 19:1 and 21:1. In the story of Genesis 34 the names Simeon and Levi stand for two constituencies in the unreformed, pre-Mosaic Israel, also known as the Bene Jacob, its worship centering on the Divine Patriarch (*'El*). The story in Genesis 34 concerns the collapse of an early treaty agreement between the Shechem city-state and the Bene Jacob. See the notice about Jacob's land purchase in Gen 33:18-20.

Only the bare outlines of the subsequent history of these two tribes can be made out. It is clear that Simeon was at last swallowed up by the mighty tribe of Judah. In the meantime it was Levite families which had been stranded in Egypt that formed the militant core, and earliest leadership, in the religious movement of Mosaic Yahwism. It was some of their offspring who returned at last to Shechem, bearing the Ark of Yahweh's Covenant.

And there were other memories attracting Yahwists to the Shechem area. Jacob on his return from Paddan-aram camped there and built an altar which he dedicated to "El, the God of Israel" (Gen 33:20). Probably his arrival had been less idyllic than the brief notice suggests, for finally he says to Joseph: "As for me, I give you, as the one above your brothers, Shechem, which I captured from the Amorites with my sword and bow" (Gen 48:22; AB 1 [1964] 356). The Shechem tradition in Genesis stems from an early period in the pre-Mosaic league, when the "house of Joseph" were also known as "sons of the left (or north)" balancing Benjamin, literally, "son of the right (or south)." See the pair of essays by Albright published posthumously: "From the Patriarchs to Moses: I. From Abraham to Joseph," *BA* 36 (1973) 5-33; "II. Moses Out of Egypt," ibid., 48-76. In those early days "Benjamin" had extended even farther south, as shown by old Benjaminite clan names absorbed in Judah.

The archaeology of Shechem is instructive. After a long and influential career in the Middle Bronze Age, especially throughout the Hyksos era, Shechem was violently suppressed in three military campaigns (possibly four). This can only be understood in relation to the Egypt's reconquest of its Asiatic realm in the sixteenth century, with the rise of the powerful Eighteenth Dynasty. This brought to an end a period of flourishing religious variety at Shechem, represented not only in the great Fortress-Temple but also in a royal chapel ("temple 7300") and an outlying mountainside sanctuary on the lower slope of Gerizim (the neighborhood formerly known as Tananir). Temple 7300 and the palace both went out of use in the last phase of Middle Bronze II C (c. 1525), when a new casemate defense system was built (Wall E). William G. Dever, *BASOR* 216 (December 1974) 31-52. This suggests the possibility of a non-monarchical form of government in the last phase of MB II C at Shechem. The Tananir building was discovered by the German team when it resumed work at Tell Balata in the late 20s. It has been reexcavated by the writer and interpreted as an outlying covenantal league sanctuary for people whose loyalty was not centered on the great Fortress-Temple or the royal chapel inside the castle walls. See Robert G. Boling, "Excavations at Tananir, 1968," in *Report on Recent Archaeological Work,* ed. George M. Landes. Campbell and Wright, "Tribal League Shrines in Amman and Shechem," *BA* 32 (1969) 104-116.

It is about a century after the Egyptian campaigns against the Hyksos strongholds that Shechem again comes into focus, in the famous Amarna

Letters. See especially Edward F. Campbell, Jr., "The Amarna Letters and the Amarna Period," *BA* 23 (1960) 2-22; reprinted in *BAR* 3 (1970) 54-75. In those letters Shechem is notorious for its resistance to directives from the foreign office in Egypt. The local prince Labayu and his sons are accused of having given the land of Shechem to the Habiru, and the sacred area at Shechem seems to be referred to as "city of God." Moreover, Labayu is bitterly accused by other city-state princes of maintaining relations with the "sons of Arzawa" (somewhere northwest of Cilicia). On the mound at Shechem, the Fortress-Temple (which itself had replaced a series of courtyard structures reflecting Anatolian design) was rebuilt on a broad-room plan. There can be no doubt that a pre-Mosaic cult of El-berit (God of the Covenant) was celebrated here. In Judges 9 it is Abimelech's attempt to exploit once again the pre-Mosaic covenant cult that explains the scorn and contempt with which Abimelech's story is told.

For this period, however, perhaps the most important archaeological results from the Joint Expedition to Balata come from its archaeological survey of the broader area that comprised the Shechem city-state. Throughout the centuries of the Middle Bronze period (2000-1525), the strongly fortified "city" of Shechem stood virtually alone as the spacious castle of the local lord. And yet it was precisely in the generally turbulent Amarna era that unwalled towns and villages sprang up for the first time all over the Shechem Valley. It had become a good and safe place to live. See the list of sites and descriptions by Edward F. Campbell, Jr., "The Shechem Area Survey," *BASOR* 190 (April 1968) 19-41.

This pacification and rapid multiplication of settlements around Shechem is paralleled a century and a half later in the uplands north of Jerusalem, stretching from Gibeah to The Ruin and on to Shiloh. At the same time the powerful Kingdom of Hazor was collapsing and new settlements were being founded all over the least accessible heights of northern Galilee (see below on chap. 11).

What then shall we make of these verses at the end of chap. 8? The usual solution is to move as quickly as possible to discussion of chap. 24. Thus Soggin rearranges the text to read 8:30-35 after 24:27. But this ignores the rhetorical structure of the finished book and obscures a nagging question about reliable historical memory.

An exceedingly complex history is involved, as indicated by an obscure reference to Gilgal in an important background passage, Deut 11:30. According to Eissfeldt's study cited above in the fifth NOTE on v 33, that Gilgal passage belongs to the first of two sets:

1) Deut 27:1-8 and Josh 8:30-35
2) Deut 11:29-32 and Deut 27:11-13

Eissfeldt concluded that the first set had originally served to link the Book of the Covenant (Exodus 20-24) with the Hexateuch narrative in a pre-Deuteronomic form. It had its setting originally in Gilgal but was secondarily transformed into a link with Deuteronomy.

Cross has considerably refined the analysis. Building upon the work of Eissfeldt and others, Cross sees in Deuteronomy, with appropriate reservations, "disintegrated materials of the old fall festival of Shechem." It was originally an annual covenant-festival which was "perhaps replaced by a seven-year cycle of pilgrimage festivals during the era when Shechem lay abandoned. Cf. Deut 31:10." *CMHE,* 84 n. 15. However, Cross continues, in the old traditions the clearest ties of the cultic traditions of Sinai are to the spring celebration of the covenant and entry into the land, at Gilgal. In other words, the confusion that Eissfeldt sought to unravel is due not so much to competition as to collaboration among sanctuaries which served as early league centers. Some such "collaboration explosion" must in fact be posited at Shechem in order to understand the reaction that came within half a century in the career of Abimelech. Surely his mid-twelfth-century destruction of Shechem is related to the prominence of Shiloh in the latter half of this period. With the subsequent destruction of Shiloh by the Philistines, in turn, the place of the Israelite muster once again became Gilgal in the days of Samuel and Saul. It was there, with Israel on the brink of expulsion from the land, that the Israelite experiment with monarchy began. In all of the unusually full tradition on the transition era in 1 Samuel, there is one institution that is most notable for its absence: the *qāhāl,* people's assembly, which had been pivotally important at the Shechem Valley Covenant.

Two hundred years of prosperity and relative peace in the Shechem Valley, from Labayu to Abimelech's massive reactionary move, was once interrupted by a violent destruction of the city. That was in the late fourteenth or early thirteenth century, when, however, there is no clearly corresponding biblical tradition. On the archaeological evidence for the destruction of Late Bronze Age Shechem, see Lawrence E. Toombs, "Problems of the Early Israelite Era," in *Symposia* I, 69-84. In our judgment the destruction of Late Bronze Shechem came too late to be associated with the story of the rape of Dinah (Genesis 34) as Toombs suggests. More likely it is to be explained in terms of rival reaction to the expansionist policies of Labayu's successors, or else as Egyptian reaction against the pre-Mosaic Israel, of the same sort that is documented in the Merneptah stele. If Genesis 49 in fact reflects Merneptah's raid, the LB destruction of Shechem might be associated with the tradition of Israel's capture of Shechem from the Amorites in Gen 48:22. So Freedman, "Early Israelite Poetry and Historical Reconstructions," *Symposia* I, 85-96.

5. THE EXCEPTIONAL ALLIANCE
(9:1-27)

Big Power Coalition

9 ¹All the western kings who were beyond the Jordan in the high country and the foothills and all along the coast of the Great Sea toward Lebanon—and the Hittites and the Amorites; the Canaanites, the Perizzites, the Hivites; and the Girgashites and the Jebusites—when they heard, ²they rendezvoused to fight Joshua and Israel under one command.

Deception

³The inhabitants of Gibeon heard what Yahweh had done to Jericho and The Ruin, ⁴and so they too acted deceptively. They packed provisions and posed as emissaries. They took worn-out sacks for their donkeys, together with worn-out, tattered and mended wineskins. ⁵On their feet were worn-out and patched sandals, they had on worn-out clothes. The bread in their food-supply was dry; it had turned to moldy crumbs.

⁶They went to Joshua in the camp at Gilgal and said to him and to Israel, "From a distant country we have come. Make a covenant with us at once!"

⁷The Bene Israel said to the Hivites, "Perhaps you really live within my territory. How then can we make a covenant with you?"

⁸They said to Joshua, "We will be your servants."

And Joshua said to them, "Who are you? Where do you come from?"

⁹They said to him, "From a very distant country your servants have come because of the fame of Yahweh your God. Indeed we have heard a lot about him and all that he did in Egypt ¹⁰and all that he did to the two Amorite kings who were across the Jordan, King Sihon of Heshbon and King Og of Bashan who was in Ashtaroth. ¹¹Our elders and all who live in our country heard and they said to us,

The bread in their food-supply was dry; it had turned to moldy crumbs   Any reconstruction must be provisional; neither LXX nor MT is satisfactory.

MT	*lḥm ṣydm ybš*	*hyh nqdym*
LXX	*lḥm ṣydm ybš wblh*	*whyh nqdym*

Recognizing that *wblh* is inappropriately referred to foodstuff, we may read as follows:

*   *lḥm ṣydm ybš*   *whyh nqdym*

6. *him*   LXX reads "Joshua," which perhaps originated in a marginal note.

to Israel   This is LXX, where MT in vv 6 and 7 has a somewhat awkward reference to *'yš yśr'l* construed collectively, "men of Israel."

7. *Bene Israel*   With LXX, against the collective "men of Israel" in MT.

said   The plural spelling of the *kethib* is supported by the bulk of the ancient versions, against the singular spelling of the *qere* found in many manuscripts and supported by Targum[L].

Hivites   So MT. LXX reads "Horites." See NOTE.

9. *a lot about him*   The only thing left unexplained by revoweling the anomalous *šom'ô* as *šim'ô*, "news of him" (Noth, Soggin, et al.), is the first vowel in MT. The form must rather be parsed as suffixed infinitive construct standing as a noun substitute: literally, "his hearing," that is, his reputation. LXX simply repeats the idiom used in the preceding phrase: *šmw*, "his fame."

all that he did in Egypt   This is not lacking in LXX (as reported by Soggin, *Joshua*, 108), but only in the L recension, and there because of homeoarkton: *w't [kl 'šr . . .* [10] *w't] kl 'šr.*

10. *who was in Ashtaroth*   This is MT. According to LXX, the speakers used the full Deuteronomic specification: *yšb b'štrwt wb'dr'y*, "who reigned in Ashtaroth and in Edrei." Compare Josh 13:12.

11. *heard*   This follows LXX, where *akousantes* probably reflects a converted imperfect (as at the beginning of 2:11) lost by haplography in MT: *wy[šm'w wy]'mrw.*

your   The pronoun is plural in MT, singular in LXX where apparently the emissaries appeal directly to Joshua.

12. *at home*   Literally, "from our houses." Lacking in LXX[AB].

look   This is not represented in the Greek.

13. *here are our clothes*   This is MT, where LXX reads simply "and our clothes."

14. *men*   Hebrew *h'nšym*, where LXX reflects *hnśy'ym*, "the leaders." The latter reading is scribal anticipation of their pivotal role and the repeated references to this group in the remainder of the chapter.

decision   Hebrew *'t py*, literally, "the mouth of," is not reflected in LXX. This is usually explained as an LXX tendency to eliminate anthropomorphisms. But here there is a mechanism for an inner-Greek lapse: *k[ai . . . k]yrion.*

15. *to guarantee their lives*   This is lacking in LXX[L] which seems rather to have emphasized the servant status being thus secured.

17. *towns*   With LXX^AB, where MT adds *bywm hšlyšy*, "on the third day," perhaps to be understood as a scribal comment or query.

18. *leaders*   Thus MT, where LXX reads "all the leaders," but lacks "of the congregation."

19. *All*   LXX^B and Syriac lack "all," but the pattern of six occurrences in vv 18-24 argues for its retention. See NOTES on v 18.

20. *to them!"*   This was dropped from LXX *Vorlage*, as a scribe's eye jumped from *h* to *h*: *n'šh* [*lhm w*]*hhyh*.

21. *And the leaders said to them*   Lacking in LXX^AB and Vulgate, after haplography: *lh*[*m* ²¹ *wy'mrw 'lyhm hnšy'y*]*m*. See NOTES.

and let them be   MT has imperfect with *waw*-consecutive *way-yihyû*, which is better revocalized as jussive with the coordinating conjunction *we-yihyû*.

And all the congregation did   Restored from LXX manuscripts, this was lost by haplography in most recensions: *l*[*kl h'dh wy'šw*] *kl h'dh*. Syriac^w continues "and they became woodcutters and water carriers for the congregation of Yahweh to this day."

22. *me*   This is LXX, where MT reads plural, under the influence of the lapse to be described next.

you'   The pronoun is singular, *mmk* according to LXX. MT shows a scribal metathesis: **mmk m'd* > *mkm m'd*.

23. *Among*   With LXX, where MT supplies a conjunction.

slaves   The noun *'bd* and the following conjunction are not reflected in the Vulgate, which probably represents the smoothing out of an awkward apposition.

woodcutter   The primary versions urge the singular, in strict apposition with *'bd*. This was the anciently adapted saying which in MT came to reflect the plural forms found in the surrounding narrative. On the other hand, the initial *waw* of MT is explicative and should be retained as a usage not always understood by LXX translators.

and water carrier   Lost by haplography in LXX^AB.

the house of   Thus MT. LXX reads "for me and my God," which seems to be evading the reference to a temple. See NOTE.

24. *all the land*   So MT. LXX "this land" may be a genuine variant.

you three occurrences   The pronoun is plural in both MT and LXX; the latter will continue the second person plural through the next verse. MT reverts to the singular.

26. *they*   The plural follows LXX. The result is an envelope construction. The first and last words in the sentence are plural verbs, shorter statements of what *they* did, framing a longer statement of what *he* did.

27. *the*   LXX reads "all" the congregation, most likely a secondary addition.

Yahweh   "God" in LXX, a substitution not often found in the Book of Joshua.

Yahweh   The repetition of the divine name has the overwhelming support of the Versions. The next unit begins with the consonant cluster *wyhy*, which helps to explain the loss of *yhwh* immediately before it.

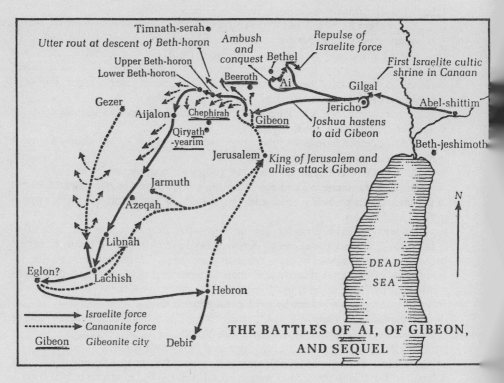

Timnath-serah •
Utter rout at descent of Beth-horon
Ambush and conquest Bethel
Repulse of Israelite force
Upper Beth-horon
Lower Beth-horon
Beeroth
Ai
Gilgal
First Israelite cultic shrine in Canaan
Gezer
Aijalon •
Chephirah
Gibeon
Jericho
Abel-shittim
Qiryath-yearim
Joshua hastens to aid Gibeon
Jerusalem
King of Jerusalem and allies attack Gibeon
Beth-jeshimoth •
Jarmuth •
Azeqah •
N
Libnah •
DEAD
Eglon? •
Lachish
SEA
Hebron •

→ Israelite force
⇢ Canaanite force
<u>Gibeon</u> Gibeonite city
Debir •

THE BATTLES OF AI, OF GIBEON, AND SEQUEL

Map D

NOTES

This chapter presents the sequel to the Shechem Valley Covenant, in two aspects: the formation of a country-wide coalition of kings and peoples (vv 1-2) and the Israelite treaty with Gibeon (vv 3-27). Together these responses exhaust the possibilities for protection of vested interests against Yahwism and Yahweh's opposition to distinctions of privilege based on social status or ethnic identity. That is, the chapter indicates that to those in Canaanite society who had most to lose materially, the alternatives to rapid and radical change were either massive military action or exceptional diplomacy.

9:1-2. The rival textual tradition in LXX places these verses just before the Shechem Valley Covenant in 8:30-35, which suggests that the actual relationship between these events was not so much one of sequence and consequence as one of concurrence and concomitance. What is claimed is that the initial successes of Joshua's units, facilitated as they were by significant events in the natural order, polarized the power elite and existing population groups throughout the land. Except for the area dominated by Shechem, the number of independent city-states and even village-states seems nearly to have doubled in the interim from Labayu to Joshua, with a corresponding diminution of the strength of each. See Bright, *A History of Israel*, 3d ed., 119.

1. *western*. Here the term *'āmōrî* must be more inclusive than the same word used later in the sentence, where it is transcribed, "Amorite." At the outset, however, it retains its etymological sense and is used generically. For this sense surviving elsewhere, see Judg 1:35 and 6:10 (*Judges*, AB 6A, 61 and 126). In Joshua it will reappear in 10:5; 11:3; and 12:8. This is the first of numerous double meanings and wordplays in this chapter.

beyond the Jordan . . . toward Lebanon. With this description of the land, compare 11:16-17 and Deut 1:7.

The reconstruction of the list of seven nations is supported by the clustering of names with and without the conjunction in the pattern: 2+3+2.

Hittites . . . Jebusites. Again in 12:8, which likewise lacks Girgashites in MT. The list is often assigned to the J source. The same seven names occur in 3:10, but in a very different order (see NOTES). There does not seem to be any direct correlation between this list of seven nations and the account of six cities (and seven kings!) defeated in 10:28-39. What this suggests is that where narrative units were lacking, the Dtr historians had to fall back on clichés. The latter were often no less firmly rooted in actual historical experience.

2. *under one command*. It is a most abrupt ending, which suggests to scholars that another battle story once followed at this point. If so, a logical candidate would be something relating to the defeat of hill-country kings to the west and north of Shechem (e.g. Tappuah, Hepher, Apheq, Lasharon in 12:17-18). It is not impossible that the LXX is correct in reading 8:30-35

next. As it stands, however, the unit poses the sharpest possible contrast with the resourceful response of the Gibeon-dwellers.

3-27. These verses separate neatly into two segments. Verses 3-15 tell of a treaty for the protection of Gibeon. Verses 16-27 add details for the suppression of Gibeon and its allied towns.

There can be no doubt about the historicity of a treaty with the Gibeonites. See F. Charles Fensham, "The Treaty between Israel and the Gibeonites," *BA* 27 (1964) 96-100. Its essential historicity is shown by the account of a plague in David's reign which was traced to Saul's blood guilt "because he put the Gibeonites to death" (2 Sam 21:1-3, where the Gibeonites are called "Amorites/Westerners"). While Saul's treatment of the Gibeonites is nowhere described in detail, it may be alluded to in connection with the murder of Saul's son and successor (2 Sam 4:2-3, and see below on "Beeroth" in v 17). The evidence is marshaled by Abraham Malamat, "Doctrines of Causality in Hittite and Biblical Historiography: A Parallel," *VT* 5 (1955) 1-12.

The second part of this story is at numerous points in strong tension with the first part. One may skip from 9:15 to 10:1ff with no sense of a gap. To this extent our analysis agrees with Yehezkel Kaufmann and others, although we do not label either part of vv 3-27 (i.e. 3-15,16-27) as specifically "priestly." We lack adequate controls for more detailed source analysis. See the survey of critical literature in Soggin, *Joshua,* 107-108.

It is not easy at first glance to know what to make of the figure of Joshua in this chapter. While one must always allow for the possibility that Joshua has been secondarily introduced into the story, the configuration here suggests rather the opposite. As in the early version of the story of The Ruin, the name of Joshua in the tradition was something of an embarrassment to Dtr 1; but the historian put down vv 3-15 in such a way as to legitimate the treaty.

3. The syntax is disjunctive, marking the beginning of a narrative unit.

The inhabitants of. The root is *yšb* and means "to dwell or inhabit" and also "to sit down." But here the sense of royalty is ruled out by the narrative context; Gibeon has no king.

Gibeon. See Map D, 260. It is located on an important east-west road from Jericho, which continues westward to descend to the coastal plain via the Beth-horon pass, which was also known as the Valley of Aijalon. The identification with el-Jib, 13 km (8 miles) northwest of Jerusalem, is clinched by the excavation of some thirty wine-jar handles stamped with the letters *gbʿn*, from the levels of the Iron II town (*ANEP,* ⚹⚹787, 810). However there seems to be a gap between this "Bordeaux of Palestine," as it has been dubbed, and the much earlier city of the Middle Bronze Age. No Late Bronze or Iron I town has been located there, although the excavated area is relatively confined. Archaeological evidence for the period of our story is unfortunately confined to the contents of a couple of tombs. It seems clear that whatever settlement was there in Joshua's day, it was, like Jericho and The Ruin, not a large one. Gibeon is not mentioned in the Amarna Letters or in any second-millennium inscriptions. But it becomes an important town, thanks no doubt to the Yahwist pacification of the region. It is assigned to Benjamin in 18:25 and designated as a Levitical town in 21:17.

There was a "high place" at Gibeon (the nearby site of Nebi Samwil?) which was important early in Solomon's career for there he received his gift of wisdom (1 Kgs 3:4-15). But otherwise little is known of it. Efforts to locate "the hill of God" (1 Sam 10:5, *RSV* "Gibeathelohim") either at Gibeon (Aaron Demsky, "Geba, Gibeah, and Gibeon—An Historico-Geographic Riddle," *BASOR* 212 [December 1973] 26-31) or at nearby Nebi Samwil (Blenkinsopp, *Gibeon and Israel*, 65-83), instead of equating it with Bethel as others have done, might help to fill a gap; but they seem to raise more problems than they solve.

It will only become clear in v 17 why the treaty with Gibeon was such a momentous event; Gibeon was part of a small four-village alliance. The term "tetrapolis" is perhaps too grandiose.

what Yahweh had done to Jericho and The Ruin. This was enough to suggest to the Gibeonites, who seem to have had no king, and thus no way of profiting from the arrangements made in vv 1 and 2, an alternative to violence. It is important to observe that while the kings were responding to the threat posed by Joshua and Israel, the Gibeonites acted on the basis of what Yahweh had done.

4. *they too acted deceptively*. The story unfolds with "disarming naiveté." McKenzie, *The World of the Judges*, 59. The trickery motif was a favorite in the formation of the patriarchal heritage: Jacob and Esau (Genesis 27), Jacob and Laban (Genesis 30), Shechem and the sons of Jacob (Genesis 34).

They packed . . . posed. On the assonance of the original, see Textual Note.

worn-out. Hebrew *bālîm*, used twice in quick succession, in anticipation of the twice-used feminine form in v 5.

"It is possible to detect, throughout the negotiations, a certain air of unreality and even detached humour especially with regard to the means chosen by the Gibeonites to authenticate their mission—as if anyone would believe that they could not have obtained fresh bread on the journey!" Blenkinsopp, *Gibeon and Israel*, 35.

6-15a. Joshua is mentioned first but the organization (Bene Israel) is first to respond (v 7). In reply to the organization, they address themselves again to Joshua, who finally enters the negotiations with a question (v 8). Then follows the consummation of this diplomatic make-believe, thanks to the pagans' use of the Deuteronomic rhetoric (vv 9-11). Thus the reader's attention might be effectively diverted from the serious responsibility which tradition had already assigned to Joshua in the Gibeon affair. It was perhaps this sort of narrative maneuver in the first edition that suggested the similar Deuteronomic rhetoric in Rahab's speech in the final edition of the book (2:9-11).

6. *at Gilgal*. Hebrew *hglgl*. LXX reflects *'l hglgl*, which looks like contamination from the four other occurrences of the same preposition in this verse.

Gilgal. After the event at Ebal and Gerizim in 8:30-35, this abrupt reference to Gilgal is jarring. The Dtr 1 informant had placed the great Shechem Valley Covenant at the end of the era (chap. 24). It was Dtr 2 who inserted the corrective, and did so in characteristic fashion, without revising what was already in the book.

Identification of this Gilgal with Tell Jiljulieh east of Shechem is ruled out by the report that the area shows no signs of ancient occupation. Edward F. Campbell, Jr., "The Shechem Area Survey," *BASOR* 190 (April 1968) 29.

Israel. Whether this reading of LXX^B or "all Israel" in LXX^A or "men of Israel" in MT, the effect is to divert responsibility from Joshua.

"From a distant country. Place of origin will be indicated in the following verse. Note other biblical examples of travel from a distance to negotiate with an advancing enemy (2 Sam 8:9; 2 Kgs 16:7). Examples from extra-biblical sources are collected by Jehoshua M. Grintz, "The Treaty of Joshua with the Gibeonites," *JAOS* 86 (1966) 122. Since the Gibeonites are "Hivites," they may in fact have arrived from the north not long before the Joshua units arrived from the east. The Gibeonites were in that case telling half of the truth.

On the matter of negotiations with cities, Deuteronomy distinguishes between cities within the inheritance and those at a distance which are "not cities of the nations here" (Deut 20:15).

Make a covenant. The Hebrew idiom is *krt bryt,* "cut a covenant." The idiom is apparently rooted in the dividing of a sacrificial victim in half. The nature of the oath is identification with the victim. See now David L. Petersen, "Covenant Ritual: A Traditio-Historical Perspective," *Biblical Research* 22 (1977) 7-18.

Judges 2:1-5 specifically singles out entangling alliances with the inhabitants of the land as violations which had brought on a policy change of major proportions; Yahweh would no longer drive them out.

at once. Hebrew *'th,* another freighted time expression; the first since 8:30.

7. *The Bene Israel.* Martin Noth took this as a sign of an older and more original element, the name of Joshua being first introduced by the collector in his framework. The question that goes unanswered, on this view, is why the collector would have wanted to introduce Joshua into such a tradition.

Here, as in the story of pell-mell rush to defeat in the first encounter at The Ruin, there is no hint of any attempt to consult the oracle or to divine Yahweh's will in the matter; and this failure is explicitly noted in v 14. Does this fact mean that the Israelites wanted to be deceived? Thus Jacob Liver, "The Literary History of Joshua IX," *JSS* 8 (1963) 227-243. This is probably to make too much of an argument from silence. Narrative structure suggests rather that their natural bumbling would cause trouble unless Yahweh intervened for them.

Hivites. They comprise one of the most influential of the six or seven "nations," and are mentioned in eighteen of the twenty-one examples of the list to be found in the Old Testament. Blenkinsopp, *Gibeon and Israel,* 14 n. 1. In fourteen occurrences of the list, they are followed by Jebusites. According to 11:3 *Hivites* were also to be found at the foot of Mount Hermon, in the land of Mizpah. In 2 Sam 21:2 the Gibeonites are "part of the remnant of the Amorites," that is, the Westerners. Moreover, the population of Shechem at some time had a significant Hivite constituency as indicated by the description of its *nāśî',* Hamor the Hivite (Gen 34:2).

Where was the Hivite homeland? The most attractive suggestion, which still awaits definitive proof, connects this gentilic name with ancient Quwe, that is, Cilicia in Asia Minor. Mendenhall, *Ten Gen,* 154. On the biblical occurrences in 1 Kgs 10:28 and 2 Chr 1:16, see A. S. Kapelrud, "Kue," in *IDB* 3, 50. Such a northern origin would in fact help to account for the rival textual tradition in Gen 34:2 (LXX) and Josh 9:7 (LXX) according to which the appropriate gentilic is "Horite" (that is, Hurrian). Although the relationship is far from clear, there is certainly an overlap to these terms that is historically grounded in contacts to the north of Canaan proper. See Blenkinsopp, *Gibeon and Israel*, 14-27.

The name of the tutelary deity of the Hivites, whom they would have invoked to witness the treaty, is unknown.

8. *your servants."* As again in vv 9,11,24, it carries a double meaning. The noun '*bd* is either "servant," a polite personal pronoun (as in v 9), or "slave" depending on context. The former sense is a standard form of modesty in writing to the foreign office in the Amarna Letters.

Where do you come from?" This is the crucial issue.

9. *Indeed.* The particle *ky* often has asseverative force.

and. The conjunction *w* is explicative.

10. *Amorite.* Here the word does not have its etymological sense of "Westerner," as in the redactor's introduction (v 1). The old Gibeon story used the word with more precise historical focus, designating Transjordan kingdoms that lay closer to the Syrian heartland of Amurru.

Sihon . . . Og. As in the speech of Rahab (2:10), it is only in reference to the earlier Transjordan successes that the negotiator with Israel is in a position to name names. The narrative background is Num 21:21-35. Cf. Deut 2:26 - 3:17 and Josh 12:1-6.

Bashan. See Map B, 112. It is the Golan Heights, as far north as Mount Hermon. A rich land.

11. *"We are your servants, so make a covenant.* Together with the appeal and assertion in vv 6 and 8, these clauses form a chiastic pattern.

13. *clothes and sandals.* Moses reminds Israel in the ceremony of covenant renewal that its clothing did not wear out during the Wanderings (Deut 29:5).

14. *The men.* At this crucial juncture the narrator makes it explicit that the responsibility for the problematical treaty had to be shared, not borne by Joshua alone. The LXX reading here mentioning "the leaders" instead of "the men" cannot be correct since this verse merely assigns fault, whereas "the leaders" are going to be the ones to salvage something out of the situation.

took some of their provisions. This seems to be a reference to the meal that is part of the treaty-making procedure.

decision of Yahweh. The narrator delays the reporting of this vital information, about the failure to consult the divine will, until it can be juxtaposed with the results. According to epic tradition, Joshua was one who had long experience, through his association with Eleazar, with the divinatory technique called "judgment of the Urim" (Num 27:21).

did not request. The Hebrew word order which this translation reproduces— verb last—makes a most emphatic declaration. Joshua had been caught in the position of having to ratify negotiations for which he was not totally responsible.

Mention of the oracle also presupposes the Ark, as in the scene of mourning with the request for an explanation of the disaster at The Ruin (7:6).

15. *peace*. Hebrew *šālôm* is a technical term in the language of treaty-making. The establishment of *šālôm* is the goal of a *běrît*.

to guarantee their lives. Hebrew *lĕhayyôtām* The form is *Pi'el* infinitive, which has iterative or durative force. It was an agreement to "prolong" their lives. It was thus more than a non-aggression treaty. Rather it would have to do with such matters as pasturelands, water rights, trade, intermarriage, and mutual military support. Weippert, *The Settlement of the Israelite Tribes in Palestine*, 19. See the stories of Isaac's dealings with the king of Gerar (Genesis 26) and especially the failure of Levi and Simeon to honor the older Shechem covenant in patriarchal days (Genesis 34).

Here in 15 is the heart of the story; the special problem with the Gibeonites in Israel began with Joshua's ratification of a treaty where he had not been fully in charge of the negotiations.

15b. *And the leaders of the congregation swore an oath to them*. Three of the four words which comprise this statement in Hebrew have not previously appeared in the chapter but are key words in what follows. This statement is therefore clearly recognizable as the redactor's splice.

16-27. This supplement to the first edition is itself excerpted from an independent and probably older account. It has been argued that the consciousness which would provide "the motive and the will to drive away the foreign ethnic elements in Gibeon and its vicinity from Israelite territory" is to be sought in the time of Saul. Liver, "The Literary History of Joshua IX," *JSS* 8 (1963) 243. In the context of the final redaction, however, when the national unity was falling apart, the old story was put to most surprising use.

16. *Three days*. That is, not long thereafter. Unlike the same length of time in 2:16, this three-day unit is not related to any longer span in the context. Compare, however, the three-day span in Judg 20:30, another old and tragic story put to later and different use by Dtr 2. R. G. Boling, "In Those Days There Was No King in Israel," in *A Light Unto My Path,* eds. Howard N. Bream, Ralph D. Heim, and Carey A. Moore, 41-44; *Judges*, AB 6A, 29-38, 280-288.

they were neighbors of theirs who lived in their midst! Hebrew *qěrôbîm hēm 'ēlāyw ubĕqirbô hēm yôšĕbîm*. The construction is chiastic.

17. *entered*. Hebrew *wyb'w*. Context indicates they did so militarily.

their towns. This is the first hint that more than one settlement might be involved. It was in fact a small but strategically located string of villages that the Hivites occupied; they controlled the entire northwest quadrant of approaches to Jerusalem.

Chephirah. See Map D. The town is assigned to Benjamin in 18:26. Tell Kefireh is northwest of Jerusalem at a point less than 8 km west of Gibeon (el-Jib). The name means "the lioness." Two Amarna Letters come from *Ba'alat-neše*, "lady of the lions," somewhere north of Jerusalem and in the vicinity of Aijalon. The logogram for *neše* is *UR-MAḤ-MEŠ* and corresponds to Hebrew *kprym*. See Blenkinsopp, *Gibeon and Israel,* 7-8. If the two Amarna Letters were written from the town that became biblical Chephirah, it would seem to indicate a continuity of population elements in the Hivite confederacy going back to the period when Shechem (another main locus of Hivite elements) was ruled by a renegade prince whose name "Labayu" also means "leonine." Tell Kefireh was not heavily settled—after a long hiatus since the Early Bronze Age —until the period of the Israelite monarchy, according to the recent surface survey. Karel J. H. Vriezen, *"Hirbet Kefire*—eine Oberflachenuntersuchung," *ZDPV* 91 (1975) 135-158.

Beeroth. "Wells." Assigned to Benjamin in 18:25. Map D, 260. Against the identification with Nebi Samwil (where there is no archaeological evidence) is the probable survival of the name in el-Bireh, the modern twin city with Ramallah. The site of Khirbet Raddana at the northern edge of el-Bireh, excavated over three seasons in 1969-1972, has produced substantial architectural remains and clear indication that the settlement there, at the very beginning of Iron I, is "contemporary and culturally related" to the village at The Ruin (J. A. Callaway, "Ai," in *EAEHL* I [1975] 38).

The most famous Beerothites were the family of one Rimmon, whose sons, Baanah and Rechab, assassinated their master Ishbaal and were executed for the crime on David's order (2 Samuel 4). In a parenthesis it is explained that the Beerothites fled to Gittaim after the incident, where they could be found in the day of the annotator (2 Sam 4:3). Beeroth was resettled after the Babylonian exile (Ezra 2:25=Neh 7:29). It is probably the place called Bereth (*RSV* "Berea") in 1 Macc 9:4. See Jonathan Goldstein, *I Maccabees*, AB 41, 372-373.

Qiryath-yearim. "Woodsville." An important town situated where the tribal territories of Judah, Benjamin, and Dan later converged. Map D, 260. The site is Tell el-'Azar above Abu Ghosh (=T. Qiryat-Ye'arim in recent Israeli publications). This name appears in Benjamin's town list (18:28 with LXX and Syriac) and is equated with "Qiryath-baal" on its southern border (18:14-15). In 15:9 it is identified with a "Baalah" on Judah's north border. Blenkinsopp thinks that the occurrence of both "Mount Yearim" and "Mount Baalah" in Josh 15:10-11 ought to suggest that Qiryath-yearim and Baalah were topographically distinct. He would then explain the name Qiryath-baal as a hybrid, formed at a later redactional stage. This would be a development without any clear parallels known to this writer. Yet another form, *ba'ălê yĕhûdâ* in 2 Sam 6:2, may not be a place name at all (cf. 1 Chr 13:6). Blenkinsopp, *Gibeon and Israel,* 10.

18. *leaders.* The spotlight has shifted. This story is our first introduction, in Joshua, to these important persons, the *nĕśî'îm.* The *KJV* translation "princes" suggests royalty, which they were not. Best known from traditions of the patriarchs and the wilderness period, in the Israel of the Book of Joshua there are ten occurrences of this noun, every one in a context that belongs to the Dtr 2 redaction (9:15,18 [*bis*],19,21; 13:21; 17:4; 22:14,30,32). From this distribution a strong rhetorical relationship between this story and the altar narrative in chap. 22 is apparent. In 13:21, recognizable on other grounds as a Dtr 2 text, the same word refers to the five Midianite chieftains.

congregation. Hebrew *'ēdâ.* This word is ubiquitous in P, but is not found at any level in Dtn. Here it is likewise used for the first time in Joshua; but here it is mentioned repeatedly in the story (9:15,18 [*bis*],19,21,27), six times in fact. In the altar story, the word occurs another six times (22:12,16,17,18, 20,30). Elsewhere in Joshua the word occurs only in the list of asylum towns (20:6,9), which also most likely belongs to Dtr 2, and in 18:1, where it may be a conflation. This usage in Joshua is to be compared with similar usage in Judges 20-21, as M. Noth observed. *Das Buch Josua,* 55; and *Das System der zwölf Stämme Israels,* 102 n. 2.

What was said above about the pre-exilic origin of "priestly" language should be kept in mind here. Such language reflects the parallel cultivation of the tradition by different Levitical families.

'*ēdâ* is, like *qāhāl*, a word for the general assembly if all free males who are subject to military service (Num 1:2-3). The assembly was summoned to consult with the executive authorities in matters of public interest (Num 10:1-7; Exod 12:3; 35:1-4). On important occasions the '*ēdâ* was granted religious and legal authority (Num 15:32-36). In unusual cases of homicide, it functioned as court of law (Num 15:32-36; Josh 20:6-9). With the transition to monarchy in Israel, this institution was replaced by royally appointed officials. Grintz, "The Treaty of Joshua with the Gibeonites," *JAOS* 86 (1966) 118.

Like its virtual synonym *qāhāl*, "assembly" (8:35), this word '*ēdâ* was mostly avoided by Dtr 1. In all of Samuel and Kings, the only certain occurrence of '*ēdâ* is 1 Kgs 12:20, where the "congregation" elects Jeroboam as king over the secessionist northern tribes.

The mention of the '*ēdâ* in 1 Kgs 8:5 at the installation of the Ark in the Jerusalem Temple is lacking in LXX[B(L)]. The presence of the '*ēdâ* at that point in the other recensions may be secondary; in the more detailed account of the same event, '*ēdâ* may also be secondary (2 Chr 5:6, where Syriac reflects '*m*, "people"). There are other signs of secondary influences on the 2 Kings account.

To summarize usage of '*ēdâ*: Dtr 1 avoids it totally in the pre-monarchy period and uses it once polemically during the monarchy. Dtr 2 revives the word to describe pre-monarchical reality for the post-monarchical context. In other words, the '*ēdâ* was an institution that had fallen into disuse or had been suppressed with the rise of the monarchy.

From the fact that in a protectorate or suzerainty-treaty, the oath was sworn by the inferior party, Blenkinsopp suspects that Israel was in fact the protected party and that the tradition was later redacted *ad maiorem gloriam Israel*. However, with so many indicators of the redactional hand of Dtr 2, we may suspect that this unit seeks also to affirm that slavish reliance upon archaic institutions should be consigned to the past. Where, on the contrary, the leaders of the congregation use their heads, they will salvage situations in which otherwise the prospects are especially grim.

had sworn. Hebrew *nšb'w*. The verb will be used three times in quick succession (vv 18,19,20), thus emphatically locating the problem, for any who might have missed it.

all. Except for three occurrences in the speech of the Gibeonites (vv 9, 10,11), this word has not been used in the chapter. It will now be used six times, so as to signal primary interests of the narrator: *all the congregation* (vv 18, and 21 [*bis*]), *all the leaders* of the congregation (v 19), *all the land* (v 24), and *all the inhabitants of the land* (v 24).

19. *"We have sworn . . . by Yahweh.* Hebrew *'nḥnw nšb'nw . . . byhwh.* Judges 21:7 (Dtr 2) uses the identical formula to express a quite analogous predicament in internal affairs.

21. *And the leaders said to them.* By repeating more compactly this formula from the beginning of v 19, the narrator shows the leaders not merely propounding the problem, but also formulating a solution—decision makers at work!

let them be woodcutters and water carriers for all the congregation." This is a most telling inversion of the covenant motif, for in Deut 29:10 (which uses exactly these designations for the sojourner) the effect of covenant is to erase distinctions of status which otherwise adhere to various occupational groups. The covenant belonged to the people-forming process, and the problem of inferior forms of membership in the community is precisely what the covenant liturgy was originally designed to counteract.

22. *Joshua.* Here he adopts the recommendation of the leaders.

'We live far away. Literally, "We are far away."

23. *You are now cursed.* For bearing false witness? On Blessing and Curse as formal treaty-elements, see 8:34 and NOTES. There are two parts to the arrangement. The Gibeonites are protected by the oath of the Israelites. For deceiving Israel, however, they must be punished. Cf. Cain who is punished by God for killing Abel but also protected (Gen 4:10-16).

the house of my God." Cf. "Yahweh's house" in 6:19. It is probable that there was a Yahwist temple at Shiloh and possible that there was one at Gilgal. Shechem involved precisely the Yahwist takeover and—for a while—reform of a patriarchal covenant-temple. We must consider the possibility that Joshua is here speaking about Gibeon's sanctuary which henceforth was going to be Yahweh's sanctuary. No doubt the referent is deliberately left vague.

24. *"It has indeed been emphatically made known.* The Gibeonites here pair the finite verb with its infinitive absolute used adverbially—and all of this preceded by asseverative *ky*—which reinforces our analysis of their speech in v 9 ("we have heard a lot about"). The two statements form a kind of *inclusio.*

25. *Well, then.* The particle *hinnēh* here signals a "logical" conclusion.

Whatever in your view is good and right. Here the Gibeonites are the ones to use the language that will furnish the last word on the era (Judg 17:6; 21:25)!

26. Joshua *delivered* the Gibeonites from the power of the Israelites and into a condition of servitude. There is here an intentionally absurd progression of great themes and phrases, ending with the famous centralization motif which in Dtr 1 had focused on Jerusalem. Dtr 2 had to contemplate the destruction of Jerusalem and the prospect of Israelites living far from Jerusalem as also expressing the will of Yahweh for the formation of his people.

27. *the place which Yahweh chooses.* Deut 12:5,11,14,18,21,26; 14:23,

24,25; 15:20; 16:2,6,7,11,15,16 (without *yhwh*); 17:8,10; 18:6; 26:2; 31:11 (without *yhwh*).

COMMENT

What historical reality lies at the base of this strange story? Even if the origin of the Gibeonites was not known to Joshua and the leaders, surely it would have been known to the people of Shechem. Is it possible that the enslavement of the Gibeonites was deliberately designed to expand territory and release manpower for the approaching struggle? There was in any case an embarrassment about the Gibeonites living in the midst of Israel. The story of the negotiations was told in vv 3-15 in such a way as to provide a coverup for the action of the newcomers in their negotiation of special status for the towns of the Hivite confederacy.

In vv 16-27 the story of the solution to the problem focuses attention on the role and significance of the popular assembly in the life of the believers. It was already an ancient institution. There was in Early Bronze Age Mesopotamia a popular assembly of such importance that it is possible to speak of a "primitive democracy" there with roots in the Sumerian Age at the very dawn of civilization (Thorkild Jacobsen, "The Cosmos as a State," *Before Philosophy,* eds. H. and H. A. Frankfort, John A. Wilson, and Thorkild Jacobsen, 137-199). But the people's assembly in Mesopotamia had disappeared by the second millennium B.C. and nothing suggests that there was any counterpart of such an assembly in the Canaanite city-states. It was Yahwism that introduced the people's assembly into Canaan for about two centuries. With the rise of monarchy in Israel, the popular assembly was eclipsed, until the rapid decline and impending collapse of the state suggested once again the viability of grassroots Yahwism for life in the midst of chaos. That which the tradition at last emphasized about Joshua can today be read with high probability as both historical truth and theological poetry. He had been "a man over the *'ēdâ*" (Num 27:16).

It would be helpful to know more about the Hivites. It is interesting that the two places where Joshua enters directly into peaceable relations with the local population were known to be significantly Hivite at some time in the past (Shechem) or in Joshua's day (Gibeon). The Hivite homelands bordered the great Hittite realm which has by chance furnished the clearest parallels to the Yahweh-Covenant form.

The unprecedented configuration of events in the crossing of the Jordan and two surprising victories (with a powerful assist from one or two timely earthquakes), and an intervening defeat, would have furnished a strong advantage in negotiations. It was, then, through a pair of "treaties" at Shechem (8:30) and Gibeon that Yahweh took over virtually the entire watershed ridge, from a point not far north of Jerusalem to the brink of the Jezreel Valley. This we may refer to as the Shechem Phase of the "conquest," the victory of a new commitment, which in turn furnished most of the manpower needed for military action in Judah (chap. 10) and Galilee (chap. 11).

The difference between events at Shechem and at Gibeon can be seen in the use to which the treaty form is put. It will become clear in the study of chapter 24 that events at Shechem must have involved religious reformation and conversion on a large scale, of such proportions in fact as to be worthy of being called a "mutation" in the evolution of the world's religions. The Shechem Covenant was the reconstitution of Israel in Canaan, following the pattern of Mosaic Yahwism.

Gibeon was different. This treaty reflects a pattern that also is well documented from Hittite archives. But it is neither a matter of parity nor vassalage. Rather it is a "pact with a protégé" (Grintz, "The Treaty of Joshua with the Gibeonites," *JAOS* 86 [1966] 113-126). In contrast to other treaty forms, the obligations of such a treaty are binding upon both parties though they are of unequal status. Two separate examples of comparable circumstances, in reports of Mursilis II, among others collected by Grintz, are especially instructive. In one the king says that "the men of Taptina, the men of Marsama, the men of Pikkurzi" have come to him after his war against three other cities and requested him to take them as slaves, for foot soldiers and horsemen in auxiliary forces, etc. In a later report the same Hittite king says that with a siege of their cities underway, "the men of Azzi were afraid" and "the elders of the land came towards me and grasped my feet and said to me, 'Lord, do not destroy us, take us into slavery and we shall give you regularly foot soldiers and horsemen.'" Because of the winter Mursilis returned home. "But, although a year passed, I established no rule in the land of Azzi, but I did make the men of Azzi swear." It seems that subsequently they broke the oath and he prepared to attack; but they then yielded and became his "slaves" (Grintz, 117).

What then shall we make of the etiological factor in understanding this chapter? Does the chapter seek to explain the origins of the later temple slaves (*nĕtînîm*) in the post-exilic period? It may have been so understood, but there is no clear evidence that it was so intended. Here it is important to have the split-level character of the Dtr corpus in view. In the story of The Ruin (chaps. 7-8), which similarly shows two strata, the etiology belongs to both levels; but there in Dtr 1 it was soberly used as a diversionary tactic which would relieve Joshua of primary responsibility for a serious error in military judgment. In those chapters it was the substantial additions by Dtr 2 that turned the Ai story into an illustration of Yahweh's rule in direct theocracy, as Divine Warrior.

With the Gibeonites the situation is similar but not identical. In the first edition (vv 1-15a, Dtr 1), there is no etiological purpose reflected. This story too is soberly told in such a way as to blunt Joshua's responsibility for a treaty which was seen to be problematical. In this chapter the etiological motif enters only in a secondary expansion (vv 15b-27, Dtr 2). There it explains not the protection but the suppression of Gibeon! Such a telling of it is either exceedingly heavy-handed, or else it deliberately presents developments as absurd. In view of the pattern elsewhere in Joshua-Judges (as well as Samuel-Kings), the latter is entirely credible.

The effect of such a unit is to startle the reader. It clears the air for a fresh look at the traditionary unit which comes next, one in which Yahweh will honor the problematical treaty.

6. IN THE WAKE OF THE GIBEON AGREEMENT
(10:1-27)

Southern Reaction

10 ¹ It happened when Adonizedeq king of Jerusalem heard that Joshua had captured The Ruin and put it under the ban—doing to The Ruin and its king as he had done to Jericho and its king—and that the inhabitants of Gibeon had made peace with Joshua and Israel though they were in their midst, ² they feared greatly. For it was known that Gibeon was a town as powerful as one of the royal towns, that it was larger than The Ruin, and that all its men were "knights"!

³ Adonizedeq king of Jerusalem sent to Hoham king of Hebron, Piram king of Jarmuth, Japhia king of Lachish, and Debir king of Eglon: ⁴ "Come up here and help me! Let us attack Gibeon because it has made peace with Joshua and the Bene Israel!"

⁵ The five western kings rendezvoused and went up—the king of Jerusalem, the king of Hebron, the king of Jarmuth, the king of Lachish, the king of Eglon—together with the entirety of their military forces. They pitched camp to fight against Gibeon.

Vindication

⁶ The men of Gibeon sent to Joshua in the camp at The Circle: "Do not withdraw your support from your servants! Come up here at once and save us! Help us! For all the western kings, who live in the hill country, have combined forces against us!"

⁷ So Joshua went up from The Circle, he and all the military force with him, all the burly warriors. ⁸ Yahweh said to Joshua, "Do not fear them, for I have given them into your power and not a man of them will stand before you!"

⁹ Joshua took them by surprise. All night long he had marched up from The Circle. ¹⁰ Yahweh confounded them before the Bene Israel! Yahweh defeated them decisively at Gibeon! He pursued them by

way of the Beth-horon Ascent. He struck them down as far away as Azeqah and Maqqedah.

11 And when they fled from the Bene Israel, while they were in the Beth-horon Descent, Yahweh threw down big stones upon them from the sky—as far off as Azeqah—and they died. Many more died because of the hailstones than the Bene Israel had put to the sword!

Lest We Forget

12 Then Joshua appealed to Yahweh, on the day God gave the Westerners into the hand of the Bene Israel.

When he attacked them at Gibeon, they were smitten before the Bene Israel.

> He said in the sight of Israel
> "Sun, over Gibeon be still,
>   Moon too, over Aijalon Valley."
> 13 Sun was stilled,
>   And Moon stood fixed
>   Until he defeated his enemies' force!

Is this not recorded in The Book of Yashar? The sun stayed in the center of the heavens and did not hurry to set for almost a whole day! 14 Never has there been a day like that before or since—God's heeding of a human voice! Surely Yahweh fought for Israel!

[15 Then Joshua returned to the camp at The Circle, all Israel with him.]

Sequel

16 Those five kings fled and hid themselves in the cave at Maqqedah. 17 It was reported to Joshua: "The five kings have been found, hidden in the cave at Maqqedah."

18 And Joshua said, "Roll some big stones to the mouth of the cave, and station some men by it to watch them. 19 But do not stay there. Go after your enemies and cut off their retreat! Do not let them enter their towns, for your God Yahweh has given them into your power!"

20 When Joshua and the Bene Israel had finished striking them

down with effect, so that they were finished off (although some survivors had got away from them and gone into the fortified towns), 21 then all the force returned safely to the camp, to Joshua at Maqqedah. No one slandered the Bene Israel!

22 Then said Joshua: "Open the mouth of the cave, and bring to me those five kings out of the cave." 23 And they did so. They brought to him from the cave the five kings: the king of Jerusalem, the king of Hebron, the king of Jarmuth, the king of Lachish, the king of Eglon. 24 When they had brought those kings to Joshua, Joshua summoned all the men of Israel and said to the commanders of the men of war . . . with him: "Come forward. Put your feet on the necks of these kings." And they came forward and put their feet on their necks. 25 Joshua said to them: "Do not be afraid of them and do not be dismayed! Be strong and be bold! For thus Yahweh will do to all the enemies whom you fight!"

26 Joshua struck them subsequently and killed them. Then he hanged them on five trees. They hung on the trees until evening. 27 Then at about the time of sunset, Joshua gave the command, and they took them down from the trees. They threw them into the cave where they had hidden and they set some big stones over the mouth of the cave: they are there unto this very day!

TEXTUAL NOTES

10 1. *Adonizedeq*   LXX reads "Adonibezeq" as in Judg 1:5-7, but that is most likely a title, "prince of Bezeq," not a name.

Joshua and   Restored from LXX, where MT has sustained a haplography: *'t [yhwš' w't] yśr'l*.

though they were in their midst   Hebrew *wyhw bqrbm*, missing in LXX^{AB}. The antecedent of "they" shifts abruptly and the use of converted imperfects at this point suggests that something else is missing.

2. *they*   Thus MT and LXX, while some lesser witnesses read the expected singular.

it was known that   This is restored from LXX and treats the verb as passive. MT shows a haplography: *ky [yd' ky] 'yr*.

that it was larger than The Ruin   This was lost by haplography from LXX^{AB} or the *Vorlage*.

3. *Hoham*   The name is, curiously, *Ailam* in LXX.

Piram   LXX *Pheidōn* shows confusion of Hebrew *d* and *r* in the script. The difference in endings between *m* and *n* is more likely auditory.

Japhia   *Iephtha* in LXX.

Debir   *Dabein* in LXX[B].

Eglon   LXX reads here and in v 23 "Odollam," essentially a difference of one letter in the Hebrew (allowing again for the auditory confusion of final *n* and *m*). Here there seems to be a confusion of *g* and *d*, which might have happened where a surface mark on poor or reused material gave the letter *gimel* the appearance of being closed on the bottom. Most witnesses support MT.

5. *western kings . . . military forces*   Thus MT where LXX shows great variation. It reads "Jebusites" for "western" (but transliterates "Amorites" in v 6), "Odollam" for "Eglon," and "people" (Hebrew *'m*) for "military force" (Hebrew *mḥnh*).

rendezvoused and   LXX[AB] shows a haplography: *wy['spw wy]'lw*.

6. *men*   Hebrew *'nšy*. LXX reflects *yšby*, "inhabitants."

camp   LXX adds "of Israel."

your support   This is the pausal form of the singular noun (**yādékā*) where the plural in MT (*yādêkā*) looks like contamination from the next word (*mē'ābādêkā*).

7. *all*   Thus LXX and Vulgate, where MT reads a conjunction, presumably a dittography: *'mw [w]kl*.

8. *and*   The conjunction survives in a few Hebrew manuscripts supported by Syriac and Targum.

you!"   Here at the end of the verse LXX switches to the plural pronoun, in direct address to Joshua, which is not implausible.

10. *the Bene*   Restored from LXX[B].

Yahweh   Restored from LXX, where in MT a scribe's eye has jumped from one *m* to another: *wykm [yhwh] mkh*.

He   This is MT, where the versions read "They."

Beth-horon   Here and in the next verse LXX reads "Horonaim," which need not be the Transjordan town of that name. The ending is dual and may be taken as referring to the "two (Beth-)Horons," upper and lower.

11. *the Bene*   Thus LXX, as also in v 10.

big   Thus MT. LXX anticipates and reads the word for "hail."

and they died   This was dropped by haplography in LXX: *w[ymtw] rbym*.

Many   LXX shows a conjunction at the outset, remnant of the lost verb as described in the preceding note.

12. *Then*   *BH*[3] apparatus for this verse is misleading. With the aid of LXX, the rubric to the old poem is seen to be perfectly chiastic. Following "the Westerners," MT shows a lengthy lapse that has wrecked the chiasm: *h'mry [byd yśr'l//bmktm bgb'wn wykw] lpny yśr'l*. Our restoration translates LXX with no remainder.

God   With LXX, where MT reads *yhwh*.

the Bene   Missing in LXX due to haplography: *lpn[y bn]y yśr'l*.

He   LXX reads "Joshua," resolving the ambiguity of MT.

13. *his enemies'*   Hebrew *'ôyĕbāw*. Whose enemies? LXX resolves the ambiguity by translating as plural, "their enemies." But see NOTE and COMMENT.

Is this not recorded in the Book of Yashar?   Lacking in LXX[AB]. See NOTE.

14. *God's*   With LXX, against MT *yhwh*.

15. [*Then Joshua returned to the camp at The Circle, all Israel with him.*] Verses 15 and 43 are missing from the best LXX witnesses. Max Margolis, *The Book of Joshua in Greek,* Part II (1931) 181 and 205. S. Holmes, *Joshua: The Hebrew and Greek Texts* (Cambridge University Press, 1914) 4. The statement is probably a gloss that seeks to understand where Joshua received the report with which the next unit begins. The glossator did not recognize the digressionary character of vv 12-14.

18. *big* This is MT *gdlwt,* which here, and again in v 27, has no reflex in LXX. Cf. v 11.

20. *and* LXX adds "all," perhaps contamination from the following verse.

from them and gone into Missing in LXX, probably an inner-Greek development.

21. *to the camp* Missing in LXX^AB, after haplography: *'l [ḥmḥnh 'l] yhwš'.*

one This is Hebrew *'yš,* omitting the initial *l* of MT as a dittography. It is awkward in Hebrew and less plausible to construe the words of MT appositionally: "No one slandered the Bene Israel, not even one of them."

22. *"Open the mouth of* This is Hebrew *ptḥw 't py,* a bit of assonance that was eliminated in the *Vorlage* of the LXX after the loss of *['t] py.* Cf. v 27.

to me Too many occurrences of *'aleph* caused the loss of a preposition in LXX *Vorlage: whmṣy'w '[ly ']t.*

23. *And they did so* Haplography in LXX *Vorlage: wy['św kn wy]wṣ'w.*

the The second "the" in the verse follows LXX^B, Syr^A, and Vulg, where MT reads "those," perhaps as a result of vertical dittography. If it was original, there is no mechanism to explain the loss.

Eglon LXX "Odollam." See fifth Textual Note at v 3 above.

24. *those kings* LXX "them."

the men of LXX omits.

said to Lacking in LXX, which instead reads "saying to them" before the quote.

men of war . . . With the preposition *'l* occurring three times, the particle *'t* four times, and two more words beginning with *'aleph,* the verse was perfectly set up for scribal accidents, which are amply attested in the versions. LXX lacks *'nšy,* "men of." There is nothing wrong with MT, except for one word. In the gap it has *hhlkw',* which is usually explained as a finite verb, with the extremely rare use of the definite article prefixed to the verb as relative particle ("who had gone," thus LXX). The final *'aleph* is explained as a dittography. An alternative would be to recognize a double dittography, *h* at the beginning and *'* at the end, in which case something more is missing.

kings" LXX omits.

26. *subsequently* Missing in LXX.

27. *big* See Textual Note at v 11 above.

the mouth of Hebrew *py* has no reflex in LXX.

they are there These words are not represented in the text. The etiological formula here appears to be loosely appended, as in 8:29.

NOTES

10:1-27. These verses clearly fall into four segments. When Gibeon is faced with the threat of the coalition headed by the king of Jerusalem (vv 1-5), Joshua and the Bene Israel fulfill their treaty obligation and repel the attackers thanks to a powerful assist from the divine Sovereign (vv 6-11). The last point is then developed in a flashback that makes it quite clear the victory was due entirely to divine participation (vv 12-14). The primary story line then resumes, with the capture of the allied kings (vv 16-27).

To all of this there is appended another old unit (vv 28-39) which focuses instead on the destruction of the allied towns. This will be treated in our next section. The old units were placed end to end in a logical sequence but without any attempt to harmonize the differences of detail between them. Of prime importance is the fact that the rapid series of victories in the south is presented as the unplanned offshoot of Yahweh's third intervention since the Bene Israel has crossed the Jordan. This time it was an intervention on behalf of the Gibeonites.

Verses 1-14 are not primarily concerned with warfare, holy or otherwise. Rather, the fighting here provides the stage upon which Yahweh works a wonder, the third and final one in the book.

1. *Adonizedeq.* "My Lord is *Ṣedeq*/Righteous." The form and meaning of this name tells nothing with certainty about the identity of the Jerusalem deity. Cross, *CMHE,* 209. In LXX this Jerusalem king has been confused with the *'ădōnîbezeq* of Judg 1:4-7. But the latter does not hail from Jerusalem; he was dispatched thither, in mutilated condition, to inspire fear. If he were the king, his capture alone would have sufficed. He was "lord of Bezeq." See *Judges,* AB 6A, 50 and 55.

Jerusalem. This is the first time the name is encountered in the Bible (cf. Gen 14:18). In Joshua's day the fortified city was largely confined to the eastern hill, south of today's Old City, although the recent excavations have indicated to Benjamin Mazar and Nahman Avigad that the City of David (tenth century) had already expanded on to the western hill, covering an area of more than fifteen acres. Benjamin Mazar, *The Mountain of the Lord* (Garden City, NY: Doubleday, 1975) 171. By Joshua's day the population of Jerusalem was highly mixed so that there would later be as much truth as poetry in Ezek 16:3—"Your father was an Amorite, and your mother a Hittite."

The supposed tension between these verses and Judg 1:5-8,21 is overstressed by scholars who have equated Adonizedeq and the lord of Bezeq. In the present chapter it is Jerusalem alone that escapes a raid even though its king is eliminated in the defeat of the coalition! This chapter offers a poor doublet for anything in Judges 1.

With the mention of Jerusalem and its allies, it becomes clear that the awareness of the opposition has increased enormously.

Joshua. He, rather than Yahweh, was perceived by the kings as the problem. Albrecht Alt concluded that Joshua was originally "at home" only in the stories of chaps. 10 and 11, which are in the form of Ephraimite hero-sagas and present Joshua as a charismatic figure of the type that we meet in the warfare stories of the Book of Judges. See Alt, "Josua," BZAW 66 (1936) 13-19; reprinted in his *Kleine Schriften* I, 176-192.

2. *they feared*. The plural is here retained as the more difficult reading. It may either anticipate the involvement of all five kings (a pentapolis?) or somehow refer to everyone around the kings.

Gibeon could be compared for strength with one of the *royal towns*, that is, one of city-states with monarchical form of government; thirty-one of them are listed for western Palestine alone in 12:7-24. Unlike them, however, Gibeon had no monarchy. By the time of the LXX translators, the city-state system had long since disappeared; instead of *the royal towns*, LXX has *mētropoleōn*.

In the Amarna period, Gibeon seems to have been a town of no particular importance in the territory of Jerusalem. "It may be suggested that the establishment of a strong Hivite enclave north-west of Jerusalem is connected with the breakup of the Mitanni empire towards the end of the Amarna period or the settlement of a group originating in Anatolia or Syria." Blenkinsopp, *Gibeon and Israel*, 30.

"knights"! Hebrew *gibbōrîm*, men trained in combat and prosperous enough to afford armament, squire, and leisure time for such activity. They were always more numerous among the opposition (Judg 5:13). Gideon was a notable Israelite *gibbōr* (Judg 6:12). With no monarchical system to support, it is not impossible that the Hivite economy in fact sustained a much larger "middle class" than royal towns.

3. See Map D, 260. Except for the convenor, Adonizedeq, it is only here that the confederate kings are mentioned by name. Similarly in Genesis 14 the allied defenders of another pentapolis are named only once (Gen 14:2), whereas the attackers are named twice (Gen 14:1 and 9). D. N. Freedman called our attention to the similarity.

Hebron. Map D, 260. In 14:13-15 it will be given to Caleb and we will learn that its name used to be Qiryat-Arba, which relates it to the Anaqim (Num 13:22). Situated in the high hills that form the north-south backbone of the country, this is the first of two towns attacked in the wake of the Gibeon and foothill victories. Very little has been learned archaeologically at Hebron; systematic excavations have yet to be carried through to publication. For the brief reports of P. C. Hammond, see *RB* 73 (1966) 566-569; *Bible et Terre Sainte* 80 (1966) 6-8; *RB* 75 (1968) 253-258. In the Amarna period the city-state centering in Jerusalem shared a border on the south with a state which encompassed at least the territory from Hebron to Keilah, some 13.6 km to the northwest of Hebron. This area was governed by the local prince Shuwardata whose involvements over the years included an alliance with Abdi-heba of Jerusalem against one who is styled as a "Hebrew man." See the compact description by Campbell, "The Amarna Letters and the Amarna Period," *BA* 23 (1960); reprinted in *BAR* 3 (1970) especially 70-71. The monarchical tradition of Hebron goes back to the early Hyksos era; the founding of Hebron is dated "seven years before Zoan in Egypt" (Num 13:22). The latter is Tanis (earlier Avaris), the Hyksos capital in the delta. It was at Hebron that David first received the title "king" and from there the monarchical tradition would be reintroduced to Jerusalem. Hebron became one of the Levitical towns (Josh 20:7) and, at last, a provincial capital (Josh 15:54).

Hebron like Jerusalem and Gibeon had a heavy concentration of non-Semitic people who had arrived mostly from the north in the Amarna and post-Amarna period. In fact the kingdoms of Canaan that were dismantled by the Yahwist revolution were mostly of recent and alien origin, as indicated by the high frequency of non-Semitic personal names.

There is no necessary contradiction between the traditions here and in Judg 1:10, where the capture of Hebron is credited to Judah, the large administrative unit to which Hebron later belonged. Judges 1 is part of a rhetorical framework to the entire Judges era, a framework which clearly exploits the "tribal" rivalry of the pre-monarchy period and caricatures it for didactic effect.

Jarmuth. Map D, 260. Khirbet Yarmuk (=Tell Yarmut), some 24 km west of Bethlehem in the Elah Valley. This is the first of three towns situated in a north-south line in the region known as the Shephelah, the foothills separating the central mountain range from the broad coastal plain. In the later administrative divisions under the monarchy, Jarmuth belongs to the second district of Judah (15:35).

Lachish. Map D, 260. Tell ed-Duweir is about 40 km southwest of Jerusalem. This fortified MB-LB town was already half a millennium old when it was destroyed c. 1200 B.C., according to recent excavations. Yohanan Aharoni et al., *Investigations at Lachish,* especially 41-43. The earliest resettlement does not appear to be earlier than the eleventh century.

In the Amarna Letters the head man at Lachish is Zimrida, succeeded at his death by Shipti-Ba'l who had been second in command. Lachish in the Amarna period was close to the center of a political storm:

> The Tell el-Amarna Letters (fourteenth century) reveal the Egyptian party in Lachish suffering the same embarrassments as their confreres in other Canaanite cities. In one letter written from Jerusalem the city is linked with Ashkelon and Gezer, and charged with having supplied the Habiru with food and oil. In another it is reported that Zimridi's servants have conspired with the Habiru against him, and perhaps killed him. Confused as the situation is . . . we can assume that the prosperity of the city and the interests of its rulers were always closely linked with the maintenance of Egyptian power. (R. W. Hamilton, "Lachish," *IDB* 3, 54.)

Debir king of Eglon. The tradition may be slightly garbled. Debir looks like a place name (15:7; 21:15). Eglon is usually placed at Tell el-Hesi (Map D, 260), but in excavations there no trace of Philistine presence has been found.

5. *western.* The survival of this etymological sense of *'ĕmōrî* (see above in 9:1) is now well-documented. In the aristocracies of these small city-states, there was no doubt a high admixture of immigrants from Asia Minor. The events reflected in this defeat of a Jerusalem force, and another raid which set

fire to the city (Judg 1:8), appear to have left a vacuum which was filled at last by the Jebusite takeover (see 3:10 and NOTE).

6. *The Circle.* This is presumably the *gilgāl* near Jericho.

7. *burly warriors.* See 1:14 and NOTE.

8. *Yahweh said.* It presupposes a consultation, presumably by means of the sacred dice called Urim and Thummim. Here they do not repeat the mistake for which they are faulted in 9:14.

"Do not fear. Compare 1:9 and 11:6. This is in contrast to the king of Jerusalem and company (v 2).

9. *All night long.* A distance of about 32 km in a straight line, mostly uphill, a strenuous twisting climb out of the Jordan valley. He had earlier used the tactic of the forced march at night, to position the ambush at The Ruin (8:3).

10. *Yahweh . . . Yahweh.* Not Joshua. And not Israel. The latter gave chase, in what may be unceremoniously described as the mopping-up phase.

Beth-horon. Two towns were sometimes distinguished (as here in LXX), as "Upper Beth-horon" and "Lower Beth-horon" in relation to this important descent. Map D, 260. The name means "House of Haurōn," the latter being a Canaanite deity. His Babylonian counterpart was the war-god Ninurta. It has recently been proposed to identify Beth-horon with Bīt Ninurta in the Amarna Letters (a town which Albright and others took to be Bethlehem, southeast of Jerusalem). The prince of Jerusalem complains of having lost Bīt Ninurta to a coalition represented by troops from Gezer, Gath, and Keilah (EA 290), which suggests rather a military interest in the approaches to Jerusalem from the coastal plain. The letter in question reflects the beginning of the breakup of the Jerusalem kingdom which in the Amarna period had extended from southern Mount Ephraim, over most of the Judean hill country, to the Shephelah in the west. "Gibeonite self-government should be explained as a remnant of their being part of the kingdom of Jerusalem. . . ." Z. Kallai and H. Tadmor, "Bīt Ninurta=Beth Horon—On the History of the Kingdom of Jerusalem in the Amarna Period," *Eretz Israel* 9 (1969); Hebrew, 138-147; English summary, 138.

The Beth-horon Pass was also known as the Valley of Aijalon, a major point of entry from the northern Shephelah to the higher hill country. The alternative route is through the next great valley to the south, the tortuous Bab el-Wad ("valley entrance") which in Israeli consciousness since 1948 has acquired a poignant significance comparable to Valley Forge in the American experience.

Azeqah and Maqqedah. The first (Map D, 260) is Tell Zakarīyeh, and the second is, surely, not far away. It was an utter rout, with part of the force fleeing downhill to the northwest and others heading south, over the hills. The biblical texts indicate that Maqqedah was in the northern Shephelah (see 12:15-16 and 15:41), somewhere in the neighborhood of Azeqah and Libnah (v 28). Eusebius, on the other hand, seems to locate it 12.8 km east of Eleutheropolis (Beit Jibrin), too far south to make sense here. Martin Noth and others have concluded that Maqqedah is a secondary addition in this verse, under the influence of v 28 where, in their judgment, a southern location offers no problem. Verses 16-27 are said to be purely etiological, serving to explain a heap of stones at the mouth of the Maqqedah cave, wherever it was. But this solution appears arbitrary, especially since Eusebius seems not to be entirely reliable. See Wright, "The Literary and Historical Problem of Joshua 10 and Judges 1," *JNES* 5 (1946) 110 n. 13. Wright finds four other instances in Eusebius where "east" would be far more intelligible as "north." The site of Maqqedah continues to resist identification. Khirbet Makdum, where the name might be represented, seems too far away from Azeqah.

11. *Yahweh threw down big stones.* In one of the most plausible attempts to explain the meteorology of the passage, it has been shown how a midsummer's cloudburst (so rare as to appear miraculous in the right circumstances) might indeed have been taken as an answer to prayer. In this case Joshua had prayed for some relief from the sun's oppressive heat and its debilitating effects on his warriors. E. W. Maunder, "A Misinterpreted Miracle," *Expositor* 10 (1910) 359-372. The major problem with this interpretation is the dubious notion that what the poem asserts is that the sun "ceased from shining." See John Bright, *IB* 2, 605. Yet the storm phenomena here are basic.

hailstones. Hail in this narrow corridor between the desert and the sea is much less of a menace than in other parts of the world. "The Coastal Plain has an average of 5-8 days of hail per year, mostly in midwinter." Efraim Orni and Elisha Efrat, *Geography of Israel,* 115. An unusually severe hailstorm—and especially an unseasonable one—seems to be in the picture. With fugitives scrambling down a narrow trail under a barrage of hailstones and probably also trapped by flash floods, there would be no credibility problem attached to this old story ending in v 11. Isaiah knew the tradition and used it for eschatological illustration: "He will be angry as in the valley of Gibeon, to do his deed—strange is his deed!" (Isa 28:21). The final redactor of Joshua would reinforce the last point, by building in the next unit, vv 12-14.

12-14. The essential preoccupation here is the thought of Yahweh's responsiveness to a human voice (vv 12 and 14). The intervening material shows how, on this occasion, he did just that: responded.

12. *Then.* Hebrew *'āz.* In the archaic poetry of Judges 5, this particle is used repeatedly, and elsewhere it is used in Num 21:17 and 1 Kgs 8:12 to introduce poetic fragments. Here, however, the particle occurs at some distance from the poetic unit. The effect is what has been noted above as a "freighted time expression" (1:2; 3:7; 4:14; 5:2; 8:30; 9:6). The particle *'āz* occurs nine times in Joshua and six of those passages are clearly in material that is shown on other grounds to be the editorial contribution of Dtr 2 (8:30; 14:10,11; 20:6; 22:1,31). Only 1:8 (where *'āz* occurs twice) seems not to be Dtr 2. This leaves 10:33 where the pattern *'āz* + perfect tense must be seen as disjunctive and digressionary within a series of converted imperfects that unite the entire section, vv 29-43.

Joshua appealed to Yahweh. It is the fact of this appeal, and especially the divine response in v 14, that is important. The content of Joshua's appeal is not even reported, according to the best textual evidence (see above, first Textual Note on v 12).

God. The shift from the divine name "Yahweh" to the generic noun *'ĕlōhîm* signals a redactor's agreement with the narrative assertion.

he attacked. That Yahweh is the subject here seems clear enough from the preceding.

He said in the sight of Israel. This is the beginning of a six-line poem; the first three lines and the second three lines are syntactically interdependent (O'Connor, private communication).

He said. Yahweh is subject. It was due to the tension between a premonarchic poem and its late monarchy setting that a tradition (represented in LXX) arose with Joshua as speaker of the poem. Scribal error perhaps assisted in the process.

"Sun. Hebrew *šemeš.* The idea that *šmš* may have been the pagan deity worshiped at Gibeon is worth keeping in mind (Blenkinsopp, *Gibeon and Israel,* 50). We seriously doubt, however, that Sun is here being told to stay out of the way.

Sun . . . Moon. It has been suggested that this pairing refers to military strategy, the attack being timed for "an early morning situation before the setting of the moon in the west, over Aijalon Valley, and after the sun had arisen in the east, over Gibeon." The enemy facing the Israelites would be looking into the blinding sun. For this and other ancient examples of the stratagem, see Abraham Malamat, "Conquest of Canaan: Israelite Conduct of War According to Biblical Tradition," in *Encyclopaedia Judaica Year Book 1975/6.*

However, sun and moon are here presented as collaborators. There is no lack of possible astronomical explanations. Least probable is a fourteenth-century shower of meteorites and the persistence of diffused light related to it. This theory of J. Phythian-Adams is adequately reported and then refuted by Soggin, who finally decides that it is "more prudent to regard the phenomenon as one of the numerous miracles of which the Bible tells us . . . a 'sign' of an extraordinary divine intervention which imparts a grace unmerited by man and inconceivable in any other way." Soggin, *Joshua,* 123. That is a theological proposition that wears well, yet the question of actual relationship between one's experience and confession of faith will not go away.

Many have thought that somewhere in the background of this poem is the experience of a total eclipse of the sun. C. R. Conder, "Notes on the Antiquities of the Book of Joshua," *PEFQS* (1899) 161-162. More recently, a date has been fixed by J. F. A. Sawyer, "Joshua 10:12-14 and the Solar Eclipse of 30 September 1131 B.C.," *PEQ* 104 (1972) 139-146. And still more recently, reinforcing Sawyer's approach, it has been urged that "the sudden disappearance of the last rays of the Sun seems to have an almost hypnotic effect on unsuspecting witnesses, making the very few minutes of totality seem like hours (and thus giving the impression of the Sun standing still in the sky, for a corresponding length of time)." F. R. Stephenson, "Astronomical Verification and Dating of Old Testament Passages Referring to Solar Eclipses," *PEQ* 107 (1975) 119.

The most serious problem with such astronomical explanations of the poem is the tension which remains with the meteorological phenomena in v 11.

It is unlikely on structural grounds that the Sun was to "cease shining." Surely the Sun has a positive mythic function here. It has been argued that the older worship of Sun and Moon is still reflected in names such as Beth-horon and Aijalon. J. Dus, "Gibeon-Eine Kultstätte des Šmš und die Stadt des benjamitischen Schicksals," *VT* 10 (1960) 353-374. What is here not made explicit is the Yahwist use of the mythic heritage. That is, Sun and Moon have already been "absorbed into Yahweh's assembly. . . ." Miller, *The Divine Warrior in Early Israel*, 126. Sun and Moon are in Yahweh's entourage. It is as his subordinates that they are addressed.

Comparison with Assyrian astronomical texts, where the simultaneous appearance in the sky of sun and moon can mean a good omen, has brought a genuine advance in understanding the poem. On this view, it is argued, the first part of the poetic excerpt resembles a prayer or incantation that the two great luminaries will stand in opposition (over Gibeon and Aijalon, that is, east and west) on a day favorable to Israel. The remainder reports a favorable outcome. John S. Holladay, Jr., "The Day(s) the *Moon* Stood Still," *JBL* 87 (1968) 166-178. This important study gives some substance to the observation by others that the nucleus here is "a remnant of an incantation." Fohrer, *Introduction to the Old Testament*, 274. What remains to be emphasized is the identity of the speaker. At the battle for the protection of Gibeon, it was Yahweh Himself who decreed the sign.

be still. Hebrew *dōm.* Usage in this passage is not much clarified by pointing to the Arabic root *dwm*, "used specifically of the sun's turning in its course" (Gaster, *MLC*, 528 n. 12). Rather, the meaning of the Hebrew verb is clearly established by its use in the next verse in parallel with '*md*, "stand." And this is confirmed by the same parallelism in 1 Sam 14:9. Blenkinsopp, *Gibeon and Israel*, 47. It is not quite the opposite of attack but means simply "stay put," to "hold a position," or "strike a pose."

13. *he . . . his.* We agree here with Miller, *The Divine Warrior in Early Israel*, 127. There is nothing in the text to signal a change of subject to "they." Yahweh is the actor here.

defeated. The verb is *nqm*, which has nothing to do here with vengeance. The latter, in the bulk of the Bible, is a strictly human activity. Rather, this "verbal root and derived nouns designate the use of force by legitimate sovereign authority. . . ." Depending on context, "the usage of the verb may demand a translation into English by the word 'defeat' or 'rescue.'" The Battle of Gibeon is a classic example of "defensive vindication." Mendenhall, *Ten Gen*, 84.

force! It is most unlikely that Hebrew *gôy* here means "the nation." The word is in construct with "his enemies." It must reflect the Amorite use of *gāwum*, the cognate word, as a military word, a usage well attested in early biblical literature. See now V. H. Matthews, *Pastoral Nomadism in the Mari Kingdom*, 63-65.

After all this it is instructive to compare a highly archaizing piece that likewise stands in a late seventh-century context—the psalm of Habakkuk. The laudatory description of Sun and Moon in Hab 3:11 suggest that they too, like Pestilence and Plague in Hab 3:5, serve Yahweh and do not form part of the opposition to the advance of the Divine Warrior on behalf of Israel in that seventh-century setting.

> On high Sun raised his arms,
> Moon stood on his lordly dais.
>
> They march by the glare of thy darts
> By the (lightning) flash of thy spear.

Cross, *CMHE*, 71, based on the study by Albright, "The Psalm of Habakkuk," in *Studies in Old Testament Prophecy*, 16 note mm.

Here, too, Sun and Moon strike the pose of the "effective victory sign." What Joshua had done to achieve a victory at The Ruin in the first edition, Yahweh in the final edition orders Sun and Moon to do for him from opposite ends of the Beth-horon battleground, while he himself goes into action.

Is this not. Soggin revowels as *lamed* affirmative and translates "Surely," but he does not explain the prefixed interrogative particle.

recorded. The poetic couplet is part of another larger work.

The Book of Yashar. Also quoted in 2 Sam 1:18-27, David's poetic lament at the deaths of Saul and Jonathan. The root *yšr* refers to what is right; compare the two uses of the cliché with which the pre-monarchy period ends, negatively in Dtr 1 (Judg 17:6) and positively in Dtr 2 (Judg 21:25). "The Book of the Upright One" might refer either to individuals whose deeds were lauded in its contents or to Israel collectively, also known in a related title as "Jeshurun." The alternative explanation recognizes *yšr* as verbal: "Let him (Israel) sing." See C. F. Kraft, "Jashar, Book of," *IDB* 2, 803.

Other "anthologies" are known to have existed, for example, the Book of the Wars of Yahweh (Num 21:14).

It is possible, however, that this question originated in a marginal query, since it is missing in the best LXX manuscripts.

The sun stayed . . . did not hurry to set. Stayed on the assignment.

14. This is the climactic statement and goal of the final edition—affirmation of Yahweh the Warrior, who wins the battle. That is what, from the very beginning, had made him the Glorious King.

God's . . . Yahweh. This reverses the pattern of the two words in v 12, thus forming a chiastic frame around the unit.

15. As explained in the Textual Note, this verse was almost certainly not a part of the original.

16-27. These verses describe the immediate sequel to the rout of the southern confederacy at the battle to protect Gibeon, which was interrupted at the end of v 11.

17. *the cave at Maqqedah."* See above on v 10.

18. *big stones to the mouth of the cave.* The stones blocking the entrance enable Joshua to post a small unit there, while he resumes the pursuit of the routed forces.

19. *cut off their retreat!* See Deut 25:18. The verb is denominative from *zānāb*, "tail." The fugitives are to be "de-tailed." It will all be done more quickly and profitably if they are not allowed access to their towns where they might fight from fortified positions.

Yahweh. In this unit, vv 16-27, he is mentioned only in Joshua's speech (again in v 25).

20. *some survivors had got away.* This parenthetical statement is in effect a considerable qualification of vv 16-21. But it was a necessary qualification made by a redactor whose tradition also included vv 28-39.

21. *No one slandered.* The idiom is, literally, "sharpen the tongue." There is no basis for *NEB*'s paraphrase: "not a man . . . suffered so much as a scratch on his tongue."

23. *the five kings.* Here they are anonymous.

24. *men of Israel.* Hebrew '*yš yśr'l* as collective.

feet on the necks. Compare "till I make your enemies your footstool" (Ps 110:1 *RSV*) and 1 Cor 15:25-28. See also the archaic poem Deut 33:29 where it is promised that with Yahweh's victory Israel will tread upon the "upper backs" (not "high places" unless a double meaning is intended) of its enemies. For the extra-biblical usage, see the Annals of Tukulti-Ninurta I (c. 1242-1206) in describing his humiliation of the captured Babylonian king Kashtiliah IV: "His royal neck I trod with my foot, like a footstool." The same action is shown in Assyrian bas-reliefs as well. Joseph De Vault, *The Book of Josue.* Pamphlet Bible Series II (New York: Paulist Press, 1960) 20. Cf. *ANEP,* ✳✳351, 355; and further 308, 319, 345, 393.

25. *"Do not be afraid.* An *inclusio* with Yahweh's usage in v 8. Compare also the exhortations in 1:7 and 9.

26. *killed them. . . . hanged them.* This is not death by hanging, nor crucifixion, but public exposure of the corpses after execution so as to inspire fear.

27. *sunset.* In 8:29 (see NOTE), the king of The Ruin receives the same treatment.

big stones over the mouth. As before (v 18), a most effective *inclusio* to the pursuit story.

unto this very day! They were not removed a second time.

COMMENT

The popular interpretation of these verses is well voiced by Joshua and Chorus in Thomas Morell's words for Handel's oratorio *Joshua* composed in 1747:

> O thou bright orb, great ruler of the day!
> Stop thy swift course, and over Gibeon stay.
> And oh! thou milder lamp of light, the moon.
> Stand still, prolong thy beams in Ajalon.
> Behold! the list'ning sun the voice obeys,
> And in mid Heav'n his rapid motion stays.

> Before our arms the scattered nations fly,
> Breathless they part, they yield, they fall, they die.

The didactic interests of the original narrators and their editors were more subtle and complex. It is a commonplace of sound historical method that religious organizations such as church and synagogue rarely cultivate historical traditions out of strictly historical interest. Rather, history is used to undergird and in some way legitimate the organization and institutions which are the carriers of the tradition. This was no less true in the ancient world.

A second guideline to our analysis is provided by the question of the different historical contexts in which the material was redacted, not once but at least twice. The question "What does it mean?" has a way of turning itself into another question: *"How* does it mean?" With a drastic change of literary and redactional context, the effect of the same statement can change from emphatically negative (Judg 17:6) to emphatically affirmative (Judg 21:25).

In these twenty-six verses we learn of the victory at Gibeon and its sequel in the south. The historicity of the latter will be examined in archaeological detail in relation to the next unit, vv 28-39. Here it will suffice to underscore the uses of history that are reflected in 10:1-27.

The main story line is carried by vv 1-11 and 16-27. Here Israel is part of a coalition opposed by a countercoalition formed under the leadership of Jerusalem. Into this larger segment is inserted a flashback on the decisive victory at the Beth-horon Pass (vv 12-14). If the first edition had displayed Joshua as a model military commander taking his signals from Yahweh in the defense of Gibeon, the effect of the second edition was to counter any extravagant claims for Joshua and give all the glory instead to Yahweh. In the finished form of the chapter Joshua makes an appeal, and in immediate response Yahweh commands Sun and Moon to do for him what in 8:18 he had commanded Joshua to do for him in the old story of the victory at The Ruin—stand still and flash the sign of Yahweh's sovereignty! In the course of time the tension was lost and the tradition came to be all about Joshua, as for example in Ecclus 46:2-4:

> How splendid he was when he raised his arms
> to brandish his sword against cities!
>
> · · · · · · · · · · · · · · · ·
>
> Was not the sun held back by his hand,
> and one day drawn out into two?

We should now answer in the negative. Nothing could be further removed from early Yahwism than the magical presupposition. Comparison with Agamemnon's prayer to Zeus not to let the sun go down at Troy, in comparable circumstances (Gaster, *MLC,* 415), only begs the textual question; see above in the apparatus and NOTES.

But the heart of the matter was never completely obscured, as the poem continues in Ecclus 46:5.

> He called on God the Most High
>   as he pressed the enemy on every side;
> And the great Lord answered him
>   with hard and violent hailstones.

This is much closer to the original where the idea seems to have been that Yahweh had commanded Sun and Moon to station themselves at opposite ends of the pass while Yahweh himself threw down the previously mentioned hailstones. It reflects an outlook on the sacral traditions of the conquest which elsewhere we recognized as characteristic of Dtr 2.

There is no "vengeance" involved, either in the story or in the poetic fragment. Vengeance is a human specialization, and it was a prime motivation for the Yahweh covenant to remove the blood feud and kindred institutions from the local scene entirely. Simply put, the story celebrates Yahweh's record, his performance in maintaining his covenant with the Israelites, and Israel's treaty with Gibeon.

The defeat of the forces from the south hill-country pentapolis that had combined against Gibeon won most of the south. It is important to remember that Gibeon in this period could not have been more than an unwalled village. Evidence for Late Bronze Age occupation at the site is limited to tombs. It was early in Iron I that Gibeon became once again a flourishing town and a strong fortification wall was built. The latter developments would seem to represent the effectiveness of the Gibeonite treaty. But the actual political situation was far too complex to be adequately represented by one story about the powerful scheming of a Jerusalem king. To tell more of the story is the burden of vv 28-39.

7. SUCCESSES IN SERIATIM
(10:28-39)

10   28 Maqqedah too Joshua captured on that day and put it to the sword, including the king. He put it under the ban, with all persons there. He left no survivor. He did to Maqqedah's king as he had done to Jericho's king.

29 Joshua moved on, all Israel with him, from Maqqedah to Libnah, and fought against Libnah. 30 Yahweh gave it too into the hand of Israel, and they captured it, with its king. He put it to the sword, with all persons there. He left no survivor. He did to its king as he had done to Jericho's king.

31 Joshua moved on, all Israel with him, from Libnah to Lachish. He pitched camp nearby and fought against it. 32 Yahweh gave Lachish into the hand of Israel. He took it on the second day and put it to the sword. He put it under the ban, including all persons there, as he had done to Libnah.

33 Then Horam, king of Gezer, went up to aid Lachish, and Joshua struck against him and his force until he left no survivor for him.

34 Joshua moved on, all Israel with him, from Lachish to Eglon. They pitched camp nearby and fought against it. 35 Yahweh gave it into the hand of Israel. They captured it that day and put it to the sword. All persons there he put under the ban, as he had done to Lachish.

36 Joshua went up, all Israel with him, from Eglon to Hebron; and they fought against it. 37 They captured it, and put it to the sword: including its king, all its towns, and all persons therein. He left no survivor. As he had done to Eglon, he put it under the ban, with all persons there.

38 Joshua turned, all Israel with him, toward Debir. He fought against it. 39 He captured it with its king and all its towns. They put them to the sword. They put them under the ban including all persons there. He left no survivor. As he had done to Hebron and its king, so he did to Debir and its king—and as he had done to Libnah and its king.

TEXTUAL NOTES

10 28. *Joshua*   LXX lacks the name and reads "he."

including the king   Lacking in LXX^AB, this might be considered to be secondary, except that it completes a chiastic pattern in the first half of the verse (direct object   verb   temporal phrase   verb   direct object).

it   Hebrew *'wth* preferred here is supported by many Hebrew and Greek manuscripts as well as Targums, against the plural of MT *'wtm*.

survivor   In vv 28,30, and 33 LXX consistently reads the longer expression: *śryd wplyṭ*, "refugee and survivor," as in 8:22.

30. *too*   Missing in some manuscripts and Versions.

and they captured it   This is restored from LXX, which reflects a plural verb (not singular as reported by Soggin, *Joshua*, 120) dropped by haplography: *w[ylkdw 'wth w]'t*.

32. *He put it under the ban, including all persons there*   There were contrasting omissions in MT and LXX *Vorlage:*

MT   w[yḥrm   'wth   w]'t   kl   hnpš   'šr   bh
LXX   wyḥrm   'wt[h   w't   kl   hnpš   'šr   b]h

as   This is *k'šr* represented by the versions against the reading of MT: *kkl 'šr*, "as in all respects." So too in vv 35 and 37, below.

33. *struck*   In LXX he did it *lpy ḥrb*, "to the mouth of the sword," but that is probably a vertical dittography since there is no way to explain the reverse process.

until he left   There is no need to revocalize *hš'yr* as infinitive construct. The negative *blty* can govern a finite verb. Cf. GKC, 152 x. LXX avoided the pileup of third person pronouns by using a passive construction: "until there was left for him."

35. *Yahweh gave it into the hand of Israel*   Restored from LXX, after an obvious haplography: *w[y . . . w]y . . .*

there   MT here repeats "on that day," clearly a dittography as shown by LXX^AB and Syriac.

36. *from Eglon*   No name appears here in LXX as a result of an inner-Greek haplography involving the prepositions: *e[k . . . e]is*. Cf. v 34 where LXX^B shows a corruption of the first word in the same pattern to read *eis . . . eis*.

37. *They captured it*   Lost by haplography in LXX^AB.

including its king, all its towns   A sizable haplography is reflected in LXX: *w['t mlkh w't kl 'ryh w]'t*. See also NOTES. This is far more plausible than the argument that the longer reading is secondary and based on a supposed but unattested prior corruption which must be posited. Orlinsky, "The Hebrew *Vorlage* of the Septuagint of the Book of Joshua," VTSup 17 (1968) 192.

39. *He*   "They" in a small number of manuscripts and LXX, and Targum.

them second occurrence   The Greek, followed here, suggests that haplography has concealed a pronoun object and conjunction in the Hebrew: *wyhrymw* ['*wtm w*]'*t*.

and its king   Thus LXX^{AB}, where the phrase is missing from other witnesses.

and as he had done to Libnah and its king   Lacking in LXX^{B}, this is generally considered to be secondary. But this is the last of six victories (seven including the Gezer force); we should expect special treatment. The phrase is thus retained, especially in view of the frequency with which LXX^{A} is proving now to be the carrier of superior readings. See *Judges*, AB 6A, 38-42 and "Appendix A," 297-301.

NOTES

10:28-39. Perhaps the most influential critical studies of this material are those of the German scholars, Kurt Elliger, "Josua in Judäa," *Palästinajahrbuch* 30 (1934) 47-71; and Martin Noth, "Die fünf Könige in der Höhle von Makkeda," *Palästinajahrbuch* 33 (1937) 22-36. On their view, vv 16-27 are purely etiological, a story told originally to explain stones at the mouth of Maqqedah Cave, wherever it was. Noth then went on to remove vv 28 and 33 as glosses and to argue that the five kings hiding in the cave were those of the other cities named in vv 29-38, which are not the same as the coalition of five kings which had attacked Gibeon at the outset of the chapter. Wright has long since shown this solution to be highly subjective and improbable. Wright, "The Literary and Historical Problem of Joshua 10 and Judges 1," *JNES* 5 (1946) 105-114.

It is in fact impossible to harmonize fully the description of the coalition (vv 1-5) with the account of the campaign in the south (vv 28-39). This is due in no small measure to the way in which an ancient editor chose to work (or was obliged to work) with preformed narrative units. It is thus not surprising that essentially the same history might be reflected with considerable differences of detail and emphasis.

It has been suggested that the foundation for this account was "a traditional itinerary which noted the sequence of victories." Miller and Tucker, *The Book of Joshua*, 88. Except for Gezer (which belongs to Joseph in 16:3), all are in the later territory of Judah.

28. *Maqqedah too*. The syntax at the outset is disjunctive. On the problem of the location of Maqqedah, see above on v 10.

under the ban. This happens to five of the seven opponents in these verses. Libnah (vv 29-30) and Gezer (v 33) are the exceptions.

with all persons there. This is specified for all opponents except that the defeat of the king of Gezer in the field was apparently not followed by an attack on the city.

as he had done to Jericho's king. The referent of this is nowhere spelled out.

The king of Jericho is not mentioned in the story of the fall of Jericho (chap. 6), but only in the story of reconnaissance (chap. 2). These verses are the most forceful description in the book highlighting Joshua's conduct of warfare.

29. *Libnah.* Tell Bornat (see Map D, 260) would appear to be the best candidate. Kh. Labnin, northeast of Lachish, despite similarity of name, is too inconspicuous and too isolated to have detained the Assyrian army after its capture of Lachish (2 Kgs 19:8). But Tell Bornat, c. 10 km NNW of Lachish, would have secured the Assyrian flank before moving against Jerusalem. Further, Joshua's force in this much earlier period is moving to secure the foothills (Maqqedah, Libnah, Lachish) before striking into the mountains (Hebron and Debir).

30. *Yahweh gave it.* This is specified only for the sites in the Shephelah (Lachish in v 32) and its outlying approaches (Eglon in v 35).

too. This brings the Shephelah location of Maqqedah under the preceding rubric.

Jericho's king. To make this comparison the narrative skips over the treatment of the king of Ai, who is mentioned nowhere outside the story in chap. 8. The comparison with Jericho at this point contributes to closure on the account of warfare in the south, chaps. 6-10.

31. *Lachish.* See above, NOTES on v 3.

33. *Then.* The syntax is disjunctive. This is the center of the chiastic pattern described below, in COMMENT.

Horam. Only now joining the action, he is the only one mentioned by name in these verses; probably, therefore, he is being identified by a redactor of the unit.

Gezer. Map D, 260. This city-state had only recently recovered from the reign of Pharaoh Merneptah, who claims the capture of Gezer in the famous stele which also reports the suppression of what was probably pre-Mosaic Israel. *ANET*[2], 378. There Gezer is mentioned in conjunction with Ashqelon. For the relation between Merneptah's claim and a thirteenth-century destruction at Tell Gezer, see Wright's "Introduction," 86-87. Apparently the old order continued at Gezer whose king comes to the aid of Lachish, against other Hebrews who have now become part of the Bene Israel.

There is no necessary contradiction between this text (which speaks only of a defeat in the field) and other passages in 16:10 and Judg 1:29 (which fault the tribe of Ephraim for failure to oust the Canaanites from Gezer). The town finally became Israelite in Solomon's time as a dowry which came with Pharaoh's daughter (1 Kgs 9:16).

went up. The verb *'lh* is used in a non-literal sense with reference to deployment for battle. So also v 36.

34. *Eglon.* Probably not to be identified with Tell el-Hesi. See G. E. Wright, "A Problem of Ancient Topography—Lachish and Eglon," *HTR* 64 (1971) 437-488; see also *BA* 34 (1971) 76-86. It is striking that extensive excavations at Hesi have yielded no evidence of any Philistine presence there although it is within Philistine territory. Wright makes a good case for understanding Hesi as belonging to a series of forts as outposts of Lachish, making a coherent conception of the area as a development of the Late Bronze Age. The most likely candidate for Eglon is Tell Aitun

1. The Jordan River, Greek Bathing Place.

II. Ai—The Wadi el-Jaya.

III. Scarabs of Thutmosis III.

IV. "Joshua gathered all the tribes of Israel at Shechem" (24:1). A western view of the remains of the Middle Bronze Age temple at Shechem, after the 1962 archaeological campaign, with the forecourt rebuilt and the great sacred stone (*massēbā*) set up again. The temple of Joshua's day was smaller, for it reused only sections of the walls of the massive Middle Bronze original.

v. Hazor, aerial view.

36. *Joshua.* In 14:6-15 it is Caleb who is credited with victory at Hebron (see also 15:13-14), but "Judah" in general gets the credit in Judg 1:10. Compare the variety of traditions regarding capture of Debir, which comes next. "In all of Judges 1 these are the only items which face us directly with that question." Wright, "The Literary and Historical Problem of Joshua 10 and Judges 1," *JNES* 5 (1946) 108-109. It is not impossible that in such tumultuous times towns changed hands (often by simply changing sides!) more than once. See the story of Abimelech at Shechem in Judges 9 which centers precisely in the tension between Abimelech's monarchist aspirations and his military service as "commander" of the forces of Bene Israel. Boling, *Judges,* AB 6A, 165-185.

Hebron. See above, NOTES on v 3.

37. *all its towns.* This specification is made only for Hebron and Debir, and reflects the military strategy used. "By conquering Libnah, Lachish, and Eglon Joshua closed the approaches to the hills from the west. . . ." Y. Elitzur in "Response" to Yigael Yadin, "Military and Archaeological Aspects of the Conquest of Canaan in the Book of Joshua," *El Ha'ayin* 1 (Jerusalem, 1965) 17.

38. *Debir.* Map D, 260. This is possibly related to Anatolian *D/Tapara,* "lord, governor." Mendenhall, *Ten Gen,* 163. In 15:15 the same place is identified as Qiryath-sepher "Town of the Treaty-Stele." In 15:15-17=Judg 1:11-13, it is Caleb's younger league-brother, Othniel, who captures it.

Where was Debir? Following Albright's epoch-making excavations from 1926-1932 at Tell Beit-Mirsim in the upper-Shephelah, which for the first time put the ceramic chronology of Palestine on a firm footing, this topographical problem was also thought by many to be solved: Tell Beit-Mirsim=Debir. The only likely alternative seemed to be Khirbet Rabûd in the higher hill country south of Hebron, a site with, however, much less impressive archaeological remains on the surface. Recent excavations at Khirbet Rabûd and especially detailed topographical study have strengthened the identification of Debir(=Qiryath-sepher) with the hill-country site. The logic of the watershed patterns, placing Rabûd clearly in the hill country and not in the Shephelah, is convincing. Moshe Kochavi, "Khirbet Rabûd=Debir," *Tel Aviv* 1 (1974) 2-33. See in further detail the story of Othniel and Achsah in 15:13-19 and the system of Judahite provinces in 15:20-62.

39. *As he had done . . . as he had done.* The clause occurs seven times in the unit, a most effective device for achieving closure.

COMMENT

When the distribution of formulaic components in the unit is fully plotted, a chiastic structure to the whole unit can be seen.

		ban	oracle	continuity (give into the hand)
A1	Maqqedah (with its king and its people)	+	—	like Jericho
A2	Libnah (with its king and its people)	—	+	like Jericho
B	Lachish (city and people)	+	+	like Libnah
C	Horam of Gezer	—	—	no comparison
B′	Eglon (city and people)	+	+	like Lachish
A′1	Hebron (with its king and its towns and its people)	+	—	like Eglon
A′2	Debir (with its king and its towns and its people)	+	—	{ like Hebron { like Libnah

Such a repetitive or balancing structure has been appropriately called a palistrophe (Greek *palin,* "again," *strophe,* "stanza"). It is characteristic of material that is found to be enjoyable by children, ancient and modern. For full discussion, see the dissertation by Sean McEvenue, *The Narrative Style of the Priestly Writer,* 1971.

The major structural elements here are the ban and the oracle reference: B=B′, and both are the opposite of C. A1 and A2 balance each other for these two features. A′1 repeats A1, and A′2 repeats both of these for the sake of closure. The comparison clause in the episodes serves to balance all the rest of the material, by moving more or less continuously forward, with a notable gap at C to mark the middle; and finally, for the sake of closure, A′2 has a reference back to the beginning. Curiously A1 (Maqqedah) is never used for the analogy, but that is probably for structural rather than historical reasons.

The didactic unit was readily incorporated by Dtr 1 because it left no uncertainty about the practical explanation for the rapid reestablishment of Israel in Canaan. The explanation as taught by these verses was, purely and simply: the military leadership of Joshua! It will be followed by a sweeping summary (vv 40-43) to make doubly sure that we do not miss the point.

Allowing, then, for a certain stylization that was appropriate to didactic effect, what can be said about the possibility of reliable historical memory behind the teaching?

It must be argued that the sequence "makes perfect sense geographically; and such archaeological evidence as we have seems to give it considerable support." Thus concluded Wright in his early article on "The Literary and Historical Problem of Joshua 10 and Judges 1," *JNES* 5 (1946) 109. The same military strategy was much later used by Sennacherib's Assyrian army at the close of the eighth century, when Lachish and Libnah were found to be the main fortresses in the Shephelah which had to be reduced before laying siege to Jerusalem.

The hill-country location of Debir (Khirbet Rabûd) makes even better geographical sense at the culmination of the unit than would another Shephelah site (Tell Beit-Mirsim). On this view, the late thirteenth-century destruction at the latter site more likely reflects the continuing power struggle of small states at the close of the Late Bronze Age, to which the formation of the peace of Yahweh was the response of early Israel. The lack of evidence for a destruction at smaller Khirbet Rabûd in this period tends to confirm our recognition of stylized generalization in the account. Clearly there was something special about the takeover of Debir (see below on 15:14-19). Its "capture" may in fact have been something of a southern parallel to that of Shechem in the north. This is the suggestion of Campbell, "Moses and the Foundations of Israel," *Interpretation* 29 (1975) 141-154.

The overall organization of this chapter (a story in some detail, followed by a rapid recapitulation of the sequel, in brief stereotyped formulations) in the first edition will be mimicked by the editor of the final edition in a chapter describing the near demise of Israel—Judges 1.

The first edition emphasized, however, that the entire region of the south had become Israelite by right of conquest. Joshua conquered all of it.

8. SUMMARY
(10:40-43)

10 40 Joshua conquered the entire land—the Highlands, the Southern Desert, the Foothills, the Slopes—with their kings. He left no survivor. Everything alive he put to the ban, as Yahweh God of Israel commanded. 41 Joshua conquered them, from Qadesh-barnea to Gaza, together with all the land of Goshen and as far as Gibeon.

42 All these kings and their land Joshua seized in a single stroke, because Yahweh God of Israel fought for Israel.

[43 Then Joshua returned to the camp at The Circle, all Israel with him.]

TEXTUAL NOTES

10 40. *Southern Desert*   Hebrew *ngb*. The spelling *Nabai* in LXX[B] perhaps reflects a metathesis of two letters in the *Vorlage: *nbg*.

their   This is the reading of LXX[AB], where MT specifies "all" the kings. The latter may be explained as a vertical dittography.

41. *Joshua conquered them*   Lacking in LXX[B] and Vulgate. See Note.

42. *these*   This is MT where in LXX the independent pronoun is displaced by a possessive suffix under the influence of "their land."

43. [*Then Joshua returned to the camp at The Circle, all Israel with him.*] As is also true of v 15, this does not appear in the Greek text, which may well be superior.

NOTES

10:40-43. This is editorial summary which, like 9:1-2 its introductory companion piece, covers both more and less than is reported in the body of the section!

40. *Joshua*. He is in the spotlight.

the Highlands. In chaps. 9 and 10, this extends from Gibeon (3-4 km to the northwest of Jerusalem) as far as Debir, the last important hill-country town before descending rapidly into the vicinity of Beersheba.

the Southern Desert. Hebrew *hngb,* increasingly familiar to English readers in transliteration: the Negeb. Its northern focus is an ancient caravan cross-roads: the Beersheba oasis.

the Foothills. Hebrew *haš-šĕpēlâ.*

Slopes. Again in 12:8. The root is *'šd,* "to pour," "flow down," "turn aside" (of a watercourse in Num 21:15). Noth thought of waterfalls and Soggin suggests "partings of water." *Joshua,* 121. See the place name "Slopes of Pisgah" in 12:3 and 13:20.

no survivor. This is the sixth occurrence in brief compass (five times in the chiastic pattern described in COMMENT on vv 28-39).

Everything alive. Hebrew *kol han-nĕšāmâ.* Literally, "every breathing thing."

the ban. Added to five occurrences in the preceding unit (second NOTE on v 28), for a mnemonic total of six. The tradition which blurs the distinction between the ban of all living things and survivor status reserved for humans reflects doctrinal developments under the monarchy. See Patrick D. Miller, Jr., "Faith and Ideology in the Old Testament," in *Mag Dei,* 471-472, with special reference to the work of Brekelmans.

as Yahweh God of Israel commanded. This echoes the language that reverberates throughout chap. 1; and in fact it forms a strong *inclusio* with 1:9.

41. *Joshua conquered them.* It is interesting that LXX[B] and Vulgate lack the first two Hebrew words and there is no mechanism for haplography in either the Hebrew or the Greek. What is left is a sort of poetic bicolon, worded chiastically, which has no direct relationship to events described in chaps. 2-10! It must have been originally a fragment of a quotation, perhaps something that Yahweh had commanded. But it has become a subordinate phrase showing how Joshua followed orders! This is the primary concern of Dtr 1 in Joshua, made explicit.

from Qadesh-barnea to Gaza. See Map B, 112. Since neither of these places has been mentioned previously this line is presumably to be taken as a general southern limit to the results of vv 28-39.

Qadesh-barnea. More than 80 km below Debir, the southernmost town previously mentioned. The editor uses a formula which probably originated in another tradition. See the account of an unsuccessful attempt to penetrate Canaan from the south (Numbers 13). That movement may well have been earlier and more successful than the later historians in Jerusalem realized, but the picture is far from clear. Located at Ain el-Qudeirat is an Iron Age fortress that was visited and drawn by Woolley and Lawrence; it was later excavated by Dothan in 1956 (*IEJ* 15 [1965]). Further excavation beginning in 1976 by Rudolph Cohen has shown that the crude handmade pottery used elsewhere in the Negeb as evidence of tenth-century date actually continued in use to the very end of Iron II (late seventh century).

Gaza. Whatever success may have been experienced here by Joshua or Judah (Judg 1:18), it was short-lived; Gaza is among the unconquered cities in 13:3.

In fact, if it is here merely the terminus of a general southwestern "border," there may well be no conquest-claim made at all in this verse. Cf. Judg 1:18.

together with all the land of Goshen and as far as Gibeon. This describes the north-south axis.

the land of Goshen. See also 11:16. It is not to be confused with the region in the northeastern Nile Delta occupied by the Hebrews at the time of the Exodus. This land of Goshen perhaps takes its name from the place listed in the southern hill-country province of Debir in 15:51.

42. *in a single stroke.* Literally, "at one time." The idea is that of a single set of military campaigns.

Yahweh God of Israel fought for Israel. Almost as an afterthought, it appears, this statement tells the truth of the old epic tradition.

43. See NOTE on v 15.

COMMENT

This is the first of three summaries (see 11:16-23 and 21:43-45) in the book. Here ends "The Conquest: Phase One." It should be compared with Judg 1:1 - 10:5 which might better be described as "The Book of Hard Times: Phase One."

The problematic character of this summary should not be minimized, but neither should the summary be dismissed out of hand, as some scholars are inclined to do: "throughout the Shephelah to Lachish (vv 28*ff*) and even to Kadesh and Gaza (v 41) is palpable exaggeration." Gray, *Joshua, Judges and Ruth,* 39. It is increasingly likely that the reason for such a generalization in the summary is that the south had been previously crisscrossed by pre-Mosaic Israelites related by caravan trade to the Qadesh-barnea junction so that it became territory inhabited and controlled by Yahwists.

With the conquest of territory that will become mostly "Benjamin" and "Judah," attention now shifts to the far north, in Galilee, without so much as a word about the "conquest" of territory that will be Ephraim and Manasseh (the powerful nucleus of the northern kingdom)! The reason that Joshua the Ephraimite can move the militia through this region without sizable opposition must be that the great Shechem convocation has already taken place (so 8:30-35, as opposed to the displaced version of the story in chap. 24).

"The Amorite attack represented an attempt to break through the cordon that had formed around Judea. And Joshua, having dispatched the allied southern forces, turned immediately north, according to the biblical accounts." Baruch Halpern, "Gibeon: Israelite Diplomacy in the Conquest Era," *CBQ* 37 (1975) 315. We may well imagine a chain-reaction effect from the series of stunning victories against surprising odds—from Jericho to Debir. Out of it came a people's militia large enough to challenge a coalition headed by one of the oldest city-states in Canaan.

C. Phase Two. THE FAR NORTH 11:1-23

1. HAZOR: FORMERLY THE HEAD
(11:1-15)

11 1 When Jabin king of Hazor heard, he sent off:
to Jobab king of Madon, to the king of Shimron, to the king of Achshaph;
2 and to all the kings in the northern Highlands, in the Arabah south of Chinneroth, in the Foothills, and in Naphath-dor to the west;
3 the Canaanites on the east and on the west the Amorites: the Hittites, the Perizzites, the Jebusites in the Highlands, and the Hivites below Hermon in Mizpah-land.
4 They came forth with all their armies accompanying them—an enormous force, as numerous as grains of sand along the seashore—with a multitude of horses and chariots. 5 All these kings rendezvoused and pitched camp together—by the Waters of Merom—to fight against Israel.
6 Yahweh said to Joshua, "Do not be afraid of them. By this time tomorrow I will hand them all to Israel on a sword. Their horses you shall hamstring. Their chariots you shall burn."
7 So Joshua and his entire fighting force with him took them by surprise at the Waters of Merom and fell upon them from the mountain. 8 Yahweh put them into the hand of Israel. They pressed the attack and gave chase. Toward Greater Sidon and Misrephoth-maim! Toward Mizpeh Valley to the east! They kept up the attack until he left no survivor for them. 9 Joshua did to them as Yahweh had told him: He hamstrung their horses and burned their chariots.
10 At that time Joshua turned to take Hazor and its king, because Hazor was formerly the head of all those kingdoms! 11 They put to the mouth of the sword all persons there. They carried out the ban. Not anything that breathed was left. And Hazor they burned!
12 All those royal towns and all their kings Joshua captured and

put to the sword; he devoted them, under the ban, as Moses the Servant of Yahweh had commanded. 13 But all the towns standing on mounds Israel did not burn, with the single exception of Hazor. That one Joshua burned.

14 All the loot of these towns, including the cattle, the Bene Israel plundered for themselves. But all the human beings they put to the sword, until they had wiped them out. They left nothing that breathed.

15 As Yahweh commanded his Servant Moses, thus Moses commanded Joshua; and thus Joshua did! He left nothing undone of all that Yahweh had commanded Moses.

TEXTUAL NOTES

11 1. *Madon*   The reading *marrōn* in LXX[B] and Syriac reflects the easy confusion of *d* and *r*, under the influence of Merom as the point of rendezvous in v 5.

2. *all*   This is LXX, where MT shows a haplography: *w'[l k]l*.

in the northern Highlands, in the Arabah south of Chinneroth   This is MT. In LXX anticipation of "Greater Sidon" in v 8 and a loss of one letter, *'ayin*, triggered the development of a very different reading which ends with "Rabah opposite Chinnereth":

| MT | *'šr mṣpwn bhr wb'rbh ngb knrwt* |
| LXX | *'šr (m?)ṣdwn (h?)rbh bhr wbrbh mngd knrwt* |

Naphath   Reading the singular in agreement with the versions and 12:23, against the plural in MT, *nāpôt dôr*.

to the west   Hebrew *mym*. LXX detached the word and read it with v 3.

3. *on the east and on the west the Amorites*   The chiastic pattern (Canaanites: east :: west: Amorites) is obscured by misdivision in LXX (where both groups are "on the west") and in MT (where a superfluous conjunction precedes "the Amorites").

Hittites, the Perizzites, the Jebusites in the Highlands, and the Hivites   LXX has these four names in reverse order. The Greek translator has simply copied off these four gentilic nouns in reverse order, but without relocating the final modifying phrase *below Hermon*.

Mizpah   Spelled "Mizpeh" in v 8. The exact coloration of the final vowel may be dependent upon phonetic context.

4. *armies*   This is Hebrew *mḥnyhm*, where LXX reads *mlkyhm*, "their kings," in anticipation of v 5 where it balances usage in vv 1 and 2.

an enormous force   Hebrew *'m rb*. Lacking in LXX.

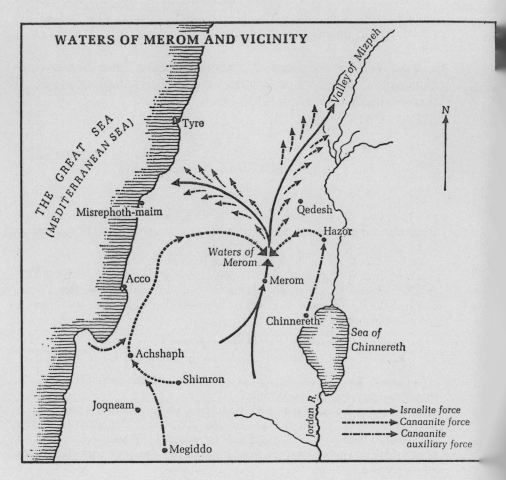

WATERS OF MEROM AND VICINITY

THE GREAT SEA
(MEDITERRANEAN SEA)

Valley of Mizpeh

N

Tyre

Misrephoth-maim

Qedesh

Hazor

Acco

Waters of
Merom

Merom

Chinnereth

Sea of
Chinnereth

Achshaph

Shimron

Joqneam

Jordan R.

Megiddo

→ Israelite force
----→ Canaanite force
-·-·→ Canaanite
      auxiliary force

Map E

5. *by*   This is the LXX reading (=Hebrew '*l*) where MT ('*l*) is a scribal assimilation to the word used four times in vv 1 and 2.

6. *all*   Hebrew '*t klm*. LXX '*tm*, "them."

7. *with him*   Lost by haplography in the *Vorlage* to LXX^(AB): '[*mw* ']*lykm*. A different haplography took place in the Syriac: '*mw* '*l*[*yhm* '*l*] *my*.

from the mountain   This follows LXX which indicates that *bhr* has been dropped following *bhm*.

8. *Misrephoth-maim!*   MT is supported by LXX^A (cf. 13:6); LXX^B reads *maserōn*.

he left no survivor for them   See 8:22, Textual Note on "he left for them"; and 10:33, Textual Note on "until he left."

10. *king*   Thus LXX^(AB). MT includes *w't mlkh* and continues *hkh bḥrb*, "and its king he put to the sword"; but this is awkward syntax, probably conflation from a variant, in the singular, for what follows.

11. *They*   In LXX^(AL), Syriac, and Vulgate "he" did it.

mouth of the   With MT and LXX^A; missing in LXX^B.

ban   LXX shows a displacement, reading "all" and omitting *kl*, "anything," in the next clause.

they   This follows LXX^(AB), which suggests that the singular finite form in MT should be revoweled as infinitive absolute, balancing *haḥărēm*.

13. *mounds*   Or "tells." This is the LXX, which reflects *tillîm*, against MT which reads *tillām*, "their tell." The latter probably originated as a plural form spelled without vowel letter.

Joshua   LXX^B reads "Israel," probably a displacement due to accidental repetition.

14. *of these towns, including the cattle*   Missing in LXX and Syriac.

15b. *Yahweh*   LXX^(BL) omit the divine name and read *ṣwh 'tw mšh*, "Moses had commanded him."

NOTES

11:1-15. The last of the stories of Joshua's military leadership to be highlighted by Dtr 1 centers in territory that will belong to the tribe of Naphtali (19:36). It appears that while the showdown with the Galilee-coalition occurred during the Shechem phase of the revolution, the effective stabilization and reorganization of the region as territory of the Bene Israel did not occur until the Shiloh phase (19:32-39). This lag may be compared to a similar situation in "Benjamin," a region apparently so weakened and disorganized by the warfare in chaps. 5-9 that it does not have an allotment until the later phase (18:11-28).

Here it is indeed "noteworthy that Hazor, and not the Israelites, took the offensive. This might have been the reaction of Hazor . . ." (Gray, *Joshua, Judges and Ruth*, 46). In fact it is only at Jericho and The Ruin (in all of chaps. 1-11) that the Bene Israel take the initiative in warfare!

1. *Jabin*. This is the shortened form of a sentence name, "the god N has created/built." It is a Hazor dynastic name, as known from an unpublished Mari text, which also yields the name of the patron deity, when it mentions "Ibni-Adad, king of Hazor." On the strong cultural and commercial relations between Mari and the two major MB kingdoms at the southwest end of its trade routes (Hazor and Laish/Dan; cf. Leshem in 19:47), see Abraham Malamat, "Northern Canaan and the Mari Texts," in *Near Eastern Archaeology in the Twentieth Century*, 20-33. See Maps B (112) and E (302).

king of Hazor. In Judg 4:2,23,24, Jabin is "king of Canaan," a title which is reminiscent of the former prominence of the great Middle Bronze Age citystate. A. Malamat, "Hazor 'The Head of All Those Kingdoms,'" *JBL* 79 (1960) 12-19. Concerning the decline of this city-state in the Late Bronze Age, we learn in Amarna correspondence (from the king of Tyre) that the king of Hazor has left his city and united with the 'Apiru, so that the land of the king is controlled by the 'Apiru (EA 148).

Hazor. Map E, 302. Tell el-Qedaḥ, c. 13.6 km north of the Sea of Galilee. In its heyday, it was a vast Middle Bronze Age city, with a strongly fortified citadel on the mound some 30 acres in size, dominating a rectangular lower city of some 175 acres protected by massive earthen embankments. The smaller upper city goes back to the third millennium B.C., but the vast lower city was founded in the eighteenth century, that is, the Mari Age. By the time of the Yahwist movement at the end of the Late Bronze Age, Hazor was once again a smaller town restricted to the area of the mound.

heard, he sent off. With no object expressed for either verb, the Hebrew describes a hurried response and evokes a sense of breathless reaction. We are left to deduce what he heard; it was either (1) news of the Shechem covenant, (2) news from the southern hill country, or (3) some combination of the two. In any event the news would be assimilated by Jabin as he looked out from his stronghold upon something quite new to the scenery of Upper Galilee:

> . . . a continuous chain of tiny settlements . . . in an area extending from Peqi'in to the Kezib brook (Wadi Qurn). These are the first permanent settlements established on virgin soil in one of the highest districts of upper Galilee, and [*sic!*] which had been completely covered by forest until then. Some . . . on the mountain tops, some on slopes or in valleys; the distances between them do not exceed 2-3 kms on the average, sometimes even less.

(Yohanan Aharoni, "The Settlement of Canaan," *WHJP* III [1971] 97. See also *EAEHL* II, 406-408.) These new, open and unfortified, settlements of people eking out a living on the small and scattered plots of cultivable land in such difficult rocky terrain cannot be unrelated to the Habiru phenomenon in general and the spread of the Yahweh movement into Upper Galilee in particular. Actually it was more widespread than the explorer himself observed. The Wadi Qurn line is breaking down, owing to subsequent discovery of Iron I sites not spotted in Aharoni's survey—for example, Har Addir alongside Kibbutz Sasa. The Sasa site, under excavation in 1975, is claimed by Danny Bahat the excavator as one of the earliest Iron I sites in the Upper Galilee (oral communication).

This setting may be compared and contrasted with the situation that had prevailed along the main highways perhaps a quarter of a century earlier. In a satirical letter from the long reign of Ramesses II (c. 1290-1224), the scribe Hori describes the Wadi 'Āra, a main branch from the coastal road linking the plains of Sharon and Esdraelon: "The narrow valley is dangerous with Bedouin, hidden under the bushes." They range from seven to nine feet tall, and they are fierce of face. "Their hearts are not mild, and they do not listen to wheedling." Trans. John A. Wilson, *ANET²*, 477. Many of the earliest re-cruits to the ranks of the Bene Israel must have been farmers who had re-treated from a combination of oppression and escalating insecurity in the more crowded and fertile plains of the coast and the Esdraelon-Jordan Valley.

Jobab. This non-Semitic name has been explained as Luwian. Mendenhall, *Ten Gen*, 166. The name illustrates the rapid influx of Anatolian peoples, after the breakup of the mighty Hittite empire, when the arrival in Canaan of vari-ous refugees and military adventurers contributed to a rapid political fragmen-tation. This was already getting under way in the fourteenth century, as the Amarna Letters make clear. As the only ally mentioned by name, this must be Jabin's most powerful neighbor.

Madon. The site is near Qarn Hattin in the heart of Lower Galilee. Map B, 112. The king of Madon will be mentioned again in the list of deposed mon-archs (12:19). Mendenhall connects this place name to the same Luwian town name (*mada*) from which he explains the name Midian. He observes that at least three of the five named kings of Midian have non-Semitic, and probably Anatolian, names: Evi, Reqem, and Reba (13:21; Num 31:8). *Ten Gen*, 167-169.

Shimron. Site uncertain. Cf. 12:20. If the text is intact, it is obscure enough that the Versions reflect names as different as "Simeon" and "Samaria" (the lat-ter may have been a genuine variant). Avi-Yonah and Aharoni find it at Kh. Sammuniyeh (Tell Shimron) in the northern portion of the Esdraelon almost due north of Megiddo.

Achshaph. See also 12:20. If it is the same place, it will belong to Asher in 19:5. The location is uncertain. The most likely candidate is et-Tell, c. 9.6 km northeast of Acco. The Galilee and Esdraelon regions were not administratively partitioned until the Shiloh phase.

2-3. These verses describe the range of Jabin's call to arms concentrically. In v 2 it is appeal to the larger Galilee area, while v 3 frames this enlarged picture with an orderly description of the region south of Esdraelon, on the one hand, and reference to the far-off Beqa Valley in Lebanon, on the other. The weight of the four-king coalition is thus considerably reinforced by a rhetorical structure from which little, if anything, can be subtracted as a secondary edito-rial accretion.

2. *the Arabah*. LXX reads instead "Rabbah," readily explained as a scribal lapse, and scarcely a reference to the Ammonite capital, as Soggin suspects (*Joshua*, 134). The Arabah in this verse is the rift into which the Esdraelon and Lake of Galilee both empty. Map B, 112.

Chinneroth. In MT, it is clear, this is the lake. LXX treats it as the name of a village (on the northwest shore of the lake) in relation to a place "Rabah" which is "opposite" it. See Textual Note.

Naphath-dor. "Dune of Dor," taking it as a reference to the famous seaport town on the coast south of Carmel. Map B, 112. Dor is mentioned along with its ruler Beder, king of the Tjeker (one of the "Sea Peoples") in the Report of Wen-Amon, c. 1100 B.C. (*ANET²*, 26). Excavations have shown that it had been settled not long before, in the Late Bronze Age. A destruction in the thirteenth century has been attributed to the Tjeker. According to literary sources Dor flourished throughout the Iron Age. Naphath-dor was the capital of Solomon's fourth administrative district (1 Kgs 4:11), important enough to be governed by the king's son-in-law. Dor became a part of the northern kingdom probably having a customs-sanctuary. The seal of one of its priests, bearing the Yahwist name Zekaryahu, was recently published, having been found near Sebaste (Samaria). Nahman Avigad, "The Priest of Dor," *IEJ* 25 (1975) 101-105. Unfortunately, the limited archaeological reports in Dor record almost nothing of the Iron Age town. See G. Foerster, "Dor," *EAEHL* I, 334-337. A new dig began there in 1980 under the direction of E. Stern.

3. *on the east and on the west.* This rendering recognizes that the mistaken reading in LXX nevertheless points in the right direction: "to the coasts of the eastern Canaanites and to the coasts of the Amorites." These "coasts" belong to Chinneroth and Mediterranean, respectively. Here "Amorite" contrasts with "eastern Canaanite" though the latter is still confined to western Palestine. Therefore the expression, "the Canaanites on the east and on the west," must originally have referred to the Arabah and the coastal plain with the outer reaches of Esdraelon, since the hill country had increasingly fallen to the Bene Israel and other newcomers.

the Amorites. Compare "Westerners" in 9:1 and 10:5 and material cited there in NOTES.

Hittites Perizzites Jebusites Hivites. Scattered along the less desirable high country of the north-south corridor between "Canaanites on the east and on the west" were people of four "nations" with non-Semitic names and backgrounds. On these names see above, NOTES and COMMENT on 3:10.

Hermon. Map B, 112. The root is the word for the ban (*ḥrm*), hence "Consecrated One," or the like. At an altitude of c. 2,743 meters, it is the tallest part of the Anti-Lebanon range, with its southern spur snowcapped all year round.

Mizpah-land. The first element means "Watchtower," "Lookout," and was very common. There was a place called Mizpah/Mizpeh in Benjamin (18:26), another one near Lachish (15:38), and still another in Gilead (Judg 10:17; Gen 31:49). This one near Mount Hermon is as elusive as the others. J. Simons suggests *Nebi Ṣafa,* in the valley called *Merj el-Qunaʻbah. Handbook for the Study of Egyptian Topographical Texts Relating to Western Asia* (Leiden: Brill, 1937) 43. It is also possible that "Lookout-land" may be a general synonym for the area that is "below Hermon."

4. *multitude of horses and chariots.* We may assume that most of these belonged to the king of Hazor; since the purpose was to plan a combined attack on terrain to the south of Esdraelon, this was probably not intended to be the staging area. Hence the success of what was probably a surprise attack.

Hazor in the Middle Bronze Age was adjacent to, if not indeed part of, the land of Amurru, which in turn was notable for export of horses. Malamat, "Hazor 'The Head of All Those Kingdoms,' " 16.

chariots. Here mentioned for the first time in Joshua. The light war chariot carrying a team of a driver and a warrior had been introduced to western Asia by the Aryans, near the beginning of the eighteenth century B.C. Such military efficiency reflects a feudal system in which the charioteers, or *maryānu,* belong to a class enjoying special privileges and performing special services for the king. The lightweight chariot, in contrast to the heavier Hittite chariot which also carried a shield-bearer, to make a three-man team, could be disassembled easily and transported for reassembly in suitable terrain. Gray, *Joshua, Judges and Ruth,* 119, with reference to the satirical letter of Hori, *ANET²,* 477.

5. *pitched camp together.* Hebrew *wyb'w wyḥnw,* literally, "and they came and camped," a verbal hendiadys.

Waters of Merom. Merom is modern Meron. Maps B, 112, and E, 302. Where were the Waters? The Wadi Meron would have provided terrain too deep and rugged to be the setting of chariot warfare. Most plausible is a location near the pond scarcely 4 km northeast of Meron, called *Birket el-Jish* (or *'Agam Daltōn*), in the plateau to the north of Jebel Jermaq. On this view "Merom" is a geographic term (meaning "elevated" or "exalted") for the local mountain region. Rösel, "Studien zur Topographie der Kriege in den Büchern Josua und Richter," *ZDPV* 91 (1975) 159-196.

6. *Yahweh said.* Only divine encouragement could account for Israel's move against such odds.

"Do not be afraid. Hebrew *'al tîrā',* as in 8:1; 10:8 (and plural form in 10:25). This formula is characteristic of the Deuteronomic corpus, which uses the particle *'al* to express immediate prohibition (with *yr'* in Deut 1:21; 3:2; 20:3; 31:6) and the particle *lō'* to express permanent prohibition (with *yr'* in Deut 7:18; 20:1; 31:8).

tomorrow. Compare Judg 20:28, which is also part of Yahweh's authorization of warfare, and the temporal expression, in foremost position, is part of a *kî*-clause, as here, laying special emphasis on the element of timing. De Vries, "Temporal Terms as Structural Elements in the Holy War Tradition," *VT* 25 (1975) especially 81-82. He concludes that the usage here is most likely a "mere conventionality in spite of its foremost position." But surely it would have been helpful to know that the victory would be "tomorrow" and not next week or next month. See NOTES on 1:2 and 3:7.

Their horses you shall hamstring. Their chariots you shall burn." These two operations presumably refer to the beginning and end of the action respectively. That is, by crippling the horses, the warriors were forced to flee on foot, leaving their unattended chariots to be subsequently consigned to flames. It was a plan that surely deserves to be called inspired. Otherwise it would require a miracle (Judges 4-5) to turn back the chariots in this era. Israel would not make use of such newfangled military equipment and organization until the imperial days of David and Solomon (2 Sam 8:4=1 Chr 18:4; 2 Sam 15:1; 1 Kgs 1:5; 9:19-22).

7. *his entire fighting force.* Recruited from Ephraim and Benjamin, accord-

ing to K.-D. Schunck, *Benjamin, Untersuchungen zur Entstehung und Geschichte eines israelitischen Stammes,* 26-28. This is surely on the right track, as explained in the COMMENT, although the thirteenth-century destruction of Hazor may have preceded the arrival of the Bene Israel militia.

by surprise at the Waters of Merom. With the horses already disabled, the opposition was put to flight.

from. Soggin recognized the archaic sense of the preposition *b* here. *Joshua,* 134.

the mountain. This was perhaps the least likely direction from which to attack a chariot encampment.

8. *Yahweh put them into the hand.* It is the fulfillment of the oracle in v 6. See 10:30 and 32.

pressed the attack and gave chase. Hebrew *wykwm wyrdpwm.* Literally, "and they smote them and pursued them," a verbal hendiadys. What it describes is more of a panicked rout than a slaughter. Compare the conclusion to the rout of the Midianite forces in the story of Gideon (Judg 7:22). *Judges,* AB 6A, 143. The force of the coalition seems to have split, some fleeing northwest toward the coastal cities.

Greater Sidon. Map B, 112. This is a distinctive designation which occurs elsewhere in the Old Testament only in 19:28. The Sidonians are mentioned in Josh 13:4 and 6.

Misrephoth-maim! Map E, 302. Mentioned again in 13:6. The second element of the name means "waters." The most likely location is Khirbet el-Musheirifeh, a Bronze Age site just south of Rosh ha-Niqra, the modern Lebanon-Israel border. It seems to be mentioned here as general southern limit to "Canaanite" coastline. If the name connection is correct then it means approximately "Eminence over the Waters," the only Hebrew use of the root *śrp*=Arabic *šrf,* "to be noble." O'Connor, private communication. An alternative interpretation takes it as a reference to a stream, the Litani River. Y. Aharoni and M. Avi-Yonah, *The Macmillan Bible Atlas,* Plate 62. There may well be a double meaning here. The same letters spell *maim* and "on the west." The word thus balances the reference to "east" in the next phrase.

Toward Mizpeh Valley to the east! In v 3 the force had assembled from east and west. Here they flee to west and east.

no survivor. The verse echoes 8:22 and 10:33.

9. Here the point of the story is made explicit: the divine plan had met with flawless performance. It began with hamstringing and ended in burning. *Inclusio* with v 6. Thus ended an old story which will now be read in a larger setting, as illustrative of Dtr 1 theology. First it is made explicit why Hazor was singled out for special attention.

10. *formerly the head of all those kingdoms!* This would rank it among the most prominent kingdoms of the Mari period, when kingdoms such as Mari, Babylon, Larsa, Eshnunna, Qatna, and Yamhad each exercised sovereignty over ten to twenty vassal kings. Malamat, "Northern Canaan and the Mari Texts," 27.

11. *carried out the ban.* Hebrew *haḥărēm.* The form is *hiph'il* infinitive absolute. With no direct object expressed, it has elative or durative force, an emphatic substitute for the finite form. Here it refers to Deuteronomic doc-

trine, not to the ad hoc decree of early Yahwist practice. This usage was lost upon the Syriac translator, who shows no trace of it.

Hazor they burned! Crucial to the history of Hazor is a small rectangular temple which originated sometime in Middle Bronze Age II, and was somewhat dilapidated by the early Late Bronze Age, though clearly still marking a holy place. A recent summary of some later strata as interpreted by the excavator may be cited:

> Stratum XIII, the last Late Bronze Age level on the mound, parallels stratum 1-a in the Lower City. With the destruction that occurred in this level, Canaanite Hazor was brought to an end in the thirteenth century B.C. As in the Lower City, few new houses were built, the ruins of the previous stratum being reconstructed and some structures erected here and there around the reservoir. A small cult installation, including stelae, found near the derelict temple, may be assigned to this stratum.
>
> Stratum XII. After a certain gap, a small settlement rose at the beginning of the Iron Age on the ruins of stratum XIII. This settlement, which can hardly be called a city, consisted mostly of deep silos, hearths, and foundations for tents and huts. The pottery is typical of the twelfth century B.C. and closely resembles that found in similar poor Israelite settlements in Upper Galilee. The settlement may be assigned to the first efforts of the Israelites to settle on the site. (Yigael Yadin, "Hazor," in *EAEHL* II [1976] 485.)

The problem is that the stratification shows a pagan temple which postdates what has been taken to be the final destruction of Canaanite Hazor. It has been plausibly argued that the destruction of Hazor in the late thirteenth or early twelfth century can as readily be traced to the Sea Peoples. Volkmar Fritz, "Das Ende der spätbronzezeitlichen Stadt Hazor Stratum XIII und die biblischer Überlieferung in Josua 11 und Richter 4," *UF* 5 (1973) 123-139. The archaeological evidence at Hazor must be considered alongside a growing list of famous towns and cities, the destruction of which during the chaos of preceding eras left only small forts to be overpowered and in fact created the conditions for the spread of unwalled villages (Jericho, Ha-Ai, Lachish), while the Yahweh army grew rapidly by conversion and negotiation (Shechem, Gibeon, possibly Debir). The forts and villages were in fact so small that a serious military blow might very well not show in the form of a "destruction layer."

12. *royal towns and all their kings.* This is a verse, presumably from another editor (the contributor of chap. 12, probably, since it lists the thirty-one dethroned kings), which seeks to correct the perspective. The "Canaanite problem" was one of a power elite.

them. Here the verb *ḥrm* has its object specified, another indication that another editor is at work. Syriac omits, as in v 11.

as Moses the Servant of Yahweh had commanded. The editor seems to be laying claim to a rival interpretation to Dtn teaching on the practice of *ḥrm*, as becomes clear in the next verse.

13. *towns standing on mounds Israel did not burn, with the single exception*

of Hazor. This is not based on any homiletical guideline but rooted in someone's memory, that opposition to the Yahweh movement in Galilee was
strongest at Hazor.

14. *the Bene Israel plundered.* See NOTES on 6:17-19.

they had wiped them out. This rendering adopts the suggestion of *BH*³ and
BHS, parsing *hšmdm* as *hiph'il* infinitive construct with object suffix.

15. *As Yahweh commanded his Servant Moses.* A strong *inclusio* with v 12
is used to conclude the account of the defeat of the northern coalition, echoing
at the same time the introductory rhetoric, according to which Joshua was to
be guided every step of the way by the teaching of Moses (1:7). In this case the
guidance is distinctive in that it has no Pentateuchal background. There is no
indication anywhere that Moses had any interest in Galilee. With the
intervening stories to serve as examples of how the teaching of Moses had been
followed, the way is prepared for a general summary in the verses which follow.

COMMENT

According to the famous historian of the First Jewish Revolt against
Rome, who was himself a traitor to that cause, it could be said that
"the Galileans are inured to war from their infancy. . . ." (Flavius
Josephus, *The Wars of the Jews,* Book III, chap. iii, 2). Scientifically accurate generalizations about any ethnic or national group are impossible
to make, and we have no way of testing the accuracy of this one. What is
clear is that the Galileans from the beginning of the Late Bronze Age to
the Roman empire had continuing experience of foreign military suppression and defensive warfare that may have been equaled elsewhere but it
was surely not surpassed. The evidence is indisputable that the majority
of the royal families and ruling aristocracies in the multitude of small city-
states that made up Canaan in the Late Bronze Age were of foreign origin in some sense—refugees and privateers moving away from the northern epicenter when the walls of the first age of internationalism had come
tumbling down. With their seizure of many of the old Hyksos castles,
which pharaohs of the early Eighteenth Dynasty had recaptured but
which their successors of the late Eighteenth Dynasty had failed to administer effectively, Canaan had entered upon a period of local city-state
warfare which, by the mid-to-late thirteenth century saw most of the castles, at least once, reduced to rubble.

From the side of the Galilean "peasants" what was needed most desperately was a new internationalism, a new ecumenical glue. This in fact
is what Yahwism seems to have been. Such in any case makes very plausi-

ble the history that has become epic in Joshua 2-10, the news of which was enough to stir into action the alarmed royal remnant that stretched from Upper Galilee, through Esdraelon, to the northern plain of Sharon.

One way or another Joshua got the word. The later loyalty of Jael (Judges 4-5), against her own clan's tradition of a covenant stemming from the days of one Jabin (the name may be a papponym), suggests that there are times when the opposite of the clan's commitment is the honorable thing (AB 6A, 92-121). And it offers a striking example of the communications network comprised largely of wandering smiths and caravaneers.

The kings were put to rout and Jabin's force destroyed because some of the Bene Israel got to the horses before the slumbering charioteers could be roused to stop them. Surely the narrator was correct; no plan could have been more truly inspired.

It was a new day in Galilee, the beginning of a period when, for about two hundred years, it would be safe to live in unwalled villages, until in the tenth century tax collectors and muster officers were once again a common sight, coming this time from Jerusalem.

2. SUMMARY OF THE WARFARE
(11:16-23)

A Complete Success

11 16 Joshua took all this land: the Highlands, all the Southern
Desert, all the territory of Goshen, the Foothills, the Arabah (the
Highlands of Israel and its Foothills). 17 From Mount Halaq that
towers over the region of Seir, as far as Baal-gad in the Lebanon
Valley below Mount Hermon—all their kings he captured. He laid
them low!
18 For years Joshua waged war with all those kings. 19 There was
not a town that secured a treaty with the Bene Israel, except the
Hivite inhabitants of Gibeon. The whole of it they took in battle.
20 Indeed, it was Yahweh's intention to bolster their hearts for the
military confrontation with Israel, to put them under the ban without
mercy being shown them—that he might destroy them, exactly as
Yahweh had commanded Moses!

A Partial Success

21 Joshua moved at that time to mow down the people of Anaq:
from the Highlands, from Hebron, from Debir, from Anab (from
all the people of Israel and from all the Highlands of Judah!).
Along with their towns, Joshua devoted them to destruction. 22 None
of the people of Anaq were left in the land of the Bene Israel. Only
in Gaza, and in Gath and in Ashdod did they remain.

End of Hostilities

23 When Joshua had taken all the land, as Yahweh had instructed
Moses, then Joshua gave it over to Israel in fief, according to their
allotments by tribes. And the land was at rest from war.

TEXTUAL NOTES

11 16. *this*   Lost from LXX^AB by haplography: *h'rṣ h[z't h]hr*.

Southern Desert   This is Hebrew *ngb*, reproduced in LXX^A, against the odd spelling *adeb* in LXX^B which may represent a mutilated copy.

17. *Halaq*   Thus MT, where the LXX reading reflects a metathesis of two letters, *hachel*.

He   Some Hebrew manuscripts read plural: "They."

18. *all*   Lost from LXX as the result of an inner-Greek haplography: *pro[s panta]s*.

19. *that secured a treaty with the Bene Israel*   LXX preserves a variant here ("that they did not take") and omits the phrase excepting the Gibeon arrangement.

with   The better reading *'t* survives in many manuscripts (cf. 10:1), whereas the anomalous *'l* in MT looks like contamination from the end of *yśr'l* just five syllables away.

20. *to put them under the ban*   Hebrew *lm'n hḥrymm*=Greek *hina eksoleuthrōsin*.

destroy   LXX instead repeats here "put under the ban," as again in v 21 in place of the verb "to mow down."

21. *Anab*   LXX reads *anabōt*.

(*from all the people of Israel and from all the Highlands of Judah!*)   This word order follows LXX where MT has the reverse sequence of geographical names and complete parallelism: "from all the highlands of Judah and from all the highlands of Israel." The latter is, however, weak since all of the places specified in the verse are in Judah. The key to these differences is the use of *genous* as a determinative in LXX, to remove from interpretation any merely geographical or merely political sense to the term *Israel;* this usage occurs also in 4:14. With *genous* recognized as determinative, the LXX *Vorlage* was: *wmkl yśr'l wmkl hr yhwdh*. Confusion entered when a scribe copied out the wrong order, providing a sequence ripe for the introduction of a scribal plus: *wmkl hr yhwdh wmkl [hr] yśr'l*.

22. *in the land of the Bene Israel*   LXX *apō tōn huiōn Israel*, "from the Bene Israel," says nothing about their land; and the differences cannot be readily explained. The lapse *b['rṣ b]ny yśr'l* would leave no preposition to be represented by *apō*. Behind the latter is perhaps the initial letter of **mbny*. This reading might well have arisen through a one-letter dittography displacing *b'rṣ*, thus: *'nqym [b'rṣ] *m-bny*.

and   The conjunction is represented in LXX, missing in MT.

in Gath and   Missing because of haplography in LXX.

> Give to Levi your Thummim
> Your Urim to your faithful one,
> Whom you tested at Massah
> Whom you tried at Meribah

Deuteronomy 33:8, translated by Cross, *CMHE*, 197. Here Moses is the faithful one placed in synonymous parallelism with Levi. This suggests that the consultation with deity via Urim and Thummim was originally a general Levitical function which was at last restricted to the office of chief priest as in Exod 28:30.

in fief. For this translation of the *nhl*-root (elsewhere "inheritance") see above, on 1:6.

And the land was at rest. This was the goal of the Yahwist reformation/revolution. The formula makes sense here, where it anticipates the related usage that is common in the Book of Judges (3:11,30; 5:31). But it scarcely makes sense where it is repeated in Josh 14:15. In Joshua, the formula is firmly in place in the oldest Greek text (as shown by Margolis, *The Book of Joshua in Greek*, 227, 276), where there are minor differences in its articulation. Such repetition with slight variation is a characteristic framing device which Shemaryahu Talmon has called the "Resumptive Repetition" and which we have discussed above and in Judg 16:31, as a classic example used by Dtr 2. See AB 6A, 252. When originally independent units were incorporated into longer texts, the ancient editor often repeated phrases or clauses—not infrequently with slight variation—as a way of marking limits to the insertion. A classic example is the two lists of David's officials used to frame the "Court History" in 2 Sam 8:16-18 and 20:23-26. The intervening material was one large preformed unit. See now James W. Flanagan, "Court History or Succession Document? A Study of 2 Sam 9-20 and 1 Kings 1-2," *JBL* 91 (1972) 172-181.

COMMENT

This summary of the warfare and transition to the redistribution of the land shows evidence of the same two main contributors we have found elsewhere in the books of Joshua and Judges.

Verses 16-20 are essentially one unit which is said to overstate the case for Joshua's conquest of "all this land." This unit from Dtr 1 needed only minimal adaptation (e.g. references to Mount Halaq and Baal-gad and "all their kings" in v 17) in order to pave the way for a major insertion, probably by Dtr 2 (see below on chaps. 12-14).

What is most striking, however, is the abrupt shift of focus in vv 21-22 concerning the elimination of the Anaqim in the southern hills (Hebron, Debir, Anab), a development which seems to have been unknown to the traditionist in 10:36-39. The partial success described in 11:21-22 may be taken, therefore, as Dtr 2's expansion indicating that the effective elimination of Anaqite control from the south was a larger and more complex process with more mixed results than the first edition had indicated.

In any case, the land was about to become "Holy Land," for ". . . wherever a member of Yahweh's community tilled his own soil under the protection of deity and the religious community, there was 'holy' (belonging to Yahweh) land." G. E. Mendenhall, "The Hebrew Conquest of Palestine," *BA* 25 (1962); reprinted in *BAR* 3 (1970) 113.

According to the ancient editors the setting for the beginning of the redistribution of the land was the Shechem Valley (8:30-35). Here by far the larger areas are assigned to two groups: Judah (chap. 15) and the Bene Joseph (chaps. 16-17). Allotments are not determined for Simeon, Benjamin, and the northern tribes until the tabernacle has been set up at Shiloh (18:1), presumably in the wake of the paganizing reaction and early destruction of Shechem (Judges 9).

The only problem with this presentation is the early prominence of Judah as a tribe of Israel. Recent studies of the early poetry have shown that Judah is most notable for its absence. Freedman, "Divine Names and Titles in Early Hebrew Poetry," in *Mag Dei,* 55-107; "Early Israelite History in the Light of Early Israelite Poetry," in *Unity and Diversity,* 3-23; "Early Israelite Poetry and Historical Reconstructions," in *Symposia,* 85-96.

It appears that, while the Bene Joseph are the older "sons of the left (north)," the powerful tribe of Judah has claimed the place of the earlier "sons of the right (south)." And in fact the names of important clans of the Mari Benjaminites occur as extinct clans of Judah. See W. F. Albright, "From the Patriarchs to Moses: I. From Abraham to Joseph," *BA* 36 (1973) 5-33. Northern Benjamin, in which most of 2:1 - 10:14 have their setting, was so devastated that it did not recover to claim its inheritance until the Shiloh phase.

In any case the account appeared far from complete, and so the later editor, Dtr 2, broke open the work of Dtr 1 to insert at this point a variety of materials in chaps. 12, 13, and 14.

III. THE INHERITANCE
12:1-19:51

A. THE FORMER KINGDOMS
(12:1-24)

12 ¹ These are the kings of the land whom the Bene Israel defeated and whose land they seized east of the Jordan, from the Gorge of the Arnon to Mount Hermon, with all of the eastern Arabah.

² Sihon the Amorite king who reigned at Heshbon: ruling from Aroer which is near the brink of the Arnon Gorge (and from the "town in the gorge") to the Gorge of the Jabboq, border of the Bene Ammon (that is, half of Gilead). ³ And the eastern Arabah as far as the Sea of Chinneroth. And, in the direction of Beth-jeshimoth, as far as the Arabah Sea (the Salt Sea). And from Teman below the Slopes of Pisgah.

⁴ And Og the king of Bashan, one of the remaining Rephaim, who reigned at Ashtaroth and Edrei: ⁵ ruling the land from Mount Hermon (actually from Salecah) over the whole of Bashan to the border of the Geshurites and the Maacathites (that is, half of Gilead), as far as the border of Sihon, king of Heshbon.

⁶ Moses the Servant of Yahweh and the Bene Israel defeated them. And Moses the Servant of Yahweh gave it as a possession to the Reubenites, the Gadites, and half of the tribe of Manasseh.

⁷ And these are the kings of the land whom Joshua and the Bene Israel defeated in the region west of the Jordan, from Baal-gad in the Lebanon Valley all the way to Mount Halaq that towers over Seir. Joshua gave it to the tribes of Israel as a possession, according to their allotments. ⁸ In the Highlands, in the Foothills, in the Arabah, on the slopes in the wilderness, and in the Negeb (Hittites, Amorites, and Canaanites; Perizzites, Hivites, and Jebusites).

[9] The king of Jericho.	One.
The king of The Ruin (which is near Bethel).	One.
[10] The king of Jerusalem.	One.
The king of Hebron.	One.
[11] The king of Jarmuth.	One.
The king of Lachish.	One.
[12] The king of Eglon.	One.
The king of Gezer.	One.
[13] The king of Debir.	One.
The king of Geder.	One.
[14] The king of Hormah.	One.
The king of Arad.	One.
[15] The king of Libnah.	One.
The king of Adullam.	One.
[16] The king of Maqqedah.	One.
The king of Bethel.	One.
[17] The king of Tappuah.	One.
The king of Hepher.	One.
[18] The king of Apheq.	One.
The king of Lasharon.	One.
[19] The king of Madon.	One.
The king of Hazor.	One.
[20] The king of Shimron-meron.	One.
The king of Achshaph.	One.
[21] The king of Taanach.	One.
The king of Megiddo.	One.
[22] The king of Qedesh.	One.
The king of Joqneam in Carmel.	One.
[23] The king of Dor (that is, Naphath-dor).	One.
[24] The king of Tirzah.	One.

. . . .

All the kings.   Thirty-one.

TEXTUAL NOTES

12 1. *Arnon*   Several Hebrew manuscripts have a prefixed conjunction: *w'd*, "and to." There is a great deal of variation involving this word in this unit.
   2. *Aroer*   LXX[B] *Arnōn*.
   near the brink of   Lacking in LXX.

the "town   Restored on the basis of uniform tradition of Deut 2:36 and Josh 13:9,16.

to   This is MT. LXX includes the conjunction: "and to."

3. *Arabah*   The prefixed conjunction at this point in two Hebrew manuscripts is clearly a case of contamination from the correct usage later in the verse.

the Slopes of   Hebrew *'šdwt*. LXX has *mēdōth*, but transliterates *asedōth* in v 8.

4. *And Og*   This agrees with LXX^AB, omitting *gĕbûl*, "boundary of," which appears in MT as contamination from the three occurrences framing this verse in vv 2 and 5.

Bashan   LXX has *basa* here, but *basan* in the following verse.

5. *ruling*   This follows LXX, where MT has a prefixed conjunction.

the Geshurites   MT *hgšwry*, where OG regularly read *hgšyry* but LXX^B mistakenly turns them into "Girgashites." Greenspoon, STBJ, 158-159.

as far as   This follows LXX^L, where the major recensions show a haplography: *hgl'd* ['d] *gbwl*.

6. *the Servant of Yahweh*   Lacking in LXX^AB, Syr^h, and Vulg. But the shorter text can be explained by haplography: *mš[h 'bd yhw]h*.

7. *land*   LXX reads instead "Amorites" (westerners), but the result is to leave the pronoun object of the next statement ("it") without an antecedent.

all   This is the reading in Hebrew manuscripts and Vulgate where MT has a prefixed conjunction.

according to   This is the preposition *k* in MT, where many manuscripts have *b*, "in," and two others have *l*, "for."

9. *One*   LXX omits the numeral throughout the list.

12. *Eglon*   Hebrew *'glwn*. LXX *ailam*.

13. *Geder*   MT *gdr*. LXX *asei*.

14. *Hormah*   The LXX spelling *hermath* reflects more closely the popular etymology from the root *ḥrm*, "ban."

Arad   LXX has a double reading which reflects alternative transliterations: "king of *airath*" and "king of *arath*."

16. *The king of Maqqedah. . . . One.* (second occurrence)   LXX reads *ēlad*, presumably in place of Maqqedah, and lacks reference to the king of Bethel.

17. *Tappuah*   MT *tpwḥ*. LXX *ataphout*.

18. *The king of Lasharon*   This takes MT at face value, although the place name is a hapax legomenon. LXX lacks the second occurrence of "The king of" (cf. v 20) and instead of "Lasharon" reads *arōk*, which is equally obscure.

19. *Madon*   This is missing from LXX^AB and many manuscripts, unless the spelling *marrōn* in v 20 involves confusion of *d* and *r*.

Hazor   MT *ḥṣwr*. LXX *hasom*.

20. *Shimron-meron*   LXX reads as two names: "the king of *symoōn*" (elsewhere for "Simeon") and "the king of *mamroth*."

21-22. The sequence is different in LXX where a number of spellings in the list do not inspire confidence. Beginning v 21 a scribe skipped ahead to "the king of *kadēs*," then returned to "the king of *zakach*" (for MT *t'nk*) and "the king of *maredoth*" (for MT *mgdw*).

23. *Dor*   LXX *eldōm* may perhaps be intended as the name of the king of Naphath-dor, but if so it violates the form of the list in being the only one named, while MT appears to be redundant (or perhaps glossed).

Naphath   A few manuscripts read the plural form Naphoth-dor. See 11:2, Textual Note.

23b. The reading in MT, *mlk gwym lglgl,* is unintelligible. LXX reads "king of the *gōim* of Galilee."

24. *Thirty-one*   This count follows MT. LXX reads "Twenty-nine."

NOTES

12:1-24. This chapter is clearly intended to serve as summary, and it surely deserves to be called "Deuteronomic." Compare the following: 12:1b and Deut 3:8b; 12:2,4 and Deut 1:4 (cf. 3:11); 12:2b,3 and Deut 3:12b plus Deut 3:16,17 (cf. Josh 13:15-16); 12:5 and Deut 3:13. These texts are collected by Magnus Ottoson, *Gilead: Tradition and History,* 119, following the analytical lead of Noth, *Das Buch Josua.*

It is equally clear that the list in this chapter did not belong to the earliest Dtr book, "because it lists kings and cities that were not mentioned in the rest of the book . . ." Fohrer, *Introduction to the Old Testament,* 203-204. Fohrer goes on to claim that the chapter shows a conception of the conquest that "does not agree with the account in [chaps.] 1-11," and this is said to be P's erudite history.

It must be admitted, however, that there is no direct evidence to show that the label "P" must be placed upon this chapter. The most that can be said is that it belongs to a secondary stage in the formation of the great historical work. It supplies additional information to plug some gaps in the first edition, but also to call attention to the larger Israel of the east-west axis which had existed before the Transjordan territories were lost to the kingdoms of Israel and Judah beginning in the ninth century. In this way the post-Josiah editor showed how the original Israel had been something much larger than the west-bank nation ruled by the great reforming king. There is no evidence that King Josiah ruled, for long, over much of the Transjordan territory; and the first editor of the historical work had no interest in territorial claims in those regions. See above on 1:12-18.

12:1-6. These verses summarize the Transjordan "conquest" under the leadership of Moses.

1. *the Gorge of the Arnon.* Maps B, 112, and F, 336. The immense Wadi el-Mujib, descending some 1.06 km through the Transjordan plateau in a distance of 48 km, is a natural northern boundary of the kingdom of Moab, and the southern limit of ancient Israel's territorial claims east of the river.

Arabah. Map B, 112. Here and in v 3, this denotes the wider Jordan Valley.

2-5. The description in these verses was composed on the basis of the document preserved in 13:9-12, or one closely related to it.

2. *Sihon.* The story is told in Num 21:21-31. Taken up in the story is an ancient song (27b-30) originally celebrating an Amorite victory over the Moabites. Ancient scribal errors in v 30, however, led to the misunderstanding of the verse and, ultimately, the entire song, when at last it was interpreted as describing instead Israel's victory over Sihon! Paul D. Hanson, "The Song of Heshbon and David's NÎR," *HTR* 61 (1968) 297-320. Objections to the historicity of the Sihon tradition based on the alleged late date of the prose texts would thus appear to be unduly skeptical; e.g. J. Van Seters, "The Conquest of Sihon's Kingdom: A Literary Examination," *JBL* 91 (1972) 182-197. See now John R. Bartlett, "The Conquest of Sihon's Kingdom: A Literary Re-examination," *JBL* 97 (1978) 347-351, which reestablishes the priority of the Numbers account. Van Seters replies in *JBL* 99 (1980) 117-119.

Amorite. This label relates him to the great state of Amurru which at the battle of Qadesh (c. 1285 B.C.) became subject to the Hittite king; see Wright's Introduction, 80-82. Immediately thereafter these allies invaded the region of Damascus and northern Transjordan. There followed a series of revolts as far south as Ashqelon. It was in this milieu that Amorite kings were established in Transjordan. Benjamin Mazar, *WHJP* III (1971) 72. The political situation in Transjordan deteriorated following the expansion of influence by the Hittites and Amurru with whom they were allied. This in turn disrupted the political alignments of Egypt and allowed for greater nomadic disruption across the northern Sinai from Seir to the land of Goshen.

> Ramses had good reasons to undertake military campaigns and send punitive forces to various districts, including the lands of Edom and Moab. His forces, that apparently reached Transjordan, fought the nomadic tribes in the lands of Moab and Seir to re-establish Pharaoh's prestige and consolidate his rule in those areas and along the vital communication arteries (ibid., 73).

who reigned. Hebrew *hay-yôšēb,* literally, "who sat enthroned."

Heshbon. Maps B, 112, and F, 336. The question of identification with *Tell Ḥesban,* which had appeared questionable as long as clear Late Bronze Age and Iron I stratification eluded the excavators, has perhaps been resolved; we are informed of "clear 13th/12th cent. B.C. material, exceedingly close to Tell Beit Mirsim B_1 and other deposits long associated by Albright with the conquest. . . ." William G. Dever, review of R. S. Boraas and S. H. Horn, *Heshbon 1973: The Third Campaign at Tell Hesban, A Preliminary Report,* in *JBL* 96 (1977) 579. For the early report on the Heshbon vicinity, see S. Douglas Waterhouse and Robert Ibach, Jr., "The Topographical Survey," *Andrews University Seminary Studies* 13 (1975) 239.

Within the organization of the Bene Israel, Heshbon became a Levitical town. See below, 21:39.

Aroer. Maps B, 112, and F, 336. Located at the edge of the desert, it has been called "the Beersheba of the East." George Adam Smith, *The Historical Geography of the Holy Land,* 377. Excavations have helped to sharpen the focus, disclosing a fortress of the Early Bronze Age, rebuilt in Iron I, after much lighter occupation in the intervening period.

"town in the gorge." A plausible explanation for this otherwise strange parenthesis is that it describes a general habitable area between the two main courses of the Arnon (Seil el-Mojib and Seil el-Heidan) which flow together on the west and also meet twice in the east. The territory thus "quasi-closed up between these two small rivers" is what is meant. Israel Ben-Shem, *The Conquest of Transjordan;* Hebrew with English summary, I.

Gorge of the Jabboq. Map B, 112. This is the second major canyon and natural boundary formed by the wadi systems that have cut into the Transjordan plateau (the third is the Yarqon, in 19:46). The Jabboq, in its lower east-west segment, marked the northern limits of Sihon's realm. The upper reaches, running from south to north, were the western limits of the early Ammonite kingdom.

the Bene Ammon. Like the Bene Israel, the Ammonites could not yet be called a kingdom. Their first biblical appearance in an active role is in collaboration with Eglon, king of Moab, Judg 3:13-14. The formal organization of an Ammonite state must be dated later than the emergence of the Amorites, Moabites, and Edomites. George M. Landes, "Ammon," *IDB* 1, 110. See also G. M. Landes, "The Material Civilization of the Ammonites," *BA* 24 (1961) 65-86=*BAR* 2 (1964) 69-88.

Gilead. The name is related to modern Jal'ad, c. 9.6 km north-northeast of es-Salt, and is probably a geographical term. The best etymology relates it to Arabic *j'd,* meaning "curly (of hair), wrinkled (of skin), pleated (of clothes), difficult (of terrain)." The territorial sense is a name for the east-Jordan countryside, "particularly the afforested hill country running from north to south which incorporates the es-Salt district." See Ottoson, *Gilead,* 29 and references given there.

3. *Sea of Chinneroth.* The Lake of Galilee, here named after the small fertile plain on its northwest shoreline.

Beth-jeshimoth. "House of wastes," an apt description for a site so near the Dead Sea, probably Tell el-'Azeimeh. Maps B, 112, and F, 336.

Arabah Sea (the Salt Sea). The Dead Sea.

Teman. This refers to one of the clans that was descended from Esau and the region where it lived in central Edom; the name is the same as that of modern Tawilan in southern Jordan. The name is a poetic equivalent of "Edom" in Amos 1:12; Jer 49:20; Ezek 25:13.

Slopes of Pisgah. Again in 13:20; Deut 3:17. It is a geographical term probably originating as name of a town or village somewhere in the Wadi 'Ayūn Mūsā, below the promontories of Pisgah and Nebo. Map B, 112.

4. *Og.* The name is non-Semitic and has been equated with Hittite and Luwian *ḫuḫḫa,* later Lycian *Kuga.* Mendenhall, *Ten Gen,* 160.

Bashan. Very productive land centering on the Golan Heights, bounded in general by Mount Hermon on the north, the hills of northern Gilead on the south, the broken lava country of Jebel Druze to the east, and the Sea of Galilee to the west. Maps B, 112, and F, 336.

one of the remaining. For others see the three or four powerful Philistine warriors who were killed by David's men in 2 Sam 21:15-22.

Rephaim. The word is best explained as referring originally to an aristocracy of professional chariot warriors, from whose ranks also came many of the Canaanite kings. The root *rp'* is used as epithet of El and the plural *rpum* refers to all the gods at El's banquet. See the essays by Conrad E. L'Heureux, "The Ugaritic and Biblical Rephaim," *HTR* 67 (1974) 265-274; "The *yĕlîdê hārāpā'*—A Cultic Association of Warriors," *BASOR* 221 (February 1976) 83-85, and his dissertation, *Rank Among the Canaanite Gods: El, Ba'al, and the Repha'im.* Harvard Semitic Monographs 21 (Missoula, MT: Scholars Press, 1979) 111-230 (esp. 218, 222). This explains a secondary meaning of Hebrew *rp'ym* as "giants" (Deut 2:11,20; 3:11,13, etc.). For another secondary meaning, "shades of the dead" (Isa 14:9; 26:14,19; Ps 88:11; Job 26:5, etc.), see Marvin H. Pope's discussion of the association for funeral feasting known as the *marzēaḥ.* M. H. Pope, *Song of Songs,* AB 7C (1977) 218-219. According to Deut 3:11, Og required an exceptionally large bedstead (another retouch by Dtr 2?). Development of the secondary sense regarding kings Sihon and Og may well have been spurred on by curiosity about extensive dolmen fields such as the one at Jourmeyet Ḥesbân, the large mountain mass lying between Tell Ḥesbân and the Middle Wadi Ḥesbân. It has yielded many Early Bronze Age sherds, prompting comparison with the EB-MB dolmens in northern Galilee and the tradition of the Rephaim as giants. See Waterhouse and Ibach, *Andrews University Seminary Studies* 13 (1975) 229-230, and references there to work by D. Bahat and Claire Epstein. That Og was the last of the Rephaim, in the original sense, may well be historically correct.

Ashtaroth and Edrei. Maps B, 112, and F, 336. Tell 'Ashtarah and Tell Der'a, respectively, reflect the toponyms of the tradition.

5. *from . . . from.* This sense of the preposition *b* is confirmed by the LXX translation, *apo.*

Salecah. Maps B, 112, and F, 336. Possibly to be identified with Salkhad, far to the east of Der'a in the broken lava country of the Jebel Druze.

the Geshurites and the Maacathites. Maps B and F. The gentilic formations name two Aramean groups at the eastern fringe of Israelite territory, a source of continuing resistance to Israel (13:13). Absalom's mother was a Geshurite princess (2 Sam 3:3). Some of the Maacathites fought against Joab at Rabbath-Ammon (2 Sam 10:6). The town of Abel or Abel-beth-maacah is probably Tell Ibn el-Qamḥ, 2.4 km south of modern Metullah. Gray, *Joshua, Judges, and Ruth,* 125. It was not incorporated into any of the recorded tribal claims.

as far as the border of Sihon. This has no precise referent in the preceding description of Og's realm. It is the one limit there not accounted for. In other words, the undefined area was a no man's land. In Iron I there was a sizable increase of settlement in the region between the Yarmuq and the Wadi el-Hasa, which flows north into the wadi system associated with the southern tip of the Dead Sea.

6. What had been the area of two other newcomer monarchies became three

parts of the one Kingdom of Yahweh, under the direct leadership of Moses the Servant of Yahweh. The heightened rhetorical effect of chiastic structure (the sequence is verb last/verb first) cannot be completely reproduced in translation.

7-8. These verses invert the order of the preceding summary. See 11:16-17 and NOTES. On the six (or seven) nations, see 3:10 and NOTES, and 9:1. Here the list does not include the Girgashites.

7. *over Seir*. Hebrew *śē'īrāh*, which the OG translated "toward Seir," but Theodotion subsequently was content to transcribe, apparently aware of the difficulty of translating the phrase. Greenspoon, STBJ, 114 and 309. This is Edom on Map B, 112.

9-24. The remainder of the chapter lists kings who were dethroned by Joshua and the Bene Israel. It makes no specific claims to the occupation or destruction of towns. These verses may very well be "the most vivid description of what happened. . . ." Mendenhall, *Ten Gen*, 26. The list is based in part on sources which Dtr 1 had omitted or only broadly summarized. The form of the list, in which each entry reads literally, "The king of N. One," suggests that the list was originally drawn up for didactic use.

9-13a. The first segment of the list is closely related to the sequence of stories in what we have called "Phase I," that is, 6:1 - 10:43. Every one of these kings has been mentioned previously.

9. *Jericho*. Chapters 2 and 6. Maps B, 112, and C, 137.

The Ruin. Chapters 7 and 8 . This is Ai on Map B.

10. *Jerusalem*. See 10:1,3 (cf. Judg 1:8,21). Map B, 112.

Hebron. See 10:36-37 (cf. 11:21; 15:13-14; Judg 1:10). Maps B, 112, and D, 260.

11. *Jarmuth*. See 10:3. Maps B and D.

Lachish. See 10:3,31-32. Maps B and D.

12. *Eglon*. See 10:3,34-35. Maps B and D.

Gezer. See 10:33. Maps B and D.

13a. *Debir*. See 10:38 (cf. 15:15-19=Judg 1:11-15). Maps B and D.

13b-16a. These verses form a supplement, related in part to chap. 10, but filled out from another source to provide four names not previously mentioned.

13b. *Geder*. Which one of the many places variously called Geder, Gederah, Gederoth, and Gederothaim is meant here is debatable. The form here, which is unique, probably reflects contamination from the name Gezer just above it, in the *BH³* format.

14. *Hormah*. Maps B, 112, and G, 364. See 15:30. This is the first two places in a region not previously dealt with, the northeastern Negeb. The epic tradition in Num 21:1-3 assigned this portion of the conquest to the period of Moses but made no claim for effective settlement. That Joshua destroyed these places is "on a par with several other reasonable inferences" of the late Dtr historians "which happen to be wrong." Albright, *YGC*, 40 n. 72. Thanks to the intensive program of exploration and excavation in the northern Negeb led by Yohanan Aharoni, the history of its major tells has become much clearer. The name Hormah ("Place of the Ban") could also refer to the larger region con-

trolled by the town of Arad (Num 21:1-3; cf. Judg 1:17). The actual place named Hormah, however, is best identified as Tell Masos, although it was unoccupied in the Late Bronze Age. See now Aharoni, "Nothing Early and Nothing Late: Re-writing Israel's Conquest," *BA* 39 (1976) 55-76.

Arad. Maps B, 112, and G, 364. For the Israelite period the identification with Tell Arad has been confirmed by the use of the name on a bowl excavated there. Y. Aharoni and R. Amiran, "Excavations at Tel Arad. Preliminary Report on the First Season, 1962," *IEJ* 14 (1964) 138-139, Fig. 3, Pl. 37:D. An Israelite sanctuary excavated at Arad was in use from the tenth to the late seventh or early sixth centuries, served by individuals whose names—many are those of known Levitical families—appear on a collection of invaluable ostraca from Arad. There is also reference to the "House of Yahweh." See D. N. Freedman and M. Patrick O'Connor, *"yhwh,"* forthcoming in *TWAT*.

It is clear, however, that Tell Arad, like Tell Masos, has no Late Bronze Age stratum. The location of Canaanite Arad has to be sought elsewhere. Aharoni concluded that in the Late Bronze Age there were "no fortified cities whatsoever in the Negeb whose kings could have stood up against the Israelite tribes swarming out of the desert." There were, however, the ruins of older Middle Bronze Age castles, and he offered nearby Tell Malhata as best candidate for Canaanite Arad. In his judgment the Patriarchal Narratives of Genesis, rather than the Conquest Narratives of Joshua-Judges, offer the clearest historical memory of the northern Negeb in the pre-monarchy period. But this is an oversimplification. It is likely that opposing forces in the period when Israel was based at Qadesh-barnea were so small as to leave scant artifactual evidence of northern Negeb confrontations.

15. *Libnah.* See 10:29-30. Maps B, 112, D, 260, and G, 364.

Adullam. Maps B and G. See 15:35; Gen 38:1; 1 Sam 22:1. Neither king nor conquest of either Libnah or Adullam is mentioned elsewhere. The site of Adullam is Tell esh-Sheikh Madhkûr, c. 16 km northeast of Beit Guvrin.

16a. *Maqqedah.* See 10:10,28 and NOTES.

16b-24. This is the third part of the list, naming kings from the central and northern regions, and closely related (except at the outset) to chap. 11.

16b. *Bethel.* Maps B, 112, and H, 398. It was, later on, an important border sanctuary of the northern kingdom. The only story of its takeover by Israel is another Dtr 2 text—Judg 1:22-26. Excavations at Beitin have shown that its destruction in the late thirteenth century was followed immediately by substantial reoccupation. It must in fact have been influential in that area where new unwalled settlements rapidly increased in number at the beginning of the Iron Age. See above on the story of The Ruin, chaps. 7-8. The early significance of Bethel (see Judges 20, another Dtr 2 text) was either forgotten or played down by the Jerusalem historian who produced the first edition of Joshua. The final editor's concern to correct an imbalance, by focusing on the north-central region, continues in vv 17 and 18.

17-18. These verses, together with the reference to Tirzah in v 24, indicate that the conversion of north-central Canaan did not proceed entirely without violence. It is significant, however, that none of the places named would be in a position to disrupt communication between Shechem and the south.

17. *Tappuah.* Previously unmentioned. It is on the border between Ephraim and Manasseh (16:8; 17:8). The site is Tell Sheikh Abū Zarad, c. 12.8 km southwest of Nablus. Maps B, p. 112, and H, p. 398. The next name in the list is likewise related to Manasseh.

Hepher. A clan of Manasseh (Num 27:1), situated north of Shechem. Map I, 408.

18a. *Apheq.* Map B, 112. It is necessary to distinguish this Apheq from several others, including those in Phoenicia east of Byblos (13:4), in Asher (19:30), and in Bashan (1 Kgs 20:26,30; 2 Kgs 13:17). The Late Bronze occupation at Ras el-'Ayin included a palace which was destroyed and robbed at the very end of LB. Survey of the surrounding area found a small Israelite settlement at Isbet Sarte (possibly Ebenezer) overlooking Apheq from the hills about 3.4 km to the east. A late LB destruction may be assigned to the Philistines who continued to control Apheq (if 1 Sam 4:1 refers to the same place), so that it was never included in specific tribal claims. See the reports by Moshe Kochavi, "Tel Aphek," *IEJ* 24 (1974) 261-262; "Tel Aphek, 1975," *IEJ* 26 (1976) 51-52; "Tel Aphek, 1976," *IEJ* 27 (1977) 54-55.

Lasharon. The Hebrew means "for the Sharon(-plain)," and is perhaps intended to cover the entire region which was very sparsely settled due to swampy and malarial conditions in antiquity. Map B, 112.

19-23. Most of these kings are either mentioned in the story of Jabin's coalition in chap. 11, or belong to the coalition's homeland.

19-20. Galilee and northern Sharon are in view here.

19. *king of Madon.* One of the few conquered kings whose name, Jobab, survived (11:1).

Hazor. Ruled by Jabin. Chapter 11 (cf. Judges 4). Maps B, 112, and J, 444.

20. *Shimron-meron.* Map B (Merom). See 11:1. This is apparently the town of Zebulun called simply "Shimron" in 19:15.

Achshaph. Map J, 444. See 11:1. It belongs to Asher in 19:25.

21-23. *Taanach. Megiddo. Joqneam in Carmel. Dor.* All are towns in Manassite territory. Concerning the first, second, and fourth of these, Manasseh is specifically faulted for failure to bring about the desired changes in land tenure. Judges 1:27.

21. *Taanach.* Maps B, 112, and H, 398. Assigned to Manasseh (17:11), and designated a Levitical town (21:25). Here the extensive and careful excavations have disclosed a sharp contrast within the twelfth-century town, between rich and poor residential quarters, suggestive of a situation where in fact Canaanites and Yahwists were living side by side. The town was finally destroyed about 1125, and the excavator was inclined to associate that destruction with the events celebrated in the Song of Deborah (Judg 5:19). Paul W. Lapp, "The 1968 Excavations at Tell Ta'annek," *BASOR* 195 (October 1969) 33-39.

Megiddo. Maps B, 112, and H, 398. Assigned to Manasseh in 17:11, the name means "Stronghold," and not inappropriately, as excavations have shown. Together with "Taanach by Megiddo's Stream" (Judg 5:19) it controlled the southern flank of Esdraelon and the most heavily traveled route through the Mount Carmel range to the Plain of Sharon. The witness of the rich cultural remains to a strong city-state continues uninterrupted in Iron I until meeting a violent end about 1130 (end of Stratum VII). This was followed by a sharp decline, with evidence of a different social organization (Stratum VI B, "Israelite"), which in turn gave way to a new public-building phase (Stratum VI A, probably Philistine) apparently lasting until the Davidic conquests. Yigael Yadin, "Megiddo," *EAEHL* III (1977) 847-851.

22. *Qedesh*. Not to be confused with the great sanctuary city in the far north of Naphtali (19:37), this one is probably to be found in the neighborhood of Tell Abu Qudeis, between Megiddo and Taanach. Map B, 112.

Joqneam. Listed on Zebulun's border with Manasseh in 19:11, and a Levitical town in 21:34. Maps B, 112, and J, 444. The site is Tell Qeimun at the western edge of the Jezreel Valley (at the tip of Zebulun's southwestern wedge). The fact that there is no mention of Joqneam among the unconquered towns in 17:11 and Judg 1:27 suggested to Aharoni that it had become Israelite at a very early stage of the conquest and settlement. *WHJP III* (1971) 119.

in Carmel. This specification of the northern border of Manasseh avoids a possible confusion with Joqmeam, a Levitical town in Ephraim. See 21:22 as reconstructed with the help of 1 Chr 6:53[6:68E].

23a. *Dor*. Map B, p. 112. See 11:2 and NOTES.

that is. Hebrew *l* introduces the parenthetical element.

23b. The LXX reading, "king of the *Gôyîm* of Galilee," suggests the name of Sisera's hometown in Judg 4:2, "Harosheth-haggoyim." The latter is perhaps to be identified with *Muhrashti* of the Amarna Letters (*Die El-Amarna Tafeln*, 335:17), which is to be sought somewhere in the Plain of Sharon. Gus W. van Beek, *IDB* 3, 526. Compare also "Galilee of the *Gôyîm*" in Isa 8:23[9:1E].

24. *Tirzah*. Also a clan of Manasseh in Num 27:1. The town is possibly Tell el-Far'ah (north), c. 10 km northeast of Shechem. Maps B, 112, and I, 408. Here we return to the north-central hill country, to a town which in fact was first favored as capital by the northern throne (1 Kings 14-16) when it moved the seat of government away from Shechem! We may assume that the latter had become a storm center of Levitical protest against the fact that the son of Solomon (Rehoboam) had been replaced in the north by the former overseer of Solomon's forced labor (Jeroboam I). The list ends abruptly with the first capital of the northern kingdom, long since destroyed by the time of the Dtr historians, who placed it last without giving it a geographical or rhetorical companion.

Thirty-one. In an area roughly the size of Vermont, this would appear to have been characteristic of political fragmentation elsewhere around the Fertile Crescent at the end of the Late Bronze and throughout Iron I. Early in Iron II Ben-hadad of Damascus headed a coalition of "thirty-two kings who helped him." 1 Kings 20:1. Ashurbanipal received tribute after his first campaign in 668 from thirty-three kings of Palestine and southern Syria (*ANET*[2], 294). See also Landes, "The Material Civilization of the Ammonites," *BA* 24 (1961) 81=*BAR* 2 (1964) 84.

COMMENT

Not content with a collection of stories which exalts a single great leader
and a rhetorical framework which resolves the tension in Yahweh's opposition to the "nations," the final editor, who was faced with the collapse
of the southern kingdom, forces the reader to reflect on the transitoriness
of kingdoms. How will it ever be possible to escape the domination of
kings?

That is precisely the question to which the original Moses-movement
had addressed itself. "The Hebrew conquest of Palestine took place because a religious movement and motivation created a solidarity among a
large group of pre-existing social units. . . ." Mendenhall, "The Hebrew
Conquest of Palestine," *BA* 25 (1962) 73=*BAR* 3 (1970) 107. The objection to this historical reconstruction has been that "local kings and
their followers took part" in the Amarna Age intrigues which provide the
nearest extra-biblical evidence for the process more than a century earlier
(Weippert, *The Settlement,* 74). But it is necessary to distinguish carefully between the bulk of the Hebrew groups involved in those earlier
struggles and those Hebrews who became converts to the religion of
Moses. At the center of the authentic religion of Israel was a trust in
ethic displacing the religious legitimation of power. Attention to the role
of ethic would enable the religion repeatedly to survive political disaster.
That is what the readers of Dtr 2 were faced with—the loss of a land and
divine-right monarchy ruling it.

B. REDISTRIBUTION OF THE LAND 13:1-19:51

1. TRANSJORDAN FLASHBACK
(13:1-33)

a. Land That Remains

13 ¹ When Joshua had reached a ripe old age, Yahweh said to Joshua: "Although you have reached a ripe old age, much of the land remains to be taken. ² This is the land that remains:

> All the districts of the Philistines and the Gezerites. ³ From the Shihor which is east of Egypt, to the Eqron border up north, it is considered Canaanite. (There were five Philistine tyrants: the Gazathite, the Ashdothite, the Ashqelonite, the Gittite, and the Eqronite.) Also the Avvim ⁴ from the south. All the Canaanite land, that is, from Arah (which belongs to the Sidonians) to Apheq, to the border of . . . ⁵ the Giblites and all of Lebanon eastward, from Baal-gad beneath Mount Hermon to the Entrance of Hamath. ⁶ All the inhabitants of the hill country, from the Lebanon to Misrephoth-maim. All the Sidonians. I will evict them before the Bene Israel.

Simply allot it to Israel in fief, exactly as I have commanded you. ⁷ Apportion this land in fief right now for the nine tribes and the half-tribe of Manasseh. From the Jordan to the Great Sea of the setting sun you shall bestow it, the Great Sea being the border."

As for the two tribes and the other half-tribe of Manasseh, ⁸ the Reubenites and the Gadites together with it had taken their fiefs which Moses gave them on the eastern side of the Jordan:

> ⁹ from Aroer at the edge of the Arnon Gorge and the "town in the gorge" (all the plateau from Madeba to Dibon; ¹⁰ all the cities of Sihon, the Amorite king, who had reigned at Heshbon) to the border of the Bene Ammon. ¹¹ Gilead, with the territory of the Geshurites and Maacathites, and all of Mount Hermon and all of Bashan, as far as Salecah; ¹² all the realm of Og in

Bashan, who had reigned at Ashtaroth and Edrei (he had remained as a survivor of the last of the Rephaim). Moses had defeated them and evicted them. 13 The Bene Israel did not evict the Geshurites and the Maacathites; and there lives a king of the Geshurites and the Maacathites in Israel to this day.

14 Only to the Levite tribe did he give no fief; offerings by fire to Yahweh God of Israel are its "fief," exactly as he promised it.

This is the division of estates which Moses worked out for the Bene Israel in the plains of Moab, in the region across the Jordan from Jericho.

b. Reuben

15 Moses made a grant to the Bene Reuben tribe, for their clans.

16 Their territory was from Aroer at the edge of the Arnon Gorge, and the "town in the Gorge," including all the plateau around Medeba; 17 Heshbon on the plateau with all its towns (Dibon, Bamoth-baal, Beth-baal-meon, 18 Jahaz, Qedemoth, Mephaath, 19 Qiryathaim, Sibmah, Zereth-shahar on Valley Mountain, 20 Beth-peor, Slopes of Pisgah, Beth-jeshimoth), 21 yes, all the towns of the plateau; that is, all from the realm of Sihon, the Amorite king who had reigned at Heshbon, whom Moses had defeated.

The Midianite chieftains (Evi, Reqem, Zur, Hur, and Reba), Sihon's princes who were enthroned in the land, 22 and the diviner Balaam ben Beor the Bene Israel also put to the sword, in addition to those already slain.

23 The boundary of the Bene Reuben was the Jordan. This is the fief of the Bene Reuben for their clans: the towns with their fenced areas.

c. Gad

24 Moses made a grant to the Bene Gad, for their clans.

25 Their territory was Jazer and all the Gilead towns (that is, half of the land of the Bene Ammon as far as Aroer which is west of Rabbah) 26 and from Heshbon as far as Ramath-mizpeh and Betonim; and from Mahanaim to the territory of Debir;

27 and in the valley Beth-haram, Beth-nimrah, Succoth, and Zaphon; the remainder of the kingdom of Sihon, king of Heshbon; with the Jordan as a border as far as the tip of the Sea of Chinnereth on the east-Jordan side. 28 This is the fief of the Bene Gad for their clans: the towns with their fenced areas.

d. Eastern Manasseh

29 Moses made a grant to the half-tribe of Manasseh for their clans. 30 Their territory reached from Mahanaim throughout Bashan, all the kingdom of Og, king of Bashan, all of Jair's tent-villages in Bashan. Sixty towns. 31 Half of Gilead, including Ashtaroth and Edrei, Og's royal cities in Bashan, belong to the descendants of Machir, a "son" of Manasseh (in other words, to the half-tribe Bene Machir) for their clans.

32 These are what Moses gave in fief beyond the Jordan in the plains of Moab east of Jericho.

33 But to the Levite tribe Moses gave no fief. Yahweh the God of Israel is himself their fief, as he promised them.

TEXTUAL NOTES

13 1. *to Joshua*   This follows LXX (*'l yhwš*) where MT has instead a pronoun object (*'lyw*).

"Although you have reached a ripe old age   With MT, where LXX shows an auditory lapse: *'t[h zqnt]h.* The spelling of *zqnth* shows the long form of the second person masculine singular ending.

2. *All*   This word is omitted in LXX. It is used twice in MT and should be deleted at its second occurrence in MT.

Gezerites   This is LXX *geseirei,* where MT reads "Geshurites" for which the LXX transcription in 12:5 is *gesouri.* Here LXX adds "and the Canaanites" under the influence of v 3.

3. *Also the Avvim* 4 *from the south*   This sentence division is based on Syr. The statement is perhaps a gloss on the preceding list.

4. *from Arah*   This division of MT *m'rh,* "cave," is proposed by Soggin, *Joshua,* 147, 149. It helps to explain LXX *gazes,* presumably=Hebrew *'zh,* "Gaza," as a confusion of names, probably due to a mutilated text, with a number of reflexes which then followed in the LXX.

. . . 5 *the Giblites*   A satisfactory connection between vv 4 and 5 cannot be

reconstructed. Verse 4 ends with "border of the Amorites." At the beginning of
v 5, MT specifies "and the land of" the Giblites, where LXX reads instead *'rṣ
glyt hplyšty,* which looks like a partial repetition from v 2.

6. *before the Bene Israel*   LXX shows a haplography: *mpn*[*y   bn*]*y   yśr'l,*
"before Israel."

7. *From the Jordan . . . half-tribe of Manasseh*   This is restored from
LXX where MT shows an omission triggered by the repetition of reference to
the "half-tribe of Manasseh."

8. *had taken their fiefs which*   Omitted from LXX.

Jordan   MT and LXX[B] continue "exactly as Moses, Servant of Yahweh,
had given them."

10. *all*   This is LXX, Syr[AW], where MT has smoothed out the transition by
adding a conjunction, "and all the cities . . ."

11. *Salecah*   LXX *acha* seems to reflect an inner-Greek haplography after
the original pronunciation had already become obscure: *heōs*[*s*]*acha.*

13. *Geshurites*   In this chapter LXX has leveled through the spelling
geseirei.

Maacathites   LXX continues formulaically "and the Canaanites."

a king of   With LXX, which is surely the more difficult reading. MT omits.

14. *he*   This is MT. LXX uses the passive verb. There is weak support in
Hebrew manuscripts and Targ[f] for the name "Moses" as subject.

offerings by fire to   This is MT *'šy,* retained as the more difficult reading,
against LXX. Cf. v 33.

he   LXX reflects *yhwh,* which removes the ambiguity of subject.

This is the division . . . across the Jordan from Jericho   This is restored
from LXX after a long haplography: *l*[*w . . . yrḥ*]*w.*

16. *the Gorge"*   LXX specifies "Arnon Gorge."

around Medeba   This is *'l mydb',* omitted in the major Greek recensions.
There is support in other manuscripts of LXX, Syriac, and Targum for reading
'd mydb', "as far as Madeba."

19. *Zereth-shahar*   LXX reads the two elements as separate names:
"Zereth" and "Shahar."

21. *from*   The text makes sense if *mmlkwt* is revocalized to read as noun
with prefixed preposition.

Reqem   LXX *Rabok.*

in the land   In place of this phrase LXX repeats the name of the overlord: "by Sihon."

22. *in addition to*   Emending *'l* to *'l,* as frequently suggested, with some
support in manuscripts.

in addition to those already slain   LXX omits.

23. *Bene*   LXX omits.

the sixth occurrence   LXX has the pronoun "their" leveled through.

their second occurrence   The pronoun suffix is feminine in the best witnesses, with the feminine noun "towns" as antecedent. Cf. v 28, where the
pattern of the evidence is just the reverse!

24. *Bene Gad*   MT is conflate: "to the tribe of Gad, to the Bene Gad."

LXX lacks the first, Syriac the second. Neither one is an exact parallel to "the Bene Reuben tribe" in v 15.

25. *Aroer which is west of Rabbah*)   In LXX this becomes "Arabah which is opposite Arad."

26. *from Mahanaim*   Haplography in LXX *Vorlage* dropped the preposition: *m[m]ḥnym.*

Debir   This agrees with LXX, Syriac, Vulgate (Greenspoon, STBJ, 203-204). MT *lidebir,* however, may be incorrectly pointed and identical with Lo-debar in 2 Sam 9:4-5; 17:27; Amos 6:13.

27. *valley Beth-haram*   LXX seems to read the first word as a noun in the construct state: "Valley of Beth-haram."

28. *their fenced areas*   Here the pronoun suffix is masculine in the strongest witnesses, apparently construed with Bene Gad as antecedent. See above, third Textual Note on v 23.

29. *Manasseh*   MT inserts "and there belonged to the half-tribe of Manasseh" in an apparently conflate text. Here we follow the OG.

30. *throughout*   Literally, "and all." LXX and Syriac reflect the conjunction that is lacking in MT.

31. *Machir*   LXX misses the covenantal nuance of "son" and repeats the specification that Machir is *bn mnśh,* presumably to be understood in the genealogical sense.

33. The verse is missing in LXX. See NOTE on v 14b.

NOTES

13:1-33. The Yahwist revolution in Transjordan occurred under the leadership of Moses (Numbers 21-25, 32). In the Book of Joshua the Transjordan events are recounted with emphasis only in chaps. 12 and 13. These chapters fall within a formulaic repetition concerning the cessation of warfare (11:23 and 14:15). They display features which mark them as a contribution by the later editor. Otherwise, the early history of the Bene Israel in Transjordan is mentioned only briefly, in 24:8-10. Chapter 24 is a much older document left largely unrevised by Dtr 1. It seems clear, in other words, that the first edition of the Book of Joshua dealt mainly with the west bank, as the area effectively ruled by King Josiah (2 Kings 22-23 // 2 Chronicles 34-35). There is in fact a tension between the epic tradition and Deuteronomistic doctrine. According to the former, the Bene Reuben and the Bene Gad had said to Moses and Eleazar and the leaders of the congregation, in effect: We want to settle here in Transjordan. The request was regarded as rebellion and the reconciliation effected was uneasy (chap. 22).

That older tradition did not serve the construction of the Josianic ideal; it was simply ignored in the first edition.

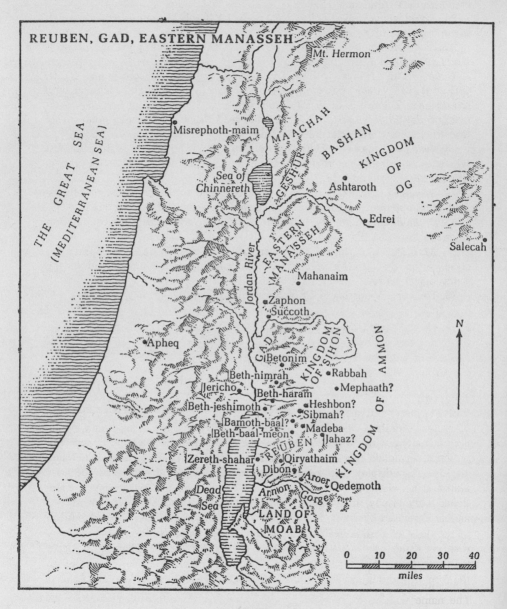

REUBEN, GAD, EASTERN MANASSEH

Mt. Hermon

MAACHAH

Misrephoth-maim

BASHAN

GESHUR

KINGDOM OF OG

THE GREAT SEA (MEDITERRANEAN SEA)

Sea of Chinnereth

Ashtaroth

Edrei

Salecah

EASTERN MANASSEH

Jordan River

Mahanaim

Zaphon
Succoth

N

•Apheq

GAD

KINGDOM OF SIHON

•Betonim

Rabbah
•Mephaath?

KINGDOM OF AMMON

Beth-nimrah

Jericho•
Beth-haram

Heshbon?

Beth-jeshimoth

Sibmah?

Bamoth-baal?

Madeba

Beth-baal-meon

Jahaz?

REUBEN

Zereth-shahar

Qiryathaim

Dibon•
Aroer

Qedemoth

Dead
Sea

Arnon
Gorge

LAND OF MOAB

0   10   20   30   40
miles

Map F

13:1-14. This introduction to the allotment of the land served the purpose of emphasizing to later exiles that Yahweh had at the outset designated the entire region—east and west—as Israel's fief. It thus affirmed that the true Israel is better represented by Moses' expectations than by Joshua's actual accomplishments.

1. *had reached a ripe old age.* Hebrew *zqn b' bymym*. Literally, "was old; he had entered into the days/years." We might say he was "getting along in years." It is a distinctive idiom which occurs again in 23:1 (Joshua's farewell address, also a Dtr 2 contribution). There it reads smoothly as part of a long conditional clause. Here, where it is not being anticipated, it is disjunctive; and the effect is to startle. Repetition of the idiom in Yahweh's speech reinforces the impression. This lengthy insert into the work of Dtr 1 will end on the upbeat with elderly Caleb still capable of going into the field against the Anaqim (14:6-15).

2-6. *the land that remains* to be redistributed to the Bene Israel is here described. For fuller discussion of the historical geography, see Aharoni, *LOB*, 215-217. There is no mention of Jerusalem, which did not come finally into Israel's control until the reign of David (2 Sam 5:6-10). The tradition of Dtr 2, however, knew of successes against the Jerusalem hills which occurred early but were inconclusive (Judg 1:8,21), and so this omission is not surprising.

2-5. *All . . . From the Shihor . . . to the Entrance of Hamath.* This most extravagant description of the extent of the Israelite conquest is perhaps to be recognized as hyperbole in Dtr 2. It was later taken literally by the Chronicler who uses the same pair of terms in 1 Chr 13:5 to encompass "all Israel." On the Chronicler's devaluation of Joshua and conquest in favor of a concern for "settlement and inhabitancy," see Sara Japhet, "Conquest and Settlement in Chronicles," *JBL* 98 (1979) 205-218.

2 and 3. *Philistine(s).* They are mentioned only here in the book, clear evidence that we are on new literary terrain in this section. They do not comprise one of the "seven nations" (3:10), but came to the southern coast of Canaan as part of a later wave of the "People of the Sea" who attacked Egypt in the reigns of Merneptah and Ramesses III (late thirteenth and early twelfth centuries B.C.), "after having ravaged the Hittite country, the Cilician and North Syrian coast, Carchemish, and Cyprus." Jonas C. Greenfield, "Philistines," *IDB* 3, 792. See especially, Wright, "Fresh Evidence for the Philistine Story," *BA* 29 (1966) 70-86.

2. *Gezerites.* The location of Gezer (Map B, 112) makes them neighbors on the north side of the Philistine pentapolis. They should not be confused with Geshurites of northern Transjordan in v 11 (see also 12:5).

3. *the Shihor.* The name probably designates "the lower reaches of the Bubastite or Pelusiac Nile arm." Thomas O. Lambdin, "Shihor," *IDB* 4, 328. The name was no longer understood by LXX translators, who rendered as "uninhabited" here; cf. "Gihon" in Jer 2:8, and "boundaries" in 1 Chr 13:5.

five . . . tyrants. Hebrew *srn* is cognate to Aegean-Anatolian *tyrannos*, "tyrant." Thus it contrasts with both *mlk*, "king," and *nś'/zqn*, "chief"/"elder," on the Canaanite scene. The great Philistine pentapolis of the southern coast was balanced by another pentapolis in the north (Beth-shean, Taanach, Dor, Ibleam, Megiddo), as recognized by D. N. Freedman. See *Judges,* AB 6A, 60.

Philistine. Nowhere in the Warfare section of the book does Joshua explicitly encounter Philistines. In 11:22, however, the three towns of Gaza, Gath, and Ashdod are occupied by Anaqim, another name that is best explained as either Anatolian or Hurrian. The Philistines, who came later, also became most successful of all the Sea Peoples; so that "Philistine" became a summary word for the non-indigenous opposition to Israel. The label was finally adopted in Rome's imperial administration for the province "Palestine."

Gittite. Person of Gath.

Avvim. Also Deut 2:23 (cf. 2 Kgs 17:31). They were settled in the neighborhood of Gaza, only to be at last attacked and displaced by people from Caphtor (Crete), that is, "Philistines." LXX here translates as *heuaiō* which also renders "Hivites" and would point to the earlier Sea Peoples for their origins. This name should probably be distinguished from the village Avvim near Bethel in Benjamin (18:23). The Benjaminite town must somehow be related to Ha-Ai, "The Ruin," in chaps. 7 and 8.

4. *Arah.* Otherwise unknown.

Apheq. Probably Afqā, east of Byblos, and thus not to be confused with the Philistine Apheq in Sharon (12:18) shown on Map F, 336.

5. *Giblites.* People of Gebal, "Byblos." Map A, 81. We are thus reminded that the "conquest and settlement" in the far north was in fact never completed, a corrective to the sweeping summary in 11:23.

Baal-gad. See 11:17 and 12:7.

to the Entrance of Hamath. Num 13:21; 34:8; Judg 3:3 (where we rendered "approach to Hamath"). The entrance or approach is the line of the Orontes River in its northwesterly course. Map A, 81. Thus Dtr 2 not only fills out the Israel of the east-west axis, but also points to a deficiency in the earlier edition's claims for the far north. Included in the region here described would be the "land of Amka" in the southern Lebanese Beqaʻ, discussed above in the fourth NOTE on 1:4.

6. This disjointed conclusion to the description, in the first half of the verse, may reflect a mutilated ending to the old source used by Dtr 2.

Misrephoth-maim. Map B, 112. See NOTES on 11:8.

I will evict . . . Simply allot it to Israel in fief. As in the earlier military organization at Mari, the sequence is gift now in exchange for the promise of future service. It was indeed a promised land which Yahweh would claim first for himself. Ancient Israel's hope for prosperity in the land and a just social order there is rooted in the assurance that God retains sole ownership: "the land is mine" (Lev 25:23).

7-33. It is possible that the boundary notices of all the tribes now listed in chaps. 13-19 derive ultimately from a single ancient document "which incorporated a unified scheme of tribal bounds." Cross and Wright, "The Boundary and Province Lists . . . ," *JBL* 75 (1956) 207. In that epoch-making study it is acknowledged that the evidence on the tribes east of Jordan is the least conclusive. It appears rather that in chap. 13 the purpose was to "give a *total* idea of

the land in Transjordan which was distributed among the eastern tribes. . . ."
Ottoson, *Gilead,* 119.

7. *Manasseh.* Maps F, 336, and H, 398. Unlike the mighty tribe of Gad,
which enjoyed the largest and best parts of Transjordan, there are many indications that this tribal name was originally at home west of the river. Numbers 26:29-33; 27:1; 32:1; 36:1-12; Josh 12:17,24; 17:1-3; 22:9; Judg 5:14,17.
See J. Liver, "The Israelite Tribes," *WHJP* II (1970) 208. It is worth noting,
therefore, that the northern component is mentioned first, although the epic
texts are concerned mainly with Reuben and Gad and the entry from the south.
This arrangement is from the hand of Dtr 2, with its deep roots in the north.

8. *Reubenites.* For evidence of their earlier presence on both sides of the
river, see below on v 15.

them. This reading in MT and Theodotion refers to the entire cluster of two
and one-half tribes in Transjordan. The Old Greek read "it," focusing attention
primarily on the eastern half of Manasseh. Greenspoon, STBJ, 160-161.

9-12. This section might well have served as documentary source for
the introduction to the larger section in 12:1-5. It is strikingly similar to
Deut 3:8,10a, which belongs to the secondary introduction to that book.
The reliability of the traditions regarding conquest of the Amorite kingdoms has been seriously questioned by Van Seters, "The Conquest of Sihon's
Kingdom: A Literary Examination," *JBL* 91 (1972) 182-197. See the response
by Bartlett, "The Conquest of Sihon's Kingdom: A Literary Re-examination,"
JBL 97 (1978) 347-351. In any case, the date of redaction or editing should
not prejudice the question of memory and reliable content. Only the most
naive would argue that a document must be untainted by ideology in order to
be regarded as a carrier of reliable historical memory. Such a totally unbiased
source is rarely encountered.

9. *Aroer.* Map F, 336. See 12:2 and NOTES. Excavations at Khirbet 'Ara'ir
have produced evidence for EB, MB, LB, Iron I; the site was most heavily
occupied in the first and last of those periods.

"town in the Gorge." See 12:2 and NOTE.

Madeba. Map F, 336. Some 11.2 km south of Ḥesbân, Madeba is archaeologically attested for the period of transition from the Late Bronze Age to Iron
I in the rich contents of one excavated tomb.

Dibon. Map F, 336. Called "Dibon-gad" in Num 33:45. Archaeologically
well-attested for EB, Iron I, and subsequent periods. See A. Douglas Tushingham, "The Excavations at Dibon (DHIBAN) in Moab, 1952-53," AASOR 40
(1972). Outside the Bible, Dibon is first mentioned in a relief at Luxor, claiming its conquest by Ramesses II (*ANET,* 242-243). This text also contains the
first reference to "Moab" in an Egyptian source. Prior to the time of Ramesses
II there is no reference in Egyptian records to any town between the Arnon
and the Jabboq. K. A. Kitchen, *JEA* 50 (1964) 53*f.*

10-13. The kingdoms of northern and central Transjordan would be separated from the Amorite homeland by the emerging Aramean kingdoms of
Syria, following the decline of the Hittite and Egyptian empires. This explains
the lack of contact between Israel and Aram throughout most of the period of

Joshua-Judges, and the eventual fate of the Amorite buffer states in Transjordan.

10. *Heshbon*. See 12:2 and NOTE. Map F, 336.

11. For all these names see 12:2-5 text apparatus and NOTES.

12. *Rephaim*. See NOTES on 12:4.

13. *did not evict*. The sentence is formulated in the style of the inventory of failure found in Judg 1:27-35, which was also an editorial contribution of Dtr 2.

lives . . . in Israel. It may have something to do with the network of dynastic marriages. Absalom's mother was a princess of Geshur, whose name was Maacah (2 Sam 3:3). Regarding the probable merger of the royal houses of Israel and Ammon, see Mendenhall, *Ten Gen*, 191.

a king of the Geshurites and the Maacathites. See Geshur and Maacah, Map F, 336. Unfortunately nothing is known of this political development.

to this day. This suggests that for Dtr 2 in Joshua, the final destruction of Jerusalem in 587 had not yet occurred.

14a. This is the first of two brief references to the tribe of Levi in the chapter. It is repeated, with less specificity, in v 33. LXX has the text of v 33 at v 14 and omits v 33 altogether. However, both verses must be retained, since v 33 cannot be explained as any kind of dittography. LXX is at least partially explainable; a scribe copied the second text in the first position, perhaps working from memory.

Levite. This class of people constitutes a major preoccupation of the Dtr editors. Usages referring to Levitical personnel are discussed above in NOTES on 3:3.

promised. Hebrew *dbr* used in this special sense (see v 33 and 22:4; 23:5,10) is Deuteronomistic. Cross cites Deut 1:11; 6:3; 9:3,28; 10:9; 11:25; 12:20; 15:6; 18:2; 26:18; 27:3; 29:12. *CMHE*, 254.

14b. With the restoration of this companion piece for v 32, the reason for the two Levite verses becomes clear; they form a chiastic framework for vv 15-31, which supplement the very meager description of Transjordan allotments in an earlier edition of the source. The origin of this frame is to be seen in Deut 18:1-2 where the explanations that the Joshua editor keeps separate ("offerings by fire" in v 14 and "Yahweh the God of Israel" as the Levitical lot in v 33) are juxtaposed. Neither half of this explanation is as important to Dtr 2 as the one he will introduce in 14:3-4 (the Levites have instead residential rights and pasturelands at certain towns of every tribe!). Thus the two statements about the Levite tribe in chap. 13 form a classic example of "repetitive resumption." Compare the repetition of "The land had rest from war," which frames the larger section into which this one is, in turn, inserted (11:23 and 14:15).

15-31. The description of the Transjordan tribes "bears a stamp of its own. This description has come down to us in its entirety, with none of the fragmentariness of c. [chap.] 19. In spite of this it contains no detail about boundaries." Kaufmann, *The Biblical Account of the Conquest of Palestine*, 26-27.

15-28. The pattern described in these verses (Reuben in the south, Gad in the north) is at odds with the epic tradition in Num 32:34-38. In the latter, Reuben's towns are clustered around Heshbon, and Gad's towns range from Dibon and Aroer in the south to include several towns located north of Heshbon, the towns of Jazer, Jogbebah, and Beth-nimrah. It is possible that the epic tradition represents the early arrangement continuing into the reign of David, but that the text in our verses reflects a reorganization under Solomon. Aharoni, *LOB*, 80.

15. *Reuben*. Map F, 336. The eponymous ancestor was the firstborn son of Jacob (his mother was Leah); he is always mentioned first. Gen 35:23; 46:8,9; Exod 1:2; 1 Chr 2:1. Restriction of Reuben came early.

> Let Reuben live, let him not die
> Let his men be beyond (*mn*) counting (*spr*)

(Deuteronomy 33:6, following M. Dahood, *Biblica* 48 [1967] 429.) For the alternative but less poetic rendering of the second line, "though his men be few," see F. M. Cross and D. N. Freedman, *JBL* 67 (1948) 193=*SAYP*, 99. In any case the lines reflect a concern for Reuben's status. The ninth-century stele of Mesha king of Moab mentions only Gad, not Reuben. In the following centuries two of the prophets will know the area only as Moabite (Isaiah 15-16; Jeremiah 48). In other words, the final editor would have the reader remember that Reuben had started out as a highly significant element in the Transjordan Yahweh movement, but under the monarchy had fallen on hard times. The latter seems somehow to be reflected in the tradition that Reuben went to bed with another matriarch, Bilhah (Gen 35:22). The archaic poetic tradition also survives:

> Reuben, my first-born
> You are my strength, and the first fruit of my vigor,
> Overweening in arrogance,
> Overweening in force.
> You are unsteady as water. You shall not excell.
> You took over the bed of your father's beloved.
> You profaned the couch of your father's beloved.

Genesis 49:3-4 after M. Patrick O'Connor, *Hebrew Verse Structure* (Winona Lake, IN: Eisenbrauns, 1980) 170. The rendering follows Dahood, redividing the consonantal text in the last line to read *ysw'-y'lh* (MT *ysw'y 'lh*). On the testament of Jacob as a whole see E. A. Speiser, *Genesis*, AB 1 (1964) 361-372. The affair of Reuben and Bilhah took place at Migdal-eder, which is in the vicinity of Bethlehem of Judah ("Tower of the Flock" translates *migdal-eder* in Mic 4:8). An important border-point between Judah and Benjamin is the "stone of Bohan ben Reuben" (Josh 15:6; 18:17). There is thus substantial evidence that the Bene Reuben once ranged widely in the mountains and plateau flanking the northern end of the Dead Sea, on both sides of the river.

their clans. Hebrew *mšphwtm*. This word is ubiquitous in the description of allotments and is often taken to be a sign of "Priestly" source or redaction. It contrasts, however, with much later Hebrew usage, not with the pre-exilic biblical usage. Avi Hurvitz, "The Evidence of Language in Dating the Priestly Code," *RB* 81 (1974) 26-28.

16. *plateau*. Hebrew *mîšōr*. This is the rich tableland east of the Jordan Valley rift, which stretches away at an altitude of some 1,216 meters above Jericho. Here it must be the name of an administrative district since several of the places lie far below, en route to the Dead Sea and Jordan River fords.

17-20. The twelve liberated towns are listed in four groups of three each, roughly spaced around the Medeba-Heshbon axis. To the south and southwest are Dibon, Bamoth-baal, Beth-baal-meon. To the southeast are Jahaz, Qedemoth, Mephaath(?). To the west of Medeba are Qiryathaim, Sibmah, Zereth-shahar(?) on Valley Mountain. West of Heshbon and northeast of the Dead Sea are Beth-peor, Slopes of Pisgah, Beth-jeshimoth.

17. (*Dibon*. See above on v 9. Only here is it clearly assigned to Reuben.

Bamoth-baal. Prominent in the setting for the Baalam stories (Num 22:41), it is simply "Bamoth" in 21:19-20. It is presumably the *bt-bmt* mentioned by the king of Moab (Mesha Stele, line 27, tr. W. F. Albright, *ANET*[3], 320-321). Khirbet el-Queiqiyeh south of Mount Nebo meets the requirements. Simons, *Handbook,* ⚹449. Map F, 336.

Beth-baal-meon. Numbers 32:38 (so also read in Num 32:3) refers to this town in the epic tradition which links it with the Bene Reuben. Mentioned in the Mesha Stele, line 30. The name survives as modern *Ma'în,* c. 7.2 km southwest of Ḥesbân. Map F, 336.

18. *Jahaz*. This was an important place which is later designated a Levitical town (21:36); it was site of the battle between Israel and Sihon's forces (Num 21:23; Deut 2:32; Judg 11:20). Later it was fortified by the "King of Israel" (probably Jehu) and used as military headquarters in the ninth-century warfare against Moab (Mesha Stele, lines 18-19). The location is possibly Khirbet el-Medeiniyeh at the desert fringe, where Glueck and Albright reported pottery of early Iron I and early Iron II. Map F, 336.

Qedemoth. Map F. Also a Levitical town (21:37); and also figuring in the showdown between Sihon and Israel (Deut 2:26), where Israel is camped "in the Qedemoth desert." The best candidate is es-Saliyeh just north of the Arnon at the edge of the desert, with occupation continuing unbroken from the Late Bronze Age through Iron II, supporting the identification proposed by A. H. van Zyl, *The Moabites,* 78, 85.

Mephaath. Another Levitical town or, more likely, village (21:37). Khirbet Nēf'ah, c. 8 km south of Amman, may preserve the name; the OT site seems most likely to have been the nearby Tell ej-Jāwah. Map F, 336.

19. *Qiryathaim*. Possibly the Qaryaten later fortified by the king of Moab (Mesha Stele, line 10). The site is identified with Qereiyat el-Mekhaiyet, the twin ruin some 9.6 km northwest of Dibon. Map F.

Sibmah. Possibly Khirbet el-Qibsh, c. 4.8 km southwest of Ḥesbān. Map F.

Zereth-shahar on Valley Mountain. Probably Zārât on Mount 'Aṭṭarus overlooking the Dead Sea (Map F); the hot springs down on the eastern seashore (Callirhoe) could not be said to be on a mountain. The specification that this one is *bĕhar hā-'ēmeq,* literally, "on a mountain of the valley," was necessary because of the wider description which included the town with "all the plateau around Medeba" (v 16).

20. *Beth-peor*. Simply "Peor" in 22:17 and Num 31:16. It was "across the valley" from the site of the Transjordan covenant encampment (Deut 3:29; 4:46) and opposite the burial place of Moses (Deut 34:6). The name is probably to be connected with the god Baal-peor, who was involved in the tragic affair concerning the plague, recounted in the epic (Numbers 25; cf. Hos 9:10 and 13:1), and echoed later in Joshua (22:17). The site is probably to be sought below the mountain massif of Pisgah. Ottoson, *Gilead*, 124. Early waves of Christian pilgrims often attracted place names to the more convenient roads. Fourth-century writers found Peor at the sixth Roman mile station (c. 8.9 km) from Esbus (earlier "Heshbon"), at a dramatic promontory called Khirbet el-Meḥaṭṭa, the western promontory of the ridge called el-Mushaqqar, along which ran the ancient road from Livias to Ḥesbân. The recent survey reports no evidence earlier than the Roman period at the site. Waterhouse and Ibach, "The Topographical Survey," *Andrews University Seminary Studies* 13 (1975) 221-225. See also Mendenhall, *Ten Gen*, 108-109.

Slopes of Pisgah. Originally a town or village; see 12:3 and NOTES. Map B, 112.

Beth-jeshimoth). See NOTE on 12:3. Map F, 336.

21. *all the towns of the plateau; . . . all from the realm of Sihon*. As described in the preceding notes, "the plateau" must be the name of an administrative unit which includes the major western approaches from the valley below, which Sihon had also controlled.

Midianite. Another "confederacy" with tumultuous history. These people are better known from the twelfth-century crisis surmounted by Gideon's leadership, where two of their "commanders" (Oreb and Zeeb) and two of their "kings" (Zebah and Zalmunnah) are named (Judges 7 and 8). The Midianite horde of Gideon's day belonged to a later wave of migration, originally from the north, probably bringing with them the domesticated camel, against which Israel was almost totally defenseless. (See Mendenhall, *Ten Gen*, especially 89 n, 108, 119, 163-173.) The earlier Midianites, however, had emerged in control of the desert trade routes, mainly as donkey caravaneers, and exercised a wide-ranging suzerainty in the days of Jethro, Midianite priest and father-in-law of Moses. W. F. Albright, "Midianite Donkey Caravans," in *Translating and Understanding the Old Testament*, 197-205; see also Robert J. Forbes, *Studies in Ancient Technology* 2, 187-204; and William J. Dumbrell, "Midian —a Land or a League," *VT* 25 (1975) 323-337.

chieftains. Hebrew *neśî'ê* (a characteristically Dtr 2 word in the Book of Joshua; see 9:18 and NOTE), not to be confused with the word for "princes" discussed below, although *nś'ym* is often translated "princes."

princes. Hebrew *nesîkê*. Translation of this word remains an educated guess, as it was for the OG translator and the subsequent Greek recensionists. Greenspoon, STBJ, 160-161. The text reflects a situation where Midianites in Transjordan were dominated by Sihon and his vassals. Here the latter were named second in a three-part series which ends with the famous Syrian seer.

(*Evi, Reqem, Zur, Hur, and Reba*). Numbers 31:8. Another alignment of five. Only the third and fourth in the series have clearly Semitic names. See Mendenhall, *Ten Gen,* 167-169, for possible northern origins.

22. *Balaam ben Beor.* Another name from eastern Anatolia? *Ten Gen,* 169. The preamble to the covenant in Josh 24:9-10 (in an old source taken up by Dtr 1), is sufficiently distinct for us to conclude that 13:22 represents another redactional stratum (Dtr 2). For the stories and poems of Balaam, see Numbers 22-24. There is no other reference to Balaam's execution by the Bene Israel. The famous diviner continued to foster a tradition outside Israel, as witnessed by the remarkable discovery of texts mentioning him (from c. 700 B.C.) in excavations at Tell Deir 'Alla in the Jordan Valley. Jacob Hoftijzer, "The Prophet Balaam in a 6th Century Aramaic Inscription," *BA* 39 (1976) 11-17; the title of this article was incorrectly translated from the German.

23. *their fenced areas.* Hebrew *haṣrêhen.* These are chiefly fields for cultivation or corrals for livestock, defined by lines of stone and brush. The word *ḥṣr* belongs to the pre-exilic stock of Biblical Hebrew and is gradually replaced in later centuries by *'zrh* according to Hurvitz, "The Evidence of Language . . . ," *RB* 81 (1974) 41-43.

24. *Gad.* Map F, 336. While in Israel it was remembered that Moses had presided over the settlement of Gad, the ninth-century king of Moab understood that "the men of Gad had always dwelt in the land of 'Aṭaroth" (Mesha Stele, line 11), that is, some distance to the south where survives the name Khirbet Aṭṭarus. No doubt there is some historical truth in both claims, if it was part of Moses' work to mediate the rivalry of the Bene Reuben and the Bene Gad.

25-27. This is an orderly description. Verse 25 gives an overall impression and sets an eastern limit. Verse 26 sets limits on south and north. Verse 27 stakes the western claims in the Jordan Valley.

25. *Jazer.* This seems to have been the name of both a town and an Amorite province (Num 21:32), promised to Gad by Moses, Eleazar, and Joshua (Num 32:28-30). It became a Levitical town in Israel (21:39). The location is uncertain. Khirbet es-Sar, c. 9.6 km west of Rabbah (Amman) is an Iron II site, according to K. Yassine in an oral communication to the writer. Kom Yajuz, c. 9.6 km north of Amman, where Glueck reported a preponderance of early Iron I sherds, yielded only a smattering of late Iron II/Persian indicators to Peterson's Levitical cities survey team (see chap. 21). A proposal to identify Jazer with Kh. es-Sireh, c. 2.4. km northeast of Kh. es-Sar, makes sense topographically but lacks archaeological documentation (George M. Landes, *BASOR* 144 [December 1956] 30-37). The most likely candidate is Kh. Jazzir, c. 3.8 km south of es-Salt, where Iron Age and Hellenistic pottery were reported by R. de Vaux, *Vivre et Penses* I (1941) 25-27.

and all the Gilead towns. Hebrew *wkl 'ry-hgl'd* is ambiguous. But v 31 rules out the possibility of meaning "all the towns in Gilead." Rather it must refer to those nearby "towns of Gilead" which center in Jazer.

(*that is.* The *w*-conjunction parses as *waw*-explicative.

half of the land of the Bene Ammon. This cannot refer to the Iron Age kingdom that came to center in the upper reaches of the Jabboq watershed. Instead it must reflect the preceding period in which the unconsolidated Bene Ammon ranged widely over the northern half of the Transjordan plateau. The establishment of the kingdom of Ammon was no doubt spurred on by Israel's surprising success at dismantling the older Amorite kingdoms, after having carefully avoided a showdown with the newer kingdoms of Edom and Moab! The result, a century after the initial Yahweh revolution in Transjordan, was an exceedingly complex network of claims and counterclaims involved in Jephthah's negotiations with a king of Ammon over a territory where the Ammonite had assumed Moabite sovereignty. Judges 11. AB 6A, 200-205.

Aroer. Not to be confused with another Aroer near the Arnon Gorge (12:2; 13:16) about 48 km to the south. The site of this one is uncertain.

west of. Hebrew *'l pny*, literally, "opposite," and not always "east."

Rabbah. Heart of the Ammonite homeland and capital of the Iron Age Ammonite kingdom, modern Amman. Map F, 336.

26. *from Heshbon.* This must be shorthand for "Heshbon, with all its towns" (v 17), the neighboring district on the south.

Ramath-mizpeh. Literally, "Lookout Height." Identification uncertain. A summit near Khirbet Jel'ad (which preserves the name "Gilead"), the equation proposed by Aharoni (*LOB,* 383), seems too far north of a line that descends, however unevenly, from the Jabboq watershed toward the next place named.

Betonim. Khirbet Batneh, c. 5.6 km southeast of es-Salt. Map F, 336.

Mahanaim. One of the Levitical towns (21:38). It served as Ishbaal's capital after the Philistines' defeat of Israel and the tragic deaths of Saul and Jonathan (2 Sam 2:8,12), the place to which David later retreats in the face of Absalom's power (2 Sam 17:24,27). Solomon made it a district center (1 Kgs 4:14). The name means "two camps" and is given two distinct popular explanations in Genesis 22; in vv 1-2, Jacob claims that he has seen the heavenly encampments, while in v 10 he exclaims that he has become "two companies." Probably reflected in the name are the twin sites on opposite sides of a dogleg bend in the Jabboq. The northernmost (but on the south bank!) is Tulul ed-dahab, ancient Penuel, the place of Jacob's dream in Gen 32:24-32. The southern site (but on the north bank!) is Tulul el-Gharbiyeh. Map F, 336. Peterson, in his study of the Levitical cities (Joshua 21), accepts Noth's alternate proposal of Tell Hejjaj, 4 km south of the Jabboq, where archaeological documentation is limited to De Vaux's general dating in the Iron Age.

Debir. Location unknown. MT *lidebîr* might be revocalized to read Lodebar (2 Sam 17:27), which was not unrelated to Mahanaim. But this would merely substitute one puzzle for another.

27. *valley.* Hebrew *'emeq* here refers to the wider rift created by the Jordan and the intersections of major wadis emptying into it.

Beth-haram. The place was strengthened by the Bene Gad before embarking on the Jordan crossing (Num 32:36 where it is spelled Beth-haran). The site is surely the imposing Tell Iktanu on the south side of Wadi Ḥesbân. Map F, 336.

Beth-nimrah. Tell el-Bleibil on the Wadi Nimrin. Map F. This site is closer to the Jordan Valley proper, where the next two locations are found.

Succoth. Literally, "booths," or "huts." This place is generally identified with Tell Deir 'Alla in the Jordan Valley a short distance north of the Jabboq. Map

F, p. 336. Destroyed by earthquake, dated by Carbon-14 to 1180 B.C. (±sixty years), the ruins were apparently used as a sanctuary by a new group of settlers, whose pottery tradition is not strictly continuous with the local Late Bronze Age material and is somewhat degenerate by comparison. H. J. Franken, *Excavations at Tell Deir 'Alla* 1, 4-8, 19-21. Only a little later the site is inhabited by other newcomers, probably Sea Peoples. Wright, "Fresh Evidence . . . ," *BA* 29 (1966) 73-74. The Balaam document was found here (see above, v 22 and NOTE). In the interim, between the assignment to Gad and the arrival of the Sea People (probably Philistines) at Succoth, must have occurred the events leading to Gideon's suppression of Succoth (Judg 8:4-16).

Zaphon. Map F. Named after the mountain in northern Syria. Richard J. Clifford, *The Cosmic Mountain in Canaan and in the Old Testament,* 137. Albright, *YGC,* 122 n. 29. The name suggests a place sacred to Baal-zaphon. It is mentioned as having a princess named "the lady of the lions" in the Amarna period. For a long time identified with Tell el-Qos on the northern edge of the Wadi Rajeb, commanding a sweep of rich lowlands about midway between Succoth and Zarethan, the identification becomes unlikely in light of the recent Jordan Valley Survey which reports no Late Bronze surface finds. M. Ibrahim, J. A. Sauer, and K. Yassine, "The East Jordan Valley Survey, 1975," *BASOR* 222 (April 1976), site 102, 50. The better candidate now is Tell el-Mazar about 3.2 km away, on the other side of the wadi and out on the valley floor (survey site 103). Zaphon is an Israelite clan name in Num 26:15, indicating something of the importance of religious conversion in the formation of early Israel.

as far as the tip of the Sea of Chinnereth. Map F, 336. Gad, it appears, inherited the most and much of the best: virtually all of the rich valley floor to go with the still heavily forested hills and plateau. The "blessing of Moses" sounds not inappropiate:

> Blessed is the Enlarger, Gad.
> Like a lion he reclines.
> He rives arm and skull.
> He seeks the best for himself
> He pants after a share of a commander.

Deuteronomy 33:20-21a as translated by O'Connor, *Hebrew Verse Structure,* 214-215, building on the study of Cross and Freedman, *JBL* 67 (1948) 195=*SAYP,* 101-102. By the same token, Gad will be vulnerable, especially from the east, with the emergence of the kingdom of Ammon, so that the "Blessing of Jacob" could be read at last as prophetic:

> Gad shall be raided by raiders,
> And he shall raid at their heels.

(Genesis 49:19, tr. Speiser, AB 1 [1964] 363.) Where Speiser redivides the consonantal text to read a suffixed form *'qb-m,* "at their heels," O'Connor recognizes emphatic *m* and renders the line "He tramples from behind." *Hebrew Verse Structure,* 175.

29-31. The description of eastern Manasseh is the sketchiest of all. Since it belongs to a document which seems to have inspired part of the introduction to the larger section, much of it has already been discussed. See above, NOTES on 12:4-6.

30. *Jair's tent-villages in Bashan.* Deut 3:14. Jair means "he enlightens." In Judg 10:3-5, where he has "thirty sons," his tent-villages are in "Gilead." See AB 6A, 186-188. In 1 Chr 2:22-23 his "twenty-three" towns are in Gilead. Map F, 336. These and other variants I have discussed in "Some Conflate Readings . . . ," *VT* 16 (1966) 295-296. The implication here is that his influence indeed ranged far and wide in northern Transjordan and Bashan, until he died and was buried in Gilead, after winning the reputation that he had "judged Israel for twenty-two years."

Sixty. This is the total for all of eastern Manasseh, a tradition that was perhaps misunderstood by the scribal commentator in 1 Kgs 4:13.

31. (*in other words.* Not "on behalf of" (*NEB*), which only introduces new unknowns. Rather, the effect of the parenthetical explanation is to imply that "Machir" belongs to the same category as "Manasseh." This will help to avert the misunderstanding of a heightened emphasis upon the twelve-tribe genealogical linkage. It is a notable concern of Dtr 2. See the problem posed by the civil war with Benjamin in Judg 21:1-6.

to the half-tribe Bene Machir). See above, NOTE on v 7. In the genealogy that finally became standard, Machir is a son of Manasseh (firstborn in 17:1-2; cf. Gen 50:23; Num 26:29; 27:1 *et passim*) and father of Gilead (1 Chr 2:21,23; 7:14). The early Yahwist tradition is reflected in Deut 3:15 ("And I gave Gilead to Machir"), where Gilead is the name of a region. At the time of Deborah's War, late twelfth century, Machir is still a prominent west-bank constituency and "Gilead" beyond Jordan is scorned for its non-participation (Judg 5:14 and 17). With the early decline of influence by the eastern tribes the standard genealogy crystallized. Y. Aharoni, "The Settlement of Canaan," *WHJP* III (1971) 94-128, offers numerous examples of clans and families split into elements that are absorbed by different clans and tribes.

32. *These are what Moses gave in fief.* Together with v 33, this forms a strong *inclusio* and editorial frame to the picture of the Transjordan "estates."

33. The repetition serves also to hold in view the Levites, among whom, no doubt, a lively controversy had developed since the reforms of King Hezekiah (c. 715-687) and King Josiah (c. 640-609). See below, COMMENT on chap. 14.

COMMENT

The first chapter on the redistribution of land is also a flashback on the settlement of Transjordan under the leadership of Moses, concerned especially with the Levites and the naming of three constituent territories. In striking contrast to the allotments in western Palestine (Canaan proper),

to be described in chaps. 15-19, there is no attempt here to depict boundaries. Except for the reference to the Jordan as a natural boundary in
v 23, the word *gĕbûl* regularly means "territory" in this chapter. The lists
in chap. 13 have regularly resisted satisfactory treatment as part of a single
evolving system or set of lists describing from the outset the entire
twelve-tribe federation. See the study by Cross and Wright, "The Boundary and Province Lists . . . ," *JBL* 75 (1956) 202-226; and the subsequent study by Zecharia Kallai, *The Tribes of Israel: A Study in the Historical Geography of the Bible* (in Hebrew); reviewed by Moshe Weinfeld,
JBL 89 (1970) 350-351.

The archaeological basis of recent topographical research in Transjordan was laid by the pioneering work of Nelson Glueck in the 1930s,
published as "Explorations in Eastern Palestine," AASOR 14 (1933-
1934), 15 (1934-1935), 18-19 (1937-1939), 25-28 (1945-1949).
Glueck concluded from the distribution of sites and their occupational
history, as they could be plotted on the basis of surface finds, chiefly
pottery, that there was a long gap in sedentary occupation, especially in
central and southern Transjordan. There was a "serious decline . . . of
permanent sedentary occupation, lasting from about the end of the nineteenth to the beginning of the thirteenth century B.C." Glueck, *The Other
Side of the Jordan*. It has turned out that Glueck was partially misled
by the relative infrequency of large tells in Transjordan. Sites occupied
in only one or two periods, which in large numbers testify surely to widespread instability and periodic social upheaval, at the same time display
a pattern of brief occupation that was not conducive to the formation of
tells. Subsequent discovery of additional Middle Bronze Age and Late
Bronze age sites has, therefore, altered the picture in some detail but
does not affect the overall impression.

The thirteenth century B.C. in fact saw a rapid increase of population in
Transjordan, when the Amorite kingdoms of the Late Bronze Age were
succeeded by Moab, Ammon, Israel, and Edom by the end of that century. There were three main sources of increment to the population.
Probably the smallest of them was the constituency arriving from the desert fringe, representing the spread of the Yahweh Covenant from Sinai.
The larger additions to the ethnic mix on the east bank came by migration: (1) from the north, on the shock waves created by the breakup of
Hittite suzerainty and the collapse of international order, and (2) from
the west bank of Canaan proper. The biblical material contains many indications of migration from west to east. The story of Ruth illustrates the
freedom of movement both ways, under the impetus of fluctuating economic conditions:

> It is becoming quite clear that, with increased research, the Transjordan
> can be clearly distinguished from Palestine. But when we examine the

distinguishing features presently available, they do not indicate poverty in contrast to Palestine. In fact, there are signs of relative prosperity and a greater similarity with more cosmopolitan metropolises of the seacoast.

(Dornemann, "The Cultural and Archaeological History of the Transjordan in the Bronze and Iron Age I, 12.)

A most prominent feature of this chapter is the abrupt reference, twice, to the Levite tribe, with the pointed assertion in each case that there is a very special relationship of responsibility between this tribe and Yahweh God of Israel. Somehow that relationship makes it unnecessary (or inappropriate, or inadvisable) for it to have a section of the land for its own support. Instead, the Levite tribe has a benefice of a different order.

If the late redactor and editor of chap. 13 thus shows a special interest in the pre-exilic Levites, it is reasonable to suspect that the book itself (and the great historical work to which it belongs) was produced under Levitical auspices.

A massive and most important recent study has vigorously challenged the whole notion of pre-exilic teaching-Levites as the original sponsors of Deuteronomy and its sequel in Dtr, that is, Joshua through 2 Kings. Weinfeld, *Deuteronomy and the Deuteronomic School*. The study tries to show that the Book of Deuteronomy plus the historical books and the redactor of Jeremiah are to be dissociated from the Levites (who are, however, mentioned repeatedly as a special concern in the nuclear Deuteronomy, our "Dtn"). Rather, these books, it is urged, are to be read as the product of a single scribal tradition, a unitary, prestigious, and influential succession of "the wise" (who are, however, not frequently mentioned in Dtr and appear but rarely in the historical corpus). In my judgment, Weinfeld's case is far stronger for Dtr 1 (which is clearly, if not uncritically, pro-monarchical) than for Dtr 2 (which is in no way supportive of the Jerusalem authorities). The continuous "school" in fact obscures a great many points of contrast and outright tension in the material. Levitical history explains one such tension.

Ideally, the Levites were to have been the only noticeable exception to the norm of the classless society in ancient Israel, and that one "class" not especially privileged. Levites were not to be tied to the land as farmers, but were to be scattered throughout the towns and villages, where they were given pasture rights and would be supported by benevolence for military and/or teaching service. See chap. 21. Not much is said about them in pre-exilic texts other than Dtn. It is possible, however, to trace an old and intense rivalry between priestly houses. This rivalry provides a key to the classification and interpretation of large blocks of Torah-tradition. An early and deep rift between southern Levitical families (generally supportive of monarchy) and northern Levitical families (generally dispossessed and alienated by Solomon and Jeroboam I) provides a key to the formation of the historical corpus in two stages: Dtr 1 and Dtr 2 respectively.

If we are on the right track in reading chaps. 12-14 as a secondary, special contribution of Dtr 2, then these two abrupt references to the unique responsibility and situation of the Levites are pointers. In the very next scene it is Eleazar, head of the principal rivals to the Jerusalem priesthood, who is mentioned ahead of Joshua at the determination of allotments (14:1-2)! This is followed immediately by the fullest statement about Levites to be found outside Dtn in the pre-exilic period (14:4).

2. CISJORDAN ALLOTMENTS: EARLY LEAGUE
14:1-17:18

a. INTRODUCTION
(14:1-15)

Eleazar and Joshua

14 ¹ Here is what the Bene Israel received in fief in the land of Canaan, which Eleazar the priest, and Joshua son of Nun, and the patriarchal chiefs of the Bene Israel tribes distributed in fief. ² Their enfeoffment was by lot, as Yahweh commanded, through Joshua, to give to the nine and one-half tribes.

³ Moses had assigned the fiefs of the two and one-half tribes beyond the Jordan, without giving to the Levites a fief among them. ⁴ Because the Bene Joseph were two tribes (Manasseh and Ephraim), they gave no division to the Levites in the land, except to live in certain towns with pasture rights, providing for their cattle and their substance.

⁵ Exactly as Yahweh had commanded Moses, so the Bene Israel did. They apportioned the land.

Caleb

⁶ The Bene Judah had gone to Joshua at Gilgal, where Caleb ben Jephunneh the Qenizzite said to him: "You know the word which Yahweh spoke to Moses, the man of God at Qadesh-barnea, in the matter of you and me. ⁷ I was forty years old when Moses, Yahweh's Servant, sent me from Qadesh-barnea to reconnoiter the land. I brought him a report of exactly what I thought. ⁸ My companions, who went up with me, undermined the morale of the people, but I completely followed Yahweh my God. ⁹ On that day Moses took an oath: 'The land on which your foot has walked shall certainly be your

fief, and your children's for ever. For you have completely followed Yahweh our God.' 10 Now Yahweh has kept me alive here, as he promised. It is forty-five years since the time Yahweh spoke this word to Moses, during which Israel has wandered in the wilderness. Now here I am today, eighty-five years old. 11 Yet I am as strong as on the day that Moses sent me. My strength now is as great as it was then for going forth and returning from the battle. 12 So give me now this hill country which Yahweh promised that day. As you yourself heard the word that day, the Anaqim are there, with huge, fortified cities. If Yaweh is with me, I shall dispossess them, as Yahweh has said."

13 Joshua blessed him; he gave Hebron to Caleb ben Jephunneh in fief. 14 Therefore Hebron belongs to Caleb ben Jephunneh the Qenizzite in fief to this day, because he completely followed Yahweh God of Israel.

15 The name of Hebron was formerly Qiryat-arba, metropolis of the Anaqim.

And the land was at rest from war.

TEXTUAL NOTES

14 2. *Joshua* This follows LXX, where the name of Moses in MT may be understood as contamination from the following verse.

to give to This follows a number of Hebrew manuscripts plus Syriac and Targ[t], where the infinitive was lost by haplography in the major recensions: *lt[t lt]š't.* See Num 34:13.

3. *beyond* This is the beginning of the verse in LXX, which shows a haplography caused by two references to a half-tribe.

4. *substance* Lost by haplography in LXX[A] and a number of manuscripts: *lmqnyh[m wlqnyn]m.*

7. *I thought* The pronoun in LXX, "he," reflects confusion of the letters *w* and *y.*

9. *certainly* LXX, which lacks this, reflects a haplography, probably caused by the frequency of the letter *'aleph: l'mr ['m l'] h'rṣ 'šr.*

our LXX is original here, where MT "my" shows contamination from the phrase at the end of the preceding verse. Greenspoon, STBJ, 164-165.

11. *as great as it was* Hebrew repeats the comparative *k* in place of which there is manuscript support at both occurrences for prepositional *b.*

for going forth and returning from the battle This word order is reflected in LXX. The awkwardness of MT ("for the battle, and for going forth and re-turning") may be attributed to a scribal lapse in copying the last word first.

12. *the word*   This is LXX, which reflects the reasonable addition of (*'t*) *hdbr*.

with me   Versions reflect *'ty*, against the object pronoun *'wty* in MT, which cannot be correct.

13. *Jephunneh*   LXX continues, identifying him again as "the Qenizzite," probably a copyist's error anticipating the next verse.

15. *Qiryath-arba*   LXX appears to have read *'rb'* as *'r'b*, to produce *Argob*.

metropolis of the Anaqim   Read with LXX. MT has "he was the great man among the Anaqim," on which see Josh 15:13-14.

NOTES

14:1-15. The recapitulation of Yahwist takeover on the east-west axis (chap. 12) and the special summary of events in Transjordan (chap. 13) are at last followed by this special introduction to the early apportionment of west-bank territories (14:6 - 17:18). After the expansion which occurs in the Shiloh phase (18:1 - 19:48), the first verse of chap. 14 will be repeated in 19:51 as part of a bracketing device.

1. *received in fief*. The root is *nḥl*, discussed above, second NOTE on 1:6. Divine ownership and redistribution of the land could be treated in song:

> The lines have fallen for me in pleasant places,
> and the Most High has traced out (*nḥlt*) my property.

Psalm 16:5, tr. Mitchell Dahood, *Psalms I*, AB 16 (1966) 86. See also Pss 105:11; 135:12; 136:21-22. Synonyms are *yrš* in Pss 25:13; 37:9,11; 105:44; and *ḥlq* in Ps 60:8-10.

the land of Canaan. Elsewhere in Joshua this designation occurs only in 21:2 and 22:9,10,11,32—all of which can be recognized on other grounds as contributions of the later historian (Dtr 2). Throughout the first edition, on the other hand, the land was occupied by "Canaanites, Hittites, Hivites, Perizzites, Girgashites, Amorites, and Jebusites" (3:10). We may suspect, therefore, that "the land of Canaan," an old provincial designation, was revived by Dtr 2, though it is rooted ultimately in Egyptian suzerainty, prior to the breakup into the "seven nations." See the remarks of Wright in the Introduction to this volume (82).

Eleazar. See the epic story of the commissioning of Joshua: "And he shall stand before Eleazar the priest, who shall ask counsel for him after the judgment of Urim before Yahweh: at his word shall they go out . . ." Num 27:21. Here Urim stands for "Urim and Thummim," the two sacred dice with which the priest might ascertain a divine "yes" or "no" in response to specific inquiry (Exod 28:30).

It is most likely that this Eleazar was head of the Bethel priesthood early in the pre-monarchy period. This priesthood would have traced its origins to Aaron, over against the rival Mushite priests of Shiloh. Cross, *CMHE*, 195-215. Here Eleazar functions in a role that understandably would not have been emphasized by the Jerusalem Aaronids (and thus Dtr 1) who claimed legitimacy through Zadoq (originally from Hebron). An ancient priestly rivalry thus evoked in chap. 14 provides the context for a most surprising combination of factors in 22:12-13, in the curious story about a confrontation over an altar at the Jordan which nearly led to civil war.

and the patriarchal chiefs. Hebrew *wr'šy h'bwt*, literally, "and the heads of the fathers' (houses)." The expression occurs elsewhere in Joshua only in 19:51 and 21:1, both of which make sense as having been put in place by the later editor, Dtr 2. The context in 21:1 makes it clear that the unit called a "father's house" is subtribal. A synonymous expression is "Israelite village chiefs" (*r'šy 'lpy yśr'l*) in 22:21,30. Both *bêt 'āb* and *'elep* also stand for small military units. In Gideon's objection to Yahweh's recruiting angel, Gideon says: "My *'elep* is the weakest in Manasseh, and I am the most insignificant in my *bêt 'āb*." Judg 6:15. Boling, AB 6A, 128 and 132.

In Num 34:17-29 the place of the patriarchal chiefs is taken by "leaders" (*něśî'îm*). One per tribe is there named, twelve in all (that is the P tradition). While the *něśî'îm* are important in Dtr 2 (see above 9:15-21), here we have the understanding that a considerably larger number of representatives had participated at this important event of partitioning the land. And this is entirely in keeping with Dtr 2's repopularizing of the tradition. While the document in Num 34:17-29 emphasized the principle of one *nāśî* per tribe, this tradition makes good on the recurring emphasis that "the land shall be divided for inheritance according to the number of names. To a large tribe . . . a larger inheritance, and to a small tribe . . . a small inheritance; every tribe shall be given an inheritance according to its numbers." Num 26:53-54; cf. 33:54.

2. *by lot.* A special Levitical responsibility was the procedure for divination by means of the sacred dice:

> "Give to Levi your Thummim
> and your Urim to your godly one. . . ."

Deuteronomy 33:8 LXX; the reading is supported by 4Q Dt[h] (unpublished). Cross, *CMHE*, 197. See the account of the discovery of Achan in 7:14-18, where the elimination is probably by lot. Later, Saul would be thus chosen to be king (1 Sam 10:19-24). Similarly Jonah's guilt would be thus established by the frightened sailors in a story that parodies the relation between cultic prophecy and temple (Jonah 1:7).

through. Hebrew *běyad*, literally, "by hand of," that is, "by the agency of."

Joshua. His military leadership had created the situation in which, however, Eleazar presided over the land distribution.

3. *Moses.* Mentioned twice in vv 3-5 (and once in the MT of v 2), thus reversing the emphasis of the earlier summary in 11:21-23 ("Joshua" four times, "Moses" once).

Levites. For general background, see above on 3:3. Of the seven explicit references to Levites in the Book of Joshua (not including chap. 21 which deals with Levitical towns), four occur in relative proximity to one another (13:14,33; 14:3,4; cf. 3:3; 8:33; and 18:7). It is clear that the first edition of the great historical work (Dtr 1) had played down the position of most Levites in the era of monarchy. For example, in all of Judges Dtr 1 did not mention Levites except to include the polemical stories devaluing the teacher-priests at northern sanctuaries (Judges 17-18). The tragicomic story of the Levite from the north in Judges 19-20 belongs to Dtr 2. References to Levites in 1 Sam 6:15 and 1 Kgs 8:4 are probably secondary, reflecting the influence of the Chronicler, by whose time the priestly caste system of the Second Temple was believed to go back in all its ramifications to King David. This leaves only a single reference, embedded in the old "Court History" (2 Sam 15:24), as the one unimpeachable reference to Levites in all of Samuel and Kings. And there they are responsible for transporting and guarding the Ark, as in Josh 8:33.

In Joshua 13-14, however, the recurring reference to Levites and their sustenance sets the stage for the inclusion of chap. 21. Here in 14:4 the list is arranged chiastically (*towns . . . pasture/cattle . . . substance*) giving emphasis to a privileged status (the Levite non-hero of Judges 19-20 appears to be very well-heeled!). It cannot be accidental that this text pertaining to the prestige and privileged status of Levites is followed by the only explicit tradition of Qadesh-barnea (14:6-15) in the book. Qadesh-barnea had been a storm center of Levitical rivalry, to judge from the welter of conflict-stories in Leviticus and Numbers, which follow the episode of Aaron's golden bull calf (Exodus 32).

5. *Yahweh had commanded Moses.* The plan is traced to its point of origin.

6-15. The fief of Caleb in the south constitutes an exception to the pattern of large tribal fiefs which was presupposed in the first edition of the book. Here in the final edition it is balanced structurally by the example of Zelophehad's daughters in the north (17:1-6).

This is the larger Caleb unit which will also be recalled briefly in Judg 1:20 ("as Moses had ordered"). *Judges,* AB 6A, 51.

The earlier edition of Joshua had another Caleb story (15:13-19), which the later historian also retained and repeated in Judg 1:12-15, probably for its less than laudatory introduction to Othniel, the first of the judges.

6. *The Bene Judah.* The clear implication is that it was only with the exercise of initiative by the Bene Judah that Joshua made good on the prior promise by Moses to Caleb.

had gone. Hebrew makes no formal distinction between the past and perfect tenses. Such use of retrospective or flashback is likewise characteristic of Dtr 2 in the Book of Judges (AB 6A, see NOTES on Judg 1:1-2 and 2:6-10).

Gilgal. The reference is probably not to the specific context of 10:15 and 43 but to the first floruit of the Jordan Valley sanctuary, reflected in chaps. 3-7.

Caleb. Hebrew *kālēb* is related to the noun *keleb,* "dog," which has a long history of use in contrasting senses. Like the noun *'ebed* ("slave, servant"), *keleb* may be applied to a person negatively (invective) or positively (implying faithfulness, humility). See Thomas, "KELEBH 'DOG': Its Origin and Some Usages of It in the Old Testament," *VT* 10 (1960) 410-427.

Caleb is one of the very few to whom the title "servant of the Lord" is applied in the pre-monarchical period (Num 14:24). Especially interesting in this connection is Amarna Letter usage, where the expression *ardu kalbu,* "the slave, the dog," or simply *kalbu,* "the dog," is applied by the vassal to himself (expression of deference) or to others (invective), a usage which continues in the Lachish Letters (*KAI* 192:4; 195:4; 196:3; cf. *ANET,* 322).

Jephunneh. Also 15:13 and 21:12. The name probably means "May he (God) turn" or perhaps "cause to turn." This is the clan name and it designates part of a more general grouping which is frequently specified when Caleb is mentioned. Num 13:6; 14:6,30,38; 26:65; 32:12; 34:19; Deut 1:36; 1 Chr 4:15; 6:41[56E].

the Qenizzite. Hebrew *haq-qenizzî.* Cf. *ben-genaz* in 15:17. This difference correlates with the alternation of "Anaqim" in 14:15 and "sons of Anaq" (i.e. Bene Anaq) in 15:14. Here the use of the old gentilic forms harks back to a period when the elements in question were not yet fully assimilated to Judah, offering further indication that our later editor is using very old material that had escaped the main seventh-century recompilation.

The name *qĕnizzî* "comes closest to a Hurrian form." Blenkinsopp, *Gibeon and Israel,* 18. See below on 15:14. References to Qenaz as one of the clans of Edom (Gen 36:9-11,15, 42) must somehow reflect subsequent migration or intertribal regrouping. Abraham Malamat, "Aspects of Tribal Societies in Mari and Israel," in *La Civilization de Mari.* XVᵉ Rencontre Assyriologique Internationale. Ed. J. R. Kupper (Liege, 1966) 138.

Yahweh. Mentioned ten times in vv 6-15, thus accounting for the later boast in Ecclus 46:9.

> The Lord gave Caleb the strength—
> which he retained right into old age—
> to tread the highlands of the country
> which his descendants still hold
> as their inheritance.

Moses. Mentioned five times in the larger unit (vv 6,7,9,10,11).

Qadesh-barnea. Maps A, 81, and G, 364. Mentioned again in the following verse, for emphasis. This large and lush oasis at the intersection of major caravan routes in the northern Sinai was strategically situated for the formation of any new alliance that might try to penetrate the Canaanite hills from the south. It must indeed be here that we should look for "the origin of that unity of Israel as the people of Yahweh, which existed quite independently of the political structures. . . ." A. D. H. Mayes, *Israel in the Period of the Judges,* 109.

7. *Yahweh's Servant.* See NOTES on 1:1,7.

to reconnoiter the land. The epic version of the story, in its priestly redaction, is found in Numbers 13. That story makes historical sense as reflecting a rift in the priestly leadership of the new federation and disagreement over strategy for God's reconquest of Canaan. On this view one influential alliance of clans (Judah) moved north from Qadesh in league with the smaller band of Simeon (which would at last be politically engulfed by Judah), and with the main body of Levites, predominantly "Aaronite." The nucleus of the Joseph tribes moved instead into Transjordan, under the leadership of a smaller group of highly militant Levites headed by Moses. We are reminded that the necessity of finding a "clear explanation of the connection of Levites with both waves of immigration" dominates the major review of conquest theories through the first half of our century. Harold H. Rowley, *From Joseph to Joshua*, 7. Some such reconstruction is necessary in order to comprehend the welter of claims and counterclaims reflected in the priestly conflict stories of Exodus-Leviticus-Numbers. In other words, in Numbers 13, we have, not a story about the early success of one major component, but a story about the failure of the mighty twelve-division army which was P's conception of early Israel on the move, a conception which was not greatly different from that of the later editors (Dtr 1 and Dtr 2).

8. *undermined the morale of the people*. Hebrew *hmsyw 't lb h'm*, literally, "they caused the heart of the people to melt." The verb here is pointed as an Aramaic form, in contrast to Deut 1:28 which has the normal Hebrew form. The latter occurs in a context where the "holy war" language is turned against Israel.

completely followed. Here and again in vv 9 and 14 the verb is *ml'* in the *pi'el* stem, which has durative or iterative force.

9. *certainly*. Hebrew *'m l'* is emphatic affirmative where an oath is expressed or implied.

12. *this hill country*. Some accompanying gesture is implied? Cf. "this Lebanon" in 1:4.

the Anaqim. According to 11:21-22 Joshua had already settled matters with the Anaqim, further evidence that chap. 14 is secondary, intended to supplement and balance the claims of the first edition. The name of this people seems originally to have been an appellative, "those who wear the necklace." Tradition described them as of awesome height (Num 13:28; Deut 2:21; 9:2). According to Num 13:33 they were descended from the union of the divine and human beings of the primeval period (Gen 6:4).

If Yahweh is with me. This was the one completely uncontrollable, yet trustworthy, variable. Everything turns upon Yahweh's faithfulness, justice, and compassion toward his covenant-partners.

I shall dispossess them. Thus the larger narrative section which begins in 13:1 with Yahweh's wry observation that Joshua has grown quite old, with much of the land yet unconquered, here ends with the story about elderly Caleb who boasts that he is still capable of military exploits, on one condition —the collaboration of Yahweh.

13. *Hebron*. For the story of Joshua's success there see chap. 10. Compare chap. 21, where Hebron is also one of the cities specified as obligated to quarter and provide pasturelands for Levites. In the case of Hebron, however, it is pointedly reported that its "farmlands and cattle enclosures" had been given to Caleb (21:11). Thus the story of Caleb's inheritance in chap. 14 survives as the reminder of an early administrative snafu regarding the very city where David would first become king.

14. *to this day*. Inasmuch as Caleb had long since passed from the scene, this

phrase is another indication that the late editor (Dtr 2) is incorporating some very much older material.

because he completely followed. Echoing vv 8 and 9. This reverses the logic of the Divine Sovereign, who bestows the land in exchange for a pledge of future service, or to keep a prior promise to the fathers. See above on 1:2.

15. *Qiryat-arba.* "Town of Four." Concerning the larger class of place names compounded with *qiryah,* see fifth NOTE on 9:17. It has been suggested that the place was one of four neighboring confederated settlements, with the families of Aner, Eshcol, and Mamre grouped around the "citadel" of Hebron (Gen 14:13 and 24). Thus Benjamin Mazar, according to *Archaeology:* Israel Pocket Library (Jerusalem: Keter Publishing House, 1974) 100. As such it would be precisely the kind of name the Hebrew storytellers loved to explain or exploit; yet we find none of the familiar etiological indicators. More likely the second element obscures a divine name having Babylonian or Hurrian roots. See C. F. Burney, *The Book of Judges,* 43*f,* and Blenkinsopp, *Gibeon and Israel,* 113 n. 19. "Arba" is father of Anaq in 15:13.

And the land was at rest from war. The statement is identical in Hebrew to the last words of 11:23. In contrast to the first occurrence, where it makes good sense as conclusion to events in chaps. 6-11, here it is most abrupt and does not seem to be clearly related to what either precedes or follows it.

was at rest. Hebrew *šqth* in both occurrences, where LXX shows a slight variation: *katepausen* in 11:23, and *ekopasen* in 14:15. This minor variation shows the latter verse as Dtr 2's mark, at the end of material which was inserted (chaps. 12-14) after Dtr 1's original use of the formula in 11:23.

COMMENT

As introduction to the allotment of tribal fiefs west of the Jordan, this chapter falls into two provocative units.

Verses 1-5 state most emphatically what had been obscured (whether by design or default is a moot point) in the first edition. That edition, lacking chaps. 13-14, had described only the west-bank allotments made under direction of Joshua with no mention of the important role of the northern Aaronite priest Eleazar. It was a version which held a large share in the eternal promise to the Davidic house. The final edition, however, which incorporated chaps. 13-14, saw the end of national existence clearly in view; and it remembered a broader base of participation (both in the fighting and in the decision-making) in the early days. It was the Dtr 2 redactor who made the Levites a matter of penultimate concern in chaps. 13-14 and in the larger work (cf. Joshua 21; Judges 17-19). This redactor's concern for participatory Yahwism and fair distribution of "tribal" lands shows clearly again in the pericopes dealing with the daughters of Zelophehad (17:1-6) and Joseph's inadequate allotment (17:14-18).

Some reminiscence of the early significance of Levites as the militant core of the Yahwist movement survives in the vocabulary used in describing their responsibility, which resists any spiritualizing interpretation, for example, "warfare" (ṣābā'). It was precisely those who could be counted on for military service that were assigned responsibility for "the work" of the desert sanctuary (Num 4:3,23,30,35,39,43). And thus the most characteristic activity of the Levites in the wilderness was guarding (not merely "keeping charge of") the portable sanctuary and the sacred things (Num 1:53; 3:28; 18:4; 31:30, et passim). The institution per se was not a Yahwist innovation. See Jacob Milgrom, "The Shared Custody of the Tabernacle and a Hittite Analogy," JAOS 90 (1970) 204-209.

Yet it would be going too far to conclude that Levi was the only constituency of Israel represented in Egypt, as argued by T. J. Meek, Hebrew Origins (Harper Torchbook Edition, 1960) 31f. In the pre-Yahwistic "Testament of Jacob" Levi is aligned with Simeon in raiding or guerrilla activity of such a character as to explain well the Jerusalem establishment's distrust of northern Levites; here the referent may well be the Shechem massacre in wake of the rape of Dinah (Genesis 34):

> Simeon and Levi are a pair;
> Their wares are the tools of lawlessness.
> My person must not enter their council,
> Or my being be joined with their company!
> For they killed men in their fury,
> And maimed oxen at their whim.
> Cursed be their fury so fierce
> And their wrath so relentless!
> I will divide them from Jacob,
> I will banish them from Israel.

Genesis 49:5-7. This is E. A. Speiser's translation in Genesis, AB 1 (1964) 361, revised in the final bicolon, where the preposition b has an archaic sense, "from." Freedman, "Early Israelite History in the Light of Early Israelite Poetry," in Unity and Diversity, 17. On the entire passage see O'Connor, Hebrew Verse Structure, 171-172.

These verses seem to be a reflection of events which led to Simeon's retreat toward the northern Negeb and the dispersion of Levitical clans, so that some of the latter were to be found later providing forced labor in Egypt. At the same time, northern Deuteronomic circles treasured a similarly ancient poem (Mosaic or early post-Mosaic) which in addition to the Levites' militancy celebrated their activity as teachers of Yahweh's judgments to Jacob, and his torah to Israel, as well as officiating at the altar (Deut 33:10-11). See especially now Campbell, *Ruth*, AB 7 (1975) 21. Many of the Levitical families after the Yahwist reformation would be suppressed or alienated (or both) by royal policies in the north and the south (see below, the Levitical cities list in chap. 21). The victory of the Zadoqite priests in Jerusalem (1 Kgs 2:26,35), Solomon's willingness to sell off northern territory including Levitical towns (1 Kgs 9:11-14), Jeroboam's expulsion of Levites and appointment of other priests in their stead (2 Chr 11:13-14), and the move of the northern capital away from Shechem all converge to explain the alienation of many Levitical families and the rise of the eighth-century Deuteronomic movement. See especially, Halpern, "Sectionalism and Schism," *JBL* 93 (1974) 519-532; "Levitic Participation in the Reform Cult of Jeroboam I," *JBL* 95 (1976) 31-42.

It has been objected that the distinction between higher-ranking altar clergy ("the Levite-priests" in Josh 3:3 and 8:33; Deut 17:9,18; 18:1; 24:8; 27:9="the priests the Levites" in older English translations) and lower-ranking teaching clergy ("the Levite," or "all the tribe of Levi") in other verses of Dtn finds no support elsewhere in the Old Testament. Emerton, "The Priests and Levites in Deuteronomy: An Examination of Dr. G. E. Wright's Theory," *VT* 12 (1962) 129-138. But the peculiar distribution of these references to Levitical persons which Wright discerned is readily explained by the dialectical relation of Josianic and post-Josianic editions. "The Levite-priests" is an old term stemming from the pre-monarchy days of Levitical prestige, a title which also served the self-understanding of Jerusalem priests in Josiah's days (Dtr 1). "All the tribe of Levi" represents the final editor's revival (Dtr 2) of another older emphasis, surviving perhaps among Levites with northern roots.

Verses 6-15, Caleb's fief, is the final unit in the long insertion (chaps. 12-14), and it offers an important correction to the view which might mistakenly be gained from the first edition. There were major exceptions to the general pattern of allotments made by Joshua to large tribes. Caleb's fief was specifically promised by Moses and was not originally assigned by Joshua (as might be inferred from 15:13 in the first edition).

b. JUDAH 15:1-63

1'. BORDERS
(15:1-12)

15 ¹ The allotment for the tribe of the Bene Judah, for their clans, extended to the border of Edom, the southern wilderness of Zin being the southern limit.

² Southern border for them was: from the tip of the Salt Sea, which is south of the Turning Tongue, ³ it followed the lowlands southward from Scorpions Pass, went around Zin, and went up from the south to Qadesh-barnea. It went around Hezron (went up to Adar), turned toward Qarqa, ⁴ went around Azmon, and followed the bed of the Egyptian Gorge. The destination of the border was toward the sea. This shall be their southern boundary.

⁵ Eastern boundary: the whole of the Salt Sea, as far as the mouth of the Jordan.

North side boundary: from the western tongue (from the Jordan's mouth), ⁶ the boundary went up to Beth-hoglah and went around to the north of Beth-araba. The boundary went up to the stone of Bohan ben Reuben. ⁷ The boundary went up, from Trouble Valley (to the north) to Debir, and went down toward The Circle opposite the Red Ascent (which is south of the gorge). The boundary went around to En-shemesh, and its destination was at En-rogel. ⁸ The boundary went up the Valley of ben Hinnom to the Jebusite ridge (that is, Jerusalem), from the south. The boundary went up to the top of the mountain opposite Hinnom Valley on the west, at the northern end of Rephaim Valley. ⁹ The boundary turned from the top of the mountain to the spring, "Waters of Nephtoah," and followed the valley out to Mount Ephron. The boundary turned toward Baalah (that is, Qiryath-yearim). ¹⁰ The boundary turned around west of Baalah to Mount Seir, went around to the northern shoulder of Mount Yearim (that is, Chesalon), descended to Beth-shemesh, and went around to Timnah. ¹¹ The boundary followed the valley to the ridge near

Eqron, to the north. The boundary turned toward Shikkeron, went around Mount Baalah, and followed the valley to Jabneel. The destination of the boundary was toward the sea.

12 The western boundary: the Great Sea is a boundary.

This is the boundary of the Bene Judah all around, for their clans.

TEXTUAL NOTES

15 1. *allotment*   Hebrew *hgwrl*, "the lot," for which LXX *horion*, "boundary," "while perhaps imprecise is nonetheless quite possible," Greenspoon, STBJ, 207.

Bene   Thus MT. LXX shows a lapse, probably auditory: *lĕmaṭṭeh* [*bĕnê*] *yĕhûdâ*.

the southern wilderness of Zin being the southern limit   LXX is quite different: "from the wilderness of Zin as far as Qadesh to the south." The first part may be explained by dittography: *'dm* [*m*] *mdbr*. Both the MT and LXX traditions seem to have contributed to Num 34:3-5.

3. *southward*   The curious phrase *'l mngb* perhaps ought to be resolved into *'l-m ngb*, recognizing enclitic *mem*. This was no longer understood by LXX, which shows no reflex of *'l* and reads *mngd*. The same consonants can be similarly analyzed in v 7.

Zin, and   MT *ṣnh w*. LXX *enak kai* is probably due to confusion of the Hebrew letters *ṣ* and ' plus a dittography of *k* in the Greek text.

toward Qarqa   MT *hqrq'h*. LXX *mdbrh qdš*, "toward the wilderness of Qadesh."

4. *their*   This is LXX, a difference of one letter from MT "your," which interrupts the third person descriptive style with an abrupt announcement that is unparalleled elsewhere.

5. *the whole of*   LXX seems to reflect Hebrew *kl*, lacking in MT. The Greek has no reference to the "mouth" of the Jordan.

North side boundary   Thus MT: *wgbwl lp't ṣpwnh*. LXX reads *wgbwlm mṣpwnh*, "Their border on the north."

from the western tongue   LXX has a prefixed conjunction, "and."

7. (*to the north*)   Lacking in LXX, due to haplography: *w*[*ṣpwnh w*]*yrd*

to Debir   Instead of Hebrew *dbrh*, LXX has *epi to tetarton*, which perhaps represents a damaged Hebrew manuscript mistakenly read as *rby'y*, "fourth."

and went down   This follows LXX (*wyrd*) where MT *pnh*, "turning," is readily understood as corrupt, partial repetition of the preceding *ṣpwnh*. But the verb *pnh* is never used with "boundary" as subject *pace* BHS. Simons, *Handbook* . . . , 137-138.

The Circle   Hebrew *hglgl*. Whence LXX *taagad*?

to En-shemesh   Thus Syriac. See also 18:17. MT and LXX "to the waters of En-shemesh" (*'l my 'n šmš*) probably obscures another enclitic mem (*'l-m 'n-šmš*).

8. *ben*   LXX omits.

9. *Mount Ephron*   This agrees with LXX, where MT, perhaps a result of partial dittography, reads "cities of Mount Ephron": [*'ry*] *hr 'prwn*. The corruption is ancient; the Old Greek reflects *'y*, "ruin," which does not appear to be an improvement. Greenspoon, STBJ, 79-81.

10. *Baalah*   Here LXX repeats the verb *wnsb*, "and turned around."

Timnah   For MT *tmnh* a few Hebrew manuscripts and LXX read *tymn(h)*, "to the south."

11. *went around Mount Baalah, and followed the valley to Jabneel*   LXX is longer, repeating the verb, but the names are garbled: "and the border went around on the south (*epi liba*) and followed the valley to Lemna."

12. *The western boundary: the Great Sea*   MT *wgbwl ym hymh hgdwl* is odd. The Targum offers some support for reading the second and third words as *ymh hym*.

is second occurrence   The conjunction of *wgbwl* in the second occurrence of the word is explicative.

NOTES

15:1-63. Here begin the delineation and allotment of territories for the tribes west of the Jordan (chaps. 15-19). Pride of place is given to the powerful tribe of Judah, which is more fully described than any of the others, thanks to the twelve-part administrative division of the southern kingdom (vv 20-63) which was presumably still in effect at the time of redaction, that is, most likely the reign of Josiah.

The major guidelines for the treatment in this chapter are given in the study by Cross and Wright, "The Boundary and Province Lists of the Kingdom of Judah," *JBL* 75 (1956) 202-226, which built upon pioneering studies by Alt and Noth. The control of archaeological and linguistic data by Cross and Wright in analysis of the material remains unsurpassed though, of course, there is an abundance of new data and adjustments contributed by many scholars to be found in the NOTES.

15:1-12. The first of the sources used by Dtr 1 dealt with tribal boundaries.

1. *The allotment.* This statement harks back to 11:23, prior to the long insertion of chaps. 12-14. On the inclusion of both "conquest" and "allotment" in Dtr 1, see Wright's discussion in the "Introduction," 58-72.

for the tribe of the Bene Judah. See Map G, 364. This verse describes the southeastern extent of a vast territorial claim.

the border of Edom. Roughly the eastern edge of the rift valley known as the Arabah, stretching from the lower end of the Dead Sea to the Gulf of Aqabah.

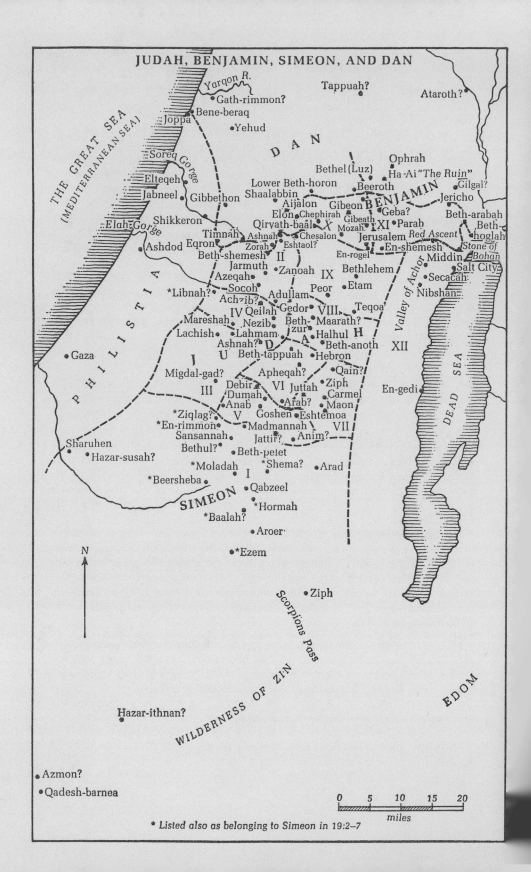

JUDAH, BENJAMIN, SIMEON, AND DAN

Yarqon R.

THE GREAT SEA (MEDITERRANEAN SEA)

Tappuah?

At_aroth?

Gath-rimmon?
Bene-beraq
Joppa
Yehud

Soreq Gorge

D A N

Ophrah
Bethel (Luz)
Ha-Ai "The Ruin"
Beeroth
Gilgal?
Jericho
Beth-arabah

Elteqeh
Jabneel
Gibbethon
Lower Beth-horon
Shaalabbin
Aijalon
Elon
Chephirah
Gibeon
BENJAMIN
Geba?
Qiryath-baal
X
Gibeath
Parah
Mozah
Jerusalem
Red Ascent
Beth-hoglah
Stone of

Elah Gorge
Shikkeron
Timnah
Ashnah
Chesalon
XI
Ashdod
Eqron
Zorah
Eshtaol?
Beth-shemesh
II
Jarmuth
Zanoah
IX
En-rogel
En-shemesh
Middin
Bohan
Salt City

P H I L I S T I A

Azeqah
*Libnah?
Socoh
Achzib?
Adullam
Peor
Etam
Bethlehem
Secacah
Nibshan

IV Qeilah
Gedor
VIII
Teqoa
Mareshah
Nezib
Beth-zur
Maarath?
Lachish
Lahmam
Halhul
H
Ashnah?
D
A
Beth-anoth
XII

Gaza
J
U
Beth-tappuah
Hebron

Migdal-gad?
Apheqah?
Qain?
Debir?
VI
Juttah
Ziph
En-gedi
III
Dumah
Carmel
Anab
Arab?
Maon

*Ziqlag?
V
Goshen
Eshtemoa
VII
*En-rimmon
Madmannah
Sansannah
Jattir?
Anim?
Bethul?
Beth-pelet

Sharuhen
*Hazar-susah?
*Moladah
I
*Shema?
Arad

*Beersheba
Qabzeel

SIMEON
*Hormah

*Baalah?

Aroer

N

*Ezem

Ziph

Scorpions Pass

DEAD SEA

Valley of Achor

EDOM

WILDERNESS OF ZIN

Hazar-ithnan?

Azmon?
Qadesh-barnea

0   5   10   15   20
miles

*Listed also as belonging to Simeon in 19:2–7

Zin. See Num 13:21 and 20:1. This is perhaps originally the name of a waterhole somewhere to the north and east of the Qadesh-barnea area, from which it is clearly distinguished in Num 34:3-4.

2. *the Turning Tongue.* Hebrew *hal-lāšōn hap-pônēh,* the tongue-shaped peninsula, opposite Masada, known as the Lisan (Arabic "tongue"). Map G.

3. *followed the lowlands.* "To follow (a wadi or lowlands)" is the sense of the verb *yṣ'* in the boundary descriptions, as shown by H. Van Dyke Parunak, "Geographical Terminology in Joshua 15-19," unpublished seminar paper, Harvard University, 1976.

from. Hebrew *l,* in archaic usage.

Scorpions Pass. Hebrew *m'lh 'qrbym.* See Map G. After climbing out of the Arabah rift, via Scorpions Pass, the border turns south.

went around Zin. The verb *'br* (again in vv 7,10, and 11) in the boundary lists describes a segment of the border which is somehow diverted from what might otherwise seem to be a more straightforward route, according to Parunak's study. See also 16:6; 18:13,18; and 19:13. Here the verb is used three times in vv 3 and 4 to show how Zin, Hezron, and Azmon were all included within Judah.

Qadesh-barnea. See Map G. The name survives at a small spring in northern Sinai, Ain Qedeis (probably the same as En-mishpat, "Spring of Judgment" in Gen 14:7). This spring is, however, very small. Not far away is the fine oasis of Ain el-Qudeirat where recent Israeli excavations have disclosed an important settlement, southern outpost of the Jerusalem monarchy, from the time of Solomon to the fall of the Judean kingdom. See Carol Meyers, "Kadesh-barnea: Judah's Last Outpost," *BA* 39 (1976) 148-151. In this respect the lush green valley watered by Ain el-Qudeirat, where the Sinai desert merges with the High Negeb, was an exception to the prevailing pattern of decline in the settlements south of Beersheba after Solomon's reign. Yet another small spring nearby is Ain Qoseimeh, formerly proposed as the location of Azmon in v 4. *Qadesh-barnea* more likely refers to the complex of the three springs.

The lack of artifactual evidence for any pre-Solomonic settlement at Qadesh-barnea is mute but suggestive reminder of the small proportions and unsettled character of "Israel" in its earliest association with this beautiful oasis.

Hezron. Also a patriarchal name in Judah (Gen 46:12; Num 26:21), Hezron is "father" of most of the families in the hill country of Judah (1 Chr 2:9-55). See J. Liver, "The Israelite Tribes," in *WHJP* II (1970) 204.

The place is probably the same as Hazar-addar, "Strong Village," in Num 34:4. Location uncertain. The root *ḥṣr* means "to encompass, surround" and derived nouns refer to enclosures both small (sheepfolds and courtyards) and large (villages). The numerous places named (or compounded with one of the following) Hazar, Hazor, Hazeroth, Hazerim, and Hezron illustrates the pastoral exploitation of even marginal regions for raising small cattle (and thus the existence of many "enclosures") in the Negeb in periods of greatest security.

(went up to Adar). The translation treats this as parenthetical restatement of the preceding clause, in view of the compound place name Hazar-addar

Opposite page, Map G

discussed above; but it may be that the verb is a mistake, the result of a later expansion.

Qarqa. Location uncertain. Aharoni tentatively proposed *'Ain el-Qoseimeh* (*LOB*, 380).

4. *Azmon.* See Map G, 364. Possibly *'Ain Muweiliḥ* which in Iron I became an important station (not a settlement) on the road to south-central Sinai. B. Rothenberg and Y. Aharoni, *God's Wilderness*, 36-37.

Egyptian Gorge. Hebrew *nḥl mṣrym.* This is presumably the great Wadi el-Arish, a natural boundary originating in the central Sinai peninsula and arching northwards to empty into the sea roughly midway between Ashdod and the isthmus of Suez, not to be confused with *nhr mṣrym,* "River of Egypt," in Gen 15:18.

destination . . . was. This is the *kethib.* Hebrew *wĕhāyāh tôṣĕ'ôt.* The final syllable is presumably the abstract ending, not the feminine plural as construed by the *qere, wĕhāyû tôṣĕ'ôt,* which MT uses elsewhere in this passage.

This shall be. The description of the borders of Judah in vv 1-12 is drawn up from a variety of fragmentary sources.

5. *western tongue.* The western shoreline of the Dead Sea has no features comparable to the great Lisan terrace. (The same part of Benjamin's border is even more obscure.) Perhaps the Hebrew *lšwn* here refers to one of the headlands along the western shore, such as Ras Feshkha.

(*from the Jordan's mouth*). The parenthetical phrase offers more precision; the border begins at a far northern point on the shoreline.

6. *Beth-hoglah.* "Partridge House." The name survives at Ain-Hajlah. See Map G, 364.

Beth-araba. "House of the Desert Rift." Map G. A northerly bulge in the border from Ain-Hajlah would encompass el-Gharabeh, which appears to reflect the ancient name, and make it a better candidate than Kh. Qumran.

stone of Bohan. Again in 18:17. The meaning of the name Bohan is not clear, though it seems to be related to the word for "thumb" and was perhaps suggested by a peculiar rock formation. In the Chicago telephone directory, there are many Hand(s), Foot(e), and Finger families, but not a single Thumb. Elsdon C. Smith, *New Dictionary of American Family Names* (New York: Harper, 1956) 511, lists both Thumm and Thum. We owe this reference to M. Patrick O'Connor, private communication. Other anatomical names for distinctive geographical features are noted above in vv 2 and 5. For other place names formed with the noun *'eben,* "stone," see Ebenezer, "Stone of Help, or succor," in 1 Sam 5:1 (cf. 1 Sam 20:19), and *'eben hazzôḥelet,* "Serpent's Stone," in 1 Kgs 1:9. In other words, we may suspect that the topographical name has displaced a personal name from a "tribe" which had long since been assigned to the east bank. The location is probably at Hajar el-Aṣbaḥ, "Rock of the Dawn." Map G, 364.

Reuben. See Map F, 336. There are a few traces of west-bank origins for at least part of this tribe which flourished for a while east of the river thanks to Moses' organizing activity (chaps. 13 and 22), but most of those who stayed behind became Judahite. See Liver, "The Israelite Tribes," *WHJP* II (1970) 204-205.

7. *The boundary went up.* This is a vivid description of geographical reality

as the elevation increases dramatically, climbing from one long and narrow semidesert "valley" to another. Trouble Valley is best known from the story of Achan in chap. 7.

Trouble Valley. Map G, 364 (Valley of Achor). On the name and location of this plain, known today as the Buqei'ah, "Little Valley," see NOTES and COMMENT on 7:24-26. On the later history of farming settlements in the valley as part of the Judahite revival in the eighth century B.C., see below on vv 61-62 (belonging to District XII).

(*to the north*). That is, along the north end of the Buqei'ah, roughly the route of the modern Jericho-Jerusalem highway. This is a helpful specification because the ancient alternative route, and probably the better and more heavily traveled one, ran from the opposite end of the Buqei'ah, via the Wadi Qidron.

Debir. Not to be confused with the southern hill-country town of the same name (15:49). A reminiscence of the name seems to survive in the Wadi Dabr and in Thoğret ed-Dabr, "Dabr Crevice," at the head of that wadi, where there used to be a ruin called Khan el-ḥatrur. Nothing of it remains today except what may be displaced or covered by the Jericho-Jerusalem highway and the Inn of the Good Samaritan. This region falls in a gap in the survey conducted by Bar-Adon et al., *Judaea, Samaria, and the Golan,* in Hebrew. Identifications proposed for this segment of the boundary are based on this writer's hikes and surveys during the winter and spring of 1976. R. G. Boling, "Where Were Debir 2 and Gilgal 3?" *ASOR Newsletter* (July-August 1976) 7-8.

and went down. This is an apt description, as one moves from the Red Ascent (see following NOTES) down into the valley-plain which centers in the Byzantine monastery ruins called Khan el-Ahmar, and up to the next point named ("The Circle") on the hills rising toward Jerusalem. This valley-plain is currently being developed under Israeli auspices as an industrial park, "Mishor Adumim." See Map G, 364.

The Circle. Hebrew *hag-gilgal.* The same place is called *gĕlîlôt* in 18:17. These appear to be variants, related to the same root *gll,* "to roll." The site cannot be Khan el-Ahmar, as generally supposed. In several hours of sherding by a half-dozen persons on each of two occasions, we found no pottery that could be earlier than Roman. Moreover, the location of the ruin squarely in the middle of the plain does not tally with the specification "opposite the Red Ascent." We are here too close to Jerusalem, in a region too heavily traveled, for there to be much imprecision in the ancient description. Little more than 1.5 km due west of Khan el-Ahmar, near the head of a wadi emptying into the plain, is a cluster of shallow caves and agricultural terraces called 'Araq ed-Deir ("the Cave of the Monastery"). Some four hundred paces farther to the south-southwest are ancient architectural remains including a substantial wall built of large boulders that describes a half circle, c. 20 meters in diameter. Pottery at these locations is predominantly Roman and Byzantine but includes sherds which are clearly from the Iron Age and some earlier materials. From the stone circle there is a clear view of the Mount of Olives and the Red Ascent.

Red Ascent. Hebrew *ma'ălê 'ădummîm.* (Arabic Tal'at ed-Damm, "Rouge Hill.") Reddish limestone showing here in the hills give the Hebrew name, which a popular etymology interpreted as derived from blood spilled there by robbers. Indeed, the hardest and most dangerous part of the climb from Jericho to Jerusalem is completed at this point, where tradition locates the Inn of the Good Samaritan, and where the Crusader fort Maldoim (a corruption of the Hebrew name) commands a view of Jericho in one direction and the Mount of Olives in the other.

(*which is south of the gorge*). The valley in question is not the broad Mishor Adummim, from which The Circle lies due west. But The Circle is in fact poised at the edge of a smaller tributary wadi (with a rich agricultural terrace) in a system which passes to the north of it.

7b-9. Suddenly we have an unusually larger number of points mentioned in the neighborhood of Jerusalem, presumably so as "to show that the territory of the city state of Jerusalem remains outside the territory of Judah. . . ." Soggin, *Joshua*, 173.

7b. *En-shemesh*. "Spring of the Sun(-god)." Geographers have generally agreed in locating this at Ain el-Hod, the "Spring of the Apostles," some 3.4 km east of Jerusalem (just east of Bethany). Map G, 364. It is not clear how the alternative proposal of Ain er-Rawabi, a "prominent spring almost directly west of Tal'at ed-Damm (grid 178.136)," is an improvement. James Maxwell Miller, "Jebus and Jerusalem: A Case of Mistaken Identity," *ZDPV* 90 (1974) 119. In this case the meaning of '*br*, "to bulge, detour," is decisive. To extend from Gilgal to Ain el-Hod, the border must circumvent numerous small valleys in the upper reaches of Wadi Og, "bulging out to the west and then returning to the east to meet the settlement." H. Van Dyke Parunak, "Geographical Terminology in Joshua 15-19." He observes that the border need not extend all the way to the spring En-shemesh, but only to a village which bore that name.

its destination. Hebrew *tṣ'tyw*. See above, v 4. It cannot here be the "terminus" (as in vv 4 and 11), but must refer to the southernmost segment of the border.

En-rogel. "Spring of the Fuller" (or "Wanderer" or "Spy"). Generally located at Bir Ayyub, "Job's Well," in the Wadi Qidron just below its junction with the Valley of ben Hinnom, at the foot of the modern village of Silwân. Map G, 364. Miller proposes instead Ain el-Madanwerah, a considerable distance north, at el-Isawiyeh on the eastern slope of Mount Scopus ("Jebus and Jerusalem," 120), but the argument is not convincing. Proximity to the wadi junction south of the city is implied by transition to the next clause.

8. *Valley of ben Hinnom*. Hebrew *gy bn hnm*. With the word *ben* omitted, the geographical name was also transliterated as "Gehenna." Regularly identified with the broad and deep Wadi er-Rababeh circling the Old City of Jerusalem on the south and west. Miller seeks to identify the Valley of ben Hinnom either with the whole of the Wadi Beit Hanina or with its easternmost branch; but this is a far less rugged and less determinative wadi system at the opposite corner, northeast of Jerusalem. Miller, "Jebus and Jerusalem," 120-121.

the Jebusite. The name belongs to one of the "Seven Nations"; see 3:10 and NOTES. On the longstanding identification of the pre-Israelite town of Jebus with pre-Israelite remains on the Ophel hill to the south of Jerusalem's sacred area, see Mazar, *The Mountain of the Lord.* Miller's alternative identifications cited above lead him to the neighborhood of the northern suburb Shafat, for an ancient Jebus which was quite distinct from ancient Jerusalem. The theory is adequately criticized by Hans Y. Priebatsch, "Jerusalem und die Brunnen-strasse Merneptahs," *ZDPV* 91 (1975) especially 24-29.

ridge. Hebrew *ktp,* "shoulder, shoulder blade, side." An apt label if it referred originally to the spur of "hill" called Ophel in later times. Miller's idea that it refers to the entire north-south range renders unintelligible the phrase with which the verse concludes: "from the south."

(that is, Jerusalem). If this is a gloss, as Miller claims, it is an ancient and helpful one, and no doubt accurate. While Jebus was at one time assigned to Benjamin (18:28 LXX), it clearly remained non-Benjaminite well into the Judges period (Judg 19:10) and later.

the mountain opposite Hinnom Valley. This is the heart of modern west Jerusalem, in the most widely accepted view. For a high spot west of Shafat, on the other hand, Miller proposes (121) Ras eṭ-Ṭabib.

Rephaim Valley. On the name Rephaim, see fourth NOTE on 12:4. This valley is the Wadi el-Ward, "Rose Wadi." It is difficult to see the reason for Miller's objection that 2 Sam 5:22-25 implies a location farther north. What that text indicates is that when David *surprised* the enemy from the rear, they fled north and were routed from positions that ranged from Geba to Gezer.

9. *"Waters of Nephtoah."* Map G, 364. Hebrew *mê neptôaḥ.* The name is perhaps reflected in modern Lifta at the northwest edge of Jerusalem, with its spring. The name may have been originally "Spring of Merneptah" (so *BHS*), though it is doubtful that such a reading should be taken as evidence for the actual presence of the campaigning Ninteenth Dynasty Pharaoh who celebrated his victory over "Israel" in the well-known stele. While it is possible that the stele narrates a campaign of the Egyptian main force, it is equally possible that the stele assimilates various local actions of Egyptian vassals and officials stationed in Canaan to the overriding suzerainty of the court back home. Priebatsch "Jerusalem . . . ," *ZDPV* 91 (1975) 29.

and followed the valley. This interpretation of *wyṣ',* as explained above (first NOTE on v 3), renders unnecessary Noth's proposed emendation to read a place name *wmṣ',* "and Moza."

Mount Ephron. The name means, roughly, "place of Apiru." Located at el-Qastel, near Mozah. Map G, 364.

Baalah (that is, Qiryath-yearim). The first name is "Wife" or "Lady," a reference to the pagan fertility goddess (Asherah, Astarte, Anat); the place is also called Qiryath-baal in 15:60 and 18:14. The parenthesis indicates how the name was demythologized in the change to "Woodsville." Located at Tell el-Azhar, "Radiant Hill." Map G, 364.

10. *Mount Seir.* Map G. Saris near Chesalon may preserve the name.

went around to the northern shoulder. See below.

Mount Yearim (that is, Chesalon). The "Wooded Mountain" also called "Back-place" is located at Kesla, c. 14.4 km west of Jerusalem in a region formerly known for its oak forests. The possibility of confusion in this segment of border was due to the use of the element Yearim, "Woods," in the renaming of a village on the northern ridge, while the same element continued in use to designate the parallel southern ridge on which Chesalon was located. The shortest route from Baalah to Chesalon would follow the Wadi Chesalon. But instead the border ran along the Baalah ridge (Mount Seir), that is, it "bulged," presumably to include in Judah some settlements there, before skipping the wadi to descend toward Beth-shemesh. (Parunak, "Geographical Terminology.")

Beth-shemesh. Map G, 364. "House of the sun" would be the Yahwist reading of "House of Shamash," the pagan deity. The site is Tell er-Rumeileh. On its history as known from excavation, see below.

went around to Timnah. This description is accurate, whether the place is to be located at Tibnah in the hills south of the Soreq (for which we have inconsistent reports on archaeological evidence) or the more likely site of Tell Butashi, on the Soreq to the northwest of Beth-shemesh. Map G, 364.

11. *Eqron*. Best located at Qatra, c. 12.8 km northeast of Ashdod. Map G.

Shikkeron. Possibly Tell el-Ful (coordinates 1325.1366) north of the Soreq. Aharoni, *LOB*, 228 and 384.

Mount Baalah. If Shikkeron is correctly located, then "Mount Baalah" is probably the long line of hills running northeast and producing a bulge to the southwest before the border reaches the next-named point.

Jabneel. Located at Yibna. See Map G, 364. Remembered as a Philistine town in 2 Chr 26:6, there called Jabne.

12. *all around*. Hebrew *sābîb*, often taken as a mark of "Priestly" language, is in any case good pre-exilic usage. Hurvitz, "The Evidence of Language in Dating the Priestly Code," *RB* 81 (1974) 39-41.

COMMENT

These verses describe the territory of the influential tribe which would later fall heir to the entire tradition of the tenth-century Monarchy centering in Jerusalem. Since the eastern, southern, and western borders of Judah described here merely reproduce the borders of the old "land of Canaan," it is often assumed that the northern border is no earlier than the Davidic or Solomonic administration. The problem with this view is the extreme care that is taken to show that Jebus (Jerusalem) lies outside Judah's border. Surely it was not by design but of necessity that the border carefully skirted that stronghold. The boundaries of Judah are old, pre-Mosaic and pre-Yahwistic, reflecting the claims of one or more of the Bene Israel clans. Together with the claims of an old southern dynasty which David acquired at Hebron they serve as the basis for the formation of the kingdom of Judah, where David ruled for seven and a half years before the takeover of Jerusalem (2 Sam 5:5). If, as archaeological evidence seems to suggest, Beth-shemesh and Qiryath-yearim were founded in the tenth century, then, of course, the archival source for our verses cannot be earlier than that time.

In other words, the "Judah" in these verses is the later political descendant of the strong pre-Yahwist Apiru-constituency celebrated in such archaic poetry as the Testament of Jacob—

> Your brothers shall praise you, O Judah,
> Your hand ever on the nape of the enemy—
> The sons of your father shall bow to you.
> A lion's whelp is Judah;
> You have fattened on prey, my son.
> He crawls like a lion recumbent,
> A lion's breed—who would dare rouse him?
> The scepter shall not move from Judah,
> Or the mace from between his feet,
> To the end that tribute be brought to him,
> And to him go the peoples' homage.
> He tethers his ass to a vine,
> His purebreed to the choicest stem;
> In wine he washes his garments,
> His robes in the blood of grapes.
> His eyes are darker than wine,
> And his teeth are whiter than milk.

(Genesis 49:9-12, tr. Speiser, *Genesis,* AB 1 [1964] 361-362. See also O'Connor, *Hebrew Verse Structure,* 172-173.)

By the time we come to the Blessing of Moses, however, Judah has entered upon a crisis of the severest nature, so that Deut 33:7 includes but a brief petition—

> Hear, O Yahweh, the voice of Judah,
>   and bring him in to his people.
> With thy hands contend for him,
>   and be a help against his adversaries.
> (Deut 33:7, RSV)

The difference between these two poems is surely related to the spread of Philistine power, to which the Davidic monarchy was at first the Judahite response. See especially, D. N. Freedman, "Early Israelite Poetry and Historical Reconstructions," in *Symposia.*

This description of Judah's borders was finally put where it is by a late seventh-century historian who recognized in the reforming, campaigning, and nation-rebuilding King Josiah the greatest of all the sons of David.

That the main lines of the northern border originated, however, long before the time of David in a forgotten kingdom of Hebron is strongly suggested by the context, in which this unit is followed immediately by notice of the takeover of Hebron (vv 13-14) and a sequel to that story (vv 15-19). The latter has been described as "the most archaic anecdote preserved in connection with the capture by the Israelites of a Canaanite town . . ." (Albright, *YGC*, 47).

2'. CALEB GETS HEBRON; OTHNIEL TAKES DEBIR
(15:13-19)

15 ¹³ To Caleb ben Jephunneh he gave a tract in the midst of the Bene Judah, according to the oracle of Yahweh to Joshua. Joshua gave him Qiryath-arba (Arba was father of the Anaq), that is, Hebron. ¹⁴ And Caleb ben Jephunneh evicted from there the three "sons of Anaq"—Sheshai, Ahiman, and Talmai (Anaq's brothers-in-arms).

¹⁵ He went up from there against the inhabitants of Debir. Debir used to be called Qiryath-sepher. ¹⁶ Caleb said, "Whoever attacks Qiryath-sepher and captures it, to him I'll give my daughter Achsah as wife. ¹⁷ Othniel ben Qenaz, Caleb's "brother," captured it; and so he gave him his daughter Achsah as wife.

> ¹⁸ When she arrived, he nagged her
> To ask tilled land from her father.
> But when she alighted from the donkey,
> And Caleb said to her: "What do you want?"
> ¹⁹ She said to him: "Give me a blessing!
> The Southland you have given me
> And you shall give me wells for water!"
> So he gave her the upper well and the lower well.

TEXTUAL NOTES

15 13. *to Joshua. Joshua gave him*   MT and LXX^B show contrasting haplographies:

MT	*lyhwš'* [	]
LXX^B	[ ] *wytn lw yhwš'*

Qiryath-arba   *Arbok* in LXX.

(*Arba was*   These words are not in the text but are supplied for sense.
father   Thus MT. LXX, as in 14:15, reads "metropolis."
14. *ben Jephunneh*   Restored from the Greek.
Ahiman, and Talmai   These two names are reversed in LXX.
(*Anaq's brothers-in-arms*)   Omitted by LXX.
15. *He*   LXX removes the ambiguity by specifying "Caleb" as subject.
18. *he nagged her*   This follows LXX and Vulgate, against MT which reads "she nagged him," a tendentious development (also in Judg 1:14) doing less damage, perhaps, to the image of the first savior-judge.
19. *wells*   Versions read the singular "a well."
he   LXX specifies the subject, "Caleb," probably under the influence of Judg 1:15.
upper well and the lower   Adjectives in the singular (Judg 1:15) are here to be preferred over the plural forms in this verse. See NOTES.

NOTES

15:13-14. In the finished Book of Joshua, the assignment of Caleb's fief at Hebron is more fully reported in 14:6-15. See NOTES and COMMENT on those verses. The first two verses in the present context permit the inference that this happened at Joshua's initiative. Thus the first edition (Dtr 1) here is supplemented by the second edition (Dtr 2) in 14:6-15 supplying more information for better recall.

13. *he gave.* The pronoun subject implicit in the verb form was perhaps originally a reference to Eleazar, who ascertained the decision of the deity which Joshua as leader implemented.

oracle. Literally, "mouth." Here the priest, if implied, is anonymous. Cf. 9:14; 17:4; 19:50.

14. *"sons of Anaq."* This is Hebrew *bĕnê 'anāq,* whereas 14:15 (Dtr 2) used the gentilic form *'anāqîm* (as also in 11:21-22, an insertion at the conclusion of the Warfare section). This contrast in usage between the two redactional strata is to be frequently noted; see below on "ben Qenaz" in v 17.

Sheshai, Ahiman, and Talmai. First met in the order of Ahiman, Sheshai, Talmai in Num 13:22. It has been suggested that the names may be Hurrian in background. Blenkinsopp, *Gibeon and Israel,* 18. More likely they are to be sought among the "pre-Philistine" Sea Peoples who had survived expulsion from the southern hill country in towns such as Gaza, Gath, and Ashdod (11:21-22).

Sheshai. One of the Hyksos rulers of Egypt bore the same name. Albright, *YGC,* 153 n. 1.

(*Anaq's brothers-in-arms*). Hebrew *yĕlîdê hā'ānāq.* In view of highly elusive identity, we suspect that this refers to a military association with membership based on adoption and initiation, like the "warrior-votaries of Rapha" described by L'Heureux, "The yĕlîdê hārāpā'—A Cultic Association of Warriors," *BASOR* 221 (February 1976) 83-85.

15-19. These verses pertain to the hill country south of Hebron, indicating how its original boundary extended also to the edge of the Negeb. Verses 16-19 will be repeated nearly verbatim in the final edition of the historical work (Judg 1:12-15; Dtr 2), presumably for their comic implications as part of a nearly disastrous "beginning" to the post-Joshua period.

15. *Debir.* See above, 10:38 and NOTE.

16. *Achsah.* The meaning of the name is uncertain, perhaps "Bangles" or the like.

17. *Othniel.* First judge in Israel according to the received tradition (Judg 3:7-11). His name is compounded with that of the patriarchal deity El. The first element is obscure but '*t(n)* may be related to the Palmyrene deity '*th*, and more generally to Middle Euphrates '*an*, the counterpart of Ugaritic '*nt*. M. Patrick O'Connor, private communication.

ben Qenaz. This usage is characteristic of the first edition—Dtr 1. On the other hand, Caleb's father Jephunneh is "Qenizzite" (gentilic form) in 14:6, that is, second edition—Dtr 2.

Qenaz. The name is plausibly related to the Luwian name "Kunz," by Mendenhall. *Ten Gen,* 162. This would point to an Anatolian origin for yet another population group in Canaan, among whom much of the so-called "conquest" took place largely by religious conversion.

17. *Caleb's "brother."* Both had joined the same Israelite cause. That Othniel was regarded as either Caleb's brother (LXX^A) or nephew (LXX^B), together with intricate Calebite genealogies in 1 Chronicles 2 and 4, implies complex tribal histories. That another text tradition specifies that Othniel was the "younger" brother (LXX^AN+MSS, Syriac, Vulgate, and Judg 1:13 MT) reflects the trend toward a literal misunderstanding of the early system.

18-19. This translation, as noted in AB 6A, 56, is adopted from that of Albright, who recognized the "scarcely disguised metrical form." *YGC*, 48.

19. *"Give.* Hebrew *tnh* has a synonymous variant *hbh* in the Judg 1:15 version, a variation suggestive of oral transmission.

a blessing! Hebrew *brkh*. In their volume on Hosea, AB 24 (Garden City, NY: Doubleday, 1980), F. I. Andersen and D. N. Freedman propose that *brkh* here is a technical term for the groom's gift to the bride and is distinct from the bride-price, which the groom here rather eccentrically supplied on the basis of his military success.

The Southland. At each of the four places in Joshua where *ngb* occurs with the definite article, the Old Greek and Theodotion transliterate, although their normal equivalent is *lips*. This suggests that *hngb* in these four passages (10:40; 11:16; 12:8; 15:19) was being taken as a place name. Greenspoon, STBJ, 37-40. Here it is not the Negeb desert, but Hebron's Southland, the hills falling away to the desert fringe. A. F. Rainey has pointed out in a private communication that the geographical setting of Rabûd and its marginal annual rainfall (c. 100-200 mm) mean "that the agricultural regimen here is identical to that of the true Negeb farther south."

gave her. In the later edition, where the story is repeated, the wells are further specified as "her heart's desire." Judg 1:15, AB 6A, 51 and 57.

upper well and the lower. Except for rainwater cisterns, the closest water supply to Kh. Rabûd is a pair of wells located about 2.5 km to the north, still known in the region by names strikingly similar to those used here: "The Upper Well of the Leech" and "The Lower Well of the Leech." Kochavi, Khirbet Rabûd . . . ," 3. Achsah's request makes excellent sense; there would be not much point in having Debir, if it was to be totally dependent upon rainwater cisterns.

COMMENT

These verses dealing with Hebron and Debir at the heart of Judah are not easily harmonized with the larger claims made for Joshua's southern campaign (esp. 10:3,36-39). There, no doubt, hyperbole has overtaken a narrator who turns another surprising guerrilla success into a sustained search-and-destroy mission. Here, however, the same editor includes another old legitimatizing unit which is somewhat in tension with the rhetoric of the lengthy "Warfare: Phase One" section (6:1 - 10:43).

3'. JUDAH'S TOWNS
(15:20-63)

15 20 This is the fief of the Bene Judah tribe, for their clans.
21 The outermost towns belonging to the Bene Judah tribe were near the border of Edom.

a'. In the Negeb

District I

Qabzeel, Arad, Jagur, 22 Qina, Dimonah, Aroer, 23 Qedesh, Hazar-ithnan, 24 Ziph, Telem, Bealoth, 25 Hazor-hadattah, Qiryoth-hezron (that is, Hazor), 26 Amam, Shema, Moladah, 27 Hazar-gaddah, Heshmon, Beth-pelet, 28 Hazar-shual, Beersheba and its dependencies, 29 Baalah, Iyim, Ezem, 30 Eltolad, Chesil, Hormah, 31 Ziqlag, Madmannah, Sansannah, 32 Lebaoth, Shilhim, En-rimmon. Altogether, thirty-three towns and their enclosures.

b'. 33 In the Shephelah

District II

Eshtaol, Zorah, Ashnah, 34 Zanoah, En-gannim, Tappuah, Enam, 35 Jarmuth, Adullam, Socoh, Azeqah, 36 Shaaraim, Adithaim, Gederah and its sheepfolds (fourteen towns and their enclosures).

District III

37 Zenan, Hadashah, Migdal-gad, 38 Dilean, Mizpeh, Joqtheel, 39 Lachish, Bozqath, Eglon, 40 Kabbon, Lahmam, Kitlish, 41 Gederoth, Beth-dagon, Naamah, Maqqedah (sixteen towns and their enclosures).

District IV

42 Libnah, Ether, Ashan, 43 Iphtah, Ashnah, Nezib, 44 Qeilah, Achzib, Mareshah (nine towns and their enclosures).

Philistia

45 Eqron and its dependencies and enclosures. 46 From Eqron sea-ward—all that are alongside Ashdod, and their enclosures. 47 Ash-dod, its dependencies and enclosures; Gaza, its dependencies and en-closures, to the Egyptian Gorge. The Great Sea is a border.

c'. 48 And in the Hill Country

District V

Shamir, Jattir, Socoh, 49 Dannah, Qiryath-sepher (that is, Debir), 50 Anab, Eshtemoh, Anim, 51 Goshen, Holon, Giloh (eleven towns and their enclosures).

District VI

52 Arab, Dumah, Eshan, 53 Janum, Beth-tappuah, Apheqah, 54 Hum-tah, Qiryath-arba (that is, Hebron), Zior (nine towns and their en-closures).

District VII

55 Maon, Carmel, Ziph, Juttah, 56 Jezreel, Joqdeam, Zanoah, 57 Qain, Gibeah, Timnah (ten towns and their enclosures).

District VIII

58 Halhul, Beth-zur, Gedor, 59 Maarath, Beth-anoth, Elteqon (six towns and their enclosures).

District IX

59 Teqoa, Ephrathah (that is, Bethlehem), Peor, Etam, Koloun, Tatam, Sores, Karem, Gallim, Bether, Manahath (eleven towns and their enclosures).

District X

60 Qiryath-baal (that is, Qiryath-yearim) and Rabbah (two towns and their enclosures).

District XI

. . . .

d'. 61 In the Wilderness

District XII

Beth-arabah, Middin, Secacah, 62 Nibshan, Salt City, En-gedi (six towns and their enclosures).
63 But the Jebusite inhabitants of Jerusalem the Bene Judah were un-

able to evict; and so the Jebusite lives with the Bene Judah in Jerusalem to this day.

TEXTUAL NOTES

15 20. *for their clans*   Lacking in LXX.

21. *towns*   LXX shows a conflation (or dittography) of "their towns" and "towns."

MT most often has the conjunction *w*, "and," connecting names in these lists, but there is wide variation. The notes here will not in general record the problems with *w* in MT and LXX since the variation is not significant except where it involves two names being merged into one, or one being split into two; and even then the variation is not decisive in reviewing the question.

Arad   With LXX^L (cf. "Ara" in LXX^B), for MT *'dr*, a simple metathesis of two letters in unpointed script.

Jagur   LXX^B reads "Asōr."

22. *Aroer*   MT *w'd'dh* must be a mistake for *w'r'rh* (cf. *b'r'r* in 1 Sam 30:28). The confusion of *d* and *r* explains in part the main LXX reading "Arouēl" ("Aroēr" in one Greek minuscule).

23. *Hazar-ithnan*   In agreement with LXX^B, where MT has the two elements as distinct names. Compare, among others, the name En-rimmon in v 32.

24. *Ziph*   Lacking in LXX^B, compounded with the preceding name in LXX^A ("Ithnaziph").

27. *Heshmon*   Lost by haplography in LXX: *w[ḥšmwn w]byt*.

28. *Beersheba and its dependencies*   This is a correction of MT *wbzywtyh* to *wbnwtyh*, on the basis of the Greek. LXX^B adds "and their enclosures."

29. *Iyim*   LXX has instead *Bakōk*.

30. *Chesil*   *Baithel* in LXX^B (see *Bethul* in MT of 19:4).

32. *En-rimmon*   With LXX, where the words are incorrectly separated by a *w* and treated as two names in MT. Compare *Hazar-ithnan* in v 23.

Altogether   Hebrew *kl* has no reflex in LXX.

34. *Zanoah, En-gannim, Tappuah, Enam*   It is not clear what the OG reading was. The names are distributed as follows:

MT	*Zanôaḥ*	*'En-gannîm*	*Tappûaḥ*	*'Ēnām*
LXX^A	*Ramen Zanō*	*Adithaim*		*Enaim*
LXX^B	*Ramen Tanō*	*Ilouthōth*		*Maiani*

The Greek begins with *Ramen/on*, a partial dittography of En-rimmon above. LXX^A has *Adithaim* displaced from v 36. The spellings in LXX^B do not inspire confidence for reconstructing the *Vorlage* of *Ilouthōth*.

35. *Adullam*   Here the Greek includes *Nemra* (LXX^A) or *Membra* (LXX^B).

36. *Gederah*   Written with the definite article in MT, *hgdrh*.

and its sheepfolds　This is the Greek reading. MT "two sheepfolds" is contamination from the Hebrew dual ending on the first two names in the verse.

40. *Lahmam*　This is the reading of numerous manuscripts and Targ[L], where MT reads *Lahmas.* In the square script the letters *s* and final *m* were easily confused.

42. *Ether　Ithak* in LXX[B].

Ashan　Lacking in LXX. Is it a partial dittography of *Ashnah* in the next verse? See NOTE. LXX[B] has "Anōch," its *Vorlage* unclear.

43. *Iphtah*　Lacking in LXX[B] and manuscripts.

44. *Achzib*　LXX[B] shows partial dittography in presenting two names for Achzib: *Akiezi* and *Kezib.*

Mareshah　The Greek has an addition: *Ailōn* in LXX[B], *Edōm* in LXX[A].

(*nine*　LXX totals "ten," correctly for its list.

47. *Ashdod, its dependencies*　Lost by haplography in LXX[A].

The Great　This is *hgdwl,* supported by manuscripts and the versions, where MT *hgbwl* is contaminated by the next word: *wgbwl.*

is　The initial *w* of *wgbwl* is explicative, as above in 15:12.

49. *Dannah*　LXX *Renna* illustrates the easy confusion of Hebrew *d* and *r.* See also *Remna/Rouma* for *Dumah* in v 52.

Qiryath-sepher　With LXX and Syr. Here MT has *Qiryath-sannah* which appears to be a corruption of the name which is also equated with *Debir* in 15:15.

50. *Eshtemoh*　MT *'štmh.* The name is alternately spelled *'štm'* (*Eshtemoa*) in 21:14; 1 Sam 30:28; 1 Chr 4:17,19.

53. *Janum*　LXX[A] supports the *qere,* against the spelling *ynym.*

54. *Qiryath-arba*　"Town of Arbok" in LXX.

55. *Maon, Carmel*　Lack of a conjunction perhaps indicates that these entries are one.

56. *Joqdeam*　Thus MT, *yqdm.* LXX *yrkm* reflects a metathesis of letters and confusion of *d* and *r.* For other examples of the latter, see vv 22 and 49.

Zanoah, [57] *Qain*　These names are mistakenly combined in the Greek: *Zanoakim* (LXX[A]) and *Zakanaim* (LXX[B]).

59. *Teqoa . . . enclosures*　This unit is restored from LXX. The names *Koulon, Tatam,* and *Sores* are textually uncertain, not known elsewhere in MT.

60. *Rabbah*　LXX has *Sotheba.*

enclosures) . . . . [61] *In the Wilderness*　See NOTES on v 60. A missing segment of the later districts of Judah has been used to describe the older territory of Benjamin in 18:21-28.

61. *Middin*　LXX[A] reads *Madōn* (LXX[B] *Ainōn*), but the place is not to be confused with the Madon in Lower Galilee (11:1).

62. *Salt City*　LXX[B] "cities of Sodom."

En-gedi　LXX *En-qadesh.*

(*six*　LXX "seven."

63. *were unable*　Reading the *qere.*

with the Bene Judah　Lacking in LXX.

NOTES

15:20-63. The format of our translation assumes the basis of these lists in an old administrative register, dividing the southern kingdom into twelve districts. Such a system would help to meet a great variety of fiscal and martial needs. That the three larger geographical groupings of the document were originally headed "In the Negeb" (v 21), "In the Shephelah" (v 33), "And in the Hill Country" (v 48) seems clear from the otherwise awkward syntax of the phrases and from the fact that the first heading was left in place and the qualifying statement pertinent only to the Negeb section, *near the border of Edom*, intruded before the heading. The list must originally have included seven districts in the hill country, but part of one (District X) and all of another (District XI) were originally assigned to Benjamin (18:21-28). The one district that follows the fourth heading, "In the Wilderness" (v 61), represents a final modification of the system. The specific numerical headings accompanying our translation are not found in the Hebrew text but are supplied here in italics for convenience.

The dagger before a place name (e.g. v 21, †*Jagur*) indicates that the place name does not occur elsewhere in the Hebrew Bible.

21b-32. Towns of the Negeb district are listed first; there appears to be no logical order to the progression of districts. The Negeb district also includes most of the towns which in 19:1-9 belong to the tribe of Simeon. In other words, by the time of this elaboration of the system in the southern kingdom, "Simeon" was mostly a memory. There are two parts to the Negeb list.

21b-25. These towns belong to a large semicircle beginning in the wilderness overlooking the Dead Sea and reaching all the way south to Qadesh-barnea.

21b. *Qabzeel*. An alternate form is "Jeqabzeel" in Neh 11:25. It is hometown of Benaiah, one of David's ranking officers. 2 Sam 23:20=1 Chr 11:22. The site is possibly Kh. Gharreh (Tell 'Ira), the "Masada of the eastern Negeb," near the Nahal Beersheba about midway between Tell Arad and Tell Beersheba. Aharoni, "Nothing Early and Nothing Late . . . ," *BA* 39 (1976) especially 74.

Arad. First mentioned in 12:14. Extensive excavations have not disclosed Late Bronze Age occupation at either Tell Arad or the next nearest site, Tell Malḥata. The former flourished in Early Bronze, apparently displaced by the latter in Middle Bronze, before it saw a revival in Iron I.

†*Jagur*. Location unknown.

22. †*Qina*. Probably to be located somewhere near Arad on the Wadi el-Qeini which may reflect the name.

Dimonah. Probably the same as "Dibon" of Neh 11:25, somewhere between Hebron and Jeqabzeel. For the alternation Dibon/Dimon, in the name of another place, in Moab, see Isa 15:2,9.

Aroer. Some 7 km south of Tell Masos. See Map G, 364. Currently under excavation, 'Ar'arah (Kh. Aroer) is now known to have flourished in the eighth and seventh centuries. One of the places relieved by David with booty taken from Amaleqite raiders (1 Sam 30:28); at that time it must have been a very small struggling outpost of Israel.

23. *Qedesh.* The name probably covers the cluster of oases known as "Qadesh-barnea" in the border description. See 15:3 and NOTES.

†*Hazar-ithnan.* The second element is a Judahite personal name in 1 Chr 4:7. The location of "Ithnan's Corral" is uncertain; Wright suggests el-Jebariyeh on the Wadi Umm Ethnan. *The Westminster Historical Atlas,* rev. ed. (1956) 124.

24. *Ziph.* Probably Kh. ez-Zeifeh, southwest of Kurnub. The name occurs again, to the north, in District VII (v 55; cf. the "Wilderness of Ziph" in 1 Sam 23:14-15 and Ps 54:1-2). A town name may also designate a good-sized district around the town.

†*Telem.* Pronounced "Telaim" in 1 Sam 15:4, where it is Saul's base of operations against the Amaleqite raiders. Abel (*Géographie,* II, 88, 478) proposed to locate it at Kh. Umm eṣ-Ṣalafe, southwest of Kurnub.

†*Bealoth.* "Ladies," a name drawn from the fertility cult. Probably the same as Simeon's Baalath-beer, "Lady of the Wells" (19:8); but Bir Yeroḥam in the north-central Negeb appears to be too far south for the Simeon group. Aharoni in *The Macmillan Bible Atlas,* maps 112 and 141.

25. †*Hazor-hadattah.* Unidentified. Perhaps "New Town/Enclosure," with a dialectical variant of *ḥdš.* M. Patrick O'Connor, private communication.

†*Qiryoth-hezron (that is, Hazor).* Possibly Kh. el-Qaryatein, about equidistant between Maon and Arad. Map G, 364. It is also possible that two distinct places are involved here, as *KJV* renders.

26-32. This is the larger group of Negeb towns and it resembles closely the Simeon list in 19:2-7, which itself is repeated in 1 Chr 4:28-32 with differences in the latter that are for the most part understandable in terms of literary transmission.

26. †*Amam.* Unknown.

†*Shema.* See 19:2 and NOTES. This appears to be the place called "Jeshua" in Neh 11:26, identified with Tell es-Sa'wi to the northeast of Beersheba. Map G, 364.

Moladah. See also 19:2. Possibly Kh. el-Waṭen, east-northeast of Beersheba. Map G. The name has to do with childbearing and kinship.

27. †*Hazar-gaddah,* †*Heshmon, Beth-pelet.* Perhaps these were originally Judahite, since they are not in the Simeon list which this section otherwise parallels. Unfortunately none of these places has been located with confidence.

Beth-pelet. Tell es-Saqati, to the northwest of Shema/Jeshua, has been suggested. Aharoni and M. Avi-Yonah, *The Macmillan Bible Atlas,* maps 94 and 165. The town was resettled in the post-exilic period. Neh 11:26.

28. *Hazar-shual.* "Fox-pen." It belongs to Simeon in 19:8 and 1 Chr 4:28. Location unknown.

Beersheba. It belongs to Simeon in 19:2. Map G, 364. Tell es-Seba' has been fully excavated. Aharoni et al., *Beer-Sheba I: Excavations* (1973). The town was a well-planned and strongly fortified administrative center of the monarchy, succeeding an Iron I fort (perhaps early eleventh century). Excavations have shed no light on the period prior to that, when it is clear that the mound itself was not occupied. The excavator suspected that the "patriarchal" town was to be sought in the vicinity of Bir es-Saba' several miles from the tell and within the modern city. Y. Aharoni, "Beersheba," *EAEHL* I (1975) 168. In the tenth-century list of Pharaoh Shishak's invasion, the town is mentioned as Beit 'Olam, "House of the Eternal One," referring to a divine name also associated with Beersheba in Gen 21:33.

dependencies. Literally, "daughter(-town)s"; again in 15:45; 17:11,16.

29. †*Baalah*. "Lady," not the same place as Bealoth in v 24. This one is the same as Balah in Simeon (19:3), and probably Bilhah in 1 Chr 4:29. Possibly Kh. Abu Tulul, southwest of Tell Masos. H. G. May et al., *Oxford Bible Atlas*, 2d ed., 63, 123.

†*Iyim*. Not in the Simeon list, this name may have been spuriously created by a partial dittography of the following name. Cross and Wright, "Boundary and Province Lists," *JBL* 75 (1956) 214.

Ezem. Assigned to Simeon in 19:3. Possibly Umm el-'Azam, southwest of Aroer. This name has turned up on a Hebrew ostracon from Tell esh-Shari'a, c. 22 km northwest of Beersheba, reported by Oren and Netzer, "Tel Sera' (Tell esh-Shari'a)," *IEJ* 24 (1974) 265.

30. *Eltolad*. "O El, you beget (us, the child, or the like)." The divine name is presumably clipped "Tolad" in 1 Chr 4:29. Given to Simeon in 19:4. Location unknown.

†*Chesil*. Possibly the same as "Bethul" in Simeon (19:4), later "Bethuel" (1 Chr 4:30). The location is unknown although Kh. el-Qaryatein, mentioned above (at v 25) as the possible site of Qiryoth-hezron, has been suggested.

Hormah. See above on 12:14, and below on 19:4 where it belongs to Simeon.

31. *Ziqlag*. A town of Simeon in 19:5; 1 Chr 4:30. The new excavations at Tell el-Khuweilfeh (Halif/Lahav) have produced no evidence of any Philistine presence or influence, which one would expect at the town given to David by Achish, king of Gath, and used by David as base for his activities as independent Habiru. (1 Sam 27:6; 2 Sam 1:1; 4:10.) This condition is met, however, by Tell esh-Shari'a, c. 15 km due west of Lahav, at the edge of the Negeb desert, with its thirteenth-century palace (eleven hieratic texts, two scarabs of Ramesses II) and, after a significant twelfth-century gap, an abundance of late Philistine pottery.

If this identification is accepted, then the location of Philistine Gath, where Achish held forth, must be reexamined. In his later studies, Wright had argued for Tell esh-Shari'a as Gath (which the clear evidence of Philistine culture would support), but that argument depended on the location of Ziqlag at Halif/Lahav. Wright, "Fresh Evidence for the Philistine Story," *BA* 29 (1966) 70-86.

Madmannah. Probably the same as Simeon's "Beth-markaboth" in 19:5; Madmannah occurs in 1 Chr 2:49. The original name seems to be reflected in Kh. Umm Deimneh, a few kilometers south of Anab. Map G, 364.

†*Sansannah*. Khirbet esh-Shamsaniyat, c. 5 km northwest of Beersheba. Map G, 364. Simeon's list has instead "Hazar-susah" in 19:5 (="Hazar-susim," 1 Chr 4:31).

32. *Lebaoth*. Simeon's "Beth-lebaoth" in 19:6 ("Beth-biri" in 1 Chr 4:31). Location unknown.

†*Shilhim*. Simeon's equivalent is Sharuhen in 19:6. The latter may be understood as based on the Egyptian transcription of the name that appears in Judah's lists (later corrupted to the Shaaraim in 1 Chr 4:31). Simon Cohen, *IDB* 4, 309 and 328. In Egyptian sources, Sharuhen is the town to which the Hyksos withdrew after being expelled from Egypt. The site is probably Tell el-Far'ah (South). For the alternative location at Tell el-'Ajjul, see A. Kempinski, "Tell el-'Ajjul—Beth-Aglayim or Sharuhen?" *IEJ* 24 (1974) 145-152.

En-rimmon. This "Pomegranate Spring" belongs to Simeon in 19:7. The ancient name is reflected in Kh. er-Ramamin, c. 3.2 km south of Lahav. At the latter site excavators found a unique ceramic form, a small bowl with a molded pomegranate in the center, thus offering a hint as to the identification of Tell Halif. Seger and Borowski, "The First Two Seasons at Tell Halif," *BA* 40 (1977) 166.

twenty-nine. Against the thirty-three that are named in the reconstructed list (thirty-two if *Iyim* in v 29 is the result of a scribal lapse). This number is apparently based on a damaged list but it shows surprisingly small variation in view of the possibilities for misdivision, annotation, and conflation of names down the centuries of transmission.

enclosures. The root is *ḥṣr*, as in the many place names formed with the same root in vv 23-28 (six occurrences), which also illustrates the process of annotation.

33. *Shephelah*. Literally, "Lowland," which is used regularly to refer to the geographically distinct western foothills through which the major wadis empty into the coastal plain and which in the south spill away to the Negeb desert. Here there were three districts. This portion of the list begins at the north end of Judah's frontier with Philistia.

33b-36. District II centers in the Soreq Valley. See Map G, 364. Here the history of territorial claims is intertwined with the tribe of Dan. Significant for its absence from the list is the town of Beth-shemesh. Cross and Wright read the archaeological evidence as pointing to a ninth-century date for the list, because of an almost total gap in the occupation of Beth-shemesh at that time. Instead other nearby towns are listed.

33. *Eshtaol*. Assigned to Dan in 19:41. The site is to be sought somewhere in the wider neighborhood of Ishwa', perhaps at Irtuf, c. 1.5 km to the south of it. Simons, *GTOT*, 146.

Zorah. Assigned to Dan in 19:41. Modern Ṣar'ah. Map G, 364.

Ashnah. Possibly Kh. Wadi Allin, just southeast of Beth-shemesh on the 1:100,000 map, section 11. Mentioned only here, it should not be confused with the town of the same name in the neighboring District IV (v 43).

34. *Zanoah*. Khirbet Zānū', 1.5 km south of modern Zanoah. Map G, 364. Also a place name in District VII (v 56).

En-gannim. "Spring of Gardens." Not to be confused with the great northern place of the same name in Issachar (19:21). The Judahite site is perhaps at Beit Jemal, c. 3.2 km south of Beth-shemesh and just west of the spring called Ain Fatir, G. W. van Beek, *IDB* 2, 101.

Tappuah. Perhaps "Quince." W. E. Reed, *IDB* 4, 517. Possibly at or near Beit Nettif, c. 5 km southeast of Azeqah. Map G, 364. There was another Tappuah on the northern border of Ephraim (12:17; 16:8; cf. 17:7-8), and a Beth-tappuah in District VI (v 53).

†*Enam*. Not well known. Genesis 38:14 may contain the same name in a different form: there the "road to Enaim" (LXX) branches from the road that runs up "from Adullam" (Kh. Sheik Madhkur) "to Timnah" (Kh. Tibnah). Simons, *GTOT*, 222.

35. *Jarmuth*. Khirbet Yarmūk. East of Azeqah. Map G, 364. Its king "Piram" belonged to the hill-country coalition opposing Joshua and Israel in 10:3,23. The place name also occurs as a Levitical town in Issachar (21:29).

Adullam. Tell esh-Sheikh Madhkūr. Map G, 364. The king of Adullam is listed in 12:15 among the thirty-one kings of Canaan defeated by Israel.

Socoh. Khirbet 'Abbad. Map G. The name occurs again in the hill country (v 48) and in the northern territory administered for Solomon by Ben-hesed (1 Kgs 4:10). This Shephelah town is probably named in a number of late Judahite royal seal impressions. Paul W. Lapp, "Late Royal Seals from Judah," *BASOR* 158 (April 1960) 19.

Azeqah. Tell ez-Zakariyeh, controlling the upland access to the Elah Valley (1 Sam 17:1). Map G, 364. Later it would be fortified by Rehoboam after the schism with the northern tribes (2 Chr 11:9) and would have a significant role to play in the resistance to Nebuchadnezzar's advance toward Jerusalem, Lachish Letter No. 4 (*KAI* 194:12-13; cf. *ANET*³, 322).

36. *Shaaraim*. Location uncertain. The name occurs again in the story of the rout of the Philistines "on the way from Shaaraim as far as Gath and Ekron" (1 Sam 17:52). Perhaps Kh. es-Sa'īreh, east-southeast from Beth-shemesh. Anson F. Rainey, "The Identification of Philistine-Gath," *Eretz-Israel* 12 (1975) 70*.

†*Adithaim*. Location uncertain.

Gederah. "Sheepfold," a common topographical label, occurring in a variety of forms as "Geder" (12:13); "Gedor" (15:58, in District VIII; 1 Chr 4:18,39), and "Gederoth" (15:41, in District III; and 1 Chr 12:5 near Gibeon). The last of these appears to be named on the stamped jar handles from el-Jib (Gibeon). A. Demsky, "The Genealogy of Gibeon (1 Chron 9:35-44): Biblical and Epigraphic Considerations," *BASOR* 202 (April 1971) esp. 20-22 n. 28.

(*fourteen*. So MT, in agreement with the critically reconstructed list.

37-41. District III, the southernmost Shephelah province, is dominated by the strongly fortified city of Lachish.

37. †*Zenan*, †*Hadashah*. The first may be equated with "Zanaan" in Mic 1:11; Micah the prophet was from Moresheth-gath, the only hint to the approximate location of these places.

†*Migdal-gad*. Possibly Kh. el-Mejdeleh, c. 6 km south of Lachish. Map G, 364.

38. †*Dilean*. Location uncertain. Identification with Tell Najila comes up

against a major gap in occupation throughout the Iron I and early Iron II periods. Ruth Amiran and A. Eitan, *EAEHL* III (1977) 894-898.

Mizpeh. "Lookout" or "Watchtower," a common place name occurring in Moab (1 Sam 22:3), in Benjamin (Josh 18:26), and in Gilead (Mizpah in Judg 10:17). This District III Lookout remains unidentified.

Joqtheel. Here spelled *yqt'l.* Location unknown, but not far from Azeqah and Socoh as shown by *yqwty'l* in 1 Chr 4:18. King Amaziah gave this name to the captured Edomite stronghold formerly called "Sela" (2 Kgs 14:7).

39. *Lachish.* The one town in the district which can be confidently located, at the impressive site of Tell ed-Duweir. Its king Japhia participated in the siege of Gibeon (10:3-5) and its sequel (10:23); the king of Lachish is listed as one of the thirty-one kings removed by Israel (12:11).

Bozqath. Unfortunately, this name is otherwise unknown except as the hometown of one of King Josiah's grandparents (2 Kgs 22:1).

Eglon. Another name figuring prominently in the coalition opposing Israel at the battle of Aijalon. On the problem of identification see fifth NOTE on 10:3.

40. †*Kabbon.* Unidentified, the name may be related to Makbenah in 1 Chr 2:49.

†*Lahmam.* Khirbet el-Laḥm near Lachish?

Kitlish. Unidentified. The same name is possibly "Kentisha" in the list of Tuthmoses III (c. 1490-1436), and as *k-n-ti-sa* on a hieratic ostracon from the reign of Merneptah nearly three centuries later found at Lachish.

41. *Gederoth.* Location uncertain. See above on *Gederah* (v 36).

Beth-dagon. Also a place name in Asher (19:27), meaning "House/Temple of Dagon." Location uncertain. Khirbet Dajun, southwest of modern Beth-Dagan, is too far to the northwest to be included in the Lachish district. The god Dagon, whose name otherwise survived as the demythologized common noun for "grain" in Israel, was exceedingly popular with the Philistines (Judg 16:23), who were famous for consuming vast quantities of beer and who built a temple for their great grain god in Ashdod (1 Sam 5:2-7). A distinctive Philistine temple has been recently excavated at Tell Qasile, on the northern bank of the Yarqon River, in a northern suburb of Tel Aviv, described by Amihay Mazar in *BA* 36 (1973) 42-48.

†*Naamah.* Unidentified.

Maqqedah. See 10:10; 12:16 and NOTES.

(*sixteen.* The list and the summary agree.

42-44. District IV is the central Shephelah region along the north-south axis.

42. *Libnah.* Defeated in 10:29; its king dethroned in 12:15. The best candidate is Tell Bornat. Map G, 364. See NOTES on 10:29. For an older view that would find Libnah at Tell es-Safi, objecting to the relatively small size of Tell Bornat, see Cross and Wright, "Boundary and Province Lists," *JBL* 75 (1956) 217-218.

Ether. Hebrew *'tr.* The presence of Ether in the Simeon list at 19:7 may account for the occurrence of the next name here by attraction from that context.

Ashan. If it is not a by-product of the dittography of Ashnah from v 43, it may have been displaced from either the preceding district ("Ashnah" in v 33) or from the Simeon list as noted above.

43. †*Iphtah.* "He (God) opens (the womb?)." Possibly Terqumiyeh, about midway between Hebron and Beit Jibrin. Simons, *GTOT,* 148. Cf. Iphtahel, "El opens," the name of a valley on the border between Zebulun and Asher.

Ashnah. Possibly Idhna, near Mareshah.

†*Nezib.* Khirbet Beit Neṣib, between Beth-zur and Mareshah. Map G, 364.

44. *Qeilah.* Khirbet Qilā, c. 13.6 km northeast of Hebron, and on the border between the fourteenth-century city-states of Jerusalem and Hebron, each of which disputes the other's occupation of Qeilah in letters to the foreign office at Amarna. Much later Qeilah appears still to be no man's land, experiencing both the protection of David against the Philistines and Saul's attack against David, forcing his withdrawal (1 Sam 23:1-13) farther south.

Achzib. "Chezib" in Gen 38:5, "Cozeba" in 1 Chr 4:22. The site is Tell el-Beida, southwest of Adullam. Map G, 364.

Mareshah. Tell Sandaḥannah. Later an important fortress city of the Judean kingdom (2 Chr 11:8; 14:9-14; 20:37). Map G.

nine. This total includes the textually questionable "Ashan."

45-47. Departure from the form which is standard throughout the bulk of vv 20-62 is obvious at a glance. Here the redactor who brought together the boundary lists and town lists of chaps. 15-19 has created his own description for an important missing segment, the Philistine plain. Never effectively controlled by Israel or Judah, it nonetheless belonged to a full description of the fairly "allotted" land. Judah's territory extended, in principle, to the coast (vv 4,11,12).

45. *Eqron.* Possibly Qatra. Map G, 364. Assigned to Dan in 19:43, it was strategically situated as the northernmost city of the Philistine pentapolis, involved in the long face-off with Israel for control of the Shephelah (Judg 1:18; 1 Sam 5-6; 7:14; 17:52), and frequently in the path of imperial armies, such as Shishak's (c. 918) and Sennacherib's (701 B.C.).

dependencies and enclosures. These are not synonymns. The first, literally "daughter(-town)s," is found in 15:28; 17:11,16; and Judg 1:27; 11:26 (*bis*). See H. Haag, "bath," in *TDOT* 2, 336. The second, sharing the root that occurs in all three town names in v 25, occurs repeatedly in chaps. 15 and 19, but elsewhere only in 13:23,28; 18:24,28. Only here, and again in v 47, do they appear in conjunction.

dependencies. An impressive example of a dependent town is the small open village excavated c. 1.5 km southeast of the strongly fortified Middle Bronze Age town of Beth-shemesh. The pattern of undefended rural villages persisted, with many more appearing in the Late Bronze Age.

46. *alongside.* Hebrew *'l yd,* lit. "at the hand of." The imprecision of the description is another indication that the historian is struggling to reconstruct an unfulfilled claim to the coastal plain.

Ashdod. Map G, 364. Archaeologically, the best known of the five leading Philistine cities. *EAEHL* I (1975) 103-118. It was the northernmost of the three that were far out in the plain, on or near the coast. The nearby harbor satellite of Ashdod was Tell Mor. On the pre-Philistine presence of the "Anaqim" in these coastal towns, see above, v 14 and NOTES and 11:21-22 and NOTES. There is increasing evidence that the Iron Age settlement of the coastal plain came in two waves. "Jaffa, Ashdod, Tel Mor, and even Gezer show evidence of having been destroyed twice—first apparently in the time of Merneptah, in hit-and-run raids from the sea; and the second, a more massive action in the time of Ramses III involving settlement . . ." Abraham Malamat, "The Egyptian Decline in Canaan and the Sea-Peoples," *WHJP* III (1971) 29. We may suspect, therefore, that the Anaqim came to Canaan as part of the "pre-Philistine" Sea Peoples.

47. *Gaza*. Map G, 364. The name sometimes evokes a sense of "deep south" (10:41).

Egyptian Gorge. See 15:4 and NOTE.

48. *And in the Hill Country*. This heading covers vv 48b-60, which seem originally to have included seven segments. The prefixed conjunction *And* helped to turn the list into a lengthy, but awkward descriptive statement.

48b-51. District V lies in the southern hills, descending toward the plateau of the northern Negeb.

48b. *Shamir*. Khirbet es-Sumara, c. 20 km west-southwest of Hebron, seems to reflect the ancient name. The name seems also to occur in the north, possibly to be equated with "Samaria," as home of the Israelite judge Tola (Judg 10:1-2).

Jattir. Map G, 364. A Levitical town (21:14), it was relieved by David with booty taken in battle with Amaleqites (1 Sam 30:27). The name is perhaps reflected as Kh. ʿAttir, which however is better related to Ether in v 42. Peterson's 1977 survey found evidence of Iron II as the earliest settlement at Kh. ʿAttir.

Socoh. Khirbet Shuweikeh. The name occurs also in the northern Shephelah district (v 35), and still farther north in Solomon's third northern district (1 Kgs 4:10).

49. †*Dannah*. Location unknown.

Debir. Map G, 364. See 10:38 and NOTES.

50. *Anab*. Map G. Formerly occupied by the Anaqim, according to 11:21. It cannot be Kh. ʿAnab el-Kebirah where there is nothing pre-Roman, but is more likely Kh. ʿAnab es-Seghirah, c. 6 km southwest of Rabûd. Kochavi, "Khirbet Rabûd=Debir," *Tel Aviv* 1 (1974) 28 n. 12.

Eshtemoh. A Levitical town (*Eshtemoa* in 21:14). The name survives at es-Semūʿ. Map G, 364.

†*Anim*. "Springs." Most likely Kh. Ghuwein el-Taḥta. Map G. Probably the same place is called Hawini in the Amarna Letters.

51. *Goshen, Holon, Giloh*. The first is possibly to be located at ed-Dahariyeh. Neither of the other two can be pinpointed with any confidence. The name "Holon" also occurs in the list of Levitical towns (21:15).

(*eleven*. LXXᴬ "ten" probably reflects an equation of two names in the list.

52-54. District VI is the area south-southwest of Hebron, administered from that city as political center of the early monarchy.

52. †*Arab, Dumah,* †*Eshan.* The first two are plausibly located at er-Rabiyeh and ed-Domeh respectively. The third is unknown unless the reading of LXX^B, "Soma," representing a different *Vorlage,* is to be connected with Kh. hallat Sama, c. 2 km west of ed-Domeh. Simons, *GTOT,* 149. We have no explanation for the differences.

53. †*Janum,* †*Beth-tappuah,* †*Apheqah.* The first is unknown. The second, "Apricot-house," seems to have given its name to *Taffūḥ* west-northwest of Hebron (Map G, 364). The third is plausibly located at the Iron Age site Kh. Marajim in a valley called Seil ed-Dilbeh, "Sycamore Torrent," c. 7 km north of Rabûd. Kochavi, *Tel Aviv* 1 (1974) 3 n. 2.

54. †*Humtah, Qiryath-arba* . . . †*Zior.* The first of these remains unidentified. For the second see 14:15 and NOTES. The third cannot be located at Si'îr because the latter lies in the middle of District VIII.

55-57. District VII is the area southeast of Hebron, the cultivable fringe of the wilderness spilling down the watershed ridge toward the Dead Sea and northeastern Negeb.

55. *Maon.* Map G, 364. Tell Ma'în is 13.6 km south of Hebron. David later hid out from Saul in the area (1 Sam 23:24-25); and here he had the run-in with Nabal, who refused him hospitality (1 Samuel 25). Note the Transjordan name Wadi Zerqa Ma'în. The name *Ma'în* occurs on an ostracon from Arad, which is interpreted as recording payment of some commodity as taxes to the fortress at Arad. Whether the name there refers to the Judahite town or to a subtribal unit of eastern Negeb clans is an open question. A. F. Rainey, "A Hebrew 'Receipt' from Arad," *BASOR* 202 (April 1971) 23-29.

Carmel. Not to be confused with the mountain overlooking the Bay of Acco. The place is identified with Kh. el-Kirmil, 11.2 km south-southeast of Hebron. Map G, 364. The place figures rather prominently in the late careers of Saul and David. 1 Samuel 25; 2 Sam 23:35=1 Chr 11:37.

Ziph. Tell Ziph. Map G, 364. This is not to be confused with the place of the same name far to the south in the Negeb district (v 24). It is this northern Ziph that is named on a large number of stamped jar handles, many of them from northern sites. H. L. Ginsberg, "Judah and the Transjordan States from 734 to 582 B.C.E.," in *Alexander Marx Jubilee Volume: English Section,* ed. Saul Lieberman (New York: Jewish Theological Seminary, 1950) 349 n. 12.

Juttah. Map G, 364. Also a Levitical town (21:16). Modern Yatta is a large village 8.8 km southwest of Hebron.

56. *Jezreel.* Location unknown. The same name occurs in the north at a famous town which also gave its name to the broad plain separating Galilee from the north-central hill country (19:18).

Joqdeam. Possibly Kh. Raqqa' near the northern Ziph.

Zanoah. Possibly Zanūtā near Jattir. Not to be confused with the place of the same name in the northern Shephelah district (v 34).

57. †*Qain.* Khirbet Yaqin, southeast of Hebron. The name is related to the clan of the metalworkers called Qenites (Num 24:22; Judg 4:11,17).

Gibeah. Cf. 2 Chr 13:2. Location unknown. The site of el-Jab'ah (6 km northwest of Beit Ummar) lies too far to the north.

Timnah. Cf. Gen 38:12-14. Again, the modern name (Tibnah in the hills southeast of Beth-shemesh) refers to a place located too far to the north.

ten. LXX reads "nine," as a result of merging two names, perhaps understanding there to be a "Zanoah of the Qenites."

58-59. District VIII is the central ridge and area to the west, 3 km or so north of Hebron. Here there is little settled life east of the watershed, where wilderness begins almost immediately.

58. *Halhul.* Modern Ḥalhul. Map G, 364.

Beth-zur. The name has Calebite connections (1 Chr 2:45). Khirbet et-Tubeiqah is well-known from excavations. Map G, 364. After a period of occupation in MB, the place was virtually abandoned for some three hundred years, until it was rebuilt at the beginning of the Iron Age. O. R. Sellers, *The Citadel of Beth-zur* (1933); Sellers et al., *The 1957 Excavations at Beth-zur,* AASOR 38 (1968).

Gedor. "Sheepfold." Khirbet Jedur. Map G, 364. For the frequency of the element *gdr* in place names, see "Gederah" in v 36 and NOTE.

59. *Maarath.* Hebrew *m'rt.* The same as "Maroth" (*mrwt*) in Mic 1:12? Khirbet Qufin, some 3.2 km north of Beth-zur? V. R. Gold, *IDB* 3, 196.

†*Beth-anoth.* "House/Temple of (the goddess) Anath." This is Beit Ainun just east-northeast of Mamre. Map G, 364. Cf. "Beth-anath" in Naphtali (19:38; Judg 1:33).

†*Elteqon.* Possibly Kh. ed-Deir, west of Etam.

The description of District IX is found in LXX, where in Hebrew a copyist had jumped from "towns and their enclosures" at the end of v 58 to the same words at the end of the restored unit. This district centers in the little town of Bethlehem, a vivid reminder of the small scale of towns and tax-paying populations in the narrow Palestinian corridor.

Teqoa. Identical with Tequ', c. 9.6 km south of Bethlehem. Map G, 364. From David's recruitment there of one of his mighty men (2 Sam 23:26)), to Joab's discovery there of a "wise woman" who would maneuver the king into a sort of "pardon" for Absalom (2 Samuel 13-14), to Yahweh's enlistment there of the prophet Amos (Amos 1:1), with many other references broadening and continuing the story on into the post-exilic and Maccabean eras, the town had a distinguished history.

Ephrathah. In the Calebite lists of 1 Chr 2:18-24 and 42-50a the names Ephrath (v 19) and Ephrathah (vv 24,50) are employed for Hezron's wife whom Caleb son of Hezron married after his father had died. This geographical term may thus be a clan name in origin. It is in any case the larger designation, to be more precisely focused in a parenthesis. See the discussion in Campbell, *Ruth,* AB 7, 54-55. The referent of the same name in Gen 35:16,19; and 48:7 (near Bethel?) is unclear.

Bethlehem). Map G, 364. Little known, archaeologically, because of continuous concentrated occupation across the centuries. See Campbell, *Ruth,* 54. The name means "house of fighting," or more likely "House of (the war god) Laḥmu." With linguistic change and spiritualizing reflection, it came to be

"House of bread." The place name also occurs in Galilee, a town in Zebulun (19:15) whence came Ibzan, one of the judges (Judg 12:8,10). The earliest mention of the famous southern town outside the Bible may be an Amarna Letter in which the prince of Jerusalem, Abdu-Heba, charges that Bit-NIN.IB has deserted Pharaoh and cast its lot with the 'Apiru. The logogram NIN.IB is read Ninurta in Mesopotamia and may have been used for West Semitic Laḫmu. But a better case can be made for interpreting the logographically written name as a reference to Beth-horon, a strategically far more important town northwest of Jerusalem (10:10 and Notes). Z. Kallai and H. Tadmor, "Bīt Ninurta=Beth Horon—On the History of the Kingdom of Jerusalem in the Amarna Period," *Eretz Israel* 9 (1969) 138-147 in Hebrew, with English summary, 138.

Peor. Map G, 364. Khirbet Fāghūr, 2.5 km southwest of Bethlehem, suggested by Aharoni, *LOB*, 296. The name also occurs in Transjordan, referring to a mountain (Peor in Num 23:27-28), to the god of the mountain (Baal-Peor in Num 25:19; Deut 4:3; Ps 106:28; Hos 9:10; cf. Josh 22:17), or his temple (Beth-peor in Deut 3:29; 4:46; 34:6).

Etam. 'Ain 'Atan just northwest of Kh. el-Khokh perhaps reflects the ancient name. Map G, 364. Later to be fortified by Rehoboam (2 Chr 11:6). The name occurs also in Simeon (1 Chr 4:32).

†*Koloun,* †*Tatam,* †*Sores.* Because the names are textually uncertain, there is little to be gained from trying to locate them.

†*Karem.* 'Ain Karim, "Vineyard Spring," lies within a suburb of modern Jerusalem.

Gallim. Location unknown, but not the place referred to in 1 Sam 25:44 and Isa 10:30; the latter is somewhere in the territory of Benjamin. This unquestioned equation is at the basis of the claim that the ancient documents were in error in equating Jerusalem and Jebus (15:63). Miller and Tucker, *Joshua,* 127.

†*Bether.* Khirbet el-Yehud, above Bittīr, which preserves the ancient name. The place is best known as Bar Kochba's capital in the war against Rome, after his recognition as messiah in 132 C.E.

Manahath. Probably Mālḥah, 4.8 km southwest of Jerusalem, near Bittīr. This is most likely the town to which certain families of Geba in Benjamin were exiled. 1 Chr 8:6. The name occurs among both the Transjordan "Horites" (Gen 36:23; 1 Chr 1:40) and the Cisjordan "Sons of Hur" ("Menuhoth" in 1 Chr 2:52).

60. Part of District X and the entirety of District XI were omitted from Judah's list by a compiler who apparently lacked adequate sources otherwise for describing the original fief of Benjamin (18:21-28).

Qiryath-baal (. . . *Qiryath-yearim*). These names and the site are discussed in Notes on 9:17. The town appears in the second of two groups of Benjamin's towns, all in this group located on the westward side of the watershed ridge (18:25-28). See Notes and Comment.

Rabbah. Literally, "The Great (One/Lady)," as used also in reference to the Ammonite capital and goddess. The location of this one remains uncertain. In order to establish an equation with Rubute, mentioned in Egyptian sources,

Aharoni proposed identification of Rabbah with Beth-shemesh. His radical solution requires removing "Eshtaol" and "Zorah" (both Shephelah towns) from the beginning of the District II list and reading them with the two names in v 60. That the result, as Aharoni admitted, made no geographical sense, he thought was overcome by "exigencies of administration and territorial tradition." *LOB,* 299-300. What remains unexplained is how the textual dislocation occurred. A far better solution is simply to observe the gap in the document and recognize the missing parts being used in 18:21-24 (eastern Benjamin) and 18:25-28 (western Benjamin), and allow that "The Great One" is a textual orphan.

61-63. District XII is the wilderness district, stretching along the northern half of the western Dead Sea shore, a desolate region very sparsely settled except near the few oases scattered along the valley floor and on a small self-contained plateau just above it.

61. *Beth-arabah.* Map G, 364. For the identification with the area of the spring called 'Ain el-Gharabeh, southeast of Jericho on the Wadi el-Qelt, see above, NOTES on 15:6. Assigned to Benjamin in 18:22.

†*Middin.* Map G, 364. This is the first of three "towns" that are most plausibly identified with the fortified farming settlements of the Buqei'ah described by F. M. Cross and J. T. Milik (see now *EAEHL* I [1975] 267-270) and studied more thoroughly by L. E. Stager, "Farming in the Judean Desert During the Iron Age," *BASOR* 221 (February 1976) 145-158. See above, concerning "Trouble Valley" in 7:24-26 and NOTES. By building terrace dams and simple sluice gates for slowing down and collecting the scant runoff from rains in the higher hill country, enough agriculture was possible to maintain a small community of perhaps a hundred persons. If the places are listed from north to south, this one is Kh. Abu Tabaq.

†*Secacah.* Map G, 364. Khirbet es-Samrah is the largest fortress and dominates a hill in the central Buqei'a. With defense walls forming a rectangle c. forty by sixty meters, and living quarters built along three sides, the fort is remarkably similar to the Iron Age forts at Qumran and En-gedi.

62. †*Nibshan.* Map G, 364. Khirbet el-Maqari is the southernmost Buqei'ah site, and the smallest of the three fortresses.

Salt City. Probably Khirbet Qumran (Map G), on the marly plateau of the wider rift, overlooking the Dead Sea south of Beth-arabah; it later served as the great Essene communal center of Dead Sea scroll fame.

En-gedi. Map G, 364. The site is perhaps Tell Jurn, near 'Ain Jidi (which preserves the ancient name), where the earliest stratum found in excavations is dated to the close of the monarchy, c. 625-580 B.C. Mazar, "Excavations at the Oasis of Engedi" (1967) 67-76.

63. *Jebusite inhabitants of Jerusalem.* For fuller discussion see NOTES on 3:10. That the failure to oust the Jebusites, here charged to the Bene Judah, is also charged to Benjamin in Judg 1:21 has been taken to mean that Jebus was in fact distinct from Jerusalem (Miller and Tucker, 128), but that conclusion is not inevitable. What the tradition seems to reflect is temporary success, on Judah's side, against the unfortified southwestern hill (Judg 1:8; cf. Joshua

10), while Benjamin on the northeast found the great walled fort on the eastern hill impregnable.

were unable to evict. This explanation is offered again in 17:12 and Judg 1:19. The stronger statement of failure is "did not evict," as in Josh 16:10 and Judg 1:21,27-28,29,33. On the origin of the Judges 1 list in a prototype which also yielded these scattered notices of continuing Canaanite land tenure, see Aharoni, *LOB,* 212-217.

COMMENT

These verses (15:20-63) reflect an administrative "province" list of the kingdom of Judah, another segment of which is similarly used to describe the allotment of Benjamin in 18:21-28. The system itself is probably much older, in which such lists originally identified the population centers which supplied troops for the tribal muster (D. N. Freedman, private communication). In its finished form the list reflects the expansionist/revivalist policies of King Josiah, in whose reign almost certainly most of the oasis forts and paramilitary settlements such as the desert farms were established and unified as a single administrative area in the wilderness (District XII). The description of Philistia in vv 45-47 is likewise not a part of the original system. With these two sections included, however, the list preserves a total of twelve divisions, after the displacement of the two Benjamin sections.

If a first major edition of the long historical work stems from the reign of the great reforming king Josiah, then the disproportionate detail in Judah's allotment as compared with all the others is understandable.

Yet it is clear that there was a pre-Josianic administrative system within which the creation of District XII was a modification. That district included Beth-arabah, at one time belonging to Benjamin (18:22). The pattern at the end of chap. 15 makes sense as reflecting the situation early in Josiah's reign, prior to his extensive activity in the territory of the old northern kingdom, but after the strengthening of the southeastern flank by settling the soldier-farmers in the Buqei'ah.

We may similarly suspect that Qiryath-yearim became Judahite (15:60) under the late monarchy; for that claim too stands in tension with an old Benjaminite identity (18:28).

Direct clues to the earlier history of the list are scant. Probably the original system already included the towns of District II that had been assigned to Dan but were not incorporated in Israel until David's victories against the Philistines. Concerning the adjacent area to the south, the

Philistine plain, the report of King Hezekiah's campaign against Philistia "as far as Gaza" (2 Kgs 18:8), might be taken as the sort of datum that would trigger the insertion of vv 45-47. Z. Kallai has thus argued for a date in the reign of Hezekiah, c. 715-687. See M. Weinfeld, review of Kallai, *The Tribes of Israel,* in *JBL* 89 (1970) 351.

Surely the original system goes back to the tenth century and earlier, reflecting in part the fiscal reorganization stemming from David's census (2 Samuel 24; 1 Chronicles 21). The Judahite system was presupposed and augmented by Solomon's creation of a comparable system for the north (1 Kings 4). See Wright, "The Provinces of Solomon," *Eretz Israel* 8 (1967) *58-*68.

Our NOTES above teem with indications of rapid change in the settlement patterns of the Negeb. The late eleventh and early tenth centuries saw an amazing rate of pacification and settlement. Beersheba and all the pre-monarchical sites known in the eastern Negeb were unwalled villages. New settlements from each of the next several centuries were finally incorporated into the list. 2 Chronicles 11:23 reports that King Rehoboam, "dealing wisely," distributed some of his sons throughout the "districts of Judah and Benjamin," perpetuating a pattern used by Solomon. Cross and Wright have pointed to tenth-century public buildings, such as the palaces and storehouses at places like Lachish and Beth-shemesh, as external evidence for the Davidic establishment of this system. Yet, they argue, the bulk of the list must be later than David because of the absence of Beth-shemesh from the list of the northern Shephelah district. This absence, they suggest, must correspond to the marked decline of Beth-shemesh in the next stratum. This in turn was correlated with the long gap at southern Tell el-Far'ah ("Shilhim" in v 32) from the ninth to the sixth centuries. Yet another significant set of data: the northern boundary of District XI (see below, 18:21-24) encompasses a strip of Israelite territory first captured for Judah by Abijah (c. 915-913), but lost again to Israel by the eighth century. Thus the administrative reforms in the reign of Jehoshaphat (2 Chr 17:2,12-13; 19:4-11) were taken as providing the life setting for a definitive form of the system and list. That Jehoshaphat's program and peaceful relations with Israel are not mentioned in the "Deuteronomic" work, is probably a reflection of Josianic bias.

A careful look at Map G (364) suggests that there was a continuing struggle over the old Benjamin territory, contiguous in the Jordan Valley with the deep-rift portion of District XII, which required periodic reorganization of the northern districts in Judah. In other words, Judah continued throughout the monarchical period to function as heir to the southern half of the old polarity between "Sons of the South" (originally Benjaminites) and "Sons of the North" (originally Bene Joseph). Not only is this reflected in the appearance of some of Benjamin's towns in the Judahite list, but also in the names of extinct Benjamin clans, known also from Mari, in Judahite genealogy. Albright, "II. Moses Out of Egypt," *BA* 36 (1973) 48-49. Perhaps Benjamin's original territory included the greater part of the south, which might reflect Saul's efforts to control the south for Benjamin.

Judah's consolidation late in the Shiloh phase has vastly overshadowed the active role of the original "southerners" in the Yahwist revolution.

If Judah in the late eleventh century is not a noteworthy participant in affairs of the league (Deut 33:7) and if Benjamin is at the same time relatively secure and peaceful (Deut 33:12), both were up to their ears in predatory violence, say, half a century earlier. The difference is that Judah's situation is celebrated at length in fourteen poetic lines (Gen 49:9-12), while Benjamin is reduced to three, and much less laudatory ones (Gen 49:27). Thus it is a vast oversimplication to posit, as many still do, a six-tribe predecessor to the Yahweh league. That the original nucleus involved a polarity of hill-country populations is implicit in the sequence of allotments. We turn directly from this fuller treatment of the later sons of the south (Judah) to the much sketchier treatment of the original sons of the north—the Joseph tribe.

c. THE BENE JOSEPH TERRITORIES 16:1-17:18

1'. SOUTHERN BORDER
(16:1-4)

16 ¹ The allotment for the Bene Joseph ran from the Jordan near Jericho, east of the Jericho spring, and went up from Jericho into the desert mountains to Bethel (that is, to Luz). ² It went out from Bethel and went around to the border of the Archites at Ataroth . . . as far as Upper Beth-horon. ³ It descended westward to the border of the Japhletites, as far as Lower Beth-horon (and as far as Gezer), and its destination was toward the sea.

⁴ The Bene Joseph—Manasseh and Ephraim—received their fief.

TEXTUAL NOTES

16 1. *allotment*   See 15:1 Textual Note.

of the Jericho spring   Lacking in LXX, by haplography: *yryḥ[w lmy yryḥ]w*.

and   With LXX, where MT lacks the conjunction.

the desert mountains   Based on LXX, where MT shows a haplography, *h[r hmdb]r*. Subsequently "the wilderness" was awkwardly restored in the middle of the verse. The reconstructed text thus accounts for all the major differences between MT and LXX:

MT	*hmdbr [ ] 'lh myryḥw bhr [ ] byt-'l*	
LXX	*w'lh myryḥw bhr hmdbr byt-'l lwzh*	
*	*w'lh myryḥw bhr hmdbr byt-'l lwzh*	

Luz)   Thus LXX which equates the two place names.

2. *Bethel*   Here MT reads "to Luz," mistakenly displaced from the end of the preceding verse.

the Archites at Ataroth   MT *h'rky 'ṭrwt*. LXX *hk(')ṭrwt*.

as far as Upper Beth-horon   Restored from v 5. See NOTE. Cf. the similarities of the following clause. "It descended westward to the border" (Hebrew *wyrd ymh 'l gbwl*) makes sense at the beginning of v 3. Not so the clause beginning v 6 in MT, "and the border follows the wadi westward" (Hebrew *wyṣ' hgbwl hymh*), which is perhaps a misplaced variant reading.

3. (*and as far as Gezer*)   Lacking in LXX, presumably as a result of haplography in its Hebrew text.

its destination   Reading the *qere tṣwtyw*.

toward the sea   MT *ymh*, literally "seawards." There is some support in Hebrew manuscripts for reading the definite article with the word: *hymh*.

NOTES

16:1-4. The verses are introduction to the early west-bank territories of the two tribes Ephraim and Manasseh who comprise the "Sons of Joseph." The introduction is a description of Ephraim's border with Benjamin and Dan, given for the most part only in very general terms.

1. *the Bene Joseph*. This is the older unit; the division into "Ephraim" and "Manasseh" may involve a replacement for "Levi" in constituencies of the old pre-Mosaic league of Israel. For the curious argument that it was the other way around (Ephraim and Manasseh early but no Levi; Bene Joseph and Levi late, i.e. post 722), see C. H. J. de Geus, *The Tribes of Israel* (Amsterdam: Van Gorcum, 1976) 69-108, 111-120. We reviewed this interesting book in *JBL* 97 (1978) 115-119 and found it extremely helpful on a great variety of other matters.

near. Expressed in Hebrew by use of apposition.

desert mountains. Hebrew *hr hmdbr*. Reference is to the barren backside of the central ridge, largely deprived of the rainfall which prevailing winds out of the west deposit on the seaward slopes.

Bethel. Map H, 398. See NOTE on 7:2. Assigned to Benjamin in 18:22.

(*that is*. The equation is established by 18:13 and Judg 1:23.

Luz). One possible verbal root means "to turn aside, depart," and figuratively refers to devious or crafty intent. But if the name truly derives from *lwḏ* (Arabic "to take refuge, seek shelter"), then it may have been an asylum-town prior to its takeover by northern tribes. See Judg 1:22-26. The change of name to Bethel is uniformly credited to Jacob (Gen 28:19; 35:6; 48:3).

2. *went out*. The verb *yṣ'* in these descriptions means to follow a wadi or lowland route, here probably the Wadi Suweinit. Parunak, "Geographical Terminology."

went around. That is, followed the northern branch of the Suweinit and continued beyond it, onto the watershed ridge. Ibid.

Archites. Hebrew *h'rky* is a gentilic formation, which refers to a clan or village population that became part of Benjamin. One of David's most loyal advisors, Hushai, was recruited from them (2 Sam 15:32; 16:16; 17:5).

Ataroth. Called Ataroth-addar, "Greater Ataroth," in v 5 and in 18:13. Not to be confused with the Ataroth on Ephraim's northern border (v 7). The

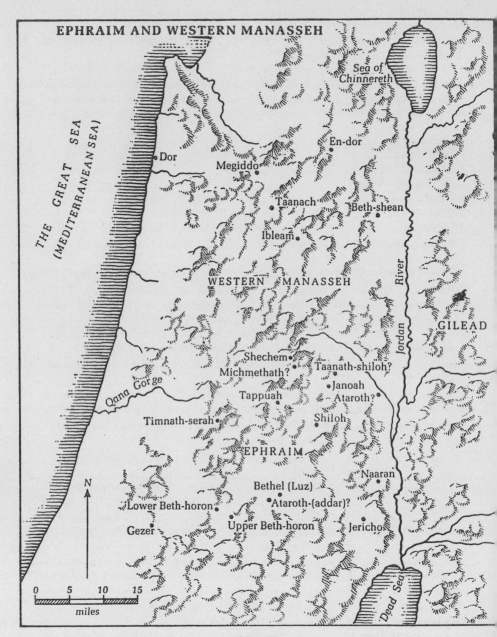

EPHRAIM AND WESTERN MANASSEH

THE GREAT SEA
(MEDITERRANEAN SEA)

Sea of
Chinnereth

Dor

En-dor

Megiddo

Taanach

Beth-shean

Ibleam

WESTERN   MANASSEH

Jordan River

GILEAD

Qana Gorge

Shechem

Michmethath?   Taanath-shiloh?

Janoah

Tappuah   Ataroth?

Shiloh

Timnath-serah

EPHRAIM

Naaran

Bethel (Luz)

N

Ataroth-(addar)?

Lower Beth-horon

Gezer   Upper Beth-horon   Jericho

Dead Sea

0   5   10   15
miles

Map H

name of southern Ataroth is reflected in Kh. Atārah, c. 3.2 km south of el-Bireh, best candidate for the ancient town. A line emerging from the northern branch of the Suweinit supports the identification. Parunak, "Geographical Terminology."

as far as Upper Beth-horon. These words are relocated from v 5, where they are clearly out of place, but make good sense here. A verb is missing.

Upper Beth-horon. Beit 'Ūr el-Fōqā. Map H. Altitude c. 533 meters above sea level. This is one of the "twin cities" overlooking the pass west of Gibeon (10:10) from opposite sides.

Beth-horon. "House/Temple of (the Canaanite god) Horon," perhaps to be identified with Bit-NIN.IB of the Amarna Letters. See above, NOTES on Bethlehem in 15:59.

3. *Japhletites.* Another clan or village population whose continuing identity helped to mark the territorial limit, but unfortunately otherwise unknown.

Lower Beth-horon. Beit 'Ūr et-Taḥta, altitude c. 320 meters above sea level. Map H.

(and as far as Gezer). The reference to Gezer may well be secondary, since that stronghold did not come into Israel's control until the pharaoh gave it to Solomon as dowry for his daughter (1 Kgs 9:16). Insertion of the phrase here may have been triggered by the brief and apparently limited success against a force from Gezer in the sequel to the Beth-horon victory (10:33). Later it became a Levitical town (21:21).

toward the sea. "Seawards." Identical construction in 15:4 and 11. This cuts across the territory of Dan as described in 19:40-48.

COMMENT

The Bene Joseph represent the "Sons of the Left" (or northerners), as opposed to the Benjaminite "Sons of the Right" (or southerners) in a social system that shows sufficient continuity with eighteenth-century Mari that Albright was at last able to make sense of the Testament of Joseph (Gen 49:22*ff*) where it was most obscure:

> Son of Euphrates is Joseph,
> Son of Euphrates, lofty of source.

The next line mentions attack on the Wall of Egypt which was built early in the second millennium as a means of controlling infiltration and repelling invasion from the desert highway routes. There Joseph was involved; in Albright's rendering:

> His bow remained steady
> And the arms of his archers were firm.

According to this reconstruction, Joseph came from the northern Euphrates Valley. He represented the Habiru "Sons of the North" and was a member of one of their tribes, the Rabbau, named after its chief occupation as Archer. He was driven out by them and was later to be found defending the Wall of Egypt. See Albright, "From the Patriarchs to Moses: I. From Abraham to Joseph," *BA* 36 (1973) 26-28.

Almost as ancient is the corresponding section in the Blessing of Moses (Deut 33:13-17), which is preoccupied with the quality of "Joseph's" fief:

> Blessed of Yahweh is his land
> From the abundance of the heavens above
> From the Deep crouching beneath
> From the abundance of harvests of the sun
> From the abundance of yields of the moon
> From the abundance of ancient mountains
> From the abundance of the eternal hills
> From the abundance of the earth and its fullness
> And the favor of the One who tented on Sinai
>   [or better, "the seneh-bush Tenter"]

Here the theme changes to that of the collaboration of deity (pre-Yahwist) and a man at war:

> May it be on the head of Joseph
> On the brow of the leader of his brethren
>   [or better, the "Nazir of his Brothers"]
> His firstborn bull, majesty is his
> The horns of the wild bull are his horns
> With them, the nations he gores
> He attacks the ends of the earth.

Almost, it appears, as an afterthought, the subdivisions are mentioned:

> Behold the myriads of Ephraim!
> Behold the thousands of Manasseh!

(Translation Cross and Freedman, "The Blessing of Moses," *JBL* 67 [1948] 194-195=*SAYP*, 100-101. See O'Connor, *Hebrew Verse Structure,* 213-214, for the alternate renderings given above and for treatment of the entire unit.)

A number of indicators suggest that the term "Bene Joseph" was authentically prior to "Ephraim and Manasseh." The description of Joseph's southern boundary, for example, lacks the kind of specificity seen in 15:2-4 and 15:5b-11, which describe the southern and northern boundaries of Judah. Here there are far fewer names, and in fact a pair of obscure ethnic-gentilic formations (Archite and Japhletite) provide key reference points. Moreover, the few reference points for Joseph's southern boundary peter out "toward the sea," approximately where a border with Dan ought to begin. Altogether this may be taken as further indication that what we have called "Warfare: Phase One" and interpreted as mostly conquest-by-covenant, from a Shechem base, was concentrated in the hill country north and south of a strip divided between Benjamin and Dan. Benjamin was caught in the middle of the upheaval and was not sufficiently consolidated to claim an allotment until the later Shiloh phase (18:11-28). Similarly Dan, whose original fief was the only one to go entirely unclaimed, is the last to be delineated (19:40-48).

2′. EPHRAIM
(16:5-10)

16 ⁵ The border was drawn for the Bene Ephraim, for their clans. The border of their fief was: to the East, Ataroth . . . ⁶ . . . Michmethath on the north . . .

The border turns east of Taanath-shiloh, and takes itself around to the east, toward Janoah. ⁷ It goes down from Janoah to Ataroth, then to Naaran, meets the Jericho area, and arrives at the Jordan.

⁸ . . . from Tappuah the border skips westward to the Qana Gorge; its destination is the sea.

This is the fief of the tribe of Ephraim for their clans, ⁹ together with the towns set apart for the Bene Ephraim within the fief of the Bene Manasseh—all the towns and their enclosures.

¹⁰ But they did not dispossess the Canaanites who inhabited Gezer. The Canaanites have lived in the midst of Ephraim to this very day— they became subjects for forced labor.

TEXTUAL NOTES

16 5. *to the east*   Syriac omits.

Ataroth . . . ⁶ . . .   Not Ataroth-addar, as in MT. In MT the description of Ephraim's remaining borders begins *'ṭrwt* (as in v 2) *'dr* (cf. 18:13) *'d byt ḥrwn 'lywn* (which we have restored in v 2), and continues *wyṣ' hgbwl hymh*, "and the border follows the wadi westward" (see 16:2, third Textual Note). LXX also so reads for the most part; it erroneously separates *'ṭrwt* and *'rk* (< *'dr*) and adds *wgzr*, "and Gezer," after *'lywn*.

6. *north* . . .   The text is apparently corrupt. MT reads nothing where LXX has *therma*. No reconstruction recommends itself. See above, on 16:3.

itself   Emending the anomalous object pronoun of MT, *'ôtô*, to read the preposition *'ittô* (reflexive sense, as in 19:14), where LXX has nothing.

7. *Naaran*   This is the spelling of the name in 1 Chr 7:28. Our text reads *n'rth*, with the directive ending. LXX took the latter to be *n'r(w)t(y)h* understood as equivalent to *bnwtyh*, "its daughter-towns, dependencies." We owe this observation to M. Patrick O'Connor in a private communication.

8. *sea*   A few Hebrew manuscripts and Vulgate mistakenly read "the Salt Sea," which regularly refers to the Dead Sea, not the Mediterranean.

Ephraim   This agrees with LXX, where MT under the influence of v 9 reads "Bene Ephraim," producing an unusually long construct chain in Hebrew.

9. *set apart*   MT has a mixed form, with the vowels of the *niph'al* (passive) participle and the consonants of the *hiph'il* (active) participle.

10. *they became subjects for forced labor*   Missing in LXX, which offers an alternative explanation for Gezer: "until Pharaoh king of Egypt went up and captured it and set fire to it. He slew the Canaanites, the Perizzites and the residents of Gezer. And Pharaoh gave it as dowry to his daughter." The source is 1 Kgs 9:16. MT is consistent in our passage.

NOTES

16:5-10. The fragmentary description of borders for the great northern tribe contrasts sharply with the description of Judah in chap. 15.

5. *The border was drawn.* This translation is not literal; MT says simply, "The border was."

to the east. It appears that the original intention was to describe a northern border, beginning near the Jordan Valley and moving west.

Ataroth. Probably Tell el-Mazār. Map H, 398. It was the occurrence of the name on the northeastern perimeter that created confusion with the town on the southern border (18:13) and triggered the textual mishap here.

6. *Michmethath.* With definite article in Hebrew, as again in description of Manasseh's southern border (17:7). Evidence from surface surveying has pointed to Kh. en-Nebi (formerly known as Kh. Makhneh el-Fōqā), 4 km south of Tell Balatah (Shechem). E. F. Campbell, Jr., "The Shechem Area Survey," *BASOR* 190 (April 1968) 35 n. 32, and 41; E. F. Campbell, Jr., James F. Ross, and Lawrence E. Toombs, "The Eighth Campaign of Balâtah (Shechem)," *BASOR* 204 (1971) 4. The syntax of 17:7, on the other hand, seems to point to a site east of Shechem such as Kh. Ibn Nasser. If the latter is correct, then "the Michmethath" was not an occupied settlement but a location visited periodically by shepherds. Kurt Elliger, "Michmethath," in *Archäologie und des Altes Testament,* 91-100.

6b-7. The eastern and northeastern perimeter is the only description that is intact. Here it is inserted between two segments of the northern border (v 6a and v 8) with the first of which it overlaps.

6b. †*Taanath-shiloh.* Map H, 398. Possibly Kh. Ta'na el-Fōqā, but the results of the archaeological surveys have not been consistent. Campbell, "The Shechem Area Survey," 31, sites 24-25, nn. 33-34.

takes itself around. That is, it produces a bulge. For this sense of '*br* in the border descriptions, see 15:3 and NOTES.

Janoah. Khirbet Janun. Map H, 398.

7. *It goes down from Janoah to Ataroth*. The topographically reasonable route is down the watershed between two wadi systems, one of which passes just north of Ataroth. The other and larger system reaches the area directly east of Taanath and Ataroth. In order to circumvent the western tributaries of the larger system the border must move back west, after passing to the east of Taanath and Janoah. This is the argument of Parunak, "Geographical Terminology," in light of which the proposal to emend *mynwḥh*, "from Janoah," to *mzrḥh*, "from the east" (Kaufmann, *The Biblical Account of the Conquest*, 33), does not commend itself.

Naaran. Khirbet el-ʿAyush. Map H, 398.

meets the Jericho area. That is, the larger area controlled by the city. The verb *pgʿ* is used to describe a meeting of boundaries, as in 19:27 and 34 (*bis*). Parunak, "Geographical Terminology."

8. This verse appears to be a continuation of the description moving from east to west that begins in v 5 but is interrupted by the description moving generally from west to east in vv 6 and 7.

Tappuah. Sheikh Abu Zarad, on a hill above the upper drainage basin of the Qana (to the west) and the southern end of the lush valley running south from Shechem (to the east). Map H, 398.

skips. The verb *hlk* in the border descriptions makes sense as "stepping" from hill to hill. Parunak, "Geographical Terminology." From the watershed ridge the border skirts, on the south, the drainage basin and the upper portion of the Qana Gorge by stepping down from one hilltop to the next.

tribe of Ephraim. This is the term for the pre-monarchy administrative division, outside of which there may also be enclaves of the "Bene Ephraim," within the administrative area of another tribe, as becomes clear in the next verse.

9-10. These two verses read like a series of two or three marginal comments, each expanding on the preceding.

9. That the constituencies named Ephraim and Manasseh did not emerge with full resolution of old local claims is here explicit. The situation becomes clearer in 17:9, when the border is described in more detail.

together with the towns. Hebrew *whʿrym*. The initial *waw*-conjunction suggested to Kaufmann that a town list once preceded this verse. Kaufmann, *The Biblical Account of the Conquest*, 34.

10. *did not dispossess*. See NOTE on 15:63.

Gezer. See 10:33 and NOTES.

forced labor. Judges 1:28,30,33,35; 1 Kgs 9:21=2 Chr 8:8. According to Deut 20:10-18 it was the people of towns at some distance from Israel that were to be so treated.

COMMENT

There is abundant evidence for the persistence of unsettled differences and deep-seated rivalry between Ephraim and other members of the league. See, for example, the stories of the Judges, especially Gideon (Judg 8:1-3) and Jephthah (Judg 12:1-7).

Chapter 16 concludes on a note of partial failure which appears sporadically throughout the description of the assignment of tribal fiefs, and which surely belonged to the first major edition (Dtr 1). These scattered notices of incomplete reforms in land tenure were seized upon, by the later redactor (Dtr 2), as a way of posing the major problem of the following era in Judges 1.

3'. WESTERN MANASSEH
(17:1-13)

d'. "Clans" 17:1-6

17 1 The allotment was made to the tribe of the Bene Manasseh. Actually he was Joseph's eldest son. To Machir, eldest son of Manasseh —the "father of Gilead"—because he was a fighting man, there already belonged Gilead and Bashan.

2 And there belonged to the remainder of the Bene Manasseh, for their clans (that is, to the Bene Abiezer, the Bene Heleq, the Bene Asriel, the Bene Shechem, the Bene Hepher, and the Bene Shemida —these were the male descendants of Manasseh ben Joseph): [. . .] for their clans.

3 Zelophehad son of Hepher, son of Gilead, son of Machir, son of Manasseh, had no sons, but only daughters. These are the names of his daughters: Mahlah, Noah, Hoglah, Milcah, and Tirzah. 4 They approached Eleazar the priest, Joshua son of Nun, and the leaders, to say, "Yahweh commanded Moses to give us a fief among our kinsmen." And so he gave them, by Yahweh's decision, a fief amidst their father's kinsfolk. 5 Manasseh's shares fell out as ten, in addition to the land of Gilead and Bashan which were beyond the Jordan, 6 because Manasseh's daughters received a fief among his sons. The land of Gilead belonged to the remainder of the Bene Manasseh.

b'. Borders 17:7-13

7 The border of the Bene Manasseh was from the Slope of Michmethath which is opposite Shechem.

The border stepped southward and turned back toward En-tappuah.

8 To Manasseh belonged Tappuah's land; but Tappuah, on the border of Manasseh, belonged to the Bene Ephraim.

9 The border went down the Qana Gorge. (In the southern corridor of the Gorge are terebinths. Do these belong to Ephraim, amidst

towns of Manasseh?) Thereafter the border of Manasseh is along the north side of the Gorge, its destination the sea.

10 To the south is Ephraim's and to the north is Manasseh's, and the sea is their border. They meet Asher on the north and Issachar on the east.

11 Near Issachar and Asher there belonged to Manasseh: Bethshean with its dependencies and Ibleam with its dependencies [. . .] the inhabitants of Dor and its dependencies [. . . ,] the inhabitants of En-dor and its dependencies, and the inhabitants of Taanach and its dependencies, and the inhabitants of Megiddo and its dependencies (*Re:* the third [Dor]. Is it Napheth?). 12 The Bene Manasseh were unable to possess these towns. The Canaanites persisted in dwelling in this land. 13 And when the Bene Israel became strong enough, they put the Canaanites into labor battalions. They never did completely evict them.

TEXTUAL NOTES

17 1. *allotment*   Hebrew *hgwrl.* LXX "The Border" (*hgbwl*) probably represents contamination from the beginning of v 7.

the Bene   With LXX, lacking in MT.

belonged   This follows LXX, where the awkward *wyhy lw* in MT reflects an attempt to bring the construction parallel with v 2 and should be deleted.

2. *Hepher, and the Bene Shemida*   These two names are reversed in LXX (as in Num 26:32), which also reads *r* for *d* in Shemida.

descendants of Manasseh ben Joseph)   Lacking in LXX.

[. . .]   This verse is a sentence fragment. Due to successive annotations, prompted by a literalizing interest in the kinship language, somewhere between two occurrences of the phrase "for their clans" what belonged to them was lost.

3. *son of Gilead, son of Machir, son of Manasseh*   Lacking in LXX. See NOTE.

his daughters   LXX reads "daughters of Zelophehad."

and   The translation conforms to English usage of the conjunction, with the last term in the series. In ancient witnesses the conjunction *w* occurs irregularly:

    MT   a w b, c d w e
    Mss   a w b, c w d, w e
    LXX   a w b w c w d w e

4. *son of Nun*   Another genealogical detail that was lacking in the OG. Greenspoon, STBJ, 136-137.

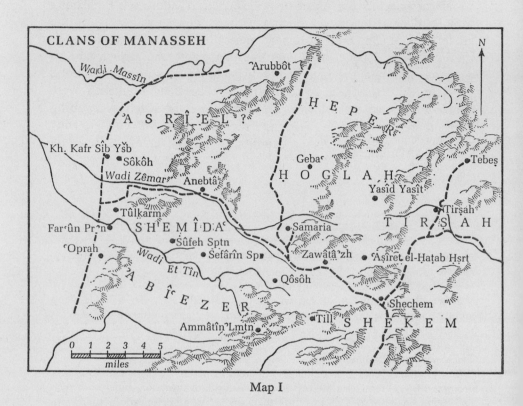

Map I

Biblical and modern Arabic place names appear in Roman type.
Clans of Manasseh are located in capital letters.
Unvoweled names occur in the Samaria Ostraca.
Geographical features are in italics.

Yahweh   LXX "God."

commanded   Where MT has '*t*, the sign of the direct object, LXX leads a group of manuscripts and versions in reading *byd*, "through" (cf. 14:2).

he   The antecedent is presumably Eleazar who would have priestly responsibility for the sacred lot.

gave them   The masculine pronoun (*lhm*) must be a mistake for *lhn*.

5. *Manasseh's*   LXX misdivides *mnšh* and reads "from Anassa," in a text which is further garbled.

as ten, in addition to the land   Hebrew '*šrh lbd m'rṣ*, for which LXX *myšr lbk m'rṣ* is unintelligible.

6. *Manasseh's daughters*   Hebrew *bnwt mnšh*. LXX *bnwt bny mnšh*, "daughters of the Bene Manasseh."

7. *the Bene*   This agrees with LXX in having *bny*, as in v 1.

the Slope   Reading '*šd* for MT '*šr* which is geographically unintelligible. Elliger, "Michmethath," in *Archäologie und des Altes Testament*, 97-98.

Michmethath   Corrupted to *Dēlanath* in LXX, with consequences to follow at the end of the sentence.

Shechem   Instead of the place name, LXX has *bny 'nt*, "sons of Anath," apparently misbegotten by the preceding scribal error.

The   Preceded by a superfluous '*l* in LXX.

and turned back toward   This is LXX, where *kai Iasseib epi* reflects Hebrew **wyšwb 'l* and is superior to MT '*l yšby*, "toward the inhabitants of."

8. *Tappuah's land*   Missing in LXX which reads "It (En-tappuah) belonged to Manasseh," distinguishing between the spring (belonging to Manasseh) and the town (belonging to Ephraim).

9. *terebinths. Do these belong*   This is based on LXX, where *Iariēl tereminthos* may be taken to reflect Hebrew '*ry'l h'lh*; we suggest that this was corrupted by anticipation of '*ry m-* three words later, to yield MT: '*rym h'lh*, "these towns." Cf. 16:9.

10. *their*   Thus LXX, restoring a suffix, *-m*, where the singular pronoun in MT, *w*, is a dittograph.

11. *and Ibleam with its dependencies*   Lost by haplography in LXX or its *Vorlage*.

the inhabitants of Dor and its dependencies   Of all the entries in the list, this one alone includes the sign of the definite direct object, suggesting that it partially fills a lacuna.

the inhabitants of En-dor and its dependencies   Lacking, after haplography, in LXX.

and the inhabitants of Taanach and its dependencies   Lacking, after haplography, in LXX[B+MSS].

third   This is LXX, where MT has the cardinal numeral, "three."

Napheth   LXX adds *wbnwtyh*, "and its dependencies."

NOTES

17:1-13. The description of Manasseh west of the river is not organized like the preceding tribal summaries. After a general introduction (v 1), it falls into two parts concerned with subgroups (vv 2-6) and the borders (vv 7-13).

1. *allotment*. As in 15:1.

tribe. This usage contrasts with the description of eastern Manasseh as "half-tribe" in 13:29 and generally. The usage in chaps. 13-14 reflects Dtr 2, who contributed the lengthy section on the Transjordan tribes. Here, in western Manasseh, we start out on the literary terrain of Dtr 1.

Actually. The asseverative particle *ky* here emphasizes the priority of Manasseh.

Joseph's eldest son. Genesis 41:51; 46:20.

Machir, eldest son of Manasseh. See NOTE on 13:31 where Machir is simply "son of Manasseh." Machir appears to be a constituency that was originally concentrated on the west bank, and then in part shifted to Transjordan; the Cisjordan element persists as late as the Song of Deborah, in which Machir's participation in the war is praised and the Transjordan constituencies, Gilead and Reuben, are denounced for their failure to show up (Judg 5:14b,15b-17a). In other words, "Machir" continued to be more effective in its original west-bank territory than in the one it was assigned to administer east of the river. The assignment served, however, to contribute to genealogy.

"father of Gilead." This honorary title is an excellent example of the influence of political history in the formation of the official genealogies. See Num 26:28-34 and cf. 1 Chr 7:14-19.

Gilead. Originally a geographical term. See 12:2,5; 13:11,25,31.

Bashan. Already mentioned in 9:10; 12:4,5; 13:11,12,30,31.

2. *the remainder*. Having briefly noted the earlier disposition of Gilead and Bashan, the historian turns to Manasseh's west-bank constituencies. In the genealogy which became normative, the six names which follow are all sons of Gilead and grandsons of Machir (Num 26:30-32).

clans. Or "families," in anthropological terms "phratries." On the difficulty of rendering Hebrew *mišpāḥâ*, see NOTES on 7:14. The following description of the territorial distribution of the subgroups follows F. M. Cross, "Epigraphic Notes on Hebrew Documents of the Eighth-Sixth Centuries B.C.," *BASOR* 163 (1961) 12-14.

Abiezer. "Iezer" in Num 26:30. Hometown of Gideon (Judg 6:11,24,34); the surrounding area is a strip running west from the neighborhood of Shechem along the border with Ephraim.

Heleq. Map I, 408. Cf. Num 26:30. This is the area to the northwest of Shechem. It is a prominent subgroup also in the Samaria Ostraca Nos. 22-24, 26-27. Cross, *BASOR* 163 (1961) 13.

Asriel. "Ashriel" in 1 Chr 7:14. Located northwest of Heleq. Map I, 408.

Shechem. Map I. See NOTES and COMMENT on 8:30-35 and 24:1-28. It is entirely in keeping with the perspective of the first edition (Dtr 1) that Shechem should figure merely as one of the clans of Manasseh, otherwise not mentioned until the end of the era (chap. 24).

Hepher. Cf. also "Epher," as name of a Manasseh subgroup living east of the river in 1 Chr 5:24; for possible Midianite connections, see Mendenhall, *Ten Gen,* 170. In this west-bank segment, Hepher is the area north of Shechem. Map I, 408. The location of Tell Hefu (Aharoni, *LOB,* 378) in the Plain of Sharon seems too far from the hill-country clustering of the other names to be intended here.

Shemida. Shechem is one of his sons in 1 Chr 7:19. This name also occurs in Samaria Ostraca Nos. 29-30. See Cross, *BASOR* 163 (1961) 14. The area is west of Heleq. Map I, 408.

these were the male descendants. The Dtr 2 material characteristically makes use of the gentilic form. The earlier edition, which preferred the more general construction with *benê,* is here explained by Dtr 2 in terms of genealogical doctrine.

3-6. These verses are an even more abrupt departure from the dominant form, that of "inheritance" by tribes and not by smaller subtribal units. This special treatment of Zelophehad's daughters in the north balances structurally the special treatment of Caleb in the south (14:6-15, Dtr 2; 15:13-14, Dtr 1).

3. *son of Gilead, son of Machir, son of Manasseh.* The absence of these genealogical details from LXX suggests that the latter reflects a Dtr 1 text. By the introduction of these details, Dtr 2 (in this case MT) focuses attention upon the tight genealogical linkage that was an increasing preoccupation toward the end of national existence. Contrary to the claim of Miller and Tucker (*Joshua,* 134), the full genealogy is in fact supported by the parallel in Num 26:28-34.

daughters. Are these "daughter-towns, dependencies" as in 15:45 and 47? More likely the text refers to social groups of distaff origin, the groups themselves being perceived as male.

Mahlah. "Weak one" if the root is *ḥlh.* Cf. also Arabic *mḥl,* "barren." The location of the subtribal unit Mahlah is unknown.

Noah. Hebrew *nʿh,* not to be confused with the Genesis flood hero, *nḥ.* Location unknown.

Milcah. "Queen." Location unknown.

Tirzah. Map I, 408. One of the former centers of Canaanite royalty, discussed above at 12:24. It is probably the great site of Tell el Farʿah (North), north of Shechem.

4. *Eleazar the priest.* He is always mentioned before Joshua when they are found together (14:1; 21:1). All three texts can be shown, on various grounds, to be contributions of the later redactor (Dtr 2).

"Yahweh commanded Moses. Cf. 14:6. The epic tradition in this case is found in Num 27:1-11 (where the inheritance is promised) and 36:1-12 (where the same subject is resumed).

Yahweh's decision. See 9:14 and NOTES. The priority of Eleazar in this passage suggests that this was a new decision, not the old one which the daughters have appealed to.

5. *shares fell out as ten*. Six clans, one of which is the grandfather of the five daughters, account for ten shares west of the river.

6. *The land of Gilead belonged to the remainder*. Together with v 2 this forms a rhetorical inclusion, framing information about the clans of Manasseh and the daughters of Zelophehad.

7-13. For the listings of the northern tribes there was apparently no archival source comparable to that for Judah (and Benjamin) in the south.

7. *Slope*. Hebrew *'šr*. See Textual Note. A reference to Manasseh's northwestern neighbor, the tribe of Asher in the broad and beautiful coastal plain north of Mount Carmel, would make no sense as part of this border.

Michmethath. See 16:6 and NOTES.

opposite. Hebrew *'al pěnê*.

Shechem. Map I, 408. This is the first direct reference to this important stronghold in Joshua (but see 8:30-35 with NOTES and COMMENT). An asylum-town (20:7) and Levitical town (21:21), it is most famous for the covenant scene that unfolds there (24:1-28).

stepped. The translation uses past tense because this is the beginning of a series of disjunctive clauses in MT, extending throughout most of v 9. If Hebrew *hlk* in these descriptions means "step" from hill to hill, then we should trace this segment of the border along the crests of mountains that overlook from the east the valley running south from Shechem.

8. *Tappuah's*. Map H, 398. See second NOTE on 16:8.

land. This must refer to fields watered by the Spring of Tappuah (LXX) and protected by the border town of Tappuah (assigned to Ephraim) which were however worked or claimed by people of the neighboring district of Manasseh.

9. At the beginning of this verse the description implies a right-angle turn in the boundary, from the vicinity of Tappuah, to start down from the mountains toward the sea.

the Qana Gorge. Map H, 398. See 16:8 and NOTES. Reference must be to the upper portion of this valley.

(*In the southern corridor of the Gorge*. Hebrew *negbāh lan-naḥal*. Reference is to sites in the valley but close to the hills which on the south serve as reference points for Manasseh's border with Ephraim.

terebinths. . . . towns of Manasseh. This balances v 8 (reflecting a trade-off?). While certain fields of Ephraimite Tappuah belonged to Manasseh for cultivation, there were forested sections in Manasseh's part of the southern Qana which were apparently claimed by Ephraim.

Do these. Hebrew *ha-'ēllēh* makes excellent sense as interrogative and renders emendation (Soggin, 168, and others) entirely unnecessary. The question is readily explained as a marginal query. See 16:9 which speaks specifically of towns belonging to Ephraim within the borders of Manasseh.

Thereafter. Hebrew has here simply the *waw*-conjunction. Apparently the border follows the south side of the valley, far enough to include certain

Ephraimite sites within Manasseh's border; then at some point it crosses the valley, thence to follow the north edge out toward the sea. That is, Manasseh and Ephraim divided the Qana between them; but Ephraim was able to retain certain places on the southern side and thus within Manasseh's half of the valley.

10. *Ephraim's. Manasseh's.* Presumably both are mentioned because the preceding verses have been concerned with some notable, and no doubt controversial, arrangements.

They. That is, the Bene Joseph.

meet. Hebrew *ypg'wn.* Note the use of the imperfect with archaic ending. This is a fragment of a very old description. On the sense of *pg'*, "to meet," see 16:7, third NOTE.

11-13. Separating the Galilee tribes from Manasseh was the Plain of Esdraelon (or Jezreel), with especially heavy concentrations of population governed by powerful and strongly fortified royal cities. With the equation of Dor and En-dor (see below), the same towns mentioned here are listed as Manasseh's responsibility (unfulfilled) in Judg 1:27.

11. *Near.* For this use of the preposition *b*, we are referred to 1 Sam 29:1; Ezek 10:15. Kaufmann, *The Biblical Account of the Conquest,* 38. The text is difficult but scarcely merits description as "grammatical nonsense" (Graeme Auld, "Judges 1 and History," *VT* 25 [1975] 280).

Bethshean. Tell el-Ḥuṣn. Map H, 398.

Ibleam. Tell Bel'ameh near Jenin. Map H. It is a Levitical city in the Greek text of 21:25 (LXX, cf. "Bileam" in the list of 1 Chr 6:55[70E]).

Dor. Hebrew *d'r.* See 11:2 and 12:23. Map H, 398. But if the name here is drawn from a parallel recension in order to fill a gap, then it may well refer to En-dor instead of the coastal town. Miller and Tucker, *Joshua,* 136.

En-dor. Hebrew *'yn dr.* "Spring of Encircling." Map H, 398. The name is perhaps reminiscent of ritual dances once performed there. D. Winton Thomas, "En-dor: A Sacred Spring?" *PEFQS* (1933) 205-206. See also 1 Sam 28:7 and especially Ps 83:11 for reference to the persistence of Canaanite culture and repeated confrontations between Israel and oppressors in the days of the Judges.

Taanach. Map H, 398. See 12:21 and NOTES. Also a Levitical town (21:25).

Megiddo. Map H. See 12:21 and NOTES.

Is it Napheth?) Naphath-dor is somehow related to the famous coastal town in 12:23. Here, therefore, we have a marginal query, addressed to the confusion introduced by the two ways of naming the same Esdraelon town (Dor/En-dor).

12-13. *were unable . . . never did completely.* The first is formulated as in 15:63 (see NOTES), regarding Judah and Jerusalem. These and other similar statements do not display merely formulaic variants. Together, they frame a statement of the solution to the problem of the leftover population.

13. *labor battalions.* Hebrew *mas.* Cf. "subjects for forced labor" (*mas 'ōbēd*) in 16:10 and NOTES.

COMMENT

The diversity of populations within the area of Western Manasseh gave rise to a complex land-tenure tradition. Here, for the first time in Joshua, the clans of a major tribe are listed, six in number. The allotment for one of the six (Hepher) is apparently divided to become the fiefs of his son's five daughters. Zelophehad was remembered as an only son, thus accounting for the total of ten.

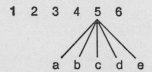

No reference is made to the institution of Levirate marriage. In the latter it is the duty of a brother to take the place of a deceased brother with whom he has been living if his brother dies without a son; he is to raise up for the deceased a male heir (Deut 25:5-10). The institution is reflected most creatively in the short story of Ruth the Moabitess. See especially the treatment by Campbell, *Ruth*, AB 7. That there is no hint of the Levirate option here reinforces the observation that a local custom of land-tenure inheritance by female heirs is being recognized. Some connection is suggested between the evidence found elsewhere for substantial Luwian presence in the Shechem region and the peculiar matrilineal customs of the Lycians (as reported by Herodotus), the latter being certainly a Luwian element. Thus Mendenhall, *Ten Gen*, 181-182.

All this was far in the past at the time the great historical work about Israel's life in the land was being compiled, in the late seventh century B.C. By then the special status of Zelophehad's daughter-towns had been long since phased out and the whole matter was irrelevant to the concerns of Dtr 1. But it was ancient tradition known to Dtr 2, who placed it so that it functioned dialectically. The result in the final redaction is that Joshua's activity as "judge" in the section to follow (vv 14-18) is upstaged by the prior activity of Moses in the same role, in a story which again, like chaps. 12 and 13, calls attention to the east-west axis formed by Cisjordan and Transjordan. The original (and therefore "ideal") Israel was something other and larger than the political state controlled briefly by Josiah, the great reforming king. The editing was undertaken with a sense of humor about the tightening genealogical linkage and with compassion for the predicament posed by being a woman in Israel. There had been a time, however brief, when thanks to negotiation with Moses, daughters had counted for as much and fared as well as sons. Compare the tragicomic portrayal of the failing genealogical connection in the story of the civil war with Benjamin and its sequel (Judges 19-21), which are likewise best understood as contributions of the post-Josianic redactor. Boling, *Judges,* AB 6A, 271-294.

On the other hand, there are scant traces of any activity by Dtr 2 in the description of Manasseh's borders (vv 7-13). The scattered references in the Joshua of Dtr 1 to "undispossessed" towns and to use of forced labor become in the later introduction to Judges a compact catalogue of failures (Judg 1:19-35).

4'. JOSHUA AS JUDGE
(17:14-18)

17 ⁱ⁴ The Bene Joseph spoke to Joshua: "Why did you make our fief but one single solitary share? We are still a numerous people whom thus far Yahweh has blessed."

¹⁵ Joshua said to them, "Because you are such a numerous people, get yourselves up to the forest. Clear space there for yourselves, in the land of the Perizzites and the Rephaim, since the hill country of Ephraim is too confining for you."

¹⁶ The Bene Joseph said: "Not enough hill country has been found for us! And there are chariots of iron among all the Canaanites who live on the valley land, those of Bethshean and its dependencies and those throughout the Jezreel Valley!"

¹⁷ Joshua said to the house of Joseph (to Ephraim and Manasseh): "You are a numerous people and you have great strength. You shall not have only one lot. ¹⁸ The hill country shall indeed be yours, though it is now a forest. You shall clear it and you shall control its approaches. You shall surely evict the Canaanites, even though they have shiny iron chariots and are powerful."

TEXTUAL NOTES

17 14. *to* This is the reading of numerous Hebrew manuscripts, *'l*, for MT *'t*.

We LXX abruptly shifts to the singular "I."

still This is a revocalization of *'ad* to *'ōd*. The former in MT is understandable as contamination from the correct use of *'ad* just two words farther on.

whom thus far Missing in LXX as a scribe's eye jumped from *b* to *b*: *rb* ['d 'šr 'd kh] *brkny*.

Yahweh LXX "God."

15. *in the land of the Perizzites and the Rephaim*   Lacking in LXX, due to haplography: *š[m b'rṣ hprzy whrp'y]m.*

16. *country*   LXX adds "of Ephraim," a carryover from the preceding verse.

chariots of iron   This is MT: *wrkb brzl bkl kn'ny.* LXX reads: *wrkb br* (less likely *bḥwr*) *wbrzl lkn'ny,* "shiny chariots, and iron (ones), to the Canaanites," awkwardly reflecting the influence of v 18.

on the valley land   LXX omits.

Jezreel   Hebrew *yzr'l.* LXX appears to be reading *yśr'l,* "Israel."

17. *house of*   This is MT *byt,* where LXX reads *bny* (Bene) under the influence of vv 14 and 16.

(to Ephraim and Manasseh)   Not in LXX, perhaps because of haplography: *l'[prym wlmnśh l']mr.* The two names may nevertheless be secondary.

18. *hill country*   LXX reads "forest" by anticipation of the next clause.

its approaches   LXX omits.

shiny   This modifier survives in LXX which reflects *rkb br,* perhaps from an original **rkb brzl br.* M. Patrick O'Connor, private communication.

and are powerful"   Hebrew *ky ḥzq hw'.* LXX instead states a contrast: *kî ḥāzaqtā minnénnû,* "for you are stronger than they," which is less intelligible in context.

NOTES

17:14-18. This is the final unit placed by the compilers in the pre-Shiloh phase, the era of Shechem. It has been treated by scholars as a conflation of two versions (vv 14-15 and vv 16-18). So Miller and Tucker, *Joshua,* 136-137. An unanswered question is how to understand the logic of the finished product. As indicated below, the evidence of literary history used to support this view can be interpreted in terms of redaction: an old story, which once served its own purpose, was added to the great historical work recounting Israel's life in the land, where it was expanded and adjusted to serve another purpose.

14. *The Bene Joseph.* As in 16:1. Here they are a single constituency (cf. the pre-Yahwist unit of Gen 49:22-26).

our . . . We. In Hebrew the pronominal forms for the Josephites in vv 14-15 are singular with one exception ("to them," v 15); in vv 16-17, the Josephites are referred to in the plural. Such variation is characteristic.

but one single solitary share? In Hebrew it is a forceful hendiadys: *gwrl 'ḥd wḥbl 'ḥd,* literally, "one lot and one portion."

15. *Perizzites.* See 3:10 and NOTES. They are found again at 9:1; 11:3; 12:8; 24:11.

Rephaim. See 12:4 and NOTES.

since. This translation is far from being literal. The argument seems to be that it is the heavily forested condition that made the area too restricted.

hill country of Ephraim. This most likely refers to the region immediately surrounding a town which gave its name to the tribe. There is such an "Ephraim" near Baal-hazor in 2 Sam 13:23, which would meet the specifications very well. In the reorganization that came with Solomon, this old designation was revived and the district of "Mount Ephraim" was redrawn to include also the eastern slopes of Manasseh (1 Kgs 4:8).

too confining. Hebrew *'āṣ,* a word very close in sound to *'ēṣ,* "tree(s)."

16. *"Not enough.* This seems to be the sense of Hebrew *l' ymṣ' lnw hhr,* literally, "the hill country has not been found for us." They imply that Joshua has misunderstood the original request. They explain that it is not the heavily forested condition of the hill country but its extent that is a problem, as it is hemmed in by the Canaanite chariotry of the plains.

Bethshean. See above, v 11 and NOTES. Map H, 398.

Jezreel Valley!" This is the broad fertile plain separating Galilee from the central hill country, a natural highway from the coast to the Jordan Valley, guarded at the east end by Bethshean. Also known as the Esdraelon Valley. Map B, 112.

17. *house of Joseph.* This contrasts abruptly with the standard designation in chaps. 16-17 as "Bene Joseph," and it is immediately glossed in terms of the early Yahwist organization mentioned in Deut 33:13-17 (see above, 401); there, too, reference to Joseph is rounded out by mention of Ephraim and Manasseh. See Freedman, "Early Israelite Poetry and Historical Reconstructions," in *Symposia* (1979) 85-96.

only one lot. Only enough of the old story is retained by the historian to serve his own purpose, which was to display Joshua making decisions regarding the disposition of northern kingdom territory and thus provide a model for Judean kings.

18. *its approaches.* Hebrew *toṣē'ôtāw.* See 15:7, eleventh NOTE.

You shall surely evict. BHS retains Noth's proposal to insert a negative; thus the Jerusalem Bible "since you cannot drive out . . ." But there is neither a mechanism nor a clear rationale to explain the dropping of the negative.

shiny. The verb *br* (or *brr*) often describes the polishing of horns or arrows.

COMMENT

There can be no doubt that the unit reflects a reality early in the premonarchical period. Palestine has experienced extensive deforestation in historical times. Originally forests covered much of Galilee, much of the watershed ridge and western slopes of the hill country which became the territories of Judah and Joseph (earlier Benjamin and Joseph), and much of Transjordan, especially north of the Jabboq. See "Map of the Flora" in M. Zohari, *Encyclopedia Biblica* I (Hebrew) (Jerusalem: Bialik Institute, 1950) cols. 651-652; ibid., III (1958) cols. 722*ff.*

The Bene Joseph demanded more agricultural land which would be tax free under the Yahwist covenant. But the clearing of forest land required enormous amounts of hard labor and the plains were too powerfully defended. See G. E. Mendenhall, "Social Organization in Early Israel," in *Mag Dei,* 138.

The scene is a very different one today.

"Almost all of the original forests that characterize the climax vegetation of the hills and mountains in the Mediterranean zone have disappeared. Man has cleared them away to extend his agriculture onto the hillsides, particularly for olive and grape cultivation. He also made extensive use of wood for fuel, charcoal production, and building materials." Lawrence E. Stager, "Ancient Agriculture in the Judean Desert: A Case Study of the Buqei'ah Valley in the Iron Age"; unpublished Ph.D. thesis, Harvard University, 1975, 2.

Today it is known that terrace agriculture was already established on the hilly slopes in Iron I; it can only have been accomplished with significant deforestation. Many of those Iron I terrace builders, surely, were the Bene Joseph of the early Yahwist league.

We are left, then, with a picture in which the "Shechem phase" of the Yahwist movement at last developed, under continued pressure from Canaanite control of the plains, into a situation where both the great northern constituencies, Manasseh and Ephraim, had their hands full trying to consolidate (Manasseh) or extend (Ephraim) their fiefs under the mediation of Joshua.

3. CISJORDAN ALLOTMENTS: SHILOH PHASE
18:1 - 19:51

a. WEST-BANK SURVEY
(18:1-10)

18 1 The entire congregation of the Bene Israel assembled at Shiloh. And there they pitched the Tent of Meeting. The land had been subdued before them. 2 There remained among the Bene Israel seven tribes whose fiefs they had not yet parceled out.

3 Joshua said to the Bene Israel: "How long are you going to dally about proceeding to take possession of the land which Yahweh, God of your fathers, has given you? 4 Choose for yourselves three men per tribe, so that I may send them forth; let them survey the land, so as to record it before me according to their fiefs, and report back to me. 5 They shall divide it among themselves into seven parts. Judah will remain at its territory in the south, and the Bene Joseph will remain at their territory in the north.

6 "You are the ones who will record the land (seven parts) and report here to me, so that I may cast the lot for you here, before Yahweh our God.

7 "But the Levites are to have no share among you, for Yahweh's priestly office is their fief. And Gad, Reuben, and half the tribe of Manasseh have already taken their fiefs east of Jordan, which Moses the Servant of Yahweh gave them."

8 The men set forth. Joshua charged those who were going out to record the land: "Go, survey the land, record it, and return to me. And here I will cast the lot for you before Yahweh in Shiloh."

9 So the men went forth and crossed through the land. They looked it over and recorded it by towns in seven parts on an inscription. Then they reported to Joshua at the camp at Shiloh.

10 Joshua cast the lot for them before Yahweh at Shiloh. There Joshua parceled out the land to the Bene Israel—according to their divisions.

TEXTUAL NOTES

18 2. *among the Bene*   Hebrew *bbny*. LXX and some Hebrew fragments lack the preposition.

3. *about proceeding*   LXX reflects a haplography: *l[bw' l]ršt*.

God of your fathers   "Our God" in LXX is probably a variant from oral tradition.

4. *so that I may send them forth*   The Hebrew word *w'šlḥm* was lost by haplography in LXX or its *Vorlage*.

before me according to their fiefs   This is based on LXX, which reflects *lpny knḥltm*, against MT *lpy nḥltm*.

me   LXX "him" reflects a dittography in its Hebrew *Vorlage: 'ly[w] w*.

5. *Bene*   This is LXX, which reflects *bny ywsp* for MT *byt ywsp*, "House of Joseph." Curiously, "Judah" is not a good match for either.

at their territory   Missing in LXX.

6. *record*   LXX reads instead "divide," repeating the idiom of v 5.

(seven parts)   This is MT *šb'h ḥlqym*, putting emphasis on description of the land. Numerous Hebrew manuscripts and versions emphasize instead the division *lšb'h ḥlqym*, "into seven parts," showing further influence of v 5.

here   Lacking in LXX, where a Hebrew copyist skipped from *l* to *l: gwrl [ph] lpny*. Grammatical parallelism favors MT.

7. *Levites*   LXX seems to read Bene Levi, which is never used in MT of Joshua.

their first occurrence   This follows LXX^A and Syriac, where MT and LXX^B "his" shows contamination from the following word.

8. *"Go, survey*   Thus MT, where LXX *Vorlage* dropped the second word by haplography: *l[kw whthl]kw*.

9. *looked it over*   This is LXX, lost by haplography in MT: *wy[r'wh wy]ktbwh*.

at the camp   Missing in LXX. MT may preserve variants: *'l yhwš'*, "to Joshua," and *'l mḥnh*, "to the camp."

at the camp at Shiloh   Lost by haplography in LXX^B *Vorlage*.

10. *There Joshua parceled out the land to the Bene Israel—according to their divisions*   Lacking in LXX.

according to   MT *k*. Many manuscripts and versions read *b*, "in, by."

NOTES

18:1-10. These verses introduce the second phase of the "settlement." It was based at Shiloh and was directly pertinent to interests and duties of seventh-century public officials in the southern kingdom. In their view it was Shiloh that had continued the wilderness tradition for a while, the only legitimate predecessor to Jerusalem as the religious center of the league (Judg 18:31). The bulk of these verses belongs therefore to the first edition (Dtr 1). The first and last verses, however, show clear signs of retouching in a manner characteristic of the later redactor (Dtr 2). The opening sentence anticipates a similar statement in 22:12 where it is embedded in a Dtr 2 story.

1. *The entire congregation of the Bene Israel assembled at Shiloh.* The congregation (*'ēdâ*) we have met in 9:15-21, the comic supplement and solution (Dtr 2) to the plight posed by hasty negotiations (Dtr 1) with the Gibeonites. But this is the first occurrence in the Book of Joshua of the important verb *qhl*, "to assemble," which together with its cognate noun (not used here) shows a distinctive distribution. The cognate noun occurs frequently in Dtn (Deut 5:19; 9:10; 10:4; 18:16; 23:2,3,4,9). The root is apparently avoided in the main edition of the historical work (Dtr 1). That historian retained the noun in an old story which he saw no reason to alter on this point (1 Sam 17:47). In 2 Sam 20:14 the text is corrupt and it is not clear who is the subject of the verb—supporters of Sheba or followers of Joab! Noun and verb occur all told six times (*sic!*) in the story of Solomon's prayer (1 Kings 8), where Solomon is the subject of the verbal uses; and only twice thereafter: once in connection with Jeroboam (1 Kgs 12:3) and once with Rehoboam as subject (1 Kgs 12:21). Only in the post-monarchical situation envisaged by Dtr 2 does the old *qāhāl* come into its own once again (Deut 4:10; 31:12,28 verb,30; Josh 8:35; 22:12 verb; Judg 20:1 verb,2; 21:5,8). Every one of these passages occurs in a context that is formally or editorially marked as distinct from the nuclear Dtn and its earliest historiographical use in relation to Joshua-2 Kings. Thus it is clear that the noun *'ēdâ* and the root *qhl* stand for the fullest possible participation by the people in the decision-making that affects their lives. However, the distribution of *qhl* can scarcely be taken as evidence of Josiah's alleged democratizing policies (Weinfeld), since it occurs only ten times in all of Samuel and Kings as compared with thirty-seven occurrences in the books of Chronicles. Most striking in this connection is its absence from the account of Josiah's reign (2 Kings 22-23). The *'ēdâ* and the root *qhl* are important in the pre-monarchical and post-monarchical contexts; both are played down by the contemporary historians of the monarchy.

Shiloh. Map H, 398. Mentioned repeatedly hereafter (vv 8,9,10 and 19:51; 21:2; 22:9,12), nothing in the book has paved the way for Shiloh's move to center stage. It was an out-of-the-way rallying point, a town site which had lain in ruins and was largely uninhabited throughout the Late Bronze Age. No doubt it became the Yahwist rallying point idealized here and depicted in the opening chapters of 1 Samuel, during the period after Abimelech's destruction of Shechem (mid-twelfth century). Shiloh fell before the Philistines late in the pre-monarchical era, as has been discovered in excavations. However, excavations at Shiloh have not uncovered the acropolis area of the town, which is the most promising location to look for ruins of a sacred area. The archaeological survey of 1967-1968 by the Israel Department of Antiquities noted small settlements in the Shiloh vicinity, dating from the Iron Age. Paul and Dever, *Biblical Archaeology*, 70.

Tent of Meeting. Hebrew *'ōhel mô'ēd.* This term for the portable sanctuary of the wilderness period (Exod 33:7; Num 11:16; 12:4; Deut 31:14) is ubiquitous in P (130 times), where it occurs alongside the term *miškān* (the key sanctuary word in Dtn). The great Canaanite god El likewise had a "tent of meeting," described with various terms, including those used here. The second word is presumably a participial formation on the root *y'd,* "to appoint." It appears to be the indigenous Canaanite word for a political assembly, in myth the deliberative assembly of the gods. In the Yahwist transformation of this theme the Tent of the heavenly court has as its earthly counterpart the site where Yahweh will meet with his people. The Tent tradition throughout the period of the monarchy was largely displaced by the notion of the Temple as permanent earthly dwelling of God. See Clifford, "The Tent of El and the Israelite Tent of Meeting," *CBQ* 33 (1971) 221-227; Cross, *CMHE,* 321-325.

2. *seven tribes.* It is impossible to be Israel without twelve tribes, whether in Canaan or elsewhere, in the story which concludes the era (Judg 21:6).

they. The antecedent is presumably Eleazar and Joshua though allusion to the congregation as a whole may be intended.

3. *Joshua said.* The landscape of Shiloh includes a sort of natural amphitheater where it is quiet enough "to hear a human voice quite distinctly at up to about 500 meters." The author of the report estimates that the place could accommodate a number of persons in the range of ten to twenty thousand. B. Cobbey Crisler, "The Acoustics and Crowd Capacity of Natural Theaters in Palestine," *BA* 39 (1976) 128-141.

"How long are you going to dally. Compare the exhortation, aimed at overcoming complacency, by Deborah near Bethel (Judges 4-5) in the post-Abimelech period. Boling, *Judges,* AB 6A, 92-93, 109, and 118-119.

proceeding to take possession. An echo of 1:11. The two Hebrew infinitives here juxtaposed form a hendiadys found together only here and in Deut 9:1,5; 11:31; Judg 18:9; Neh 9:15,23.

4. *Choose.* Hebrew *hābû,* the same verb with which Moses secures the nomination of leaders in Deut 1:13.

so that I may send. Not merely declarative (EVV), in Hebrew the simple conjunction followed by the imperfect signals purpose or result.

let them survey. Hebrew *wyqmw wythlkw,* literally, "let them arise and walk back and forth," another verbal hendiadys continuing the statement of purpose.

5. *They shall divide it among themselves.* Hebrew *whthlqw.* It is thus made clear that the delineation of tribal fiefs was no one person's unilateral action. Note wordplay in the assonance of walking and dividing in Hebrew.

territory. Hebrew *gĕbûl,* normally "border."

Judah. south. Joseph. north. The objection has been made that this would only make sense if spoken from the perspective of Gilgal, rather than Shiloh which is within the territory already assigned to Ephraim. Miller and Tucker, *Joshua*, 139. But the point is that they are north and south in relation to each other; it must have made sense to the contributor of vv 2 and 10.

6. *"You are the ones.* Word order in the original gives this emphasis. Joshua turns to address directly the cartographic team.

the lot. See 14:1 and NOTES; 15:1; 16:1.

In Num 27:21 Joshua is to take his questions to Eleazar who "shall inquire for him by the judgment of the Urim." This is the only means of divination that the biblical texts explicitly name as legitimate. The reader is totally unprepared to find Joshua (not Eleazar) casting the lot.

before Yahweh. This seems to imply the presence of the Ark of the Covenant in the Tent of Meeting at Shiloh. Toward the end of the era it is the temporary presence of the Ark at Bethel that makes Bethel the place of reliable inquiry (Judg 20:27).

7. *the Levites.* Here they have as fief only the honor of priestly status. There is no mention of provisions for their livelihood. See 13:14 and 33 and NOTES; and chap. 21 NOTES and COMMENT.

Gad, Reuben, and half the tribe of Manasseh. Joshua 13:8-32.

Moses the Servant of Yahweh. As in 1:2,7.

8. *to record the land.* Literally, "to write the land (up/down), inscribe the land (in a registry)." Hebrew uses the *qal* infinitive, for which the OG (*chōrobatēsai*) and Theodotion (*diagrapsai*) reflect independent translations. Greenspoon, STBJ, 122-123, 310.

10. *Joshua cast the lot.* Joshua gets the credit, though the action was probably performed by the priest Eleazar (see 19:51). One Eleazar the Aaronite is father of Phinehas who presides at the Ark in Bethel (Judg 20:27-28). We suggest that the picture of Joshua wielding the lot reflects the success of rival Aaronite priests in Jerusalem.

parceled. The Hebrew root is *ḥlq;* "their divisions" is a cognate accusative.

their divisions. See above, 11:23 and 12:7. This usage is found elsewhere only in the Ezekiel torah (48:29). This word *mḥlqwt* became a technical term for the organization of priests and Levites. 1 Chr 23:6; 24:1; 26:1,12,19, *et passim;* and cf. Luke 1:5,8.

COMMENT

Shiloh was conveniently situated but somewhat off the beaten path, "north of Bethel, east of the main road that goes up from Bethel to Shechem, and south of Lebonah" (Judg 21:19, AB 6A, 290). This location is roughly opposite the Timnath-serah that became Joshua's fief (24:30). These two sites form, together with Shechem to the north and

Gibeon to the south, a long narrow "diamond" astride the watershed ridge, within which many new settlements, small and unwalled, sprang up at the beginning of the Iron Age. These are discussed above, in relation to The Ruin, in chaps. 7 and 8.

It was probably in the wake of Abimelech's counterrevolution and eventual destruction of Shechem that the leadership of the alliance established itself at Shiloh; on one decisive occasion the charismatic leadership came from the neighborhood of Bethel (Deborah in Judges 4).

The Shiloh phase, which eventually added seven allotments, mostly around the edges but with Benjamin insecurely sandwiched between Joseph and Judah, was considerably longer than the Shechem phase. It is doubtful that the historical Joshua actually lived to see the end of Phase One. But it is not impossible that he saw it coming and engineered the move to Shiloh before the reaction had set in at Shechem.

By the end of the seventh century, all this was far in the past. What seems to have impressed the late redactor was the difference between Phases One and Two. The former (chaps. 13-17) began with partitioning of land already under Israel's control. The latter (chaps. 18-19) deals with division of land yet to be pacified. In this way the sense of the land as gift, sheer grace, is elevated and that of possession by right of conquest is played down. And the lot (vv 6,8,10) is seen to place the distribution beyond the possibility of any human manipulation. The holy Ark as war palladium yields pride of place to the Tent of Meeting, which stood at least during the Wanderings, for God's freedom and ability to be present wherever his people assemble.

b. BENJAMIN
(18:11-28)

Borders

18   11 The lot turned up first for the tribe of Benjamin, for their clans. The border of their allotment went out between the Bene Judah and the Bene Joseph.

12 Their border on the north side began at the Jordan. The border went up to the ridge north of Jericho, climbing westward into the hill country, and its destination was the wilderness of Beth-aven. 13 From there the border went around to Luz, to the southern ridge of Luz (that is, Bethel). The border went down from Ataroth-addar, to the mountain which is to the south of Lower Beth-horon.

14 The border turned sharply and, on the west side, came around to the south, from the mountain which is on the south of Beth-horon. Its destination was Qiryath-baal (that is, Qiryath-yearim), a town belonging to the Bene Judah. This was the west side.

15 The south side began at the town limit of Qiryath-baal. The border took the lower route . . . and followed the watercourse to the spring of Me-Nephtoah. 16 The border went down to the foot of the mountain opposite the valley of Ben Hinnom (which is adjacent to the valley of Rephaim, on the north of it); and it descended into the valley of Hinnom, to the south of the Jebusite ridge, and descended to En-rogel. 17 It turned sharply northward and followed the watercourse to En-shemesh, then down the watercourse to Geliloth which is across from the Red Ascent, and went down to the stone of Bohan ben Reuben. 18 It went around on the ridge overlooking Beth-arabah from the north, and descended into the Arabah. 19 The border went around to the northern shoulder of Beth-hoglah. The destination of the border was at the northern side of the Tongue of the Salt Sea, at the southern end of the Jordan. This was the southern border.

20 The Jordan bounds it on the east side.

This was the fief of the Bene Benjamin for their clans, according to its borders all around.

Towns

21 The towns that belonged to the tribe of the Bene Benjamin for their clans were: Jericho, Beth-hoglah, Emeq-qeziz, 22 Beth-arabah, Zemaraim, Bethel, 23 Ha-avvim, Parah, Ophrah, 24 Kefar-ammoni, Ophni and Geba (twelve towns and their enclosures).

25 Gibeon, Ramah, Beeroth, 26 Mizpeh-marom, Chephirah, Mozah, 27 Reqem, Irpeel, Taralah, 28 Zela-eleph, the Jebusite (that is, Jerusalem), Gibeath, Qiryath-yearim (thirteen towns and their enclosures). This was the fief of the Bene Benjamin for their clans.

TEXTUAL NOTES

18 11. *turned up*   This is Hebrew *wy'l*, for which LXX has a variant, probably originating in oral formulations: *wyṣ'*, "went to."

first   LXX *prōtos* seems to represent *r'šwn*, lost by haplography in MT: *gwrl* [*r'šwn l*]*mṭh*.

Benjamin   With LXX. Here MT "Bene Benjamin" seems to represent the influence of v 21.

Bene   With MT, where LXX has used the short form of the names.

12. *wilderness*   Hebrew *midbārāh*, which LXX took as a place name "Madbaritis"! See COMMENT on 5:15.

13. *ridge of Luz*   Lacking in LXX^L, OL, Vulgate, a simple haplography: *l*[*wzh 'l ktp l*]*wzh*.

from   With no preposition expressed in MT, we suspect another haplography, perhaps spurred on by archaic use of *l*, "from": *wyrd hgbwl* [*l*]*'ṭrwt 'dr*. In LXX the spelling *m'ṭrwt-'rk* (<*'dr*) may in fact represent the preposition *m*, "from," in another recension.

14. *which is*   LXX reflects haplography: *hh*[*r 'š*]*r*.

15. *Qiryath-baal*   With LXX, where MT's Qiryath-yearim has assimilated to the parenthetical element in v 14.

. . .   According to MT the border at this point does something "to the west" (*ymh*) which is unintelligible. OG offers *Gain*. No solution commends itself.

16. *of the mountain*   LXX omits.

Ben   LXX omits.

adjacent to the   This is LXX, where one word has dropped out of MT: *b*[*qṣh*] *'mq*.

Hinnom   Syriac and Targum read "Ben Hinnom."

17. *turned sharply northward*   Lacking in LXX, haplography of *w/kai* in Greek or in its *Vorlage*.

En-shemesh   Beth-shemesh in LXX.

Bohan ben Reuben   LXX reads *bhn bny r'wbn*, "Bohan (of the) Bene Reuben."

18. *Beth*   Restored from LXX.

into the Arabah   Lacking in LXX.

19. *went around*   Thus MT. In LXX the verb has been replaced by a repetition of the preposition *'l*.

Beth-hoglah   LXX reads *ym*, "sea."

20. *bounds it*   Revoweling *ygbl* as causative (cf. Exod 19:12). LXX translators produced no reflex of the object pronoun.

21. *the tribe of*   LXX omits.

23. *Ophrah*   Thus MT. LXX has *Ephrata*.

24. *Kefar-ammoni*   The beginning of the verse in LXX reflects *whkprh*, "and Chephirah," attracted from v 26 by the following place name, *kpr h'mny*.

Ophni   Lacking in LXX, after haplography.

26. *Mizpeh-marom*   Literally, "High Lookout." The reading is based on LXX which reflects *wmrwn* at the beginning of the verse and which the translator mistakenly took as a separate name. Thus M. Patrick O'Connor, private communication.

27. *Taralah*   MT *tr'lh*, which a Cairo Geniza text spells *tr'lh*.

28. *Zela-eleph*   This follows LXX^A, where MT reads as two names "Zela and Ha-eleph," and LXX^B shows the results of haplography.

Gibeath, Qiryath-yearim   This is based on LXX where, however, two elements are transposed; while there has been a haplography in MT:

| MT | gb't | qryt | [ ] | 'rym |
| LXX | wqry(w)t | wgb'(w)t | y'rym | 'rym |

(*thirteen*   This is LXX, where MT reads "fourteen," after the division of Zela-eleph as two names.

NOTES

18:11-28. The section on Benjamin's fief returns to the pattern displayed in describing Judah (15:1-63), with a description of the borders (18:11-20) followed by a list of towns (18:21-28).

11-20. Beginning at the Jordan, and facing north, the borders are described counterclockwise.

12. *on the north*. This segment uses different wording but corresponds in structure to the beginning of the allotment to the Bene Joseph in 16:1-2.

the ridge north of Jericho. This must be the Wadi Makkuk, which opens into the Arabah north of Jebel Qarantel.

Beth-aven. By popular etymology, "House of Iniquity." Possibly Tell Maryam, 5 km south of et-Tell ("The Ruin" in chaps. 7-8). Map G, 364.

13. *went around to Luz.* The border describes an arc, starting out due north of Beth-aven, far enough perhaps to include the vicinity of "The Ruin" before bending around to the west.

Bethel). Map G, 364. The verse seems to be designed to leave this town clearly within Ephraim, against the listing in v 22.

from Ataroth-addar. See "Ataroth" in 16:2 and NOTES. A segment of the border connecting Bethel and Ataroth-addar, presumably along the watershed ridge, is not described. This place should not be confused with the Ataroth of 16:7 on Ephraim's northeastern border.

Lower Beth-horon. Map G, 364. See 16:2-3 and NOTES.

14. *side.* Hebrew *p'h.* Cf. 15:5. The Benjamin descriptions are distinctive in their use of this word (vv 12,14 [*bis*],20) to refer to each of the four "quarters" of the border.

Qiryath-baal (*that is, Qiryath-yearim*). Map G, 364. See 15:60. This is the one clear overlap with Judah's "District X."

15-19. *The south side.* This boundary is described in somewhat lesser detail than is Judah's corresponding northern border (15:5b-9).

15. *at the town limit.* The town itself is in Judah (according to the preceding verse) and a member of the old Hivite confederacy (9:17).

took the lower route. This is the verb *yṣ'.* The final segment of this border is described in 15:9, with reference to the upper Soreq Valley and its tributaries. But to go from Qiryath-yearim to the Soreq one must cross the line of hills running southwest from Qastil. A route "between hill 788 and hill 791 could still be termed a lowland route." Parunak, "Geographical Terminology," with reference to the 1:100,000 map of Israel, Sheet 11.

and followed the watercourse. Again, the verb is *yṣ'* contextually nuanced. In this case, to follow a wadi or lowland route is to go steadily up. Perhaps it was the several slightly different uses of *yṣ'* in the immediate context of v 15 that triggered the textual corruption noted above.

Me-Nephtoah. See 15:9. Probably modern Lifta at the northwestern edge of modern Jerusalem. Literally, "Waters of Nephtoah," which yields a redundancy in this context.

16. *valley of Ben Hinnom.* See also 15:8. The Wadi er-Rababi runs north-south along the west side of Jerusalem's old city, then turns sharply to enter the Qidron valley.

valley of Rephaim. See also 15:8. This is most likely the plain of *Baqa',* now in the southwest suburbs of modern Jerusalem. G. A. Barrois, *IDB* 4, 35-36. On the background of "Rephaim" see NOTES on 13:12.

Jebusite. On this name, see 3:10 and NOTES.

ridge. This is the eastern hill of Jerusalem extending south from the site that would become the Jewish Temple Mount.

En-rogel. Map G, 364. See 15:7 and NOTES.

17. *followed the watercourse.* Hebrew *yṣ'.* In 15:7 the cognate noun *tṣ'wt* describes the same segment.

En-shemesh. See 15:7 and NOTE.

Geliloth. This is "The Gilgal" in 15:7 and the Targum so reads here. See NOTES. Map G.

stone of Bohan ben Reuben. See 15:6 and NOTES.

18. *It went around.* Here the verb *'br* describes a bulge or detour from the expected straight descent to the floor of the Arabah, a detour made desirable by the configuration of cliffs represented by the "Thumb" (Bohan). Parunak, "Geographical Terminology."

Beth-arabah. Map G, 364. See 15:6,61 and NOTES.

19. *went around to the northern shoulder of Beth-hoglah.* See the description of Judah's northern border, 15:6 and NOTES.

at the northern side of the Tongue. The latter is apparently the distinctive geological terrace jutting into the Dead Sea from Transjordan. There is no bay or "inlet" (*NEB*) on the north or northwest shoreline to match this description which is extremely odd as a point of reference for the border. The description in 15:5 is only slightly more intelligible.

20. *all around.* Hebrew *sābîb* is allegedly P. See the NOTE on 15:12.

21-28. The towns of Benjamin are numerous and close together. They are concentrated in the area which was the center of the action in the warfare recounted in chaps. 2-9, which must have left them thoroughly weakened and unable to consolidate until the second phase of "settlement." The towns are listed in two groups, one crowded onto the attractive watershed ridge north and west of Jerusalem (vv 25-28), and the other beginning on the less desirable eastern part of the ridge and falling away to Jericho and the Jordan (vv 21-24). This list of towns in two groups is clearly related to the administrative document which served as the basis of Judah's description in 15:20-62; the source which was the basis of both 15:20-62 and 18:21-28 comes from a period when Judah and Benjamin were united under one administration. If the Benjamin units are fitted into the appropriate spot (where Qiryath-baal in 15:60 overlaps with the Benjamin list), then it is clear that the area called "Benjamin" had become two districts, under Judahite administration, by the time the present text was drafted.

21-24. The eastern half of the territory of Benjamin became Judahite District XI.

21. *Jericho.* The name may be derived from the tribe of Yarihu, a minor subdivison of the Banu-Yamin in the Mari documents. Albright, "From the Patriarchs to Moses: II. Moses Out of Egypt," *BA* 36 (1973) 49. On the archaeology and tradition of Jericho, see chaps. 2 and 6 with NOTES and COMMENT.

Beth-hoglah. Map G, 364. See 15:6 and NOTES.

† *Emeq-qeziz.* Mentioned only here, location unknown.

22. *Beth-arabah.* Map G, 364. This Benjaminite border town was finally assigned to Judah's District XII (15:61); the reassignment reflects the Judahite revival in the reign of Josiah, to judge from the archaeological evidence.

Zemaraim. Possibly Rās ez-Zeimara near eṭ-Ṭaiyibeh.

Bethel. Map G, 364. Here and in v 23 the territory of Benjamin includes an area elsewhere assigned to Joseph (16:1-2) and including this famous royal sanctuary town of the northern kingdom.

23. *Ha-avvim.* "The Avvites." The name looks like a gentilic formation in

13:3, referring to a people displaced by the Philistines. Here, however, the name may be a variant of *hā-'ai*, "The Ruin," in chaps. 7-8.

†*Parah*. Khirbet 'Ain Farah, northeast of Anathoth.

Ophrah. Not to be confused with the same place name in Manasseh (Judg 6:11,24; 8:27,32; 9:5). This one is identified with eṭ-Ṭaiyibeh, some 6.4 km northeast of Bethel. Map G, 364.

24. †*Kefar-ammoni*. "Ammonite Village." Possibly Kafr 'Ana, southeast of Baal-hazor.

†*Ophni*. Another gentilic form. The name is perhaps reflected at Jifneh, about 4.8 km north-northwest of Bethel.

Geba. This is best identified with Jaba', where however surface exploration produced no evidence of occupation earlier than the eighth century. John Peterson, private communication. The same name in other contexts is a short form of "Gibeah" (Tell el-Fūl) and even "Gibeon" (el-Jīb). Aaron Demsky, "Geba, Gibeah, and Gibeon—An Historico-Geographic Riddle," *BASOR* 212 (1973) 26-31. Cf. the similar name "Gibeath" in v 28. For the Levitical status of the town of Geba, see 21:17 and NOTES.

25-28. The western half of Benjamin became Judahite District X.

25. *Gibeon*. Map G, 364. A Hivite population. On the archaeology and history of tradition, see NOTES and COMMENTS on chaps. 9 and 10.

Ramah. "Height." The site is er-Ram.

Beeroth. "Wells." Possibly Kh. Raddana at the northern edge of Bireh, Ramallah's twin city. Beeroth was one of the towns in league with Hivite Gibeon (9:17). Map G, 364.

26. Each of the three names in this verse has the definite article in MT.

Mizpeh-marom. Also spelled Mizpah, and meaning "Watchtower." The site is probably Tell en-Naṣbeh, just south of modern Ramallah. Map G, 364. It appears to have been a new small town settlement in the late thirteenth and early twelfth centuries. Y. Aharoni, "The Settlement of Canaan," *WHJP* III (1971) 113.

Chephirah. "Lioness." Map G, 364. On its Hivite prehistory and alliance with Gibeon see 9:17 and NOTES.

Mozah. The name occurs on stamped jar handles discovered at Jericho and Tell en-Naṣbeh (probably Mizpeh). Located at Qalōniyeh, 6.4 km northwest of Jerusalem, near Me-Nephtoah.

27. †*Reqem*, †*Irpeel*, †*Taralah*. These are otherwise unattested as place names. Reqem is also the name of a Midianite chieftain in 13:21 (cf. Num 31:8). Irpeel is a form of the name Raphael, "El heals."

28. *Zela-eleph*. "Rib(=slope) of the *'eleph*." The *'eleph* here is perhaps the muster unit of the clan or village. Or does this signify the first settlement of that name with a Zela-beth somewhere else? D. N. Freedman, private communication. Cf. 2 Sam 21:14.

the Jebusite. Another gentilic form (see 3:10 and NOTES; cf. 15:8,63), here used in reference to the place itself.

Gibeath. It is generally agreed that this is the town made famous as residence of King Saul, elsewhere known as "Gibeah," spelled here with the *t* of the original feminine ending. This place is clearly to be distinguished from

"Geba" in v 24, since they belong to separate districts. The name means "hill" (there was also a Gibeah in Judah—15:57) and might be read together with the following name in our list as "Hill of Qiryath-yearim." Thus Y. Aharoni identifies "Gibeah of Qiryath-yearim" with Abu Ghosh as distinct from neighboring Deir el-'Azar, which he identifies as the Qiryath-yearim of Judah in 15:60. In other words, the tribal boundary ran between Qiryath-yearim and the neighboring hill which bore a similar name. This ingenious proposal raises more questions than it answers. Most seriously, it eliminates from the description of Saul's tribe the name of the town that he had made famous. The best location for Gibea(t)h is Tell el-Fūl. See Lawrence A. Sinclair's report of earlier excavations by Albright and the subsequent work by Lapp, in *EAEHL* II (1976) 444-446. This "Hill" was another of the new, unwalled villages first flourishing in the twelfth century. The identification of Tell el-Fūl with the Gibeah of Saul has recently been challenged by J. M. Miller, "Geba/Gibeah of Benjamin," *VT* 25 (1975) 1-22. But his alternative equation with Geba runs into serious archaeological problems. See above.

Qiryath-yearim. See NOTES on 9:17.

COMMENT

Benjamin is the first of seven tribes whose territories are not described until it has been made clear that the setting for the apportionment is Shiloh. Benjamin's towns are numerous and close together, clustered in two groups.

The eastern cluster in vv 21-24 includes a portion of territory that extends considerably north of the border with Joseph, as that is outlined in the description in 16:1. Here it is not a matter of making explicit exception for residential enclaves or grazing (perhaps farming) rights of one tribe within the allotment of another (as in 16:9 and 17:8, for example), but clearly contradictory claims.

The description of Benjamin presupposes a time after the split of the monarchy when Benjamin and southeastern Ephraim were both administered from Jerusalem. Albrecht Alt dated the passage to the reign of Josiah who extended his control into the north, to include Bethel and other northern towns (2 Kgs 23:15-19). Cross and Wright have argued on the other hand that the border drawn in this chapter lies too far south to be a reflection of Josiah's power in the north. They point instead to the late tenth century when Abijah the son and successor of Rehoboam invaded the north and took control of a number of towns, including two that appear in our list: Bethel and Ephron(=Ophrah). 2 Chronicles 13:19. It is not clear when the towns in question were restored to Israel, but that had clearly happened by the mid-eighth century when the flourishing northern sanctuary at Bethel was denounced by famous prophets (Amos 7:13; Hos 8:6; 10:15).

An alternative explanation would see the northern group of Benjaminite towns as a continuation of the Solomonic district of Benjamin (1 Kgs 4:18) after the split of the nation. Aharoni, *LOB,* 302. The problem with this interpretation is that there is no evidence that Benjamin was ever effectively partitioned between the north and the south. On the contrary it appears that what Solomon tried to administer as one long east-west corridor between Judah and Ephraim was subsequently divided into two districts by the southern administration. There is a perfectly plausible explanation for the transfer of Beth-arabah (v 22) to Judah's District XII (15:61). The latter (the "wilderness district") was a late seventh-century concentration of paramilitary settlements (including a number of new sites) established by the nation-rebuilding King Josiah.

Thus our lists are far removed from the early era in which Benjamin acquired a reputation for its militancy and independent attitude. See the characterizations of Ehud in Judg 3:15-30 and his tribe in Judges 20, the story of the pre-monarchical Civil War. The early prestige and success of Benjamin "son of the south" flanking Joseph "son of the north" is brightly reflected in the archaic Testament of Moses—

> The beloved of Yahweh encamps in safety
> The Exalted One hovers over him
> And between his shoulders he tents

(Deuteronomy 33:12, tr. F. M. Cross and D. N. Freedman, *JBL* 64 [1948] 194)=*SAYP,* 100.

It seems clear enough that Benjamin had, very early, ranged much farther south than the border which was eventually drawn with Judah, since the names of certain groups known best among the Banu-yamin at Mari survive only as extinct clans in Judahite tradition. Albright, "From the Patriarchs to Moses: I. From Abraham to Joseph," *BA* 36 (1973) 7-8. It is not clear what significance is to be assigned the curious fact that Benjamin alone, of the twelve sons of Jacob, is born in Canaan. James Muilenburg, "The Birth of Benjamin," *JBL* 75 (1956) 194-201.

But the original Banu-yamin were only one element in the rich social and cultural mix of the towns that were grouped together to consolidate the territory of the Yahwist "tribe." This is clear from the unusually high percentage of gentilic formations and related indicators in the place names, as observed in the NOTES. It is also clear from the clustering and content of the Warfare stories, precisely in the area that would become Benjamin (chaps. 2-9), and with the sequel in chap. 10 which points to early continuity with the southern hill country which later became the "tribe" of Judah.

In the other pre-monarchical collection of testaments, perhaps a quarter to half a century earlier than the Testament of Moses, we are reminded that

> Benjamin is a wolf on the prowl.
> Mornings he devours the prey.
> And evenings he distributes the spoils.

(Genesis 49:27, tr. Speiser, *Genesis,* AB 1 [1964] 364.) Here are a mere three lines for Benjamin, almost as an afterthought, following nineteen lines devoted to Joseph (49:22-26) and seventeen to Judah (49:8-12), a contrast that is scarcely offset by the intrinsic importance of being in the concluding position in the list of Genesis 49.

Benjamin's early preeminence was eclipsed by the career of Judah, so that in the received form of the tradition the description of Benjamin's fief must await the second phase, as part of the sequel to Judah's consolidation. The Benjaminites were at last crowded to the north in a narrow corridor across the watershed and down to the Jordan, just as certain elements of Reuben were inclined to retreat, it appears, across the river (13:15-23). Simeon, whose allotment comes next, fled south to flourish for a significant time on the desert fringe before being surrounded by Judah (19:1-9).

c. SIMEON
19:1-9

19 1 The second lot went to Simeon for their clans. Their fief was within the fief of the Bene Judah.

2 They had in their fief Beersheba, Shema, Moladah, 3 Hazar-shual, Balah, Ezem, 4 Eltolad, Bethul, Hormah, 5 Ziqlag, Beth-marcaboth, Hazar-susah, 6 Beth-lebaoth, Sharuhen: thirteen towns and their fenced areas.

7 En-rimmon, Tochen, Ether, Ashan: four towns and their fenced areas 8 scattered around those towns. (As far away as Baalath-beer, the Ramah of the Negeb?)

This is the fief of the tribe of the Bene Simeon for their clans. 9 Part of the territory of Judah is the fief of the Bene Simeon tribe; for the portion belonging to the Bene Judah was too large for them alone, and so the Bene Simeon received a fief within their fief.

TEXTUAL NOTES

19 1. *to Simeon* This follows LXX^A, where LXX^B reflects one variant ("to the Bene Simeon") which MT conflates with another one ("to Simeon, to the Bene Simeon tribe").

for their clans Lacking in LXX.

2. *They had in their fief* This is MT *wyhy lhm bnḥltm.* LXX appears to have read only *wyhy nḥltm.*

Shema This is the reading of LXX^B and OL, in agreement with 15:26, against MT and LXX^A *Sheba* (contamination from the preceding name) in this verse.

6. *Sharuhen* LXX omits.

7. *En-rimmon* LXX^{B+MSS} support this reading where MT vocalization and LXX^A read two names, as in 1 Chr 4:32.

Tochen Not in MT, restored on the basis of LXX^B *Thalcha.* The vocalization is preserved in 1 Chr 4:32.

8. *scattered around* This follows LXX. MT adds at the beginning of the

verse *wkl-ḥṣryhn,* "and all their fenced areas" (a variant of the preceding phrase). The next word in MT, *'šr,* though not represented in LXX, is presumably original.

(*As far away as Baalath-beer, the Ramah of the Negeb?*)   This takes MT at face value, although its sense is far from clear: *'d b'lt b'r r'mt ngb.* LXX seems to be reading *'d brk b'ym bmt ngb,* which yields no sense.

9. *territory of Judah*   This is LXX, where MT has assimilated to the following phrase and reads "territory of the Bene Judah."

tribe   With LXX which reflects *mṭh.* MT omits.

NOTES

19:1-9. Simeon's fief falls entirely within the larger area of Judah. There are no traces of boundary descriptions. What appears instead, after the usual introductory rubric (v 1), is a list of towns in two segments (vv 2-6 and 7-8a) with the usual concluding rubric (v 8b) plus a substantial explanation of the peculiar situation of Simeon (v 9).

1. *Simeon.* A Semitic explanation of the name is uncertain. It has been provisionally related to the Anatolian place name Šamḫuna. Mendenhall, *Ten Gen,* 163 n. 62. Simeon is the second son of Leah in the genealogy that became normative. It appears that in an earlier period the precursors who bore the same name ranged into the north-central hill country where their history is intimately connected with that of Levi. See the Testament of Jacob (Gen 49:5-6) and the story of the rape of Dinah and the retaliatory raid by Simeon and Levi, which surely left the great Shechem castle in ruins (Genesis 34). In this description of allotments based on town lists from a later era, however, there is no hint of that prehistory in the more desirable Shechem region. On the contrary, Simeon lost its holdings in the north and had been living at the northern Negeb oases, or digging deep wells, ever since the era of Shiloh, for such had been the determination by lot in the tribal assembly.

2-8a. This list of towns is very closely related to the second part of Judah's District I, the northern Negeb area around Beersheba (15:26-32). And it is even more closely related to the list of Simeonite towns in 1 Chr 4:28-32. On the latter see Jacob M. Myers, *I Chronicles,* AB 12, 25-31. The relationships are clearest when the three lists are lined up in parallel as follows:

JUDAH DISTRICT I		SIMEON	
15:26-32		19:2-7	1 Chr 4:28-32
v 28 Beersheba		v 2 Beersheba	v 28 Beersheba
v 26 Amam			
Shema		Shema	
Moladah		Moladah	Moladah
v 27 Hazar-gaddah			

	Heshmon				
	Beth-pelet				
v 28	Hazar-shual	v 3	Hazar-shual		Hazar-shual
v 29	Baalah		Balah	v 29	Bilhah
	Iyim				
	Ezem		Ezem		Ezem
v 30	Eltolad	v 4	Eltolad		Tolad
	Chesil		Bethul	v 30	Bethuel
	Hormah		Hormah		Hormah
v 31	Ziqlag	v 5	Ziqlag		Ziqlag
	Madmannah		Beth-marcaboth	v 31	Beth-marcaboth
	Sansannah		Hazar-susah		Hazar-susim
v 32	Lebaoth		Beth-lebaoth		Beth-biri
	Shilhim		Sharuhen		Shaaraim
				v 32	Etam
	En-rimmon	v 7	En-rimmon*		Ain
					Rimmon
			Tochen		Tochen
			Ether		
			Ashan		Ashan

Differences between the two Simeon lists are mainly scribal, while differences between Simeon and Judah District I are far more striking and must reflect distinct political and demographic realities, adjustments which came with consolidation of the larger tribe of Judah, as implicitly acknowledged in v 9. See Cross and Wright, "The Boundary and Province Lists," 214-215.

2. *Beersheba.* See 15:28 and NOTES. This is obviously the key town of the area.

Shema. See 15:26 and NOTES. The different order in the chap. 15 list (and the significant additions to it) stand in striking contrast to the list in 1 Chronicles 4.

Moladah. See 15:26 and NOTES.

3. *Hazar-shual.* See 15:28 and NOTES.

Balah. See "Baalah" in 15:29 and NOTES.

Ezem. See 15:29 and NOTES. This town is named on a Hebrew ostracon from Tell esh-Shari'a (Ziqlag?), reported by Oren and Netzer, *IEJ* 24 (1974) 265.

4. *Eltolad.* See 15:30 and NOTES.

Bethul. See "Chesil" in 15:30 and NOTES.

Hormah. See 15:30; 12:14 and NOTES.

5. *Ziqlag.* See 15:31 and NOTES.

Beth-marcaboth. "House of chariots." Compare Solomon's construction of chariotry posts according to 2 Chr 9:25. This town is not mentioned in Judah District I unless its older name is given there as Madmannah (15:31).

Hazar-susah. "Corral of the mare." Also in 1 Chr 4:31 ("corral of the

* See Textual Note.

horses"). The location is possibly Sabalat Abu Susein. Its place in the list is taken by "Sansannah" in Judah District I (15:31).

6. *Beth-lebaoth.* "Lions' House." It is simply "Lebaoth" in 15:32, "Beth-biri" in 1 Chr 4:31.

Sharuhen. This seems to be the Egyptian spelling of the place name "Shilhim" in 15:32. The same name appears as "Shaaraim" in 1 Chr 4:31, presumably a corruption of *šr'm.*

thirteen. The list has fourteen names. Perhaps the simplest explanation is to suppose that the annotator was mistakenly counting the two chariot towns, Beth-marcaboth and Hazar-susah, listed side by side as one and the same.

fenced areas. The noun *ḥṣr* refers to enclosures in general, formed of stone and/or brush, used for grazing or cultivation.

7. The second segment of the list contains four names, all of which are probably to be located in the area north and northwest of Beersheba. The last three places are not listed in Judah District I.

En-rimmon. Here the translation is based on LXX. In MT the vocalization as two distinct names probably originated as an adjustment after the loss of Tochen. In 1 Chr 4:32 the division into two names was reinforced by the annotated summary "five towns."

Tochen. As in 1 Chr 4:32. This is the only name in the second segment for which there is no topographical or linguistic clue to location.

Ether. 1 Chronicles 4:32 has instead "Etam," *'yṭm,* but there is scarcely any way that either name could have been accidentally created from the other one. Ether may be Kh. 'Attir south of Lahav. It should not be confused with another Ether located in the fourth district of Judah (15:42).

Ashan. Location uncertain. A site that was known to earlier geographers as Kh. 'Asan, said to be 3.2 km north of Beersheba, remains archaeologically unknown; it seems to have been built over by expansion of the modern city. The occurrence of "Ashan" in 15:42 is a separate problem, already noted above. See also W. F. Albright, "The Topography of Simeon," *JPOS* 4 (1924) 160.

8. (*As far away as.* This rendering treats the parenthetical element as a marginal query concerning a site in neighboring tribal territory during the period prior to Judah's consolidation, the area known elsewhere as the Negeb of the Jerahmeelites, scene of David's retaliatory forays against the Amaleqites in 1 Sam 27:10.

†*Baalath-beer.* "(Divine) Lady of the Well." Identification with Bir Rakhmeh 30 km southeast of Beersheba would indeed make sense out of the preceding phrase.

the Ramah of the Negeb?) Hebrew *ra(')mat-negeb,* "Southern Height," spelled with plural ending in 1 Sam 30:27, *rāmôt-negeb,* "Southern Heights." The latter is listed as one of the towns supplied by David with booty taken in the Amaleqite warfare. The list of recipients also includes a general reference to "the towns of the Jerahmeelites" (1 Sam 30:29). If the location is Bir Rakhmeh, then the name is readily explained by its situation in the low mountains of the north-central Negeb.

9. *territory.* Hebrew *ḥebel.* The sense is quite clear. These towns were under-

stood as Judahite turf. To be sure, it had been precisely the genius of Mosaic religion to dissolve the unsanctified marriage between "blood and soil." But it is probably going too far to suggest that because the towns were not *entirely* inhabited by Simeonites they should be understood mainly as marking territory from within which Simeonites continued to move out as partial nomads as late as the eighth century B.C. Kempinski, "Tell el-'Ajjul—Beth-Aglayim or Sharuhen?" *IEJ* 24 (1974) especially 151-152.

This conclusion to the unit makes it look as though what happened at Shiloh was mainly an agreement to abide by divine confirmation (by lot) of "tribal" areas that were already largely staked out or at least formulated as ideal. It is highly probable that at that time Judah had not yet become the principal southern tribe, and thus had not acquired the political position it would use to displace the original "Sons of the South," Benjamin, in the Cisjordan allotments. It is in fact now possible to speak with considerable clarity about the pre-monarchy heyday of Simeon.

COMMENT

How came Simeon to be situated in the edge of the desert where it was at last entirely surrounded by Judah? It is clear from the story of the rape of Dinah in Genesis 34 that Simeon had once ranged much farther north, from a position where in collaboration with a highly militant "Levi" it could successfully attack a major fortified stronghold such as Shechem, in violation of an agreement with the local lord.

In a recent restudy of the Testament of Jacob it has been urged that the pairing of Simeon and Levi there involves more than merely poetic license. They are both being banished from the pre-Mosaic (that is, pre-Yahwist) league of El-worshipers called "Israel" (Gen 49:5-7). D. N. Freedman, "Early Israelite History in the Light of Early Israelite Poetry," in *Unity and Diversity* (1975) especially 16-17.

Jacob's pronouncement on Simeon and Levi is the very opposite of a blessing.

> Simeon and Levi are a pair;
> Their wares are the tools of lawlessness.
> My person must not enter their council,
> Or my being be joined with their company!
> For they killed men in their fury,
> And maimed oxen at their whim.

(Genesis 49:5-6. Tr. E. A. Speiser, *Genesis,* AB 1 [1964] 361.)

It is the next line which can be sharpened in translation. To speak of both tribes being dispersed "in Israel" yields a picture that might at best be true of only one of them. Freedman reads the preposition *b* as "from" in both occurrences in v 7 and renders

> Cursed be their wrath—how fierce it was!
> And their rage—how cruel it was!
> I will divide them from Jacob,
> And I will banish them from Israel.

The result of whatever tribal condemnation stands behind the Patriarch's curse was that Simeon sought refuge at the edge of the desert, while Levi abandoned all territorial claim and, in substantial numbers, eventually made its way to Egypt.

What was the cause of the curse? Yet another recent study by the same author connects Merneptah's campaign with the events which account for the absence of Simeon and Levi from the Song of Deborah (Judges 5) and of Simeon from the Testament of Moses (Deuteronomy 33). Freedman, "Early Israelite Poetry and Historical Reconstructions," in *Symposia* (1979) 85-96.

Such a course of events would account very well for the literary configuration: Simeon retreated too far south to figure effectively in the events celebrated in Judges 5, while elements of Levi had undergone religious conversion to emerge at the militant core of Yahwism (as had, we may suspect, the poet of Judges 5). In the eleventh century, however, unwalled settlements were safely flourishing in the northern Negeb, where Simeon was to enjoy a brief comeback.

Out of a total eighteen "towns" listed for Simeon (Map G, 364), all but five can be certainly or approximately located (the five unknowns being Hazar-shual, Eltolad, Bethul/Chesil, Beth-lebaoth, and Tochen). All the others are concentrated in the general vicinity of Beersheba and the northeastern Negeb fringe, where oases are not numerous and where deep wells such as the famous one at Beersheba are essential to continuous settlement. Thus concentrated, Simeon can be recognized as the western part of a larger area which extends east to Arad and which displays a common and distinctive demographic pattern. Throughout the period of MB II (c. 1800-1550) this area was dominated by only two fortified towns, at the sites of Masos and Malhata, probably Hormah and Canaanite Arad respectively. The destruction of these two towns left the northeastern Negeb nearly uninhabited by any settled population throughout the Late Bronze Age, in contrast to the northwestern fringe of sites such as Tell esh-Shari'a (Ziqlag?), which in the thirteenth century was apparently an Egyptian administrative outpost, abandoned in the next century (see NOTES on 15:31).

What comes as a complete surprise, therefore, is the sudden establishment of permanent unwalled settlements at the beginning of the Iron Age all across the northern Negeb. Beersheba was one of them and its next neighbor to the east, Masos, was of more than village proportions. These and others, such as the new settlement at Tell Arad (with Malhata now abandoned) must represent the spread of the peace created by the Yahwist organization called Israel. In the tenth century virtually all of the settlements were destroyed and eventually replaced by a few strongly fortified towns such as Beersheba, Hormah (moved now to nearby Tell Ira), and Arad. This development represents the crisis posed by Sea Peoples (Philistines) and Amaleqite raiders from the desert, with the response of a strong central government which was rapidly formed in the careers of Saul and David.

While the area of Beersheba and its northwestern environs was predominantly "Simeonite," the areas to the east and northeast ("Negeb of the Jerahmeelites" and "Negeb of the Calebites") became strictly Judahite by virtue of David's military success. The preformed unit "Simeon," in other words, by its support of the Davidic kingship, found itself literally surrounded by the "tribe" of Judah.

d. ZEBULUN
(19:10-16)

19 ¹⁰ The third lot turned up for the Bene Zebulun for their clans.

The border of their fief lay as far south as Sedud. ¹¹ Their border went up westward to Mareal, met Dabbesheth, and met the gorge which is opposite Joqneam.

¹² In the opposite direction from Sedud, that is, eastward toward the sunrise, it ran to the border of Chisloth-tabor, followed the watercourse to Daberath and went up to Japhia. ¹³ From there it went around eastward to Gath-hepher, to Eth-qasin. It followed the watercourse to Rimmon and turned a corner toward Neah. ¹⁴ The border on the north bent around to Hannathon, and its destination was the valley of Iphtahel ¹⁵ (Qattah, Nahalal, Shimron, Idalah, and Bethlehem): twelve towns and their enclosures.

¹⁶ This was the fief of the Bene Zebulun tribe for their clans—these towns and their enclosures.

TEXTUAL NOTES

19 10. *turned up*   This is Hebrew *wy'l*, for which LXX reflects the variant "came out" (*wyṣ'*).

Bene   Thus MT. LXX reflects a haplography in its *Vorlage: hšlyšy l[bny l]zbwln.*

Sedud   This spelling of the name is suggested by LXXᴸ, Syr, and OL. MT and LXXᴬ read "Sarid" (cf. LXXᴮ "Esedek" where the *k* is actually a remnant of the conjunction *k[ai]*).

11. *westward to Mareal*   MT *lymh wmr'lh.* The conjunction *w* suggests that something may have dropped out between these two words, for the first of which LXXᴸ reads *Lacha* and OL *Lancha.*

Dabbesheth   LXX reads *Beth-arabah!*

met   This is the second occurrence of *pg'*, which is nowhere else construed with the preposition *'l.* It is not reflected in LXX which may therefore be superior. Parunak, "Geographical Terminology."

12. *eastward toward the sunrise   qdmh mzrḥ hšmš* may be conflate (cf. the pattern of prepositional phrases in v 13). The LXX translator was perhaps confused by the pileup of *h* locale endings in these verses and emended *hšmš* to *byt-(h)šmš,* "Beth-shemesh."

13. *eastward*   Here the text is clearly conflate: *qdmh mzrḥh* (both words with *h* locale), no doubt a repetition of the second word from the similar sequence in the preceding verse.

to Gath-hepher, to Eth-qasin   Hebrew uses the *h* locale in these names and no conjunction between them: *gth-ḥpr 'th-qṣyn.*

to Rimmon and turned a corner   Reading *rimmōnāh* (with LXX) *wĕ-tā'ar* for the unintelligible *rimmōn ham-mĕtō'ār* in MT.

14. *around*   Repointing the anomolous *'ōtô* (which LXX omits) to read a reflexive pronoun *'ittô* as in 16:6.

15. *Shimron*   LXX consistently uses "Simeon" for *šmrwn.*

Idalah   Thus MT. *Iralah* in Syriac and Vulgate (cf. "Jericho" in LXX[B]) illustrates the easy confusion of *d* and *r* in Hebrew script.

twelve towns and their enclosures   Lacking in LXX (cf. vv 22,30,38 for similar omissions in LXX).

16. *tribe*   Thus several Hebrew manuscripts along with LXX and Vulgate. MT omits.

these   Lacking in LXX[B] and Vulgate. See vv 31 and 48 for similar omissions in LXX and Vulgate.

NOTES

19:10-16. Zebulun's fief was a part of the poorer southern flank of the Galilee mountains together with a contiguous wedge out of the Jezreel plain.

10. *lay.* Literally, "was," in the Hebrew construction.

south. This word has no counterpart in the Hebrew text but is supplied to make intelligible in English what is clearly intended by the original.

†*Sedud.* This is probably Tell Shadud at the northern edge of the Jezreel Valley, c. 9.6 km northeast of Megiddo, with clear LB-Iron I occupation. Map J, 444.

11. †*Mareal.* Possibly Tell Ghalta, north of Megiddo.

met. Hebrew *pg',* as in 16:7, describes the meeting and running together of one boundary with another (whether of tribe or town), in this case leaving Dabbesheth outside the tribe of Zebulun. Parunak, "Geographical Terminology."

†*Dabbesheth.* Possibly Tell esh-Shamman, near Joqneam. Map J, 444.

Joqneam. Map J. See second NOTE on 12:22.

12. *In the opposite direction . . . it ran.* The verb *šb* here refers to a reversal of direction. Parunak, "Geographical Terminology."

Chisloth-tabor. The same town is called "Chesuloth" in v 18 (Issachar).

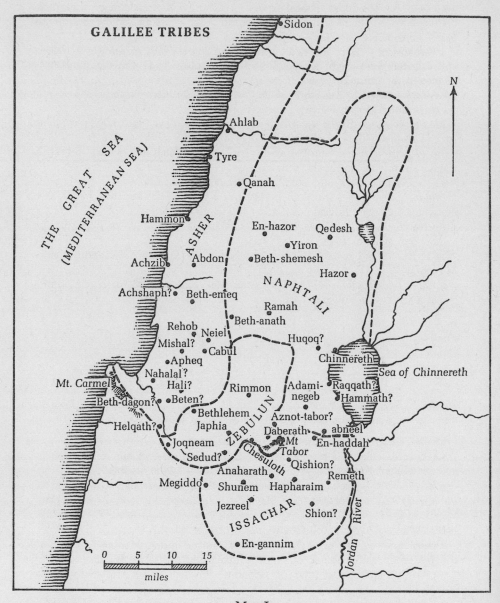

GALILEE TRIBES

THE GREAT SEA
(MEDITERRANEAN SEA)

Sidon

N

Ahlab

Tyre

Qanah

Hammon

ASHER

En-hazor

Qedesh

Yiron

Beth-shemesh

Achzib

Abdon

Hazor

NAPHTALI

Achshaph?

Beth-emeq

Ramah

Beth-anath

Rehob

Neiel

Huqoq?

Mishal?

Cabul

Chinnereth

Apheq

Sea of Chinnereth

Nahalal?

Hali?

Rimmon

Adami-negeb

Raqqath?

Mt. Carmel

Beten?

Hammath?

Beth-dagon?

ZEBULUN

Bethlehem

Aznot-tabor?

Helqath?

Japhia

Daberath

abneel

Joqneam

Mt

En-haddah

Sedud?

Chesuloth

Tabor

Qishion?

Anaharath

Remeth

Megiddo

Shunem

Hapharaim

Jezreel

Shion?

ISSACHAR

Jordan River

En-gannim

0   5   10   15

miles

Map J

It is identified with the village of Iksal, c. 6.4 km west of Mount Tabor near the northern edge of Jezreel Valley. Map J.

Daberath. This is Debūriyeh, northwest of Mount Tabor. A Levitical town in 21:28. Map J.

†*Japhia*. The name may be reflected at Yāfā, southwest of Nazareth. However, a good case can be made that the Hebrew verbs lead to Mishad, northeast of Nazareth. Parunak, "Geographical Terminology." The town is "Yapu" in the Amarna Letters, required by Pharaoh to supply corvee labor after Labayu the master of Shechem had destroyed Shunem (*ANET*[2], 485).

We are immediately reminded of a couplet in the Blessing of Jacob—

> Rich shall be the yield of Asher,
> And he shall furnish dainties for kings

(Genesis 49:20. Tr. E. A. Speiser, *Genesis*, AB 1 [1964] 363.) Indeed we should probably be justified in reading "Zebulun" here, for it is clear from Gen 49:13 that the latter name has displaced Asher "by the seashore." For some reason the two testaments are simply reversed. Albright, *YGC*, 265-266.

13. *went around*. That is, bulged. For this meaning of *'br* in the border descriptions, see 15:6,10 and NOTES (also 16:2,6; 18:13,19).

to Gath-hepher, to †*Eth-qasin*. That is, somewhere toward Kafr Kanna (=NT "Cana"). The names may be variants, or the second one a gloss on the first. The first is, literally, "Hepher's Winepress."

followed the watercourse. Hebrew *yṣ'*. If Mount Tabor is included in Zebulun, then its location between two branches of Naḥal Ṭabor readily explains the use of this verb, to encircle it on the south and east via the two branches. Parunak, "Geographical Terminology."

Rimmon. "Pomegranate." This is Rummaneh, 9.6 km northeast of Nazareth. It is probably the Levitical town of 21:35 called "Dimnah" in MT. Map J. There was another Rimmon in Judah's first district (15:32).

†*Neah*. Location unknown.

14. †*Hannathon*. Twice mentioned in Amarna Letters (EA 8, EA 245, *ANET*[2], 485), and once in the annals of the Assyrian king Tiglath-pileser III. Tell el-Bedeiwiyeh, c. 9.6 km north of Nazareth, was occupied in MB, LB, and Iron I. The alternative identification is el-Harbaj, at the southern edge of the Plain of Acco. G. W. van Beek, *IDB* 2, 522-523.

valley of Iphtahel. This is the Wadi el-Melek (or Sahl el-Baṭṭof). The name means "El (God) opens (the womb?)." There was a Judahite town with the same verbal element for its name (15:43). The latter was also the personal name of a great savior-judge (Judg 11:1).

15. (*Qattah*. This is probably "Qitron" in Judg 1:30, but is otherwise unknown. Khirbet Qoṭeina c. 8 km southwest of Joqneam has been suggested.

Nahalal. Possibly Tell en-Hahl, north of the Qishon in the southern Plain of Acco. A Levitical town in 21:35.

Shimron. Somewhere in the northern part of Esdraelon. See seventh NOTE on 11:1 where the king of Shimron is in league with Jabin of Hazor.

†*Idalah*. Possibly Kh. el-Hawārah, south of Zebulunite Bethlehem.

Bethlehem). Beit Laḥm. Map J, 444. This is not to be confused with the little town in Judah (15:59a LXX).

twelve towns. This seems to be an ancient annotation, since it counts Joqneam (not clearly in Zebulun) and does not count the five names inserted in v 15. It is not clear what purpose such a list, of border towns only, originally served.

COMMENT

In a classic study which has been the foundation for later work, Alt argued persuasively that a single document underlay the various tribal boundary descriptions. That document presented a system that came from the old tribal league and originated in the official deliberations and decisions made in settling disputes by the league leaders. It was a system which laid claim to lands not yet being administered by the Yahwists. See Albrecht Alt, "Das System der Stammesgrenzen im Buche Josua," reprinted in his *Kleine Schriften* I (1959) 193-202.

In an important subsequent study, M. Noth thought he discerned as the basic document not a connected description but a list of boundary points and frontier towns. These were secondarily connected up with verbs ("goes up," "goes down," "turns a corner") to produce the extant text. See Noth, "Studien zu den historisch-geographischen Dokumenten des Josuabuches," *ZDPV* 58 (1935) 185-255.

Alt's view has held up better than his student's on this point, but it is now possible to go beyond both Alt and Noth. The precision with which it is often possible to track the route described by the verbs '*br, yṣ', pg'*, etc. argues for a much tighter set of boundary descriptions for most of the tribes than has been recognized by critical scholarship. The boundary descriptions now look less like approximations created out of town lists and fixed border points, and more like fragmentary survivals that vary greatly in their degree of preservation.

In the earliest period of the Yahwist movement, the various territorial claims were doubtless a combination, in various degrees, of fact and ideal. Surely Zebulun's finest hour is the one celebrated in song in Judges 5, the resolution of the crisis that called forth the leadership of Deborah and Baraq and the muster of the militia at Tabor.

> Zebulun is a troop
> That scorned death

(Judges 5:18. Tr. AB 6A, 103.) There too, as in many other texts, it is explicit that the fluctuating fortunes of this tribe are related to those of its neighbor to the southeast—

> Exult, Zebulun, in thy going forth
> Rejoice, Issachar, in thy tents

(Deuteronomy 33:18, tr. Cross and Freedman, *JBL* 67 [1948] 195= *SAYP*, 101.) Issachar's fief is the next to be described.

e. ISSACHAR
(19:17-23)

19 ¹⁷ For Issachar came out the fourth lot. ¹⁸ Their border was as far south as Jezreel.

Chesuloth, Shunem, ¹⁹ Hapharaim, Shion, Anaharath, ²⁰ Dabeiron, Qishion, Ebez, ²¹ Remeth, En-gannim, En-haddah, Beth-pazzez.

²² The border met Tabor.

Shahazumah, Beth-shemesh.

The limit of their border was the Jordan. Sixteen towns and their enclosures. ²³ This was the fief of the tribes of the Bene Issachar for their clans, the towns and their enclosures.

TEXTUAL NOTES

19 17. *lot*   This follows LXX, where MT adds, reflecting the influence of the concluding formula used in v 16, "for the Bene Issachar for their clans."

18. *Chesuloth*   A Cairo Geniza fragment vocalizes *kislôt* as in v 12.

19. *Anaharath*   The Greek has two names after Shion: *Renath* and *Arraneth* in LXX^A, *Reērōth* and *Anachereth* in LXX^B. To judge from the spellings in LXX^A, it is likely that the first name of the pair arose as a corruption or partial dittography of the second name. Soggin's proposal (*Joshua,* 188) to reinstate *Reērōth* on the basis of LXX^B thus does not carry conviction.

20. *Dabeiron*   This is LXX *w(h)dbr(w)n*, for MT *whrbyt*.

21. *Remeth*   "Jarmuth" in 21:29. Cf. Ramoth in 1 Chr 6:58.

En-gannim   LXX^B reads as two names.

22. *Shahazumah*   This is the *kethib* *šḥšwmh*. Several manuscripts plus Syriac, Targum, Vulgate display the *qere* *šḥṣymh* (LXX^A *Sasima;* LXX^B *Vorlage, šlm 'l ymh!*), reflecting the easy confusion of *w* and *y* in the evolution of the script.

Sixteen towns and their enclosures   Lacking in LXX by homoioteleuton: *hyrd[n . . . wḥṣryh]n.*

NOTES

19:17-23. Issachar's fief will be the center of continuing struggle to control the fertile fields and strategic crossroads in the Jezreel, not finally won until the careers of Deborah and Baraq (Judges 4-5). Here there is no effort to trace a border. Instead there are three fixed reference points given (Jezreel in v 18, and in v 22 Tabor and the Jordan River) with two segments of a town list intervening.

17. *Issachar*. Perhaps literally, "Hired Man." It is a name which may refer to corvee labor in the fields and caravans of Jezreel. We would now render the Testament of Issachar in Genesis 49 as follows:

> 14 Issachar is a (resident-)alien donkey driver
> Who camps between the (campfire) hearths.
> 15 When he saw how good was the homestead,
> And how very pleasant the country,
> He bent his shoulder to burdens
> And became a willing serf.

This is Albright's improvement of the rendering in v 14 (*YGC*, 266), with Speiser's translation of v 15 (AB 1, 362). The "settlement" of Issachar, as local labor force, as Albright observes, probably began well before the fourteenth century B.C.

18. *as far south as*. Hebrew has here simply the directive ending in a non-verbal construction. Compare the similar phrase in v 10 which uses instead the preposition *'ad*.

Jezreel. "El (God) sows," or "Let El (God) make fruitful." Map J, 444. The village Jezreel (modern Zer'in) at the foot of Mount Gilboa looks out upon the entire fertile plain of Jezreel, from a strategic location where the major trade routes intersect. The next town mentioned is at the northern border!

Chesuloth. Also known as "Chisloth-tabor" in description of Zebulun's border (v 12). The name survives at Iksāl. Map J, 444. The next site is in the southwest again.

Shunem. It is identified with Solem, c. 14.4 km north of Jenin. It had stood in the path of Thutmose III (c. 1490-1435); a century later it was destroyed by Labayu of Shechem and rebuilt by Biridiya of Megiddo. Issachar's claim will not settle the matter, as the Philistines will encamp there for the face-off with Saul and his forces (1 Sam 28:4). Map J, 444. The next two towns named lie toward the southeast.

19. †*Hapharaim*. This is almost certainly et-Ṭaiyibeh, some 14 or so km northwest of Bethshean. Map J, 444.

†*Shion.* Possibly located at Sirim, c. 22.4 km southeast of Mount Tabor. Map J, 444.

†*Anaharath.* This also lay in the path of Thutmose III, located at Naʿūrah, 3.2 km south of En-dor, in the heart of Issachar. Map J.

20. *Dabeiron.* This is most likely the "Daberath" listed as a Levitical town (21:28) and previously mentioned in description of Zebulun's border (v 12). The location is Debūriyeh. Map J, 444.

Qishion. Also conquered by Thutmose III. It will become a Levitical town in 21:28. The most probable location is Tell el-Muqarqash, east of En-dor. Map J. It is a "dominant Late Bronze-Iron I site." John L. Peterson, "A Topographical Surface Survey," 155. After a tenth-century gap, the surveyors found clear ninth-century indicators, followed by another gap, in the eighth century.

†*Ebez.* Location unknown.

21. *Remeth.* This is the Levitical town called "Jarmuth" in 21:29. The location is probably Kōkab el-Hawā. Map J, 444.

En-gannim. "Spring of Gardens." Khirbet Beit Jann near Jenin. Map J. A similar name also occurs in the Judean Shephelah (15:34). A Levitical town (21:29).

†*En-haddah.* Probably el-Hadetheh, c. 9.6 km east of Mount Tabor (Tel ʿEn Ḥadda on Israeli maps).

†*Beth-pazzez.* Location unknown.

22. *met.* On the use of the verb *pgʿ*, see above, second NOTE on v 11. It indicates that Tabor itself lies beyond the border, in Zebulun.

Tabor. According to 1 Chr 6:62[77E], there was in Zebulun a Levitical town by this name, which does not show up in the parallel list of Joshua 21. It must lie somewhere near the foot of that impressive mountain which rises all by itself to an altitude of c. 519 meters, from the floor of the northeastern stretch of the Jezreel plain.

†*Shahazumah.* Location unknown. It may be a conflation of two names, Shahaz and Yammah. G. W. van Beek, *IDB* 4, 303.

Beth-shemesh. "House/Temple of the Sun(-god)." There was one similarly named place on the northern border of Judah (15:10) which will be assigned to Dan (19:41); and another in Naphtali (19:38). The location in Issachar is uncertain; possibly it is el-Abeidiyeh, east of Kh. Shamsawi, which would preserve the name, and near the Jordan.

Sixteen. This is correct if Tabor is counted, or if Tabor is not counted but Shahazumah is divided.

COMMENT

Situated at the most strategic crossroads in the entire land, Issachar suffered most from the annual parade of ancient armies. And like Benjamin in the south it was much less successful in consolidating its territorial control than its league neighbors. Among the latter there seems to have been a condecension and scorn toward the "hired man" that is paralleled by an attitude toward Benjamin in the south, an attitude that is warmly repudiated by use of comic irony in telling the stories of Ehud (Judg 3:12-30) and the tragic Civil War against Benjamin (Judges 19-21).

f. ASHER
(19:24-31)

19 24 The fifth lot came out for the tribe of the Bene Asher for their clans. 25 Their border was: Helqath, Hali, Beten, Achshaph, 26 Alamelech, Amad, and Mishal.

On the west it met Carmel and Shihor-libnath. 27 It returned eastward at Beth-dagon, to meet Zebulun and the valley of Iphtahel to the north. The border stepped north to Beth-emeq and Neiel, and proceeded north to Cabul, 28 Abdon, Rehob, Hammon, and Qanah, as far as Greater Sidon.

29 The border returned to Ramah, then out as far as the fortified city Tyre.

The border returned to Hosah. Its destination was the sea (from Ahlab to Achzib).

30 Ummah, Apheq, Rehob.

Twenty-two towns and their fenced areas.

31 This was the fief for the tribe of the Bene Asher, for their clans —these towns and their fenced areas.

TEXTUAL NOTES

19 24. *the tribe of the Bene*   Thus MT. The shorter text of LXX "for Asher" is explained by haplography: *hḥmyš[y lmṭh bn]y 'šr*.

25. *Helqath*   LXX^B reads "from Helqath" which seems to reflect a dittography: *gbwlm [m]ḥlqt*.

26. *Alamelech*   Lacking in LXX^A.

Shihor-libnath and 27 *the valley of Iphtahel*   Some versions read each of these as two names connected by the conjunction.

27. *The border stepped north*   There has been a haplography in MT, here restored on the basis of LXX: *ṣpwnh [whlk hgbwl ṣpwn] byt-'mq*.

28. *Abdon*   This is the reading in a few Hebrew manuscripts, supported by the evidence of 21:30 and 1 Chr 6:59 (*pace BHS*). The spelling of MT *'brwn* shows the easy confusion of *d* and *r*.

29. *the fortified city Tyre*   Repunctuating to read '*yr-mbṣr ṣr* (MT '*yr mbṣr-ṣr*, "a city, fortification of Tyre"). LXX, curiously, reads *b'r*, "well," for '*yr*, "city."

(*from Ahlab*   The authority for this spelling is Judg 1:31. MT shows the elision of '*aleph* and metathesis. **m'ḥlb* > *mḥbl*. The original is partially reflected in LXX[B].

to   After the confusion in the preceding word, the directive ending of '*kzybh* made no sense, and thus it is not reflected in LXX.

30. *Ummah*   LXX[B] has *Archōb*, presumably reflecting, in part, Hebrew '*kw*.

Twenty-two towns and their fenced areas   Lacking in LXX[B], OL. Cf. vv 15 and 22.

31. *these*   Lacking in LXX, Vulg. See v 16.

NOTES

19:24-31. One of the most prosperous areas in the league, and the one most exposed to continuing Canaanite influence, fell to Asher. It was the lush plain of Acco and its narrowing northern extension as far as Rosh ha-niqra (the ancient Ladder of Tyre), together with territory inland from the great Canaanite cities farther north along the Lebanese coast. It is not clear that Tyre and Sidon were considered part of Israelite territory. The description is not highly unified.

24. *Asher.* In the fully developed genealogical tradition, this ancestor is son of Zilpah, handmaid to Leah (Gen 30:9-13). His only full brother among the twelve is Gad, settled in Transjordan. Zebulun and Issachar are Leah's Galilean offspring.

25. *Their border was.* Here there follows a list of seven names, probably an insert; the number is mnemonically significant and the names do not connect up to form a coherent "border."

Helqath. This is *ḥrgt* in the list of Thutmose III. It will become a Levitical town in 21:31. The site is perhaps Tell Qassis at the west bank of the Qishon River just after it flows through a spur in the northern scarp of Carmel to enter the plain of Acco. Map J, 444.

†*Hali.* Possibly Khirbet Ras 'Ali.

†*Beten.* The name is reflected in Abṭun, approximately 17.6 km south of Acco. Map J, 444.

Achshaph. Probably et-Tell, some 9.6 km northeast of Acco. Map J. Better known than many others, Achshaph's history offers a window on the world of the Late Bronze Age. Its king was in league with Jabin of Hazor (11:1) and was removed by the Bene Israel (12:20). In the fifteenth century Achshaph had been disciplined by Thutmose III. And in the fourteenth century it figures in Amarna politics and is mentioned in Papyrus Anastasi I.

26. †*Alamelech,* †*Amad.* These places are otherwise unknown and have not been located.

Mishal. This is a Levitical town (21:30). It is *msh'r* in the list of Thutmose III. It is most likely Tell Kisan, approximately 9.6 km southeast of Acco. Map J, 444.

Carmel. The Mount Carmel range juts to the coast just south of Haifa Bay (Map J, 444), presenting steep and precipitous slopes to the northeast, a decisive natural boundary.

Shihor-libnath. "Swamp of Libnath" in *NEB*. Whether this is one place or two remains an open question.

27. *It returned.* Here the verb *šûb* appears to be used as in v 12 to signal a 180° turn from a central reference point along the southern boundary.

at. This is implicit in use of the verb *šûb* without prepositional complement. The usage occurs again in v 34.

Beth-dagon. "House/Temple of Dagon." Probably Tell Regeb, about 1 km southwest of Abtun. Map J, 444. For another town known for its Dagon temple, located in the Lachish district of Judah, see 15:41.

north. . . . *north* . . . *north.* The direction is expressed differently in the third occurrence: *ṣpwnh.* . . . *ṣpwn* . . . *mśm'l.* In the allotment descriptions the latter occurs only here, adding its evidence to suggest that vv 27b-28 are a fragment drawn from a minor source.

†*Beth-emeq.* "House (temple) of the Valley." Possibly Tell Mimas, approximately 9.6 km east-northeast of Acco. Map J, 444.

†*Neiel.* Probably Kh. Ya'nin, east of Acco and just north of Cabul. Map J.

Cabul. About 14.4 km east-southeast of Acco, in the low hills overlooking the maritime plain. Map J, 444. Cabul became the center of a district of twenty towns, including several Levitical towns, which Solomon traded to Hiram of Tyre in exchange for temple-building materials (1 Kgs 9:13). According to 2 Chr 8:2 there were other towns in need of rebuilding which Solomon acquired by trade with Hiram and which were used for resettlement of Israelites after the work of building the temple was complete. This was part of the process resulting in the alienation of many Levitical families and the rise of the Deuteronomic movement.

28. *Abdon.* Map J, 444. Khirbet Abdeh (Tel Avdon) founded in MB inland from Achzib in foothills of western Galilee, occupying a position relative to Achzib comparable to the relation of Rehob and Acco. M. W. Prausnitz, "The Planning of the Middle Bronze Age Town at Achzib and Its Defenses," *IEJ* 25 (1975) 202.

Rehob. This is most likely Tell el-Gharbi(=T. Bira in Israeli publications), about 11.2 km east-southeast of Acco, with LB and Iron I occupation. Map J, 444. Designated a Levitical town in 21:31, it too continued to display the Canaanite socioeconomic structure (Judg 1:31).

Hammon. "Hot Spring"? Perhaps it is Umm el-'awāmīd, near the Lebanese coast about 8 km northeast of Rosh ha-niqra.

Qanah. "Reed." Modern Qana is about 9.6 km southeast of Tyre. Map J, 444.

as far as Greater Sidon. This was the plan, never fully carried out (Judg 1:31).

29. *The border returned.* Another turn of 180° is envisaged. That is, the *gĕbûl* seems to have been drawn by the writer on the basis of limited information so as to include the handful of place names known to him. This does not rule out the possibility that already in the Shiloh phase the Bene Israel believed themselves to be in control of access routes to the towns thus listed.

Ramah. "Height." Location unknown. It is doubtful that this is the same as Ramah in Naphtali (v 36). Rather it must be a point somewhere near the projected line from Sidon to Qanah. Ramia, approximately 17.6 km east of Rosh ha-niqra, is too far south.

then out. A more or less right-angle turn toward the sea is implied.

the fortified city Tyre. Map J, 444. This description seems to specify the great fortified island capital of the famous maritime kingdom, "Old Tyre," as distinct from its sibling city on the shore. The "border" then backtracked to the mainland.

Hosah. This is most likely Tell Rashīdīyeh. Topographical indications favor the identification of Hosah with the town of Usu (or *Uzu*) mentioned in texts ranging from Papyrus Anastasi I and inscriptions of Seti I (thirteenth century) to the annals of Sennacherib's campaign of 701 B.C.

(from Ahlab to Achzib). As the preceding phrase about the destination (the "end") of a border segment is normally a concluding formula, these two names look like a secondary addition. Without them the total of twenty-two in v 30 is accurate.

Ahlab. Probably Kh. el-Maḥâlib, about 6.4 km northeast of Tyre. Map J, 444. In Judg 1:31 Asher is faulted for failure to implement league policy at Ahlab and at "Helbah" which is either an error for the preceding name or a variant spelling of it.

Achzib). A fair-weather port on the coast, 14.4 km north of Acco. Map J, 444. It is another of Asher's failures in Judg 1:31. Its defenses in the earlier MB period enclosed a city of about seventy dunams (17.5 acres); anchorages took up another fifty dunams.

30. Two towns known as fief for the Bene Asher were left over, after the attempt to describe Asher's *gĕbûl.*

Ummah. It is widely accepted that this is an error for Acco. See Judg 1:31.

Apheq. Tell Kūrdaneh (T. Afeq on Israeli maps), approximately 9.6 km southeast of Acco. It continued to be Canaanite (Judg 1:31).

Rehob. The reason for its repetition here is obscure.

Twenty-two. Not counting the two in parenthesis at the end of v 29, this is correct.

COMMENT

The enviable richness of the area that was to be the fief of the Bene Asher was celebrated in the archaic "Blessing of Moses":

> Most blessed of the sons is Asher
> He is the favorite of his brothers
> He dips his feet in oil

(Deuteronomy 33:24. Tr. Cross and Freedman, *JBL* 67 [1948] 196= *SAYP*, 102.) The earliest extra-biblical reference is not clear. There is a fabled man named "Qazardi, the Chief of Aser" in Papyrus Anastasi I (*ANET²*, 477), who may belong to a pre-Mosaic constituency called Asher. On the other hand the identification with *i-s-r* in the list of Seti I (Simons, *Handbook,* 147) is doubtful. (W. F. Albright, *JAOS* 74 [1954] 222*ff.*)

No doubt the earliest concentration of the Bene Asher was on the western slopes of Lower Galilee (Qazardi's territory has deep ravines), from which position they might in fact scan the plain with a certain yearning to settle by the sea.

> ———— shall dwell by the seashore,
> Which shall be a haven for ships;
> And his flank shall be based on Sidon.

This is Gen 49:13 in the translation by Speiser (*Genesis,* AB 1, 362) with the name "Zebulun" omitted. Enter instead Asher, for somehow their testaments got exchanged. See NOTES on 19:10-16.

g. NAPHTALI
(19:32-39)

19 ³²For Naphtali came out the sixth lot—for their clans. ³³Their border was: from Heleph and from the Sacred Tree at Zaananim, by way of Adami-neqeb and Jabneel, then to Laqqum. Its destination was the Jordan.

³⁴The border returned, on the west, at Aznot-tabor. From there it followed the watercourses to Huqoq, meeting Zebulun along the south and meeting Asher along the west, and the Jordan is on the east.

³⁵The fortified towns are [. . .]: Hammath, Raqqath, Chinnereth, ³⁶Adamah, Ramah, Hazor, ³⁷Qedesh, Edrei, En-hazor, ³⁸Yiron, Migdal-el, Horem, Beth-anath, and Beth-shemesh.

(Nineteen towns and their fenced areas.)

³⁹This was the fief of the Bene Naphtali tribe for their clans—the towns and their fenced areas.

TEXTUAL NOTES

19 32. *For Naphtali*   This is LXX, where MT has a conflation of variants with the first of them partially assimilated to the second one: *l[bny] nptly yṣ' hgwrl hššy [lbny nptly].* LXX lacks the final phrase *lmšpḥtm.*

34. *and* second occurrence   With LXX, omitting MT's specification "in Judah" which makes no sense.

35. [. . .]   In the gap here MT reads *hṣdym ṣr,* which looks like a corruption originating in a partial repetition of preceding *h'ry mbṣr,* "the fortified towns"; cf. v 29. LXX then levels through the *r* and renders "the (cities of) Tyrians: Tyre, . . ."

38. *Horem*   The vocalization of this name is uncertain.

(*Nineteen towns and their fenced areas.*)   Lacking in LXXᴮ, OL. Cf. vv 15,22,30 for similar omissions.

39. *for their clans—the towns and their fenced areas*   Also lacking in

LXX, presumably the result of a sizable haplography: *nptly l[mšpḥtm . . .* ⁴⁰ *l]mṭh bny dn.*

NOTES

19:32-39. The area described in these verses is the heartland of Galilee. The major trade routes connecting the port of Acco and the coastal plains with all points north and northeast passed through this long and narrow corridor.

32. *Naphtali.* The meaning of the name is not clear; Gen 30:7-8 gives a folk etymology which explains it in terms of Rachel's quick-witted success in contest with her "sister." Naphtali is the second son of Bilhah, Rachel's handmaid. His only full brother is Dan, who finally comes to occupy territory in the north contiguous with Naphtali (see below, v 47; and Judges 18). It is not clear that Naphtali's name is Semitic. K. Elliger, "Naphtali," *IDB* 3, 509.

33. *Their border.* This verse projects a line which runs more or less direct along the eastern crests of Galilee (but including the little plain of Chinnereth, as v 35 makes clear), until it turns more abruptly at Jabneel.

†*Heleph.* We expect a site rather far to the north at the head of this description, which would rule out Kh. 'Arbathah just northeast of Mount Tabor. The place is otherwise unknown, unless the construction in MT is meant to identify Heleph with the next name in the list.

the Sacred Tree. This is surely a very special oak tree (Hebrew *'ēlôn*), which figures in the story of Deborah and is situated "near Qedesh" (Judg 4:11). On the possible derivation of *'ēlôn* from "El," via the minor deities associated with fine shade trees, see Albright, *YGC,* 189-191.

Zaananim. This is in the area once controlled by Jabin, king of Hazor (Judg 4:11,17). There Heber the Qenite had settled, by treaty with Jabin. And thither Sisera fled after Yahweh's victory celebrated in Judges 4-5. The tree must belong to a minor sanctuary somewhere hard by the great northern Qedesh, whose very name marks the area as one of "Holiness." A site farther south would have Sisera retreating directly into the heart of Israelite strength. Boling, *Judges,* AB 6A, 96-97.

†*Adami-neqeb.* This is most likely Khirbet Damiyeh, about 8 km southwest of the Sea of Galilee, on the ancient highway from Acco to Damascus. One might object that it is a long way from the vicinity of Tell Qades to Adami-neqeb, with no other places named along the way. But this is comparable to the long and narrow description of Asher (south to north) (v 28), where there is likewise no northern border. What was important was control of the highways! Map J, 444.

Jabneel. Possibly Khirbet Yemma, west-southwest of the Sea of Galilee. Map J. Not to be confused with the famous town near the coast on the northern border of Judah (15:11).

then to. Hebrew *'ad* signals a change of direction, as in v 29, "then out."

†*Laqqum*. The best candidate is Kh. el-Mansura, about 4.8 km south-west of Kh. Kerak at the southern tip of the Sea of Galilee.

34. *returned*. The verb is *šûb*. The western border started back to the north, and the previously described *gĕbûl* of Issachar is here presupposed.

at. See above, second NOTE on 19:27.

†*Aznot-tabor*. Possibly Umm Jebeil north of Mount Tabor, which has produced LB sherds. Parunak, "Geographical Terminology." Map J, 444.

followed the watercourses. Hebrew *yṣ'*, literally, "went out," means more precisely to take the lowland route, in the boundary descriptions, as shown by Parunak.

Huqoq. The location of Yaquq seems too far east to fit this description. Aharoni tentatively proposed Kh. el-Jemeijmeh, about 3.2 km west of Sakhmin. Map J, 444. The route would thus follow, for a significant stretch, wadis and lowlands, though some higher terrrain must also be crossed. Parunak, "Geographical Terminology."

35. *fortified towns*. As in 10:20; cf. 19:29 which singles out Tyre as "fortified." Otherwise the word "fortified" is not used in the Book of Joshua. In other words, the area that became the fief of Naphtali was remembered as especially formidable.

Hammath. "Hot Springs." One of Naphtali's Levitical towns is "Hammoth-dor" (21:32). Since there is no evidence of Iron Age occupation at the famous Hammam Ṭabiriyeh, "the Tiberias Hotsprings," a better location is Tell Raqqat, 1 km north of Tiberias, where Peterson found LB and Iron Age pottery, the latter clustering in the eleventh century and the eighth century, but not confined to them.

†*Raqqath*. The name is reflected in Tell Raqqat, about 2.4 km north of Tiberias. Map J, 444. Was it, at some time, also known as Hamath(-dor)? This is the implication of Peterson's study.

Chinnereth. Tell el-Oreimeh, on a hill commanding a view of the small but fertile plain on the northwestern shore of the Sea of Galilee. It was previously visited by Thutmose III and is known to have been occupied from MB to Iron I.

36. *Adamah*. Location unknown. It should not be confused with Adami-neqeb (v 33) or with Adam (3:9-17), although confusion with Adami-neqeb may have taken place in antiquity. See below, final NOTE on v 38.

Ramah. "Height." The site is er-Rameh, about 24 km west of Safed. Map J, 444. Not to be confused with the Ramah on Asher's *gĕbûl* (19:29).

Hazor. Sixteen km north of the Sea of Galilee was "the head of all those kingdoms" (11:10).

37. *Qedesh*. It will become a refuge-city in 20:7 and a Levitical city in 21:32. There was also a Qedesh in southwestern Issachar (1 Chr 6:57[72E]) and another one in what is described as southern Naphtali (Kh. Qedesh near the southwestern tip of the Sea of Galilee). But Tell Qades in the hills approximately 11.2 km northwest of Hazor is perhaps the most impressive archaeological site in the entire land of Israel. It is definitely not "in the Huleh valley" as described by Miller and Tucker, *Joshua*, 151. Hazor's neighbor is far more suitable than the much smaller site of Kh. Qedesh (though the latter may be

the referent of Judg 4:6), for the same reasons given above regarding the location of Zaananim (v 33).

Edrei. Otherwise unknown, it is not to be confused with one of Og's royal cities in Bashan which has the same name (13:12).

En-hazor. Possibly Kh. Ḥaṣireh near Hazzūr in the hills of Upper Galilee.

38. †*Yiron*. The name is reflected in Yārūn in southern Lebanon, c. 2.5 km north-northwest of Barʿam (Israel survey 1:100,000 map, Sheet 2).

Migdal-el. "Fortress-temple of El." This is possibly Mejdel Islim, approximately 16 km northeast of Yārūn. On the form and function of the "fortress-temple," see Wright, *Shechem*, 80-102, 123-133; Boling, *Judges*, AB 6A, 180-182 regarding Shechem's Tower.

†*Horem*. Otherwise unknown.

Beth-anath. "House/Temple of Anath." It is possibly Safed el-Battik, roughly 3.2 km southwest of Mejdel Islim. The rival candidate (el-Baʿneh, east of Acco) appears to be too far south of the rest of this cluster. Beth-anath is mentioned in lists of several campaigns by New Kingdom pharaohs, and in Dtr 2's little catalogue of failures (Judg 1:33). While this town has been suggested as the home of Shamgar (Judg 3:31), the specification that he is "ben Anath" may serve primarily to identify him as a mercenary, as P. C. Craigie suggests. See discussion in *Judges*, AB 6A, 89.

Beth-shemesh. "House/Temple of the Sun(-god)." The name occurs also on Judah's northern border (15:10) and in Issachar (19:22). This town is most likely to be found at Kh. Tell er-Ruweisi (Tell Rosh) just northeast of Elqosh in Upper Galilee. It continues to be Canaanite in Judg 1:33.

(*Nineteen*. Our best efforts find twenty (if Hammath and Raqqath are equated) or twenty-one. Perhaps the annotator was equating Adami-neqeb (v 33) with Adamah (v 36), or Hazor (v 36) with En-hazor (v 37). See above on the possible equation of "Heleph" with "the Sacred Tree of Zaananim."

COMMENT

It is surely not going too far to say that Naphtali must have been the nerve center of the Yahwist movement in Galilee. The densely forested mountains give the area an almost indescribable attractiveness that is both aesthetic and political. It was here in the southern part of Upper Galilee that the new, small, unfortified settlements of the Iron I period were first discovered. See above on 11:1-15 and 17:14-18, and note the evocation of villages in Jacob's Testament.

> Naphtali is a hind let loose
> That brings forth lovely fawns.

(Genesis 49:21. Tr. Speiser, *Genesis*, AB 1 [1964] 363.) If the treatment of Naphtali here is "very archaic," and if it "points to nomadic atmosphere" (Albright, *YGC*, 265-266), the rapid settlement pattern that produced the new villages seems to be clearly enough reflected in the other archaic testament of Naphtali.

> Naphtali is sated with favor
> He is full of the blessing of Yahweh
> He takes possession west and south.

(Deuteronomy 33:23. Tr. O'Connor, *Hebrew Verse Structure*, 215-216. Cf. Cross and Freedman, *JBL* 67 [1948] 195=*SAYP*, 102.)

It is now clear that new Upper Galilean settlements of the Iron I period ranged beyond the concentration of them that was first discovered, south of the Brook Kezib (Wadi Qurn). It is interesting in this respect that Naphtali is expected to spread out "west and south." The latter is clearly spoken from the perspective of northern Galilee. And in fact the expansion of Naphtali, a Bilhah tribe, is curtailed chiefly by the fiefs of Zebulun and Issachar, the two Leah tribes of Galilee and the Jezreel plain, and by the fief of Asher, whose mother was handmaid to Leah.

h. DAN
(19:40-48)

19 40 For Dan came out the seventh lot. 41 The territory of their fief was: Zorah, Eshtaol, Ir-shemesh, 42 Shaalabbin, Ammon, Ithlah, 43 Elon, Timnah, Eqron, 44 Elteqeh, Gibbethon, Baalath, 45 Yehud, Bene-beraq, Gath-rimmon.

46 On the west: from the Yarqon all the way to the border in front of Joppa.

47 This was the fief of the tribe of the Bene Dan, for their clans: these towns and their fenced areas.

The Bene Dan did not dispossess the Westerners, who crowded them into the hills. The Westerners did not allow them to move down to the plain.

And their territory became too confining for them.

48 The Bene Dan went up and fought against Leshem; and they captured it. They put it to the sword. They took possession of it and settled there. Leshem they renamed Dan, in honor of Dan their founding father.

The Westerners continued to live in Aijalon and Shaalabbin. When Ephraim acquired superior strength, they were put to forced labor.

TEXTUAL NOTES

19 40. *For Dan*   This follows LXX, where MT has assimilated to the longer concluding formula, "the tribe of the Bene Dan, for their clans." Cf. v 32.

41. *Ir-shemesh*   Also called "Beth-shemesh" (Targ^L and some Hebrew MSS), but "En-shemesh" in a handful of manuscripts is no doubt rooted in a scribal error.

42. *Shaalabbin*   Spelled "Shaalbim" in Judg 1:35; 1 Kgs 4:9.

Ammon   Thus LXX^B, where the reading Aijalon in MT and LXX^A appears to be a variant of Elon at the beginning of v 43; cf. 21:24.

44. *Elteqeh*   Hebrew '*ltqh*. The name is alternately spelled '*ltq*', Elteqe, in 21:23.

46. *On the west*   Thus LXX (*wmym*) where MT has lost the final *m*, reading "waters of" the Yarqon.

the Yarqon   This is *hyrqwn*. MT continues *whrqwn*, which looks like a partial dittography.

all the way to   The reading *'d* (some Hebrew manuscripts and Syriac) is here adopted against MT *'m*. LXX represents neither.

47. *This*   In LXX, which is considerably longer than MT, v 47=MT v 48; and LXX v 48=MT v 47. We follow LXX. Following the paragraphing of our translation, we can summarize the differences between LXX and MT. LXX refers to (i) the Dan fief, (ii) the Westerners on the plain, (iii) the confining of Dan, (iv) the conquest of Leshem (but see first Textual Note at v 48), and (v) the Amorites in Aijalon and Shaalabbin. MT omits (ii) and (v), and rearranges the others in the order (iii), (iv), and (i). The texts of (iv) in LXX and of (iii) in MT are so defective as to be incoherent in context.

these   *h'lh* is lacking in LXX^A and Vulgate (as in vv 16 and 31). In MT, however, this fuller formula alternates with the shorter one used in vv 23 and 39.

The Bene Dan . . . into the hills. The Westerners . . . to the plain   The translation here follows LXX, where MT has a sizable gap. Both these statements are necessary, however, to make sense of what follows. It was probably the influence of the border formula recurring frequently in these chapters that triggered the corruption noted next.

And their territory became too confining for them   This is the first clause of v 47 in MT and the last clause of v 47 in LXX. The Greek reflects *wy'ṣ* (cf. 17:15) which gave rise to the unintelligible *wyṣ'* in MT.

48. *Bene Dan went up and fought against Leshem*   Curiously, LXX has in place of this a notice about the Bene Judah taking over Lachish!

They took possession of it   Lacking because of haplography in LXX or its *Vorlage: wy*[*ršw 'wth wy*]*šbw*.

in honor of Dan their founding father   This is lacking in LXX, presumably a result of haplography caused by too many *m*-endings in the vicinity: *llšm dn* [*kšm dn 'byhm*].

The Westerners . . . forced labor   LXX here parallels Judg 1:35 and is probably original; from the MT of Judg 1:35, LXX here deletes *bhr-ḥrs;* MT uses *byt-ywsp* for *'prym*. Holmes, *Joshua: The Hebrew and Greek Texts* (1914). Auld, "Judges 1 and History: A Reconsideration," *VT* 25 (1975) 277.

NOTES

19:40-48. Dan's entry in the list of the Shiloh-phase allotments is structurally distinctive in having two parts. Only the first part (vv 40-47a), which describes the southern Danite fief, resembles the form that has been in use throughout, describing separate tribal fiefs in terms of border elements and specific lists of

towns, in various combinations. The second part (vv 47b-48) details resistance
to Dan's settlement and reports its eventual relocation, to center in one town in
the far north. History is often reflected in genealogy. Dan was the fifth son of
Jacob. Born of Bilhah, Rachel's maid (Gen 30:1-6), his only full brother was
Naphtali, to whose northern fringe Dan finally moved (Judges 18). Along the
way Dan acquired a somewhat less than complimentary reputation—

> Dan is a lion's whelp
> Who shies away from a viper

(Deuteronomy 33:22. Tr. Cross and Freedman, *JBL* 7 [1948] 195=*SAYP*,
102.) Or again—

> Dan is a serpent by the roadside,
> A horned snake by the path,
> That bites the horse's heel,
> So that backward is tossed the rider.

(Genesis 49:17. Tr. Speiser, *Genesis*, AB 1 [1964] 362.) These lines must be
studied against the background of a strategic territorial claim.

41-46. In his pioneering study, Alt considered this to be part of a larger administrative document that had been broken apart to describe three "tribal"
sections: Judah (15:21-62), Benjamin (18:21-28), Dan (19:41-46). While
the main lines of the study hold good for Benjamin, Wright and Cross objected
that there is no obvious slot in the town list of Joshua 15 where these Danite
towns might be fitted. In fact these verses look, upon closer examination, more
like the mixed tribal lists that precede them in the chapter than they do the
uniform town lists for Judah and Benjamin.

41-45. The list moves in a general east-west direction from the Aijalon and
Soreq valleys, but the names do not link up to form a coherent border or segments of borders.

41. *their fief was.* For the same formulation see 19:10 (Zebulun); 19:17 (Issachar); and 19:24 (Asher). This leaves only Benjamin (18:11) and Simeon
(19:1) with a slightly different formulation among the allotments of the
Shiloh phase.

Zorah. The name survives at Ṣar'ah, on the north side of the Soreq Valley,
about 3.2 km north of Beth-shemesh. Map G, 364. Cf. 15:33, where the town
belongs to Judah, District III.

Eshtaol. This is probably Irtuf, about 1.6 km south of Ishwa'. Simons, *Handbook*, 146. Cf. 15:33, where this town too is assigned to Judah's second district.

Ir-shemesh. "City of the Sun(-god)." Better known as Beth-shemesh, which
was previously listed on Judah's north border (15:10). It became a Levitical
town (21:16). It is probably the same as Har-heres, "Mountain of the Sun," in
Judg 1:35 where Dan is faulted for failure to carry through the "conquest"
there. The site is well-known from excavations at Tell er-Rumeileh. Map G, 364.

42. *Shaalabbin.* Spelled "Shaalbin" in the little catalogue of failures (Judg
1:35). The location is probably Selbît, 12.8 km north of Beth-shemesh, on the
north side of the Aijalon Valley. Map G, 364. It is only by an arbitrary re-

versal of position with the next name in the list that the text can be said to be "tracing a line northward from Beth-shemesh" Miller and Tucker, *Joshua*, 153).

†*Ammon*. The Hebrew spelling of this name is uncertain and location unknown.

†*Ithlah*. Location unknown.

43. *Elon*. This is another Levitical town, named in 21:24 where the alternative pronunciations "Elon" and "Aijalon" are represented as *kethib* and *qere*. It is probably Tell Qoqa on the south side of the Aijalon Valley, southwest of the site of Yalo. Map G, 364.

Timnah. "Allotted Portion." A town on Judah's border (15:10) which became famous as a center of Philistine occupation in the Samson story (Judg 14:1,2,5). The same name seems to be reflected at Kh. Tibnah, about 3.2 km south-southwest of Beth-shemesh. However it is best identified with Tell el-Batashi, approximately 6.4 km northwest of Beth-shemesh, in the Soreq Valley. Map G, 364. Not to be confused with the town in Judah's seventh district (15:57), nor with Joshua's burial place in Ephraim (24:30).

Eqron. See NOTES on 13:3 and 15:11. Best located at Qatra, since Kh. el-Muqenna' is preempted by the next town in the list.

44. *Elteqeh*. A Levitical town (21:23). The site of Kh. el-Muqenna' at the eastern edge of the coastal plain, roughly 6.4 km west of Tell el-Batashi. The recently favored location at Tell esh-Shalaf is ruled out by Peterson's surface survey and study of the Levitical towns. Map G, 364.

Gibbethon. Another Levitical town (21:23). Tell Malat, nearly 8 km north of Khirbet el-Muqenna' and similarly situated at the eastern edge of the plain (4.8 km west of Gezer). Map G, 364.

Baalath. Location uncertain, not to be confused with Baalah in 15:10 (contra Miller and Tucker, *Joshua*, 153).

45. †*Yehud*. Modern Yehud, some 4.8 km south of Petah Tikvah. Map G, 364.

†*Bene-beraq*. In the northeastern Tel Aviv suburbs.

Gath-rimmon. Levitical town in 21:24. Most scholars have favored Tell Jerishe on the Yarqon River in a northern suburb of Tel Aviv. John Peterson holds open the possibility that it might be 3.2 km farther to the northeast, at Tell Abu Zeitun. The same name listed as another Levitical town in Western Manasseh (21:25) is probably a scribal error.

46. *in front of*. Use of Hebrew *mûl* relative to a piece of *gĕbûl*, "border," does not occur elsewhere in the book. But cf. use of *mûl* in other contexts (8:33; 9:1; 18:18; 22:11). It here refers to some well-known point, near Joppa, on the coast between the terminus of Dan's northern border (well marked by the Yarqon) and the southern border (less clearly defined because of Philistine presence).

Joppa. The town had a late thirteenth-century occupation and it was clearly Philistine in the twelfth century, with nearby Tell Qasile and Tell Qudadi as contemporary ports; a distinctive Philistine temple at Qasile was recently excavated. A fair-weather point of entry for shipping into Israel and Judah in later centuries, it was not incorporated in either one, until it was conquered during the Maccabean Revolt and annexed to the Jewish state.

47-48. Much of this is secondary to the bulk of the chapter. But it is too extensive to be understood as a pileup of unoriginal comments. The shorter text of MT and the longer text of LXX may be correlated with the interests of Dtr 1 and Dtr 2 respectively. The most serious revision of the settlement plan had involved the relocation of an entire "tribe," which therefore called for special treatment. A related narrative is found in Judges 18 (mainly Dtr 1).

47. *This was the fief.* In the original sequence of verses (found in LXX) the form seen throughout the description of the Shiloh phase also obtains here. There is thus the sharpest possible contrast drawn between what was planned and what was implemented.

towns and their fenced areas. Only here is there no number specified.

did not dispossess. As in 16:10 and NOTE.

the Westerners. The Hebrew *Vorlage, h'mry,* evokes this sense in 9:1; 10:5; 12:8.

crowded them into the hills. Cf. Judg 1:34-35. This will be part of the climactic statement of the non-settlement offered as a catalogue of failures in Judges 1, the final (or Dtr 2) edition. There is, however, no word-for-word repetition.

48. *Leshem.* The final *m* may be enclitic; the name is Laish in Judg 18:29 (cf. 18:7), meaning "Lion." It was known by the same name in the Mari texts, in the later Execration Texts (*ANET²*, 329), and in the list of Thutmose III (*ANET²*, 242). A. Malamat, "Northern Canaan and the Mari Texts," in *Near Eastern Archaeology in the Twentieth Century,* 20-23.

Aijalon. This is presumably the Elon of v 43.

Ephraim. The claim seems to be that sometime after the move of Dan to the far north, Ephraim was able to move into at least part of the relinquished area to augment its labor force. "Ephraim" is here perhaps a synonym of "Israel" as frequently in poetic usage.

COMMENT

The northern border of Judah already described (15:10-11) together with the southern border of Joseph (16:2) bracket an area within which falls the fief of the Bene Dan. Here, however, description of borders is even more vestigial than in the case of Issachar (19:17-23). That there was once a fuller description of Dan's borders seems clear from the forced use of the noun *gĕbûl,* "territory," in v 41, over against the use that is normal for these chapters, "border, boundary," in v 46.

The territory in question spans the two major western access routes to Jerusalem and the neighborhood immediately to the north of it: the wadis known as the Soreq and Aijalon valleys. It is not surprising, therefore, that while the later historians would refer to the opposition as "Canaanite" or more generally "Westerners," the older narrative units would know them as Philistines (Judges 13-16). Samson was a Danite. His home base was Mahaneh-dan, "Dan's Camp," somewhere between Zorah and Eshtaol (Judg 13:25).

That the opposition came in fact in the form of Philistine domination of the southern coast is the most plausible background for the line deriding Dan's failure to answer the muster, when the league was at last able to check the Sea Peoples' expansion through Esdraelon. Thus Deborah sings:

> Why did Dan take service on ships? (Judg 5:17)

Part of the answer to Deborah's question may be that in pre-Philistine days Dan had itself been a maritime "tribe." W. F. Albright, "The Earliest Forms of Hebrew Verse," *JPOS* 2 (1922) 82 n.; Rowley, *From Joseph to Joshua,* 83.

In fact it has been argued that it was a remnant of the older "Sea People" called Dananu that became the Israelite "tribe." The move to the far north can be correlated with destruction of Tell Qasile (which was founded by Sea People) and its resettlement by another Sea People, probably the Shardan. Yigael Yadin, "And Dan, Why Did He Remain in Ships?" *Australian Journal of Biblical Archaeology* 1 (1968) 9-23.

Identification of the famous northern town of Dan with Tell el Qadi at the southern foot of Mount Hermon is confirmed by the discovery of an inscription there (third-second centuries B.C.), containing an oath to "the god who is in Dan." A. Biran, "Tell Dan, 1976," *IEJ* 26 (1976) 202-206. The town has become well-known from excavations conducted since 1966 by Dr. Avraham Biran, who now believes that "the Danite takeover probably took place in the middle of the twelfth century." *EAEHL* I (1975) 316. This would seem to correlate significantly with the evidence for Abimelech's destruction of Shechem likewise in the mid-twelfth century; so that Dan's allotment and relocation understandably belongs to the Shiloh phase.

i. CONCLUSION
(19:49-51)

19 ⁴⁹ They completed the distribution of the land in fief, according to its boundaries. And the Bene Israel gave a fief to Joshua ben Nun in their midst. ⁵⁰ By Yahweh's decision they gave him the town which he requested, Timnath-serah in the hill country of Ephraim. He rebuilt the town and settled there.

⁵¹ These are the fiefs which Eleazar the priest and Joshua ben Nun and the patriarchal chiefs assigned by lot to the tribes of Israel at Shiloh, before Yahweh at the opening of the Tent of Meeting. They completed the apportionment of the land.

TEXTUAL NOTES

19 50. *Yahweh's* Replaced by "God's" in LXX[B].
 Timnath-serah "Timnath-heres" in LXX[B], OL, and Judg 2:9.

NOTES

19:49-51. This is the wrap-up to the lengthy section on the distribution of the land into newly determined tribal fiefs (chaps. 13-19). The unit is given a strong rhetorical frame: "They completed the distribution (root *nḥl*) of the land" in v 49; "They completed the apportionment (*root ḥlq*) of the land" in v 51. LXX uses *embateusai* for both.

49. *according to its boundaries.* The idiom *lgbwltyh* is used elsewhere in the book only to describe the fief of Benjamin (18:20), and it is specified that the boundaries enclose the area. In other words, the historian here emphasizes that the Bene Israel as a whole stayed strictly within the land that was Yahweh's gift in fief to them. On the other hand, it is a matter of internal boundaries that will pose a problem in chap. 22.

50. *Yahweh's decision.* Literally, "by the mouth of Yahweh." See above,

9:14 and NOTES; also 15:13; 17:4; 21:3; 22:9. This is another idiom which contributes to the dialectical relationship between elements of the first and second editions (see COMMENT).

Timnath-serah. "Leftover portion." Here and in 24:30 this form of the name reflects a popular etymology playing upon the original form, Timnath-heres, "Sun's portion" (Judg 2:9). Khirbet Tibnah is located some 24 km southwest of Shechem. Map H, 398.

He rebuilt. The evidence from the recent survey is that the place had been mostly abandoned since MB II and was reoccupied in Iron I. *Judaea, Samaria, and the Golan: Archaeological Survey 1967-1968,* ed. M. Kochavi. Jerusalem: Carta, 1972; Ephraim and Manasseh site ⁑220, 234.

rebuilt the town and settled there. This clause will also contribute dialectically to the last word on the entire pre-monarchy era (Judg 21:23).

51. The first half of this verse forms a strong inclusion with 14:1, where this same list of leaders is found. The two verses thus enclose a redactor's expanded account of the process and results of reforms in land tenure west of the Jordan. At the same time it echoes 18:1 (the beginning of the Shiloh phase) by referring to the new league center and the much older Tent of Meeting which lent its legitimation to the site and the assembly.

Eleazar the priest. See above on 14:1 and 17:4. From this point on he will be mentioned with surprising frequency (21:1; 22:13,31,32; 24:33). All other references to Eleazar in Joshua occur in markedly Dtr 2 contexts. This, combined with the fact that Eleazar is not mentioned at the beginning of the Shiloh-phase allotments, suggests that his presence here is another sign of that later historian at work.

the patriarchal chiefs. See 14:1 and NOTE. This distinctive group of leaders will appear again in 21:1.

Shiloh. Second NOTE on 18:1.

before Yahweh. Third NOTE on 18:6.

Tent of Meeting. Third NOTE on 18:1.

They completed. Hebrew *wyklw.* The subject is plural, forming a strong redactional inclusion with the first word in the unit (v 49). There too the verb form was plural though the focus abruptly shifted to the reward for the leader of the conquest.

the apportionment. The root *ḥlq* here in MT echoes its use in 18:2, "parceled out."

COMMENT

The lengthy section on the impartial division and distribution of the land appears to end twice. In vv 49-50 the focus is on Joshua and the legitimation of his personal fief, a long abandoned or lightly occupied village site. This conclusion to the section, highlighting the figure of Joshua and by implication the reward for his kind of leadership, may be confidently assigned to the first edition (Dtr 1), and it stands in dialectical relation to the echoes of it which occur at the end of the sequel (Judg 21:23-24).

In the second ending (v 51), Joshua takes second place, between Eleazar the priest and the patriarchal chiefs. Here everything coheres to evoke a memory of the way it was in the wilderness setting of the pre-conquest era. This we may recognize as the handiwork of Dtr 2, living during a time of rapid transition to a period of something like pre-conquest conditions.

There remains only to describe the establishment of two institutions for which Moses had made preliminary specification. The first of them was designed to remove blood vengeance from the life of the Bene Israel.

IV. PROVISIONS FOR KEEPING THE PEACE
20:1-21:45

A. ASYLUM-TOWNS
(20:1-9)

20 1 Yahweh spoke to Joshua: 2 "Tell the Bene Israel, 'Make your selection of asylum-towns, concerning which I spoke to you through Moses, 3 so that anyone who kills by striking down a person accidentally (that is, unintentionally) may flee thither. You shall have them as towns for asylum. And thus the killer will not die because of the blood-redeemer. 4 He shall flee to one of these towns, stand at the entrance to the towngate, and state his case in the hearing of that town's elders. They shall gather him to them in the city and give him sanctuary, and he shall reside with them. 5 If the blood-redeemer pursues him, they shall not hand over the killer to him, because it was unintentionally that he struck down his neighbor. He had not at any time harbored hatred for him. 6 He shall reside in that town until he has stood fair trial before the congregation—until the death of whoever is chief priest at the time. Then the killer may return and go in, to his own town and to his own house, to that town from which he had fled.'"

7 They selected Qedesh-in-Galilee in the mountains of Naphtali, Shechem in the hill country of Ephraim, and Qiryath-arba (that is, Hebron) in the mountains of Judah.

8 From the region beyond the Jordan, to the east of Jericho, they had already selected Bezer on the desert plateau from the tribe of Reuben, Ramoth-in-Gilead from the tribe of Gad, and Golan in Bashan from the tribe of Manasseh.

9 These were the towns designated for all the Bene Israel and for any resident alien in their midst, so that anyone who killed by striking down a person accidentally might flee there and thus not die

by the hand of the blood-redeemer without standing before the congregation.

TEXTUAL NOTES

20 3. (*that is, unintentionally*)   Hebrew *bbly-d't*, literally, "unknowingly." Lacking in LXX.

as towns   Restored from LXX, after haplography in MT: *lk[m h'ry]m lmqlṭ*. Cf. Num 35:12 MT.

And thus the killer will not die   Restored from LXX. Cf. Num 35:12 MT.

4. *entrance*   LXX^A omits.

in the city   This is MT *h'yrh*. LXX^A reflects *h'dh*, "the congregation," in anticipation of v 6, a mistake spurred on by the confusion of *d* and *r*. Not until late pre-exilic times would *h'yrh* have been spelled with *y* as the sign of a long vowel.

6. *to that town*   Hebrew *'l-h'yr*, missing in the Cairo Geniza manuscript.

7. *selected Qedesh*   This is LXX which reflects *wyqrw 't qdš* where MT reads *wyqdšw 't qdš*, another example of contamination facilitated by the similarity of *d* and *r*. While the use of cognate accusative in MT "They sanctified Qedesh (the sacred place)" is a possible explanation, usage in Num 35:11 favors LXX here.

8. *to the east of Jericho*   Lacking in LXX.

they had already   Or possibly "he" (referring to Moses) had done so, if LXX^B rightly reads the singular. The translation follows the substantial reading of LXX^B and takes the same consonantal text to be infinitive absolute used as emphatic substitute for a finite verb.

9. *all*   Lacking in LXX *Vorlage*, as a scribe's eye jumped from one *l* to another: *[lk]l bny*.

congregation   This agrees with MT, where LXX and Syriac show assimilation to v 6 and add that the refugee stands there "for a fair trial." Such a longer form is more likely secondary in v 9, because neither the MT nor the Greek shows a mechanism for haplography.

NOTES

20:1-9. This chapter introduces the first of two public institutions in ancient Israel which had high symbolic value for the last redactors of the book. These institutions were the system of Levitical towns, to be described in chap. 21, and the special group of six towns in these verses which served to provide refuge for anyone who might become the innocent target of private vengeance.

The system of asylum-towns has recently been treated as a seventh-century development. Henry McKeating, "The Development of the Law on Homicide in Ancient Israel," *VT* 25 (1975) especially 53-55. By that time, however, Transjordan was lost to the Jerusalem throne and any successes of Josiah in reclaiming portions of it were very short-lived. *The Jerusalem Bible* (268) is surely closer to the mark in describing the system as "an institution of great antiquity." The list, itself drawn from ancient records, functioned paradigmatically for the late redactor. It shows how in the early days tribes, cities, congregations, and a chief priest were supposed to have functioned for the well-being of individuals first and foremost. Both institutions, the asylum-towns and the Levitical towns to which system they also belonged, were no doubt long since defunct by the time of the seventh-century historians. There is not a single reference to either one of these institutions in the historical books of 1 and 2 Samuel, 1 and 2 Kings, and 1 and 2 Chronicles; and nowhere are they clearly presupposed.

1. *Yahweh spoke.* Hebrew *dbr.* The setting that is presupposed is the Tent of Meeting, as in the preceding verse, at Shiloh.

2. *"Tell.* Hebrew *dbr* as in the preceding verse. The transition to the chapter is not smooth. The editorial work was largely a matter of prefixing v 1 to a preformed unit telling about the asylum-towns.

'Make your selection of. Literally, "Give to/for yourselves."

asylum-towns. The plan is announced in the epic narrative at Num 35:9-34. The three Transjordan towns are so designated in Deut 4:41-43, leaving the appointment of the three to the west of the Jordan as a matter for exhortation by Moses in Deut 19:1-13. (The relation of the "three cities" in Deut 19:7 to the "three other cities" in Deut 19:9 is not at all clear.) The institution is rooted ultimately in the principle, implicit in the Covenant Code, of the inviolability of the altar of God as place of refuge (Exod 21:12-14). But the altar-asylum was at an early period replaced by this system, in the Solomonic period at the latest. See a forthcoming paper by Jacob Milgrom, "Sancta Contagion and Altar/City Asylum" (used with permission).

3-6. The translation follows MT and LXX^A, where LXX^B+MSS lack all of vv 4-5 and most of v 6. Verse 3 is represented and its last clause is joined to the single remaining clause of v 6: "⁸ The killer shall not die by the agency of the blood-redeemer ⁶ until he has stood fair trial before the congregation." This is coherent and probably represents a parallel but shorter recension.

3. *accidentally.* For example, "as when a man goes into the forest with his neighbor to cut wood, and his hand swings the ax to cut down a tree, and the head slips from the handle and strikes his neighbor so that he dies—he may flee to one of these cities and save his life" (Deut 19:5 *RSV*).

the blood-redeemer. Hebrew *gō'ēl had-dām.* Not "avenger of blood." While the law in Israel included the death penalty for willful and premeditated murder, the didactic "Codes" of the Bible are at pains to eliminate abuses that accompany retaliatory vengeance for accidental manslaughter. Numbers 35 makes it explicit more than once that only by forsaking the asylum-town or by being found guilty in a fair trial there did an accused manslayer run the risk of being hunted down by the blood-redeemer. Biblical law does not anywhere promote private vengeance, but seeks everywhere to restrain it. The blood-redeemer becomes, in effect, the executioner, not also the court. Cain is indeed the exception, the guilty one who is nevertheless protected by the deity. But Cain was not "Israelite" and lived, as it were, in prehistory. His mark may in fact represent a negotiated exception for one of the early constituencies. Mendenhall, *Ten Gen*, 89.

4. *at the entrance to the towngate*. This is not redundant. A number of towngates from Iron Age sites have now been excavated (Shechem, Gezer, Dan, to mention three of the best preserved). The towngate was an elaborate structure at least two stories high, with guardrooms flanking a tunnel-like opening, and bench-lined court(s) guarded by towers. The outer court at Dan, for example, is a relatively spacious plaza (c. 20.4 by 9.4 meters), with benches in the right angle formed by two walls and having a remarkable structure which has been interpreted as the foundation for a ceremonial chair or throne, in other words, a seat of judgment. Matt 27:19; John 19:13. It has been offered as a natural setting for the kind of civil proceeding narrated, for example, in Ruth 4 (Campbell, *Ruth*, AB 7, 154-155); it would serve as well for "criminal" cases. Many other references to "the gate" depict it as the place where the elders gather, court is held, arguments are negotiated, disputes are arbitrated or tried, and refuge is sought.

elders. Not frequently met in the body of the book (7:6; 8:10,33; 9:11 [Gibeonite elders]), they are especially important in these concluding chapters (see 23:2; 24:1,31).

They. The plural verbs refer back to the elders.

sanctuary. Hebrew *māqôm*, "place," but evoking the sense of "holy place" as in the stipulation of the old Covenant Code concerning the "place" of refuge. Exod 21:13.

5. *unintentionally*. Is this the source of the same expression used as a gloss, apparently redundant, in v 3?

6. *fair trial*. Hebrew *lmšpṭ*, literally, "at custom(ary law)."

the congregation. Hebrew *hā-ʿēdâ* is a key word in this unit, repeated in v 9 as the last word. Clearly this "congregation" (the adult male Yahwists of the town) is of pivotal importance.

until the death. The granting of this prolonged asylum presumes that the case did not involve intentional homicide. The second specification is thus consequent on, but otherwise independent of, the first "until" clause.

death of whoever is chief priest. The death of the high priest was apparently the occasion for a general amnesty; it would then be safe for the fugitive to return home (Num 35:25,28). At the heart of the story in chap. 22 is the action of "congregation" and chief "priest" in dealing with a sanctuary dispute that nearly escalated into civil war. The problem there is a "tribal" manifestation of the problem behind private vengeance.

Then. Hebrew *ʾāz* is a marker of Dtr 2 in Joshua, discussed above, first NOTE on 10:12.

7. *They selected Qedesh*. The list runs from north to south in Cisjordan, then from south to north in Transjordan.

Qedesh-in-Galilee. Probably the great mound of Tell Qades, far to the north in Upper Galilee. See first NOTE on 19:37. A Levitical town (21:32). Map K, 477.

Shechem. Map K. In the heart of the north-central hill country. See NOTES on 8:30-35; 17:2,7; 24:1,25,32. A Levitical town (21:21).

hill country of Ephraim. This may well be an administrative area of the United Monarchy, not strictly coinciding with the tribal fief of the Bene Ephraim, but drawn in such a way as to include Shechem. See 17:2 and 7.

Qiryath-arba (that is, Hebron). Map K, 477. The center of the southern hills. On the equation and change of names, see 14:15; 15:13,54 and NOTES.

8. *From the region beyond.* The syntax in Hebrew is disjunctive. The words introduce a flashback.

had already selected. The use of the perfect tense in Hebrew here contrasts sharply with the converted imperfect at the beginning of the preceding verse. This flashback is to be correlated with Deut 4:41-43 which credits Moses with the appointment of the three towns. It is not by coincidence that those verses comprise part of the Dtr historians' secondary introduction to the old "Book of the Law," our Dtn.

Bezer. The best prospect is Umm el-Amad, 14 km northeast of Madeba. Map K, 477. See the Levitical town list and NOTES on 21:36. The town is mentioned by Mesha king of Moab as one of the places that he refortified (*ANET*², 320-321), but it is not mentioned above in chap. 13. Was it already in ruins in Joshua's time when it was designated to be rebuilt as a place of refuge?

Ramoth-in-Gilead. Tell er-Rumeith. Map K, 477. See Levitical town list, 21:38 and NOTES. On the excavations, see Paul W. Lapp, "Tell er-Rumeith," *RB* 70 (1963) 406-411; "Tell er-Rumeith," *RB* 75 (1968) 98-105. The destruction of Stratum VIII (early ninth century) is associated with the Aramaean expansion (see below on Golan and Ashtaroth in 21:27). The evidence of Strata VI and V indicates that a significant resurgence of Israelite control in Transjordan had taken place by the eighth century.

Golan. Possibly Saḥem el-Jolan in southern Syria. Map K, 477. Levitical town in 21:27.

9. *were.* The tense is clear. The asylum-towns are here regarded as part of the past, the way it was supposed to have been.

designated. Hebrew *hmw'dh* evokes thought of the subject implied here, "the congregation" (*h'dh*) and the setting at the Tent "of Meeting" (*mw'd*).

for all . . . and for any. As is made explicit in Num 15:15, there is to be "one statute for you and the stranger who sojourns with you, a perpetual statute . . ."

before the congregation. This ending is abrupt and totally unexpected. Why? The simplest and most likely answer is that the "congregation" no longer served the asylum function. Yet it was "the congregation," the hometown assembly, that continued to be (or had recently come again to be) the all-important center of a redactor's thought. That development is surely not unrelated to the imminent collapse of state and temple security at the end of the seventh century B.C.

COMMENT

It is not easy to imagine a plight more terrifying than that of the innocent homicide in a society where the practice of private vengeance is deeply rooted and very much alive, as it surely was in the highly fragmented society of Canaan in the Late Bronze Age. The promise of safety at the sanctuary for such persons, in the old village law that was taken over as the Covenant Code, was strengthened and federalized in the creation of a system of asylum-towns. This may be taken as another product of the mutation in religion which was Mosaic Yahwism: the well-being of individuals is the highest good and a corporate responsibility called *mišpaṭ*, "justice."

For a couple of hundred years, in any case, the ideology and system of asylum-towns must have been highly effective, for we know exceedingly few cases of attempts to execute private vengeance in the Hebrew Bible. Classic examples are seen in the stories of Gideon in Judges 8 and the anonymous Levite in Judges 19-20, both of whom are presented as scathing caricatures, probably for this very reason.

In these nine verses on the asylum-towns, in other words, we get the first glimpse of a rather delicate literary superstructure that is supported by three massive foundational pillars: the Mobilization (1:1 - 5:12), the Warfare (5:13 - 11:23), and the Inheritance (12:1 - 19:51). Here it is recognized that there can be no continued well-being for the hunted individual (Israelite or otherwise) apart from refuge within the "congregation." When it is first encountered in this book, the "congregation" is part of a somewhat comic scene; premature action by the "leaders of the congregation" had led Joshua into using his wits rather than force in dealing with the Gibeonites (chap. 9). Here, however, toward the end of the post-Joshua era of monarchy, there is nothing comic about the establishment of asylum-towns. Here the functioning of the congregation is soberly and straightforwardly presented as "Exhibit A" of how it had been intended. The next chapter presents "Exhibit B," provision for the militant teacher-priests.

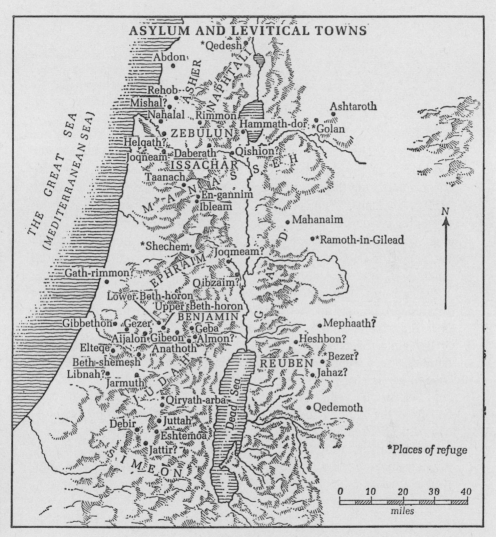

ASYLUM AND LEVITICAL TOWNS

*Qedesh
Abdon
ASHER NAPHTALI
Rehob
Mishal?
Nahalal Rimmon
Ashtaroth
Hammath-dor *Golan
ZEBULUN
Helqath?
Joqneam Daberath Qishion?
ISSACHAR S E H
Taanach
M A N A S
En-gannim
Ibleam
THE GREAT SEA (MEDITERRANEAN SEA)
Mahanaim
*Shechem *Ramoth-in-Gilead
Joqmeam?
Gath-rimmon?
EPHRAIM
Qibzaim?
Lower Beth-horon
Upper Beth-horon
Gibbethon Gezer BENJAMIN
Mephaath?
Aijalon Gibeon Geba
Elteqe Anathoth Almon?
Heshbon?
Beth-shemesh
*Bezer?
Libnah? J U D A H
REUBEN
Jarmuth
Jahaz?
Dead Sea
*Qiryath-arba
Qedemoth
Debir Juttah
Eshtemoa
S I M E O N Jattir?

N

GAD

*Places of refuge

0 10 20 30 40
miles

Map K

B. LEVITICAL TOWNS
(21:1-42d)

Three Families

21 ¹ The patriarchal chiefs of the Levites converged upon Eleazar the priest, and Joshua ben Nun, and the patriarchal chiefs of the tribes comprising the Bene Israel. ² They said to them at Shiloh in the land of Canaan: "Yahweh gave orders through Moses to assign us towns for residence, with access to their common-lands for our livestock." ³ So the Bene Israel assigned for the Levites, out of their fiefs by Yahweh's decision, these towns, with access to their common-lands.

⁴ Here is how the lot came out for the Qohathite families. For those Levites who comprised the Bene Aaron, the priests, there were by lot, from the tribe of Judah and the tribe of the Simeonites and the tribe of Benjamin thirteen towns. ⁵ For the rest of the Bene Qohath, from families of the Ephraim tribe, and from the tribe of Dan and half the tribe of Manasseh, there were by lot ten towns.

⁶ And for the Bene Gershon, from families of the Issachar tribe and from the Asher tribe and the Naphtali tribe and from the half-tribe of Manasseh in Bashan, there were by lot thirteen towns.

⁷ And for the families of the Bene Merari, from the tribe of Reuben and the tribe of Gad, and the tribe of Zebulun, there were twelve towns.

Forty-eight Towns

⁸ The Bene Israel assigned for the Levites these towns with access to their common-lands in the way Yahweh ordered through Moses, that is, by lot.

Qohathite Priests

9 From the Bene Judah tribe and from the Bene Simeon tribe and from the Bene Benjamin tribe, they assigned the towns which are here named individually. 10 They were for members of the Bene Aaron who were from the families of the Qohathites, part of the Bene Levi, because the lot fell first to them.

11 They assigned them Qiryath-arba (the father of Anaq), that is, Hebron in the hill country of Judah, with access to the common-lands around it. 12 The town's fields and its enclosures Joshua had assigned to Caleb ben Jephunneh as his holding.

13 To the Bene Aaron they assigned along with the asylum-town for the unconvicted killer, Hebron with its common-lands: Libnah with its common-lands, 14 and Jattir with its common-lands, and Eshtemoa with its common-lands, 15 and Holon with its common-lands, and Debir with its common-lands, 16 and Ashan with its common-lands, and Juttah with its common-lands, and Beth-shemesh with its common-lands (nine towns out of these two tribes).

17 And from the Benjamin tribe: Gibeon with its common-lands, Geba with its common-lands, 18 Anathoth with its common-lands, and Almon with its common-lands (four towns).

19 All the towns of the Bene Aaron, the priests: thirteen towns with their common-lands.

Other "Qohathites"

20 As for the remaining Levitical families of the Bene Qohath, the towns of their allotment were as follows:

From the tribe of Ephraim 21 they assigned them the asylum-town for the unconvicted killer, Shechem with its common-lands in the hill country of Ephraim, and Gezer with its common-lands, 22 and Qibzaim with its common-lands, and Joqmeam with its common-lands, and Beth-horon with its common-lands (four towns).

23 And from the tribe of Dan: Elteqe with its common-lands, and Gibbethon with its common-lands, 24 Aijalon with its common-lands, Gath-rimmon with its common-lands (four towns).

25 And from half the tribe of Manasseh: Taanach with its common-lands, and Ibleam with its common-lands (two towns).

26 Altogether, ten towns with their common-lands for the rest of
the families of the Bene Qohath.

"Gershonites"

27 For the Levitical families of the Bene Gershon, from one half
of the Manasseh tribe: the asylum-town for the unconvicted killer,
Golan in Bashan with its common-lands, and Ashtaroth with its
common-lands (two towns).

28 And from the Issachar tribe: Qishion with its common-lands,
Daberath with its common-lands, 29 Jarmuth with its common-lands,
En-gannim with its common-lands (four towns).

30 And from the Asher tribe: Mishal with its common-lands,
Abdon with its common-lands, 31 Helqath with its common-lands,
and Rehob with its common-lands (four towns).

32 And from the Naphtali tribe: the asylum-town for the unconvicted killer, Qedesh-in-Galilee with its common-lands, and Hammoth-dor with its common-lands, and Qartan with its common-lands
(three towns).

33 All the towns of the Gershonites for their families: thirteen towns
with their common-lands.

"Merarites"

34 For the families of the Bene Merari (the rest of the Levites),
from the Zebulun tribe: Joqneam with its common-lands, Qartah
with its common-lands, 35 Rimmon with its common-lands, Nahalal
with its common-lands (four towns).

36 And out of the region beyond the Jordan opposite Jericho, from
the Reuben tribe: the asylum-town for the unconvicted killer, Bezer
in the wilderness on the plateau with its common-lands, and Jahaz
with its common-lands, 37 Qedemoth with its common-lands, and
Mephaath with its common-lands (four towns). 38 And from the Gad
tribe: the asylum-town for the unconvicted killer, Ramoth-in-Gilead
with its common-lands, and Mahanaim with its common-lands,

³⁹ Heshbon with its common-lands, Jazer with its common-lands (four towns).

⁴⁰ All these towns were for the Bene Merari for their families (the rest of the Levitical familes). Their allotment was twelve towns.

⁴¹ All the Levitical towns within the holding of the Bene Israel: forty-eight towns with their common-lands surrounding these towns. ⁴² These towns had each its own common-lands surrounding it. So it was for all these towns.

⁴²ᵃ So Joshua finished the distribution of the land within its boundaries. ⁴²ᵇ The Bene Israel gave a fief to Joshua, according to the decision of Yahweh. They gave him the town he asked for. They gave him Timnath-serah in the hill country of Ephraim. ⁴²ᶜ Joshua rebuilt the town and there he settled. ⁴²ᵈ Joshua took the flint knives with which he circumcised the Bene Israel who came out of the wilderness, and he deposited them in Timnath-serah.

TEXTUAL NOTES

21 1. *Levites*   LXX reads Bene Levi.

the Bene   LXX omits.

2. *common-lands*   The compound noun is Hebrew *mgrš*=Greek *perisporion*.

3. *out of their fiefs*   MT is preferable to the OG "in their fief," which reflects a participle *mmnḥltm* used as noun substitute, probably resulting from dittography of *m* in the *Vorlage*. Greenspoon, STBJ, 179.

these   Lacking in LXX, perhaps by assimilation to the standard LXX concluding formula in the tribal fief descriptions of chaps. 18 and 19.

4. *the priests*   This follows LXX, Syriac, Vulgate where MT "Aaron the priest" probably represents a haplography: *hkhn[m] mn hlwym*. This solution yields the better syntax and an *inclusio* with v 19.

the Simeonites   MT has the gentilic form with the definite article: *hšm'ny*. LXX reads without the *y*, conforming to the references to Judah and Benjamin in the series.

5. *families*   Missing in LXX after haplography: *m[mšpḥt] mṭh 'prym*.

there were   Not in the text, which is in list form; these words are supplied in vv 5,6, and 7.

6. *from families of the Issachar tribe*   See Textual Note on "families" in v 5.

7. *And*   Reading with a few Hebrew manuscripts and the major versions. MT omits.

were   In LXX it happens "by lot," which is readily understood as contamination from the preceding and following verses, whereas the shorter MT text cannot easily be derived from the longer one.

8. *these*   See Textual Note at v 3.

9. *From*   Lost by haplography in the first two of three occurrences in LXX: [*m*]*mṭh*.

and from the Bene Benjamin tribe   This is restored on the basis of LXX, after an obvious haplography in MT.

the   This follows the shorter reading of the versions; MT reads "these."

named   If the text is intact, *yiqrāʾ* parses as an impersonal passive use of the indicative.

individually   Literally, "by name." Lacking in LXX which also lacks the following verb.

10. *first*   Lost in some Hebrew manuscripts and LXX.

11. *Anaq*   This vocalization (cf. 15:13) is supported by several Hebrew manuscripts and versions against MT.

12. *Joshua*   Thus LXX, where MT has assimilated to v 13, "they assigned." *Caleb*   LXX has "Bene Caleb."

13. *Aaron*   This follows LXX^B, OL, supported by 1 Chr 6:42, where MT has assimilated to its own corrupted form in v 4, by adding *hkhn*.

they assigned   Missing in LXX^B.

14. *Jattir*   *Ailōm* in LXX^B.

common-lands   For the Hebrew noun *mgrš*, LXX^B here switches to *aphorisma*.

15. *Holon*   *ḥlm* in MT, for which 1 Chr 6:43 has *ḥyln* in MT and many manuscripts.

16. *Ashan*   This name is read here on the authority of 1 Chr 6:44[59E] (see also 15:42; 19:7), in place of MT "Ain."

and third occurrence   Read the conjunction with abundant support in the versions.

18. *Almon*   Spelled "Almon" in LXX^A, "Amala" in LXX^B, "Alemeth" in LXX^MSS, OL, and 1 Chr 6:45[60E]. All three forms are close to the modern name.

19. *with their common-lands*   Lacking in LXX, presumably due to haplography: *w*[*mgršyhn w*]*lmšpḥwt*.

20. *Levitical families of the Bene Qohath*   The text is conflate in both MT and LXX: "Levitical Qohathite (*bny qht*) families of the Bene Qohath."

their allotment   For MT *gwrlm* the alternative is *gbwlm*, "their border/territory" in LXX^A+MSS, which represents a corruption in the *Vorlage* of OG. LXX^B, "their priests," is a further corruption. Greenspoon, STBJ, 205-207.

21. *in the hill country of Ephraim*   Lacking in LXX.

Gezer   LXX has a plus: *kai ta pros autēn*, perhaps=*wsbybtyh*, "and its surroundings."

22. *and Joqmeam with its common-lands*   This is restored on the basis of the list in 1 Chr 6:53. The stereotyped pattern produced a situation ripe for haplography. In the LXX^B *Vorlage* it was "Qibzaim" that was dropped. Less likely is either of the alternative explanations: that one name is a corruption of the other, or else represents an actual change of name.

23. *Elteqe*   MT *ʾltqʾ*, alternative spelling with *-h* in 19:44.

24. *Aijalon*   Some manuscripts have as a *kethib Elon*, in agreement with some LXX texts. Cf. 19:42 and NOTES.

25. *Ibleam*   This is based on 1 Chr 6:55[70E] with some support in LXX[B], *Iebatha*. MT shows a duplication from the Dan section: "Gath-rimmon."

26. *common-lands*   LXX seems to add *sbyb*, "surrounding (it)."

27. *Ashtaroth*   Thus Syriac and 1 Chr 6:56[71E] (*'štrt*) for the odd form of the name in MT which also shows the influence of narrative usage (13:12), with a prefixed preposition, *bĕ'ĕštĕrā*.

28. *Qishion*   "Qedesh" in 1 Chr 6:56[72E].

29. *Jarmuth*   "Ramoth" in 1 Chr 6:58[73E].

En-gannim   Thus MT. LXX reads *nḥl s(w)prym*, "Book (or Scribe's) Gorge."

31. *Helqath*   "Huqoq" in 1 Chr 6:60[75E].

32. *Hammoth-dor*   "Hammat" in LXX[B+MSS], Syriac[u] (cf. 19:35). "Hammon" in 1 Chr 6:61[76E].

Qartan   "Raqqat" in 19:35. "Qiryathaim" in 1 Chr 6:61[76E].

33. *towns* second occurrence   The plural ending was easily lost from both MT and LXX in such a context: *'r[ym] wmgršyhn*.

34. *families*   Manuscripts and versions read the singular.

Qartah   Thus MT. LXX reads "Qedesh."

35. *Rimmon*   Where MT *dmnh* shows confusion of *d* and *r* (LXX omits), this name is taken from 19:13; cf. *rmwnw* in 1 Chr 6:62[77E].

36-37. These verses are lacking in various witnesses, or differently positioned. Found in the majority of Hebrew manuscripts (though not the best), they are "necessary to the completeness of the narrative." H. B. Swete, *An Introduction to the Old Testament in Greek*, 244.

36. *region beyond the Jordan opposite Jericho*   Restored from LXX, after haplography in Hebrew: *m['br lyrdn lyryḥw m]mṭh*.

the asylum-town for the unconvicted killer   Restored from LXX.

in the wilderness on the plateau   This is LXX, missing in MT: *bṣr [bmdbr bmyšr]*.

39. *(four towns)*   This follows Syriac and Vulgate, where MT ("all towns: four") is contaminated by anticipation of the first two words in the next verse, *kl h'rym*.

40. *allotment*   See Textual Note at 15:1.

41. *surrounding these towns.* [42] *These towns*   Contrasting omissions seem to have obscured the end of v 41 in MT and the beginning of v 42 in LXX[B]:

MT	[*sbybt*	*h'rym*	*h'lh*]	*thyynh*	*h'rym* *h'lh*
LXX[B]	*sbybt*	[*h'rym*	*h'lh*	*thyynh*]	*h'rym* *h'lh*

42. *each its own common-lands surrounding it. So it was for all these towns*   Confusion is further compounded by haplography in LXX[B]:

MT	*'yr*	*'yr*	*wmgršyh*	*sbybtyh*	*kn*	*lkl*	*h'rym*	*h'lh*
LXX[B]	[ ]	*'yr*	*wmgršyh*	*sbybt*		*h'yr* *lkl*	*h'rym*	*h'lh* "a

town and its common lands around the town, for all these towns."

42a-42d. A long gap in MT is here filled from LXX.

42d. *out of the wilderness*   Greek *en tō hodō en tē erēmō*=Hebrew *bdrk bmdbr*, where the second *b*="from."

NOTES

21:1-42. This chapter on the institution of Levitical towns occupies a position of penultimate significance in the structure of the book. Three separate questions must be addressed in NOTES and COMMENT, in seeking to grasp the significance of the chapter. These are questions of (1) the origin and purpose of the system in which certain towns have an obligation to provide Levites with residence and grazing rights; (2) the date of the actual list used in Joshua 21; and (3) the effect in context of its redactional use. Within the format of a commentary it is appropriate to pursue these questions simultaneously, giving attention to whatever relevant information the text offers. The examination is greatly aided by the list that parallels vv 10-42 in 1 Chr 6:39-66[54-81E]. See Jacob M. Myers, *I Chronicles*, AB 12, 47-48. That these are two scribal recensions of a single list, rather than separate and distinct traditions, was shown by W. F. Albright, "The List of Levitic Cities," in *Louis Ginzberg Jubilee Volume* (New York: American Academy for Jewish Research, 1945) 49-73.

A deeply rooted scholarly tradition that this chapter is another piece of the literary source P is rooted in Wellhausen's analysis of the material as based on Ezekiel's programmatic vision (Ezek 45:1; 48:8-14). Julius Wellhausen, *Prolegomena to the History of Ancient Israel*. Tr. W. Robertson Smith (New York: Meridian Books, 1957) 152-168.

That P, however, does not figure as a source in Joshua, in any way comparable to P in the first four books of the Pentateuch, is adequately shown by Wright in the Introduction to this volume, 54-59.

1-3. These verses are an editorial introduction to a preformed list, adapting it to the narrative setting.

1. *patriarchal chiefs*. This treats Levi as socially and politically comparable to the other tribes, which originally it must have been. See now Freedman, "Early Israelite History in the Light of Early Israelite Poetry," in *Unity and Diversity* (1975) 17. The eleventh-century poem in Genesis 49 recalls a time when Simeon and Levi were banished from the league, on a single charge:

> Cursed be their wrath—how fierce it was!
> And their rage—how cruel it was!
> I will divide them from Jacob,
> and I will banish them from Israel

(Genesis 49:7 as rendered by Freedman, ibid.) The Israel from which Levi and Simeon were banished must have been the pre-Mosaic league based on the cult of the patriarchal god El.

Levites. Hebrew here uses the gentilic form (as in 3:3; 8:33; 14:3,4;

18:7—never "Bene Levi"), a characteristic of many sections redacted by the later editor (Dtr 2) incorporating some very old material. A number of elements in the makeup and history of the Levites can be best understood in terms of Anatolian (specifically Luwian) origins. Mendenhall, *Ten Gen*, 163.

converged upon. The verbal root is *ngš*, "draw near," which in this case happened from all sides. The Levites had to take the initiative and remind the leaders to implement the Lord's directive.

Eleazar. Joshua. chiefs. As in 14:1 and 19:51 (the framework around description of the Cisjordan tribes) and in 17:4 (Cisjordan towns for daughters of Zelophehad, a Transjordan chief). I.e. the redactor who used this formula was interested in the east-west axis of the early league.

Eleazar the priest. He represents almost certainly the Bethel branch of the Bene Aaron (Judg 20:28) who lost out in the post-Solomonic "reforms" of Jeroboam I (1 Kgs 12:31-32). For his presence only at points that are otherwise marked as the work of Dtr 2, see NOTES on 14:1; 17:4; and 19:51.

2. *Shiloh in the land of Canaan.* This is the first occurrence of a formula which clusters with other indicators to point to Dtr 2 in Joshua (again in 22:9) and Judg 21:12. See *Judges*, AB 6A, 292.

"Yahweh gave orders through Moses. See Num 35:1-8. The claim suggests that Moses had anticipated a time when Levites would no longer be serving only the function for which they are noted in the epic sources—guarding the portable palace and throne of the divine king. See above, on the priestly porters of the Ark at the Jordan crossing (chaps. 3 and 4) and the Shechem Valley ceremony (8:30-35).

towns for residence. The mention of special arrangements for Levites in 13:14,33 and 14:4 (all clearly Dtr 2) or special status in 18:7 (the sole reference to Levites in the earlier edition of Joshua!) has prepared the way.

common-lands. The word *mgrš* makes scattered appearances in Ezekiel, Numbers, Leviticus, but is ubiquitous in the Chronicles and in Joshua 21. Elsewhere in this book, however, it occurs only in 14:4, another Levite text.

3. *the Bene Israel assigned.* Not the leadership, confirming the nuance noted at the outset in v 1.

by Yahweh's decision. Again the use of the lot is implied. For the expression *py yhwh*, literally, "mouth of Yahweh," see 9:14; 15:13; 17:4; 19:50; 22:9.

with access to their common-lands. City houses had no economic function in the society presented in the epic sources. There can be no well-being without access to land outside the village limits or city wall. See Menahem Haran, "Studies in the Account of the Levitical Cities," *JBL* 80 (1961) 45-54 and 156-165. He concluded that a historical institution lies at the basis of what is essentially a utopian creation in this list. But there are too many territorial gaps, and too many known cult towns missing for the list to be a later composition. Aharoni, *LOB*, 269.

4-7. The families are obviously listed in descending order of size, influence, and importance, presumably reflecting the era of the redaction.

4-5. First provision is for "the priests," all in towns of the three southern tribes. The seemingly segregated pattern that results (priests in the south, all other Levites in the north) should not be taken as evidence of the list's "utopian character" (as first suggested by Kaufmann, *The Biblical Account* . . . , 43). The chapter was compiled from lists which were not all assembled on the same organizing principles. These lists reflected the shifting fortunes and prestige of various Levitical families. Since the verses seem to imply that there are no Bene Aaron north of Benjamin, they may presuppose the divided kingdom in which the northern Aaronides of Bethel had been displaced by Jeroboam's appointments; later tradition asserted that they were expelled from the north. See the discussion by Baruch Halpern, *JBL* 95 (1976) 31-42.

To the most influential branch of Levi thirteen towns are assigned for support of the priests, compared to ten towns for all the rest of that same Levitical "family."

4. *the Qohathite.* Another gentilic formation. This became a most important Levitical family over the years. As "father" of Amran, Izhar, Hebron, and Uzziel (Exod 6:18; Num 3:19; 1 Chr 5:28[6:2E]; 6:3[18E]; 23:12) he came to be regarded as grandfather of Aaron, Moses, and Miriam (Exod 6:20; Num 26:59). Qohathites guarded the Ark (Num 3:29-31; 4:1-3,34-37; 1 Chr 15:5) and participated in the later reforms of Jehoshaphat (2 Chr 20:19), Hezekiah (2 Chr 29:12), and Josiah (2 Chr 34:12).

Bene Aaron, the priests. This makes it explicit for any who might miss the contrast that is implicit with the following verse.

Judah. See chap. 15.

Simeonites. Note the gentilic form, used within an envelope formed by two uses of the non-gentilic form. See NOTES and COMMENT on 19:1-9 for Simeon's fief.

Benjamin. See 18:11-28.

5. *For the rest.* The shift to disjunctive syntax here (repeated at beginning of vv 6 and 7) shows a strong distinction being made between those families which in fact produced "the priests" and all other families of lower clergy at the end of the national era.

the rest of the Bene Qohath. The implication is that the priests (Bene Aaron) were the original Qohathites, perhaps those to whom the gentilic as such first properly referred. There were no doubt many other members of the Bene Qohath who could not claim the same origin or prerogatives.

Ephraim. See 16:5-10 (cf. 17:14-18).

Dan. The southern location is meant; see 19:40-48.

Manasseh. In Cisjordan, 17:1-13.

6. *Bene Gershon.* Alternatively "Gershom" as in the name of the elder son of Moses. "Sojourner there," the popular explanation of the name given in Exod 2:22; 18:3, puns on *gēr,* "sojourner." It is important to note at this point that the Levite in Israel was to have precisely the same status (social and legal) as the *gēr,* "resident alien," and was to receive the same benevolence in Israel as the widow and the orphan.

Issachar. Asher. Naphtali tribe. Manasseh in Bashan. At one point or another, they are contiguous. At one time "Gershom/n" was the dominant Levitical family, to judge from this distribution and from its frequent appearance in first position where all three families are listed (Gen 46:11; Exod 6:16; Num 3:17; 26:57; 1 Chr 6:1,16; 23:6). In other texts, however, they are in lower or subordinate positions relative to the sons of Aaron (Num 3:23-26; 4:24-27; 10:17). The first group of texts suggests that there were priestly families who claimed Mosaic (that is, Mushite or Gershonite) ancestry in the pre-monarchy era. One explicit reference to such a priesthood, headed by "Jonathan, son of Gershom, son of Moses," locates it precisely in the far north at the town of Dan (Judg 18:30). "The patronymic of Gershom is probably to be understood as the clan name, suggesting that Gershom—in traditional genealogies the first son of Levi, as well as the name of Moses' son—was a Mushite clan." Cross, *CMHE*, 197-198.

Issachar. See 19:17-23.

Naphtali tribe. For the fief, see 19:32-39.

Manasseh in Bashan. See 13:29-31.

7. *And for the families of the Bene Merari*. Hebrew (*w*)*lbny mrry lmšpḥtm*, literally, "(And) for the Bene Merari, for their families." This was the weakest of the three Levitical families.

Reuben. Gad. See 13:8-28.

Zebulun. See 19:10-16. It is separated from the two preceding tribes by the territory of Issachar and eastern Manasseh.

8-41. The backbone of the chapter is the list naming the towns which were designated to fill out the quotas established in vv 4-7.

8. *these towns*. In study of the list and attempt to identify each of the forty-eight, the recent work by John L. Peterson is pivotal. Peterson's archaeological study is based on careful surface surveys (and repeated visits to a number of sites) at each of the possible locations for a given Levitical town. See John L. Peterson, "A Topographical Surface Survey of the Levitical 'Cities' of Joshua 21 and 1 Chronicles 6: Studies on the Levites in Israelite Life and Religion."

9-19. First are listed the towns for those Qohathites who comprised the Bene Aaron.

9-10. This introduction to the Qohathite segment rings the changes on a pre-occupation with tribal identity.

9. *Bene Benjamin*. This brings the number of *Bene* groups to a total of five in the two-verse unit.

which are here named individually. This is a striking clause, completely without parallel in the rest of the book. Is it possible that the form used here reflects the Levitical teaching function, in other words, that the list is derived from a school exercise?

10. This is the compiler's explanation for the preeminence of the Bene Aaron in the south.

the Qohathites. To the narrator it is not surprising that Qohath just happened to come out on top, because to him God is behind the system.

the lot fell first to them. "Judah first" (chap. 15) will be a major theme of the framework to the Book of Judges (chaps. 1 and 19-21).

lot. An ironic echo of the end of v 8.

11. *Qiryath-arba*. Map K, 477. See 14:15 and NOTES.

Anaq). See above, first NOTE on 11:21 and second NOTE on 14:12.

that is, Hebron. The first place to be named is precisely "the most prominent priestly city in Judah." Haran, "Studies in the Account of the Levitical Cities," *JBL* 80 (1961) 161. He considers it likely that the Zadoq family of Aaronite priests originated at Hebron. See now Cross, *CMHE*, 195-215, on the priestly houses of early Israel.

Albright argued that Hebron and Shechem (v 21), both priestly towns and asylum-towns, were not originally in this list. This would not be surprising if it stems from a period when Shechem was being suppressed in favor of the new Jerusalem capital at which the Hebron leadership was established, that is, United Monarchy or early southern kingdom. The updating (rather "correction") to include both makes sense as the work of Dtr 2, when incorporating the list in its structurally key position.

12. *Caleb.* The correction of the list to include Hebron also made it possible to evoke the compiler's own expansion (14:6-15, Dtr 2) on the compact notice of a predecessor (15:13-14, Dtr 1), reinforcing the critical awareness of a distinct perspective.

his holding. Hebrew *'ḥztw.* This is the first occurrence of the noun in the Joshua book. It will be echoed in the summary to the chapter (v 41) and the root is a key element in the story to follow (22:4,9,19), in which the focus shifts rapidly.

13. The asylum-town is always first to be named (vv 21,27,32,36,38).

unconvicted killer. In this context the sense of *hrṣḥ,* "the killer," is limited by reference to the place of refuge while trial is pending.

13b-16. Beginning with the name of Libnah, this is a preformed list which a redactor has taken up intact as proved by the parenthetical summary at the end. The list displays an envelope structure; the first and last named are in the foothills (Hebrew *šephēlā*), framing the list of seven that are concentrated along the southern watershed ridge, from Hebron to the neighborhood of Beersheba.

Libnah. In Judah's fourth district (15:42). Map K, 477. For its identification with Tell Bornat, see NOTE on 10:29.

14. *Jattir.* In Judah District V. Map K, 477. See 15:48 and NOTES. Peterson's survey found evidence for Iron II as the earliest period of occupation.

Eshtemoa. In Judah District V. Map K, 477. See second NOTE on 15:50.

15. *Holon.* In Judah District V, location uncertain. See NOTE on 15:51.

Debir. In Judah District V. Map K, 477. See second Note on 15:49. Cf. 10:38-39; 12:13; 15:15-17.

16. *Ashan.* This is the one town listed in the fief of Simeon. See 19:7 and fifth NOTE there.

Juttah. Judah District VII. See 15:55 and fourth NOTE. Map K, 477.

Beth-shemesh. On Judah's northern border. See 15:10 and fourth NOTE. Map K, 477.

two. This agrees with MT of v 9, which lacks reference to Benjamin. It is possible that the LXX translator counted the territory of Judah and Simeon as one and retained the numeral "two."

17-18. *Benjamin.* With four more towns in the neighboring territory of Dan, the narrow east-west strip just north of Jerusalem has a higher concentration of Levites than any other area in the country. It is an "important region, which formed a wedge between Ephraim and Judah." B. Mazar (Maisler), "The Cities of the Priests and the Levites," *VTSup* 7 (1960) 203. It included the region of the heaviest fighting in the first phase of the west-bank revolution (Benjamin), flanked by the coastal region of total and successful resistance to the expansion of Israel (Dan).

17. *Gibeon*. Map K, 477. On its Hivite background, see second NOTE on 9:7. *Geba*. Map K. Third NOTE on 18:24.

18. *Anathoth*. Map K, 477. The most likely candidate is Ras el-Kharrubeh, a kilometer southwest of Anata, which preserves the ancient name. This town is not mentioned in the description of Benjamin's fief. The name is probably a shortened form of Beth-anathoth, "Shrine of the great Anath" (plural of majesty); i.e. the place was formerly sanctified by the great Canaanite goddess. It is one of the priestly towns where Mosaic Yahwism put down deep roots. Abiathar was the last chief priest from the old Mushite line at Shiloh and he held property in Anathoth to which he was at last confined by Solomon, with the ascendancy of the Zadoqite (Aaronid) line (1 Kgs 2:26). The prophet Jeremiah comes from "the priests who were in Anathoth," probably tracing their lineage to Abiathar. Jer 1:1.

†*Almon*. Map K, 477. Otherwise not mentioned, the name is reflected in Khirbet 'Almit, c. 1.5 km northeast of Anata. Peterson's pottery includes a twelfth-century pithos and ninth-century jug, but mostly eighth-seventh century forms.

19. *All the towns*. That this is not a complete list of towns in the south with sizable Levite presence is shown by discovery of ostraca at Arad bearing a number of Levitical names; the ostraca came from the last fortress at Arad of the First Temple period. Yohanan Aharoni, "Hebrew Ostraca from Tel Arad," *IEJ* 16 (1966) 1-7.

20-26. The second segment of the town list provides for other Qohathites who did not at last enjoy the high status of priests.

21. *Shechem*. Map K, 477. See NOTES on 17:2 and 7 (concerning the clans of Manasseh), and 20:7 (the asylum-town in the hill country of Ephraim).

the hill country of Ephraim. On the possible administrative gerrymandering of tribal areas, such as would in effect reassign Shechem to Ephraim, see fourth NOTE on 20:7.

Gezer. Map K, 477. Third NOTE on 10:33. This stronghold was at last turned over to Solomon with his marriage to Pharaoh's daughter (1 Kgs 9:16). Although it suffered heavily in the Shishak invasion, Gezer continued to be occupied in the period from the ninth to seventh century (Strata VII-V). *EAEHL* II (1970) 441-442.

22. †*Qibzaim*. It is otherwise unknown, but there is no solid ground for considering it a doublet (or rival tradition) for the next place named. It is possibly to be located at Tell el-Mazar in the mouth of the Wadi Far'ah where it empties into the Jordan Valley. Map K, 477.

Joqmeam. The town is also mentioned in 1 Kgs 4:12 and is not to be confused with *Joqneam* in Zebulun (v 34 and 19:11). Mazar proposed to explain the name as due to the assignment of Levites there who would trace their lineage to Jeqameam, fourth son of Hebron (1 Chr 23:19; 24:23). Mazar,

*VT*Sup 7 (1960) 198. This may well be true, but it is doubtful that the same place is here called Qibzaim.

Regarding location, both the Archaeological Survey of Israel (Chalcolithic, EB I, EB II, MB II, Israelite and later) and Peterson's survey (EB, Iron II and later) support a location at Tell esh-Sheikh Dhiab, c. 22 km north of Jericho at the foot of the Ephraim hills. Like its companion farther north, Tell el-Mazar (Qibzaim), it overlooks a major access from the Jordan Valley to the hill country.

Beth-horon. There were twin towns called Upper Beth-horon and Lower Beth-horon. Map K, 477. See NOTES on 16:3 and 18:13; and cf. 10:10.

(*four.* It is not surprising to find the later annotation out of phase with the original list after the loss of Joqmeam.

23-24. *from the tribe of Dan.* It was not until the days of David and Solomon that this area was actually administered as "Israelite." Administrative needs in relation to newly captured territory have been advanced as the prime motivation for the creation of this whole system in the tenth century. Mazar, *VT*Sup 7 (1960) 201. Though Mazar rightly recognizes the zeal and militancy of the Levites, the history of the system is more complex than he allows.

23. *Elteqe. Gibbethon.* Map K, 477. See 19:44 and NOTES.

24. *Aijalon.* Map K. See 19:42 and NOTES.

Gath-rimmon. See third NOTE on 19:45.

25. The two towns assigned in Western Manasseh remained Canaanite well into the post-Joshua period (Judg 1:27).

Taanach. Map K, 477. See 12:21 and NOTES. It is assigned to Western Manasseh in 17:11.

Ibleam. Map K, 477. Third NOTE on 17:11.

27-33. *the Bene Gershon.* This third segment of the list deals with the second major family of Levites and includes towns ranging much farther to the north.

27. The two towns named here were probably taken by Benhadad (1 Kgs 15:20) in the early ninth century as recognized by W. F. Albright, "The List of Levitic Cities," in *Louis Ginzberg Jubilee Volume* (1945) 57 nn. 19,20, indicating a rapid and sharp decline of Israelite power in Transjordan. That was the beginning of a tumultuous era there, with significant Israelite recovery in Transjordan coming at last in the eighth century.

Golan. See the asylum-town (20:8 and NOTES). This site has been out of reach in recent years because of proximity to international borders; and so it remains archaeologically uncertain.

Ashtaroth. This was the old Amorite city of King Og (12:4 and NOTES; compare 9:10 and 13:31).

28. *Qishion.* Map K, 477. See second NOTE on 19:20; this is the only accessible location in the entire list that has not yet yielded evidence of eighth-century occupation.

Daberath. Map K, 477. Third NOTE on 19:12.

29. *Jarmuth.* Elsewhere "Remeth." See first NOTE on 19:21. The name is related to Mount Yarmuta (probably in Lower Galilee) where various Habiru

groups settled according to the second stele of Seti I at Bethshean. Aharoni, *LOB*, 175.

En-gannim. Map K, 477. Second NOTE on 19:21.

30-31. *from the Asher tribe*. Here are four towns in the rich and most desirable Plain of Acco.

30. *Mishal*. Map K, 477. Second Note on 19:26.

Abdon. Map K. First NOTE on 19:28.

31. *Helqath*. Map K. Possibly Tel Qassis. The alternative site of Tel Regev (Tell el-Harbaj) is tentatively identified with Beth-dagon (19:27).

Rehob. Map K. Second NOTE on 19:28. This too continued to be Canaanite in the post-Joshua period (Judg 1:31).

32. *Naphtali*. Here the Gershonites had residential rights in only three towns, spread far apart.

Qedesh. Map K, 477. First NOTE on 19:37. See also 20:7.

Hammoth-dor. If it is "Hot Springs of Encircling," the name "perpetuates the custom of the sacred dance . . . in honor of the spirit who was invoked to keep up the fire and heat the waters." D. Winton Thomas, "The Meaning of the Name Hammath-Dor," *PEFQS* (1934) 147-148. It is thus to be equated with Naphtali's town Hammath in 19:35 and has nothing to do with either the coastal town of Dor (12:23; cf. 11:2) or the Esdraelon town (17:11).

Qartan. Khirbet el-Qureiyeh, said to be in the Lebanese-Upper Galilean hills, remains archaeologically unknown, the one prospective Levitical town site in western Palestine which could not be found by Peterson's team.

33. *Gershonites*. Note the gentilic formation, in contrast with use of "Bene" in v 27. A relatively high frequency of gentilic forms is characteristic of the material used by the later redactor (Dtr 2).

34-39. *the Bene Merari*. The third Levitical family is for some reason assigned to two widely separated areas: Zebulun (vv 34-35) and central Transjordan (vv 36-39).

34. *Zebulun*. See 19:10-16.

Joqneam. Formerly head of a small city-state (12:22). For its location in Zebulun's fief, see fourth NOTE on 19:11.

†*Qartah*. Without a parallel in 1 Chronicles 6 and not mentioned elsewhere, this is very possibly a partial dittography of Naphtali's "Qartan" (v 32), displacing a reference to "Tabor" in 1 Chr 6:62[77E]. Mount Tabor is clearly within the *gĕbûl* of Zebulun as that border is described in 19:12. But the town of "Tabor" cannot be equated with Chisloth-tabor (19:12), which is just as clearly within Issachar where it is also called Chesuloth (19:18). The town called "Tabor" remains to be found.

35. *Rimmon*. Map K, 477. See third NOTE on 19:13.

Nahalal. Map K. Second NOTE on 19:15. This is yet another town which held out against the movement (Judg 1:30).

36-39. *the region beyond the Jordan*. Here the Bene Merari were to be found in four towns from Reuben (vv 36-37) and four from Gad (vv 38-39). And thus the first region to be "conquered" by the Moses movement is the last to be assigned by lot to have a continuing Levitical presence.

36. *the Reuben tribe.* See 13:15-23.

Bezer. Map K, 477. See third NOTE on 20:8. This place seems to have been in ruins when Mesha king of Moab captured it in the ninth century.

Jahaz. Map K, 477. See first NOTE on 13:18. This too was taken from Israel by Mesha king of Moab, but its subsequent history is not clear.

37. *Qedemoth.* Map K, 477. Second NOTE on 13:18.

Mephaath. Map K. Third NOTE on 13:18.

38-39. *the Gad tribe.* See 13:24-28.

38. *Ramoth-in-Gilead.* Map K, 477. See fourth NOTE on 20:8, for its eighth-century revival.

Mahanaim. Map K. Fourth NOTE on 13:26.

39. *Heshbon.* Map K, 477. Fourth NOTE on 12:2.

Jazer. Location uncertain. See first NOTE on 13:25.

40. *these.* The definite article in Hebrew often has demonstrative force.

41. *the holding.* See above, second NOTE on v 12.

forty-eight. After the textual mishap in v 22, the annotator counted four towns per tribal unit except for Naphtali (three) and Judah/Simeon (nine).

42. This is a most emphatic summary, underscoring precisely the provision of supporting common-lands.

42a-c. Together with 19:50,51b, this makes a frame around the two institutional supplements: asylum-towns (chap. 20) and Levitical towns (21:1-42). With the distribution of fiefs for tribes complete and with the appointment of asylum-towns and the dispersion of the Levites, all is in readiness for Israel to live in the conquered land. How will it go? The one remaining statement in the chapter suggests that the answer to the question will create a need for comic relief.

42d. *the flint knives with which he circumcised.* This is Joshua's penultimate act in the finished "book of the Shechem covenant," as we may now surely subtitle the Book of Joshua (for he does not figure at all in the story of chap. 22), and it turns back upon Joshua's penultimate act in preparation for the western offensive (5:1-9). The one move is as unexpected, and therefore structurally significant, as the other. Together they signal an ancient dissatisfaction with the reliance upon external and ritual marks of religious identity that developed during the monarchy.

COMMENT

If we look for a single period when all the towns in the list were likely to have been occupied, the trail leads directly to the eighth century. The following chart is based on the results of Peterson's survey, updating earlier work with improved pottery chronology. Our only disagreements concern the dubious textual integrity of "Qartah" in Zebulun (v 34), the location of Helqath in Asher (v 31), and the locations of "Mahanaim" in Gad (v 38). Question marks in our chart indicate a lack of success by Peterson's team in finding confirmatory evidence for a previous dating of a site. In some cases the presence of a sizable modern village (Juttah, Daberath), or modern urban expansion (Ashan, Hebron), or nearby international borders (Golan, possibly Qartan) have either reduced the value of surface sherding or rendered it impossible for the time being. The occupational history of the towns in the tenth to eighth centuries, based on extensive surface surveys, especially the recent work of Peterson, and in light of numerous excavations, appears as follows.

			TENTH	NINTH	EIGHTH
JUDAH/SIMEON					
v 11	Hebron	(Jebel er-Rumeida)			x
v 13	Libnah	(Tell Bornat)		x	x
v 14	Jattir	(Khirbet Attir)			x
	Eshtemoa	(es-Semu‘)		?	?
v 15	Holon	(Khirbet Alin)	?	?	?
	Debir	(Tell Rabud)	x	x	x
v 16	Ashan	(Khirbet Asan)	inaccessible		
	Juttah	(Yatta)	unclarified see 15:55 fourth NOTE		
	Beth-shemesh	(‘Ain Shems)	x	x	x
BENJAMIN					
v 17	Gibeon	(el-Jib)		x	x
	Geba	(Jeba)			x
v 18	Anathoth	(Ras el-Kharrubeh)		x	x
	Almon	(Tell Almit)		x	x
EPHRAIM					
v 21	Shechem	(Tell Balatah)	x	x	x
	Gezer	(Tell Jezer)	x	x	x
v 22	Qibzaim	(Tell el-Mazar)		x	x
	Joqmeam	(Tell esh-Sheikh Dhiab)	x	x	x
	Beth-horon	(Beit ‘Ur)			
	Upper	(el-Foqa)	x	x	x
	Lower	(et-Taḥta)	x	x	x
DAN					
v 23	Elteqe	(Khirbet el-Muqenna‘)		x	x
	Gibbethon	(Tell Malat)		x	x
v 24	Aijalon	(Tell Qoqa + Yalo)	x	x	x
	Gath-rimmon				
		(Tell Abu Zeitun)	x	x	x
		(Tell Jerishe)		x	x
MANASSEH (WEST)					
v 25	Taanach	(Tell Ta‘annak)	x	x	x
	Ibleam	(Tell Bel‘ameh)	x	x	x

MANASSEH (EAST)		TENTH	NINTH	EIGHTH
v 27 Golan	(Sahem el-Jolan)	inaccessible		
Ashtaroth	(Tell Ashtarah)	x	x	x
ISSACHAR				
v 28 Qishion	(Tell el-Muqarqash)		x	
Daberath	(Deburiyeh)	Iron Age: unclarified		
v 29 Jarmuth	(Kokab el-Hawa')		x	x
En-gannim	(Khirbet Beit Jann)	x	x	x
ASHER				
v 30 Mishal	(Tell Kisan)		x	x
Abdon	(Tell Abdon)		x	x
v 31 Helqath	(Tell el-Qassis)	x	x	x
Rehob	(Tell el-Gharbi)	x	x	x
NAPHTALI				
v 32 Qedesh	(Tell Qades)			x
Hammoth-dor	(Tell Raqqat)			x
Qartan	(Khirbet el-Qureiyeh)		unclarified	
ZEBULUN				
v 34 Joqneam	(Tell Qeimun)		x	x
Qartah/Tabor	(?)			
v 35 Rimmon	(Rummaneh)	?	?	x
Nahalal	(Tell en-Nahl)	x	x	x
REUBEN				
v 36 Bezer	(Umm el-Amad)	x	x	x
Jahaz	(Khirbet el-Medeiyineh)	LB-Iron I: unclarified		
v 37 Qedemoth	(es-Saliyeh)	Iron Age: unclarified		
Mephaath	(Tell ej-Jawah)	x	x	x
GAD				
v 38 Ramoth-in-Gilead	(Tell er-Rumeit)	x	x	x
Mahanaim	(el-Gharbiyeh)	Iron Age: unclarified see 13:26 fourth NOTE		
v 39 Heshbon	(Tell Ḥesban)	x	x	x
Jazer	(Khirbet Jazzir)	Iron Age: unclarified		

From the archaeological evidence, which is considerable and impressive, we conclude that these particular forty-eight or forty-nine towns could not have been part of one system earlier than the eighth century B.C. The middle and late decades of the eighth century were precisely the sort of period in which such a system might flourish. It was an era which saw the long and brilliant reigns of Uzziah (c. 783-742) in the south and Jeroboam II (c. 786-746) in the north, rapidly eclipsed by the swift decline and fall of the northern kingdom, with severe vassalage imposed at the same time upon the south. The great eighth-century prophets who were active in the north and the south are increasingly recognized as having had close connections to the same Levitical circles from which comes the core of Deuteronomy (our Dtn). That work was originally the platform of a vigorously transmonarchical (not necessarily "antimonarchical") reform movement intellectually akin to northern prophecy as represented especially by Hosea.

A support system for the network of Levitical teachers of Torah which embraced both north and south and extended to both sides of the river in the eighth century B.C. is one which does not acknowledge the divisions and has not made peace with the redefinition of the Bene Israel in terms of the nation-state. The rationale is beyond doubt Mosaic in origin.

A clear precedent for the system used in Israel is in fact recognizable in Egypt's Late Bronze Age administration of domestic affairs. Certain "cities had been confiscated . . . turned into royal estates and dedicated by Pharaoh to the great gods of the Egyptians." Mazar, VTSup 7 (1960) 204-205. It is impossible, however, to argue for a Solomonic date for the creation of the system, although it is obvious that towns such as Gezer and the outlying towns in Dan could not have been part of the system any earlier than the tenth century. A uniformly monarchical-administrative approach to this institution is inadequate in that it fails to account for subsequent Levitical history, which was very different in the north and in the south. For the Egyptian parallel to be valid, we should insist that it was Yahweh as King of Israel who instituted the system, in imitation of Pharaoh his administrative counterpart. It does in fact appear that it was manipulation of an existing system by Solomon and the impoverishment of northern Levites by Jeroboam I that nourished Levitical discontent and generated a movement for reform. See above, fourth NOTE on 3:3.

How different had Levi's role been in the pre-monarchy heyday of its prestige and influence—handling the priestly lot, guarding the oracle, protecting the covenant, teaching tôrâ ("ethic") and mišpaṭ ("judgment"/"justice"). Deuteronomy 33:8-10 seems to voice a hope based on late eleventh-century reality as shown by Freedman, "Divine Names and Titles in Early Hebrew Poetry," in Mag Dei.

This Levi in turn was different from the one that is denounced and dismissed from the pre-Mosaic Israel, in tandem with Simeon, in the earlier Testament of Jacob (see above, first NOTE on v 1). In other words the oldest poetic reference is to the "patriarchal" or pre-Yahwist tribe of Levi, a significant portion of which found its way, after expulsion from the league, to Egypt where it later experienced religious conversion and was reconstituted at the core of the Yahwist movement. Apparently its institutional charisma from the days of the pre-Yahwist league left it predisposed toward the role of "palace guard" in the newborn Kingdom of Yahweh.

At the same time, the deeply rooted teaching function of the Levites demands recognition, in some such manner as proposed by Wright and more recently his student Merlin Rehm (see fourth NOTE on 3:3). And it has recently been suggested most cogently that it was the rural Levites as storyteller custodians of the tradition who created the distinctive old Israelite short-story form (used in purest state, for example, in the books of Judges and Ruth) and whose work fostered the survival of Yahwist ethic against the increasing paganization that came with kingship in Israel. See Campbell, *Ruth,* AB 7, 21-22.

The revolution led by Moses and Joshua was nearly five hundred years in the past when the two kingdoms created out of the Bene Israel experienced their revival and expansion under King Uzziah in the south and Jeroboam II in the north. As it turned out, the second quarter of the eighth century was only the lull before the storm, strictly comparable to the reign of Josiah a century later. It is precisely this mid-eighth-century era that is represented by the list of towns providing especially for Levites, surely in their capacity as teachers of torah, guidelines for right-living.

By no means all the Levites were thus employed, as is clear from such extra-biblical sources as the Arad ostraca, where person with Levitical names are involved in fiscal administration and accounting for stores of wine, flour, and oil on behalf of the "House of Yahweh" (a temple at either Arad itself or Jerusalem) toward the end of the period of the monarchy. Aharoni, "Hebrew Ostraca . . . ," *IEJ* 16 (1966) 1-7. Here there is considerable data that lends credibility to the report of King Jehoshaphat's reforms in Judah, a century earlier than our list (c. 873-849). A team of eight Levites and two priests was dispatched to "all the cities of Judah," with the purpose of teaching the people from the book of Yahweh's Torah (2 Chr 17:7-9), while in Jerusalem the king had Levites and priests announcing the decisions of Yahweh (by lot?) and adjudicating cases.

And yet Jerusalem is not included in the list of Levitical towns. Why not? In his unpublished dissertation John Peterson concluded that the Levitical cities were teaching centers of the Yahweh Covenant, where the Levites taught what was involved in covenantal living, so that there was a basis for understanding prophetic critique when it erupted. On this view it was the continuing Yahwist movement, and most decidedly not royal administrative fiat, that created the system of Levitical towns; it had no sponsorship other than the word of Yahweh.

Such a roster of towns would surely tend to fluctuate (consult any church executive with responsibility for targeting new church developments seeking to succeed withering old ones and to promote growth).

Jehoshaphat's teaching Levites were no doubt related to those who had fled from the north late in the tenth century, expelled by Jeroboam I but welcomed by the son of Solomon because, as the post-exilic historian put it, they "walked in the ways of David and Solomon" and regarded the Jerusalem throne as the legitimate one (2 Chr 11:13-17). In other words, there were in both of the divided kingdoms elements of two major Levitical factions, divided primarily over the legitimacy of the Jerusalem establishment.

If our list represents a distribution of major Levitical centers roughly a century after the reforms of Jehoshaphat, the assignments made for the Bene Aaron are extremely interesting. Although the list reflects the priority and southern predominance of the Bene Aaron, no special importance is attached to them. In fact the Bene Aaron appear to have no special relation to Jerusalem and they have no support towns at all in the heartland north of Hebron. The Bene Aaron are included here because the historical reality of the Levitical centers had been omitted from the first edition. Probably by the reign of Josiah it had been long since defunct, so that Dtr 1 saw no need to include such a list.

By the time of the final (post-Josianic) redactor, the list was more than a hundred years old; the redactor took it as recording the actual assignments made by Eleazar, Joshua, and the Bene Israel. In the view of the final redactor, the list of Levitical towns had high symbolic value. And as the following chapter makes clear, the point of view represented by the list is anything but utopian.

Now that the land has been fairly allotted, with institutions in place for eliminating private vengeance (chap. 20) and for the public teaching of ethic (chap. 21), how will the Bene Israel conduct themselves as citizens of the Yahweh kingdom?

With the record now filled out to the satisfaction of the final redactor, the transition is effected in a characteristic way, by adding another tragi-comic story (chap. 22); at the end of Judges there are two such (Judges 19-20, and 21). But first comes a summary emphasizing the quality of Yahweh's faithfulness to his promise and oath.

C. SUMMARY: THE GOOD WORD
(21:43-45)

21 ⁴³ Yahweh entrusted to Israel all the land which he had promised on oath to their ancestors to give. They took possession of it, and there they settled down. ⁴⁴ Yahweh brought about a cessation of hostilities toward them from every side, in strict conformity to the ancestral promise. And no one successfully withstood them—out of all their enemies! All their enemies Yahweh subjected to them. ⁴⁵ Not a word of all the Good Word which Yahweh had spoken to the house of Israel proved untrue. It all happened.

TEXTUAL NOTE

21 44. *in strict conformity*   Thus MT, where LXX and Syr show a loss of one word: *k[kl] 'šr*.

NOTES

21:43-45. This summary makes no reference, direct or otherwise, to the asylum-towns (chap. 20) or Levitical towns (21:1-42). It follows coherently the end of chap. 19, from which it has no doubt been detached in the final edition to make room for two key institutions.

43-44. *entrusted . . . to give. . . . subjected.* The verses display three uses of the verb *ntn*, with three distinct nuances, thus underscoring the free and gracious initiatives of Yahweh toward the house of Israel.

43. The first sentence of this summary forms the strongest possible *inclusio* with 1:6.

all the land. The later redactor was interested especially in calling attention, through materials such as chaps. 12-14, to the east-west axis of early Israel, which provides the alignment for the story which follows in chap. 22.

promised on oath. Used twice in quick succession, to underscore it. See third NOTE on 1:6.

to give. The dangling infinitive, although undesirable in English style, is good Hebrew usage. Here however it may be the result of seeing the promise of land for the fathers (1:6) finally made good in the generation of Joshua.

They took possession of it, and there they settled down. This full formula in Joshua first appears in the note about Dan's takeover at Laish (19:48).

took possession. The verb is *yrš* as in 1:11,15; 12:1; 18:3; 19:47; 23:5; 24:4,8. The negative formula occurs in 15:63 and 17:12; cf. Judg 1:27-33.

44. *brought about a cessation of hostilities toward them.* The phrase means literally "he gave rest for them," and here it turns back on the repeated use of the same verb in 1:13 and 15.

ancestral promise. Concerning the identity of the fathers in the Book of Joshua, see fifth NOTE on 1:6.

And no one successfully withstood. This recalls directly the strong assurance given by Yahweh at the outset in 1:5.

all their enemies! The repetition yields a forceful chiastic pattern.

subjected to them. Literally, "gave into their hand." Concerning this idiom, see third NOTE on 6:2, where Yahweh thus decrees the first of the Cisjordan victories.

45. *the Good Word.* Hebrew *had-dābār haṭ-ṭôb* sums up the promise made by Yahweh in 1:1-9 and fulfilled by Yahweh in the body of the book. In these verses there is no mention of Joshua or Eleazar. Yahweh and his promise-keeping share the stage with no one else.

had spoken. This is the third occurrence, in quick succession, of the *dbr* root, producing a most emphatic wrap-up to the motif of divine initiative in arranging for Israel's life in the land.

house of Israel. Used only here in the Book of Joshua, this metaphor gives climactic expression to the hard-won unity that was Yahweh's gift in the reformation of Israel and which is promptly threatened with collapse in the very next scene.

proved untrue. Literally, "fell."

COMMENT

It was a major theme of the Deuteronomic Historical Work (Dtr in both the early and late editions) that the promises to the fathers had been publicly fulfilled with the careers of Moses in Transjordan and Joshua in Cisjordan. We cannot stress too emphatically this theme of amazing grace which Wright in his Introduction traces throughout the transformations of the Divine Warrior motif.

In the finished edition of the book, crafted at the brink of Babylonian domination, this emphasis upon the faithfulness of Yahweh casts into high relief the comic squabbling of his people over an internal (or was it external?) boundary, which comes next.

V. HOW TO AVOID CIVIL WAR
(22:1-34)

Concluding Exhortation to the Transjordan Tribes

22 ¹ Then Joshua summoned the Reubenites, the Gadites, and the Manasseh half-tribe. ² He said to them:

"You have attended to everything that Moses as Servant of Yahweh commanded you, and you have obeyed my voice in everything that I have commanded you. ³ You have not deserted your brothers in all this time. Up to this day you have scrupulously kept the commandment of Yahweh your God. ⁴ But now Yahweh your God has given rest to your brothers, as he promised them. Turn back now and go to your tents, to the land of your own possession which Moses as Servant of Yahweh assigned to you beyond the Jordan. ⁵ Just be absolutely sure to implement the Commandment and the Treaty-Teaching which Moses as Servant of Yahweh enjoined upon you: loving Yahweh your God, walking in all his ways, keeping his stipulations, clinging to him, and serving him with all your heart and your very being."

Blessing and Dismissal of the Transjordan Tribes

⁶ Joshua blessed them and sent them on their way. They went to their tents. ⁷ To the one half of the Manasseh tribe Moses had made the assignment: in Bashan. And to the other half Joshua had made the assignment, together with their brothers: in the region beyond the Jordan, to the west. Moreover, Joshua sent them to their tents with his blessing. ⁸ He said to them, "With great wealth, return to your tents—and with an abundance of cattle, with silver and gold, with

bronze, with iron, and with a plenitude of clothing. Share the plunder of your enemies with your kinfolk."

Alternative Altar or Visual Aid?

9 The Bene Reuben, the Bene Gad and the Manasseh half-tribe turned back and made their departure from the Bene Israel, from Shiloh which is in the land of Canaan, to go to the land of their own possession, the land of Gilead, which they held by Yahweh's decision made through Moses. 10 They entered the Jordan districts (which are in the land of Canaan?). And there the Bene Reuben, the Bene Gad and the Manasseh half-tribe built an altar beside the Jordan, a conspicuously large altar! 11 And the Bene Israel heard of it:

"Attention! The Bene Reuben and the Bene Gad and the Manasseh half-tribe have built an altar out in front of the land of Canaan, near the Jordan districts, near the region on the other side of the Bene Israel!"

12 When the Bene Israel heard, the entire congregation of the Bene Israel assembled at Shiloh to go to war against them. 13 To the Bene Reuben and the Bene Gad and the Manasseh half-tribe (that is, to the land of Gilead) the Bene Israel sent Phinehas ben Eleazar the Priest. 14 With him were ten chiefs, each one a chief of an ancestral house representing all the tribes of Israel. Each was head of the house of their fathers. They were from the village-units of Israel.

15 They went to the Bene Reuben and the Bene Gad and the Manasseh half-tribe in the land of Gilead and spoke to them as follows:

16 "Thus says the entire congregation of Yahweh: What means this treachery which you have committed against the God of Israel, turning away from Yahweh at this time, by building for yourselves an altar so as to rebel at this time against Yahweh? 17 Was the crime of Peor too small a thing for us, from which we have not cleansed ourselves to this day? There came the plague on the congregation of Yahweh! 18 But you, you have in this day turned away from Yahweh. If you rebel at this time against Yahweh, then in the future he will be enraged against the entire congregation of Israel.

19 "However, if the land you have seized is unclean, get yourselves over to the land that Yahweh has seized, where Yahweh's Tent is pitched, and take a possession in our midst. But do not rebel against Yahweh. Do not rebel against us, by building for yourselves an altar apart from the altar of Yahweh our God. 20 Did not Achan ben Zerah commit a treacherous violation of the ban? And there was wrath upon the entire congregation, although he was only one man! Did he not perish for his iniquity?"

21 The Bene Reuben and the Bene Gad and the Manasseh half-tribe responded and said to the heads of the village-units in Israel:

22 "God of gods is Yahweh
God of gods is Yahweh
Let him make known
Let Israel learn:
Whether by rebellion
Or by treachery against Yahweh.

"Do not save us today 23 for building ourselves an altar to turn away from Yahweh. If it was in order to present there burnt offerings or cereal offerings, or to perform there sacrificial peace offerings, let Yahweh himself investigate!

24 "Yes, we did this fearfully, telling ourselves that in the future your children would say to our children, 'What is the bond between you and Yahweh the God of Israel? 25 Yahweh has established a border between us, namely the Jordan. You have no share in Yahweh!' Your children might cause our children to stop fearing Yahweh!

26 "So we said, 'Let's act on our own in building this altar—not for burnt offerings or for sacrifice.'

27 "Instead it is a witness between us and you, and between our descendants after us, to perform the service of Yahweh in his presence with our burnt offerings and our sacrifices and our peace offerings.

"And so your children would not be able to say to our children sometime in the future, 'You have no share in Yahweh.' 28 We said, 'Whenever they speak to us or to our descendants in the future, we will say: Look at the replica of Yahweh's altar which our fathers made. It is not for burnt offering nor for sacrifice. Instead it is a witness between us and you.'

29 "But we are damned if it was to rebel against Yahweh or to

turn away from Yahweh at this time, by building an altar for burnt offering or cereal offering or sacrifice, apart from the altar of Yahweh our God which is front of his Tent!"

30 Phinehas the Priest and all the chiefs of the congregation, the heads of the village-units who accompanied him, heard what the Bene Reuben and the Bene Gad and the Bene Manasseh had to say. In their view it was satisfactory. 31 Said the Priest Phinehas ben Eleazar to the Bene Reuben and the Bene Gad and the Bene Manasseh:

"Today we have recognized that Yahweh is in our midst. Because you have not committed this treachery against Yahweh, you have rescued the Bene Israel from Yahweh's hand."

32 The Priest Phinehas ben Eleazar returned with the chiefs, from the Bene Reuben and the Bene Gad and from the Manasseh half-tribe (from the land of Gilead), to the land of Canaan, to the Bene Israel. They reported the word. 33 And the word was satisfactory in the view of the Bene Israel. The Bene Israel blessed God and no longer spoke of going to war against them to despoil the land where lived the Bene Reuben and the Bene Gad and the Manasseh half-tribe.

34 The Bene Reuben and the Bene Gad and the Manasseh half-tribe gave a name to the altar:

"There is a witness between us
Yahweh is truly God!"

TEXTUAL NOTES

22 1. *Reubenites, the Gadites*   LXX reflects "Bene Reuben and Bene Gad."
   half-tribe   The words *mṭh* (MT) and *šbṭ* (many MSS and often below) are interchangeable. Similarly *mnšh* (MT) and *hmnšh* (a great many MSS and often below) are interchangeable.
   2. *You have attended to*   This follows MT, where the idiom is *šmr 't*. LXX *šm' 't* has partially assimilated to the verb in 2b where the correct idiom for "obey" is *šm' b*.
   3. *in all this time*   Literally, "this many days." It is the end of the first statement in a chiastic pair, as the omission of the conjunction (*w*)*šmrtm* in LXX makes clear.
   you have scrupulously kept   This follows LXX in omitting MT's initial *w* and thereafter MT, where LXX and Syriac show that a haplography has wrecked a construct chain: *šmrtm '[t mšmr]t mṣwt.*

4. *your*   Two first occurrences here and first in v 5. LXX "our" is a variant stemming from oral transmission of material or from the process of scribal dictation.

tents   LXX *oikous* has the sense of "dwellings," an adequate rendering of Hebrew *'hl*.

to   LXX reads "and to."

as Servant of Yahweh   LXX reflects a haplography: *mš[h 'bd yhw]h*.

5. *you*   LXX "us."

walking in all his ways   Syriac reflects a haplography here: *wl[lkt bkl drkyw wl]šmr*.

clinging to him   The OG (*kai proskeisthai*) and Theodotion (*kai kollasthai*) represent the same Hebrew text (*wldbqh*). Greenspoon, STBJ, 123-124.

7. *in the region beyond the Jordan*   This is the *kethib m'br hyrdn*, while the *qere* and the versions read the synonymous preposition *b'br hyrdn*. The expression normally refers to the territory east of the Jordan. LXX^A+MSS omit, but it is the more difficult reading and is thus retained.

8. *He said to them*   This is lacking in LXX, which also adjusts the verbs and pronouns to the third person and lacks the first word in v 9. In other words there is no command by Joshua in the Greek version, simply a declarative sentence. It may very well reflect a more original form of the story. Greenspoon, STBJ, 181. Possibly there existed a fuller text which had both MT and LXX, in that order, as command and fulfillment.

return   Instead of imperative, OG read the same consonantal text (in the pre-exilic spelling, without internal vowel letters) as indicative.

your   LXX reads "their" throughout the verse.

with bronze   Missing by haplography in LXX: *wbzhb wb[nhšt wb]brzl*.

with bronze, with iron   Missing by haplography in LXX^A+MSS: *wb[nhšt wbbrzl wb]šlmwt*.

9. *Manasseh*   LXX reads "Bene Manasseh."

turned back   Lacking in LXX, where the action has already taken place in v 8.

from   Second instance. Hebrew *mn*. LXX reflects *b*, which would give the same sense.

10. *districts*   This is Hebrew *glylwt*, for which LXX^B and Syriac read the place name "Gilgal."

(which are in the land of Canaan?)   Contrary to the recommendation of *BH³*, there is no evidence that this should be omitted.

altar   This is another example of different renderings in OG (*bōmon*) and Theodotion (*thysiastērion*) for the same Hebrew text (*mzbḥ*). Greenspoon, STBJ, 125.

11. *out in front*   Hebrew *'l mwl* is a somewhat curious expression, from which LXX removes all ambiguity by reading "outside the territory" (*mgbwl*). It appears, however, that lack of clarity belongs to the structural integrity of this story.

districts   For Hebrew *glylwt*, LXX this time reads "Gilead."

12. *When the Bene Israel heard*   Missing in LXX^B, Syriac, Vulgate, presumably due to haplography: *wy[šm'w bny yśr'l wy]qhlw*.

13. *the Manasseh half-tribe*   LXX has the same addition as in NOTE 9

above, but at the wrong point: *bny ḥṣy šbṭ mnšh,* "sons of the Manasseh half-tribe."

Eleazar   LXX continues with "ben Aaron," which looks like an addition (but a correct one), and makes Eleazar an *archieros,* "high priest," a correct rendering of *hkhn.*

14. *of an ancestral house* and *of the house of their fathers*   The two references to patriarchal organization in this verse (*lbyt 'b* and *byt 'bwtm*) are omitted in Syriac and should perhaps be deleted, as recommended in *BHS.*

15. *Bene Reuben and the Bene Gad*   LXX reverses the order of these two tribal names.

16. *Yahweh*   First occurrence. Thus MT and major LXX recensions. There is some evidence in minor manuscripts and versions for "Israel" or "Bene Israel."

at this time   The phrase was removed by haplography in the *Vorlage* of LXX and Syriac: *lmrdk[m hyw]m.*

17. *Was . . . for us*   Hebrew *hm'ṭ lnw 't 'wn p'wr,* with anomalous use of the object marker *'t* in this non-verbal construction. Perhaps the original narrative had a form of *ṭm',* "to be or become unclean."

18. *But you, you have in this day turned away from Yahweh*   This statement in its entirety was dropped from the Syriac or its *Vorlage: b'dt y[hwh . . . m'ḥry y]hwh.*

If   This follows LXX, reading the particle *'m* where MT *'tm,* "you," is perhaps the remnant of *'t[m ']m.*

he will be enraged   Hebrew *yqṣp.* This ending to the verse is emphatic. LXX has assimilated to the form of idiom used in v 20, *hyh qṣp.*

19. *unclean*   Hebrew *ṭm'h.* LXX manuscripts uniformly reflect *m'ṭ,* "small." In LXX it is a disagreement over the adequacy of allotments; in MT it is a question concerning the enormity of an alleged offense.

midst   LXX *Vorlage* seems to insert here *w'l thyw mrd b'lhym,* "But do not be in rebellion against God," a parallel or variant for what follows.

Do not   Reading *'al* with numerous manuscripts against the vocalization *'el* given in L. The latter perhaps shows the influence of *'lhym* in the longer LXX reading.

against us   Hebrew *'tnw* has no reflex in LXX. Targum seems to reflect *wbnw,* which may have originated in anticipation of *bbntkm* three words later in MT.

20. *Did he not perish for his iniquity?*   The unmarked interrogative form can only be recognized from context. LXX^A did so recognize it; LXX^B did not.

21. *to*   This reading in a great many manuscripts (*wydbr 'l*) is superior to MT (*wydbr 't*) which is probably the result of contamination from the idiom used above in v 15.

22. *Whether by rebellion/Or by treachery*   MT *'m bmrd w'm bm'l.* LXX obscures the poetic form, reading *'m bmrd m'lnw,* "If in rebellion we have acted treacherously."

Do not save us   LXX reflects a one-letter difference: "Let him not save us."

23. *for building*   See first NOTE on v 23.

ourselves   LXX reads "themselves."

Yahweh   LXX adds "our God."

24. *fearfully*   This is Hebrew *md'gh*. The translation omits the following *mid-dābār* (with Syriac), which is either the remnant of a variant or rationalization.

25. *us*   This follows LXX and Syriac where MT specifies in apposition "Bene Reuben and Bene Gad." The addition was no doubt triggered by the preceding consonant cluster of *bynnw wbynykm*, "between us and you."

26. *own*   The Hebrew is awkward and evidence of the versions (Syr[A], Targ[L]) suggests that something has dropped out.

this   Restored from LXX.

28. *we*   Old Greek "they."

29. *we*   MT appears to be conflate: *lnw mmnw*. Syriac omits the latter.

Yahweh or to turn away from Yahweh   LXX reads "at this time" after the first occurrence of the divine name and omits it after the second occurrence.

altar   LXX adds *lnw*, "for ourselves."

cereal offering or sacrifice   MT *mnḥh* and *zbḥ* respectively. LXX reads *thusiais salamein* (*Vorlage* uncertain) and *thusia tou sōtēriou* (=Hebrew *šelem*, "peace offering").

our God   Lost by haplography in LXX[B]: '[*lhynw* ']*šr*.

30. *all*   Missing in MT. This follows LXX which thereafter, however, shows a complex chain of development:

MT	w[ ]	nśy'y	h'dh		wr'šy 'lpy	yśr'l	'šr 'tw
LXX[A]	wkl	nśy'y	'dh yśr'l wr'šy 'lpym			[ ]	'šr 'tw
LXX[B]	wkl	nśy'y (?)'dh [				] yśr'l	'šr 'tw

It appears that in LXX[A] *yśr'l* was entered at the wrong place creating a situation ripe for haplography in a "corrected" text which must be posited to understand the omission in LXX[B].

Bene Manasseh   This is the first occurrence in the chapter. Major versions uniformly reflect the familiar expression "Manasseh half-tribe."

31. *ben Eleazar*   Lacking in LXX, but MT regularly includes this datum.

Bene   Third instance. LXX reads the formula "one half of."

32. *the Manasseh half-tribe*   Also in vv 33 and 34. Restored from LXX.

33. *And the word was satisfactory in the view of the Bene Israel*   Thus MT. LXX omits *hdbr*, "the word," which reappears in part as a verb, "he (Eleazar?) spoke," in a new clause:

MT	wyyṭb hdbr	b'yny bny	yśr'l	
LXX	wyyṭb	b'yny bny	yśr'l wdbr 'l bny yśr'l	

34. *gave* and *us* and *God!*   In OG it is Joshua who gives the name, which is appropriately formulated in the third person:

There is a witness in their midst,
Yahweh is truly their God!

NOTES

22:1-34. The chapter was put together in three segments. Verses 1-5 are Joshua's concluding exhortation to the Transjordan tribes just prior to their dismissal and departure to rejoin their families and settle down as Yahweh's tenants in Transjordan. As such, these verses form a concluding framework piece, balancing the introduction to the Transjordan tribes in 1:12-18, which we have analyzed above as contribution of the later redactor (Dtr 2). Certain contrasts in vocabulary and style set this final address to the Transjordan tribes apart from the old story of the altar at the Jordan (vv 9-34), for which these verses now stand as the dialectical preparation. The intervening vv 6-8 are the redactional transition made, presumably, by Dtr 2.

1-5. This is one of a number of speeches "in pure Deuteronomistic style patterned after Deuteronomy" which together comprise the major framework for the historical work. Cross, *CMHE*, 274. Cross cites Josh 1:11-15 and chap. 23, Samuel's address in 1 Sam 12:1-24, the oracle of Nathan and David's prayer in 2 Sam 7:1-29, and Solomon's prayer in 1 Kgs 8:12-51. The major distinctive feature of this speech is that in it Joshua speaks to a particular segment of the organization, not to all Israel as in the next chapter.

1. *Then Joshua summoned.* Hebrew *'āz yiqrā' yĕhôšûa'*. An expansive opening to a climactic unit. Elsewhere in the Book of Joshua the pattern *'az*+imperfect introducing a unit occurs only at 8:30, the beginning of the brief notice about the great Shechem Valley ceremony (also Dtr 2; see NOTES and COMMENT on 8:30-35).

Reubenites. Gadites. The use of gentilic forms at the outset suggests the hand of the later redactor, whose contributions frequently show this preference. The use of gentilic formations here contrasts startlingly with the *bny* forms used in MT in the old story which begins in v 9.

2-5. There is a rhetorical grandeur to Joshua's speech.

2. *Moses as Servant of Yahweh.* Repeated in vv 4 and 5, use of this name and title forms an inclusion with 1:1 (where the title is first applied to Moses), and 1:2,7 (where Yahweh twice refers to Moses as "my Servant").

commanded. commanded. The repetitive use harks back to the opening verses of the book. See fifth NOTE on 1:7.

3. *brothers.* In current idiom these are "soul brothers," many of whom will, of course, be kinsmen.

you have scrupulously kept. The narrator uses a cognate accusative, *wšmrtm 't mšmrt.* Literally, "you have guarded the guardianship." The activity called *mišmeret* was originally "guard duty" in the era of the Ark and Tabernacle, to protect and defend the portable palace and throne of the invisible but approachable King. Is this speech rooted ultimately in a charge to Levites who were being assigned work in the Transjordan territories?

4. *But now.   now.* The syntax is disjunctive.

has given rest to. That is, has given a solid base to, has established. See 1:13,15; 21:44 and NOTES.

promised. For this sense of the root *dbr*, see fourth NOTE on 13:14.

to your tents. The preposition is *l*, as in Judg 19:9, another sign of rhetorical relationship between these stories. Here the reference to tents is repeated in vv 6 and 7. The same expression used as exclamation, "To your tents!" in 1 Kgs 12:16, means that the tribal assembly is adjourned and the northerners are separating themselves from further alliance with Judah. Here, however, the crisis develops on the east-west axis.

your own possession. The verbal root is *'ḥz*, "to seize, take hold." It will be repeated in vv 9 (twice) and 19 (thrice).

5. The rhetorical structure of this one long verse establishes it as the key to the entire chapter. The verse begins with a reverse expanded synecdoche. The Commandment is the synecdoche proper (part of Torah used for the whole), and then the synecdoche proper is followed by the expansion of it, the Torah. Expanded synecdoches usually have the order whole+part. O'Connor, private communication. Here the Commandment and the Treaty-Teaching encompass all that is necessary for right living and abundant living.

the Commandment. The singular noun *miṣwâ* can stand as surrogate word for the entire covenant relationship in Dtn/Dtr, as shown by Kamol Aryaprateep, "Studies in the Semantics of the Covenant Relationship in Deuteronomic Teaching," 1974. This singular "Commandment" is elsewhere in scripture called a *bĕrît*, "covenant."

the Treaty-Teaching. Hebrew *tôrâ*. In conjunction with the "Commandment" this must be the summary word for instruction in right living which was the special responsibility of Levites down the years. The indispensable significance of the covenant and the teaching derived from it is next displayed in a chiasm of action words, with loving/walking and clinging/serving separated in the middle by the plural *miṣwôt*, "stipulations," which is governed by a form of *šmr*, the verb used in v 3.

loving Yahweh your God. See the farewell address to all Israel, 23:11. The referent is Exod 20:6=Deut 5:10, a prime Deuteronomic concern (Deut 6:5; 10:12; 11:1,13,22; 13:4; 19:9; 30:6,16,20). The love of God in the Old Testament has its primary definition in terms of the benevolent and therefore trustworthy Suzerain. William L. Moran, "The Ancient Near Eastern Background of the Love of God in Deuteronomy," *CBQ* 25 (1963) 77-87. Those who celebrate Yahweh's victory in the ancient Song of Deborah and Baraq are, in its climactic and concluding verse, precisely and literally "his lovers." (Judg 5:31, AB 6A, 105.) In that situation they had shown the love of Yahweh by performing faithfully in the struggle. It was the struggle to dismantle the structures of oppression and put in their place the operation of law which itself would stand under divine judgment.

walking in all his ways. See Deut 5:33; 8:6; 10:12; 11:22; 19:9; 26:17; 30:16.

keeping his stipulations. Hebrew *miṣwôt*, literally, "commandments." This concern reverberates through some thirty-seven occurrences, in one form or another, in Deuteronomy alone. The commandments are the guidelines for the two forms of action just mentioned and two more now to be specified.

clinging to him. See also 23:8,12. It is another Dtn/Dtr favorite, as seen in Deut 4:4; 10:20; 11:22; 13:5; 28:21; 30:20. This is older English "cleaving" (Hebrew *dbq* as used of the man and the woman in Gen 2:24, another distinctly covenantal context).

serving him. See also 24:14. This is a prime Dtn/Dtr objective. Deut 6:13; 10:12,20; 11:13,20; 13:5; 1 Sam 12:14,20,24. Weinfeld, *Deuteronomy and the Deuteronomic School,* 332.

with all your heart and your very being. See also 23:14. Deut 4:29; 6:5; 10:12; 11:13; 13:4; 26:16; 30:2,6,10; 1 Kgs 2:4; 8:48; 2 Kgs 23:3,25. For Dtn/Dtr the covenant is like doing the Hokey-Pokey: sooner or later "you put your whole self in."

6-8. These verses form the transition, from the Deuteronomic exhortation addressed to the Transjordan tribes into the old story of the altar at the Jordan. They make the point that Yahweh did not restrict his providence to teaching theology and ethics. Rather, the Transjordan militiamen could return from the Cisjordan warfare sufficiently enriched to be able to share the booty with relatives left behind. It would make for a splendid homecoming.

6. *to their tents.* Here and in v 8 the preposition is *'l.*

7. *had made the assignment.* Literally, "gave," Hebrew *ntn* with no object expressed. The same usage is found in 13:15, another Dtr 2 text. In other words, Dtr 2 emphasizes not the acquisition of land but the activity of the leaders, Moses and Joshua.

in the region beyond the Jordan, to the west. Juxtaposition of these two phrases introduces the ambiguity which is at the heart of the story to follow.

8. *an abundance of. a plenitude of.* Hebrew *rb m'd . . . hrbh m'd.* These related expressions are used to form an envelope construction: an abundance of cattle and a plenitude of clothing frame four kinds of metal assets.

Share. In the unpointed text the same letters (*ḥlqw*) could be taken as perfect tense, "they shared" (LXX). In this chapter the Greek text shows a time sequence that has been skewed by the unrecognized comic vision in MT. The story deals with matters that are far more profound when they are taken hilariously. With the peace secured and the plunder in hand, what could possibly go wrong?

your kinfolk." Hebrew *'ḥykm* sounds like a broader category than just the wives and children of 1:14. The old story used by Dtr 2 was not the redactor's own creation.

9-34. Scholars are nearly unanimous: this "warning against illegitimate forms of cult and cultic sites constitutes a concluding admonition characteristic of P." Georg Fohrer, *Introduction to the Old Testament,* 204. But here the total configuration is obviously not characteristic of P. It is, rather, a caricature of some major priestly preoccupations, such as genealogy and tribal identity. Specification of the two and a half tribes in Transjordan occurs eleven times in vv 9-34!

9-11. The unilateral action by the Transjordan tribes in building a Jordan Valley sanctuary is taken as posing a problem of "all Israel" proportions which will develop to the very brink of civil war.

9. *Bene Reuben. Bene Gad.* Compare the use of gentilic forms ("Reuben-ites," "Gadites") in v 1. This is clear indication that we have suddenly moved onto literary terrain that is distinct from vv 1-8.

Shiloh. This has been the assumed setting for everything since 18:1 (see second NOTE there).

which is in the land of Canaan. A distinctive way of locating the venerable place of the Tent and, presumably, the Ark of the Covenant. A variation of the formula occurs in 21:2, "Shiloh in the land of Canaan." The formula in its full form is found elsewhere only in Judg 21:12, a story in which Dtr 2 provides comic resolution to the tragic aftermath of all-out civil war (*Judges,* AB 6A, 289-294).

Gilead. Again in vv 13,15, and 32, it is mentioned with a frequency which recalls the five rapid-fire occurrences of "Gilead" in the story of an inheritance for the daughters of Zelophehad (17:1-6).

10. *Jordan districts.* The precise referent is unclear, and probably intended to be so.

(*which are in the land of Canaan?*) This is generally read as indicative. But in view of the outright contradiction with the following verses which place the altar somewhere on the east bank, this looks like a marginal query.

Bene Reuben. Bene Gad. built. The Hebrew is highly alliterative: *wybnw bny r'wbn wbny gd.*

an altar beside the Jordan. It is not easy to understand how the twelve stones "in the middle of the Jordan" (4:9) might be this "altar" as suggested by Joanne N. M. Wijngaards, "The Dramatization of Salvific History in the Deuteronomic Schools," *Oudtestamentische Studien* 16 (1969). The cultic disunity represented here, with the river as divider, is inversely related to the picture of cultic unity at the dividing of the river in chaps. 3-4. Indeed, since the old Dtr 2 material seems to have been cultivated and treasured in the circles of northern Levites, we may wonder if the altar in question was not to be found at Shittim (2:1 and NOTES). For the late redactional use of the story it is important that the precise location of the site that nearly caused civil war had long since been forgotten. Compare in this respect the way the elders of the congregation struggle to recall the exact location of Shiloh in the companion piece (Judg 21:19).

conspicuously large. Literally, "large for seeing." It could not be overlooked or easily forgotten, an ironic touch, in view of the ambiguity regarding the location.

We may suspect that the institution of a dominant league sanctuary is here in view. Since it was the place of the tribal muster, a "central sanctuary" for the east bank situated so far off-center as to be near the border, perhaps even in violation of the border, was taken to be a serious threat to west-bank league security. Historical parallels for prestigious and economically powerful off-center sanctuaries abound. Most interesting for its Old Testament counterparts (e.g. especially Dan and Bethel in the northern kingdom) is the border-sanctuary at Anthela in northern Greece sharing the spotlight with Delphi in the old Thessalian League. That league was the Iron Age predecessor to the Great Amphictyony centering in Delphi and a most instructive parallel to the early

Yahwist alliance known as the Bene Israel (see our discussion in *Judges*, AB 6A, 18-23).

11. *the Bene Israel.* Membership is suddenly, without any explanation, restricted to the west-bank tribes. In the same manner, the "sons of Israel" in Judges 20 are all those who comprise the militia arrayed against one of the constituent tribes. The two stories swarm with incongruities which suggest that the purpose is to tell the painful truth in an entertaining way and thus to be edifying.

out in front. The reference could be to any point in the Jordan Valley, on either side of the river. Each succeeding phrase, ostensibly written to further pinpoint the area, only sustains the obscurity of the location.

the other side of the Bene Israel! Use of the Hebrew construct chain here yields the crowning ambiguity. Is it "the other side" that is outside the area of Israel? Or is it "the other side" which is in fact the area occupied by the Bene Israel in this story?

the Bene Israel! Nine occurrences of this label, crammed into the compact framework for a pair of lengthy speeches, contribute to the sense of disproportion and incongruity in the chapter. The question posed concerns the true identity of Israel, the congregation.

12. *the Bene Israel heard.* The verse presupposes the summons to the militia by an agency unspecified. Cf. the action of the anonymous Levite at the outset of the later full-scale civil war (Judg 19:29-30).

the entire congregation of the Bene Israel assembled. The wording is almost identical to that of 18:1 but the situation is inverted. There it was for the purpose of peacefully taking fiefs in Yahweh's land. Here it is for the purpose of civil war (as in Judg 20:1 where the same vocabulary is used).

congregation. This is a key word in Dtr 2, occurring five times in this story (vv 12,16,18,20,30), five times in the solution to the problem posed by the Gibeonite hoax (9:18 [*bis*],19,21,27), and twice in relation to the asylum-towns (20:6,9)—twelve occurrences in all and all twelve contributions by Dtr 2. This leaves only 18:1, which probably reflects the late retouch too.

to go to war. This decision, which ignores the fact that Yahweh is Commander in Chief, would appear to be somewhat premature. But it corresponds very well to the presumptuous action of the militia against Benjamin in Judges 20 where the organizing key to the story seems to be: fight first and inquire later. In this case, however, violence was avoided by the choice of the right man to head the delegation bearing the declaration of war.

13. *Phinehas ben Eleazar.* See also Num 25:6-18, where he wins a "perpetual priesthood" (*khnt 'wlm*) by virtue of his decisive action in the crisis concerning the god of Pe'or. The name Phinehas is Egyptian and means "the Nubian." This one should not be confused with the son of Eli (whose brother Hophni also has an Egyptian name) in 1 Sam 1:3; 2:34; 4:4,11,17. This is instead a predecessor of the ranking priest at Bethel whom the Bene Israel will tardily consult in the warfare against Benjamin (Judg 20:27-29) to receive a reliable oracle in that account.

Eleazar. See third NOTE on 14:1.

the Priest. Obviously a chief priest is intended by the syntax. And a most uncommon one, for he will function as the bearer of indictment by the Bene Israel, much as the prophet in later Israel and Judah is the bearer of indictment by Yahweh for breach of covenant, the dominant form of classical prophecy in the Old Testament which was in effect a declaration of war. The name and title of Phinehas will occur twice again, in rapid succession (vv 30,32). In other words, we are to observe that, when the congregation assembled at the Mushite sanctuary (Shiloh), they elected as the negotiator the chief Aaronite priest of Bethel the non-Mushite sanctuary (Phinehas ben Eleazar) who would be the one to salvage the larger league! The other persons in the delegation are significant as well.

14. *chiefs.* Hebrew *nĕśî'îm.* It is a key word in this story (again in vv 30,32), as in other Dtr 2 contexts. See for example the solution to the problem posed by the Gibeonite hoax (9:15b-27) where the word occurs six times. See also their role in 17:4 where with Eleazar the Priest and Joshua they hear the petition of Zelophehad's daughters and produce a solution in the form of an exception to the rule.

each one a chief of an ancestral house. Syntactically compare Num 1:4, "each man is head of his ancestral family." Francis I. Andersen, *The Hebrew Verbless Clause in the Pentateuch,* ⁂164.

ancestral house. Hebrew *bêt 'āb,* literally, "house(hold) of a father." The unit is "based on patriarchal rule, all the offspring—including the adults—being subject to the father's authority, and all together forming a compact social unit. Upon his death, the 'father's house' disintegrates. By contrast, the 'family' . . . is a permanent group persisting down the generations." J. Liver, "The Israelite Tribes," in *WHJP* II (1971) 184.

the house of their fathers. Hebrew *bêt 'ăbôtām.* The phrase is as inelegant in Hebrew as it is in English.

village-units of Israel. Hebrew *'lpy yśr'l.* These are the locally functional units in Israel. At the time of the muster lists in Numbers 1 and 26, each *'elep* was responsible for sending anywhere from five to fourteen militiamen. Mendenhall, *JBL* 77 (1958) 52-66. The exact figure would depend upon quotas established in the council of the chiefs.

16-20. In these verses Phinehas functions in a role analogous to the Judges in the immediately following era (compare especially Jephthah's negotiations with the king of the Ammonites in Judg 11:12-28) and especially the prophet in the era of the monarchy. The prophet was ambassador, representative of the court of Yahweh, delivering the communique which brings the Sovereign's indictment for breach of treaty. In the final version of the Jordan Altar story, it is the Aaronite priest of northern-kingdom fame who goes into the breach to confront the rebellious ones and bring about a peaceful settlement.

16. *Thus says.* The plural counterpart of the prophet's *kô 'āmar,* the messenger formula signaling the self-understanding of the speaker as diplomatic representative of the very highest authority.

the entire congregation of Yahweh. In this case, not quite the highest authority.

treachery which you have committed. MT here uses the verb *m'l* and its cognate noun, as in the Achan story (7:1) which incident is cited using the same construction again in v 20. The noun also occurs in vv 22 and 31.

at this time. Not a specific day but a general reference to the present time of the participants.

17. *the crime of Peor.* The mere construction of an impressive and potentially rival altar—precise location unknown—is now compared with one of the most infamous developments during the period of wilderness life, the apostasy to the Baal of Peor (see Beth-peor in 13:20), narrated in Numbers 25 (recalled in Deut 4:3, which is generally recognized as a secondary chapter, that is, Dtr 2). It apparently involved the fertility rites of sexual intercourse with outsiders to the covenant community, either an attempt to arrest the spread of bubonic plague or to replace those who died of the plague, but with the reverse effects which were interpreted as the operation of curses for treaty violation. See Mendenhall, *Ten Gen,* 105-121. On that occasion, according to the Numbers story, it was Phinehas whose decisive action stayed the plague.

18. *the entire congregation.* Forming an inclusion with the same expression at the beginning of v 16, this phrase concludes part one of the speech—the accusation. While it is assumed at the outset of the speech that the Transjordan tribes are no longer part of "the entire congregation," it now turns out that divine wrath triggered by former members can thus erupt against all the members! The purport seems to be that the east-bank tribes aren't acting like members but the west-bank tribes are stuck with them and still have to behave. In their own way, the west-bank tribes will oversimplify the course of the conquest in the next verse.

19. *land you have seized. land that Yahweh has seized.* This distinction must be rooted in Yahweh's winning of Canaan from Pharaoh at the Reed Sea, when Pharaoh's Canaan did not include Transjordan (Exod 15:15); the latter Yahweh took with Moses in charge. But Phinehas gets it all turned around.

unclean. Scholars often appeal to "primitive conceptions" that only land west of the Jordan (and more specifically land around Shiloh in the hill country of Ephraim) was Yahweh's land.

But the original referent, surely, was to the lingering effects of the plague, still observable in Israel at the time the new altar was built. The story was at last used to suggest an artificial distinction between Transjordan (human conquest) and Cisjordan (divine conquest); or was it the other way around? The effect of the incongruity is to challenge the notion that Israel must have geographical definition. This was written for the benefit of believers who were living at the brink of exile from the beloved homeland. The finally redacted story makes the point that "Israel" is wherever believers talk things through in order to avoid violence and secure a peaceful solution.

Tent. Hebrew *miškan* (cf. Tent of Meeting, *'ōhel mô'ēd* in 18:1). Another reference to this venerable institution, the shelter for the Ark of the Covenant and thus the place of highest legitimacy for oracular inquiry (Judg 20:27-28), will be the very last word in the rebuttal to this indictment (v 29).

take a possession. The *niph'al* imperative of *'ḥz* can also be rendered "be seized," i.e. "get caught."

Do not rebel against us. This is called blurting out the truth. What was put initially in terms of apostasy and rebellion against Yahweh (vv 16-18) is now expressed in MT as a repudiation of a certain supposedly constituted authority.

20. *Achan.* This is the only mention of Achan in all of scripture outside chap. 7, which makes the literary connection between these stories, already observed in terms of vocabulary and comic exaggeration, certain.

commit a treacherous violation. As told in chap. 7, Achan had tried to enrich himself by ignoring the ad hoc decree regarding the plunder from Jericho, a decree prompted by the danger of debilitating disease, physical contamination, and ritual impurity.

entire congregation. As in vv 16 and 18.

21-29. The defense will be about twice as long as the indictment.

21. *said to the heads of the village-units.* Apparently they address themselves to the people who bear arms; there is no mention of Phinehas.

22. *God of gods.* The Hebrew superlative. The defense begins by reciting strict confessional orthodoxy.

Let him make known. Reading Hebrew *yd'* as *hiph'il* jussive. They are ready to submit the truth of their claim to adjudication by oracle.

Let Israel learn. Hebrew *wyśr'l hw' yd'.* The initial *w* is emphatic, which forces the verb to the end of its clause. In this story vigorous argument over religious intentions is being positively commended as an alternative to religiously rooted violence, with Yahweh as final arbiter.

23. *for building.* This is a literal translation where it is not absolutely certain that the transition from v 22 to v 23 is intact. There are far more textual problems in the defense speech than in the indictment.

If. Hebrew *wĕ-'im.* The initial *w* is the explicative conjunction. Here rebellion or treason is caricatured by being reduced to a matter of sacrifice at the wrong place.

burnt offerings. cereal offerings. sacrificial peace offerings. Will the discussants ever get around to holding up the ethic which Joshua had commended to them in v 5?

sacrificial peace offerings. Hebrew *zbḥy šlmym.*

24. *Yes.* Hebrew *'im lô',* with an oath expressed or implied, is emphatic affirmative.

25. *share.* Hebrew *ḥeleq.* This forms an inversion with the instruction given by Joshua at the end of v 8.

in. The preposition *b* may instead retain here the sense of "from."

fearing Yahweh! This was the prime covenantal stipulation in Deuteronomy, as recognized by Aryaprateep, "Studies in the Semantics of the Covenant Relationship in Deuteronomic Teaching." Here, however, it has become synonymous with "sacrificial worship at the right place." As such it caricatures Jerusalem's preoccupation with being the place chosen by Yahweh.

27. *Instead it is.* Here the comic transformation of the story becomes transparent. The exceptionally large altar which was to be seen somewhere near the Jordan was designed from the outset to be nonfunctional except as a visual aid to the unity of Israel and Dtn's teaching on the "central sanctuary."

witness. This anticipates another stone serving as witness in 24:27.

to perform the service. Hebrew *l'bd 't 'bdt,* another narrative use of the cognate accusative.

burnt offerings. sacrifices. peace offerings. This is mostly a repetition of the list in v 23, omitting "cereal offerings" and reading *zbḥynw* and *šlmynw* as distinct categories. For the importance of the Ark of the Covenant in relation to such activities, see Judg 20:26-28.

29. *But we are damned if.* It is now their turn to blurt out the truth. The force of this oath of clearance can only be approximated in paraphrase: *ḥālîlā lānû,* "defilement (or 'profanation') is ours." But this is treated as one word and followed by *mmnw;* thus "the curse on us is from us alone!"

his Tent! Hebrew *miškānô.* Second and last occurrence in this book.

30. *Bene. Bene. Bene.* This sustains the focus on the total "family" (Israel) to the very end.

31. *Phinehas.* Having been sent on an unnecessary mission, he will now make an unnecessary ruling.

Because you have not committed. An odd logic, but an effective way of telling the truth, this idea that by having done nothing wrong these people had rescued all the rest.

this treachery. It is the root *m'l* again, as in vv 16 and 22. Phinehas and his team are represented as assuming that Yahweh will treat all Israel as guilty unless the board of inquiry can be satisfied about the innocence of the ones accused. This attitude has nothing to do with lingering traces of a primitive notion called "corporate personality," but is a caricature which originates in the perennial ability of *homo religiosus* to put ultimate trust in cultic activity.

33. *the word was satisfactory.* Hebrew *wyṭb hdbr,* which turns back upon "the Good Word" in 21:45.

34. *gave a name.* The practice of giving commemorative names to altars is not fiction. See Gen 33:20; 35:7; Judg 6:24. The end of Joshua 22, however, reads like an etiological adaptation of a story told originally to serve another purpose.

There is a witness. The translation treats the last line as a poetic bicolon (Hebrew syllable count 7:7), which gives the name of the altar. The truce between Jacob and Laban, which likewise had its setting in Transjordan, established a peaceful boundary between them and was also marked by a monument called "Witness" (Gen 31:43-54).

Yahweh is truly God! And truer words were never spoken. The redactor of the story and the speeches has made the point that it is better to talk than to fight.

truly. The asseverative particle *kî* is repeated in both segments of the poetic line.

COMMENT

Here is a story that originated in some obscure altar-building program which very nearly developed into all-out civil war pitting "brothers" against "brothers." The conflict started out to be most unpromising, but it ended to everyone's satisfaction. And violence was avoided. As such this story prefigures the tragic story of the Benjaminite war in Judges 19-21 which was likewise told with the later redactor's characteristic sense of humor. There the crowning touch is the recommendation made by the elders of the congregation to kidnap two hundred young women at the Shiloh festival. This is in order to maintain Benjamin's reproductive capacity and thus perpetuate the twelve-tribe structure. That Shiloh caper is given a theologically foolproof, if curiously inverted, rationale. The complaining fathers and brothers were to be told that it was sheer grace, the plan that the elders thought up! See Judg 21:22 in AB 6A, 290-294.

Similarly the Transjordan rebuttal to the accusation made by the Cisjordan delegation is theologically unobjectionable. And so the chapter moves to one of the most profound etiological explanations in all of scripture (v 34). Yet the very location of the place thus made legitimate is entirely unknown (see second NOTE on v 10). Probably it had been long since forgotten when the story was put into its present form.

It was the later redactor, looking out at the prospects for life in exile, who rang the changes on slavish attachment to cultic places. Life with Yahweh would go on wherever there was a congregation of Yahweh! The actual altar at the Jordan was no concern of his but the story about the naming of it would make for life among believers, about any group of whom it might also be said:

> There is a witness between us
> Yahweh is truly God!

In some such way we would explicate the hope of Dtr 2, who turns in the next chapter to Joshua's concluding exhortation and largely negative expectation for all Israel, in the final edition of the book.

VI. THEOLOGY BY JOSHUA
(23:1-16)

Introduction

23 1 Much later, after Yahweh had given rest to Israel from all their enemies on every side and Joshua had reached a ripe old age, 2 Joshua summoned all Israel (that is, their elders, their chiefs, their judges, and their officers) and said to them:

Concerning the Past

"I have reached a ripe old age. 3 And you have witnessed everything that Yahweh our God has done to all these nations on our behalf. Yahweh is truly our God. He is The One Who Fights For Us.

4 "Attention! To you I have allotted in fief these remaining nations for your tribes: from the Jordan . . . and all the nations which I have mowed down, and from the Great Sea that is the sunset boundary. 5 Yahweh our God is the one who will drive them out on our behalf until they are totally destroyed. He will send wild beasts against them until they are evicted on your behalf, along with their kings. Then you shall seize their land, as Yahweh our God promised you.

6 "Be strong, carefully to carry out all that is written in the Book of the Mosaic Treaty-Teaching without deviating from it one way or the other, 7 without mingling with these nations that are left with you. In the name of their god(s) you shall neither pronounce an invocation nor administer an oath. Do not serve them, and do not bow down to them. 8 You shall cling exclusively to Yahweh our God, just as you have done down to this day.

9 "Yahweh has dispossessed on your behalf great and powerful nations. As for you, no one has withstood you, down to this day.

10 Each one of you stampedes a village-unit! Yahweh is truly your God. He is The One Who Fights For Us, as he promised us.

Regarding the Future

11 "Be exceptionally careful for your own sakes to love Yahweh our God. 12 For if in fact you turn away and cling to the remnant of these nations that are left with you (arrange marriages with them and go in to them—and they to you), 13 you may be absolutely sure that Yahweh your God will no longer evict these nations on your behalf. To you they will be a snare, a trap, and a scourge on your ribs and thorns in your eyes, till you perish from this good land which Yahweh your God has entrusted to you.

14 "Here I am now going the way of everything earthly. And you know with all your heart and your very being that not one thing has failed of all the good things Yahweh our God promised concerning you. All has come true for us. Not a bit of it has failed—not one word.

15 "But as surely as everything good which Yahweh your God promised has come true for us, so Yahweh will likewise bring upon you every bad thing, until he has destroyed you from this good land that Yahweh has given you. 16 When you deviate from the covenant of Yahweh our God which he commanded us, to go and serve other gods and bow down to them, then Yahweh's wrath will be kindled against you. You will quickly disappear from this good land that he has entrusted to you."

TEXTUAL NOTES

23 2. *Israel*   LXX reads "Bene Israel," which is unlikely in view of the following parenthesis.

(*that is*   The explicative *w* is here restored from LXX, Syriac. In MT a scribe's eye jumped from *l* to *l: ysr'l* [*w*]*lzqnyw*.

judges, and their officers   LXX reverses the order of "officers" and "judges."

3. *our* and *us*   This is LXX ("our" three times in vv 3 and 5, once in vv 8,11,14,16; "us" once in vv 3,14, and 16, twice in v 10). MT uses second person.

4. *these remaining nations*　　MT and the versions in vv 4,7, and 12 reflect a most bewildering array of differences. But it is essentially a matter of two readings in various stages of conflation. R. G. Boling, "Some Conflate Readings in Joshua-Judges," *VT* 16 (1966) 296-297.

and all the nations　　The text is not intact. In LXX "and" is omitted before "all" and inserted before "which."

from　　This is LXX: *wmhym*. MT omits the preposition *m*.

boundary　　This is restored on the basis of LXX, after a haplography in MT: *hgdw*[*l gbw*]*l mbw' hšmš*.

5. *until they are totally . . . along with their kings*　　This is restored from LXX, after a lengthy haplography in MT: *mpnyk*[*m . . . wmlkyh*]*m*.

7. *with these nations that are left*　　This is Syriac *bgwym h'lh hnš'rym*, where LXX reads *bgwym hnš'rym h'lh* and MT is conflate. Cf. Textual Note at v 4 above.

nor administer an oath　　This was dropped by haplography from LXX or its *Vorlage: wl*['*tšby'w wl*]'. Syriac seems to have read the same consonants as a *niph'al*, which would be rendered as middle voice: "you shall not swear."

9. *you* second occurrence and [10] *your*　　LXX reads first person, a rather consistent preference in this chapter, most likely a secondary development in this verse. Greenspoon, STBJ, 186.

10. *Each*　　LXX shows another haplography: '[*yš* ']*ḥd*.

11. *for your own sakes*　　This was lost by haplography in LXX *Vorlage: l*[*npštykm l*]'*hbh*.

12. *these nations that are left with you*　　This follows Syriac, where the major Greek recensions show contrasting haplographies and MT is conflate. Cf. Textual Note above at v 4.

13. *your God*　　Not in LXX. Cf. v 15.

14. *now going the way of everything earthly*　　This is MT. Cf. LXX.

MT	*hwlk hywm bdrk*		*kl h'rṣ*
LXX	*kwlk*	*drk* [*kn? w*]*kl b'rṣ*	

Here LXX omits the temporal modifier and relocates the preposition *b* following a plus that is not entirely clear: "going the way of *kn*(?) and of(?) everything on earth."

good　　The adjective was lost by haplography in LXX *Vorlage: hdbry*[*m hṭby*]*m*.

concerning you. All has come true　　This is MT. Cf. LXX.

MT	'*lykm hkl b'w*
LXX	'*l* *kl hb'w*

LXX has lost a suffix and transposed the article: "concerning everything that has come true."

15. *Yahweh*　　LXX reads "Yahweh God."

Yahweh　　Third instance. This is LXX, Syriac, where MT adds "your God."

16. *then Yahweh's wrath . . . entrusted to you"*　　LXX lacks all of v 16b, presumably because of haplography, *lh*[*m . . . lk*]*m*, and reads v 16a as the protasis for which v 15 is the apodosis.

NOTES

23:1-16. Concerning the form and function of the edifying discourses made by the great leaders which give structure to the historical work of Joshua-2 Kings, see the NOTES on 22:1-5.

1-2. These verses introduce a period, however brief, when the Israelite take-over of Canaan is far from complete, but hostilities have pretty much ceased, and Joshua has grown old.

1. *Yahweh had given rest.* It is the fifth and final occurrence of the idiom in the Book of Joshua (1:13,15; 21:44; 22:4), all in passages which on other grounds are recognized as belonging to the later redaction. Thus Dtr 2 especially emphasized peace in the land as Yahweh's gracious gift.

and Joshua had reached a ripe old age. This is exactly what is specified in 13:1, the introduction to the allotments of Transjordan and the unconquered land.

2. *Joshua summoned.* The location is not specified. Presumably the central Tent-sanctuary is intended, still at Shiloh. Compare 24:1, set at Shechem; the book seems to approach a conclusion twice.

all Israel. The larger definition of Israel in former days, with Transjordan and Cisjordan tribes interacting and interdependent, is a special concern of Dtr 2. Here again the tribes of all Israel are represented by the leaders.

elders. As in 7:6; 8:10,33; 9:11 (Gibeonites); 20:4 (asylum-towns); 24:1,31.

chiefs. Literally, "heads," as in 21:1; 24:1; and the related idioms "patriarchal chiefs" (14:1; 19:51) and "heads of the village-units" (22:21,30).

judges. Elsewhere in this book, only 8:33 and 24:1, both relating directly to the Shechem Valley events.

officers. As in 1:10; 3:2; 8:33; 24:1.

2b-16. Joshua's speech is in two parts for which we have supplied the italicized headings; each part displays a form of envelope construction. The first part is framed by a description of the Divine Warrior (vv 3 and 9-10). It focuses on the recent past, emphasizes that Yahweh has indeed kept his promises (vv 4-5) as the motivation for Israel to continue doing likewise (vv 6-8). In other words, in the first half of the speech the Suzerain's promise and the reality of the treaty blessings are seen to have been operative alongside Israel's loyalty throughout the lifetime of Joshua.

The second half of the speech reverses the envelope pattern. Here instead is a thunderous warning in two stages (vv 11-13,15-16) separated by a compact echo of the first half (v 14). The warning is just as clearly rooted in the oath of the vassal and the reality of the treaty curses which will continue in force in the post-Joshua era. It is possible that these two emphases are to be assigned to two redactors, Dtr 1 and Dtr 2 respectively, as suggested by Cross, *CMHE*,

249-250 n. 129; 287. It is more likely that both themes were present in the first edition and that their distinctive configuration now is the work of the later redactor. The curses were coming to frightful fulfillment in the total collapse of the state and temple institutions in the post-Josiah years.

3-10. These verses hark back to the promise in 1:10-11, here seen to be fulfilled.

3. *all these nations.* It is apparently a time of relatively peaceful coexistence after many of the local kingdoms have been dismantled while others remain effectively cowed before the power of Yahweh.

truly our God. This statement evokes the punch line of the preceding unit (22:34).

The One Who Fights For Us. Hebrew *han-nilḥām, niph'al* participle used as a noun, repeated at the end of v 10 to form an *inclusio* around the first half of the speech.

4. *"Attention!* Hebrew *rě'û,* literally, "See!"

these remaining nations. This picks up a theme that was only secondarily introduced into the book (by Dtr 2, we have suggested) in chaps. 13 and 14. Here it is once again explicit. The first edition, with its sweeping summaries, had implied too much.

the Jordan. the Great Sea. This looks like the remnant of an envelope construction, but the result is a somewhat garbled description.

I have mowed down. Hebrew *hkrty,* literally, "I have cut off." The verb is a Deuteronomic favorite (see, for example, Deut 12:29; 19:1). The first person claim by Joshua is somewhat surprising in the wake of the sustained rhetoric about the Divine Warrior. Probably these affirmations were part of a Yahweh speech which Joshua is quoting.

5. *Yahweh our God is the one who will drive them out.* He will be the only one to do so, according to this chapter. When Joshua dies, it will be the end of an era: no more expansionist warfare. All of Israel's expansionist warfare is past (Judg 2:1-5).

He will send wild beasts. The haplography described in the Textual Note at v 5 dropped from MT this key to the entire section. Since all the land has been allotted and all the warfare is past—though not all the land has been won—how will the promise be fulfilled? Verse 5 provides an answer.

wild beasts. Is this an interpretation of "the Hornet(s)" to be mentioned in 24:12 (cf. Exod 23:28 and Deut 7:20)? It is not clear whether the referent is strictly zoological or possibly mythological. In light of the Exodus passage we suspect the latter, a reference to the transnatural battalions of the Divine Warrior which can manifest themselves in defeat, disease, and all forms of calamity.

promised. See below, final NOTE on v 10.

6. *"Be strong.* This imperative is a rhetorical echo of 1:6 and 9.

carefully to carry out. The verbal hendiadys formed by two infinitives, *lšmr wl'śwt,* harks back to similar usage in the introductory exhortation (1:7).

all that is written in the Book of the Mosaic Treaty-Teaching. Compare "the entire Treaty-Teaching which Moses my Servant commanded you" (1:7), "the Book of the Treaty-Teaching" and "all that is written in it" (1:8), and "the text of God's Treaty-Teaching" (24:26).

one way or the other. Literally, "right or left." See 1:7.

7. *without mingling.* The grass-roots origin of most Israelites within Canaanite society has long since been forgotten among the Deuteronomists' audience. A national militancy is commended in Dtr 1, leading to a preoccupation with ethnic identity and genealogical descent that is caricatured in Dtr 2.

you (bis). The emphasis of this chapter is on responsible leadership (as displayed especially in Joshua 9 and 22; and Judges 21), thanks to the later redactor.

administer an oath. See second Textual Note at v 7. We have retained MT; since it is the leadership that is being addressed, the two commands given in the verse are both expressed in causative form.

do not bow down. The prohibition evokes a central covenant stipulation (Exod 20:5=Deut 5:9). It is a recurring emphasis in epic, Dtn, and Dtr texts. Exod 23:24; Deut 8:19; 11:16; 29:25; Judg 2:19; 1 Kgs 9:9; 22:54; 2 Kgs 17:35; 21:3,21. This is the first occurrence in this book of another word deeply rooted in rules of courtly etiquette. Samuel E. Loewenstamm, "Prostration from Afar in Ugaritic, Accadian and Hebrew," *BASOR* 188 (December 1967) 41-43. In early Israel it described behavior which was recognized as appropriate for the presence of Yahweh alone. In the present context it is the action which will constitute the rhetorical climax in v 16.

8. *cling exclusively.* To achieve this emphasis, the sentence begins with asseverative *kî* which thrusts the verb *dbq* to the end of the clause. On this verb see 22:5 and seventh NOTE.

as you have done down to this day. Yahweh's promise-keeping has always been conditional.

9. *powerful.* Hebrew *'ṣwmym* indicates that strength is here reckoned in numbers, size of populations or armies.

no one has withstood you. The assurance given in 1:5 has proved to be reliable.

10. This verse converts the old poetic question of Deut 32:30 into descriptive prose.

stampedes. Hebrew *yirdōp*, literally, "pursues." The imperfect form here describes habitual or customary rather than future action. For in this chapter the conquest is complete, so far as Israel's military participation is concerned.

a village-unit! Hebrew *'elep.*

Yahweh is truly. The last two sentences of v 10 form the strongest possible *inclusio* with v 3b.

promised. This is Hebrew *dbr* with special nuance, as in 13:14,33; 22:4; and 23:5—five times in Joshua and all five in passages recognized on other grounds as Dtr 2. In the era of divine judgment, it was even more important to stress the priority of the divine promises having been kept.

11-16. The second half of Joshua's speech accentuates the negative, advocating a form of enlightened self-interest.

11. *"Be exceptionally careful.* The *niph'al* of *šmr* (cf. *qal* infinitive in v 6)

expresses the middle voice. This expression occurs elsewhere only in Deut 4:15, another Dtr 2 text. Levenson, "Who Inserted the Torah?" *HTR* 68 (1975) 220.

to love Yahweh. Exclusive loyalty. See fourth NOTE on 22:5.

12. *in fact you turn away.* The Hebrew infinitive absolute is here used to reinforce the finite form adverbially.

(*arrange marriages with them.* Except for the mingling in v 7, this is the first time in the book that this subject has come up. It clearly anticipates the situation at the end of the following era (Judges 21).

go in. Both Hebrew *b'* and Greek *mignumi* are used for a broad range of symbiotic relations as well as more specifically for the sexual act.

13. *you may be absolutely sure.* Another infinitive absolute is used adverbially to balance precisely the emphatic conditional in the preceding verse.

God will no longer evict. they will be a snare. trap. scourge. thorns. This too was understood to be rooted in the teaching of Moses (Num 33:55). What it means is that the "nations" left behind would be available to Yahweh as agents for implementing the curses of the covenant. Hillers, *Treaty-Curses and the Old Testament Prophets,* 69-70. These warnings were seen to be confirmed in Judg 3:1-6.

entrusted. The verb *ntn,* root meaning "to give" (rendered "assigned" in 22:4,7 where Joshua and Moses are subjects) here evokes this sense which is technically correct since they are in the land and all allotments from Yahweh have been determined.

14. *"Here.* Hebrew *wĕhinnēh* emphasizes the immediacy of the situation.

I am now going the way of everything earthly. In saying so Joshua sounds like a king, for elsewhere it is only David who uses this formula. 1 Kgs 2:2.

with all your heart and your very being. See Joshua's previous farewell to all Transjordan tribes (22:5).

Not a bit. not one word. This translation assumes that the force of the negative carries over to the last two words.

15. *everything good. every bad thing.* The former summarizes the blessings, and the latter the curses, of the covenant.

until he has destroyed you. The temporal construction here uses the infinitive construct, with a suffix that has contaminated the vowel of the following object pronoun: *'d-hšmydw '(w)tkm.*

16. *When you deviate.* Here again we have the suffixed infinitive construct in the temporal construction, and the result is a grammatical chiasm with v 15.

covenant. Hebrew *bĕrît.* It is used elsewhere in Joshua only in 7:15, apart from references to the Ark of the Covenant. The Mosaic treaty is, however, the presupposition of the entire value system that pervades the final edition, after a monumental effort in the first edition to harmonize that system with what was also taken to have been political necessity.

serve other gods and bow down. See fourth NOTE on v 7. The picture is that of performing in public (serving) and reporting in person (bowing down).

You will quickly disappear. That is, the collectivity that is "all Israel" will fall apart, with the abrogation of the covenant; and the land will revert to con-

ditions of the patriarchal era. "A perishing Aramean was my father . . ."
(Deut 26:5).

COMMENT

The delivery of a farewell speech by Joshua puts him in a small and most
distinguished company in the Old Testament. The series begins with
Moses, for whom the entire Book of Deuteronomy is "last words," and
continues with Samuel (1 Sam 12:1-24) and David (1 Kgs 2:1-9; cf.
2 Sam 23:1-7). There are no others in all of the Dtr corpus.

Such speeches are not to be dismissed as pious fraud. Chapter 24, for
example, surely reflects a fully developed liturgical scene in which a duly
qualified person reenacted or represented the role of Joshua at Shechem,
just as most of the material in Deuteronomy requires a covenant mediator. And the interest of the Jerusalem kings in functioning as priests is
amply documented. It is thus not surprising to find the speeches of great
public figures reported on, from time to time, and with different nuances
from various distinct Levitical circles.

As will be seen from even a cursory glance at chap. 24, the last two
chapters of the book are heavily redundant, with an address modeled on
the blessings and curses of the covenant (chap. 23) now serving as hortatory preparation for participating in renewal of the covenant at Shechem,
where again those two elements of the form are most prominent (chap.
24). The explanation must lie in the independent antiquity of the
Shechem account, as concluded by Wright in the Introduction, 70-71.
It is most likely that the original speech of Joshua 23 in Dtr 1 was at
last overwritten in Dtr 2, under the influence of the account now found in
chap. 24. Gray, *Joshua, Judges and Ruth*, 8.

The result is a speech that seems to end on a devastatingly negative expectation for the future of Israel in the land, as though the ax has already
fallen. It is indeed critical orthodoxy to date the speech in the exilic period or later and to find some way of dismissing it, in Latin if possible, as
vaticinium ex eventu. That it is an example of prophecy after the event is,
of course, not impossible. But the setting for the speech need be no later
than the last decades of Judah for it to become relevant and plausible.
Those schooled in the tradition that led from Hosea and Dtn to Jeremiah
could very well read the signs of the times. For existence in the coming
time of exile there could perhaps be no more forceful way of underscoring
the need for covenantal living than to hear Joshua as an old man speaking on the subject of the divine prerogative to dismantle a nation-state
should it get in the way of abundant life for each and all.

VII. THE SHECHEM COVENANT, AND POSTSCRIPTS
(24:1-33y)

The Peace

24 1 Joshua gathered all the tribes of Israel at Shechem. He summoned Israel's elders, chiefs, judges, and officers; and they presented themselves before God. 2 Joshua said to all the people: "This is what Yahweh God of Israel has to say—

'A long time ago your ancestors lived beyond The River—that is, Terah the father of Abraham and of Nahor. And they served other gods. 3 I took your ancestor Abraham from the far side of The River. I made him travel through the whole land of Canaan. I multiplied his progeny and gave him Isaac. 4 To Isaac I gave Jacob and Esau. I allowed Esau to have possession of the hill country of Seir, but Jacob and his sons went down to Egypt. There they became a great nation, strong and numerous, and the Egyptians oppressed them. 5 I sent Moses and Aaron. I assailed Egypt with the signs that I performed in it, and after that I brought you out. 6 I brought your ancestors out from Egypt and you came to the sea. Egypt pursued your ancestors with chariotry and horsemen, to the Reed Sea!

7 'When they cried out to Yahweh, he put a cloud between you and the Egyptians. Then he brought the sea on them, and it covered them.

'You saw with your own eyes what I did in Egypt, and you lived in the wilderness for a long time. 8 I brought you to the land of the Amorites who lived on the other side of the Jordan, and they fought you. I put them in your power, and you took possession of their land. I destroyed them on your behalf. 9 Balaq ben Zippor, king of Moab, made a stand and "fought"

Israel. That is, he sent to summon Balaam ben Beor so as to curse you. 10 But I was not willing to listen to Balaam. He emphatically blessed you! I rescued you from his power.

11 'You crossed the Jordan and came to Jericho. The Jericho lords ganged up on you (the Amorites, the Perizzites, the Canaanites, the Hittites, and the Girgashites; the Hivites and the Jebusites), but I put them in your power.

12 'I sent before you The Hornet, and it drove them out on your behalf—the two Amorite kings. It was not by your sword or by your bow.

13 'I presented to you a land for which you had not labored and towns which you did not build, but on which you live. From vineyards and olive orchards which you did not plant, you eat.'

14 "So now, fear Yahweh and serve him with complete honesty. Put aside the gods your ancestors served on the other side of The River and in Egypt. But serve Yahweh!

15 "If in your view it is a bad thing to serve Yahweh, then choose today whom you will serve, either the gods your ancestors served from the region beyond The River or the gods of the Amorites on whose land you are living. But as for me and my household, we are going to serve Yahweh."

16 The people said in response, "We are damned if we are going to desert Yahweh so as to serve other gods.

17 "Yahweh is our God! He it is who brought up our ancestors from the land of Egypt and from slaves' barracks, who performed before our eyes those great signs. He has watched over us all along the route that we have traveled and among the peoples in the midst of whom we have passed. 18 Yahweh has expelled for our sake the Amorites (that is, all the peoples) who were living in the land. We too are going to serve Yahweh. He is truly our God."

19 Joshua said to the people: "You will never be able to serve Yahweh. For he is a holy God! He is El the Zealous! He will not put up with your disloyalty and your sinning. 20 When you desert Yahweh and enter the service of foreign gods, he will turn around and do you harm. He will finish you off, after he has done you good."

21 The people said to Joshua, "Never! It is Yahweh we will serve!"

22 Joshua said to the people, "You are witnesses against yourselves that you yourselves have chosen for yourselves Yahweh—that is, to serve him."

They said, "We are witnesses."

23 He said, "So now repudiate the foreign gods which are in your midst and give your assent to Yahweh God of Israel."

24 The people said to Joshua, "Yahweh we will serve, and his command we will obey."

25 Joshua concluded a covenant for the people that day, and established for it legal precedent at Shechem. 26 Joshua recorded these stipulations in the text of God's Treaty-Teaching; he took a large stone and set it up there beneath the oak which was in the sacred place of Yahweh. 27 Joshua said to all the people, "This stone will indeed be a witness against us, for it has heard all the words of Yahweh which he has negotiated with us today. It will be a witness against you, lest you deceive Yahweh your God."

28 Joshua dismissed the people, each man to his own fief. 31 Israel served Yahweh throughout Joshua's days and throughout the days of the elders who survived Joshua, who had experienced all the works of Yahweh which he had performed on behalf of Israel.

Various Burial Notices

29 After these things, Joshua ben Nun, the Servant of Yahweh, died at the age of a hundred and ten years. 30 They buried him inside the border of his fief at Timnath-serah, which is in the hill country of Ephraim, to the north of Mount Gaash. 30ˣ They laid with him there, in the tomb where they buried him, the flint knives with which he had circumcised the Bene Israel at Gilgal, when he brought them out of Egypt, as Yahweh commanded them. There they are to this very day.

32 Joseph's bones, which the Bene Israel had brought from Egypt, they buried at Shechem in the plot of ground which Jacob had purchased from the Bene Hamor (father of Shechem) for a hundred *qesitah*. It belongs to the fief of the Bene Joseph.

33 After these things Eleazar ben Aaron died and they buried him in the Gibeah belonging to Phinehas his son, which had been assigned to him in the hill country of Ephraim. 33ˣ At that time the Bene Israel had the Ark of God traveling in their midst; and Phinehas was priest in place of Eleazar his father, until he died and was buried in his Gibeah.

33ʸ Then the Bene Israel went away, each to his hometown sanctuary! The Bene Israel worshiped Astarte (the "Lady") and the gods of the nations surrounding them. And so Yahweh delivered them into the power of Eglon king of Moab, who oppressed them for eighteen years.

TEXTUAL NOTES

24 1. *Shechem*   LXX reads "Shiloh" here and again in v 25.

Israel's elders, chiefs, judges, and officers   Thus MT, reading *lzqny yśr'l wlr'šyw wlšpṭyw wlšṭryw*. LXX shows a loss of two words, "Israel" and "chiefs," and transposition of the other two words: *lzqnyw wlšṭryw wlšpṭyw*. The same sequence occurs in LXX 23:2.

3. *of Canaan* and ⁴*I gave*   Lacking in LXX.

multiplied   This is the converted imperfect as represented in the *kethib*.

4. *There they became . . . oppressed them*   Restored from LXX, after a haplography triggered by repetition of "Egypt(ians)": *mṣrym w[yhy šm lgwy gdwl w'ṣwm wrb wy'nwnw hmṣrym w]'šlḥ*. LXXᴮ contains a third clause which says: "and he [LXXᴬ: the Lord] smote Egypt with what he did to them." This is presumably a corruption or variant of the text "I assailed Egypt with what I did in it," after a preceding haplography and a further, internal haplography (see respectively first and second Textual Notes at v 5 below). That is to say, MT and LXX show contrasting omissions. With the aid of both, a text is restored that is superior to either one.

5. *I sent Moses and Aaron*   This is lacking in LXX which reflects a haplography in a series of clauses, each beginning with the identical consonant cluster of the converted imperfect form.

the signs   The reading is based on LXXᴬ⁺ᴹˢˢ, which support *b'twt 'šr*. Cf. Num 14:11. Haplography perhaps best accounts for LXXᴮ *b'šr* which by a common scribal lapse became *k'šr* in MT.

you out. ⁶*I brought*   Lacking in LXXᴮ which may be correct. But see below.

6. *I brought your ancestors*   Lacking in LXXᴹˢˢ, showing, it seems, another example of contrasting haplographies. Here the fuller of the Greek texts reads "our ancestors" (cf. chap. 23, Textual Notes at vv 3 and 9).

7. *they* and *you*   LXX has first person throughout, continuing the review by Joshua in that version.

cloud   MT perhaps shows a one-letter dittography: *wyśm [m]'pl* (so BHS). For "cloud" LXX reads *nephelēn kai gnophon*, which suggests that there was a gloss in its text.

I   LXX "the Lord." Also in v 8 (second occurrence) and v 11.

8. *I brought*   Following the *qere*. In LXX "He" (the Lord) is the subject.

and they fought you   Another haplography is reflected in LXXᴮ: *wy[lḥmw 'tkm wy]tn*.

I second occurrence   LXX "you."

9. *you*   Also in v 10 twice; v 11 (second occurrence) and "your"; v 12 and "your" (first occurrence); v 14 "your." LXX first person.

10. *I*   LXX "your (singular in LXX^B) God," sustaining the third person narrative form.

to listen to Balaam   LXX reads instead "to destroy you," which may be an attempt to make sense out of a mutilated copy by reading *lbl'm* as infinitive of *bl'* "to destroy." But the pronoun suffix (*m*="them") would remain unexplained. Greenspoon, STBJ, 186-189.

power   LXX has a plus, reflecting *wntn 'tm*, "and he gave them."

11. *Jericho lords*   MT *b'ly yryḥw* for which LXX reflects *yšby yryḥw*, "the inhabitants [or "the enthroned (ones)] of Jericho."

Amorites, the Perizzites, the Canaanites, the Hittites, and the Girgashites; the Hivites and the Jebusites)   LXX has the same seven in different sequence: Amorites, Canaanites, Perizzites, Hivites, Jebusites, Hittites, Girgashites.

12. *'I*   LXX "He."

two   This number is the more difficult reading and should be retained. LXX "twelve" assumes mistakenly that it must refer to events of chaps. 2-10.

your (bis)   Syriac reads plural suffixes, where MT shifts momentarily to singular in this weaponry formula.

13. *From*   The preposition was a victim of haplography: *bhm* [*m*]*krmym*.

14. *gods*   In LXX "foreign gods," as in v 23.

15. *Yahweh"*   Second instance. LXX adds "for he is holy" in anticipation of v 19.

16. *The people*   "All the people" in Syriac.

17. *"Yahweh is our God! He it is*   This is MT; cf. LXX.

MT	*ky yhwh 'lhynw h'w*
LXX	*ky yhwh 'lhynw h'w 'lhym h'w*

The addition of two words shifts the focus from the act of decision to monotheistic declaration: "Yahweh our God is God. He . . ."

our ancestors   MT and LXX read *'bwtynw* in conjunction with a preceding *'tnw*, "us." But that object pronoun may be explained as originating in a partial dittography in an early text written without internal vowel letters (*'btnw*). Syriac omits "and our ancestors," which looks like a secondary attempt at improvement by choosing between the two.

the land of   Lost by haplography in LXX^B+MSS: *m*['*rṣ*] *mṣrym*.

from slaves' barracks, who performed before our eyes those great signs   Lacking in LXX.

18. *the Amorites (that is, all the peoples)*   This word order is based on LXX. MT reverses the conjuncts.

19. *El the Zealous!*   Hebrew *'l qnw'*. LXX omits the first word.

22. *you yourselves have chosen for yourselves*   Literally, "you have chosen for yourselves." It is shorter in LXX, due to haplography: *'tm bḥrt*[*m lk*]*m*.

They said, "We are witnesses."   This is lacking in LXX, after haplography: *'wtw w*[*y'mrw 'dym w*]*'th*.

23. *He said*   These words are not in MT or LXX but are supplied for clarity in the translation.

24. *"Yahweh*   Thus LXX, where MT adds "our God."

25. *Shechem*   LXX reads "at Shiloh" (cf. Textual Note at v 1); it also adds: *lpny mškn 'lhy yśr'l*, "before the Tent of the God of Israel."

26. *Joshua recorded these stipulations in the text of God's Treaty-Teaching; he took a large stone and set*   In LXX the name is omitted at the beginning of the verse and appears instead with the third verb in the verse.

there   Hebrew *šm* has no counterpart in LXX and Syriac. It may have arisen in misunderstanding *śm*, a variant for the preceding verb.

oak   MT *hā-'allâ* has the consonantal spelling of "terebinth" (*'ēlâ*) but the stem pattern of "oak" (*'allôn*).

in the sacred place of Yahweh   Hebrew *bmqdš yhwh* where LXX reflects *lpny yhwh*, "before Yahweh." Possibly both are correct and we have contrasting haplographies.

27. *all* first occurrence   LXX reflects a haplography which dropped this word: *'[l k]l*.

all the words of Yahweh   Thus MT: *kl 'mry yhwh*. It is not clear what lies behind LXX *panta ta lechthenta autō hupō kyriou*, "all that was spoken to it on behalf of the Lord."

today   This is restored on the basis of LXX.

you first occurrence   LXX adds *ep eschatōn tōn hēmerōn*, "to the end of days"=Hebrew *'d 'wlm* or *'d qṣh hymym*.

Yahweh   Syriac and Vulgate read the full formula, "Yahweh your God." LXX reads "Yahweh my God."

31. From here on our translation follows the verse order of LXX (but numbered as in MT) which is considerably less disjointed than MT.

29. *After these things*   Hebrew *wyhy 'ḥry kn*=LXX *kai egeneto met' ekeina*.

30. *Timnath-serah*   The second element is variously represented as *srḥ* (MT), *shr* (LXX), and *ḥrs* (Judg 2:9).

30ˣ. *They laid with him there . . . There they are to this very day*   Restored from LXX. For the reconstructed Hebrew text, see *BH³*. Presumably this was lost in connection with the displacement of v 31 in the tradition of MT.

32. *Hamor (father of Shechem)*   LXX confused "Hamor" with "Amorites" and read *yšby škm*, "who were living at Shechem." Cf. Textual Note on "Jericho lords" in v 11.

It belongs   Reading *wyhy* (thus Syriac and Vulgate) against the anomalous plural form in MT. LXX has a variant: "He had given it" (presumably Hebrew *wytn*).

Bene   LXX omits *bny*, but the longer formula seems to be characteristic of these concluding verses.

33. *After these things*   Missing in MT, restored from LXX which reads *kai egeneto meta tauta*; cf. v 29 and Textual Note.

Eleazar   Syriac adds *hkhn*, "the priest."

Aaron   Some Syriac manuscripts add *hkhn* and LXX gives *archiereus*, "chief priest," a correct rendering of *hkhn*, as noted above in 22:13 where the same readings occur.

33x-33y. Verses restored from LXX. There is no reason to doubt that this material was translated from the Hebrew.

33y. *Astarte* (*the "Lady"*)   This is LXX *Astartēn kai Astarōth*. The latter=Hebrew *'štrwt*, which may be taken as a plural of majesty, perhaps a variant for the name of the goddess in a conflate text.

NOTES

24:1-33. This final chapter has two parts. The first and major section describes the Shechem Covenant (vv 1-28+31). This is followed by a collection of notes on the burials of several famous persons plus the flint knives used for the circumcision at Gilgal. The book ends with brief description of the apostasy that introduces the following era.

1-28+31. These verses are a fuller description of events first reported in 8:30-35. There the focus was on the liturgical action which was rooted in the Shechem Valley treaty. In our NOTES and COMMENT on the end of chap. 8, those verses were interpreted as the later editor's contribution, offering a corrective to the possible misunderstanding of the first edition which had placed this chapter on the Shechem Covenant at the end of the era. And indeed, as seen above, that placement earlier in the era makes much better sense historically. The reason for the displacement in the first edition is that, as these verses show clearly, they originated in an older document which the historian could simply append to the description of the warfare and redistribution of land because the covenant was assumed to refer to all of the area ruled by the late seventh-century Judean throne. The document has had a long history, perhaps starting out as the holy word or text, "the *hieros logos* of the celebration of the constitution of the sacral confederacy of the Twelve Tribes in Canaan." Weiser, *The Psalms*, 27.

1-25. A key to the pre-Deuteronomic account here is dialogical structure: seven occurrences of *'mr* in the converted imperfect (vv 1,2,16,19,21,22 [*bis*], 24); seven occurrences of the name Joshua (vv 1,2,19,21,22,24,25); seven references to the people (vv 2,16,19,21,22,24,25); and seven imperatives (four in v 14, one in v 15, two in v 23). These patterns underscore the literary unity of vv 1-25, with scant traces of any internal Dtr editing. See Charles H. Giblin, "Structural Patterns in Joshua 24:1-25," *CBQ* 26 (1964) 50-69.

1. *all the tribes of Israel.* In the pre-Shiloh phase only the tribes of Joseph, Reuben, and Gad had attained any territorial definition, to which we should probably add a tribe of Benjamin ranging south into what becomes Judah. In 8:33 and 8:35, in fact, there is no mention of tribes.

Shechem. The LXX reading "Shiloh" appears to be the result of harmonization with 18:1. It is equally possible that it reflects a developing anti-Samaritan bias, since it is known that Shechem was rebuilt by Samaritan refugees in the Hellenistic period. Wright, *Shechem*, 170-181. Thus MT remains the more difficult reading and is more likely to be original, although the matter cannot be solved on text-critical grounds.

Except for this text there has been a major effort in the Book of Joshua to play down the role of the Shechem Valley. See above on 17:7.

elders, chiefs, judges, and officers. See 23:2 and NOTES. All but the chiefs are also listed in 8:33.

before God. MT has the definite article: *lpny h'lhym*. The phrase implies the presence of the Ark. G. Henton Davies, "The Ark in the Psalms," in *Promise and Fulfillment*, 61. In 8:33 the elders, officers, and judges are explicitly said to be flanking the Ark, before the Levite-priests who are the porter-guardians of the Ark.

2. *"This is what Yahweh God of Israel has to say.* Hebrew *kōh 'āmar yahweh 'ĕlōhê yisrā'ēl*. It is the familiar messenger formula best known from usage by the prophets in Israel and Judah. It introduces Joshua as ambassador, representative of the court of Yahweh, delivering the communique which is offered as ground and motivation for the vassal's acceptance of the treaty. See NOTES on 22:16-20.

2b-13. A number of parallel recitals are also clearly related to covenant ceremonies. Exod 19:3b-6; Deut 6:20-25; 26:5-9. The treaty is grounded in the prior benevolent acts of the Suzerain toward the vassal and thus there is no mention of Sinai and/or Shechem in the recital itself. Covenant formation (or reformation) is the social presupposition of the speech.

2b. *ancestors. father.* These are the same key Hebrew word, its precise sense depending on context. Here it is used in an envelope construction: six times in the Hebrew text of vv 2-6 and three times in vv 14-17. The intervening passages speak about (or address themselves) to "you." Yahweh, Sovereign in the Shechem Covenant, is encountered as the God of a great variety of individuals and clans, each of whom makes its own identification with the Bene Israel.

The River. This is the Euphrates which is explicitly "The Great River" in the Deuteronomic introduction to the book (1:4).

Terah. Gen 11:24-32. It is likely that his roots were in northern Mesopotamia; one of the Ebla tablets is said to have disclosed a town called Ur that is actually located in Haran. Paul Maier, "Discovery of Ancient Ebla," *Christian Herald* (March 1977) 29. It was with the general eclipse of third-millennium Syrian culture that the hometown was interpreted to be the Babylonian Ur in the south.

Terah the father of Abraham and of Nahor. It appears that the name of Terah has been awkwardly introduced so as to exempt Abraham and Nahor from the charge implied with the specification that comes next.

they served other gods. See third NOTE on 23:16.

3. *your ancestor Abraham.* The abrupt shift to the singular means that the tradition of the common ancestor has become functional. The chapter reflects the social change and adaptation of the covenant that came in the tenth century. Mendenhall, *Ten Gen,* 180. But the lingering awareness that the fathers had served other gods means that the source took shape prior to development of the full-blown royal theology. Thus it reflects the Davidic—not yet Solomonic—establishment, as described by Cross, *CMHE,* 219-273.

through the whole land of Canaan. This is not the cyclical movement, season after season, of pastoral nomads, but describes the development of a wide-ranging network of effective control, which Albright concluded was economic in essence. *YGC*, 53-73.

I multiplied his progeny. Gen 12:1-3; 15:4-5. This is a way of fulfilling promises to the fathers that is not stressed in the bulk of the Joshua book, another indication that chap. 24 had a prior and independent history down to the compilation by Dtr 1.

4. *Jacob and Esau*. Genesis 25*ff*.

Seir. Joshua 11:17; 12:7; 15:10.

5. *sent Moses and Aaron*. Exodus 4-6.

assailed Egypt with the signs. Exodus 7-13.

5-6. *you. your ancestors. you. your ancestors*. The alternation here is stylistic, not a sign of mixed sources. After the complete merging of the generations in v 7 there is no more reference to *'ābôt* until we come back to "ancestors" in v 14.

6-7. The two verses read like a compact paraphrase of Exodus 14.

6. *to the sea*. Hebrew *hymh* permits the hearing of mythological overtones, however muted. Used again but without the directive ending in v 7, the two references to the sea form an envelope around the more specific designation that occurs at the end.

to the Reed Sea! Mythological overtones are suddenly converted to sharp historical memory. Here the referent must be a papyrus marsh somewhere in the isthmus of Suez.

7. *'When they cried out to Yahweh*. The divine initiative is correlated to the cry of stark human despair. See also use of this motif in Ps 107:6,13,19,28.

they. you. them (*bis*). *You. your. you*. The rhetorical appeal in MT continues. The text thus invites any reader to make personal identification with those whose story is recounted.

Yahweh, he. he. To focus attention on the nub of the matter, the divine communique itself resorts to third person description.

a cloud. Hebrew *ma'ăpēl* is a hapax legomenon. The word generally used in epic texts is *'ānān*, as in the pillar "of cloud." The latter is Israel's counterpart, in narratives of theophany, to the winged sun-disk in pagan art. That is, it makes visible the hidden presence of the one who holds the sovereignty and legitimate power to act, in this case over against the illegitimate claims of Pharaoh. See Mendenhall, *Ten Gen*, 32-66.

Then he brought. Out of the dark cloud, executive action!

the sea on them. This is the prose text that stands in closest relation to the archaic Song of the Sea (Exodus 15) and shows little if any evidence of influence by the tradition of the Jordan River crossing. See Cross, *CMHE*, 134.

'You saw with your own eyes what I did. In the biblical tradition theophany reveals the God who acts.

and you lived. In the wilderness especially, long life is the salvific gift of Yahweh to those whose roots were not in the desert.

8. *Amorites. on the other side*. That is, east of the Jordan. The epic tradition is Numbers 21: cf. Deuteronomy 2-3. See above, NOTES and COMMENT on 12:1-6 and 13:8-31.

9. *Balaq. Zippor.* Two names with possible explanations from Anatolian dialects but only forced explanation, if any, from Semitic languages. Mendenhall, *Ten Gen,* 169-170; the name Balaam which he also discusses may however be Semitic, a short form of the name Ibleam.

Balaq. made a stand and "fought." Either the text is in total contradiction to Judg 11:25, where Jephthah asserts just the opposite, or else the reference to Balaq is made with a twinkle in the eye that reflects a sense of humor in the epic sources, Numbers 22-24 (cf. Deut 23:4-5). That is, Balaq's belligerence was exercised and exhausted in his employment of a famous diviner to pronounce curses against the advancing Yahwists.

Balaam ben Beor. See 13:22 and NOTE.

10. *I rescued you from his power.* What actually happened to blunt Balaq's mobilization against Israel remains unclear. The assertion of the text is that when Balaq opposed Israel, Yahweh won the war, apparently without much violence. It may well reflect a certain mythologizing of the tradition by the invincible monarchy.

his power. Whose power? Probably Balaq as the one who was ultimately responsible for Balaam's activity against Israel.

11. The Yahwist takeover west of the Jordan is here represented by the capture of Jericho, but it is surely an oversimplification to conclude that in this tradition "the whole conquest was accomplished physically at Jericho." D. J. McCarthy, "The Theology of Leadership in Joshua 1-9," *Biblica* 52 (1971) 174. Much more plausible is Wright's argument above, stressing the formative influence of celebrations at the Gilgal sanctuary near Jericho. See the Introduction, 24-26.

The Jericho lords. Hebrew *ba'ălê yĕrîḥô.* Cf. "Shechem lords" in Judg 9:2 and "Qeilah lords" in 1 Sam 23:11-12. Compare Amarna usage of *bêl ālīm* to refer to the loyal military government of a vassal city-state. Mendenhall, *Ten Gen,* 128 n. 31.

ganged up on you. This tradition is much closer to the spy story (2:1-24 and 6:22-26) than to the bulk of the familiar story which represents the conquest of Jericho in the highly stylized form of liturgical action (6:1-21).

the Amorites, the Perizzites, etc. A local liturgy reenacting the capture of a single oasis in the Jordan Valley is here transferred to Shechem and properly glossed to illustrate the power of Yahweh throughout the tiny land of the many nations. For these seven, see NOTES on 3:10. One side effect of the insertion, however, was to obscure the rhetoric of another envelope construction; for the communique immediately returns to the subject of the east-bank territory, linking v 12 to vv 8-10.

12. *The Hornet.* See also Deut 7:20. The Hornet was sent as promised in Exod 23:28. Is this an allusion to the power of Pharaoh who was represented in symbols of the bee or hornet? John Garstang, *Joshua-Judges,* 258-260. If so, the tradition suggests that repeated Egyptian campaigns of the fourteenth and thirteenth centuries had so weakened the land as to prepare the way for the Yahwist takeover. But why such a veiled reference to Egypt? An alternative interpretation sees The Hornet as visible representative of the "terror" that Yahweh is regularly said to send upon the enemy, within the Holy War, to im-

mobilize the opposition (for example, 2:9-11,24; 5:1; 6:27; and at greatest length, Exod 15:14-16). Still more likely is the explanation in terms of actual use of insects in warfare episodes which were already part of a far distant past at the time of Joshua. See Edward Neufeld, "Insects as Warfare Agents in the Ancient Near East (Ex. 23:28; Deut. 7:20; Josh. 24:12; Isa. 7:18-20)" in *Orientalia* 49 (1980) 30-57.

drove . . . out. See Exod 23:28-31; 33:2; 34:11; Judg 2:3; 6:9. Hebrew *grš* is "almost a technical term for Yahweh's activity in the conquest." Miller, *The Divine Warrior in Early Israel*, 85.

two Amorite kings. This returns to the east-bank victories, first mentioned in v 8, forming the envelope around "Jericho." The reference is thus to Sihon (12:2; 13:10,27) and Og (12:4; 13:12,30-31). There is no need to emend the text to "thirty-two," as sometimes suggested, on the strength of thirty-one kings listed in chap. 12. The reading "twelve" in LXX may be the symbolic number closest to eleven, which is the total number of kings figuring in the narratives down through chap. 10; as such it would be a tertiary development, after the transfer to Shechem and the specification of the seven nations had obscured the original structure.

sword. bow. The same formulaic pairing of the two weapons occurs in the patriarch's reference to the capture of Shechem. Genesis 48:22.

13. *'I presented to you a land.* The supremely legitimating achievement of the great Savior-King. Here the second person pronouns revert to plural form except for one verb.

you had not labored. Second person singular.

you live. you eat.' The well-being of ancient Israel originated solely in Yahweh's sovereign initiatives. Thus ends the communique which is at last presented as the Sovereign's invitation to join in a new Israel.

14. *fear Yahweh.* That is, "revere, give allegiance." This is the prime covenant stipulation, establishing an exclusive relationship in the healthy attitude of awe. See the usage in 4:14 and 24 and fifth NOTE on the latter.

serve. The verb *'bd* occurs seven times in vv 14-15.

serve him. This imperative is parallel with "fear Yahweh" at the beginning and together they form an envelope construction centering in the transfer of loyalties to Yahweh.

with complete honesty. Hebrew *bĕtāmîm ûbe'ĕmet,* literally, "in completeness and in truth," another example of hendiadys. This covenantal formula occurs otherwise only in Judg 9:16-19, the summary of Jotham's fable which turns it into an indictment for covenantal failure. AB 6A, 174.

Put aside. Hebrew *whsyrw.* In v 23 the same verb will be the next-to-last imperative before the concluding declaration of allegiance. It has been argued that this element "would find a better background in the late monarchy period" under domination of Assyria or even Babylonia. Mayes, *Israel in the Period of the Judges,* 38. Such an explanation might account for the redactional use of the Shechem document by Dtr 1, but it scarcely accounts for its genesis in the historical process.

Put aside the gods. There was precedent in a patriarchal tradition for the renunciation of old gods at Shechem. Gen 35:2-4. That it was still happening as late as the career of Joshua stands in the strongest possible tension with the tradition that became normative in the Jerusalem monarchy.

15. *bad thing.* Hebrew *ra‘*, generally "evil." This verse is rhetorical repetition of the preceding, with inverted order of elements.

choose. The issue is not monotheism in the abstract but allegiance in concrete particularity. Compare Exod 20:3.

from the region beyond. This sense is proved by variants in the initial preposition: *b* and *m*. A number of gods had moved west with patriarchal families.

beyond The River. Joshua's usage forms an *inclusio* with Yahweh's opening statement in v 2.

living. The same form means "sitting." Without the acknowledgment of Yahweh's non-metaphorical kingship, which the covenant serves to secure, many Israelites are in fact squatters.

me and my household. Joshua is first to make the move that no responsible adult, male, head of household can make for another. Ruth 1:16 offsets any notion that such decision-making is only the prerogative of male family heads.

16-18. In this response to Joshua's challenge, the people indicate that they have already made up their minds. Yahweh is going to continue to be their God. That there is nothing said here about a union of diverse groups in an expanding federation is an argument from silence. There is no question that the chapter comes to us in a monarchical redaction and that the seventh-century historians would have taken the group of people involved to represent the entirety of the state west of the Jordan.

16. *"We are damned.* Compare 22:29. They thus place themselves under the sanction of the covenant curses before they have even entered into the covenant! It is an incongruity worthy of the narrator of the Jordan altar story, who will have the last word in chap. 24 as well.

to desert Yahweh so as to serve other gods. That is, to be guilty of treason in the kingdom of God, which the Transjordanians, in the story to which this now is sequel, had reduced to a matter of offering sacrifice at the wrong altar (22:22-23). This is a case of defending against the threat of treason before there has been any opportunity to be loyal! The final redactor was not going to leave anyone with any excuse for saying "I told you so." It was time for a new covenant.

17-18. The bulk of the people's response is a polished rhetorical piece, probably a preformed liturgical unit taken over intact by the historian. It stands now as the irreducible minimum of Joshua's historical review in vv 2b-13.

17. *"Yahweh is our God!* See also 22:34; 23:3,10. Here the clause forms an *inclusio* with the last clause in v 18.

God! The introductory particle *ky* gives exclamatory force to the Hebrew sentence.

our ancestors.   our eyes. This compact unit employs the same technique that was noted in alternation between second and third person forms in the initial communique (vv 2b-13), to elicit and signal identification with the experience of others.

18. (*that is, all the peoples*). The plain appositional construction in MT suggests that this is a secondary element corresponding to the list of seven nations

in v 11. The parenthesis was made necessary by the initial and original use of "Amorites" in this chapter to refer to kingdoms east of the Jordan (v 8). That is to say, the liturgy was updated with the move from Gilgal to Shechem.

19-20. Joshua returns to the fray and restates his challenge to the people.

19. *For he is a holy God! He is El the Zealous!* Exclamatory force of *ky* at the beginning of the first statement carries over to the second one; both are formulated to give emphasis to the identity of Yahweh.

El the Zealous! Cf. "El the Living" in 3:10. This is another apparently poetic epithet referring to the god of the early league; see Exod 20:5; 34:15; Deut 5:9. Joshua goes directly to the heart of the matter. Yahweh is zealously different. His holiness and zeal are further specified in the next sentence.

put up with. Hebrew *nś'* is variously rendered: "forgive" (*RSV/NEB*), "bear" (Soggin).

disloyalty. sinning. In the covenant perspective these are synonymous.

20. *foreign.* Hebrew *nēkār*, used again in v 23. It seems to assume that the God of Israel has national or tribal identity. As such it continues the caricature with which the book now concludes.

finish. The root is *klh.* The sentence is hyperbole and inexact. Not the people but the structure of state and temple would be "finished."

21-24. Here is another envelope construction. The people's declaration of allegiance in the first and last verses is the frame to Joshua's final admonition to the effect that it will be necessary to keep an eye on one another. At the center of the unit, they agree.

21. *serve!"* The asseverative *kî* thrusts the verb to the end of the sentence.

that is, to serve him. At the last moment Joshua rules out the possibility of choosing Yahweh for any other reason.

22. *"We are witnesses."* Hebrew *'dym.* The affirmative response in Hebrew may repeat only the key word which stands for the whole sentence. For the same formula where it is clear that the distinction between civil law and religious law is completely blurred and where Yahwist behavior within the guidelines of ethic is being commended, see Ruth 4:9-11 and discussion by Campbell, *Ruth,* AB 7, 150-152.

23. *gods which are in your midst.* While the people have been protesting their firm preference for Yahweh, Joshua knows that in fact there are some "patriarchal" deities to be discarded.

give your assent. Literally, "incline your heart." Joshua calls upon the decision-making center, for the heart in ancient understandings of the organism was the seat of mind and will.

24. Hebrew puts the direct object first for emphasis, in grammatically parallel clauses, a most emphatic wrap-up to the negotiations.

25-27. In these verses Joshua makes final arrangements for the future of relationships among the people, chief of which is a large stone at Shechem which will betoken the internal-surveillance function.

25. *for the people. for it.* Joshua was Yahweh's negotiator for a covenant with many new people.

legal precedent. Hebrew *ḥōq umišpāṭ,* literally, "statute and judgment." It is another hendiadys, representing the general content of the agreement.

26. *stipulations*. Hebrew *dbrym*, "words" or "commandments," in a familiar Dtn/Dtr usage. Is this another reference to the Decalogue of Exodus 20 and Deuteronomy 5? Certainly the Shechem treaty was modeled on the Sinai one, extending benefits of the latter to peoples many of whom had long been at home in Canaan. Most likely the specific stipulations of the Shechem covenant which would establish for Canaan the peace of God have not survived unless they have been displaced to serve as the Code of the Covenant made at Sinai (Exod 20:22-23:19). In any case the stipulations at Shechem are broadly represented in the narrative by the prime imperatives to fear and to serve (vv 14-15). Campbell, "Moses and the Foundations of Israel," *Interpretation* 29 (1975) 150.

text. Hebrew *sēper*, perhaps "inscription" here (not precisely "book"). See 1:8; 8:31,34; 23:6.

God's. In narrative texts where the divine name Yahweh predominates, the sudden shift to the generic noun *'ĕlōhīm* often signals a value judgment and tacit agreement with the assertion of the story.

Treaty-Teaching. Hebrew *tôrā* as in 1:7,8; 8:31,32,34; 22:5; 23:6. It is neither mere teaching nor strictly law. It is perhaps best paraphrased as the negotiated guidance and support for right living. A record of it was to be publicly displayed.

a large stone. This clause is so closely joined to the preceding that it is a fair inference that the record of the stipulations was made on the large stone. The parallel unit is apparently a bit garbled in describing the torah as written on the undressed stones of the Mount Ebal altar (8:31-32). For other monuments as implicit witnesses to explicit covenants, see Gen 31:43-54 (cf. Gen 28:18). The stone of Joshua's covenant should be compared with the great standing-stone excavated in front of the Shechem Fortress-Temple of the Late Bronze Age, and its two smaller predecessors of an earlier phase. Since the use of sacred pillars is condemned in the strongest terms by the Mosaic guidelines (Deut 16:22), we may conclude that this one was "depaganized" by having the covenant stipulations inscribed on it, probably in a fresh coat of plaster. No doubt there are very real Yahweh-Covenant steles at the basis of this Shechem account and the one concerning the altar by the Jordan (for "witness," not for sacrifice) in chap. 22.

the oak which was in the sacred place. Compare the "Oak of Moreh" (Gen 12:6) and the "oak which survives at the palisade in Shechem" (Judg 9:6). The work of the Joint Expedition to Tell Balatah has shown that there can scarcely be any location for this other than the temenos area in front of the Fortress-Temple.

27. *indeed*. Hebrew *hinnēh* at the outset of the clause signals "a fact upon which a following statement or command is based." Lambdin, *Introduction to Biblical Hebrew*, 169.

witness. The inscribed stone would be a public reminder to worshipers and pilgrims, a common point of reference in the lives of those who had themselves become witnesses in v 22.

words of Yahweh. Hebrew *'imrê yahweh*, literally, "statements of Yahweh."

negotiated with. A distinctive idiom, *dbr 'm,* "to speak with," i.e. "to discuss."

us. At the conclusion of the covenant which he has negotiated, Joshua restates in this pronoun his own identification with the covenant community; he had first declared himself in an earlier phase of negotiations (v 15).

lest you deceive. The caricature of religion that has turned inward to the maintenance of distrust is thus sustained to the last word.

28 and 31. MT is in disarray. Missing parts survive in LXX, and the doublet in Judg 2:6-9 helps to restore order.

28. *Joshua dismissed the people.* His work was satisfactorily finished (first edition) if curiously so (second edition). In the first edition he provides a model for the two great achievements of King Josiah, military conquest and covenant renewal. In the second edition he offers a vision indispensable for life in exile.

31. *experienced.* Hebrew root *yd',* "to know," in this case empirically. They were the last of the first generation.

works. Reading the plural (LXX, Syriac, Vulgate) instead of the singular as in MT. For the latter, cf. Deut 11:7 and Judg 2:7,10.

31,29-30. We may suspect that the first edition of the book continued with a notice of Joshua's death and burial (vv 29-30), as transition to the era of the Judges. As it stands now, the ending has attracted to it a variety of other burial notices.

29. *After these things.* Hebrew *wyhy 'ḥry hdbrym h'lh.* It is a distinctive temporal construction, used only here in the MT of Joshua (but cf. v 33, LXX). It marks an emphatic pause and transition, as is clear from the related formula used at the outset of the following era in Judg 1:1.

Joshua. Servant of Yahweh. Given the frequency of the servant title in reference to Moses (1:1,2,13; 8:31,33; 9:24; 11:12,15; 12:6; 13:8; 14:7; 18:7; 22:2,4,5), it is somewhat surprising that it is not used of Joshua until now. It must be deeply rooted in the reality of the covenant in which a servant is the diplomatic representative of God. In other words, it was not as guerrilla-warfare genius but as covenant-negotiator that Joshua bore, like Moses, the title of Servant of Yahweh.

30. *Timnath-serah.* See NOTES and COMMENT on 19:50, regarding the name, location, and archaeology of this town.

Mount Gaash. Hebrew *har gā'aš.* One of David's "thirty" would be recruited from a place or region called *naḥălê gā'aš,* "the Gorges of Gaash." 2 Sam 23:30=1 Chr 11:32.

30x. Perhaps originating in some relatively "late local tradition" (Bright, *IB* 2, 672), this continues the story and sustains the interest that is present in 5:2-9 and 21:42d. There should be no difficulty in recognizing its presence in the book as a contribution of Dtr 2, lost later on (as were a number of Dtr 2 elements) perhaps because their sense of humor was not appreciated.

to this very day. This use of the familiar etiological formula explains nothing. The resulting absurdity of noting the safe burial of these particular tools of circumcision signals the presence of the final redactor.

32. *Joseph's bones. Bene Joseph.* This forms an envelope construction with Gen 50:25 (cf. Exod 13:19) tying the end of the Joshua book to the end of

Genesis and showing that the Tetrateuch is presupposed as one long epic, preface to the Dtr historical work.

plot of ground. Literally, "portion of the field."

Jacob had purchased. See Gen 33:18-20. Compare Abraham's acquisition of the cave in the field at Machpelah in Genesis 23.

Hamor (father of Shechem). See COMMENT on 8:30-35.

qesitah. Genesis 33:19; Job 42:11. Value (weight) unknown.

the fief of the Bene Joseph. The redactor was content to let the burial of Joseph remain a matter of local northern tribal interest. This is perhaps the end of the first edition. But it was not to be the last word.

33,33x,33y. These concluding verses are loosely connected to the preceding as indicated by the disjunctive syntax of subject-first word order at the beginning. The verses display characteristic interests of the later "stratum" and show a telltale overlapping with framework material in the following Book of Judges.

33. *Eleazar ben Aaron died.* This priest and Phinehas ben Eleazar we have encountered only in Dtr 2 contexts (17:4; 21:1; 22:13,30-32; cf. Judg 20:28).

in the Gibeah. It may mean "on the hill." Does this reflect a "local tradition of Shechem"? Gray, *Joshua, Judges and Ruth,* 36-37. More likely the carriers of this tradition came from Bethel, the old rival to the Jerusalem sanctuary, where Phinehas ben Eleazar presides in Judg 20:26-28.

belonging to Phinehas his son, which had been assigned to him. Assigned to whom? Presumably to Eleazar, to whom Phinehas was heir. But the verse is not clear and this is the kind of syntactical ambiguity which abounds in the story of the altar at the Jordan (22:6-34). We have returned for the last words to the redactional turf of Dtr 2.

33x. *At that time.* Literally, "in that day." The same formula in its plural construction connects Phinehas ben Eleazar and "the Ark of the Covenant of God" at Bethel in Judg 20:27. The latter belongs to a collection of old stories about early Israel which the later redactor used to put a frame around the picture of the Judges era.

the Ark of God. With the imminent collapse of the state which had been ideologically supported by the permanent and immovable temple-palace of the deity, the latter having begun as a splendid royal chapel for the Jerusalem king, the old portable throne of the One who led the way through the wilderness was liberated for high symbolic value once again.

Phinehas. he died. The final edition makes the point that it was not so much the death of Joshua as it was the passing of Phinehas that marked the unhappy turning point in Israel's covenant-living before Yahweh.

33y. Scholars are generally agreed that this concluding matter, surviving in LXX but not MT, was not original. We may suspect that it entered as part of the redactional work of Dtr 2. Perhaps this is what brought about the division of Joshua and Judges into separate books; with the sizable contributions made by the later redactor, the account of the pre-monarchical period was too long for a single scroll. Certain repetitions were inevitable as the original transition underwent two transformations to become a conclusion in one book and introduction in the other.

to his hometown sanctuary. Literally, 'to his place and to his town." Here the Greek clearly represents a hendiadys, beginning with Hebrew *māqôm* which often means more precisely "holy place." That the same is intended here becomes clear in the next sentence.

Astarte (the "Lady") and the gods of the nations. Compare Judg 2:11-15; 3:7; 10:6 on this formulation of the charge against Israel.

Astarte. First is specified the beautiful fertility goddess, chief consort of the Lord of storm and warfare Baal-Haddu, and no mean fighter in her own right.

(the "Lady"). Here LXX represents Hebrew *'štrwt* which seems to be a plural of "Astarte" used apparently to refer to the plurality of local manifestations of the goddess.

gods of the nations surrounding them. Compare Judg 2:12-13. In that context they are also called "the Baals" (that is, "the Lords").

Yahweh. LXX does not distinguish between the title "Lord" and the personal name Yahweh which surely stood in the Hebrew here.

delivered. Literally, "gave over." This is an inversion with the many examples of Israel as beneficiary of the same action by the sovereign. The effect is that of another incongruity, with the result that the reader of the "book" of Joshua was encouraged at once to study the following era of the Judges.

Eglon king of Moab. Judges 3:12-30. This looks like another corrective inserted by Dtr 2. For the first edition of Judges began the era with the oppression by the mysterious "Cushan-rishathaim" (Judg 3:8-10). The latter story in fact looks like a carefully crafted unit made to serve as "Exhibit A" for the Judges era in the first edition. Boling, *Judges,* AB 6A, 80-83.

COMMENT

We have attempted to help our reader track the logic of the Book of Joshua and trace its origins. The subsequent history of Israel left its mark on this record of the takeover of twelfth-century Canaan. In the tenth century came a transformation from covenant-community to nation-state and briefly flourishing empire, a status soon lost and only approximately recovered by the great reforming King Josiah three hundred years later. We have recognized in Josiah's reign the most probable setting for the first edition of Joshua (Dtr 1). But the reformation was followed by the disastrous collapse of the state after Josiah's death, and this was the life-setting for the final edition. Closing comments may be brief.

We have concluded that vv 1-28 stem ultimately from a great revolutionary gathering at Shechem, more correctly referred by the final editor to the earlier part of the era, as represented by the covenant-liturgy fragment inserted at the end of chap. 8. This was the formative period, when there were already many social units which could be attracted by the story of Yahweh's past deeds and three recent surprises (Jordan River,

Jericho, Ai), and by the life of his community, to abandon inherited tribal religion or petty statist ideology derived from it.

But the final redactor left the full account of Shechem negotiations at the end of the book and turned it into an example of covenant renewal, with a characteristic twist. It is not done in any legalistic way, and it is done without moralizing comment.

The final editor would not let us have chap. 24 without also reflecting on the close brush with civil war in chap. 22 and Joshua's devastatingly negative "farewell" in chap. 23. The representation of tragic human failure in terms of comic reality is then sustained to the very last word where the motivation for the Shechem treaty-stele is put entirely in negative terms: it is necessary thus carefully to protect Yahweh from the deceitfulness of Israel (v 27)!

The reason for such a transformation is not far to seek (compare the conclusion to the following era, the Benjaminite War and its sequel in Judges 19-21). The Josianic attempt to use the power of the throne in reactivating the authority of Moses collapsed with the death of the king himself. As the reality of exile became inevitable, it was time for persons to do once again what the founding fathers did at Shechem: Choose!

The book thus originates and culminates with a revolution that is also a mutation in religion; the community of believers puts at the center of all decision-making the value of the individual, the quality of responsible life as response to a gracious gift, and the willingness of the individual to be governed by ethic, to be ruled by the One who is himself the ever-free and ever-reigning Lord. It is an exercise of sovereignty which transforms into everlasting relativity all forms of coercive power: political, economic, ecclesiastical.

The historical Joshua can only have been a man who held such convictions and behaved accordingly. Working as critical historians to penetrate the haze that hovers over political and ecclesiastical reuses of the past, we see a clear and somewhat different image of the hero of the conquest come into focus. Yahweh won far more towns with Joshua in the role of ambassador than with Joshua as field commander of the militia. To get a clear answer to the question, "What sort of man was Joshua?" the persons to ask would be not Dtr 1 or Dtr 2 but persons such as the family of Rahab, the residents of the Hivite town of Gibeon, and the participants in the convocation at Shechem. That assembly, it was finally recalled, was actually the prelude to Israel's relief of Gibeon, which in turn led to the suprising defeat of a southern hill-country coalition. With historical Joshua, we may be sure, persons came first and mattered most. That is the heart of Mosaic Torah. And that was perhaps the discovery of Dtr 1, which did its best to present Joshua-with-the-law-of-Moses as model for the Jerusalem king. It is a point that wears well: without serious attention to the teaching of Moses, life is a bad scene. Dtr 2 had, however, to come to grips with the historical refutation of a theology which would impose covenant renewal by using the power of the state.

For the exiles Dtr 2 commends an outlook that will let the past be past. The burial of the "tools" of recircumcision is highly symbolic when read alongside the caricature of slavish dependence upon archaic institutions with which the next era also concludes in the final redaction (Judges 19-21).

The value system that is rooted in the experience of the Exodus-Sinai-Shechem participants is imperishable, no matter how systematic the effort may be to suppress it. There is still much to be learned about ourselves from observing the tension between Dtr 1 and Dtr 2; deep-rooted ecclesiastical rivalries will sooner or later be buried just as surely as were the obsolete tools for the superficial maintenance of religious identity.

What began with Yahweh's conquest (read "pacification") of Canaan had issued most recently in Yahweh's defeat and destruction of the northern nation-state (Dtr 1). After the death of good King Josiah, the same was in process for the southern kingdom. It was about time to make a new start—with Yahweh the King of Israel.

INDEX OF PLACE NAMES

INDEX OF BIBLICAL REFERENCES INCLUDING
APOCRYPHA AND QUMRAN MANUSCRIPTS

INDEX OF AUTHORS

INDEX OF SUBJECTS